The Child Psychotherapy
Progress Notes Planner
Sixth Edition

Wiley Practice*Planners*® Series

Treatment Planners

The Complete Adult Psychotherapy Treatment Planner, Sixth Edition
The Child Psychotherapy Treatment Planner, Sixth Edition
The Adolescent Psychotherapy Treatment Planner, Sixth Edition
The Addiction Treatment Planner, Sixth Edition
The Continuum of Care Treatment Planner
The Couples Psychotherapy Treatment Planner, with DSM-5 Updates, Second Edition
The Employee Assistance Treatment Planner
The Pastoral Counseling Treatment Planner
The Older Adult Psychotherapy Treatment Planner, with DSM-5 Updates, Second Edition
The Behavioral Medicine Treatment Planner
The Group Therapy Treatment Planner, with DSM-5 Updates, Third Edition
The Gay and Lesbian Psychotherapy Treatment Planner
The Family Therapy Treatment Planner, with DSM-5 Updates, Second Edition
The Severe and Persistent Mental Illness Treatment Planner, with DSM-5 Updates, Second Edition
The Intellectual and Developmental Disability Treatment Planner, with DSM-5 Updates, Second Edition
The Social Work and Human Services Treatment Planner, with DSM-5 Updates
The Crisis Counseling and Traumatic Events Treatments Planner, with DSM-5 Updates, Second Edition
The Personality Disorders Treatments Planner, with DSM-5 Updates, Second Edition
The Rehabilitation Psychology Treatment Planner
The Special Education Treatment Planner
The Juvenile Justice and Residential Care Treatment Planner, with DSM-5 Updates
The School Counseling and School Social Work Treatment Planner, with DSM-5 Updates, Second Edition
The Sexual Abuse Victim and Sexual Offender Treatment Planner, with DSM-5 Updates
The Probation and Parole Treatment Planner, with DSM-5 Updates
The Psychopharmacology Treatment Planner
The Speech-Language Pathology Treatment Planner
The Suicide and Homicide Risk Assessment and Prevention Treatment Planner, with DSM-5 Updates
The Co-Occurring Disorders Treatment Planner, with DSM-5 Updates
The Parenting Skills Treatment Planner, with DSM-5 Updates
The Early Childhood Education Intervention Treatment Planner
The College Student Counseling Treatment Planner
The Complete Women's Psychotherapy Treatment Planner
The Veterans and Active Duty Military Psychotherapy Treatment Planner, with DSM-5 Updates

Progress Notes Planners

The Child Psychotherapy Progress Notes Planner, Sixth Edition
The Adolescent Psychotherapy Progress Notes Planner, Sixth Edition
The Adult Psychotherapy Progress Notes Planner, Sixth Edition
The Addiction Progress Notes Planner, Sixth Edition
The Severe and Persistent Mental Illness Progress Notes Planner, Second Edition
The Couples Psychotherapy Progress Notes Planner, Second Edition
The Family Therapy Progress Notes Planner, Second Edition
The Veterans and Active Duty Military Psychotherapy Progress Notes Planner

Homework Planners

Couples Therapy Homework Planner, Second Edition
Family Therapy Homework Planner, Second Edition
Grief Counseling Homework Planner
Group Therapy Homework Planner
Divorce Counseling Homework Planner
School Counseling and School Social Work Homework Planner, Second Edition
Child Therapy Activity and Homework Planner
Addiction Treatment Homework Planner, Sixth Edition
Adolescent Psychotherapy Homework Planner, Sixth Edition
Adult Psychotherapy Homework Planner, Sixth Edition
Child Psychotherapy Homework Planner, Sixth Edition
Parenting Skills Homework Planner
Veterans and Active Duty Military Psychotherapy Homework Planner

Client Education Handout Planners

Adult Client Education Handout Planner
Child and Adolescent Client Education Handout Planner
Couples and Family Client Education Handout Planner

Complete Planners

The Complete Depression Treatment and Homework Planner
The Complete Anxiety Treatment and Homework Planner

Wiley Practice*Planners*®

The Child Psychotherapy Progress Notes Planner

Sixth Edition

Arthur E. Jongsma, Jr.

Katherine Pastoor

David J. Berghuis

Timothy J. Bruce

WILEY

Library of Congress Cataloging-in-Publication Data

Names: Jongsma, Arthur E., Jr., 1943- author. | Pastoor, Katherine, author. | Berghuis, David J., author. | Bruce, Timothy J., author.
Title: The child psychotherapy progress notes planner / Arthur E. Jongsma, Jr., Katherine Pastoor, David J. Berghuis, Timothy J. Bruce.
Description: Sixth edition. | Hoboken, NJ : John Wiley & Sons, Inc., 2023. | Series: Wiley practice planners | Revised edition of: The child psychotherapy progress notes planner / Arthur E. Jongsma, Jr., L. Mark Peterson, William P. McInnis, David J. Berghuis. Fifth edition. [2014].
Identifiers: LCCN 2022029478 (print) | LCCN 2022029479 (ebook) | ISBN 9781119840893 (paperback) | ISBN 9781119840909 (adobe pdf) | ISBN 9781119840916 (epub)
Subjects: LCSH: Child psychotherapy.
Classification: LCC RJ504 .J663 2023 (print) | LCC RJ504 (ebook) | DDC 618.92/8914—dc23/eng/20220713
LC record available at https://lccn.loc.gov/2022029478
LC ebook record available at https://lccn.loc.gov/2022029479

Cover Design: Wiley
Cover Images: © Ryan McVay/Getty Images

Set in 12/14 pts and Times New Roman MT Std by Straive, Chennai, India

SKY 10042292_020223

To Bob and Ruth Knoll,
who have been good friends longer than we all care to remember.

—Arthur E. Jongsma, Jr.

To my good friend, Ronn Koehler.
Thanks for your friendship and support through the years.

—David J. Berghuis

To my daughter, Gloria.
May you grow up courageous and kind.

—Katherine Pastoor

To our new granddaughter, Nora.
Welcome to your loving family.

—Timothy J. Bruce

CONTENTS

PRACTICE*PLANNERS*® SERIES PREFACE

Accountability is an important dimension of the practice of psychotherapy. Treatment programs, public agencies, clinics, and practitioners must justify and document their treatment plans to outside review entities in order to be reimbursed for services. The books in the Practice*Planners*® series are designed to help practitioners fulfill these documentation requirements efficiently and professionally.

The Practice*Planners*® series includes a wide array of treatment planning books including not only the original *Complete Adult Psychotherapy Treatment Planner*, *Child Psychotherapy Treatment Planner*, and *Adolescent Psychotherapy Treatment Planner*, all now in their sixth editions, but also *Treatment Planners* targeted to specialty areas of practice, including:

- Addictions
- Behavioral medicine
- College students
- Co-occurring disorders
- Couples therapy
- Crisis counseling
- Early childhood education
- Employee assistance
- Family therapy
- LGBTQIA+ community
- Group therapy
- Juvenile justice and residential care
- Intellectual and developmental disabilities or Neurodiverse community
- Neuropsychology
- Older adults
- Parenting skills
- Pastoral counseling
- Personality disorders
- Probation and parole
- Psychopharmacology
- Rehabilitation psychology
- School counseling and school social work
- Severe and persistent mental illness
- Sexual abuse victims and offenders
- Social work and human services
- Special education
- Speech-language pathology

- Suicide and homicide risk assessment
- Veterans and active military duty
- Women's issues

In addition, there are three branches of companion books that can be used in conjunction with the *Treatment Planners*, or on their own:

- *Progress Notes Planners* provide a menu of progress statements that elaborate on the client's symptom presentation and the provider's therapeutic intervention. Each *Progress Notes Planner* statement is directly integrated with the behavioral definitions and therapeutic interventions from its companion *Treatment Planner*.
- *Homework Planners* include homework assignments designed around each presenting problem (such as anxiety, depression, chemical dependence, anger management, eating disorders, or panic disorder) that is the focus of a chapter in its corresponding *Treatment Planner*.
- *Client Education Handout Planners* provide brochures and handouts to help educate and inform clients on presenting problems and mental health issues, as well as life skills techniques. The handouts are included on CD-ROMs for easy printing from your computer and are ideal for use in waiting rooms, at presentations, as newsletters, or as information for clients struggling with mental illness issues. The topics covered by these handouts correspond to the presenting problems in the *Treatment Planners*.

The series also includes adjunctive books, such as *The Psychotherapy Documentation Primer* and *The Clinical Documentation Sourcebook*, which contain forms and resources to aid the clinician in mental health practice management.

The goal of our series is to provide practitioners with the resources they need in order to provide high-quality care in the era of accountability. To put it simply: We seek to help you spend more time on patients, and less time on paperwork.

ARTHUR E. JONGSMA, JR.
Grand Rapids, Michigan

PROGRESS NOTES INTRODUCTION

ABOUT PRACTICE*PLANNERS*® PROGRESS NOTES

Progress notes are not only the primary source for documenting the therapeutic process but also one of the main factors in determining the client's eligibility for reimbursable treatment. The purpose of the *Progress Notes Planner* series is to assist the practitioner in easily and quickly constructing progress notes that are thoroughly unified with the client's treatment plan.

Each *Progress Notes* Planner:

- Saves you hours of time-consuming paperwork.
- Offers the freedom to develop customized progress notes.
- Features over 1,000 prewritten progress notes summarizing client presentation and treatment delivered.
- Provides an array of treatment approaches that correspond with the behavioral problems and *DSM-5* diagnostic categories in the corresponding companion *Treatment Planner*.
- Offers sample progress notes that conform to the requirements of most third-party payors and accrediting agencies, including The Joint Commission, Council on Accreditation, Commission on Accreditation of Rehabilitation Facilities, and National Committee for Quality Assurance.

HOW TO USE THIS *PROGRESS NOTES PLANNER*

This *Progress Notes Planner* provides a menu of sentences that can be selected for constructing progress notes based on the behavioral definitions (or client's symptom presentation) and therapeutic interventions from its companion *Treatment Planner*. All progress notes must be tied to the client's treatment plan—session notes should elaborate on the problems, symptoms, and interventions contained in the plan.

Each chapter title is a reflection of the client's potential presenting problem. The first section of the chapter, "Client Presentation," provides a detailed menu of statements that may describe how that presenting problem manifested itself in behavioral signs and symptoms. The numbers in parentheses within the Client Presentation section correspond to the numbers of the Behavioral Definitions from the *Treatment Planner*.

The second section of each chapter, "Interventions Implemented," provides a menu of statements related to the action that was taken within the session to assist the client in making progress. The numbering of the items in the Interventions Implemented section follows exactly the numbering of Therapeutic Intervention items in the corresponding *Treatment Planner*.

All item lists begin with a few keywords. These words are meant to convey the theme or content of the sentences that are contained in that listing. The clinician may peruse the list of keywords to find content that matches the client's presentation and the clinician's intervention.

It is expected that the clinician may modify the prewritten statements contained in this book to fit the exact circumstances of the client's presentation and treatment. To maintain complete client records, in addition to progress note statements that may be selected and individualized from this book, the date, time, and length of a session; those present within the session; the provider; provider's credentials; and a signature must be entered in the client's record.

A FINAL NOTE ABOUT PROGRESS NOTES AND HIPAA

Federal regulations under the Health Insurance Portability and Accountability Act (HIPAA) govern the privacy of a client's psychotherapy notes, as well as other protected health information (PHI). PHI and psychotherapy notes must be kept secure and the client must sign a specific authorization to release this confidential information to anyone beyond the client's therapist or treatment team. Further, psychotherapy notes receive other special treatment under HIPAA; for example, they may not be altered after they are initially drafted. Instead, the clinician must create and file formal amendments to the notes if they wish to expand, delete, or otherwise change them.

Does the information contained in this book, when entered into a client's record as a progress note, qualify as a "psychotherapy note" and therefore merit confidential protection under HIPAA regulations? If the progress note that is created by selecting sentences from the database contained in this book is kept in a location separate from the client's PHI data, then the note could qualify as psychotherapy note data that are more protected than general PHI. However, because the sentences contained in this book convey generic information regarding the client's progress, the clinician may decide to keep the notes mixed in with the client's PHI and not consider it psychotherapy note data. In short, how you treat the information (separated from or integrated with PHI) can determine if the progress note planner data are psychotherapy note information. If you modify or edit these generic sentences to reflect more personal information about the client or you add sentences that contain confidential information, the argument for keeping these notes separate from PHI and treating them as psychotherapy notes becomes stronger. For some therapists, our sentences alone reflect enough personal information to qualify as psychotherapy notes and they will keep these notes separate from the client's PHI and require specific authorization from the client to share them with a clearly identified recipient for a clearly identified purpose.

ACADEMIC UNDERACHIEVEMENT

CLIENT PRESENTATION

1. **History of Underperformance (1)***
   A. The client's teachers and parents report a history of overall performance that is below the client's chronological age, given the client's measured intelligence or performance on standardized achievement tests.
   B. The client verbally admitted that their current academic performance is below their chronological age.
   C. The client has started to assume more responsibility for increasing academic performance to an age-appropriate level.
   D. The client has taken active steps (e.g., studying at routine times, seeking outside tutor, consulting with teacher before or after class) to improve academic performance.
   E. The client's academic performance has improved to a level expected for their chronological age.

2. **Academic Underachievement (2)**
   A. The client's teachers and parents reported a history of academic performance that is below the expected level, given the gifted client's measured intelligence or performance on standardized achievement tests.
   B. The client verbally admitted that current academic performance is below the expected level of functioning.
   C. The client has started to assume more responsibility for completing school and homework assignments.
   D. The client has taken active steps (e.g., studying at routine times, seeking outside tutor, consulting with teacher before or after class) to improve academic performance.
   E. The client's academic performance has improved to the expected gifted level.

3. **Incomplete Homework Assignments (3)**
   A. The client has consistently failed to complete classroom or homework assignments in a timely manner.
   B. The client has refused to comply with parents' and teachers' requests to complete classroom or homework assignments.
   C. The client expressed a renewed desire to complete classroom and homework assignments on a regular basis.
   D. The client has recently completed classroom and homework assignments on a consistent basis.
   E. The client's regular completion of classroom and homework assignments has resulted in higher grades.

---

*The numbers in parentheses correlate to the number of the Behavioral Definition statement in the companion chapter with the same title in the *Child Psychotherapy Treatment Planner*, Sixth Edition, by Jongsma, Peterson, McInnis, & Bruce (Wiley, 2023).

4. Disorganization (4)

A. The parents and teachers described a history of the client being disorganized in the classroom.

B. The client has often lost or misplaced books, school papers, or other important things necessary for tasks or activities at school.

C. The client has started to take steps (e.g., using a planner or agenda to record school/homework assignments, consulting with teachers before or after school, scheduling routine study times) to become more organized at school.

D. The client's increased organizational abilities have contributed to improved academic performance.

5. Poor Study Skills (4)

A. Parents and teachers reported that the client has historically displayed poor study skills.

B. The client acknowledged that lowered academic performance is primarily due to the lack of studying.

C. The client has recently spent little time studying.

D. The client reported a recent increase in study time.

E. The client's increased study time has been a significant contributing factor to improved academic performance.

6. Procrastination (5)

A. The client has repeatedly procrastinated or postponed doing classroom or homework assignments in favor of engaging in social, leisure, or recreational activities.

B. The client has continued to procrastinate doing classroom or homework assignments.

C. The client has agreed to postpone social, leisure, or recreational activities until completing homework assignments.

D. The client has demonstrated greater self-discipline by completing homework assignments before engaging in social, leisure, or recreational activities.

E. The client has achieved and maintained a healthy balance between accomplishing academic goals and meeting social and emotional needs.

7. Lack of Motivation (6)

A. The client verbalized little motivation to improve academic performance.

B. The client has often complained of being bored with or disinterested in schoolwork.

C. The client verbally acknowledged that their academic performance will not improve unless the client shows more interest and puts forth greater effort.

D. The client has shown more interest in schoolwork and put forth greater effort.

E. The client's renewed interest and motivation have contributed to improved academic performance.

8. Depression (7)

A. The client's feelings of depression, as manifested by apathy, listlessness, and lack of motivation, have contributed to and resulted from lowered academic performance.

B. The client appeared visibly depressed when discussing lowered academic performance.

C. The client expressed feelings of happiness about improved academic performance.

D. The client's academic performance has improved since their depression has lifted.

9. **Low Self-Esteem (7)**

A. The client's low self-esteem, feelings of insecurity, and lack of confidence have contributed to and resulted from lowered academic performance.

B. The client displayed a lack of confidence and expressed strong self-doubts about being able to improve academic performance.

C. The client verbally acknowledged a tendency to give up easily and withdraw in the classroom when feeling insecure and unsure.

D. The client verbalized positive self-descriptive statements about academic performance.

E. The client has consistently expressed confidence in their ability to achieve academic goals.

10. **Disruptive/Attention-Seeking Behavior (8)**

A. The client has frequently disrupted the classroom with negative attention-seeking behavior instead of focusing on schoolwork.

B. The parents have received reports from teachers that the client has continued to disrupt the classroom with negative attention-seeking behavior.

C. The client acknowledged tending to engage in disruptive behavior when they begin to feel insecure or become frustrated with schoolwork.

D. The client has started to show greater self-control in the classroom and inhibit the impulse to act out in order to draw attention to self.

E. The client has demonstrated a significant decrease in disruptive and negative attention-seeking behavior.

11. **Low Frustration Tolerance (8)**

A. The client has developed a low frustration tolerance as manifested by a persistent pattern of giving up easily when encountering difficult or challenging academic tasks.

B. The client's low frustration tolerance has resulted in patterns of acting out, disruptions, and negative attention-seeking behaviors.

C. The client's frustration tolerance with schoolwork has remained very low.

D. The client has started to show improved frustration tolerance and has not given up as easily or as often on classroom or homework assignments.

E. The client has demonstrated good frustration tolerance and consistently completed classroom/homework assignments without giving up.

12. **Test-Taking Anxiety (9)**

A. The client described a history of becoming highly anxious before or during tests.

B. The client's heightened anxiety during tests has interfered with academic performance.

C. The client shared that test-taking anxiety is related to fear of failure and of meeting with disapproval or criticism by significant others.

D. The client has begun to take steps (e.g., deep breathing, positive self-statements, challenging irrational thoughts) to reduce anxiety and feel more relaxed while taking tests.

E. The client reported a significant decrease in the level of anxiety while taking tests.

13. Excessive Parental Pressure (10)

A. The client has viewed parents as placing excessive or unrealistic pressure on the client to achieve academic success.

B. The parents acknowledged that they have placed excessive or unrealistic pressure on the client to achieve academic success.

C. The parents denied placing excessive or unrealistic pressure on the client to achieve; instead, they attributed the client's lowered academic performance to lack of motivation and effort.

D. The client reported that parents have decreased the amount of pressure they placed on the client to achieve academic success.

E. The parents have established realistic expectations of the client's level of capabilities.

14. Family History of Academic Problems (11)

A. The client and parents described a family history of academic problems and failures.

B. The client's parents have demonstrated little interest or involvement in the client's schoolwork or activities.

C. The client expressed a desire for parents to show greater interest and involvement in schoolwork or activities.

D. The parents verbalized a willingness to show greater interest in and to become more involved in the client's schoolwork or activities.

E. The parents have sustained an active interest and involvement in the client's schoolwork and have implemented several effective interventions to help the client achieve academic goals.

15. Environmental Stress (12)

A. The client's academic performance has markedly declined since experiencing stressors within personal and/or family life.

B. The client's academic performance has decreased since the family moved and the client changed schools.

C. The client has not been able to invest sufficient time or energy in schoolwork because of having to deal with environmental stressors.

D. The client has begun to manage stress more effectively so that they have more time and energy to devote to schoolwork.

E. The client's academic performance has improved since resolving or finding effective ways to cope with environmental stressors.

INTERVENTIONS IMPLEMENTED

1. Establish Rapport (1)*

A. Caring was conveyed to the client through support, warmth, and empathy.

B. The client was provided with nonjudgmental support and a level of trust was developed.

---

*The numbers in parentheses correlate to the number of the Therapeutic Intervention statement in the companion chapter with the same title in the *Child Psychotherapy Treatment Planner*, Sixth Edition, by Jongsma, Peterson, McInnis, & Bruce (Wiley, 2023).

C. The client was urged to feel safe in expressing academic issues.

D. The client began to express feelings more freely as rapport and trust level have increased.

E. The client has continued to experience difficulty being open and direct about the expression of painful feelings; the client was encouraged to use the safe haven of therapy to express these difficult issues.

2. Focus on Strengthening Therapeutic Relationship (2)

A. The relationship with the client was strengthened using empirically supported factors.

B. The relationship with the client was strengthened through the implementation of collaborative approach, agreement on goals, demonstration of empathy, verbalization of positive regard, and collection of client feedback.

C. The client reacted positively to the relationship-strengthening measures taken.

D. The client verbalized feeling supported and understood during therapy sessions.

E. Despite attempts to strengthen the therapeutic relationship, the client reports feeling distant and misunderstood.

F. The client has indicated that sessions are not helpful and will be terminating therapy.

3. Coordinate Psychoeducational Testing (3)

A. The client received a psychoeducational evaluation to rule out the presence of a learning disability that could be contributing to academic underachievement.

B. The client was cooperative during the psychoeducational testing and appeared motivated to do their best.

C. The client was uncooperative during the psychoeducational testing and did not appear to put forth good effort.

D. The client's resistance during the psychoeducational testing appeared to be due to feelings of insecurity and opposition to possibly receiving special education services.

E. The client, family, and school officials were provided with feedback regarding the psychoeducational evaluation.

4. Coordinate Psychological Testing for Attention-Deficit/Hyperactivity Disorder (ADHD)/ Emotional Factors (4)

A. The client received a psychological evaluation to help determine whether they have ADHD, which may be contributing to low academic performance.

B. The client received psychological testing to help determine whether emotional factors are contributing to low academic performance.

C. The client was uncooperative and resistant during the evaluation process.

D. The client approached the psychological testing in an honest, straightforward manner and was cooperative with the examiner.

E. The client, family, and school officials were provided with feedback regarding the psychological evaluation.

5. Obtain Psychosocial History (5)

A. A psychosocial assessment was completed to gather pertinent information about the client's past academic performance, developmental milestones, and family history of educational achievements and failures.

    B. The client and parents were cooperative in providing information about the client's early developmental history, school performance, and family background.

    C. A review of the client's background revealed a history of developmental delays and low academic performance.

    D. The psychosocial assessment revealed a family history of academic underachievement and failures.

    E. The psychosocial assessment revealed a history of strong expectations being placed on family members to achieve academic success.

6. Assess Level of Insight (6)

    A. The client's level of insight toward the presenting problems was assessed.

    B. The client was assessed in regard to the syntonic versus dystonic nature of their insight about the presenting problems.

    C. The client was noted to demonstrate good insight into the problematic nature of the behavior and symptoms.

    D. The client was noted to be in agreement with others' concerns and is motivated to work on change.

    E. The client was noted to be ambivalent regarding the problems described and is reluctant to address the issues as a concern.

    F. The client was noted to be resistant regarding acknowledgment of the problem areas, is not concerned about them, and has no motivation to make changes.

7. Assess for Correlated Disorders (7)

    A. The client was assessed for evidence of research-based correlated disorders.

    B. The client was assessed in regard to the level of vulnerability to suicide.

    C. The client was identified as having a comorbid disorder, and treatment was adjusted to account for these concerns.

    D. The client has been assessed for any correlated disorders, but none were found.

8. Assess for Culturally Based Confounding Issues (8)

    A. The client was assessed for age-related issues that could help to better understand their clinical presentation.

    B. The client was assessed for gender-related issues that could help to better understand their clinical presentation.

    C. The client was assessed for cultural syndromes, cultural idioms of distress, or culturally based perceived causes that could help to better understand their clinical presentation.

    D. Alternative factors have been identified as contributing to the client's currently defined "problem behavior," and these were taken into account in regard to treatment.

    E. Culturally based factors that could help to account for the client's currently defined "problem behavior" were investigated, but no significant factors were identified.

9. Assess Severity of Impairment (9)

    A. The severity of the client's impairment was assessed to determine the appropriate level of care.

B. The client was assessed in regard to impairment in social, relational, and educational endeavors.

C. It was reflected to the client that impairment appears to create mild to moderate effects on the client's functioning.

D. It was reflected to the client that impairment appears to create severe to very severe effects on the client's functioning.

E. The client was continuously assessed for the severity of impairment, as well as the efficacy and appropriateness of treatment.

10. **Assess for Pathogenic Care (10)**

A. The home, school, and community of the client were assessed for pathogenic care and concerns.

B. The client's various environments were assessed for the persistent disregard of the child's needs, repeated changes in caregivers, limited opportunities for stable attachment, harsh discipline, or other grossly inept care.

C. Pathogenic care was identified and the treatment plan included strategies for managing or correcting these concerns and protecting the child.

D. No pathogenic care was identified and this was reflected to the client and caregivers.

11. **Refer for Hearing/Vision/Medical Examination (11)**

A. The client was referred for a hearing and vision examination to rule out possible problems that may be interfering with school performance.

B. The client was referred for a medical evaluation to rule out possible health problems that may be interfering with school performance.

C. The hearing examination results revealed the presence of problems that are interfering with the client's academic performance.

D. The vision examination revealed the presence of problems that are interfering with the client's school performance.

E. The medical examination revealed the presence of health problems that are interfering with the client's school performance.

F. The client has not been evaluated for hearing, vision, or medical concerns and the parents were redirected to coordinate this evaluation.

12. **Attend Individualized Educational Planning Committee Meeting (12)**

A. The client's Individualized Educational Planning Committee (IEPC) meeting was held with the parents, teachers, and school officials to determine the client's eligibility for special education services, to design educational interventions, and to establish educational goals.

B. The recommendation was made to the IEPC that the client receive special education services to address learning problems.

C. At the IEPC meeting, it was determined that the client is not in need of special education services because they do not meet the criteria for a learning disability.

D. The IEPC meeting was helpful in identifying specific educational goals.

E. The IEPC meeting was helpful in designing several educational interventions for the client.

13. Arrange for Appropriate Classroom (13)

A. Based on the IEPC goals and recommendations, arrangements were made for the client to be moved to an appropriate classroom setting to maximize learning.

B. The client has been moved to a more appropriate classroom setting, and the benefits of this were reviewed.

C. Despite specific recommendations, the client has not been moved to a more appropriate classroom setting, and further advocacy was provided in this area.

14. Consult About Teaching Intervention Strategies (14)

A. A consultation was held with the client, parents, and school officials about designing effective teaching programs for intervention strategies that build on the client's strengths and compensate for weaknesses.

B. The client, parents, and teachers were assisted in identifying several learning or personality strengths that the client can use to improve academic performance.

C. The consultation meeting with the client, parents, and school officials identified the client's weaknesses and intervention strategies that they can use to overcome problems.

15. Assign Helpful Books (15)

A. The client's parents were instructed to read books to help the client overcome learning weaknesses or patterns of underachievement.

B. The client's parents were assigned *The Motivation Breakthrough: 6 Secrets to Turning on the Tuned-Out Child* (Lavoie), *Solve Your Child's School-Related Problems* (Martin & Greenwood-Waltman), or *How to Help Your Child with Homework* (Schumm).

C. The client's parents read the assigned material and key factors were reviewed.

D. The client's parents have not read the assigned material and were redirected to do so.

16. Arrange School Conference (16)

A. Arrangements were made for a school conference for the underachieving gifted client to identify factors contributing to underachievement, design appropriate education curriculum, identify relevant school assignments and establish reasonable educational goals.

B. A school conference for the client was held, yielding reasonable educational goals.

C. A school conference was not held for the client, and barriers to this were managed.

17. Refer to Private Learning Center (17)

A. The client was referred to a private learning center for extra tutoring in the areas of academic weakness and for assistance in improving study and test-taking skills.

B. The client reported that the extra tutoring and support provided by the private learning center have helped improve performance in the areas of academic weakness; the benefits of this improvement were reviewed.

C. The client reported that performance in the areas of academic weakness has not improved since attending the private learning center but was encouraged to continue.

D. The client reported that study and test-taking skills have improved since attending the private learning center, and the benefits of this improvement were reviewed.

E. The client's study skills and test performances have not improved since attending the private learning center, and a discussion was held about whether to continue the use of the private learning center.

18. Establish Regular Homework Routine (18)

A. The parents and client were encouraged to create a regular homework routine.

B. The parents and client were assisted in identifying factors of a regular homework routine, such as a set time to study in the same place or working with the same adults.

C. The parents and client have engaged in a regular homework routine; the benefits were highlighted, and barriers were managed.

D. The parents and client have not engaged in a regular homework routine, and they were redirected to do so.

19. Teach Study Skills (19)

A. The client was assisted in identifying a list of good locations to study.

B. The client was instructed to remove noise sources and eliminate as many distractions as possible when studying.

C. The client was instructed to outline or underline important details when studying or reviewing for tests.

D. The client was encouraged to use a tape recorder to help with studying for tests and reviewing important facts.

E. The client was instructed to take breaks in studying when they become distracted and have trouble staying focused.

20. Utilize Peer Tutor (20)

A. The recommendation was given to parents and teachers that the client be assigned a peer tutor to improve study skills and address areas of academic weakness.

B. The client verbalized a desire and willingness to work with the recommended peer tutor to improve study skills and academic performance.

C. The client expressed opposition to the idea of working with a peer tutor to improve study skills and academic performance but was encouraged to use this resource.

D. The client reported that peer tutoring has helped to improve study skills and academic performance, and the benefits of this resource were highlighted.

E. The client reported that peer tutoring has not helped to improve study skills and academic performance but was encouraged to continue.

F. The client has not taken advantage of working with and learning from the peer tutor and was redirected to use this resource.

21. Maintain Communication Between Home and School (21)

A. The parents and teachers were encouraged to maintain regular communication via phone calls or written notes regarding the client's academic progress.

B. The client's teachers were asked to send home daily or weekly progress notes informing the parents about the client's academic progress to help the client remain organized and keep up with school assignments.

C. The client was informed of their responsibility to bring home daily or weekly progress notes from school, allowing for regular communication between parents and teachers.

D. The parents were supported as they identified the consequences for the client's failure to bring home a daily or weekly progress note from school.

E. It was noted that the increased communication between teachers and parents via phone calls or regular progress notes has been a significant contributing factor to the client's improved academic performance.

F. The parents have not maintained regular contact with the child's teachers and were redirected to do so.

22. Assign Self-Monitoring Checklists (22)

A. The client was encouraged to utilize self-monitoring checklists to increase completion of school assignments and improve academic performance.

B. The client was directed to read portions of *How to Do Homework Without Throwing Up* (Romain).

C. The client reported that the use of the assigned self-monitoring checklists has helped them to become more organized and to complete school assignments on time.

D. The client's teachers were consulted about the use of self-monitoring checklists in the classroom to help with completing school and homework assignments on a regular, consistent basis.

E. Parents and teachers were instructed to use a reward system in conjunction with the self-monitoring checklists to increase the client's completion of school and homework assignments and improve academic performance.

F. The client has failed to consistently use self-monitoring checklists and as a result has continued to have trouble completing school and homework assignments; the client was encouraged to use the checklists.

23. Use Assignment Planner or Calendar (23)

A. The client was strongly encouraged to use a planner or calendar to record school and homework assignments and plan ahead for long-term assignments.

B. It was noted that the client's regular use of a planning calendar has helped with completing classroom and homework assignments on a consistent basis.

C. The client reported that the use of a planning calendar has helped with planning ahead for long-term assignments, and the client was encouraged to continue.

D. The client has failed to use a planning calendar consistently and has continued to struggle to complete school/homework assignments; the client was redirected to use this technique.

E. It was noted that the client's ADHD symptoms have contributed to failure to use a planner or calendar on a regular basis.

24. Monitor Assignment Completion (24)

A. The client's completion of school and homework assignments was monitored.

B. The "Establish a Homework Routine" program from the *Child Psychotherapy Homework Planner* (Jongsma, Peterson, McInnis, & Bruce) was used to help the client complete school and homework assignments on a consistent basis.

C. The parents and teachers were encouraged to use daily or weekly school reports from the "Establish a Homework Routine" program to help them communicate regularly about how well the client is doing at completing school and homework assignments.

D. Regular communication between the parents and teachers was noted to have helped the client to complete school and homework assignments on a consistent basis.

E. The client, parents, and teachers were encouraged to use the reward system outlined in the "Establish a Homework Routine" program to help the client complete school and homework assignments on a regular basis.

F. The reward system has helped motivate the client to complete school and homework assignments.

25. Develop Study and Recreation Schedule (25)

A. The client and parents were assisted in developing a routine schedule to help the client achieve a healthy balance between completing homework assignments and engaging in independent play or spending quality time with family and peers.

B. The client has followed the agreed-on schedule and has been able to successfully complete homework assignments and engage in independent play or spend quality time with family and peers.

C. The client has failed to consistently complete homework assignments because they have not followed the agreed-on schedule.

26. Encourage Positive Reinforcement (26)

A. The parents and teachers were encouraged to provide frequent positive reinforcement to maintain the client's interest and motivation in completing school/homework assignments.

B. The parents and teachers were challenged to look for opportunities to praise the client for being responsible or successful at school, instead of focusing on times when the client failed to behave responsibly or achieve success.

C. Today's session explored the contributing factors or underlying dynamics that prevent the parents from offering praise and positive reinforcement on a consistent basis.

27. Identify Rewards to Maintain Motivation (27)

A. The client and parents were helped to develop a list of possible rewards or positive reinforcers that would increase the client's interest and motivation to complete school assignments.

B. The client signed a written contract specifying the positive reinforcers that are contingent on completion of school assignments.

C. The rewards and positive reinforcers have helped to maintain the client's interest and motivation in completing school assignments.

D. The client and parents have not used rewards to maintain motivation and were redirected in this area.

28. Teach Test-Taking Strategies (28)

A. The client was asked to review a list of effective test-taking strategies to improve academic performance.

B. The client was encouraged to review classroom material regularly and study for tests over an extended period of time.

C. The client was instructed to read the instructions twice before responding to questions on a test.

D. The client recognized the need to recheck work to correct any careless mistakes or improve an answer; the client was praised for this helpful technique.

29. **Teach Guided Imagery or Relaxation Techniques (29)**

   A. The client was trained in the use of guided imagery and deep-muscle relaxation techniques to help reduce the level of anxiety before or during the taking of tests.

   B. The client reported a positive response to the use of guided imagery and deep-muscle relaxation techniques to help decrease anxiety before and during the taking of tests.

   C. The client appeared uncomfortable during the therapy session when being instructed on the use of guided imagery and deep-muscle relaxation techniques.

   D. The client was encouraged to continue to practice the use of guided imagery and deep-muscle relaxation techniques, even though the client reports little or no improvement in the reduction of level of anxiety or frustration since the previous therapy session.

30. **Teach Stress-Coping Strategies (30)**

   A. The client was taught guided imagery and relaxation techniques to help decrease the level of anxiety and frustration when encountering difficult or challenging school assignments.

   B. The client was encouraged to utilize positive self-talk as a means of decreasing anxiety and managing frustration when encountering difficult or challenging school assignments.

   C. The client was taught cognitive restructuring techniques to decrease anxiety and frustrations associated with schoolwork.

   D. The client reported that the use of the assigned positive coping mechanisms (e.g., relaxation techniques, positive self-talk, cognitive restructuring) has helped to decrease the level of anxiety and frustration when encountering difficult or challenging school assignments.

   E. The client reported experiencing little or no reduction in the level of anxiety or frustration through the use of the assigned relaxation techniques, positive self-talk, or cognitive restructuring.

31. **Explore Family Stress (31)**

   A. A family therapy session was held to explore the dynamics that may be contributing to the client's lowered academic performance.

   B. The family members were asked to list the stressors that have had a negative impact on the family.

   C. The family members were asked to identify the things that they would like to change within the family.

   D. The parents were supported as they acknowledged how their marital problems are creating stress for the client and agreed to seek marital counseling.

   E. The parents refused to follow through with the recommendation for marital counseling.

32. **Assign Reading Materials (32)**

   A. The client was assigned to read books that teach effective ways to deal with anxiety, frustration, or difficulty with schoolwork.

   B. The client was assigned *My Name Is Brain Brian* (Betancourt), *The Junkyard Wonders* (Polacco), or *The Flunking of Joshua T. Bates* (Shreve).

   C. The client read the assigned material and key points were processed.

   D. The client has not read the assigned material and was encouraged to try again.

33. Encourage Parental Involvement (33)

A. The parents were strongly encouraged to demonstrate regular interest in and involvement with the client's school activities and homework.

B. The parents were encouraged to attend the client's school conferences.

C. The parents were encouraged to read aloud or alongside the client on a regular basis to improve reading skills.

D. The parents were encouraged to use flashcards on a regular basis to improve the client's math skills.

E. The parents were encouraged to work with the client each school night to improve spelling abilities.

F. Despite encouragement, the parents have not become more involved in the client's schoolwork and were reminded about the necessity of this involvement.

34. Explore/Confront Unrealistic Parental Expectations (34)

A. A family therapy session was held to explore whether the parents have developed unrealistic expectations or are placing excessive pressure on the client to perform.

B. The client and parents were supported as they discussed and identified more realistic expectations about the client's academic performance.

C. The parents were confronted and challenged about placing excessive pressure on the client to achieve academic success.

D. Today's family therapy session explored the reasons why the parents have placed excessive pressure on the client to achieve academic success.

E. The client was seen individually to allow them to express thoughts and feelings about excessive pressure placed on them by parents.

F. A family therapy session was held to provide the client with an opportunity to express anger, frustration, and hurt about parents placing excessive pressure on them.

35. Encourage Parents to Set Firm Limits for Homework Refusal (35)

A. The parents were strongly encouraged to set firm, consistent limits and use natural, logical consequences for the client's refusal to do homework.

B. Positive feedback was provided as the parents identified a list of consequences to use for the client's refusal to do homework.

C. The parents reported that the client has responded positively to their limits or consequences and has begun to complete homework assignments on a regular, consistent basis; the benefits of setting limits and consequences were reviewed.

D. The client has refused to comply with parents' request to complete homework assignments, even though the parents have begun to set firm limits; the parents were encouraged to continue.

E. The parents were instructed to follow through with firm, consistent limits and not become locked into unhealthy power struggles or arguments with the client over homework each night.

F. The client was asked to repeat the rules surrounding homework to demonstrate an understanding of parents' expectations of the client.

36. Assess Parents' Overprotectiveness (36)

A. A family therapy session was conducted to explore whether the parents' overprotectiveness or infantilization of the client contributes to the client's academic underachievement.

B. The parents were helped to see how their pattern of overprotectiveness or infantilization contributes to the client's academic underachievement.

C. The client and parents were helped to recognize the secondary gain that is achieved through the parents' pattern of overindulging or infantilizing the client.

D. The parents were instructed to expect some resistance (e.g., crying, complaining, exhibiting temper outbursts) when they begin to terminate their pattern of overprotectiveness or infantilization.

E. The parents were encouraged to remain firm and follow through with consistent limits when the client tests them about doing homework.

F. The parents were helped to develop realistic expectations of the client's learning potential.

G. The client and parents were assisted in developing realistic academic goals that were in line with the client's learning potential.

37. Consult School Officials to Improve On-Task Behavior (37)

A. The therapist consulted with school officials about ways to improve the client's on-task behavior.

B. The recommendation was made that the client sit toward the front of the class or near positive peer role models to help them stay focused and on task.

C. The teachers were encouraged to call on the client often during the class to maintain the client's interest and attention.

D. The teachers were instructed to provide frequent feedback to the client to maintain interest and motivation to complete school assignments.

E. The recommendation was given to teachers to break the client's larger assignments into a series of smaller tasks.

38. Assign Reading Material on Organization and Study Skills (38)

A. The client was assigned to read material designed to improve organizational and study skills.

B. The client was instructed to read *13 Steps to Better Grades* (Silverman) to improve organizational and study skills.

C. The client's reading of *13 Steps to Better Grades* was processed in today's therapy session.

D. After reading *13 Steps to Better Grades*, the client was able to identify several positive study skills that will help them remain organized in the classroom.

E. The client has not read the information on improving organizational and study skills and was redirected to do so.

39. Reinforce Successful School Experiences (39)

A. The parents and teachers were encouraged to reinforce the client's successful school experiences.

B. The client was given the homework assignment of making one positive statement about school each day.

    C. All positive statements by the client about school were noted and reinforced.

    D. The client was helped to realize how their negativistic attitude about school interferes with the ability to establish peer friendships.

40. Record Positive Statements About School (40)

    A. The client was assigned the task of making one positive statement daily about school and either recording the statement in a journal or writing it on a sticky note to place in the kitchen or bedroom.

    B. The client was assigned the exercise "Positive Self-Statements" from the *Child Psychotherapy Homework Planner* (Jongsma, Peterson, McInnis, & Bruce).

    C. The client complied with the homework assignment to record at least one positive statement daily about school experiences.

    D. After reviewing the positive statements about school recorded in the journal, the client was encouraged to engage in similar positive behaviors that would help make school a more rewarding and satisfying experience.

    E. The client did not cooperate with the homework assignment to record at least one positive statement daily about school experiences.

41. Confront Self-Disparaging Remarks (41)

    A. The client was confronted about the self-defeating pattern of making derogatory comments about self and giving up easily when encountering difficulty with schoolwork.

    B. The client was instructed to use positive self-talk when encountering difficult or challenging tasks at school instead of making disparaging remarks about self and giving up easily.

    C. The client was directed to verbalize at least one positive self-statement around others at school.

    D. The client has not made positive self-descriptive statements around others at school and was redirected to use this positive self-talk on a regular basis.

42. Teach Self-Control Strategies (42)

    A. The client was taught deep-breathing and relaxation techniques to inhibit the impulse to act out or engage in negative attention-seeking behaviors when encountering frustration with schoolwork.

    B. The client was encouraged to use positive self-talk when encountering frustration with schoolwork instead of acting out or engaging in negative attention-seeking behaviors.

    C. The client was taught mediational self-control strategies (e.g., "stop, listen, think, and act") to inhibit the impulse to act out or engage in negative attention-seeking behaviors when encountering frustration with schoolwork.

43. Review Past Periods of Academic Success (43)

    A. The client was assisted in exploring periods of time when they completed schoolwork regularly and achieved academic success.

    B. The client was encouraged to use strategies or organizational skills similar to those used in the past to achieve academic success.

C. The client shared the realization that involvement in extracurricular or positive peer group activities increased motivation to achieve academic success.

D. The session revealed that the client was more disciplined with study habits when the client received strong family support and associated with positive peer groups.

E. The client was helped to recognize that they achieved greater academic success in the past when they scheduled routine times to complete homework.

44. **Review Past Successful Coping Strategies (44)**

A. The client was assisted in exploring other coping strategies previously used to solve other problems.

B. The client was encouraged to use coping strategies similar to those used successfully in the past to overcome current problems associated with learning.

C. The session revealed that the client overcame past learning problems when they sought extra assistance from teachers, parents, or peers.

D. The client recognized that they were more successful in completing school assignments in the past when they used a planning calendar to record homework assignments and long-term projects; the client was encouraged to return to these techniques.

45. **Identify Resource People Within School (45)**

A. The client was assisted in developing a list of resource people within the school to whom they can turn for support, assistance, or instruction when encountering difficulty or frustration with learning.

B. After identifying a list of school resource people, the client was directed to seek support at least once from one of these individuals before the next therapy session.

C. The client reported that the extra assistance they received from other individuals in the school helped with overcoming difficulty and learning new concepts or skills; the benefits of this technique were highlighted.

46. **Encourage Reward System for Independent Reading (46)**

A. The parents were encouraged to use a reward system to reinforce the client for engaging in independent reading.

B. The parents were encouraged to use the "Reading Adventure" program from the *Child Psychotherapy Homework Planner* (Jongsma, Peterson, McInnis, & Bruce) to increase the client's motivation to read on a regular basis.

C. The parents were instructed to use the reward system in the "Reading Adventure" program to reinforce the client for engaging in independent reading.

D. The parents reported that the "Reading Adventure" program has increased the client's interest and enjoyment with reading.

E. The reward system helped the client reach the goal of reading for a specific period of time each day or week.

F. The parents have not used the reward system to reinforce the client for engaging in independent reading and were directed to do so.

47. Use Individual Play Therapy (47)

A. An individual play therapy session was conducted with the client to help with working through and resolving painful emotions, core conflicts, or stressors that have impeded academic performance.

B. A psychoanalytic play therapy approach was used to explore the core conflicts that are impeding the client's academic performance.

C. The client made productive use of the individual play therapy session to express painful emotions surrounding core conflicts or significant stressors.

D. Client-centered play therapy approaches were used to help the client identify and express painful emotions surrounding the core conflicts or significant stressors that impede academic performance.

48. Use Mutual Storytelling Techniques (48)

A. The mutual storytelling technique was used to model appropriate ways for the client to manage frustration related to learning problems.

B. The mutual storytelling technique was used to show how achieving one's academic goals leads to improvements in feelings of self-worth.

C. The mutual storytelling technique was used to show the client the benefits of completing homework before engaging in social or recreational activities.

D. The client found the mutual storytelling technique to be an enjoyable way to learn how to manage frustrations related to learning problems.

E. The client created a story through the use of puppets, dolls, or stuffed animals that was noted to be reflective of feelings of insecurity and frustration about their struggles to learn.

49. Use Art Therapy Techniques (49)

A. The client was instructed to draw a variety of pictures that reflected how personal and family life would be different if the client completed homework on a regular basis.

B. After completing the drawings, the client was helped to verbalize how academic underachievements or failures have negatively affected self-esteem and family relationships.

C. The completion of the client's drawings led to a discussion about what steps the client can take to improve academic performance.

D. The client's artwork was noted to be reflective of their perception of the parents being overly critical or placing excessive pressure on the client to achieve academic success.

ADOPTION

CLIENT PRESENTATION

1. **Infant Adoption (1)***
   A. The client was adopted into the present family during infancy.
   B. The adoptive parents eagerly desired the adoption to occur directly after the client's birth.
   C. The client was 1 to 2 years old when adopted into the family.

2. **Adoption After Age 2 (2)**
   A. The client was adopted into the present family after age 2.
   B. The client was adopted into the present family after having lived with the biological family for 2 years or more.

3. **Adoption of Special-Needs Children (3)**
   A. The parents have recently adopted a special-needs child/sibset.
   B. The parents expressed feeling overwhelmed by the demands of the children.
   C. The parents asked for support and resources to assist them in coping with the special needs of the adopted child/children.
   D. The parents have gradually adjusted to, and are becoming accepting of, the special-needs child/children.

4. **Relates to Others in a Withdrawing/Rejecting Way (4)**
   A. The parents indicated that from the beginning the client has shown withdrawing and rejecting behaviors toward them.
   B. It has been observed by caregivers and professionals that the client relates in a detached manner with everyone.
   C. Evaluations have noted that the client rarely makes any eye contact and physically keeps away from others.
   D. The client has started to relate more closely with others and is allowing others to get physically closer.

5. **Hoarding or Gorging Food (5)**
   A. The parents have discovered that the client has stashes of food in various hiding places in their bedroom.
   B. It has been observed that the client eats quickly to ensure that they can get more.
   C. The parents reported that the client often eats so much that they become physically sick.
   D. The client has been seen sneaking food at home and school to save for eating at a later time.

---

* The numbers in parentheses correlate to the number of the Behavioral Definition statement in the companion chapter with the same title in the *Child Psychotherapy Treatment Planner*, Sixth Edition, by Jongsma, Peterson, McInnis, & Bruce (Wiley, 2023).

E. The parents indicated that the client now eats more normal amounts of food and no longer hides food for later consumption.

6. **Aggressive Behaviors (6)**
   A. Records of the client reflected a long, clear history of aggressive acts toward siblings, peers, and caregivers.
   B. The parents indicated that they are dealing on a daily basis with the client's aggressive actions toward siblings, peers, and themselves.
   C. School officials have reported intervening with the client on a frequent basis for aggressive actions toward peers.
   D. The client showed little, if any, concern about aggressive behaviors.
   E. The client has reduced aggressive behaviors toward siblings, peers, and parents.

7. **Frequent Lying (7)**
   A. The parents reported that the client frequently lies about everything.
   B. It has been observed by teachers and caregivers that the client often lies even when there is no obvious reason for doing so.
   C. The client's record reflected that they often lie about their behavior.
   D. The client shows little remorse when caught in a lie.
   E. The client's frequency of lying has decreased and is now showing remorse when caught in a lie.

8. **Stealing Unneeded Items (7)**
   A. Records reflect that the client has a history of stealing.
   B. On several occasions, the client has been caught stealing items that they don't need.
   C. The client acknowledged not having a reason or explanation for stealing.
   D. The client has stopped stealing.

9. **Becomes Friendly Too Quickly (8)**
   A. The parents report that the client quickly becomes too friendly and affectionate with any adult.
   B. The client has rapidly become very friendly and affectionate with the therapist.
   C. The client has been observed becoming very friendly and somewhat affectionate with strangers they meet in public places.
   D. The client has stopped being overly friendly and affectionate with strangers.

10. **Parental Frustration with Child's Development and Achievement Level (9)**
   A. The parents expressed frustration with the child's level of achievement and development.
   B. The parents expressed unrealistic expectations of where they felt the child should be in terms of development.
   C. The parents expressed disappointment about the child's achievement level and noted that they had expected much more from the child.
   D. The parents have worked to adjust their expectations of the child to more realistic levels.

11. Parents Anxious/Fearful of Client's Adoption Questions (10)

A. The parents have voiced anxiety and fear about the client raising questions about being adopted.

B. The parents have sought advice from numerous experts on how to handle an adopted child's questions regarding their background.

C. The parents have looked for ways to avoid, ignore, or shut down the client's inquisitiveness about their background.

D. The parents have become more comfortable and less anxious and fearful about the client's questions concerning their background.

E. The parents have developed reasonable responses to the possible future questions of the client regarding the adoption, and this preparation has reduced their concern in this area.

12. History of Adverse Childhood Experiences (11)

A. The client has an identified history of multiple adverse childhood experiences.

B. The client has identified the symptoms they experience related to adverse childhood experiences.

C. The client has been involved in processing their history of adverse childhood experiences.

D. The client has experienced relief from symptoms related to adverse childhood experiences.

INTERVENTIONS IMPLEMENTED

1. Establish Rapport (1)*

A. Caring was conveyed to the client through support, warmth, and empathy.

B. The client was provided with nonjudgmental support and a level of trust was developed.

C. The client was urged to feel safe in expressing concerns related to adoption.

D. The client began to express feelings more freely as rapport and trust level have increased.

E. The client has continued to experience difficulty being open and direct about the expression of painful feelings; the client was encouraged to use the safe haven of therapy to express these difficult issues.

2. Focus on Strengthening Therapeutic Relationship (2)

A. The relationship with the client was strengthened using empirically supported factors.

B. The relationship with the client was strengthened through the implementation of collaborative approach, agreement on goals, demonstration of empathy, verbalization of positive regard, and collection of client feedback.

C. The client reacted positively to the relationship-strengthening measures taken.

---

*The numbers in parentheses correlate to the number of the Therapeutic Intervention statement in the companion chapter with the same title in the *Child Psychotherapy Treatment Planner*, Sixth Edition, by Jongsma, Peterson, McInnis, & Bruce (Wiley, 2023).

D. The client verbalized feeling supported and understood during therapy sessions.

E. Despite attempts to strengthen the therapeutic relationship, the client reports feeling distant and misunderstood.

F. The client has indicated that sessions are not helpful and will be terminating therapy.

3. **Conduct Psychosocial Assessment (3)**

   A. The parents and their child(ren) participated in a psychosocial assessment.

   B. All parties cooperated fully in the psychosocial assessment, providing in detail all of the information that was requested.

   C. The parents were generally cooperative with the psychosocial assessment but the information they provided was lacking in detail.

   D. The parents' barriers to providing information were confronted, addressed, and resolved.

4. **Conduct Trauma-Specific Evaluation (4)**

   A. A trauma-specific evaluation was conducted with the client and parents to obtain a more complete picture of the number of traumas experienced and how they have impacted the client.

   B. The *Adverse Childhood Experiences Questionnaire (A.C.E.)* was conducted as a portion of this evaluation.

   C. The rationale for the *A.C.E.* was accepted by the client and parents.

   D. The *A.C.E.* was not completed due to lack of information provided by the client and parents.

5. **Conduct Psychological Evaluation (5)**

   A. A psychological evaluation was conducted with the client to assess behavioral/emotional functioning, cognitive style, and intelligence.

   B. The client cooperated fully in all areas of the evaluation.

   C. The parent's questions about the need for a psychological assessment were addressed and answered to their satisfaction.

   D. The psychological evaluation was only partially completed due to lack of the client's cooperation.

6. **Assess Level of Insight (6)**

   A. The client's level of insight toward the presenting problems was assessed.

   B. The client was assessed in regard to the syntonic versus dystonic nature of their insight about the presenting problems.

   C. The client was noted to demonstrate good insight into the problematic nature of the behavior and symptoms.

   D. The client was noted to be in agreement with others' concerns and is motivated to work on change.

   E. The client was noted to be ambivalent regarding the problems described and is reluctant to address the issues as a concern.

   F. The client was noted to be resistant regarding acknowledgment of the problem areas, is not concerned about them, and has no motivation to make changes.

7. **Assess for Correlated Disorders (7)**

    A. The client was assessed for evidence of research-based correlated disorders.

    B. The client was assessed in regard to the level of vulnerability to suicide.

    C. The client was identified as having a comorbid disorder, and treatment was adjusted to account for these concerns.

    D. The client has been assessed for any correlated disorders, but none were found.

8. **Assess for Culturally Based Confounding Issues (8)**

    A. The client was assessed for age-related issues that could help to better understand their clinical presentation.

    B. The client was assessed for gender-related issues that could help to better understand their clinical presentation.

    C. The client was assessed for cultural syndromes, cultural idioms of distress, or culturally based perceived causes that could help to better understand their clinical presentation.

    D. Alternative factors have been identified as contributing to the client's currently defined "problem behavior," and these were taken into account in regard to their treatment.

    E. Culturally based factors that could help to account for the client's currently defined "problem behavior" were investigated, but no significant factors were identified.

9. **Assess Severity of Impairment (9)**

    A. The severity of the client's impairment was assessed to determine the appropriate level of care.

    B. The client was assessed in regard to impairment in social, relational, and educational endeavors.

    C. It was reflected to the client that the impairment appears to create mild to moderate effects on the client's functioning.

    D. It was reflected to the client that the impairment appears to create severe to very severe effects on the client's functioning.

    E. The client was continuously assessed for the severity of impairment, as well as the efficacy and appropriateness of treatment.

10. **Assess for Pathogenic Care (10)**

    A. The home, school and community of the client were assessed for pathogenic care and concerns.

    B. The client's various environments were assessed for the persistent disregard of the child's needs, repeated changes in caregivers, limited opportunities for stable attachment, harsh discipline, or other grossly inept care.

    C. Pathogenic care was identified and the treatment plan included strategies for managing or correcting these concerns and protecting the child.

    D. No pathogenic care was identified and this was reflected to the client and caregivers.

11. **Summarize Evaluation Results (11)**

    A. Assessment results and recommendations were presented and explained to the family.

B. The family's questions regarding the assessment and recommendations were clarified and addressed.

C. The parents were asked to make a verbal commitment to follow through on all of the recommendations that evolved from the assessment.

D. The parents' reluctance to verbally commit to following through on the recommendations was explored, processed, and resolved.

E. The parents were monitored for follow-through on recommendations generated from the evaluation.

F. The client's parents have not followed through on the recommendations, and the reasons for this were identified and resolved.

12. Assess Unresolved Infertility Grief (12)

A. The parents' unresolved grief associated with their infertility was assessed.

B. The grief assessment indicated that the parents have worked through most of the issues related to their infertility.

C. The grief assessment revealed that the parents have many unresolved issues surrounding their infertility, and they were given a referral to a counselor who specializes in these issues.

D. The referral of the parents for grief counseling was monitored for their follow-through and for their overall satisfaction with the service provided.

E. The parents reported many positive outcomes from the grief counseling.

F. The parents have not availed themselves of grief counseling for infertility issues and were reminded about this resource.

13. Establish a Wellness Plan for Family (13)

A. The purpose and benefits of establishing and following through with a wellness plan were explained to the family.

B. A wellness plan was developed with the family, and the parents were asked to make a verbal commitment to implementing it.

C. The family was monitored for implementation of the wellness plan, with redirection being given as needed.

D. The family has actively participated in each of their quarterly wellness checkups.

14. Refer Parents to Skills-Based Marital Program (14)

A. The possible gains for parents of attending a program to strengthen their marriage were identified and explored.

B. The parents were referred to a skills-based marital program that teaches personal responsibility, communication skills, and conflict resolution (e.g., "PREP" in *Fighting for Your Marriage* by Markman et al.).

C. The parents' follow-through on completing the recommended marriage enrichment program was monitored, and positive gains were reinforced.

D. The parents completed the recommended marital program and indicated they gained many new skills that have improved their marital relationship.

E. The parents' dropping out of the recommended marriage enrichment program was addressed and processed.

15. **Assign Book on Parent Communication (15)**

   A. The parents were assigned to read *Peaceful Parents—Happy Kids* (Markham).

   B. The parents discussed key concepts learned from the assigned reading and identified one idea to implement into their daily life.

   C. Parents were reinforced and supported for implementing one idea from the assigned reading.

   D. Parents were redirected to attempt one new idea from the assigned reading.

16. **Explain Attunement (16)**

   A. The client and parents were provided with education on the concept of attunement.

   B. The client and parents were taught the value of attunement for their family, such as understanding, concern, and closeness.

   C. The client and parents were willing to learn more about attunement.

   D. The client and parents were uninterested in attunement concepts.

17. **Conduct Attunement Exercise (17)**

   A. The family was invited to participate in an attunement exercise in which the therapist taps out three notes that each family member replicates in turn.

   B. The family found usefulness in this exercise, and this was repeated at the start of all family sessions.

   C. The family did not find the attunement exercise to be useful and would not participate in this.

18. **Provide Brain Development Psychoeducation (18)**

   A. The family was provided with psychoeducation on how the brain develops and works.

   B. The family displayed an understanding of how the brain develops and works, and affect management skills were introduced.

   C. The family struggled with understanding of how the brain develops and works and were provided with remedial feedback.

19. **Provide Psychoeducation on Triggers (19)**

   A. The family was provided with psychoeducation on "triggers."

   B. The family displayed an understanding of the concept of "triggers" and processed how these relate to impulsive actions.

   C. The family struggled with understanding the concept of "triggers" and were provided with remedial feedback.

20. **Complete *Whole Brain* Exercise (20)**

   A. The client was assisted in completing an exercise from the *Whole Brain Child Workbook* (Siegel & Bryson).

   B. Ideas from the *Whole Brain Child Workbook* (Siegel & Bryson) exercise were processed and the client was able to identify one or two things learned.

   C. The client was assisted in sharing new concepts learned with parents/caregivers.

   D. The client struggled to understand new concepts and was provided with additional support.

21. **Conduct Filial Therapy Sessions (21)**

   A. The purpose of filial therapy was explained to the parents, and their involvement was solicited and encouraged.

   B. Role-playing was used with the parents to give them opportunities to practice empathetic responses to the client's angry ones.

   C. Filial-therapy sessions were conducted in which both the client and the parents took active roles.

   D. In filial sessions, parents responded empathetically to angry feelings expressed by the client.

   E. Active participation by the parents and the client in filial therapy sessions has reduced the client's level of anger and increased their bond with the parents.

22. **Conduct Psychoanalytic Play Therapy (22)**

   A. A psychoanalytic play therapy session was conducted to explore the issues, fixations, and developmental arrests that contribute to the client's acting-out behaviors.

   B. The client actively and freely participated in the psychoanalytic play therapy.

   C. Transference issues that emerged in the session were worked through to resolution.

   D. The feelings expressed in the psychoanalytic play therapy session were interpreted and connected to the client's acting-out behaviors.

   E. The client's participation in the psychoanalytic play therapy has reduced the frequency and intensity of acting-out behaviors.

   F. Despite the use of psychoanalytic play therapy, the client's frequency and intensity of acting out behaviors has not decreased.

23. **Conduct Individual Play Therapy (23)**

   A. Individual play therapy was conducted with the client to help with expressing and working through feelings of loss, neglect, and abandonment.

   B. The client actively participated in the play-therapy session.

   C. The feelings the client expressed through play were affirmed, reflected, and validated.

   D. The supportive environment of the play therapy has helped the client express and work through feelings of loss, neglect, and abandonment.

24. **Employ ACT Model of Play Therapy (24)**

   A. The ACT model of play therapy (Landreth) was conducted to acknowledge the client's feelings, communicate limits, and target appropriate alternatives to acting-out or aggressive behaviors.

   B. Positive verbal affirmation was given in ACT play therapy when the client displayed or verbalized appropriate alternatives to acting-out or aggressive behaviors.

   C. The client willingly and actively participated in ACT play therapy.

   D. The client's involvement in the ACT play therapy session has helped decrease the frequency and intensity of acting-out or aggressive behaviors.

   E. Despite use of the ACT model of play therapy, the client's frequency and intensity of acting-out or aggressive behavior has not decreased.

25. **Connect Painful Feelings to Acting-Out Behavior (25)**

   A. The client was helped to make key connections between painful feelings of loss, rejection, and abandonment and acting-out and/or aggressive behaviors.

   B. Verbal praise and affirmation were given to the client for each connection made between feelings and behaviors.

   C. The client's progress in connecting painful feelings and behaviors has helped to reduce the frequency of acting-out behaviors.

   D. The client has not connected painful feelings to acting-out behavior and was provided with tentative interpretations in this area.

26. **Use Puppets to Tell Loss Story (26)**

   A. A story of another's loss, rejection, and/or abandonment was told to the client using puppets and/or stuffed animals.

   B. The client was asked to create a story about their loss, rejection, and/or abandonment using puppets and/or stuffed animals.

   C. The client was given positive affirmation for telling the story of their loss, rejection, and/or abandonment.

   D. The feelings that the client expressed through the story were affirmed and validated.

   E. The client has been guarded about using puppets to tell the story of their loss and was encouraged and supported in this area.

27. **Assign Drawing of Self (27)**

   A. The client was assisted in drawing a self-outline on a sheet of paper and then told to fill the outline with objects and pictures that reflect what fuels acting-out behaviors.

   B. The completed self-portrait was described and explained by the client and then processed.

   C. Verbal affirmation and validation were given to the client for each connection made between what was inside them and the acting-out behaviors.

   D. The client completed the self-portrait exercise and was helped to make the connection between emotions and acting-out behaviors.

28. **Use Art Therapy Techniques (28)**

   A. Expressive art materials (e.g., Play-Doh, clay, and fingerpaints) were used with the client to create pictures and sculptures.

   B. The client's active involvement in creating pictures and sculptures has helped with expressing feelings of rage, rejection, and loss.

   C. The feelings that the client expressed through artwork were identified, reflected, and validated.

   D. The client's work with various art materials has been noted to help with beginning to express and resolve feelings of rage, rejection, and loss.

29. **Read Books on Anger Management (29)**

   A. Books on anger management were read with the client.

   B. The client was asked to read with therapist the book *Don't Rant and Rave on Wednesdays!* (Moser) and/or *A Volcano in My Tummy* (Whitehouse & Pudney) to assist in identifying ways to handle angry feelings.

C. The client was assisted in processing the various ways suggested in the book to handle angry feelings and in identifying two that they could implement in coping with angry feelings.

D. Ways to implement the identified anger management strategies were developed with the client and they committed to using them in daily life when feeling angry.

E. The client has consistently and effectively used the anger management strategies gained from the reading of anger management stories and has had fewer problems with inappropriately expressing angry feelings.

30. **Play Therapeutic Games (30)**

A. The "Talking, Feeling, and Doing" game (Gardner; available from Childswork/Childsplay) and/or the "Anger Control" game (Berg) was played with the client to help with learning to identify emotions.

B. Feelings and thoughts that were identified by the client during the game(s) were affirmed and validated.

C. The parents were given access to the game(s) and encouraged to play them at home with the client one or two times between sessions.

D. The client's active involvement in playing the therapeutic game(s) has increased their ability to identify and express thoughts and feelings.

31. **Use Feelings Chart (31)**

A. Feelings charts and cards were used with the client to increase their ability to identify specific feelings.

B. The client received positive verbal affirmation and reinforcement for identifying specific feelings during sessions.

C. The client's resistance to identifying feelings was gently confronted, addressed, and resolved.

D. Through the client's work with feelings charts and cards, they have increased their ability to identify, understand, and express feelings.

32. **Process Thoughts About Adoption (32)**

A. The client was asked to share thoughts about being adopted.

B. The client was assigned the exercise "Questions and Concerns About Being Adopted" from the *Child Psychotherapy Homework Planner* (Jongsma, Peterson, McInnis, & Bruce).

C. The client was assisted in processing thoughts and feelings about being adopted.

D. The client's expressed uncertainty about expressing thoughts and feelings about adoption was acknowledged and worked through.

33. **Read Books on Adoption (33)**

A. The client was assigned to read books on adoption.

B. The client was asked to read *How It Feels to Be Adopted* (Krementz) or *Adoption Is for Always* (Girard) and make a list of key concepts gathered from the reading.

C. The feelings the client identified with from the adoption book were processed.

D. The client was noted to have successfully worked through the feelings of rejection and abandonment and has come to see their bioparents as possibly having their best interest at heart when they released the client for adoption.

E. The client has not read *How It Feels to Be Adopted* and was redirected to do so.

34. Affirm Health of Family (34)

  A. The parents were given verbal affirmation and validation for the health and strength of the family system.

  B. The parents were educated on triangulation and undermining of authority by children and their effect on family functioning.

  C. Ways to cut off or prevent triangulation and undermining were explored, identified, and developed with the parents.

  D. The parents gained an understanding and awareness of triangulation and undermining and how to effectively counter them.

35. Refer to Support Group (35)

  A. Options for possible support groups were explored with the parents and the client.

  B. The parents and the client were given information on the various support groups and asked to make a commitment to attend one.

  C. The family questioned their need for support outside of therapy and were noncommittal about even trying one meeting.

  D. The client and parents have begun attending a support group and have reported that it has been beneficial to them.

  E. The client and parents have not attended an adoption support group and were redirected to do so.

36. Reframe Acting-Out Behaviors (36)

  A. The parents were worked with in conjoint sessions to understand the client's acting-out behavior as opportunities for them to reparent the client.

  B. The parents' barriers to accepting the acting-out behavior as opportunities to reparent were explored, addressed, and resolved.

  C. The parents were assisted in developing and implementing new interventions for the client's problem behaviors.

  D. The parents were given positive reinforcement for implementing new interventions and for their accepting reparenting opportunities.

  E. The parents have reported positive results on the client's acting-out behavior as a result of their new intervention techniques.

  F. The parents have not reframed acting-out behaviors as opportunities to reparent the child and were reminded about using this technique.

37. Assign Parents to Read Books on Adoption (37)

  A. The parents were directed to read material to increase their knowledge and understanding of adoption.

  B. The parents were asked to read *Helping Children Cope with Separation and Loss* (Jewett) and/or *Adoption Wisdom* (Russell) to increase their knowledge and understanding of adoption.

  C. The parents were encouraged to read *The Whole Life Adoption Book* (Schooler), *Why Didn't She Keep Me?* (Burlingham-Brown),or *Making Sense of Adoption* (Melina) to advance their knowledge and understanding of adoption's effects on identity.

  D. The key concepts of the parents' readings on adoption were processed and reinforced.

E. The parents' questions about adoption that were raised by their reading were discussed and answered.

F. The parents increased their knowledge and understanding of adoption from reading and processing the assigned books.

G. The parents' failure to read the suggested books on adoption was addressed and processed.

38. **Refer Parents to Internet Information (38)**

A. The parents were referred to reliable internet sites that provide information and support to adoptive parents.

B. The parents were referred to internet sites (e.g., https://adoption.com, www.adoption.about.com, www.olderchildadoptions.com, local adoption and government websites).

C. The parents have used internet sites to obtain additional information and support, and the benefits of this information were reviewed.

D. The parents have not accessed reliable internet sites for additional information and support and were reminded about this resource.

39. **Educate Parents on Affirming Client's Identity (39)**

A. The parents were educated on the importance of affirming the client's entire history.

B. The parents were assisted in listing the possible ways that they could affirm the client's entire history.

C. The parents' list for affirming the client's identity was processed and specific ways were developed to implement each suggestion on the list.

D. The parents were monitored for their implementation of the ways they developed to affirm the client's identity and were given verbal reinforcement for their consistent efforts.

E. It was noted that the client has responded very positively to the parents' affirmations of their entire history.

40. **Assign *Life Book* (40)**

A. The parents were educated on the key benefits for the client in having a *life book*.

B. The parents and the client were given instructions on how to create a *life book* and then assigned to put one together.

C. The parents were directed to use the "Create a Memory Album" exercise in the *Child Psychotherapy Homework Planner* (Jongsma, Peterson, McInnis, & Bruce).

D. The parents and the client were monitored in their completing the assignment of creating a *life book*.

E. The parents reviewed the completed *life book* with the client in order to give the client perspective and knowledge of their history; the results of this technique were reviewed.

F. The parents have not completed a *life book* and were redirected to do so.

41. **Clarify Needs and Desires (41)**

A. The client was assisted in clarifying and expressing needs and desires.

B. The client was asked to complete and process the "Three Wishes Game" or "Some Things I Would Like You to Know About Me" from the *Child Psychotherapy*

Homework Planner (Jongsma, Peterson, McInnis, & Bruce) to help with beginning to express needs and desires.

C. The completed exercise was processed with the client and verbal validation was given for each expressed need and desire.

D. The client was asked to construct and present a list of needs based on results from the exercise.

E. The client presented the needs list and received verbal recognition of each identified need.

F. The client has increased the ability to recognize and express needs and desires as a result of the exercises to express needs and desires.

42. Assign Self-Esteem Exercise (42)

A. The client was assigned a self-esteem-building exercise that develops self-knowledge, acceptance, and confidence.

B. The client was asked to complete a *SEALS+Plus* (Korb-Khara et al.) exercise directed at assisting in developing self-knowledge, acceptance, and confidence.

C. The client reported that the self-awareness exercise was helpful in building confidence.

D. The client has not followed through on completing the self-awareness exercise and was redirected to do so.

43. Process Parents' Expectations of Behavior (43)

A. The parents' expectations regarding the client's behavior and adjustment were explored, identified, and processed.

B. The parents' unrealistic expectations were confronted and modified to more realistic standards.

C. The parents' resistance to modifying certain unrealistic expectations were addressed, processed, and resolved.

D. The parents were noted to have adjusted their expectations to be more appropriate to the client's developmental level and to the adoption process.

44. Utilize Theraplay Approach (44)

A. The parents were educated in the Theraplay approach (Jernberg & Booth) to building a relationship with the client.

B. A verbal commitment was elicited from the parents to be active cotherapists using the Theraplay approach.

C. The Theraplay attachment-based approach was used as the focus of therapy to entice the client into a relationship and to steer away from intrapsychic conflicts.

D. The parents were given specific therapeutic assignments to do at home with the client between therapy sessions.

E. The parents' follow-through as co-therapists on the assignments was monitored and any needed redirection was given.

F. The Theraplay approach appears to be effective because the client has started to form a relationship with parents and with the therapist.

G. The Theraplay approach does not appear to be effective because the client has continued to act out and does not seem to be forming a better relationship with parents and therapist.

45. **Assign Parents One-on-One Play with Client (45)**

   A. The value of spending time in one-on-one daily play with the client was explored and processed with the parents.

   B. The parents were asked to commit to spending consistent one-on-one time playing with the client.

   C. A daily schedule of one-on-one time, with each parent playing with the client, was developed and implemented.

   D. The parents were monitored, encouraged, and redirected in their follow-through on one-on-one daily playtime with the client.

   E. The parents reported seeing visible gains in the client's bonding through spending daily one-on-one time with the client.

   F. The parents have not spent one-on-one time with the client and were redirected to do so.

46. **Encourage Verbal Reinforcement/Physical Affection (46)**

   A. The positive values of providing large doses of genuine verbal reinforcement and physical affection were identified with the parents.

   B. The parents were assisted in exploring ways they could give the client large doses of reinforcement or affection, and specific ways were selected for them to implement.

   C. The parents were assigned "Clear Rules, Positive Reinforcement, Appropriate Consequences" in the *Adolescent Psychotherapy Homework Planner* (Jongsma, Peterson, McInnis, & Bruce).

   D. The parents were encouraged, supported, and monitored in their efforts to provide the client with large daily doses of genuine verbal reinforcement and physical affection.

   E. The parents were reinforced for consistently providing the client with large doses of reinforcement and affection, to which the client has responded by showing signs of increased attachment.

   F. The parents have not consistently provided the client with large doses of reinforcement and affection and were redirected to do so.

47. **Discourage Negative Bioparent References (47)**

   A. The potential negative consequences of the adoptive parents making negative references about the client's bioparents were explored, identified, and processed.

   B. The parents were given instructions on how to respond to the client's questions about the bioparents.

   C. The parents were confronted when making any negative references to the bioparents.

   D. The parents were sensitized to how negative references about the bioparents adversely affect children who are adopted.

   E. The parents were provided with reinforcement as they terminated making any negative references about the client's bioparents.

48. **Answer Parents' Adoption Questions (48)**

   A. The parents were given an opportunity to raise adoption-specific concerns and questions.

   B. The parents received direction and support for each question or issue they raised.

C. The parents were given permission, encouragement, and reinforcement to ask any question and raise any issue.

D. Open opportunities for the parents to ask questions or raise issues have helped to reduce their anxiety and concerns about adoption.

49. Provide Parents with Education on Discipline (49)

A. The parents were provided with education regarding discipline methods.

B. Ways to implement the discipline that is consistent to the offense were explored with the parents.

C. The parents were recommended to read portions of *The Kazdin Method for Parenting the Defiant Child* (Kazdin).

D. The parents were recommended to read portions of *Parenting the Strong-Willed Child* (Forehand & Long).

E. The parents' implementation of the discipline system was encouraged, supported, and monitored.

F. The parents' consistent use of the discipline system has been noted to reduce the frequency and intensity of conflict with the client.

G. The parents have not consistently used the discipline system and were redirected to do so.

50. Assign *The 7 Habits of Highly Effective Families* (50)

A. The parents were asked to read *The 7 Habits of Highly Effective Families* (Covey) to obtain ideas for increasing the family's health and interconnectedness.

B. The parents' suggestions for increasing family health and bonding were processed and ways to implement them were explored and developed.

C. The parents were assisted in implementing suggestions to increase the family's health and sense of unity.

D. The parents' implementation of the suggestions gained from *The 7 Habits of Highly Effective Families* was encouraged, supported, and monitored for its effectiveness.

E. The parents' implementation of the new ideas gained from *The 7 Habits of Highly Effective Families* has been noted to be helpful in increasing the family's health and strengthening their sense of unity.

F. The parents have not implemented the new ideas from *The 7 Habits of Highly Effective Families* and were redirected to use ideas appropriate for their family.

51. Assign Parents One-on-One Time with Other Children (51)

A. The value of spending one-on-one time with each of their other children was explored with the parents and the benefits were identified and processed.

B. The parents were reinforced as they committed to spend one-on-one time with all of the children in the family.

C. A weekly schedule of parents spending one-on-one time with each child was developed and implemented.

D. The parents were monitored, encouraged, and redirected in their follow-through on spending weekly one-on-one time with all of the children in the family.

E. The parents reported seeing less conflict and attention-seeking behaviors from their children since starting to spend one-on-one time with each child, and the benefits of this improvement were reviewed.

F. The parents have not followed up on their commitment to spend one-on-one time with all of the children in the family and were redirected to do so.

52. Refer Family to Initiative Weekend (52)

A. The positive benefits of attending an initiative weekend were identified, explained, and processed with the family.

B. The parents were given information on several initiative programs and encouraged to choose one to attend.

C. The family arranged for and attended an initiative weekend.

D. The experience of a family initiative weekend was processed, with positive gains in trust and cooperation and connections being identified, confirmed, and reinforced.

E. The parents have not used a family initiative weekend and were reminded about the use of this resource.

53. Construct a Genogram (53)

A. A genogram was constructed with the family that included each member's origin and how each is connected.

B. The family was actively involved in constructing the genogram.

C. Each family member's origin and present place in the family were identified, affirmed, and validated.

D. The family work on constructing the genogram has helped each member visualize the family and how each is connected to it.

ANGER CONTROL PROBLEMS

CLIENT PRESENTATION

1. **Episodic Excessive Anger (1)***
   A. The client described a history of loss of temper in response to specific situations.
   B. The client described a history of loss of temper that dates back many years, including verbal outbursts and property destruction, typically related to specific emotional themes.
   C. As treatment has progressed, the client has reported increased control of situational episodic excessive anger.
   D. The client has had no recent incidents of episodic excessive anger.

2. **Cognitive Biases Toward Anger (2)**
   A. The client shows a pattern of cognitive biases commonly associated with anger.
   B. The client makes demanding expectations of others.
   C. The client tends to generalize labeling the targets of anger.
   D. The client tends to have anger in reaction to perceived slights.
   E. As treatment has progressed, the client displays a decrease in patterns of cognitive biases associated with anger.

3. **Evidence of Physiological Arousal (3)**
   A. The client displayed direct evidence of physiological arousal in relation to feelings of anger.
   B. The client displays indirect evidence of physiological arousal related to feelings of anger.
   C. As treatment has progressed, the client's level of physiological arousal has decreased as anger has become more managed.

4. **Angry/Tense Body Language (4)**
   A. The client presented with verbalizations of anger as well as tense, rigid muscles and glaring facial expressions.
   B. The client expressed anger with bodily signs of muscle tension, clenched fists, and refusal to make eye contact.
   C. The client appeared more relaxed, less angry, and did not exhibit physical signs of aggression.
   D. The family reported that the client has been more relaxed within the home setting and has not shown glaring looks or pounded fists on the table.

---

*The numbers in parentheses correlate to the number of the Behavioral Definition statement in the companion chapter with the same title in the *Child Psychotherapy Treatment Planner*, Sixth Edition, by Jongsma, Peterson, McInnis, & Bruce (Wiley, 2023).

5. Overreaction to Perceived Negative Circumstances (5)

A. The client seems to overreact to perceived disapproval, rejection, or criticism.

B. The client can become angry even when no disapproval, rejection, or criticism exists.

C. The client tends to have a bias toward their experience of disapproval, rejection, or criticism.

D. As treatment has progressed, the client has decreased the pattern of overreaction to disapproval, rejection, or criticism.

E. The client has decreased angry overreaction to perceived disapproval, rejection, or criticism.

6. Rationalization and Blaming (6)

A. The client has a history of projecting blame for angry outbursts or aggressive behaviors onto other people or outside circumstances.

B. The client did not accept responsibility for recent angry outbursts or aggressive behaviors.

C. The client has begun to accept greater responsibility for anger control problems and blame others less often for angry outbursts or aggressive behaviors.

D. The client verbalized an acceptance of responsibility for the poor control of anger or aggressive impulses.

E. The client expressed guilt about anger control problems and apologized to significant others for loss of control of anger.

7. Angry Outbursts (7)

A. The client has exhibited frequent angry outbursts that are out of proportion to the degree of the precipitating event.

B. The client appeared angry, hostile, and irritable during today's therapy session.

C. The client has recently exhibited several angry outbursts at home and school.

D. The client has started to show greater control of anger and does not react as quickly or intensely when angry or frustrated.

E. The client reported a significant reduction in the frequency and intensity of angry outbursts.

8. Verbally Abusive Language (8)

A. The client has a history of yelling, swearing, or becoming verbally abusive when needs go unmet or when asked to do something that the client does not want to do.

B. The client began to yell and swear during today's therapy session.

C. The frequency and intensity of the client's screaming, cursing, and use of verbally abusive language has decreased.

D. The client has begun to express feelings of anger in a controlled fashion.

E. The client has consistently demonstrated good control of anger and has not yelled or become verbally abusive toward others.

9. Physical Aggression/Violence (9)

A. The client described a history of engaging in acts of physical aggression or violence.

B. The client has recently been physically aggressive or violent.

C. The client has gradually started to develop greater control of anger and has not become involved in as many fights in the recent past.

D. The client has recently exercised good self-control and not engaged in any physically aggressive or violent behaviors.

10. Verbal Threats/Intimidation (10)

A. The client has a history of threatening or intimidating others to meet their own needs.

B. The client became verbally threatening during today's therapy session.

C. The client has continued to threaten or intimidate others at home, at school, and in the community.

D. The client reported a mild reduction in the frequency and intensity of verbal threats and acts of intimidation.

E. The client has recently displayed good anger control and reported that they have not threatened or intimidated others.

11. Destructive Behaviors (11)

A. The client described a persistent pattern of becoming destructive or throwing objects when angry or frustrated.

B. The client described incidents in which they were destructive of property.

C. The client has started to control the impulse to destroy or throw objects when angry.

D. The client reported that they have not thrown any objects or been destructive of property in the recent past.

12. Blaming/Projecting (12)

A. The client has a history of projecting the blame for angry outbursts or aggressive behaviors onto other people or outside circumstances.

B. The client did not accept responsibility for recent angry outbursts or aggressive behaviors.

C. The client has begun to accept greater responsibility for anger control problems and blames others less often for angry outbursts or aggressive behaviors.

D. The client verbalized an acceptance of responsibility for the poor control of anger or aggressive impulses.

E. The client expressed guilt about anger control problems and apologized to significant others for loss of control of anger.

13. Passive-Aggressive Behavior (13)

A. The parents and teachers described a persistent pattern of the client engaging in passive-aggressive behaviors (e.g., forgetting, pretending not to listen, dawdling, procrastinating).

B. The client verbally acknowledged that they often deliberately annoy or frustrate others through passive-aggressive behaviors.

C. The client has started to verbalize anger directly toward others instead of channeling angry or hostile feelings through passive-aggressive behaviors.

D. The client expressed feelings of anger in a direct, controlled, and respectful manner.

E. The client has recently demonstrated a significant reduction in the frequency of passive-aggressive behaviors.

14. Poor Peer Relationships (14)

A. The client's anger control problems have been a significant contributing factor to strained interpersonal relationships with peers.

B. The client has often projected the blame for interpersonal problems onto peers and refused to acknowledge how anger control problems contribute to the conflict.

C. The client has started to recognize how anger control problems interfere with the ability to establish and maintain peer friendships.

D. The client reported that effective anger control has led to improved relations with peers.

15. Feelings of Depression and Anxiety (15)

A. The client's anger control problems have often masked a deeper feeling of depression and/or anxiety.

B. The client expressed feelings of depression and anxiety about the struggles to control angry or hostile feelings.

C. The client verbally recognized how they often react with anger and aggression when beginning to feel depressed or anxious.

D. The client expressed feelings of happiness and contentment about the ability to control anger more effectively.

E. The client has taken active steps (e.g., expressed feelings of sadness to supportive individuals, faced anxiety-producing situations, socialized with positive peer groups) to reduce feelings of depression and anxiety.

16. Low Self-Esteem (15)

A. The client's angry outbursts and aggressive behaviors have often masked deeper feelings of low self-esteem, insecurity, and inadequacy.

B. The client's persistent anger control problems have resulted in development of a negative self-image and feelings of low self-esteem.

C. The client verbally recognized how angry outbursts and aggressive behaviors are often associated with feelings of inadequacy and insecurity.

D. The client expressed positive self-statements about improved ability to control anger.

E. The client has taken active steps to improve self-esteem and build a positive self-image.

INTERVENTIONS IMPLEMENTED

1. Establish Rapport (1)*

A. Caring was conveyed to the client through support, warmth, and empathy.

B. The client's concerns were closely listened to and their feelings were reflected to the client.

C. The client was provided with nonjudgmental support and a level of trust was developed.

D. The client was urged to feel safe in expressing anger issues.

---

*The numbers in parentheses correlate to the number of the Therapeutic Intervention statement in the companion chapter with the same title in the *Child Psychotherapy Treatment Planner*, Sixth Edition, by Jongsma, Peterson, McInnis, & Bruce (Wiley, 2023).

E. The client began to express feelings more freely as rapport and trust level have increased.

F. The client has continued to experience difficulty being open and direct about expression of painful feelings; the client was encouraged to use the safe haven of therapy to express these difficult issues.

2. Focus on Strengthening Therapeutic Relationship (2)

A. The relationship with the client was strengthened using empirically supported factors.

B. The relationship with the client was strengthened through the implementation of collaborative approach, agreement on goals, demonstration of empathy, verbalization of positive regard, and collection of client feedback.

C. The client reacted positively to the relationship-strengthening measures taken.

D. The client verbalized feeling supported and understood during therapy sessions.

E. Despite attempts to strengthen the therapeutic relationship, the client reports feeling distant and misunderstood.

F. The client has indicated that sessions are not helpful and will be terminating therapy.

3. Assess Anger Dynamics (3)

A. The client was assessed for various stimuli that have triggered anger.

B. The client was helped to identify situations, people, and thoughts that have triggered anger.

C. The client was assisted in identifying the thoughts, feelings, and actions that have characterized anger responses.

4. Assess Parents' Reaction to Anger (4)

A. The parents' reaction to the client's anger was assessed.

B. A focus was given to the level of reinforcement that the parents' reaction may hold for the client's anger outbursts.

C. It was reflected that the parents' reaction to the client's anger outbursts reflects some pattern of reinforcement for the client's anger.

D. It was reflected to the parents that they seemed to have steered clear of inadvertently reinforcing the client's anger.

5. Assess Parents' Consistency (5)

A. The parents' approach and consistency were assessed in regard to how they address their child's anger control problems.

B. A specific focus was held on the conflicts that may arise between parents in regard to parenting practices for the child's anger control problems.

C. Conflicts regarding the parents' approach to the child's anger control problems were identified and processed to resolution.

D. It was reflected to the parents that their approach seems to be consistent and there appear to be no significant conflicts between them arising from parenting practices.

6. Refer for Physical Examination (6)

A. The client was referred to a physician for a complete physical examination to rule out organic contributors (e.g., brain damage, tumor, elevated testosterone levels) to anger.

B. The client has complied with the physical examination, and the results were shared with the client.

C. The physical examination has identified organic contributors to poor anger control, and treatment was suggested.

D. The physical examination has not identified any organic contributors to poor anger control, and this was reflected to the client.

E. The client has not complied with the physical examination to assess organic contributors and was redirected to do so.

7. Refer/Conduct Psychological Testing (7)

A. A psychological evaluation was conducted to determine whether emotional factors or attention-deficit/hyperactivity disorder (ADHD) is contributing to the client's anger control problems.

B. The client was reinforced as they approached the psychological testing in an honest, straightforward manner and was cooperative with any requests presented to the client.

C. The client was uncooperative and resistant to engage during the evaluation process and was encouraged to comply with the testing.

D. The client was resistive during the psychological testing and refused to consider the possibility of having ADHD or any serious emotional problems; support and redirection were provided.

E. Feedback was provided to the client and parents regarding the results of the psychological testing.

8. Assess Level of Insight (8)

A. The client's level of insight toward the presenting problems was assessed.

B. The client was assessed in regard to the syntonic versus dystonic nature of their insight about the presenting problems.

C. The client was noted to demonstrate good insight into the problematic nature of the behavior and symptoms.

D. The client was noted to be in agreement with others' concerns and is motivated to work on change.

E. The client was noted to be ambivalent regarding the problems described and is reluctant to address the issues as a concern.

F. The client was noted to be resistant regarding acknowledgment of the problem areas, is not concerned about them, and has no motivation to make changes.

9. Assess for Correlated Disorders (9)

A. The client was assessed for evidence of research-based correlated disorders.

B. The client was assessed in regard to the level of vulnerability to suicide.

C. The client was identified as having a comorbid disorder, and treatment was adjusted to account for these concerns.

D. The client has been assessed for any correlated disorders, but none were found.

10. Assess for Culturally Based Confounding Issues (10)

A. The client was assessed for age-related issues that could help to better understand their clinical presentation.

   B. The client was assessed for gender-related issues that could help to better understand their clinical presentation.

   C. The client was assessed for cultural syndromes, cultural idioms of distress, or culturally based perceived causes that could help to better understand their clinical presentation.

   D. Alternative factors have been identified as contributing to the client's currently defined "problem behavior," and these were taken into account in regard to treatment.

   E. Culturally based factors that could help to account for the client's currently defined "problem behavior" were investigated, but no significant factors were identified.

11. Assess Severity of Impairment (11)

   A. The severity of the client's impairment was assessed to determine the appropriate level of care.

   B. The client was assessed in regard to impairment in social, relational, and educational endeavors.

   C. It was reflected to the client that their impairment appears to create mild to moderate effects on the client's functioning.

   D. It was reflected to the client that their impairment appears to create severe to very severe effects on the client's functioning.

   E. The client was continuously assessed for the severity of impairment, as well as the efficacy and appropriateness of treatment.

12. Assess for Pathogenic Care (12)

   A. The home, school, and community of the client were assessed for pathogenic care and concerns.

   B. The client's various environments were assessed for the persistent disregard of the child's needs, repeated changes in caregivers, limited opportunities for stable attachment, harsh discipline, or other grossly inept care.

   C. Pathogenic care was identified and the treatment plan included strategies for managing or correcting these concerns and protecting the child.

   D. No pathogenic care was identified and this was reflected to the client and caregivers.

13. Refer for Medication Evaluation (13)

   A. The client was referred to a physician for an evaluation for psychotropic medication to help in controlling the anger symptoms.

   B. The client complied with the medication evaluation referral and has attended the appointment.

   C. The client refused to attend an evaluation appointment with the physician for psychotropic medication; the client was encouraged to proceed with the evaluation as they feel capable of doing so.

14. Monitor Medication Adherence/Effectiveness (14)

   A. The issues of medication adherence and effectiveness were addressed with the parents and the client.

   B. The client's resistance to taking medication was processed and addressed.

C. Information related to the client's medication adherence and its effectiveness was communicated to the physician.

D. The client's responsible adherence with medications was verbally reinforced.

E. The client reported that the use of the psychotropic medication has been effective in reducing their experience of anger.

15. **Use Motivational Interviewing (15)**

A. Motivational interviewing techniques were used to help the client clarify their stage of motivation to change.

B. Motivational interviewing techniques were used to help move the client to the action stage in which the client agrees to learn new ways to conceptualize and manage anger.

C. The client was assisted in identifying dissatisfaction with the status quo and the benefits of making changes.

D. The client was assisted in identifying level of optimism for making changes.

16. **Challenge Lies and Blaming (16)**

A. Therapeutic care was taken while challenging statements in which the client lies and/ or blames others for their misbehaviors.

B. The client was gently confronted when having failed to accept responsibility for their actions.

C. The client was guided toward acceptance of responsibility and willingness to change anger control problems.

D. The client was reinforced for gradual acceptance of responsibility for anger control problems.

E. The client has not accepted responsibility for anger control problems and was encouraged to do so.

17. **Explore Parents' Willingness for New Techniques (17)**

A. The parents were explored in regard to their willingness to learn and implement new parenting techniques.

B. The parents were encouraged to use new techniques designed to manage their child's anger control problems.

C. The parents were reinforced for their commitment to trying new techniques to manage their child's anger control problems.

D. The parents seemed cautious about any new techniques to try to manage their child's anger control problem, and were provided with additional feedback in this area.

18. **Use Parent Management Training (18)**

A. Parent Management Training was used.

B. The parents were taught how parent and child behavioral interactions can encourage or discourage positive or negative behavior.

C. The parents were taught about how changing key elements of parent-child interactions can be used to promote positive change.

D. The parents were taught techniques as described in *Defiant Children* (Barkley), *Parent Management Training* (Kazdin), and *Handbook of Parent–Child Interaction Therapy* (Niec).

E. The parents were provided with specific examples of how prompting and reinforcing positive behaviors can be used to promote positive change.

F. The parents were provided with positive feedback for the use of Parent Management Training approaches.

G. The parents have not used the Parent Management Training approach and were redirected to do so.

19. Assign Parent-Training Manuals (19)

A. The parents were directed to read parent-training manuals.

B. The parents were directed to read *Parenting the Strong-Willed Child* (Forehand & Long) and *The Explosive Child* (Greene).

C. The parents were directed to watch videotapes demonstrating the techniques used in parent-training sessions.

D. The parents' study of pertinent parent-training media was reviewed and processed.

E. The parents have not reviewed the assigned pertinent parent-training media and were redirected to do so.

20. Teach Parents to Define Aspects of Situation (20)

A. The parents were taught how to specifically define and identify their child's problem behaviors.

B. The parents were taught how to identify their reactions to their child's behavior, and whether the reaction encourages or discourages the behavior.

C. The parents were taught to generate alternatives to their child's problem behavior.

D. Positive feedback was provided to the parents for their skill at specifically defining and identifying problem behaviors, reactions, outcomes, and alternatives.

E. The parents were provided with remedial feedback as they struggled to correctly identify their child's problem behaviors and their own reactions, responses, and alternatives.

21. Teach Consistent Parenting (21)

A. The parents were taught about how to implement key parenting practices on a consistent basis.

B. The parents were taught about establishing realistic, age-appropriate roles for their child's acceptable and unacceptable behavior.

C. The parents were taught about prompting positive behavior and use of positive reinforcement.

D. The parents were taught about clear direct instruction, time out, and other loss-of-privilege techniques for their child's problem behaviors.

E. The parents were taught about negotiation and renegotiation with children.

F. The parents were provided with positive feedback because they have been able to develop consistent parenting practices.

G. The parents have not developed consistent parenting practices and were redirected to do so.

22. Assign Home Exercises to Implement Parenting Technique (22)

A. The parents were assigned home exercises in which they implement parenting techniques and record the results of the implementation exercises.

B. The parents were assigned "Clear Rules, Positive Reinforcement, Appropriate Consequences" in the *Adolescent Therapy Homework Planner* (Jongsma, Peterson, McInnis, & Bruce).

C. The parents' implementation of homework exercises was reviewed within the session.

D. Corrective feedback was used to help develop improved, appropriate, and consistent use of skills.

E. The parents have not completed the assigned homework and were redirected to do so.

23. **Identify Positive Consequences of Anger Management (23)**

A. The client was asked to identify the positive consequences they experienced in managing anger.

B. The client was assisted in identifying positive consequences of managing anger (e.g., respect from others and self, cooperation from others, improved physical health).

C. The client was encouraged to learn new ways to conceptualize and manage anger.

24. **Use Anger Control Training (24)**

A. Anger control training was used to assist the client in reconceptualizing frustration and anger as involving different domains of response and predictable sequences.

B. The client was assisted in identifying cognitive, physiological, effective, and behavioral response domains.

C. The client was assisted in identifying stages of anger, including demanding expectations not being met leading to increased arousal and anger, leading to acting out.

D. It was emphasized to the client that anger can be managed by intervening in the domains.

25. **Teach Calming Techniques (25)**

A. The client was trained in the use of muscle relaxation, paced breathing, and calming imagery.

B. The client reported a positive response to the use of calming techniques taught to help control anger.

C. The client appeared uncomfortable and unable to relax when being instructed in the use of calming techniques.

26. **Explore Self-Talk (26)**

A. The client's self-talk that mediates angry feelings was explored.

B. The client was assessed for self-talk such as demanding expectations, reflected in "should," "must," or "have to" statements.

C. The client was assisted in identifying and challenging biases and in generating alternative self-talk that correct for the biases.

D. The client was taught about how to use correcting self-talk to facilitate a more flexible and temperate response to frustration.

E. The client was assigned "Replace Negative Thoughts with Positive Self-Talk" in the *Child Psychotherapy Homework Planner* (Jongsma, Peterson, McInnis, & Bruce).

27. **Assign Thought-Stopping Technique (27)**

A. The client was directed to implement a thought-stopping technique on a daily basis between sessions.

B. The client and parents were assigned the exercise "Thought-Stopping" from the *Adolescent Psychotherapy Homework Planner* (Jongsma, Peterson, McInnis, & Bruce).

C. The client's use of the thought-stopping technique was reviewed.

D. The client was provided with positive feedback for helpful use of the thought-stopping technique.

E. The client was provided with corrective feedback to help improve use of the thought-stopping technique.

28. Teach Assertive Communication (28)

A. The client was taught about assertive communication through instruction, modeling, and role-playing.

B. The client was assigned "Becoming Assertive" in the *Adolescent Psychotherapy Homework Planner* (Jongsma, Peterson, McInnis, & Bruce).

C. The client was referred to an assertiveness training class.

D. The client displayed increased assertiveness and was provided with positive feedback in this area.

E. The client has not increased level of assertiveness and was provided with additional feedback in this area.

29. Teach Conflict-Resolution Skills (29)

A. The client was taught conflict-resolution skills through modeling, role-playing, and behavioral rehearsal.

B. The client was taught about empathy and active listening.

C. The client was taught about "I messages," respectful communication, assertiveness without aggression, and compromise.

D. The client was assigned the "Problem-Solving Exercise" in the *Child Psychotherapy Homework Planner* (Jongsma, Peterson, McInnis, & Bruce).

E. The client was reinforced for clear understanding of the conflict-resolution skills.

F. The client displayed a poor understanding of the conflict-resolution skills and was provided with remedial feedback.

30. Construct Strategy for Managing Anger (30)

A. The client was assisted in constructing a strategy for managing anger.

B. The client was encouraged to combine somatic, cognitive, communication, problem-solving, and conflict-resolution skills relevant to needs.

C. The client was reinforced for comprehensive anger management strategy.

D. The client was redirected to develop a more comprehensive anger management strategy.

31. Select Challenging Situations for Managing Anger (31)

A. The client was provided with situations in which they may be increasingly challenged to apply new strategies for managing anger.

B. The client was asked to identify likely upcoming challenging situations for managing anger.

C. The client was urged to use strategies for managing anger in successively more difficult situations.

32. Assign Practice Exercises (32)

   A. The client was assigned a homework exercise to help practice newly learned calming, assertion, conflict-resolution, or cognitive-restructuring skills.

   B. The client's use of homework exercises was reviewed and processed, toward the goal of consolidation.

   C. The client was provided with positive feedback for mastery of homework exercises related to newly learned coping skills.

   D. The client has not participated in homework exercises to practice newly learned coping skills and was redirected to do so.

33. Monitor/Decrease Outbursts (33)

   A. The client's reports of angry outburst were monitored, toward the goal of decreasing their frequency, intensity, and duration.

   B. The client was urged to use their new anger management skills to decrease the frequency, intensity, and duration of the anger outburst.

   C. The client was assigned the "Anger Control" exercise in the *Child Psychotherapy Homework Planner* (Jongsma, Peterson, McInnis, & Bruce).

   D. The client was assigned the "Child Anger Checklist" exercise in the *Child Psychotherapy Homework Planner* (Jongsma, Peterson, McInnis, & Bruce).

   E. The client's progress in decreasing angry outbursts was reviewed.

   F. The client was reinforced for success at decreasing the frequency, intensity, and duration of anger outbursts.

   G. The client has not decreased the frequency, intensity, or duration of anger outbursts, and corrective feedback was provided.

34. Encourage Disclosure (34)

   A. The client was encouraged to discuss anger management goals with trusted persons who are likely to support their change.

   B. The client was assisted in identifying individuals who are likely to support their change.

   C. The client has reviewed anger management goals with trusted persons, and their response was processed.

   D. The client has not discussed anger management goals and was redirected to do so.

35. Conduct Parent–Child Interaction Therapy (35)

   A. Parent–Child Interaction Therapy (McNeil & Hembree-Kigin) was used to teach appropriate child behavior and parent behavior management skills.

   B. Child-directed sessions focused on teaching the child appropriate child behavior.

   C. Parent-directed sessions focused on teaching parental behavior management skills (e.g., clear commands, consistent consequences, and positive reinforcement).

36. Facilitate Parent Skills Training (36)

   A. The parents' enrollment in an evidence-based parent skills training program was facilitated.

B. The parents were referred to an evidence-based parent skills training program and key concepts were reviewed.

C. The parents have not followed up on involvement with an evidence-based parent skills training program and were redirected to do so.

37. Design Contingency/Reward System (37)

A. A reward system was developed with the client.

B. A contingency contract was developed with the client.

C. A meeting was held with school officials to help reinforce identified positive behaviors.

D. The client was encouraged to participate in the reward system/contingency contract in order to deter impulsive or rebellious behaviors.

E. Fine-tuning was done to the reward system/contingency contract in order to reinforce identified positive behaviors at home and school.

38. Explore Family Abuse History (38)

A. The client's family background was explored for a history of physical, sexual, or substance abuse that may contribute to the emergence of anger control problems.

B. The client was assisted in developing a timeline in the therapy session where they identified significant historical events, both positive and negative, that have occurred in the family.

C. The client's parents were confronted and challenged to cease physically abusive or overly punitive methods of discipline.

D. The parents were asked to identify how physically abusive or overly punitive methods of discipline negatively affect the client and siblings.

E. The parents were supported as they apologized to the client for abusive behaviors and overly harsh methods of discipline.

F. The parents were taught how aggressive discipline promotes the client's aggression and poor anger management.

G. The parents were referred to a parenting class.

39. Protect the Client from Abuse (39)

A. The physical abuse of the client was reported to the appropriate protective services agency.

B. A recommendation was made that the abuse perpetrator be removed from the home and seek treatment.

C. A recommendation was made that the client and siblings be removed from the home to ensure protection from further abuse.

D. The client and family members were supported as they identified necessary steps to take to minimize the risk of abuse occurring in the future.

E. The nonabusive parent was supported for verbalizing a commitment to protect the client and siblings from physical abuse in the future.

40. Emphasize Respect (40)

A. The client was taught about the basics of treating others respectfully.

B. The client was taught the principle of reciprocity, focusing on treating others the way that the client would wish to be treated.

C. The client was asked to conduct an experiment to treat everyone in a respectful manner for a 1-week period to see if others will reciprocate by treating the client with more respect.

D. The results of the client's experiment in treating others with respect were reviewed.

41. Use Puppets, Dolls, and Stuffed Animals (41)

A. A mutual storytelling technique using puppets, dolls, or stuffed animals was implemented to model appropriate ways to manage anger and resolve conflict.

B. The mutual storytelling technique helped the client learn effective ways to manage anger and resolve conflict.

C. The client was encouraged as they created a story through the use of puppets, dolls, or stuffed animals that reflected strong feelings of anger and aggression.

D. Games (e.g., checkers) were used to help model appropriate ways to manage anger and resolve conflict.

42. Encourage Benevolent Acts (42)

A. The client was directed to engage in three altruistic or benevolent acts.

B. The client was provided with examples of altruistic and benevolent acts (e.g., reading to a developmentally disabled student, mowing an elderly person's lawn).

C. The client's experience of using altruistic or benevolent acts was reviewed.

D. An emphasis on how the client can develop empathy and sensitivity to the needs of others through altruistic or benevolent acts was emphasized.

E. The client has not done the assigned altruistic or benevolent acts and was redirected to do so.

43. Encourage Allowing Client to Be in Charge of Tasks (43)

A. The family was encouraged to allow the client to be in charge of tasks at home.

B. Specific examples of areas in which the client might be able to be in charge of tasks at home were reviewed (e.g., preparing and cooking a special dish for a family get-together, cleaning a room, helping make a salad).

C. The family was urged to demonstrate confidence in the client's ability to act responsibly.

D. The family's experience of the client being in charge of tasks at home was reviewed and processed.

E. The family has not allowed the client to be in charge of any significant tasks at home and was redirected to do so.

44. Uncover Feelings Associated with Neglect or Abuse (44)

A. The client was given the opportunity to express feelings about past neglect, abuse, separation, or abandonment.

B. The client was instructed to draw pictures that reflect feelings about past neglect, abuse, separation, or abandonment.

C. The client was instructed to use a journal to record thoughts and feelings about past neglect, abuse, separation, or abandonment.

D. The empty-chair technique was employed to facilitate expression of feelings surrounding past neglect or abuse.

E. The client was assigned "The Lesson of Salmon Rock ... Fighting Leads to Loneliness" from the *Child Psychotherapy Homework Planner* (Jongsma, Peterson, McInnis, & Bruce).

45. Assess Marital Conflicts (45)

A. The marital dyad was assessed for possible conflict and/or triangulation that places the focus on the client's anger control problems and away from marital problems.

B. The marital dyad was assessed for possible substance abuse.

C. The parents recognized how their marital problems are creating stress for the client and agreed to pursue marital counseling.

D. The parents refused to follow through with the recommendation to pursue marital counseling.

46. Conduct Family Therapy Sessions (46)

A. Family therapy sessions were conducted to explore the dynamics that contribute to the emergence of the child's anger control problems.

B. The family therapy sessions identified several dynamics that contribute to the client's anger control problem.

C. Family dynamics were addressed within the family therapy session.

47. Employ Family-Sculpting Technique (47)

A. The family-sculpting technique was utilized within the session to help gain greater insight into the roles and behaviors of each family member.

B. The client and family members were assisted in using the family-sculpting technique to identify positive changes they would like to see take place in the family.

C. The family-sculpting technique was noted to reveal how the client perceives the parents as being distant and unavailable.

48. Challenge Disengaged Parent Involvement (48)

A. The disengaged parent was challenged to spend more time with the client in leisure, school, or work activities.

B. The client was supported as they verbalized the need to spend greater time with the disengaged parent.

C. Today's therapy session explored the factors contributing to the distant relationship between the client and the disengaged parent.

D. The disengaged parent was reinforced for verbalizing a commitment to spend increased time with the client.

E. The client and the disengaged parent were assisted in developing a list of activities that they would both enjoy doing together.

F. The disengaged parent has not regularly increased the level of involvement with the client and was reminded of their commitment to do so.

ANXIETY

CLIENT PRESENTATION

1. **Excessive Worry (1)***
   A. The client presented for the session upset and worried about recent events.
   B. The client was upset and worried to the point where they could not be easily settled down by the therapist.
   C. The client was able to work on the core issues that have caused them to be upset.
   D. The client reported having been significantly less worried and less preoccupied with anxieties in the recent past.

2. **Fearful/Urgent (1)**
   A. The client revealed a strong sense of urgency and sought any possible reassurance for their fears.
   B. The urgency surrounding the client's fear is overwhelming.
   C. The client's sense of urgency is not diminished by reassurance from the therapist.
   D. The sense of urgency that surrounds the client's fears is no longer existent, and the client no longer presses for reassurance.

3. **Restless/Tense (2)**
   A. The client was restless and tense, making it difficult to sit in session or to complete thoughts or activities.
   B. The client is becoming less tense and is now able to respond to questions attentively.
   C. The client is more relaxed and able to focus throughout the session, even when addressing issues that cause anxiety.

4. **Autonomic Hyperactivity Symptoms (3)**
   A. The client presented as being very anxious and experiencing a rapid heartbeat and shortness of breath.
   B. The client has been plagued by nausea and diarrhea brought on by anxiety, as all physical reasons have been medically ruled out.
   C. The client complained of having a dry mouth and frequently feeling dizzy.
   D. The client indicated that they have not experienced symptoms of a rapid heartbeat or shortness of breath since they started to talk about what makes them anxious.

5. **Hypervigilant (4)**
   A. The client presented in a tense, on-edge manner.
   B. The client's level of tension and anxiety was so high that they were unable to concentrate on anything and were irritable.

---

*The numbers in parentheses correlate to the number of the Behavioral Definition statement in the companion chapter with the same title in the *Child Psychotherapy Treatment Planner*, Sixth Edition, by Jongsma, Peterson, McInnis, & Bruce (Wiley, 2023).

C. The client reported sleep disturbance related to anxious worry.

D. The client's anxiety has diminished and they are significantly more relaxed.

6. Specific Fear/Phobia (5)

A. The client presented as being anxious over the specific stimulus situation to the point of being able to function only on a limited basis.

B. The client reported that the phobic anxiety gradually increased to where it now interferes with their daily life and family's life as well.

C. The client indicated having no idea of why the phobic fear has come to dominate their daily existence.

D. The client's daily ability to function has increased steadily as they have begun to face the phobic fear.

7. Parental Causes for Anxiety (6)

A. The client complained of being worried and anxious about the constant arguing of their parents.

B. The parents reported that they restrict the client's freedom and physical activity to protect the client from the dangers present today.

C. It was observed that the parents' use of excessive guilt and threats of abandonment caused worry and anxiety in the client.

D. The client indicated now feeling less anxious because their parents have stopped arguing so often.

E. The parents' relaxing their restrictions and control has reduced the client's level of worry and anxiety.

INTERVENTIONS IMPLEMENTED

1. Establish Rapport (1)*

A. Caring was conveyed to the client through support, warmth, and empathy.

B. The client was provided with nonjudgmental support and a level of trust was developed.

C. The client was urged to feel safe in expressing anxiety symptoms.

D. The client began to express feelings more freely as rapport and trust level have increased.

E. The client has continued to experience difficulty being open and direct about the expression of painful feelings; the client was encouraged to use the safe haven of therapy to express these difficult issues.

2. Focus on Strengthening Therapeutic Relationship (2)

A. The relationship with the client was strengthened using empirically supported factors.

---

*The numbers in parentheses correlate to the number of the Therapeutic Intervention statement in the companion chapter with the same title in the *Child Psychotherapy Treatment Planner*, Sixth Edition, by Jongsma, Peterson, McInnis, & Bruce (Wiley, 2023).

B. The relationship with the client was strengthened through the implementation of collaborative approach, agreement on goals, demonstration of empathy, verbalization of positive regard, and collection of client feedback.

C. The client reacted positively to the relationship-strengthening measures taken.

D. The client verbalized feeling supported and understood during therapy sessions.

E. Despite attempts to strengthen the therapeutic relationship, the client reports feeling distant and misunderstood.

F. The client has indicated that sessions are not helpful and will be terminating therapy.

3. **Assess Fear and Worry (3)**

A. An objective fear survey was administered to the client to assess the depth and breadth of their phobic fear.

B. The client was assisted in completing "Finding and Losing Your Anxiety" in the *Child Psychotherapy Homework Planner* (Jongsma, Peterson, McInnis, & Bruce).

C. The *Anxiety Disorders Interview Schedule for Children—Parent Version or Child Version* (Silverman & Albano) was used to assess the level of phobia symptoms.

D. The fear survey results indicated that the client's phobic fear is extreme and severely interferes with their life.

E. The fear survey results indicate that the client's phobic fear is moderate and occasionally interferes with daily functioning.

F. The fear survey results indicate that the client's phobic fear is mild and rarely interferes with daily functioning.

G. The results of the fear survey were reviewed with the client.

4. **Administer Client- or Parent-Report Measure (4)**

A. A client/parent-report measure was used to further assess the depth and breadth of the client's anxiety responses.

B. A parent-report measure was used to further assess the depth and breadth of the client's anxiety responses.

C. The *Revised Children's Manifest Anxiety Scale* (Reynolds & Richmond) was used to assess the depth and breadth of the client's anxiety responses.

D. The *Fear Survey Schedule for Children–Revised* (Ollendick) was used to assess the depth and breadth of the client's anxiety responses.

E. The client/parent-report measure indicated that the client's anxiety is extreme and severely interferes with their life.

F. The client/parent-report measure indicated that the client's anxiety is moderate and occasionally interferes with their life.

G. The client/parent-report measure indicated that the client's anxiety is mild and rarely interferes with their life.

5. **Assess Level of Insight (5)**

A. The client's level of insight toward the presenting problems was assessed.

B. The client was assessed in regard to the syntonic versus dystonic nature of their insight about the presenting problems.

   C. The client was noted to demonstrate good insight into the problematic nature of the behavior and symptoms.

   D. The client was noted to be in agreement with others' concerns and is motivated to work on change.

   E. The client was noted to be ambivalent regarding the problems described and is reluctant to address the issues as a concern.

   F. The client was noted to be resistant regarding acknowledgment of the problem areas, is not concerned about them, and has no motivation to make changes.

6. Assess for Correlated Disorders (6)

   A. The client was assessed for evidence of research-based correlated disorders.

   B. The client was assessed in regard to the level of vulnerability to suicide.

   C. The client was identified as having a comorbid disorder, and treatment was adjusted to account for these concerns.

   D. The client has been assessed for any correlated disorders, but none were found.

7. Assess for Culturally Based Confounding Issues (7)

   A. The client was assessed for age-related issues that could help to better understand their clinical presentation.

   B. The client was assessed for gender-related issues that could help to better understand their clinical presentation.

   C. The client was assessed for cultural syndromes, cultural idioms of distress, or culturally based perceived causes that could help to better understand their clinical presentation.

   D. Alternative factors have been identified as contributing to the client's currently defined "problem behavior," and these were taken into account in regard to treatment.

   E. Culturally based factors that could help to account for the client's currently defined "problem behavior" were investigated, but no significant factors were identified.

8. Assess Severity of Impairment (8)

   A. The severity of the client's impairment was assessed to determine the appropriate level of care.

   B. The client was assessed in regard to impairment in social, relational, and educational endeavors.

   C. It was reflected to the client that the impairment appears to create mild to moderate effects on the client's functioning.

   D. It was reflected to the client that the impairment appears to create severe to very severe effects on the client's functioning.

   E. The client was continuously assessed for the severity of impairment, as well as the efficacy and appropriateness of treatment.

9. Assess for Pathogenic Care (9)

   A. The home, school, and community of the client were assessed for pathogenic care and concerns.

B. The client's various environments were assessed for the persistent disregard of the child's needs, repeated changes in caregivers, limited opportunities for stable attachment, harsh discipline, or other grossly inept care.

C. Pathogenic care was identified and the treatment plan included strategies for managing or correcting these concerns and protecting the child.

D. No pathogenic care was identified and this was reflected to the client and caregivers.

10. Refer for Medication Evaluation (10)

A. The client was referred to a physician for an evaluation for psychotropic medication to help in controlling the anxiety symptoms.

B. The client complied with the medication evaluation and has attended the appointment.

C. The client refused to attend an evaluation appointment with the physician for psychotropic medication; the client was encouraged to proceed with the evaluation as they feel capable of doing so.

11. Monitor Medication Adherence/Effectiveness (11)

A. The issues of medication adherence and effectiveness were addressed with the parents and the client.

B. The client's resistance to taking medication was processed and addressed.

C. Information related to the client's medication adherence and its effectiveness was communicated to the physician.

D. The client's responsible adherence with medications was verbally reinforced.

E. The client reported that the use of the psychotropic medication has been effective in reducing the experience of anxiety.

12. Discuss Anxiety Cycle (12)

A. The client was taught about how anxious fears and worries typically involve excessive concern about unrealistic threats, various bodily expressions of tension, overarousal, hypervigilance, and avoidance of what is threatening.

B. The client was taught about the interrelated physiological, cognitive, emotional, and behavioral components of anxiety.

C. The client was taught about how treatment breaks the anxiety cycle by encouraging positive, corrective experiences.

D. The client was reinforced as they displayed a better understanding of the anxiety cycle of unwarranted fear and avoidance and how treatment breaks the cycle.

E. The client displayed a poor understanding of the anxiety and was provided with remedial feedback in this area.

13. Discuss Target of Treatment (13)

A. A discussion was held about how treatment targets the interrelated components of anxiety to help the client manage worry effectively.

B. The reduction of overarousal and unnecessary avoidance were emphasized as treatment targets.

C. The client displayed a clear understanding of the target of treatment and was provided with positive feedback in this area.

D. The client struggled to understand the target of treatment and was provided with specific examples in this area.

14. **Assign Reading on Anxiety (14)**

A. The parents were assigned to read psychoeducational chapters of books or treatment manuals on anxiety.

B. The client and parents were assigned to read psychoeducational sections of *The Coping C.A.T. Workbook* (Kendall & Hedtke).

C. The parents were assigned information from *Helping Your Anxious Child* (Rapee et al.).

D. The parents have read the assigned information on anxiety, and key points were reviewed.

E. The parents have not read the assigned information on anxiety and were redirected to do so.

15. **Teach Relaxation Skills (15)**

A. The client was taught relaxation skills.

B. The client was taught progressive muscle relaxation, guided imagery, and slow diaphragmatic breathing.

C. The client was taught how to discriminate better between relaxation and tension.

D. The client was taught how to apply relaxation skills to daily life.

E. The client was provided with feedback about use of relaxation skills.

16. **Assign Relaxation Homework (16)**

A. The client was assigned to do homework exercises in which they practice relaxation on a daily basis.

B. The client was assigned the "Deep Breathing Exercise" from the *Child Psychotherapy Homework Planner* (Jongsma, Peterson, McInnis, & Bruce).

C. The client was assigned "Progressive Muscle Relaxation" from the *Adolescent Psychotherapy Homework Planner* (Jongsma, Peterson, McInnis, & Bruce).

D. The client has regularly used relaxation exercises, and the helpful benefits of these exercises were reviewed.

E. The client has not regularly used relaxation exercises and was provided with corrective feedback in this area.

F. The client has used some relaxation exercises but does not find these to be helpful; the client was assisted in brainstorming how to modify these exercises to be more helpful.

17. **Assign Reading on Relaxation and Calming Strategies (17)**

A. The parents were assigned to read about progressive muscle relaxation and other calming strategies in relevant books and treatment manuals.

B. The parents were directed to read about muscle relaxation and other calming strategies in *New Directions in Progressive Relaxation Training* (Bernstein et al.).

C. The client and parents were assigned to read portions of *The Relaxation and Stress Reduction Workbook for Kids* (Shapiro & Sprague).

D. The client and parents were assigned to read portions of *The Coping C.A.T. Series* (Kendall et al.).

E. The parents have read the assigned information on progressive muscle relaxation, and key points were reviewed.

F. The parents have not read the assigned information on progressive muscle relaxation and were redirected to do so.

18. Use Biofeedback Techniques (18)

A. Biofeedback techniques were used to facilitate the client's success in learning relaxation skills.

B. The client was provided with consistent feedback about physiological responses to relaxation skill training.

C. The client was reinforced for increasing use of relaxation skills through biofeedback training.

D. The client has not increased success at learning skills through biofeedback techniques, and remedial instruction was provided.

19. Discuss Estimation Errors (19)

A. In today's session, examples were discussed about how unrealistic worry typically overestimates a probability of threats.

B. It was noted that unrealistic worry often underestimates the client's ability to manage realistic demands.

C. The client was assisted in identifying specific examples of how unrealistic worry involves estimation errors.

D. The client was reinforced for insightful identification of unrealistic worry and inappropriate estimation.

E. The client has struggled to identify estimation errors in regard to unrealistic worry and was provided with tentative examples in this area.

20. Develop Insight into Worry as Avoidance (20)

A. The client was assisted in gaining insight into how worry is a form of avoidance of a fear problem and that it creates chronic tension.

B. The client was assisted in understanding that avoidance precludes learning that fears and worries may be unwarranted, needlessly distressing, and addressable.

C. The client was reinforced for insightful understanding about how worry creates avoidance and tension.

D. The client struggled to understand the nature of worry as a form of avoidance and was provided with remedial information in this area.

21. Journal Anxiety Experiences (21)

A. The client was asked to self-monitor or journal instances where they experience anxiety.

B. The client was provided with a framework to record the intensity, concurrent thoughts, physiological sensations, and actions taken.

C. The client was assisted in reviewing their record and learning the role of cognitive appraisal in the process and the interaction of thoughts, feelings, and actions.

D. The client was able to identify repeated patterns and begin targeting therapeutic change options.

E. The client was unable to identify repeated patterns of anxiety and was provided with additional support.

22. **Identify Fearful Self-Talk (22)**

A. The client was assisted in identifying the self-talk, underlying assumptions, and schema that mediate anxiety responses.

B. The client was taught the role of fearful self-talk in precipitating emotional responses.

C. The client was reinforced as they verbalized an understanding of the biased beliefs and messages that mediate anxiety responses.

D. The client was assisted in replacing fearful self-talk with reality-based alternatives and positive self-talk that will increase self-confidence in coping with irrational fears and worries.

E. The client failed to identify fearful self-talk and was provided with tentative examples in this area.

23. **Assign Exercises on Self-Talk (23)**

A. The client was assigned homework exercises in which they identify fearful self-talk and create reality-based alternatives.

B. "Tools for Anxiety" from the *Adolescent Psychotherapy Homework Planner* (Jongsma, Peterson, McInnis, & Bruce) was assigned to help the client identify fearful self-talk.

C. The client's replacement of fearful self-talk with reality-based alternatives was critiqued.

D. The client was reinforced for successes at replacing fearful self-talk with reality-based alternatives.

E. The client was provided with corrective feedback for failure to replace fearful self-talk with reality-based alternatives.

F. The client has not completed assigned homework regarding fearful self-talk and was redirected to do so.

24. **Challenge Fears (24)**

A. The client was assisted in challenging fear or worry by examining the actual probability of the negative expectation occurring, the real consequences of it occurring, the ability to manage the likely outcome, the worst possible outcome, and the ability to accept it.

B. The client was reinforced for regular use of challenging thoughts regarding fear or worry and was provided with positive feedback in this area.

C. The client has not regularly challenged fears and worries and was redirected to do so.

25. **Read About Cognitive Restructuring of Fears (25)**

A. The parents were assigned to read and discuss about the cognitive restructuring of fears or worries in books or treatment manuals.

B. *The Coping C.A.T. Series* (Kendall et al.) was assigned to the parents to help teach about cognitive restructuring.

C. *Helping Your Anxious Child* (Rapee et al.) was assigned to the parents to help teach about cognitive restructuring.

D. Key components of cognitive restructuring were reviewed.

E. The client and parents have not done the assigned reading on cognitive restructuring and were redirected to do so.

26. **Use Worry Time (26)**

A. The client was taught about how the use of a "worry time" limits the association between worrying and environmental stimuli.

B. The client was assisted in setting a worry time and place to be implemented.

C. The client's experience of the use of worry time was processed.

D. The client has not implemented the worry time technique and was redirected to do so.

27. **Delay Worry Until Worry Time (27)**

A. The client was taught to recognize and delay worrying until the agreed-upon time and place.

B. The client was taught about skills such as thought-stopping, relaxation, and redirecting attention.

C. The client was assigned the exercise "Worry Time" from the *Adolescent Psychotherapy Homework Planner* (Jongsma, Peterson, McInnis, & Bruce).

28. **Teach Worry Time Techniques and Skills (28)**

A. During worry time, the client was asked to distinguish which worries are capable of being resolved and which are not.

B. The client was taught cognitive defusion techniques to let go of unsolvable worries.

C. The client was taught problem-solving skills to apply to solvable worries.

D. The client repeatedly used techniques and skills instead of engaging in unproductive worry and was reinforced for success.

E. The client was unable to use techniques and skills to address worries, and obstacles were problem-solved.

29. **Construct Anxiety Stimuli Hierarchy (29)**

A. The client was assisted in constructing a hierarchy of anxiety-producing situations associated with two or three spheres of worry.

B. It was difficult for the client to develop a hierarchy of stimulus situations because the causes of anxiety remain quite vague; the client was assisted in completing the hierarchy.

C. The client was successful at creating a focused hierarchy of specific stimulus situations that provoke anxiety in a gradually increasing manner; this hierarchy was reviewed.

30. **Select Initial Exposures (30)**

A. Initial exposures were selected from the hierarchy of anxiety-producing situations, with a bias toward the likelihood of being successful.

B. A plan was developed with the client for managing the symptoms that may occur during the initial exposure.

C. The client was assisted in rehearsing the plan for managing the exposure-related symptoms within their imagination.

D. Positive feedback was provided for the client's helpful use of symptom management techniques.

E. The client was redirected for ways to improve symptom management techniques.

31. Assign Imagination Exercises (31)

A. The client was asked to vividly imagine anxiety-producing situation, holding the worries in mind until the anxiety associated with them weakens.

B. The client was supported as they maintained a focus on the anxiety-producing situation until the anxiety has weakened.

C. The client was assisted in generating reality-based alternatives to the worry scenarios and these were processed within the session.

32. Assign Homework on Situational Exposures (32)

A. The client was assigned homework exercises to perform worry exposures and record the experience.

B. The client was assigned situational exposures homework from *Phobic and Anxiety Disorders in Children and Adolescents* (Ollendick & March).

C. The client was assigned "Gradually Facing a Phobic Fear" from the *Adolescent Psychotherapy Homework Planner* (Jongsma, Peterson, McInnis, & Bruce).

D. The client's use of worry exposure techniques was reviewed and reinforced.

E. The client has struggled in implementation of worry exposure technique and was provided with corrective feedback.

F. The client has not attempted to use the worry exposure techniques and was redirected to do so.

33. Develop List of Key Conflicts (33)

A. The client was asked to develop a list of key conflicts that trigger fear or worry.

B. The client's list of conflicts was processed toward resolution.

C. Problem-solving skills and assertiveness techniques were used to help the client resolve key conflicts.

D. Techniques of acceptance and cognitive restructuring were used to help the client reduce the emotional dysregulation that occurs from key conflicts.

E. The client was assigned "What Makes Me Anxious" in the *Adolescent Psychotherapy Homework Planner* (Jongsma, Peterson, McInnis, & Bruce).

F. It was noted that the client has significantly decreased fear and worry by resolving some of their key conflicts.

G. The client continues to have significant conflicts despite the use of problem-solving, assertiveness, acceptance, and cognitive-restructuring skills; the client was provided with remedial feedback in this area.

34. Assign Problem-Solving Exercise (34)

A. The client was assigned a homework exercise in which they solve a current problem.

B. The client was assigned "An Anxious Story" from the *Child Psychotherapy Homework Planner* (Jongsma, Peterson, McInnis, & Bruce).

C. The client was provided with feedback about use of the problem-solving assignment.

35. Encourage Increased Activities (35)

A. The client was encouraged to strengthen their new nonavoidant approach by using distraction from anxious thoughts through increased activities.

B. The client was encouraged to use social and academic activities to help distract from anxious thoughts.

C. The client was encouraged to use their own list of potentially rewarding experiences to use as a distraction from anxious thoughts.

D. The client was reinforced for use of distraction from anxious thoughts.

E. The client has not regularly used distraction techniques for anxious thoughts and was redirected to do so.

36. Involve Parents in Treatment (36)

A. A discussion was held with the client about the extent to which parents should be involved in treatment.

B. The parents were encouraged to participate in selective activities of the client's treatment.

37. Conduct Cognitive Behavioral Group Therapy (37)

A. Group therapy was conducted in accordance with the concepts espoused by Flannery-Schroeder and Kendall in *Cognitive Behavioral Therapy for Anxious Children* or the *Therapist Manual for Group Treatment* (Flannery-Schroeder & Kendall).

B. Cognitive behavioral group therapy was conducted in which the client was taught about the cognitive, behavioral, and emotional components of anxiety.

C. Cognitive behavioral group therapy was conducted in which the client learned and implemented skills for coping with anxiety and practiced new skills in several anxiety-provoking situations.

D. The client has actively participated in cognitive behavioral group therapy and benefits of this were reviewed.

E. The client has not actively participated in cognitive behavioral group therapy and was reminded to do so.

38. Conduct Cognitive-Behavior Family Therapy (38)

A. Cognitive-Behavioral Family Therapy was conducted in accordance with the concepts espoused by Howard et al. in *Cognitive-Behavioral Family Therapy for Anxious Children* and the *Therapist Manual for Group Treatment* (Flannery-Schroeder & Kendall).

B. Cognitive-Behavioral Family Therapy was conducted in which family members were taught about the cognitive, behavioral, and emotional components of anxiety.

C. Cognitive-Behavioral Family Therapy was conducted in which family members learned and implemented skills for coping with anxiety, practiced the new skills, and parents learned parenting skills to facilitate therapeutic progress.

39. Teach Parents Management of Child's Anxiety (39)

A. The parents were taught constructive skills for managing the child's anxiety.

B. The parents were taught about how to prompt and reward courageous behavior.

C. The parents were taught about empathetically ignoring excessive complaining and other avoidant behaviors.

D. The parents were taught about managing their own anxieties and modeling the behaviors being taught in session.

40. Conduct Family Anxiety Management Sessions (40)

A. The family was taught how to prompt and reward courageous behavior.

B. The family was taught how to empathetically ignore excessive complaining and other avoidant behaviors.

C. The family was taught to manage their own anxieties and model behavior being taught in session.

41. Differentiate Between Lapse and Relapse (41)

A. A discussion was held with the client regarding the distinction between a lapse and a relapse.

B. A lapse was associated with an initial and reversible return of symptoms, fear, or urges to avoid.

C. A relapse was associated with the decision to return to fearful and avoidant patterns.

D. The client was provided with support and encouragement as they displayed an understanding of the difference between a lapse and a relapse.

E. The client struggled to understand the difference between a lapse and a relapse and was provided with remedial feedback in this area.

42. Discuss Management of Lapse Risk Situations (42)

A. The client was assisted in identifying future situations or circumstances in which lapses could occur.

B. The session focused on rehearsing the management of future situations or circumstances in which lapses could occur.

C. The client was reinforced for appropriate use of lapse management skills.

D. The client was redirected in regard to poor use of lapse management skills.

43. Encourage Routine Use of Strategies (43)

A. The client was instructed to routinely use the strategies learned in therapy (e.g., cognitive restructuring, exposure).

B. The client was urged to find ways to build new strategies into their life as much as possible.

C. The client was reinforced as they reported ways in which they have incorporated coping strategies into their life and routine.

D. The client was redirected about ways to incorporate new strategies into their routine and life.

44. Develop a Coping Card (44)

A. The client was provided with a coping card on which specific coping strategies were listed.

B. The client was assisted in developing the coping card in order to list helpful coping strategies.

C. The client was encouraged to use the coping card when struggling with anxiety-producing situations.

45. Conduct Cognitive-Behavioral Family Therapy (45)

A. Cognitive-Behavioral Family Therapy was conducted.

B. Parents were taught about skills for managing the child's anxious behavior and to help facilitate the client's progress.

C. The client was taught anxiety management skills.

46. Use Child-Centered Play Therapy Approach (46)

A. A child-centered play therapy approach was used with the client to help work through and resolve anxiety.

B. In the child-centered play therapy session, the client's feelings were mirrored, reflected, and validated.

C. In session, the client's feelings were reflected back to the client in an affirming, non-judgmental manner to promote working through anxieties.

D. The child-centered play therapy approach has helped the client reduce and resolve most of their unconscious conflicts and core anxieties.

E. Despite the use of a child-centered play therapy approach, the client has not been able to reduce and resolve most of their unconscious conflicts and core anxieties.

47. Draw Anxious Situations (47)

A. The client was asked to draw two or three situations that generally make them anxious.

B. Active listening skills were used as the client explained and processed each picture, telling in detail what situations cause anxiety.

C. Options for handling the client's anxious feelings were explored for each of the drawings.

D. The client has tried each coping option when they encountered anxiety situations in daily life and reported reduced distress.

E. The client has not tried the coping mechanisms when encountering an anxious situation and was reminded about each of the drawings and the options available to deal with that anxiety.

48. Conduct Psychoanalytic Play Therapy (48)

A. Using a psychoanalytic play therapy approach, the client's core conflicts were identified, processed, and resolved.

B. In the psychoanalytic play therapy session, the client was allowed to take the lead and explore the sources of unconscious conflict and/or core anxieties.

C. Resistance issues that emerged in the psychoanalytic play therapy session were worked through to resolution.

D. The client's active involvement in the psychoanalytical play therapy session has helped with working through to resolution of unconscious conflicts and core anxieties.

E. Despite the use of psychoanalytic play therapy, the client has not been able to work through unconscious conflicts and core anxieties to resolution.

49. Model Positive Cognitive Responses to Anxiety (49)

A. Using puppets, the sand tray, or felts, the client was encouraged to create scenarios that provoke anxiety.

B. Support was provided as the client actively took part in creating and explaining the various scenarios that create anxiety.

C. For each scenario created by the client, a positive cognitive response was modeled that would help reduce the anxiety of the situation.

D. The positive cognitive responses modeled for the client have been put to successful use in handling situations that cause anxiety.

E. The client has not used positive cognitive messages as a response to anxiety and was redirected to use this helpful therapeutic technique.

50. Play the "My Home and Places" Game (50)

A. The "My Home and Places" game (Flood) was played with the client, who participated without resistance.

B. As the client played "My Home and Places," the client was assisted in identifying what made them anxious.

C. The client played "My Home and Places" with the therapist under duress and gave only partial and minimal responses.

51. Teach Narrative Approach to Anxiety (51)

A. The client was assigned the task of writing out the story of their anxious feelings.

B. The client was instructed to act out the story that they created about anxiety.

C. The externalized anxiety story was processed with the client after they completed acting it out.

D. The client was assisted in developing effective coping resolutions to the story that could be implemented in daily life.

E. The client was helped to identify ways to implement strategies to reduce fear in daily life.

F. The strategies developed and implemented from the narrative exercise have helped reduce the client's fear in daily life.

G. The client has not implemented strategies to reduce fear in daily life and was reminded to implement these strategies on a regular basis.

52. Focus on Anxiety-Producing Situations (52)

A. The client used storytelling techniques, drawing, and viewing pictures of anxiety-producing situations to help talk about and reduce the level of anxiety.

B. The client has gradually been able to tolerate more of the anxiety-producing situations and talk more freely about anxiety.

C. The client was given encouragement and support in exploring stories, drawing, and viewing pictures of anxiety-producing situations.

D. The client reported an increased ability to tolerate anxiety-producing situations as they occur; the benefits of this success were reviewed.

E. Despite the focus on anxiety-producing situations through storytelling techniques, drawing, and viewing pictures of anxiety-producing situations, the client's anxiety level has not been significantly reduced.

53. Utilize Mutual Storytelling Technique (53)

A. The client was encouraged to tell the story of an anxiety-producing situation utilizing a mutual storytelling technique.

B. The client readily told their story about anxiety, which was interpreted for its underlying meaning.

C. The client was told a story that used the same characters and settings as their story but woven in healthy ways to demonstrate how to handle, cope with, and resolve anxieties.

D. The client verbalized that the mutual storytelling technique was helpful in providing ways to handle and resolve anxieties.

54. Prescribe a Prediction Task (54)

A. The client was instructed to predict each night the anxiety that would bother them the next day, along with key elements that would make it a good day.

B. The experience of predicting the anxiety was processed with the client, and key elements that were part of making a good day were affirmed and reinforced.

C. A solution was formed from the data gathered by the client about elements that led to good days; this solution was assigned to the client to implement in order to increase the frequency of good days.

D. The client's active embracing of the prediction task has increased the number of good days they have had in managing anxiety.

E. The client has not embraced the prediction task and was urged to use this on a regular basis.

ATTENTION-DEFICIT/HYPERACTIVITY DISORDER (ADHD)

CLIENT PRESENTATION

1. **Short Attention Span (1)***
   - A. The parents and teachers reported that the client displays a short attention span and has difficulty staying focused for extended periods of time.
   - B. The client had trouble staying focused in today's therapy session and often switched from one topic to another.
   - C. The client remained focused and was able to discuss pertinent topics for a sufficient length of time.
   - D. The client's attention span has improved in structured settings where they receive supervision and greater individualized attention.
   - E. Both parents and teachers report that the client has consistently demonstrated good attention and concentration at home and school.

2. **Distractibility (2)**
   - A. The parents and teachers report that the client is easily distracted by extraneous stimuli and their own internal thoughts.
   - B. The client appeared highly distractible during today's therapy session and often had to be redirected to the topic being discussed.
   - C. The client often has to be redirected to tasks at home or school because of distractibility.
   - D. The client appeared less distractible and more focused during today's therapy session.
   - E. The client has appeared less distractible and more focused at home and school.

3. **Poor Listening Skills (3)**
   - A. The client has often given others the impression at home and school that they are not listening to what is being said.
   - B. The client did not appear to be listening well to the topics being discussed in today's therapy session.
   - C. The client listened well during today's therapy session.
   - D. The client has recently demonstrated improved listening skills at home and school.

4. **No Follow-Through on Instructions (4)**
   - A. The parents and teachers reported that the client does not consistently follow through on instructions.

---

*The numbers in parentheses correlate to the number of the Behavioral Definition statement in the companion chapter with the same title in the *Child Psychotherapy Treatment Planner*, Sixth Edition, by Jongsma, Peterson, McInnis, & Bruce (Wiley, 2023).

B. The client's repeated failure to follow through on instructions has interfered with the ability to complete school assignments, chores, and job responsibilities in a timely manner.

C. The client has generally been able to follow single or simple instructions but has had trouble following through on multiple, complex instructions.

D. The client has begun to demonstrate improvement in the ability to follow through on instructions.

E. The client has recently followed through on instructions from parents and teachers on a consistent basis.

5. **Incomplete Classroom/Homework Assignments (4)**

A. The client has consistently failed to complete classroom and homework assignments in a timely manner.

B. The client has often rushed through classroom work and does not fully complete assignments.

C. The client has recently demonstrated mild improvements in the ability to complete classroom and homework assignments.

D. The client has completed classroom and homework assignments on a consistent basis.

6. **Unfinished Chores (4)**

A. The client has often failed to comply with parents' requests to complete chores at home.

B. The parents reported that the client often becomes sidetracked and does not complete chores.

C. The client has demonstrated mild improvements in the ability to finish chores or household responsibilities.

D. The client has been responsible in completing chores on a consistent basis.

7. **Poor Organizational Skills (5)**

A. The client has displayed poor organizational skills and often loses or misplaces important things necessary for tasks or activities at home and school.

B. The client has a tendency to become more disorganized and impulsive in responding in unstructured settings where there is a great deal of external stimuli.

C. The client has recently taken active steps (e.g., using a planner, consulting with teachers about homework, performing homework and chores at routine times) to become more organized at home and school.

D. The client has demonstrated good organizational skills at home and school on a regular basis.

8. **Hyperactivity (6)**

A. The parents and teachers described the client as being a highly energetic and hyperactive individual.

B. The client presented with a high energy level and had difficulty sitting still for extended periods of time.

C. The client has trouble channeling high energy into constructive or sustained, purposeful activities.

D. Both parents and teachers reported a decrease in the client's level of hyperactivity.

E. The client has consistently channeled energy into constructive and purposeful activities.

9. **Restless Motor Movements (6)**

A. Both parents and teachers described the client as being highly restless and fidgety in motor movements.

B. The client was restless and fidgety in motor movements during today's therapy session.

C. The client has frequently annoyed or antagonized peers because of a difficulty in keeping their hands to themselves.

D. The client exhibited a decrease in the amount of motor activity during today's therapy session.

E. The client has demonstrated greater control of motor movements on a regular basis.

10. **Impulsivity (7)**

A. The client presents as a highly impulsive individual who seeks immediate gratification of needs and often fails to consider the consequences of their actions.

B. The client has considerable difficulty inhibiting impulses and tends to react to what is going on in the immediate environment.

C. The client has begun to take steps toward improving impulse control and to delay the need for immediate gratification.

D. The client has recently displayed good impulse control, as evidenced by an improved ability to stop and think about the possible consequences of actions before reacting.

11. **Disruptive/Attention-Seeking Behavior (8)**

A. The parents and teachers described a history of the client frequently disrupting the classroom with silly, immature, and negative attention-seeking behaviors.

B. The client has often disrupted the classroom by blurting out remarks at inappropriate times.

C. The client has started to exercise greater self-control and recently has not disrupted the classroom as much.

D. The client has demonstrated a significant reduction in the frequency of disruptive or negative attention-seeking behaviors at home and school.

12. **Angry Outbursts/Aggressive Behavior (8)**

A. The client reported a history of losing control of anger and exhibiting frequent angry outbursts or aggressive behaviors.

B. The client appeared angry and hostile during today's therapy session.

C. The client reported incidents of becoming easily angered over trivial matters.

D. The client has begun to take steps to control anger and aggressive impulses.

E. The client has recently demonstrated good control of anger and has not exhibited any major outbursts or aggressive behavior.

13. **Careless/Potentially Dangerous Behavior (9)**
    A. The client described a history of engaging in careless or potentially dangerous behavior, whereby the client shows little regard for the welfare or safety of self and others.
    B. The client's impulsivity has contributed to their propensity for engaging in careless, risky, or dangerous activity.
    C. The client verbally recognized a need to stop and think about the possible consequences of actions for self and others before engaging in risky or potentially dangerous behaviors.
    D. The client has not engaged in any recent careless or potentially dangerous behaviors.

14. **Blaming/Projecting (10)**
    A. The client has often resisted accepting responsibility for the consequences of actions and has frequently projected the blame for poor decisions or problems onto other people or outside circumstances.
    B. The client appeared defensive and made excuses or blamed others for poor decisions and behavior.
    C. The client has slowly begun to accept greater responsibility for actions and has placed the blame less often for wrongdoing on other people.
    D. The client admitted to wrongdoing and verbalized an acceptance of responsibility for actions.

15. **Low Self-Esteem (11)**
    A. The client expressed feelings of low self-esteem and inadequacy as a consequence of poor decisions and impulsive actions.
    B. The client's defensiveness and unwillingness to accept responsibility for the consequences of actions have reflected deeper feelings of low self-esteem, inadequacy, and insecurity.
    C. The client verbalized an awareness of how feelings of inadequacy contribute to an increase in disruptive and impulsive behaviors.
    D. The client verbalized positive self-descriptive statements during today's therapy session.
    E. The client has taken active steps to improve self-esteem and develop a positive self-image.

16. **Poor Social Skills (11)**
    A. The client historically has had difficulty establishing and maintaining lasting peer friendships because of poor social skills and impulsivity.
    B. The client frequently becomes entangled in interpersonal disputes because of failure to pick up on important social cues or interpersonal nuances.
    C. The client's interpersonal relationships are strained by intrusive behaviors.
    D. The client has begun to take steps (e.g., listen better, compliment others, allow others to go first) to improve social skills.
    E. The client has recently demonstrated good social skills and related well to siblings, peers, and adults on a consistent basis.

INTERVENTIONS IMPLEMENTED

1. **Establish Rapport (1)***
   A. Caring was conveyed to the client through support, warmth, and empathy.
   B. The client was provided with nonjudgmental support and a level of trust was developed.
   C. The client was urged to feel safe in expressing attention-deficit/hyperactivity disorder (ADHD) symptoms.
   D. The client began to express feelings more freely as rapport and trust level have increased.
   E. The client has continued to experience difficulty being open and direct about the expression of painful feelings; the client was encouraged to use the safe haven of therapy to express these difficult issues.

2. **Focus on Strengthening Therapeutic Relationship (2)**
   A. The relationship with the client was strengthened using empirically supported factors.
   B. The relationship with the client was strengthened through the implementation of collaborative approach, agreement on goals, demonstration of empathy, verbalization of positive regard, and collection of client feedback.
   C. The client reacted positively to the relationship-strengthening measures taken.
   D. The client verbalized feeling supported and understood during therapy sessions.
   E. Despite attempts to strengthen the therapeutic relationship, the client reports feeling distant and misunderstood.
   F. The client has indicated that sessions are not helpful and will be terminating therapy.

3. **Identify Targets (3)**
   A. The various stimuli that have triggered the client's ADHD behavior were assessed, including situations, people, and thoughts.
   B. The thoughts, feelings, and actions that have characterized the client's ADHD behaviors and their consequences were reviewed.
   C. The client was assisted in identifying target behaviors, antecedents, consequences, and the appropriate implementation of interventions.
   D. Placement of interventions was prioritized in school-based situations, and to a lesser extent, home-based and peer-based situations.
   E. Placement of interventions was prioritized in home-based situations and, to a lesser extent, school-based and peer-based situations.
   F. Placement of interventions was prioritized in peer-based situations and, to a lesser extent, home-based and school-based situations.

4. **Rule Out Alternative Conditions (4)**
   A. Alternative conditions that could cause inattention, hyperactivity, and impulsivity were reviewed.

---

* The numbers in parentheses correlate to the number of the Therapeutic Intervention statement in the companion chapter with the same title in the *Child Psychotherapy Treatment Planner*, Sixth Edition, by Jongsma, Peterson, McInnis, & Bruce (Wiley, 2023).

B. Behavioral, physical, and emotional problems were reviewed in regard to the effect on the client's inattention, hyperactivity, and impulsivity.

C. The client's level of normal developmental behavior was reviewed.

5. Obtain Psychological Testing to Assess ADHD (5)

A. A psychological evaluation was conducted to determine whether the client has ADHD, or whether emotional factors are contributing to impulsive or maladaptive behaviors.

B. The client was uncooperative during the evaluation and did not appear to put forth good effort; the client was encouraged to comply with the testing.

C. The client was cooperative during the psychoeducational evaluation and appeared motivated to do their best.

D. The examiner provided feedback on evaluation results to the client, parents, or school officials and discussed appropriate interventions.

E. The evaluation results supported the diagnosis of ADHD.

F. The evaluation revealed the presence of underlying emotional problems that contribute to the client's problems with inattentiveness, distractibility, and impulsivity.

G. The evaluation process did not reveal the presence of any learning disability, emotional problems, or ADHD that has contributed to the client's problems with attention, distractibility, or impulsivity.

6. Assess Level of Insight (6)

A. The client's level of insight toward the presenting problems was assessed.

B. The client was assessed in regard to the syntonic versus dystonic nature of their insight about the presenting problems.

C. The client was noted to demonstrate good insight into the problematic nature of the behavior and symptoms.

D. The client was noted to be in agreement with others' concerns and is motivated to work on change.

E. The client was noted to be ambivalent regarding the problems described and is reluctant to address the issues as a concern.

F. The client was noted to be resistant regarding acknowledgment of the problem areas, is not concerned about them, and has no motivation to make changes.

7. Assess for Correlated Disorders (7)

A. The client was assessed for evidence of research-based correlated disorders.

B. The client was assessed in regard to the level of vulnerability to suicide.

C. The client was identified as having a comorbid disorder, and treatment was adjusted to account for these concerns.

D. The client has been assessed for any correlated disorders, but none were found.

8. Assess for Culturally Based Confounding Issues (8)

A. The client was assessed for age-related issues that could help to better understand their clinical presentation.

B. The client was assessed for gender-related issues that could help to better understand their clinical presentation.

C. The client was assessed for cultural syndromes, cultural idioms of distress, or culturally based perceived causes that could help to better understand their clinical presentation.

D. Alternative factors have been identified as contributing to the client's currently defined "problem behavior," and these were taken into account in regard to treatment.

E. Culturally based factors that could help to account for the client's currently defined "problem behavior" were investigated, but no significant factors were identified.

9. **Assess Severity of Impairment (9)**

A. The severity of the client's impairment was assessed to determine the appropriate level of care.

B. The client was assessed in regard to impairment in social, relational, and educational endeavors.

C. It was reflected to the client that the impairment appears to create mild to moderate effects on the client's functioning.

D. It was reflected to the client that the impairment appears to create severe to very severe effects on the client's functioning.

E. The client was continuously assessed for the severity of impairment, as well as the efficacy and appropriateness of treatment.

10. **Assess for Pathogenic Care (10)**

A. The home, school, and community of the client were assessed for pathogenic care and concerns.

B. The client's various environments were assessed for the persistent disregard of the child's needs, repeated changes in caregivers, limited opportunities for stable attachment, harsh discipline, or other grossly inept care.

C. Pathogenic care was identified and the treatment plan included strategies for managing or correcting these concerns and protecting the child.

D. No pathogenic care was identified and this was reflected to the client and caregivers.

11. **Refer for Medication Evaluation (11)**

A. The client was referred for a medication evaluation to improve attention span, concentration, and impulse control.

B. The client was referred for a medication evaluation to help stabilize moods.

C. Positive feedback was provided to the client and parents as they agreed to follow through with a medication evaluation.

D. The client was strongly opposed to being placed on medication to help improve attention span and impulse control; the client's feelings were acknowledged.

12. **Monitor Medication Adherence and Effectiveness (12)**

A. The client reported that the medication has helped to improve attention, concentration, and impulse control without any side effects, and the benefits of this were reviewed.

B. The client reported little to no improvement on the medication; the client and parents were redirected to the prescriber.

C. The client has not adhered with taking medication on a regular basis and was redirected to do so.

D. The client and parents were encouraged to report any side effects of the medication to the prescribing physician or psychiatrist.

E. A consultation was held with the prescribing clinician.

13. Educate Family About ADHD (13)

A. The client's parents and siblings were educated about ADHD and its impact on individuals vulnerable to it.

B. The therapy session helped the client's parents and siblings gain a greater understanding and appreciation of the impact of ADHD.

C. The family members were given the opportunity to express their thoughts and feelings about having a child or sibling with ADHD.

14. Discuss Treatment Options (14)

A. The various treatment options available for ADHD were discussed with the client and/or parents.

B. The options regarding behavioral parent training, classroom-based behavioral management programs, peer-based programs, medication, organizational training, and self-verbalization were reviewed.

C. Pros and cons of each of the various treatment options were reviewed.

D. Risks and benefits of each treatment option were reviewed to assist the parents in making fully informed decisions.

15. Assign Parents to Read ADHD Information (15)

A. The parents were assigned reading material to increase their knowledge about symptoms of ADHD.

B. The client's parents were directed to read *Taking Charge of ADHD* (Barkley).

C. The parents were assigned to read *The ADD/ADHD Checklist* (Rief).

D. The parents were assigned to read *The Family ADHD Solution* (Bertin).

E. The parents have read the information about ADHD, and key points were processed.

F. The client's parents have not read the information about ADHD and were redirected to do so.

16. Assign Children's Books on ADHD (16)

A. The client was assigned readings to increase knowledge about ADHD and the ways to manage related behavior.

B. The client was assigned to read *Putting on the Brakes* (Quinn & Stern) to learn more about ADHD.

C. The client and parents were assigned to read *Sometimes I Drive My Mom Crazy, But I Know She's Crazy About Me* (Shapiro) to help them be more aware and accepting of the symptoms of ADHD.

D. The client was assigned to read *The ADHD Workbook for Kids* (Shapiro).

E. The reading of the book(s) on ADHD was processed.

F. The client reported having learned more effective organizational and study skills after reading *Putting on the Brakes*.

G. The client was able to identify more effective ways to control impulses after reading the children's book(s) on ADHD.

17. Explain Benefit of Behavioral Parent Management Training (17)

A. Today's session focused on how parent and child behavioral interactions can reduce the frequency of impulsive, disruptive, and negative attention-seeking behaviors and increase desired prosocial behavior.

B. The use of prompting and reinforcing positive behaviors was reviewed.

C. An emphasis was also placed on the use of clear instruction, time out, and other loss-of-privilege practices for problem behavior.

D. *The Kazdin Method for Parenting the Defiant Child* (Kazdin) was recommended to the parents.

E. *Parenting the Strong-Willed Child* (Forehand & Long) was recommended to the parents.

F. *Living with Children* (Patterson) was recommended to the parents.

18. Teach Parents to Define Aspects of Situation (18)

A. The parents were taught how to specifically define and identify their child's problem behaviors.

B. The parents were taught how to identify their reactions to their child's behavior, and whether the reaction encourages or discourages the behavior.

C. The parents were taught to generate alternatives to their child's problem behavior.

D. Positive feedback was provided to the parents for their skill at specifically defining and identifying problem behaviors, reactions, outcomes, and alternatives.

E. Parents were provided with remedial feedback as they struggled to correctly identify their child's problem behaviors and their own reactions, responses, and alternatives.

19. Teach About Functions of ADHD Behavior (19)

A. The parents were taught about the possible functions of ADHD behavior.

B. Alternative functions for ADHD behavior, such as avoidance, attention-seeking, to gain a desired object/activity, or to regulate sensory stimulation were reviewed.

C. Parents were assisted in reviewing how to test which function is being served by the behavior.

D. The parents were taught about how to use parent training methods to manage behavior depending on the function it serves.

20. Assign Home Exercises to Implement Parenting Techniques (20)

A. The parents were assigned home exercises in which they implement parenting techniques and record results of the implementation exercises.

B. The parents were assigned "Clear Rules, Positive Reinforcement, Appropriate Consequences" in the *Adolescent Psychotherapy Homework Planner* (Jongsma, Peterson, McInnis, & Bruce).

C. The parents' implementation of homework exercises was reviewed within the session.

D. Corrective feedback was used to help develop improved, appropriate, and consistent use of skills.

E. The parents have not completed the assigned homework and were redirected to do so.

21. Refer to Parent Management Training Course (21)

A. The parents were referred to a Parent Management Training course.

B. The parents have completed the Parent Management Training course and the key concepts were reviewed.

C. The parents have not used the Parent Management Training course and were redirected to do so.

22. Consult with Teachers (22)

A. Consultation was held with the client's teachers to implement strategies to improve school performance.

B. The client was assigned a seat near the teacher or in a low-distraction work area to help the client remain on task.

C. The client, teacher, and therapist agreed to use a prearranged signal to redirect the client to task when attention begins to wander.

D. The client's schedule was modified to allow for breaks between tasks or difficult assignments to help maintain attention and concentration.

E. The teachers were encouraged to obtain and provide frequent feedback to help maintain the client's attention, interest, and motivation.

F. The client was directed to arrange for a listening buddy.

23. Institute Behavioral Classroom Management Interventions (23)

A. The parents and pertinent school personnel were consulted in order to implement an age-appropriate behavioral classroom management intervention.

B. The behavioral classroom management interventions were focused to reinforcing appropriate behavior at school and at home, using time out for undesirable behavior, and a daily report card for monitoring progress.

C. The client was assigned "Getting It Done" in the *Child Psychotherapy Homework Planner* (Jongsma, Peterson, McInnis, & Bruce).

D. The behavioral classroom management program has been utilized and the benefits were reviewed.

E. The behavioral classroom management program has not been utilized and problems with this intervention were resolved.

24. Refer for Behavioral Peer Intervention (24)

A. Behavioral peer intervention as described by Pelham et al. in *Summer Treatment Programs for ADHD* was utilized.

B. Behavioral Peer Intervention was utilized that involves brief social skills training, followed by coached group play.

C. Contingency Management Systems were used as a portion of the behavioral peer intervention, including point systems and time outs.

D. Objective observations, frequency counts, and adult ratings of social behavior were used as outcome measures.

25. Model Self-Verbalization (25)

A. The client was taught the use of self-verbalization involving the use of self-statements during tasks that help them stay focused, thorough, thoughtful, and self-reinforcing.

B. Self-verbalization was modeled to the client and/or parents.

C. The client practiced self-statements such as "What is it I have to do?," "What is the next step?," "Have I completed it all?," and "I'm doing well!"

D. The client used self-statements in gradually more difficult tasks.

E. The client did not use self-statements to help stay focused and was redirected to try again.

26. Implement Organizational System (26)

A. The parents were assisted in developing an organizational system to increase the client's on-task behavior and completion of school assignments, chores, or work responsibilities.

B. The parents were encouraged to communicate regularly with the teachers through the use of notebooks or planning agendas to help the client complete school or homework on a regular, consistent basis.

C. The client and parents were encouraged to use organizational aids and strategies such as calendar, charts, and notebooks to help remind the client of when they are expected to complete chores or household responsibilities.

D. The client and parents were instructed to ask the teacher for a course syllabus and to use a calendar to plan large or long-term projects by breaking them into smaller steps.

E. The client and parents were encouraged to purchase a notebook with binders to help the client keep track of school or homework assignments.

F. The client and parents have not implemented an organizational system to increase the client's on-task behavior and were redirected to do so.

27. Develop Routine Schedule (27)

A. The client and parents were assisted in developing a routine schedule to increase the completion of school/homework assignments.

B. The client and parents were assisted in developing a list of chores for the client and identified times and dates when the chores are expected to be completed.

C. A reward system was designed to reinforce the completion of school, household, or work-related responsibilities.

D. The client was assigned "Getting It Done" in the *Child Psychotherapy Homework Planner* (Jongsma, Peterson, McInnis, & Bruce).

E. The client, parents, and the therapist signed a contingency contract specifying the consequences for success or failure in completing school assignments or household responsibilities.

F. The client and parents have not developed a routine schedule to increase the completion of school/homework assignments and were redirected to do so.

28. Teach Effective Study Skills (28)

A. The client was assisted in identifying a list of good locations for studying.

B. The client was instructed to remove noise sources and clear away as many distractions as possible when studying.

C. The client was instructed to outline or underline important details when studying or reviewing for tests.

D. The client was encouraged to use a tape recorder to help study for tests and review important facts.

E. The client was instructed to take breaks in studying when they become distracted and start to have trouble staying focused.

29. Teach Test-Taking Strategies (29)

A. The client and therapist reviewed a list of effective test-taking strategies to improve academic performance.

B. The client was encouraged to review classroom material regularly and study for tests over an extended period of time.

C. The client was instructed to read the directions twice before responding to the questions on a test.

D. The client was taught to recheck work to correct any careless mistakes or to improve an answer.

30. Assign Information About Study Skills (30)

A. The client was directed to read information about study skills to improve organizational and study skills.

B. The client was instructed to read *13 Steps to Better Grades* (Silverman) to improve organizational and study skills.

C. After reading *13 Steps to Better Grades,* the client was able to identify several positive study skills that will help the client remain organized in the classroom; these were reviewed and summarized.

D. "Establish a Homework Routine" from the *Child Psychotherapy Homework Planner* (Jongsma, Peterson, McInnis, & Bruce) was assigned to the client.

E. The client has not read the information about study skills and was redirected to do so.

31. Develop Homework Routine (31)

A. The parents were assisted in developing a routine schedule to help the client complete other responsibilities and prioritize homework.

B. The family was assigned "Establish a Homework Routine" from the *Child Psychotherapy Homework Planner* (Jongsma, Peterson, McInnis, & Bruce).

C. The client has developed a standard routine for completing responsibilities with a prioritization of homework; the client was positively reinforced for this.

D. The client has struggled to establish a routine homework schedule, while still completing other responsibilities and was provided with corrective feedback in this area.

32. Teach Self-Control Strategies (32)

A. The client was taught mediational and self-control strategies (e.g., relaxation techniques, "stop, listen, think, and act") to help delay the need for immediate gratification and inhibit impulses.

    B. The client was encouraged to use active-listening skills to delay the impulse to act out or react without considering the consequences of actions.

    C. The client was asked to identify the benefits of delaying the need for immediate gratification in favor of longer-term gains.

    D. The client was assisted in developing an action plan to achieve longer-term goals.

33. Facilitate Delay of Gratification (33)

    A. The therapy session focused on helping the parents increase the structure in the home to help the client delay needs for immediate gratification in order to achieve longer-term goals.

    B. The parents were supported as they established the rule that the client is unable to engage in social, recreational, or leisure activities until completing chores or homework.

    C. The parents were supported as they identified consequences for the client's failure to complete responsibilities; client verbalized recognition of these consequences.

    D. The client and parents were encouraged as they designed a schedule of dates and times when the client is expected to complete chores and homework.

34. Identify Periods of Good Impulse Control (34)

    A. The client was helped to identify periods when they demonstrated good impulse control in the past and engaged in significantly fewer impulsive behaviors.

    B. The client was encouraged to use coping strategies similar to those used successfully in the past to control impulses.

    C. The therapy session revealed that the client exercised greater self-control and was better behaved during periods of time when they received strong family support and affiliated with positive peer groups.

35. Teach Problem-Solving Skills (35)

    A. The client was taught effective problem-solving skills (i.e., identify the problem, brainstorm alternate solutions, select an option, implement a course of action, and evaluate) in the therapy session.

    B. The client was assigned the exercise "Problem-Solving Exercise" from the *Child Psychotherapy Homework Planner* (Jongsma, Peterson, McInnis, & Bruce).

    C. The client was encouraged to use effective problem-solving strategies to solve or overcome a problem or stressor that the client is facing.

    D. The client was given a directive to use problem-solving strategies at home or school on at least three occasions before the next therapy session.

    E. The client has not used the problem-solving strategies at home or school and was redirected to do so.

36. Teach Communication and Assertiveness Skills (36)

    A. The client was taught effective communication and assertiveness skills to learn how to solve problems and express feelings in a controlled fashion and meet needs through more constructive actions.

    B. Role-playing and modeling techniques were used to teach the client effective ways to control emotions, solve problems, and identify appropriate ways to meet needs.

C. The client was assigned "Stop, Think, and Act" in the *Child Psychotherapy Homework Planner* (Jongsma, Peterson, McInnis, & Bruce).

D. The therapeutic game "Stop, Relax, and Think" (Bridges) was played to help the client develop greater problem-solving.

E. The client identified the therapeutic game as being helpful in teaching problem-solving strategies.

F. The client was given the homework assignment to practice the problem-solving strategies that they learned from playing the therapeutic game before the next therapy session.

37. Build Communication Skills (37)

A. Instruction, modeling, and role-playing techniques were used the help build the client's general social and communication skills.

B. The client was assisted in practicing general social and communication skills.

C. The client was reinforced for increasing social and communication skills.

D. The client was redirected in areas in which they continue to struggle with communication and social skills.

38. Assign Books/Manuals of Building Social Skills (38)

A. The parents were assigned to read about general social and/or communication skills in books or treatment manuals on building social skills.

B. The client was assigned the "Social Skills" exercise in the *Child Psychotherapy Homework Planner* (Jongsma, Peterson, McInnis, & Bruce).

C. The client was assigned the exercise "Greeting Peers" from the *Child Psychotherapy Homework Planner* (Jongsma, Peterson, McInnis, & Bruce).

D. Key points from the parents' reading material were reviewed and processed.

E. The parents have not read the assigned information on social and communication skills and were redirected to do so.

39. Teach Parents to Reinforce Positive Behaviors (39)

A. The parents were encouraged to observe and record three to five positive behaviors by the client between therapy sessions.

B. The parents were encouraged to reinforce the client for engaging in positive behaviors.

C. The client was strongly encouraged to continue to engage in positive behaviors to build self-esteem, gain parents' approval, and receive affirmation from others.

40. Assign One-on-One Time with Parents (40)

A. The client and parents acknowledged that there have been many negative interactions between them in the recent past and were directed to spend one-on-one time together to provide an opportunity for positive experiences.

B. The client and parents were instructed to spend 10 to 15 minutes of daily one-on-one time together to increase the frequency of positive interactions and to help create a closer parent-child bond.

C. The parents were directed to allow the child to take the lead in selecting a task or activity during their one-on-one time together.

D. The client and parents reported that the one-on-one time together has helped them develop a closer relationship.

E. The client and parents have not spent one-on-one time together and were redirected to do so.

41. Identify Strengths or Interests (41)

A. The client was given a homework assignment to identify 5 to 10 strengths or interests.

B. The client was assigned the exercise "Show Your Strengths" from the *Child Psychotherapy Homework Planner* (Jongsma, Peterson, McInnis, & Bruce).

C. The client's interests or strengths were reviewed, and they were encouraged to use strengths or interests to establish friendships.

D. The client reported having been able to establish a greater number of friendships by using strengths and interests.

E. The client has not completed the homework related to identifying 5 to 10 strengths or interests and was redirected to do so.

42. Assign Demonstration of Empathy and Kindness (42)

A. The client was given the homework assignment of performing three altruistic or caring acts before the next therapy session to increase empathy and sensitivity to the thoughts, feelings, and needs of others.

B. The client was encouraged to volunteer in a community service organization or fundraising activity to demonstrate empathy and concern for others.

C. Feedback was provided for the client as they described altruistic acts and demonstrations of empathy and kindness.

D. The client was unable to identify any demonstrations of empathy and kindness toward others and was redirected to complete these types of tasks.

43. Identify Trigger Events to Impulsivity (43)

A. The therapy session explored the stressful events or contributing factors that frequently lead to an increase in the client's hyperactivity, impulsivity, and distractibility.

B. The client was supported as they identified the stressful events or contributing factors that have contributed to an increase in hyperactivity, impulsivity, and distractibility.

C. Role-playing and modeling techniques were used to teach appropriate ways to manage stress or resolve conflict more effectively.

D. The "stop, listen, think, and act," relaxation, and positive self-talk techniques were taught to the client in order to help manage stress more effectively.

E. The client and parents were assisted in identifying more effective coping strategies that could be used to manage stress or meet important needs instead of responding impulsively to a situation.

F. The client was unable to identify trigger events for impulsivity and was offered some examples in this area.

44. **Explore Future Stressors or Roadblocks (44)**

   A. The client was helped to explore possible stressors, roadblocks, or hurdles that might cause impulsive and acting-out behavior to increase in the future.

   B. The client was supported as they identified successful coping strategies that could be used in the future when facing similar stressful events, roadblocks, or hurdles.

   C. Guided imagery techniques were employed to help the client visualize how to solve potential problems or stressors in the future.

   D. The client was encouraged to consult and/or enlist the support of family members or significant others when facing problems or stressors in the future.

45. **Develop Coping Strategies for Relapse Risk (45)**

   A. Coping strategies were identified to assist the client and family in coping with or overcoming stressors, roadblocks, or hurdles.

   B. Techniques such as "stop, look, listen, and think," guided imagery, and utilizing "I messages" to communicate needs were identified as effective coping strategies.

46. **Refer to ADHD Parental Support Group (46)**

   A. The parents were referred to an ADHD support group to increase their understanding and knowledge of ADHD symptoms.

   B. Active listening was used as the parents verbalized that their participation in the ADHD support group has increased their understanding and knowledge of ADHD.

   C. The parents reported that they have learned new strategies for how to deal with the client's impulsive behavior through attending the ADHD support group; these were reviewed and summarized.

   D. The client's parents have not attended the ADHD parental support group and were reminded about this useful resource.

47. **Use EEG Biofeedback (47)**

   A. The client was referred for EEG Biofeedback for ADHD.

   B. EEG Biofeedback (neurotherapy) was conducted.

48. **Clarify Effects of High Energy Level (48)**

   A. The client was given a homework assignment to identify the positive and negative aspects of high energy level.

   B. The client completed assigned homework and identified the positive and negative aspects of high energy level.

   C. The client was encouraged to channel energy into healthy physical outlets and positive social activities.

AUTISM SPECTRUM DISORDER (ASD)

CLIENT PRESENTATION

1. **Aloof/Unresponsive (1)***
   A. The client presented in an aloof, unresponsive manner.
   B. The client showed virtually no interest in the counseling process or in even small interactions with the therapist.
   C. All attempts to connect with the client were met with no discernable response.
   D. The client has begun to respond in small ways to the therapist's interaction attempts.

2. **Detached/Uninterested (1)**
   A. The client presented in a detached manner with no interest in others outside of self.
   B. The parents reported that the client has a history of pervasive disinterest in other people.
   C. The client has started to acknowledge others on a somewhat consistent basis.
   D. The client has shown more interest in relating with the therapist in sessions.

3. **Social Connectedness (2)**
   A. The client has little to no interest in social relationships.
   B. The parents indicated that the client from an early age has not shown interest in friendships or other social relationships.
   C. With encouragement, the client has started to interact on a limited basis with a selected peer.
   D. The client has started to show somewhat more interest in connecting with the therapist, family members, and selected peers.

4. **Lack of Social/Emotional Spontaneity (3)**
   A. The client exhibited virtually no spontaneity in mood or behavior.
   B. The client remains unchanged in emotional presentation when others show emotion.
   C. The client has at times shown glimmers of spontaneity.

5. **Language Deficits (4)**
   A. The parents reported significant delays in the client's language development.
   B. The client has developed only a few words, at far below developmental language expectations.
   C. The client has engaged in very limited verbalizations with the therapist during sessions.
   D. There has been a slight increase in the client's skill and use of language with others.
   E. There has been a significant increase in the client's skill and use of language with others.

---

* The numbers in parentheses correlate to the number of the Behavioral Definition statement in the companion chapter with the same title in the *Child Psychotherapy Treatment Planner*, Sixth Edition, by Jongsma, Peterson, McInnis, & Bruce (Wiley, 2023).

6. Conversation Deficits (5)

A. The parents report significant delays in the client's language development.

B. The parents reported that the client has never demonstrated conversational skills with family members.

C. The parents reported that the client has given brief responses to their inquiries on occasion.

D. The parents reported slight improvements in the client's ability to initiate conversations and verbalize single-word responses to their initiatives.

7. Speech and Language Oddities (6)

A. The client presented with a variety of speech oddities (e.g., echolalia, pronominal reversal).

B. The client used metaphorical language as their primary speech pattern throughout the therapy session.

C. The client frequently echoed sounds and words heard from the therapist during the session.

D. The parents indicated that the client's language oddities have increased and intensified as the client has grown older.

E. The parents report that all their attempts, with the help of professionals, to interrupt and advance the client's speech patterns have been frustrating and nonproductive.

F. The client's speech oddities have decreased as they have started to communicate with others in a didactic manner.

8. Inflexible/Repetitive Behavior (7)

A. The parents and school officials reported that the client demonstrates an inflexible adherence to repetition of nonfunctional rituals or stereotyped motor mannerisms.

B. The parents reported that the client becomes upset if their behavioral routine is changed or interrupted.

C. The client has started to decrease repetitive behaviors and seems more open to trying some different activities.

D. The client was willing to engage in a new activity during today's therapy session.

E. The client did not exhibit stereotypical motor movements during today's therapy session.

9. Preoccupied/Focused (8)

A. The parents reported that the client appears to be preoccupied nearly all of the time and focused on narrowly selected objects or areas of interest.

B. It has been nearly impossible to intrude on the client's preoccupation or break focus.

C. The client has started to allow others to interrupt preoccupation and focus.

D. The client has recently been less focused and preoccupied with only one thing and has been open to new outside stimuli.

10. Impaired Intellectual/Cognitive Functioning (9)

A. The client exhibits marked impairments in intellectual and cognitive functioning.

B. The parents indicated that it is difficult to follow and understand the client's thought process.

C. The client's thinking has often been unaffected by the thoughts and feedback from others.

D. The client has begun to show some positive improvements in intellectual and cognitive functioning.

11. **Intellectual Variability (9)**

A. The client has demonstrated considerable variability in the level of intellectual functioning.

B. The client demonstrated severe deficits in language and verbal comprehension skills, but has shown significant advances in very focused areas.

12. **Resistance to Change (10)**

A. The client has been resistant to outside stimulation and attempts to engage the client.

B. Both parents and teachers reported that the client is very resistant to any changes in daily schedule, routine, or behaviors.

C. The client has started to tolerate small changes in routine without becoming resistant.

D. The client has recently begun to try new things with the therapist without any show of resistance.

13. **Overreaction to Change (10)**

A. The client's mood and behavior are often punctuated by angry and aggressive outbursts.

B. The client has often reacted to others with anger and aggression when they have attempted to interact or connect with the client.

C. The client has often overreacted with anger and aggression to minor changes in their routine or environment.

D. The client has recently started to react with less anger and aggression to changes in their routine or environment.

14. **Flat Affect (11)**

A. The parents reported that the client's affect often appears flat and constricted.

B. The parents reported that the client only becomes animated and spontaneous in emotional presentation on rare occasions.

C. The client has begun to show more affect in interacting with the therapist.

D. The client became animated in emotional presentation when discussing a topic of interest.

15. **Self-Abuse (12)**

A. The client has exhibited a pattern of self-abusive behaviors (e.g., head banging, hitting self).

B. The parents reported that the client becomes self-abusive when the client is frustrated.

C. The client demonstrated self-abusive behaviors in today's therapy session.

D. The client has decreased the frequency of episodes of self-abuse.

E. The client did not engage in any self-abusive behavior in today's therapy session.

INTERVENTIONS IMPLEMENTED

1. **Establish Rapport (1)***
   A. Caring was conveyed to the client through support, warmth, and empathy.
   B. The client was provided with nonjudgmental support and a level of trust was developed.
   C. The client was urged to feel safe in expressing autism symptoms.
   D. The client began to express feelings more freely as rapport and trust level have increased.
   E. The client has continued to experience difficulty being open and direct about the expression of painful feelings; the client was encouraged to use the safe haven of therapy to express these difficult issues.

2. **Focus on Strengthening Therapeutic Relationship (2)**
   A. The relationship with the client was strengthened using empirically supported factors.
   B. The relationship with the client was strengthened through the implementation of collaborative approach, agreement on goals, demonstration of empathy, verbalization of positive regard, and collection of client feedback.
   C. The client reacted positively to the relationship-strengthening measures taken.
   D. The client verbalized feeling supported and understood during therapy sessions.
   E. Despite attempts to strengthen the therapeutic relationship, the client reports feeling distant and misunderstood.
   F. The client has indicated that sessions are not helpful and will be terminating therapy.

3. **Assess Autism (3)**
   A. An initial clinical interview was held with the child and parents to assess the history of the autism.
   B. The need for additional assessments was identified and referrals were made to have these conducted.
   C. The results of the initial clinical interview indicated mild autism concerns.
   D. The results of the initial clinical interview indicated moderate autism concerns.
   E. The results of the initial clinical interview indicated severe autism concerns.

4. **Assess Cognitive and Intellectual Functioning (4)**
   A. An intellectual and cognitive assessment was conducted on the client to determine strengths and weaknesses.
   B. The client was uncooperative and resistive in the assessment process and was encouraged to be more open to the evaluation.
   C. The client was cooperative during the intellectual and cognitive assessment and appeared to put forth satisfactory to good effort.
   D. Feedback was provided to the parents and the client regarding the results of the intellectual and cognitive assessments.

---

*The numbers in parentheses correlate to the number of the Therapeutic Intervention statement in the companion chapter with the same title in the *Child Psychotherapy Treatment Planner*, Sixth Edition, by Jongsma, Peterson, McInnis, & Bruce (Wiley, 2023).

5. **Refer for Vision/Hearing Examination (5)**

   A. The client was referred for a vision and/or hearing examination to rule out problems that may be interfering with social and speech/language development.

   B. The findings from the vision examination did not reveal any problems with the client's vision, and this was reflected to the family.

   C. The findings from the hearing examination did not reveal any problems with the client's hearing, and this was reflected to the family.

   D. The vision examination revealed the presence of vision problems, and this was reflected to the family.

   E. The hearing examination revealed the presence of a hearing loss, and this was reflected to the family.

6. **Refer for Medical Examination (6)**

   A. The client was referred for a medical examination to rule out possible health problems that may be interfering with speech/language development.

   B. The parents followed through with the recommendation to seek a medical examination to rule out possible health problems that may be contributing to the client's speech/language development.

   C. The findings from the medical examination did not reveal the presence of any health problems that may be interfering with the client's speech/language development, and this was reviewed with the family.

   D. The findings from the medical examination revealed that the client's health problems and/or physical condition have interfered with speech/language development, and this was reviewed with the family.

   E. The parents have failed to follow through with seeking a medical examination and were encouraged to do so to rule out possible health problems that may be interfering with the client's speech/language development.

7. **Refer for Speech/Language Evaluation (7)**

   A. The client was referred for a speech and language evaluation.

   B. The client was praised for cooperation throughout the entire speech and language evaluation process.

   C. Because of client resistance, the speech and language evaluation could not be completed.

   D. With urging of the parents and the therapist, the client followed through with the speech and language evaluation with only minimal resistance.

   E. The results of the speech/language evaluation were shared with the client and parents.

   F. Speech/language evaluation results indicate the need for ongoing services to improve the client's speech and language abilities.

8. **Refer for Neurological/Neuropsychological Evaluation (8)**

   A. The client was referred for neuropsychological testing to rule out organic factors.

   B. The client was cooperative during the neurological evaluation or neuropsychological testing.

    C. With parental encouragement, the client followed through and completed the neurological evaluation.

    D. Neuropsychological testing could not be completed because the client was not cooperative.

    E. The parents were helped in seeing the need for neuropsychological testing.

    F. The results of the neurological evaluation or neuropsychological testing were reviewed with the client and parents.

9. **Assess Level of Insight (9)**

    A. The client's level of insight toward the presenting problems was assessed.

    B. The client was assessed in regard to the syntonic versus dystonic nature of their insight about the presenting problems.

    C. The client was noted to demonstrate good insight into the problematic nature of the behavior and symptoms.

    D. The client was noted to be in agreement with others' concerns and is motivated to work on change.

    E. The client was noted to be ambivalent regarding the problems described and is reluctant to address the issues as a concern.

    F. The client was noted to be resistant regarding acknowledgment of the problem areas, is not concerned about them, and has no motivation to make changes.

10. **Assess for Correlated Disorders (10)**

    A. The client was assessed for evidence of research-based correlated disorders.

    B. The client was assessed in regard to the level of vulnerability to suicide.

    C. The client was identified as having a comorbid disorder, and treatment was adjusted to account for these concerns.

    D. The client has been assessed for any correlated disorders, but none were found.

11. **Assess for Culturally Based Confounding Issues (11)**

    A. The client was assessed for age-related issues that could help to better understand their clinical presentation.

    B. The client was assessed for gender-related issues that could help to better understand their clinical presentation.

    C. The client was assessed for cultural syndromes, cultural idioms of distress, or culturally based perceived causes that could help to better understand their clinical presentation.

    D. Alternative factors have been identified as contributing to the client's currently defined "problem behavior," and these were taken into account in regard to treatment.

    E. Culturally based factors that could help to account for the client's currently defined "problem behavior" were investigated, but no significant factors were identified.

12. **Assess Severity of Impairment (12)**

    A. The severity of the client's impairment was assessed to determine the appropriate level of care.

B. The client was assessed in regard to impairment in social, relational, and educational endeavors.

C. It was reflected to the client that the impairment appears to create mild to moderate effects on the client's functioning.

D. It was reflected to the client that the impairment appears to create severe to very severe effects on the client's functioning.

E. The client was continuously assessed for the severity of impairment, as well as the efficacy and appropriateness of treatment.

13. **Assess for Pathogenic Care (13)**

A. The home, school, and community of the client were assessed for pathogenic care and concerns.

B. The client's various environments were assessed for the persistent disregard of the child's needs, repeated changes in caregivers, limited opportunities for stable attachment, harsh discipline, or other grossly inept care.

C. Pathogenic care was identified and the treatment plan included strategies for managing or correcting these concerns and protecting the child.

D. No pathogenic care was identified and this was reflected to the client and caregivers.

14. **Refer for Medication Evaluation (14)**

A. The client was referred for a medication evaluation to assess the potential benefit of psychotropic medication in the treatment plan.

B. Positive feedback was provided to the client and parents as they agreed to follow through with a medication evaluation.

C. The client was strongly opposed to being placed on medication; the client's feelings were acknowledged.

15. **Educate About Autism Spectrum Disorders (15)**

A. The client's parents and family members were educated about the nature of autism spectrum disorders, treatment options, challenges, and supports.

B. The parents were encouraged to share their thoughts and feelings about their child's autism diagnosis.

C. The parents were assigned the exercise "Initial Reactions to Diagnosis of Autism" from the *Child Psychotherapy Homework Planner* (Jongsma, Peterson, McInnis, & Bruce).

D. The parents and family were assisted in processing the information and feelings regarding the autism diagnosis.

16. **Assign Teaching Materials on Autism (16)**

A. The parents were assigned to view or read information regarding autism.

B. The parents were directed to view the videotape *Straight Talk About Autism with Parents and Kids* (ADD Warehouse).

C. The parents have reviewed the information regarding autism, and key points were processed within the session.

D. The parents have not reviewed the information about autism and were redirected to do so.

17. **Use Lovaas Model (17)**

   A. The Lovaas model of applied behavioral analysis for autism was used.

   B. The client was referred to a provider trained in the Lovaas model of applied behavioral analysis for autism.

   C. Parent training, positive reinforcement, shaping and chaining, functional behavior assessment, and peer integration were used to develop skills, in accordance with the Lovaas model.

   D. Communication skills, speech and language skills, academic skills, self-help skills, and play skills were developed using the Lovaas model.

   E. The client was assisted in generalizing the use of new skills across various settings and integrating them into the school environment.

18. **Tailor Behavioral Interventions (18)**

   A. Behavioral interventions were tailored to the client's particular autism spectrum disorder profile.

   B. Information from *Individualized Autism Intervention for Young Children* (Thompson) was used in tailoring behavioral interventions.

   C. The parents were assisted in understanding and using the tailored behavioral interventions.

19. **Teach Pivotal Response Intervention (19)**

   A. The parents were taught how to use behavior management skills to increase their child's motivation to respond to and self-initiate social interactions in a context of play.

   B. The parents were taught the pivotal response intervention technique as described in "Pivotal Response Treatments for Autism Spectrum Disorder" and *The PRT Pocket Guide* (Koegel & Koegel).

   C. The parents were urged to use natural reinforcers and child-selected stimulus materials.

   D. Feedback was provided to the parents to move them toward improvement of the pivotal response intervention techniques.

20. **Train in Power Card Strategy (20)**

   A. The parents were trained in the use of the Power Card strategy (see *Power Cards* by Gagnet) to help increase the child's motivation.

   B. The child's special interests were incorporated in various skill-building activities.

   C. The parents were assisted in reviewing their use of the Power Card strategy, with affirmation for appropriate use and redirection for situations in which they struggled to use the technique.

21. **Practice Pivotal Response Training and Power Card Technique (21)**

   A. The parents and client practiced pivotal response training and Power Card techniques throughout the day and across multiple settings.

   B. The parents were reinforced for using the techniques for skill-building, reaching 80% correct use criteria.

   C. The parents were redirected to improve their correct use of the skill-building techniques.

22. **Consult with Teachers (22)**

   A. Teachers were consulted regarding implementation of a school-based, teacher implemented intervention based on applied behavioral analysis.

   B. The child's teacher was willing to implement interventions based on applied behavioral analysis.

   C. The teacher was willing to promote social communication and interaction by being responsive to the child, such as imitating, expanding on, or joining into play activities that the child initiates.

   D. The child has progressed in social communication and interaction through the use of interventions by the teacher and this was encouraged to continue.

   E. The child has not progressed in social communication and interaction through the use of interventions by the teacher, and this use was reviewed for problems to solve.

23. **Begin Therapy Early (23)**

   A. The parents were encouraged to begin in-home and school-based therapy as early as possible after a diagnosis is made.

   B. The parents, school officials, and mental health professionals were consulted in order to establish in-home and school-based therapy.

   C. The parents were referred to a specialist to provide intensive treatment.

   D. The parents have begun in-home, school-based, and/or intensive therapy for the client soon after a diagnosis was made.

   E. The parents have not made steps toward in-home, school-based, or intensive therapy for the client and were encouraged to begin this as soon as possible.

24. **Maintain Communication (24)**

   A. Ongoing communication was maintained with the client's primary care physician and other involved providers to ensure that the client's current needs are being met in all areas.

   B. Follow-up was conducted with school-based providers, audiologists, neurologists, and home-based therapists/tutors to make certain that the client's needs for medical, psychological, and educational services were provided.

   C. Information was provided to appropriate clinicians to assist in determining services and appropriate referrals.

   D. Follow-up was conducted with other professionals to ensure that care is coordinated.

25. **Complete an IEPC Review (25)**

   A. An Individualized Educational Planning Committee (IEPC) meeting was held to determine the client's eligibility for special education services, to design educational interventions, and to establish goals.

   B. The decision was made at the IEPC meeting that the client is eligible to receive special education services under the classification of Autistic Impaired.

   C. The decision was made at the IEPC meeting that the client is not eligible to receive special education services.

D. A consultation was held with the client's parents, teachers, and other appropriate professionals about designing educational interventions to help the client achieve academic goals.

E. The client's academic goals were identified at the IEPC meeting.

26. Design Effective Teaching Program (26)

A. The client's parents, teachers, and other appropriate school officials were consulted about designing effective teaching programs or interventions that build on the client's strengths and compensate for weaknesses.

B. The client's learning strengths and weaknesses were identified in the consultation meeting with parents, teachers, and other appropriate school officials.

C. The client's parents, teachers, and other appropriate school officials were consulted about ways to maximize the client's learning strengths.

D. The client's parents, teachers, and other appropriate school officials were consulted about ways to compensate for the client's learning weaknesses.

E. The effectiveness of previously designed learning programs or interventions was evaluated and adjustments were made where indicated.

27. Conduct Functional Analysis (27)

A. A functional analysis of the reasons for an unwanted behavior was conducted, followed by the development of a positive plan for teaching appropriate functional behavior.

B. The client and family were assigned the exercise "Reaction to Change and Excessive Stimulation" from the *Child Psychotherapy Homework Planner* (Jongsma, Peterson, McInnis, & Bruce).

C. The functional analysis has been used to develop an understanding of the reasons for unwanted behaviors.

D. Skills were taught to the client to serve as replacement behaviors for the unwanted behavior, based on the functional analysis.

28. Teach Behavioral Management Techniques (28)

A. Behavioral management techniques (e.g., prompting behavior, using reinforcement schedules, ignoring off-task behavior) were taught to the parents to assist them in handling the client's difficult behaviors.

B. Plans were developed with the parents for implementing behavioral management techniques into their day-to-day parenting of the client.

C. Role-playing and behavioral rehearsal techniques were used with the parents to give them the opportunity to practice new skills.

D. The parents were verbally reinforced for their consistent use of behavioral management techniques.

E. Behavioral management techniques were reinforced and evaluated for their effectiveness with the client.

F. The parents have not used the behavioral management techniques on a consistent basis and were redirected to do so.

29. Develop Tailored Social Skills (29)

A. The client was assessed in regard to specific social skills.

B. The client was trained on developing specific social skills.

C. The parents were included in the client's social skills training, with a gradual transfer of the training role to the parents.

D. The parents were directed to conduct social skills training in various settings to facilitate generalization.

30. Assist Parents in Social Skill Training (30)

A. The parents were assisted in arranging meaningful, age-appropriate learning activities to assist the child in learning social/communication skills.

B. Training opportunities were selected with the ability to use behavior management techniques while the child learns social/communication skills.

C. Naturalistic teaching methods and didactic, mass trial, adult directed, one-on-one teaching approaches were used.

31. Apply Behavior Management Techniques to Temper Outbursts (31)

A. The parents were taught to apply behavior management techniques to decrease the client's temper outbursts.

B. The parents were taught to apply behavior management techniques (e.g., prompting behaviors, using reinforcement schedules, ignoring off-task behaviors).

C. "Clear Rules, Positive Reinforcement, Appropriate Consequences" from the *Adolescent Psychotherapy Homework Planner* (Jongsma, Peterson, McInnis, & Bruce) was assigned to the family.

D. Positive feedback was provided for the parents' application of behavior management techniques.

E. The parents have not regularly used behavior management techniques and were directed to do so.

32. Apply Behavior Management Techniques to Self-Abusive Behaviors (32)

A. The parents were taught to apply behavior management techniques to decrease the client's self-abusive behaviors such as scratching and hitting self.

B. The parents were taught to apply behavior management techniques (e.g., prompting behaviors, using reinforcement schedules, ignoring off-task behaviors).

C. "Clear Rules, Positive Reinforcement, Appropriate Consequences" from the *Adolescent Psychotherapy Homework* (Jongsma, Peterson, McInnis, & Bruce) was assigned to the family.

D. Positive feedback was provided for the parents' application of behavior management techniques.

E. The parents have not regularly used behavior management techniques and were directed to do so.

33. Encourage Self-Care Skills (33)

A. Various ways to teach the client self-care skills were processed with parents.

B. The parents were reinforced for committing to actively working with the client on a daily basis to teach and develop self-care skills.

C. The parents' work with the client has produced significant gains in hygiene and self-care skills, and they were encouraged to continue.

D. The parents have not regularly taught the client self-care skills and were redirected to do so.

34. Use Modeling and Operant Conditioning Principles (34)

A. Modeling and operant conditioning principles and response-shaping techniques have been used to develop the client's self-help skills and improve personal hygiene.

B. The parents were taught response-shaping techniques to improve the client's self-help skills and personal hygiene.

C. A reward system was designed to improve the client's self-help skills and personal hygiene.

D. The client and parents were assisted in identifying a list of rewards to reinforce the client's self-help skills and personal hygiene.

E. The reward system and response-shaping techniques were noted to have helped to improve the client's self-help skills and personal hygiene.

35. Use Personal Hygiene/Self-Help Program (35)

A. The parents were directed to use a reward system to improve the client's personal hygiene and self-help skills.

B. The parents were directed to use the reward system in the "Activities of Daily Living" program from the *Child Psychotherapy Homework Planner* (Jongsma, Peterson, McInnis, & Bruce) to improve the client's personal hygiene and self-help skills.

C. The parents were strongly encouraged to praise and reinforce the client for improvements in personal hygiene and self-help skills.

D. The parents reported that the "Activities of Daily Living" program has helped to improve the client's personal hygiene and self-help skills.

E. The parents reported that the client has demonstrated little to no improvement in personal hygiene and self-help skills since using the "Activities of Daily Living" program, but were encouraged to continue the technique.

F. The parents have not used a personal hygiene/self-help skills program and were redirected to do so.

36. Encourage Structured Family Interaction (36)

A. Family members were encouraged to include structured work time and playtime with the client in their daily routine.

B. Positive feedback was provided as the parents developed and implemented structured work time and playtime with the client.

C. Structured playtime and work time have improved the client's social initiation and interest in others; the continued use of these techniques was emphasized.

D. The client was assigned a task to perform in the family to provide a sense of responsibility or belonging.

E. The client was given praise in today's therapy session for the successful completion of the assigned task.

F. The family has not used structured interaction times with the client and was redirected to do so.

37. Strengthen Parent–Child Bond Through Singing (37)

A. The parents were encouraged to sing songs (e.g., nursery rhymes, lullabies, popular hits, songs related to client's interests) with the client to help establish a closer parent–child bond.

B. The parents were encouraged to sing songs with the client to help increase verbalizations in the home.

C. The parents reported that singing songs with the client has helped them to connect with the client; they were encouraged to continue this technique.

D. The parents reported that singing songs with the client has helped to increase verbalizations at home; they were encouraged to continue this technique.

E. The parents reported that they have not been able to connect with the client by singing songs with the client but were encouraged to continue.

38. Involve Detached Parent (38)

A. The detached parent(s) was (were) strongly encouraged to increase involvement in the client's daily life, leisure activities, or schoolwork.

B. The detached parent was instructed to spend [fill in number] minutes daily with the client in social or physical interaction.

C. The detached parent was given the assignment of helping the client with homework assignments.

D. The detached parent was praised and reinforced for increasing involvement in the client's everyday life.

E. Despite efforts to increase involvement, the detached parent has become only slightly more involved.

39. Build Mutual Trust (39)

A. A task was assigned to the client and parents to build mutual trust.

B. The parents and client were helped to identify a list of activities they could perform (e.g., swimming, riding a bike) to build trust and mutual dependence.

C. The parents and family members were strongly encouraged to include the client in outings or activities on a regular basis.

D. A family-therapy session was held to explore family members' resistance or objections to including the client in some outings or activities.

E. It was noted that the level of trust and mutual dependence between the client and parents has increased as they continue to follow through on the recommendation to engage in regular activities together.

40. Consult to Increase Client's Social Contacts (40)

A. The parents and teachers were consulted about ways to increase the frequency of the client's social contacts with peers.

B. A recommendation was made that the client be assigned a student aide in the classroom.

C. The parents were encouraged to talk to their minister or church leaders about placing the client in a Sunday school class or other small group.

D. The parents were encouraged to register the client for the Special Olympics to increase social contacts with peers.

E. The client was referred to a summer camp program for special-needs children to foster social contacts.

F. The parents were reinforced as they have followed through with the recommendations to increase the frequency of the client's social contacts with peers.

41. Generalize Social Skills (41)

A. The client was assisted in generalizing new social skills by arranging their use in a variety of different activities and settings.

B. The client's use of social skills was coordinated with multiple adults and children throughout the day.

C. The client was reinforced for positive use of new social skills.

D. The client was assisted with redirection for social skills that were difficult to generalize into new areas.

42. Teach Parents About Monitoring Progress (42)

A. The parents were taught about how to monitor the child's progress and incorporate the data into ongoing clinical decision-making.

B. The parents were taught about how to rate the frequency and severity of unwanted behaviors, disruptions in sleep and eating, and measures reflecting the acquisition and generalization of new skills.

43. Provide Support (43)

A. The parents and siblings were provided with nonjudgmental and empathic support.

B. The parents were encouraged to review balancing the needs of each member of the family toward increasing family well-being.

44. Recommend Reading for Parents (44)

A. The parents were recommended to read *Helping Your Child with Autism Spectrum Disorder: A Step-by-Step Workbook for Families* (Lockshin et al.).

B. The parents were recommended to read *Making Sense of Autism* (Thompson).

C. The parents were recommended to read *An Early Start for Your Child with Autism* (Rogers et al.).

D. The parents have read the assigned material and key concepts were reviewed.

E. The parents have not read the assigned material and were encouraged to do so.

45. Allow Family Members' Expression of Feelings (45)

A. A family-therapy session was held to provide the parents and siblings an opportunity to share and work through their feelings pertaining to the client's autism spectrum disorder.

B. The family members were educated about the client's symptoms of autism spectrum disorder.

C. The parents were given the opportunity to express their thoughts and feelings about raising a child with autism spectrum disorder.

D. The parents and siblings were given support in verbalizing their feelings of sadness, hurt, anger, and disappointment about having a child or sibling with an autism spectrum disorder.

E. The parents were helped to work through their feelings of guilt about raising a child with an autism spectrum disorder.

46. **Employ Filial Play Therapy (46)**

A. Filial play therapy approaches have been employed to help increase the parents' awareness of the client's thoughts, feelings, and needs.

B. The parents' involvement in the play therapy sessions was noted to have helped them establish a closer bond with the client.

C. The filial play therapy sessions have helped increase the parents' awareness of the client's thoughts, feelings, and needs.

D. The parents demonstrated empathy and support for the client's expression of thoughts and feelings in today's filial play therapy session.

47. **Assist in Managing Family Stress (47)**

A. The client and family members were encouraged to manage relevant stressors through supportive stress management interventions.

B. The family members were taught about calming, cognitive, time management, and conflict-resolution techniques.

C. The family members were encouraged to facilitate social support for managing their stress.

48. **Refer to Support Group (48)**

A. The parents' opinions and feelings about support groups were explored.

B. The client's parents were referred and encouraged to attend a support group for families of individuals with developmental disabilities.

C. Active listening skills were used as the parents attended an autism/developmental disability support group and indicated that they found the experience positive and helpful.

D. Despite encouragement, the parents have continued to be resistive to any involvement in an autism/developmental disability support group.

49. **Use Respite Care (49)**

A. Options for respite care were given and explained to the parents.

B. Advantages to using respite care were identified and the parents were encouraged to use this resource regularly.

C. Resistance on the parents' part to respite care was confronted and resolved.

D. The parents were asked to develop a regular schedule for respite care.

50. Employ Art Therapy Techniques (50)

A. Art therapy techniques were employed to help the client express basic needs or emotions.

B. Art therapy techniques were employed to help the client establish rapport with the therapist.

C. Art therapy techniques were employed to facilitate a closer parent–child relationship.

D. Art therapy techniques helped the client express basic emotions and identify needs.

E. The client was uncooperative and resistant to engage during the art therapy session.

51. Use Feelings Poster (51)

A. The Feelings Poster (available from Childswork/Childsplay, LLC) was used to help the client identify and express basic emotions.

B. The parents were encouraged to use the Feelings Poster at home to help the client identify and express basic emotions.

C. The parents were encouraged to use the Feelings Poster at home when the client starts to become agitated or angry to help prevent an outburst.

D. The parents report that the Feelings Poster has helped the client identify and express basic emotions, and they were encouraged to continue to use this technique.

E. Use of the Feelings Poster has produced little to no improvement in the client's ability to identify and express feelings.

BLENDED FAMILY

CLIENT PRESENTATION

1. **Angry/Hostile (1)***
   A. Anger and hostility have dominated the client's manner since the parents have blended their two families.
   B. The client was extremely angry and hostile about having to be a part of the new blended family.
   C. The client's level of anger and hostility has started to diminish as they have accepted being a part of the new blended family.
   D. The client has dropped anger and hostility and has become a cooperative member of the blended family.

2. **Frustrated/Tense (1)**
   A. There was a deep sense of frustration and tension present in the client as they talked of the blended family situation.
   B. The client reported being frustrated and tense about feeling pushed into a new blended family.
   C. The client's level of tension has subsided as they are feeling more comfortable with the idea of being a part of a stepfamily.

3. **Resistant Toward Stepparent (2)**
   A. The client presented in a defiant manner toward the stepparent.
   B. In a defiant way, the client reported they will have nothing to do with the new stepparent.
   C. The client threatened to make it difficult for the new stepparent.
   D. The client has dropped some of the resistance and seems to be warming a little to the new stepparent.

4. **Defiant of Stepparent (2)**
   A. The client showed a pattern of making alliances and causing conflicts in an attempt to have a degree of control over the new stepparent.
   B. The client reported no interest in taking direction or accepting limits from the stepparent.
   C. Gradually, the client has begun to give up rebellion toward the stepparent and to accept some direction from them.

5. **Stepsibling Conflict (3)**
   A. The siblings have engaged in ongoing conflict with one another.
   B. The two sibling groups stated clearly their dislike of and resentment toward one another.

---

*The numbers in parentheses correlate to the number of the Behavioral Definition statement in the companion chapter with the same title in the *Child Psychotherapy Treatment Planner*, Sixth Edition, by Jongsma, Peterson, McInnis, & Bruce (Wiley, 2023).

C. The parents indicated their frustration with the siblings' apparent attempt to sabotage their efforts to form a new family group.

D. The two sibling groups have stopped their open conflicts and started to tolerate and show basic respect for each other.

6. **Threats of Moving to Other Parent's House (4)**

A. The parents reported feeling like hostages to children's threats to move to the other parent's home whenever the children were crossed or told no.

B. The children presented as being ambivalent and manipulative regarding where they would like to live and why.

C. The children indicated they have changed their minds several times regarding where they want to reside and are presently still undecided.

D. The children have decreased their threats of going to the other parent's home and have started to join the new family unit.

7. **Ex-Spouse Interference (5)**

A. Each spouse reported frequent incidents of interference in their new family by their ex-spouses.

B. Ex-spouse interference has caused ongoing conflict and upheaval in the new family unit.

C. Efforts to keep ex-spouses out of the new family's business have been unsuccessful and sabotaged by the siblings.

D. Efforts to keep ex-spouses out of the daily life of the new family have started to be effective and the new family has started to solidify and become connected.

8. **Parental Anxiety (6)**

A. The client's parents presented with anxiety about the blending of their two families.

B. The parents seemed unsure about how to respond to issues being raised by the new blended family.

C. The parents looked for reassurance and some sense of security about how best to respond to blended family issues.

D. Parental anxiety has decreased as both parties have become more comfortable with working toward forming a new blended family.

9. **Lack of Responsibility Definitions (7)**

A. The family presented as very chaotic, lacking clear boundaries, rules, and responsibility definitions for members.

B. The parents reported they have struggled in their attempts to establish clear definitions of expectations of responsibility for family members.

C. Siblings indicated that they are not clear about their roles, responsibilities, or expectations in their new family.

D. The family has begun to develop and institute clear areas of responsibility for all members, which has also reduced the chaos and confusion for all.

INTERVENTIONS IMPLEMENTED

1. **Establish Rapport (1)***
   A. Caring was conveyed to the client through support, warmth, and empathy.
   B. The client was provided with nonjudgmental support and a level of trust was developed.
   C. The client was urged to feel safe in expressing blended family concerns.
   D. The client began to express feelings more freely as rapport and trust level have increased.
   E. The client has continued to experience difficulty being open and direct about the expression of painful feelings; the client was encouraged to use the safe haven of therapy to express these difficult issues.

2. **Focus on Strengthening Therapeutic Relationship (2)**
   A. The relationship with the client was strengthened using empirically supported factors.
   B. The relationship with the client was strengthened through the implementation of collaborative approach, agreement on goals, demonstration of empathy, verbalization of positive regard, and collection of client feedback.
   C. The client reacted positively to the relationship-strengthening measures taken.
   D. The client verbalized feeling supported and understood during therapy sessions.
   E. Despite attempts to strengthen the therapeutic relationship, the client reports feeling distant and misunderstood.
   F. The client has indicated that sessions are not helpful and will be terminating therapy.

3. **Employ Cooperative Family Drawing (3)**
   A. Each family member took part in interpreting and listening to others' interpretations of a drawing that was made through the cooperative effort of all family members.
   B. All family members were willing to take part in making the family drawing, but were resistant to interpreting it.
   C. The family drawing exercise revealed that the family members have a very difficult time cooperating with each other, as there was resistance to the exercise and bickering within the family during the exercise.

4. **Address Family and Marital Issues (4)**
   A. Family sessions were conducted that focused on addressing and facilitating relationship building and joining rituals.
   B. Family members were assigned the exercise "Blended Family Sentence Completion" from the *Child Psychotherapy Homework Planner* (Jongsma, Peterson, McInnis, & Bruce).
   C. Each family member was asked to make a list of recent losses to share with other members in a family session.
   D. The parents were educated in the dynamics of stepfamilies and how they work.
   E. Conflict-negotiation skills were taught to family members and practiced in role-play situations particular to stepfamilies.

---

*The numbers in parentheses correlate to the number of the Therapeutic Intervention statement in the companion chapter with the same title in the *Child Psychotherapy Treatment Planner*, Sixth Edition, by Jongsma, Peterson, McInnis, & Bruce (Wiley, 2023).

F. It was identified that family members have gained information and understanding about stepfamilies, learning to use negotiation skills and building relationships with each other.

G. Despite attempts to address family and marital issues, conflicts continue to occur on a frequent basis.

5. **Assess Level of Insight (5)**

A. The client's level of insight toward the presenting problems was assessed.

B. The client was assessed in regard to the syntonic versus dystonic nature of their insight about the presenting problems.

C. The client was noted to demonstrate good insight into the problematic nature of the behavior and symptoms.

D. The client was noted to be in agreement with others' concerns and is motivated to work on change.

E. The client was noted to be ambivalent regarding the problems described and is reluctant to address the issues as a concern.

F. The client was noted to be resistant regarding acknowledgment of the problem areas, is not concerned about them, and has no motivation to make changes.

6. **Assess for Correlated Disorders (6)**

A. The client was assessed for evidence of research-based correlated disorders.

B. The client was assessed in regard to the level of vulnerability to suicide.

C. The client was identified as having a comorbid disorder, and treatment was adjusted to account for these concerns.

D. The client has been assessed for any correlated disorders, but none were found.

7. **Assess for Culturally Based Confounding Issues (7)**

A. The client was assessed for age-related issues that could help to better understand their clinical presentation.

B. The client was assessed for gender-related issues that could help to better understand their clinical presentation.

C. The client was assessed for cultural syndromes, cultural idioms of distress, or culturally based perceived causes that could help to better understand their clinical presentation.

D. Alternative factors have been identified as contributing to the client's currently defined "problem behavior," and these were taken into account in regard to treatment.

E. Culturally based factors that could help to account for the client's currently defined "problem behavior" were investigated, but no significant factors were identified.

8. **Assess Severity of Impairment (8)**

A. The severity of the client's impairment was assessed to determine the appropriate level of care.

B. The client was assessed in regard to impairment in social, relational, and educational endeavors.

C. It was reflected to the client that the impairment appears to create mild to moderate effects on the client's functioning.

D. It was reflected to the client that the impairment appears to create severe to very severe effects on the client's functioning.

E. The client was continuously assessed for the severity of impairment, as well as the efficacy and appropriateness of treatment.

9. **Assess for Pathogenic Care (9)**

A. The home, school, and community of the client were assessed for pathogenic care and concerns.

B. The client's various environments were assessed for the persistent disregard of the child's needs, repeated changes in caregivers, limited opportunities for stable attachment, harsh discipline, or other grossly inept care.

C. Pathogenic care was identified and the treatment plan included strategies for managing or correcting these concerns and protecting the child.

D. No pathogenic care was identified and this was reflected to the client and caregivers.

10. **Utilize Child-Centered Play Therapy (10)**

A. Child-centered play therapy sessions were conducted with the client to assist in resolving issues of adjusting to and cooperating with a new stepfamily.

B. A child-centered play therapy approach was utilized to display trust in the client's capacity to resolve the issues surrounding adjustment to a new family.

C. The client actively participated in the child-centered play therapy sessions.

D. The client's active involvement in the child-centered play therapy sessions has helped the client to begin to resolve the issues of being a part of a new stepfamily.

E. Despite the use of child-centered play therapy sessions, the client has not begun to actively resolve the issues of being part of a new stepfamily.

11. **Encourage Expression of Feelings (11)**

A. Play therapy sessions were conducted to provide the client with an opportunity to express the feelings surrounding loss and changes in their life.

B. The client was given the opportunity to express feelings about loss and changes in their life in today's therapy session.

C. The client was guarded and resistant to expressing any feelings about loss and changes in their life in the play therapy session; the client was gently prompted to express these feelings.

D. The client was reinforced as they have effectively used the play therapy session, openly expressing feelings connected to loss and/or changes in their life.

E. The client remained guarded about expressing feelings surrounding the loss and changes in their life and was urged to express these feelings as they felt able to do so.

12. **Emphasize Respect and Cooperation (12)**

A. The need for respect and cooperation among all family members was emphasized in play-, sibling-, and family-therapy sessions.

B. Respect and cooperation were modeled for the family and emphasized in family-therapy sessions.

C. Gentle, respectful confrontation and redirection were utilized when members were disrespectful of each other or uncooperative in sibling- and family-therapy sessions.

D. Puppets were used in play therapy sessions to create scenarios that could provide opportunities to emphasize respect and cooperation among family members.

E. Barriers to respect and cooperation were explored, identified, and resolved with the family members.

F. The positive value and benefits of respect and cooperation between family members were identified, emphasized, and reinforced in family-therapy sessions.

13. **List Expectations for New Family (13)**

A. Each family member was asked to list expectations for the new family.

B. Each family member's list or expectations regarding the future of the blended family was shared and processed in family session, with common realistic expectations being affirmed and reinforced.

C. Unrealistic expectations of family members were gently confronted and reframed into more realistic and attainable expectations.

14. **Remind Family of Instant Love Myth (14)**

A. The family was reminded of the myth of "instant love" between new members.

B. Family members' expectations of instant love and connections between blended family members were confronted with the reality that time is necessary for relationships to grow.

C. All the family members have become more realistic regarding the time necessary for meaningful relationships to develop between them, and this was noted to be a healthy response.

D. Although the family members have been reminded that instant love is a myth, they continue to expect an immediate harmonious relationship.

15. **Reinforce Kindness and Respect (15)**

A. The family was reminded that new members need not love or like each other but that they need to treat each other with kindness and respect.

B. Family members were confronted when they failed to treat each other with kindness and respect.

C. The parents were taught ways to model respect and kindness for all members and to confront and give consequences for disrespectful interactions.

D. It was noted that there is a discernable growth of respect and consideration among new family members that is being positively reinforced by the parents.

16. **Read *Changing Families* (16)**

A. The family was asked to read *Changing Families* (Fassler et al.) to identify and reinforce the recent changes each has experienced in family life.

B. The family members struggled to identify the losses and changes that each had experienced, even after reading *Changing Families*.

C. The family was reminded that change is an opportunity to grow and thrive, not just survive.

D. After reading *Changing Families,* the family members have a better understanding of the difficult process they have gone through recently in forming the blended family.

E. The family members have not read *Changing Families* and were redirected to do so.

17. List Losses and Changes (17)

A. Each sibling was asked to make a list of all the losses and changes experienced in the past year.

B. Each sibling's list of losses was shared with other family members and similarities between the lists were identified.

C. Reviewing each sibling's list of losses enhanced the degree of understanding and the feeling of similarity between the siblings.

18. Play Games to Promote Self-Understanding (18)

A. The family was directed to play either "The Ungame" (Ungame Company) or the "Talking, Feeling, and Doing" game (Gardner; available from Childswork/Child-splay) to increase members' awareness of themselves and their feelings.

B. Expressions of self-awareness and identification of feelings were reinforced in family sessions.

C. The family members were very uncomfortable during the playing of therapeutic games together and most of them had significant difficulty in identifying and expressing feelings; they were assisted in becoming more at ease with this task.

19. Use Feelings Charts (19)

A. Feelings charts, cards, and felt board were utilized to help the family increase their skills in identifying and expressing feelings.

B. The parents were encouraged to use a feelings chart and cards with children at home as a family activity.

C. Positive verbal recognition and reinforcement were given to the family members when they identified or expressed feelings in sessions.

D. Each family member has been noted to show an increased ability to recognize and appropriately express feelings.

20. Practice Identifying and Expressing Feelings (20)

A. Various feelings exercises were used with the family to help expand their ability to identify and express feelings.

B. Positive affirmation was given to family members when they identified and expressed their feelings appropriately.

C. Family members were confronted and reminded when they were not identifying and expressing their feelings.

21. Assign Material on Stepfamilies (21)

A. The parents were assigned to read material to expand their knowledge of step families and their development.

B. The parents were asked to read *Stepfamily Realities* (Newman), *How to Win as a Stepfamily* (Visher & Visher), or *Building Love Together in Blended Families* (Chapman & Deal).

C. Key concepts from the reading material on stepfamilies were identified and reinforced.

D. The children were assigned to complete the workbook *Twice the Love* (Winnett).

E. Several ideas learned from the reading on stepfamilies were implemented by the parents in their present situations; these were reviewed and processed.

F. The parents have not completed the assignment to read information about stepfamilies and were encouraged to do so.

22. **Refer to Stepfamily Association (22)**

A. The parents were referred to the Stepfamily Association of America in order to gather information on the process of blending families.

B. Information gathered from the Stepfamily Association of America was processed and incorporated into a more realistic view of the reality of stepfamilies.

C. The reality that stepfamilies are not inferior to regular families, just different, was introduced, along with the new information the parents received from the Stepfamily Association of America.

D. The parents have not followed through on obtaining further information from the Stepfamily Association of America and were again encouraged to do so.

23. **Assign "Tearing Paper" Exercise (23)**

A. The "Tearing Paper" exercise (Daves) was given and the guidelines were explained to the family.

B. The family actively participated in the "Tearing Paper" exercise and followed the guidelines set for the exercise.

C. The experience of doing the "Tearing Paper" exercise was processed with the family regarding the positive aspects of releasing energy and emotion.

D. The family was given positive verbal feedback for their follow-through and cooperation with cleaning up after the "Tearing Paper" exercise.

24. **Train Family in Problem-Solving Skills (24)**

A. The family members were trained in the use of problem-solving skills.

B. Family members were taught about identifying and pinpointing problems, brainstorming solutions, evaluating pros and cons, compromising, agreeing on a solution, and making an implementation plan.

C. Family members were assigned the "Problem-Solving Exercise" from the *Child Psychotherapy Homework Planner* (Jongsma, Peterson, McInnis, & Bruce).

D. The family was assisted in practicing problem-solving skills on issues present in the family session.

25. **Assign "Negotiating a Peace Treaty" Exercise (25)**

A. The siblings were asked to specify their conflicts and suggest solutions.

B. The siblings were asked to complete and process the "Negotiating a Peace Treaty" exercise from the *Child Psychotherapy Homework Planner* (Jongsma, Peterson, McInnis, & Bruce).

C. Through the use of the "Negotiating a Peace Treaty" exercise, the clients were assisted in identifying their conflicts and exploring a variety of solutions.

D. The siblings were asked to select, commit to, and implement one of the solutions they identified in the negotiation exercise.

E. The siblings' completion of the negotiation exercise revealed how far apart they are in terms of having any common ground, and this was reflected to them.

26. Explain Attunement (26)

A. The client and parents were provided with education on the concept of attunement.

B. The client and parents were taught the value of attunement for their family, such as understanding, concern, and closeness.

C. The client and parents were willing to learn more about attunement.

D. The client and parents were uninterested in attunement concepts.

27. Conduct Attunement Exercise (27)

A. The family was invited to participate in an attunement exercise in which the therapist taps out three notes that each family member replicates in turn.

B. The family found usefulness in this exercise and this was repeated at the start of all family sessions.

C. The family did not find the attunement exercise to be useful and would not participate in this.

28. Use Humor to Decrease Tension (28)

A. Humor was injected into sessions when it was appropriate to decrease tension and to model balance and perspective.

B. Each family member was directed to tell one joke daily to other family members.

C. Positive feedback was given to family members who created appropriate humor during a session.

D. It was reflected to the family members that they have extreme difficulty being light and humorous toward each other because tension levels are high and teasing is reacted to angrily.

29. Use "Cloning the Perfect Sibling" Exercise (29)

A. A family sibling session was held in which each child was asked to list and verbalize an appreciation of each sibling's unique traits and abilities.

B. Siblings were asked to complete the "Cloning the Perfect Sibling" exercise and the "Interviewing My New Family Member" exercise from the *Child Psychotherapy Homework Planner* (Jongsma, Peterson, McInnis, & Bruce).

C. In processing the cloning exercise, siblings were assisted in identifying and affirming the positive aspects of individual differences.

D. Siblings continued to argue and bicker with each other, complaining about unique traits and characteristics, despite the use of the cloning exercise.

30. Normalize Conflict as a Stage (30)

A. A brief solution-focused intervention was utilized with the family to normalize conflict as a stage.

B. Family members were assisted in identifying the next stage after conflict and how they might begin to move in that direction.

C. The intervention of normalizing the conflict as a stage has, according to family reports, reduced the frequency of conflicts.

D. The family was unwilling to embrace any reframing or normalizing interventions.

31. **Process Feelings About New Parent (31)**

A. The client was encouraged to express feelings about the bioparent's new partner/spouse.

B. The client was asked to identify how feelings could be changed to be more positive.

C. The client was assigned the exercise "Thoughts and Feelings About Parent's Live-In Partner" from the *Child Psychotherapy Homework Planner* (Jongsma, Peterson, McInnis, & Bruce).

D. The client was assisted in processing thoughts and feelings about the biological parent's new partner.

32. **Read *The Sneetches* (32)**

A. The story *The Sneetches* (Dr. Seuss) was read and discussed with the family.

B. The folly of perceiving people as top dog/low dog and insider/outsider was seeded with family members.

C. Family members were asked to list each way they felt better than or superior to new members.

33. **Encourage Parenting Role for Biological Parent (33)**

A. The parents were educated in the positive aspects of each biological parent taking the main role with their children.

B. The parents were assisted in developing ways to redirect the parenting of the stepchildren.

C. The parents were asked to refrain from all negative references to ex-spouses.

D. Incidents of a parent making negative references to ex-spouses were confronted and processed.

34. **Refer to Parenting Group (34)**

A. The parents were referred to a parenting group designed for stepparents.

B. The parents were assisted in implementing new concepts that were learned from the parenting group.

C. The parents were confronted about their poor attendance at the stepparenting group.

35. **Institute Family Meeting (35)**

A. The parents were assisted in developing a process for and scheduling a weekly family meeting.

B. Family meetings were monitored, and the parents were assisted in solving conflictual issues.

C. The parents were given positive verbal support and encouragement for their follow-through on implementing weekly family meetings.

D. The parents have not followed through on implementing regularly scheduled meetings, and a commitment for this scheduling was obtained from them.

36. Develop Family Rituals (36)

A. The positive aspects of family rituals were taught to the parents.

B. The parents were asked to develop a list of possible rituals for their new family unit.

C. The parents were assisted in selecting family rituals and developing a plan for their implementation.

D. Family rituals were monitored for their implementation and effectiveness.

E. Verbal affirmation and encouragement were given to the parents for their effort to implement and enforce new family rituals.

37. Select Past Family Rituals (37)

A. The family members were asked to make a list of rituals that were followed in their previous family.

B. Rituals from previous families were discussed, and key rituals were chosen to implement in the new family.

C. Plans were developed to implement the chosen rituals from previous families.

D. The family members were assisted in establishing the new rituals and making the necessary adjustments to increase their effectiveness.

38. Create Birthday Rituals (38)

A. The family was given the assignment of creating new birthday rituals for the new family.

B. The parents were asked to implement the new birthday rituals at the first opportunity.

C. The value of birthday rituals was reinforced with the parents.

D. A new birthday ritual has been implemented, and the family members have responded very favorably to this recognition of their special status.

E. New birthday rituals have not been developed by the family, and they were redirected to complete this task.

39. Teach Patterns of Family Interactions (39)

A. The parents were taught key aspects and patterns of family interaction.

B. Past family interaction patterns were explored and identified, with a special focus on those involving triangulation.

C. A family genogram was developed that denotes the family's pattern of interaction.

D. The parents were assisted in blocking patterns of triangulation that are occurring within the family.

E. The episodes of triangulation within the family have diminished significantly.

F. The parents have not identified patterns of triangulation within the family and were provided with tentative examples of how this occurs.

40. Refer for Marital Therapy (40)

A. The parents were referred to a skills-based marital therapy program.

B. Gains made in marital therapy were affirmed and reinforced with the parents.

C. The parents were asked to identify the gains they achieved in the skills-based therapy program and how they would improve parenting.

D. The parents have not obtained marital therapy and were urged again to do so.

41. Identify Individual Parental Needs (41)

A. The parents were assisted in exploring and identifying their individual needs within the relationship and family.

B. The needs of each partner were recognized and affirmed, and plans were developed for meeting these needs on a consistent basis.

C. The parents were confronted when they failed to take care of their individual needs and did not follow through on the plans developed to do this.

D. The importance of meeting individual needs in a relationship was reinforced with the parents.

42. Process Sharing of Affection (42)

A. The ways the parents show affection to each other were explored with them in a conjoint session.

B. The negative aspects of blatant displays of parental physical affection were processed with them.

C. The parents were assisted in identifying appropriate ways to show affection to each other when in the presence of their children.

D. The parents were confronted about blatant displays of affection between them, which reminded them of the negative impact this could have on their children.

43. Assign Book on Parent Communication (43)

A. The parents were assigned to read *Peaceful Parents–Happy Kids* (Markham).

B. The parents discussed key concepts learned from the assigned reading and identify one idea to implement into their daily life.

C. Parents were reinforced and supported for implementing one idea from the assigned reading.

D. Parents were redirected to attempt one new idea from the assigned reading.

44. Draw Family Genogram (44)

A. A genogram was developed with the family that included all members and how they are connected.

B. From the genogram, the family was asked to identify the ways in which they see themselves being connected.

C. Constructing the family genogram revealed that some family members are virtually unconnected to other family members; ways to reverse this fact were discussed.

45. Recommend Initiatives Camp (45)

A. The family was asked to attend an initiatives weekend to build trust, cooperation, and the conflict-resolution skills of each family member.

B. The initiatives experience was processed with the family, and each member identified the positive gains he/she received from the weekend.

C. The family was assisted in identifying how they could continue to use and expand on the gains from the weekend.

46. Complete Coat of Arms Exercise (46)

    A. The family was asked to create a coat of arms for their new family by drawing a collage on poster board.

    B. The experience of creating the coat of arms was processed with the family, and both old and new identities were acknowledged and reinforced.

    C. The parents were asked to display the coat of arms in their new home.

47. Plan One-on-One Time (47)

    A. The parents were encouraged to build time into their schedules for one-on-one contact with each child and stepchild.

    B. The parents were reminded of the importance of taking the time to build parent-child relationships.

    C. The parents have not developed one-on-one contact with each child and stepchild and were encouraged to coordinate this.

48. Emphasize That Relationships Build Slowly (48)

    A. Allowing relationships to build slowly was emphasized to the family in family sessions.

    B. Ways to build trust in relationships were explored with the parents to help them slowly build relationships with stepchildren.

    C. The parents exhibiting patience in allowing relationships to build was verbally reinforced.

BULLYING/AGGRESSION PERPETRATOR

CLIENT PRESENTATION

1. **Seeks Control (1)***
   A. The client has a history of calculated, repetitive threatening or intimidation of younger or weaker peers to gain control.
   B. The client has threatened to hurt younger or weaker peers if they do not meet the client's needs.
   C. The client reported a mild reduction in the frequency and intensity of controlling behavior.
   D. The client has recently displayed good anger control and reported that they have not threatened or intimidated younger or weaker peers.

2. **Physical Aggression (2)**
   A. The client engages in physical encounters that have injured others or have threatened serious injury to others.
   B. The client showed little or no remorse for causing pain to others through behavior such as hitting, punching, kicking, or tripping.
   C. The client projected blame for aggressive encounters onto others.
   D. The client has a violent history and continues to interact with others in a very intimidating, aggressive style.
   E. The client has shown progress in controlling aggressive patterns and seems to be trying to interact with more assertiveness rather than aggression.

3. **Verbal Abuse (3)**
   A. The client acknowledged that they frequently engage in verbally aggressive statements as a means of intimidating or demeaning peers.
   B. Peers of the client have indicated that they have been hurt through teasing, mocking, taunting, threatening, or name-calling.
   C. The client has shown little empathy toward others for the pain that they have caused because of verbal aggression.
   D. The client has become more aware of their pattern of verbal aggression and is becoming more sensitive to the negative impact of this behavior on others.
   E. There have been no recent incidents of verbal aggression toward others by the client.

4. **Relational Bullying (4)**
   A. The client engages in bullying that destroys or threatens to destroy social relationships.
   B. The client acknowledged using behaviors such as telling falsehoods/lies, gossiping, and excluding others that have had a negative effect on social relationships

---

* The numbers in parentheses correlate to the number of the Behavioral Definition statement in the companion chapter with the same title in the *Child Psychotherapy Treatment Planner*, Sixth Edition, by Jongsma, Peterson, McInnis, & Bruce (Wiley, 2023).

C. The client continues to use relational bullying with no improvement in social relationships.

D. The client has decreased behaviors that destroy social relationships.

E. The client no longer engages in relational bullying behaviors.

5. **Cyberbullying**

A. The client described a history of engaging in cyberbullying acts in an attempt to demean, embarrass, or isolate peers through the use of electronic devices.

B. The client admitted to engaging in online behaviors such as posting embarrassing pictures, encouraging peers to drop friends, and sending derogatory or threatening messages.

C. The client has gradually reduced cyberbullying behaviors toward peers.

D. The client has recently exercised good self-control and has not engaged in any cyberbullying behaviors.

6. **Takes and/or Breaks Victim's Objects (6)**

A. The client has often stolen objects belonging to others.

B. The client has purposely broken objects belonging to the victim of their bullying.

C. The client has recently engaged in taking and/or breaking objects belonging to the victim of their bullying.

D. The client has not recently engaged in any theft from others as a means of intimidating them.

E. The client has stopped breaking objects belonging to the victim of their bullying.

7. **Feelings of Inadequacy (7)**

A. The client's bullying behaviors have often masked or compensated for deeper feelings of inadequacy, helplessness, and vulnerability.

B. The client's bullying behaviors have helped them achieve a maladaptive or false sense of power.

C. The client verbally recognized how bullying is often associated with feelings of inadequacy, helplessness, and vulnerability.

D. The client expressed decreased feelings of inadequacy and fewer bullying behaviors.

E. The client has resolved negative feelings about self and their bullying behaviors have been eliminated.

8. **Externalizing Behaviors (8)**

A. The client has a history of using externalizing behaviors to cope with life's stressors or threats to self-esteem.

B. The client used intimidating, blaming, or aggressive acts to cope with life's stressors or threats to self-esteem.

C. The client did not accept responsibility for externalizing behaviors.

D. The client has begun to cope more appropriately with life's stressors or threats to self-esteem.

E. The client apologized to others for intimidating, blaming, and aggressive acts.

9. **Intimidates When Reinforced by Others (9)**

A. The client tends to bully and intimidate others to elicit approval, affirmation, or acceptance from others.

B. The client's intimidating behavior usually happens when in a group setting.

C. The client acknowledged the reinforcing effects of others in regard to intimidating behavior and has decreased the frequency of the intimidating behavior.

10. **Lack of Sensitivity (10)**

A. The parents reported that the client shows a lack of empathy or sensitivity regarding how bullying behaviors negatively affect other people.

B. The client demonstrated little empathy or sensitivity for the thoughts, feelings, and needs of vulnerable or weaker peers discussing interpersonal problems during today's therapy session.

C. The client has usually sought immediate gratification of needs and failed to consider how their actions may affect others.

D. In today's therapy session, the client verbalized an understanding of how their bullying behaviors negatively affect others.

E. The client has recently started to verbalize empathy and sensitivity to the thoughts, feelings, and needs of others.

11. **Family-of-Origin Models (11)**

A. Members of the client's family of origin have provided models of threatening, intimidating, or aggressive behavior.

B. The client alluded to threatening, intimidating, or aggressive family members as examples of the way they have learned to relate to others.

C. Members of the client's family of origin have discontinued modeling threatening, intimidating, and aggressive behaviors and have directed the client to discontinue these behaviors as well.

D. The client no longer looks to family-of-origin members as models for threatening, intimidating, or aggressive behavior.

12. **Acts of Aggression (12)**

A. The client often acts with aggression to cause intentional harm.

B. The client uses direct or indirect acts of aggression in order to elevate their status in the eyes of peers.

C. As the client has developed better peer relationship skills, acts of aggression have decreased.

D. The client has ceased acts of aggression in order to elevate their status in the eyes of peers.

INTERVENTIONS IMPLEMENTED

1. **Establish Rapport (1)***

A. Caring was conveyed to the client through support, warmth, and empathy.

B. The client was provided with nonjudgmental support and a level of trust was developed.

C. The client was urged to feel safe in expressing bullying behaviors.

*The numbers in parentheses correlate to the number of the Therapeutic Intervention statement in the companion chapter with the same title in the *Child Psychotherapy Treatment Planner*, Sixth Edition, by Jongsma, Peterson, McInnis, & Bruce (Wiley, 2023).

    D. The client began to express feelings more freely as rapport and trust level have increased.

    E. The client has continued to experience difficulty being open and direct about the expression of painful feelings; the client was encouraged to use the safe haven of therapy to express these difficult issues.

2. Focus on Strengthening Therapeutic Relationship (2)

    A. The relationship with the client was strengthened using empirically supported factors.

    B. The relationship with the client was strengthened through the implementation of collaborative approach, agreement on goals, demonstration of empathy, verbalization of positive regard, and collection of client feedback.

    C. The client reacted positively to the relationship-strengthening measures taken.

    D. The client verbalized feeling supported and understood during therapy sessions.

    E. Despite attempts to strengthen the therapeutic relationship, the client reports feeling distant and misunderstood.

    F. The client has indicated that sessions are not helpful and will be terminating therapy.

3. Gather Peer Interaction Data (3)

    A. The client was asked about their pattern of interaction with peers.

    B. The client was helped to focus on interaction with peers when they are trying to control the situation or intimidate others.

    C. The client was supported as they were open and honest about the situations that they are trying to control through intimidation.

    D. The client was gently confronted about defensiveness regarding providing information about their pattern of interaction with peers.

4. Obtain Input from Adults (4)

    A. The client's parents/caregivers were asked for their input regarding the client's pattern of bullying or intimidating peers.

    B. The client's teachers were asked for their input regarding their pattern of bullying or intimidating peers.

    C. The parents'/caregivers' and teachers' input was summarized and it reflected a pattern of bullying or intimidation of peers.

5. Assess Level of Insight (5)

    A. The client's level of insight toward the presenting problems was assessed.

    B. The client was assessed in regard to the syntonic versus dystonic nature of their insight about the presenting problems.

    C. The client was noted to demonstrate good insight into the problematic nature of the behavior and symptoms.

    D. The client was noted to be in agreement with others' concerns and is motivated to work on change.

    E. The client was noted to be ambivalent regarding the problems described and is reluctant to address the issues as a concern.

    F. The client was noted to be resistant regarding acknowledgment of the problem areas, is not concerned about them, and has no motivation to make changes.

6. Assess for Correlated Disorders (6)

A. The client was assessed for evidence of research-based correlated disorders.

B. The client was assessed in regard to the level of vulnerability to suicide.

C. The client was identified as having a comorbid disorder, and treatment was adjusted to account for these concerns.

D. The client has been assessed for any correlated disorders, but none were found.

7. Assess for Culturally Based Confounding Issues (7)

A. The client was assessed for age-related issues that could help to better understand their clinical presentation.

B. The client was assessed for gender-related issues that could help to better understand their clinical presentation.

C. The client was assessed for cultural syndromes, cultural idioms of distress, or culturally based perceived causes that could help to better understand their clinical presentation.

D. Alternative factors have been identified as contributing to the client's currently defined "problem behavior," and these were taken into account in regard to treatment.

E. Culturally based factors that could help to account for the client's currently defined "problem behavior" were investigated, but no significant factors were identified.

8. Assess Severity of Impairment (8)

A. The severity of the client's impairment was assessed to determine the appropriate level of care.

B. The client was assessed in regard to impairment in social, relational, and educational endeavors.

C. It was reflected to the client that the impairment appears to create mild to moderate effects on the client's functioning.

D. It was reflected to the client that the impairment appears to create severe to very severe effects on the client's functioning.

E. The client was continuously assessed for the severity of impairment, as well as the efficacy and appropriateness of treatment.

9. Assess for Pathogenic Care (9)

A. The home, school, and community of the client were assessed for pathogenic care and concerns.

B. The client's various environments were assessed for the persistent disregard of the child's needs, repeated changes in caregivers, limited opportunities for stable attachment, harsh discipline, or other grossly inept care.

C. Pathogenic care was identified and the treatment plan included strategies for managing or correcting these concerns and protecting the child.

D. No pathogenic care was identified, and this was reflected to the client and caregivers.

10. Confront with Facts (10)

A. The client was confronted with facts that have been reported by others that indicate the client does engage in intimidating behavior toward peers.

    B. The client was assigned the exercise "Bullying Incident Report" from the *Child Psychotherapy Homework Planner* (Jongsma, Peterson, McInnis, & Bruce).

    C. The client was praised for the ability to accept and acknowledge the truth about their intimidating behavior toward peers.

    D. The client continued to deny any intimidating behavior toward peers and was more directly confronted with this information.

11. Role-Play Bullying (11)

    A. The client was engaged in several role-plays of social interactions in which the therapist played the role of the client and used bullying behavior to intimidate others.

    B. The client was asked to acknowledge that they do behave in the bullying manner displayed in the role-play.

    C. Support and encouragement were provided as the client admitted to their pattern of bullying behavior as displayed in the role-play situation.

    D. The client continued to deny their pattern of bullying behavior and was more directly confronted with this information.

12. Establish Consequences (12)

    A. The client, parents, and school officials were consulted to identify appropriate consequences for bullying/intimidation behavior.

    B. The client, parents, and school officials were assisted in establishing clearly defined consequences for lying and manipulative behavior.

    C. The parents gave rather vague rules and consequences for the client's lying or manipulative behavior and were assisted in making these clearer and more specific.

    D. The client was informed of the rules and consequences for lying or manipulative behavior.

    E. The client was asked to repeat the rules and consequences in order to demonstrate understanding of these guidelines.

13. Assign Apology (13)

    A. The client was directed to offer or write a sincere apology to individuals the client has bullied.

    B. The client was educated on expectations of an apology, including describing the nature of the bullying behavior, identifying factor(s) contributing to bullying behavior, accepting responsibility for actions, placing blame for behavior on self, and identifying changes needed to make to prevent future bullying.

    C. Positive feedback was provided for the client's use of apologies.

    D. The client has not made apologies to those whom they have bullied and was redirected to follow through on this expectation.

14. Teach About Empathy (14)

    A. The client was taught about empathy for the victim of intimidating behavior.

    B. The client was asked to list the feelings generated in the victim due to the client's bullying behavior.

C. The client was assigned the exercise "Apology Letter for Bullying" from the *Child Psychotherapy Homework Planner* (Jongsma, Peterson, McInnis, & Bruce).

D. The client was supported as they identified feelings generated in the victim (e.g., fear, rejection, anger, helplessness, social withdrawal) because of the client's bullying behavior.

E. The client could not identify the emotions generated in the victim because of the client's bullying and was provided with tentative examples in this area.

15. Acts of Kindness (15)

A. The client was given the homework assignment of performing kind or compassionate acts toward the bullying victim before the next therapy session to increase empathy and sensitivity to thoughts, feelings, and needs.

B. Feedback was provided for the client as they described kind or compassionate acts toward the bullying victim and demonstrations of empathy and kindness.

C. The client was unable to identify any demonstrations of kindness or compassion toward the bullying victim and was redirected to complete these types of tasks.

16. Role-Play Regarding Emotional Effects of Bullying (16)

A. The client was engaged in a role-playing session in which they were the victim of bullying from a peer (played by the therapist).

B. The role-play was periodically stopped to explore and identify feelings generated in the victim because of being bullied by the client.

C. Support and encouragement were provided as the client identified feelings that the victim may experience.

D. The client was provided with specific examples of feelings that might be experienced by the victim of bullying.

17. Teach an Understanding of Feelings (17)

A. The client was asked to list the feelings generated in the victim because of bullying.

B. The client was assigned the exercise "Building Empathy" from the *Child Psychotherapy Homework Planner* (Jongsma, Peterson, McInnis, & Bruce).

C. The client was able to identify feelings and actions the victim may experience, such as fear, rejection, anger, helplessness, or social withdrawal.

D. The idea of how the client would like to be treated by others was explored, along with what they would need to do to make this possible.

E. The client was unable to identify feelings or actions of the bullying victim and was provided with additional information.

18. Assign Observation of Bullying (18)

A. The client was assigned to be alert to observing instances of bullying perpetrated by others.

B. The client was asked to specifically note the feelings experienced by the victim.

C. The client identified instances of bullying being perpetrated by others and the feelings of the victim; these experiences were processed.

D. The client has not identified instances of bullying being perpetrated by others and was directed to continue to be alert for examples in this area.

19. **Explore Capacity for Empathy (19)**

A. The client's capacity for empathy was explored.

B. Indicators of conduct disorder were explored (e.g., cruelty to animals).

C. Conduct disorder indicators were identified, and the focus of treatment was shifted to this area.

D. The client has been assessed for indicators of conduct disorder but does not display them; the client displays a significant capacity for empathy.

20. **Assess Self-Perception (20)**

A. The client was asked to write a list of words that were self-descriptive.

B. The client's list of self-descriptive words was reviewed to help assess self-perception.

C. The client's self-descriptors were interpreted as indicative of low self-esteem, isolation, and feeling unloved.

D. The client's self-descriptors were interpreted as indicative of aggression.

E. The client's self-perception was judged to be distorted and unrealistic because they did not acknowledge their pattern of intimidation of others.

21. **Assign Drawing Pictures of Self (21)**

A. The client was asked to draw pictures that reflect how they perceive self when engaging in bullying behavior.

B. The client drew detailed pictures about how they feel about self when engaging in bullying behavior, and these were processed.

C. With encouragement, the client drew several vague, undetailed pictures of self.

D. The client willingly talked about each of the pictures they drew, identifying specific feelings about self, and these were processed.

E. The client refused to draw pictures and was reminded of the benefits of these techniques.

22. **Explore Thoughts, Feelings, and Circumstances (22)**

A. The client was assisted in exploring thoughts, feelings, and circumstances that preceded the bullying/intimidation incident.

B. The client was reinforced for insight into the connection between thoughts, feelings, and circumstances, and the bullying/intimidation incident.

C. The client struggled to make a connection between thoughts, feelings, and circumstances, and the bullying/intimidation incident.

23. **Journal Incidents of Bullying (23)**

A. The client was instructed to journal past or present incidents of bullying.

B. The client journaled past or present incidents of bullying and was assisted in identifying maladaptive thoughts or cognitive distortions.

C. The client did not accurately journal past or present incidents of bullying and was redirected to do so.

D. Upon reviewing the journal, the client was assisted in replacing maladaptive thoughts or cognitive distortions with more adaptive cognitions.

E. The client struggled to identify and replace maladaptive thoughts or cognitive distortions and was given remedial feedback.

24. Teach Appropriate Feeling Expression (24)

A. The client was taught about more appropriate ways to express feelings and resolve conflict with peers.

B. The client was given examples of ways to replace thinking errors or distorted thoughts that encourage bullying with more reality-based statements.

C. The benefits of expressing feelings and reality-based statements were reinforced with the client.

D. The client was resistive to identifying thinking errors or distorted thoughts; tentative examples were identified and offered to the client.

25. Explore Goal of Intimidation (25)

A. The client was assisted in exploring their goal when the client engages in intimidation of others.

B. The client was assisted in identifying the desire to impress peers and gain acceptance as the goal of intimidation.

C. The client was assisted in identifying how intimidation is directed toward the goal of controlling others.

D. The client was assisted in identifying that intimidation of others is used to resolve a conflict through aggressive means.

E. The client had difficulty understanding the goal of intimidation of others and was provided with tentative examples in this area.

26. Role-Play Goal of Bullying (26)

A. Social interactions were role-played in which the client is the bully.

B. The role-play interaction was periodically stopped in order to have the client verbalize their goal or intent.

C. Support and feedback were provided as the client identified their goal and intent of their bullying behavior.

D. The client struggled to identify the goal or intent of their bullying behavior and was provided with tentative interpretations, based on their actions within the role-play.

27. Identify Social Rewards (27)

A. The client was asked to identify social rewards they achieve through bullying, such as smiles, laughter, or words of affirmation.

B. The client was asked to identify more adaptive ways to achieve social rewards.

C. The client was able to identify social rewards received through bullying and new adaptive ways to achieve social rewards.

D. The client was unable to identify social rewards of bullying and was provided with tentative examples.

E. The client was unable to identify more adaptive ways to achieve social rewards and was provided with tentative examples.

28. Identify Prosocial Means to Attain Goals (28)

A. The client was assisted in identifying prosocial means of attaining healthy interaction goals.

B. The client was recommended to read excerpts from *Cool, Calm and Confident: A Workbook to Help Kids Learn Assertiveness Skills* (Schab).

C. The client was assisted in identifying how they can attain respect by being kind, honest, and trustworthy.

D. The client was assisted in identifying how they can attain leadership through assertiveness and respect of others rather than aggression.

E. The client was assisted in identifying how they can use effective problem-solving techniques rather than intimidation.

F. The client was defensive and unwilling to identify prosocial means of attaining healthy interaction goals and was provided with tentative examples in this area.

29. List Ways to Achieve Empowerment (29)

A. The client was instructed to list appropriate ways to achieve a sense of empowerment among peers.

B. The client was provided with initial examples of appropriate ways to achieve a sense of empowerment among peers.

C. The client listed realistic, appropriate ways to achieve a sense of empowerment among peers.

D. The client was unable to list realistic, appropriate ways to achieve a sense of empowerment and was assisted in brainstorming this.

30. Recommend Mentor (30)

A. It was recommended that the client be assigned an adult or peer mentor.

B. The client was accepting of an adult or peer mentor to help teach effective conflict resolution, assertiveness, and positive social skills.

C. The client was unwilling to engage with an adult or peer mentor and unhealthy beliefs were challenged.

31. Role-Play Assertiveness (31)

A. Conflict situations were role-played with the client, first using bullying, then using assertiveness and problem-solving techniques.

B. The client was assigned the "Problem-Solving Exercise" from the *Child Psychotherapy Homework Planner* (Jongsma, Peterson, McInnis, & Bruce).

C. The client successfully replaced bullying with assertiveness and problem-solving techniques and was provided with feedback.

D. The client was supported as they identified ways to use assertiveness or problem-solving techniques in situations in which they have used bullying.

E. The client has failed to use assertiveness and problem-solving as a substitute for bullying, and the client was provided with further encouragement in this area.

32. Refer to Social Skills Training Group (32)

A. The client was referred to a social skills training group to improve the demonstration of respect and compassion for peers.

B. The client was given the directive to self-disclose at least one time during the group-therapy session.

C. The client was encouraged to demonstrate respect and compassion for the thoughts, feelings, and needs of others during the group therapy sessions.

D. The client has regularly attended group therapy sessions, and the benefits of these sessions were reviewed.

E. The client has not regularly attended group social skills training and was redirected to do so.

33. Utilize Small Group Intervention Approaches (33)

A. Parents and school officials were consulted about utilizing small group intervention approaches.

B. Small group intervention approaches were employed to assist the client in building social skills, increasing empathy for victim(s), and improving conflict-resolution skills with peers.

C. Small group intervention approaches have been useful in improving the client's social skills, empathy, and conflict-resolution skills.

D. Small group intervention approaches have not been useful for the client, and barriers were problem-solved.

34. Play the "Social Conflict" Game (34)

A. The "Social Conflict" game (Berg) was played with the client.

B. Through the use of the "Social Conflict" game, the client was able to develop behavioral skills to decrease antisocial interactions with others.

C. The client was open and verbal when playing the "Social Conflict" game and was encouraged for this progress.

D. The client was guarded and defensive when playing the "Social Conflict" game and was urged to be more open in order to learn the skills to decrease interpersonal conflict.

35. Connect Painful Feelings to Acting-Out Behavior (35)

A. The client was helped to make key connections between painful feelings of loss, rejection, and abandonment and acting-out and/or aggressive behaviors.

B. Verbal praise and affirmation were given to the client for each connection they made between feelings and behavior.

C. The client's progress in connecting painful feelings and behaviors has helped to reduce the frequency of acting-out behaviors.

D. The client has struggled to connect painful feelings to acting-out behavior and was provided with remedial assistance in this area.

36. Use Puppets to Model Constructive Conflict Management (36)

A. A story of another's use of constructive ways to handle/manage conflicts with peers was told to the client using puppets, dolls, and stuffed animals.

B. The client was asked to use the puppets, dolls, or stuffed animals to tell a story about constructive ways to handle/manage peer conflicts.

C. The client appeared to internalize the conflict-management techniques because they were able to describe these techniques through playing with puppets, dolls, and stuffed animals.

37. Use a Therapeutic Game for Anger Control (37)

A. A therapeutic game was used to help expand the client's ways to manage aggressive feelings.

B. "The Anger Control Game" (Shore) was used to help expand the client's ways to manage aggressive feelings.

C. The client was provided with positive feedback as they were active and involved in the therapeutic game and learned ways to manage aggressive feelings.

D. The client was guarded and defensive when participating in the therapeutic game and was urged to be more open.

38. Teach About Bullying Causes and Effects (38)

A. Books were read with the client to teach about the causes and effects of bullying.

B. Books were read with the client, including *Sometimes I Like to Fight, But I Don't Do It Much Anymore* (Shapiro) and *Confessions of a Former Bully* (Ludwig).

C. Games were used to teach the client about the causes and effects of bullying.

D. The "No More Bullies" game (Courage to Change) or "The Anti-Bullying Game" (Searle & Streng) was used to teach the client about the causes and effects of bullying.

E. The principles learned through books and games were applied to the client's daily life.

39. Conduct Family Therapy to Explore Contributing Dynamics (39)

A. Family therapy sessions were held to explore the dynamics that contribute to the emergence of the client's bullying/intimidating behavior.

B. Family dynamics were investigated, including parental modeling of aggressive behavior; sexual, verbal, or physical abuse of family members; substance abuse in the home; and neglect.

C. Specific family dynamics were identified within the home and appropriate treatment was coordinated for these issues.

D. The family therapy session did not uncover dynamics that contribute to the emergence of the client's bullying/intimidating behavior, and issues were left to be reviewed again at a later time.

40. Explore Family Interaction Patterns (40)

A. Family interaction patterns were explored with the family members to identify whether aggression, intimidation, and threats are often used during times of conflict.

B. Family members were supported as they identified that aggression, intimidation, and threats are often used during times of conflict with others outside the family.

C. Family members were provided with support as they identified that aggression, intimidation, and threats are typically used to resolve most conflicts within the family.

41. Assign a Family Task (41)

A. In a family therapy session, the family was assigned the task of resolving a conflict.

B. The family was assigned the "Problem-Solving Exercise" from the *Child Psychotherapy Homework Planner* (Jongsma, Peterson, McInnis, & Bruce).

C. The family's conflict-resolution skills were assessed for the use of effective and respectful problem-solving techniques.

D. The client's family was provided with positive feedback for their use of effective and respectful problem-solving techniques.

E. It was reflected to the family that authoritarian and aggressive techniques were used rather than respectful problem-solving.

42. **Teach Respectful Family Conflict-Resolution Techniques (42)**

A. Family members were taught respectful conflict-resolution techniques, in which the parents' authority is recognized but not flaunted without regard to the feelings of others.

B. The family was provided with specific examples of how respectful conflict-resolution techniques can be used within a family.

C. Positive feedback was provided as the family displayed a clear understanding of respectful conflict-resolution techniques.

D. The family members failed to understand the use of respectful conflict-resolution techniques and the recognition of the parents' authority without sounding authoritarian; they were provided with additional information in this area.

43. **Encourage Emotional Expression (43)**

A. The client was encouraged to express feelings associated with experiences of neglect, abuse, separation, or abandonment.

B. The client was supported as they expressed feelings associated with experiences of neglect, abuse, separation, or abandonment.

C. The client was guarded about expressing feelings associated with experiences of neglect, abuse, separation, or abandonment and was urged to express these as the client feels safe in doing so.

44. **Give Permission for Crying (44)**

A. The client was given specific permission to cry about losses, separation, or abandonment.

B. The client was educated about the healing nature of crying.

C. The client was taught about how crying provides an opportunity to express sadness, takes the edge off of anger, and helps to induce calm.

D. The client was supported as they cried about past losses, separation, or abandonment.

E. Despite encouragement and support, the client remained guarded about crying about losses, separation, or abandonment; the client was encouraged to cry about this as they feel able to do so.

BULLYING/AGGRESSION VICTIM

CLIENT PRESENTATION

1. **Repeated Victimization Experiences (1)***
   A. The client and parents reported that the client has been victimized by peers.
   B. The client reported verbal/physical aggression, relational bullying, and/or cyberbullying.
   C. Experiences of aggression and/or bullying from peers has decreased over time.
   D. The client reported no longer experiencing aggression and/or bullying from peers.

2. **Intense Negative Emotions (2)**
   A. The client has experienced intense negative emotions related to the bullying/intimidation from an older or stronger peer.
   B. The client was visibly distressed and upset when discussing the bullying/intimidation.
   C. The intensity of the client's emotional distress has decreased when discussing the bullying/intimidation.
   D. The client has been able to talk about the bullying/intimidation without displaying a significant amount of emotional distress.

3. **Feelings of Shame (2)**
   A. The client expressed strong feelings of shame about the bullying/intimidation.
   B. The client has continued to experience strong feelings of shame about the bullying/intimidation, despite being given reassurance that they are not responsible for the bullying/intimidation.
   C. The client's feelings of shame have started to decrease as they now recognize that the perpetrator is responsible for the bullying/intimidation.
   D. The client has successfully worked through and resolved feelings of shame about the bullying/intimidation.

4. **Fear of Assault (3)**
   A. The client experiences a strong fear of being physically assaulted, ridiculed, embarrassed or forced to do something against their will.
   B. The client's fear of being physically assaulted, ridiculed, embarrassed, or forced to do something against their will has altered their day-to-day life.
   C. The client's fear of being physically assaulted, ridiculed, embarrassed, or forced to do something against their will has reduced in frequency.
   D. The client no longer experiences a strong fear of being physical assaulted, ridiculed, embarrassed, or forced to do something against their will.

---

*The numbers in parentheses correlate to the number of the Behavioral Definition statement in the companion chapter with the same title in the *Child Psychotherapy Treatment Planner*, Sixth Edition, by Jongsma, Peterson, McInnis, & Bruce (Wiley, 2023).

5. **Negative Self-Image (4)**
   A. The client has developed a negative self-image of being weak and powerless.
   B. The client verbalized several self-derogatory remarks and compared self unfavorably to others.
   C. The client shared their viewpoint of self as being weak and powerless.
   D. The client's increased confidence in self has helped them be more outgoing and independent.
   E. The client has consistently verbalized positive self in the presence of others.

6. **Social Isolation (5)**
   A. The client described a persistent pattern of withdrawing or self-isolating from most social situations.
   B. The client acknowledged that social withdrawal interferes with the ability to establish and maintain friendships.
   C. The client has gradually started to socialize with a wider circle of peers.
   D. The client has become more outgoing and interacts with peers on a regular, consistent basis.

7. **Passivity (6)**
   A. The client is viewed to be passive in peer relationships.
   B. The client's passive nature contributes to a reluctance to talk about victimization with adults, school staff, or peers.
   C. The client has become more confident and been able to share experiences of victimization with trusted adults and peers.

8. **Lack of Assertiveness (6)**
   A. The client has much difficulty being assertive in social situations where it is indicated.
   B. The client has generally avoided any social situations that involve the potential for conflict.
   C. The client is beginning to be assertive more often instead of withdrawing from interpersonal problems or conflicts.
   D. The client has recently been assertive in an effective manner during conflict with others.

9. **Intense Emotional Distress (7)**
   A. The parents indicated the client experiences intense emotional distress when faced with going to school in the morning.
   B. The client reported thinking about going to school in the morning has caused intense distress.
   C. The client's intense emotional reactions to school have interfered with academic abilities and friendships at school.
   D. The client and parents report that the client is experiencing fewer periods of intense emotional distress before going to school.
   E. The client and parents reported no recent experiences of intense emotional distress before going to school.

10. **Psychosomatic Ailments (8)**
    A. The client has demonstrated a significant increase in psychosomatic complaints related to going to school.
    B. The client complained of not feeling well when discussing school.
    C. The client was resistant to the interpretation that psychosomatic complaints are related to underlying painful emotions about going to school.
    D. The client verbalized an understanding of the connection between psychosomatic complaints and school conflicts.
    E. The client has demonstrated a significant reduction in the frequency of psychosomatic complaints.

11. **Suicidal Ideation (9)**
    A. The client verbalized suicidal ideation.
    B. The client reported feeling very hopeless and helpless regarding the future.
    C. Suicidal thoughts and feelings seemed to dominate the client at the present time.
    D. The client revealed a plan along with a backup plan for suicide.
    E. The client has gradually started to feel more hopeful and less despondent.

12. **Victimization Due to Academic Performance (10)**
    A. The client's parents reported that the client's learning disability or lowered academic performance contributes to bullying/intimidation by peers.
    B. The client reported low self-esteem due to peers' bullying related to their grades.
    C. The client has gained self-confidence regarding their learning disability or academic performance.

13. **Poor Social Behaviors (11)**
    A. The client has engaged in poor social behaviors that have set up the client for bullying.
    B. The client has lacked awareness of annoying, disruptive, or immature social behaviors.
    C. The client has started to develop an awareness of appropriate social behaviors.
    D. The client has displayed good social behaviors in recent interactions with peers and adults.
    E. The client has developed a number of essential social behaviors that have reduced the bullying/intimidation from peers.

INTERVENTIONS IMPLEMENTED

1. **Establish Rapport (1)***
    A. Caring was conveyed to the client through support, warmth, and empathy.
    B. The client was provided with nonjudgmental support and a level of trust was developed.

---

*The numbers in parentheses correlate to the number of the Therapeutic Intervention statement in the companion chapter with the same title in the *Child Psychotherapy Treatment Planner*, Sixth Edition, by Jongsma, Peterson, McInnis, & Bruce (Wiley, 2023).

C. The client was urged to feel safe in describing experiences of being bullied or intimidated by others.

D. The client began to express feelings more freely as rapport and trust level have increased.

E. The client has continued to experience difficulty being open and direct about the expression of painful feelings; the client was encouraged to use the safe haven of therapy to express these difficult issues.

2. Focus on Strengthening Therapeutic Relationship (2)

A. The relationship with the client was strengthened using empirically supported factors.

B. The relationship with the client was strengthened through the implementation of collaborative approach, agreement on goals, demonstration of empathy, verbalization of positive regard, and collection of client feedback.

C. The client reacted positively to the relationship-strengthening measures taken.

D. The client verbalized feeling supported and understood during therapy sessions.

E. Despite attempts to strengthen the therapeutic relationship, the client reports feeling distant and misunderstood.

F. The client has indicated that sessions are not helpful and will be terminating therapy.

3. Assess Nature of Victimization Experiences (3)

A. The client was given encouragement and support to tell the entire story of the bullying/intimidation experiences and to express feelings experienced during and after the victimization

B. Support was provided as the client described the sequence of events before, during, and after the bullying/intimidation incidents, including their response to this behavior but neither showed nor talked of any feelings.

C. Client-centered principles were used to encourage and support the client in expressing feelings surrounding the past bullying/intimidation experiences.

D. The client has not been able to tell the entire story of the bullying and intimidation that they experienced and was redirected to do so.

4. Obtain Input from Adults (4)

A. The client's parents/caregivers were asked for their input regarding the effects of bullying/intimidation on the client's moods and behaviors.

B. The client's teachers were asked for their input regarding the effects of bullying/intimidation on the client's moods and behaviors.

C. The parents'/caregivers' and teachers' input about bullying/intimidation was summarized, and it reflected a significant pattern of mood or behavior concerns.

5. Conduct/Refer for Psychoeducational Evaluation (5)

A. The client received a psychoeducational evaluation to rule out the presence of a possible cognitive/intellectual deficit or learning disability that may be contributing to low self-esteem, social anxiety, and passivity in peer relationships.

B. The client appeared anxious and seemed to lack confidence in their abilities during the psychoeducational evaluation.

C. The client was uncooperative during the psychoeducational evaluation and did not appear to put forth good effort.

D. Rapport was easily established with the client, and they appeared motivated to do their best during the psychoeducational testing.

E. Feedback from the psychoeducational testing was provided to the client, parents, and school officials.

6. Assess Level of Insight (6)

A. The client's level of insight toward the presenting problems was assessed.

B. The client was assessed in regard to the syntonic versus dystonic nature of their insight about the presenting problems.

C. The client was noted to demonstrate good insight into the problematic nature of the behavior and symptoms.

D. The client was noted to be in agreement with others' concerns and is motivated to work on change.

E. The client was noted to be ambivalent regarding the problems described and is reluctant to address the issues as a concern.

F. The client was noted to be resistant regarding acknowledgment of the problem areas, is not concerned about them, and has no motivation to make changes.

7. Assess for Correlated Disorders (7)

A. The client was assessed for evidence of research-based correlated disorders.

B. The client was assessed in regard to the level of vulnerability to suicide.

C. The client was identified as having a comorbid disorder, and treatment was adjusted to account for these concerns.

D. The client has been assessed for any correlated disorders, but none were found.

8. Assess for Culturally Based Confounding Issues (8)

A. The client was assessed for age-related issues that could help to better understand their clinical presentation.

B. The client was assessed for gender-related issues that could help to better understand their clinical presentation.

C. The client was assessed for cultural syndromes, cultural idioms of distress, or culturally based perceived causes that could help to better understand their clinical presentation.

D. Alternative factors have been identified as contributing to the client's currently defined "problem behavior," and these were taken into account in regard to treatment.

E. Culturally based factors that could help to account for the client's currently defined "problem behavior" were investigated, but no significant factors were identified.

9. Assess Severity of Impairment (9)

A. The severity of the client's impairment was assessed to determine the appropriate level of care.

B. The client was assessed in regard to impairment in social, relational, and educational endeavors.

C. It was reflected to the client that the impairment appears to create mild to moderate effects on the client's functioning.

D. It was reflected to the client that the impairment appears to create severe to very severe effects on the client's functioning.

E. The client was continuously assessed for the severity of impairment, as well as the efficacy and appropriateness of treatment.

10. Assess for Pathogenic Care (10)

A. The home, school, and community of the client were assessed for pathogenic care and concerns.

B. The client's various environments were assessed for the persistent disregard of the child's needs, repeated changes in caregivers, limited opportunities for stable attachment, harsh discipline, or other grossly inept care.

C. Pathogenic care was identified and the treatment plan included strategies for managing or correcting these concerns and protecting the child.

D. No pathogenic care was identified and this was reflected to the client and caregivers.

11. Assess for Depression (11)

A. A structured assessment was conducted to help identify the severity of depression, social anxiety, and presence of suicidal ideation.

B. No symptoms of depression, social anxiety, or suicidal ideation were identified, and this has been reflected to the client and parents.

C. Symptoms of depression, social anxiety, and suicidal ideation have been identified as mild and this was reflected to the family members.

D. Symptoms of depression, social anxiety, and suicidal ideation have been identified as severe and this was reflected to the family members.

E. Treatment has been focused onto the client's depression, social anxiety, and/or suicidal ideation symptoms.

12. Refer for Medication Evaluation (12)

A. Arrangements were made for the client to have an evaluation for the purpose of considering psychotropic medication to alleviate social discomfort symptoms.

B. The client has followed through with seeing a prescriber for an evaluation of any organic causes for the anxiety and for the need for psychotropic medication to control the anxiety response.

C. The client has not cooperated with the referral to a prescriber for a medication evaluation and was encouraged to do so.

13. Assess for Suicide Plan (13)

A. The client was assessed for specific thoughts, desire for, or plans for suicide.

B. The client was assessed as having a high risk for suicide and hospitalization was arranged.

C. The client was assessed as having a low risk for suicide and was provided with resource in case this risk increases.

14. **Consider Informing Parents (14)**

   A. A discussion was held with the client regarding informing parents of the suicide potential as well as precautions that should be taken.

   B. The client made a plan to tell their parents about their suicide potential and was aided by the therapist in this discussion.

   C. The client did not want to tell their parents about their suicide potential and was provided with feedback regarding this decision.

   D. Although the client did not want to tell their parents about their suicide potential, the therapist was compelled to inform them and provide resources.

15. **Encourage Informing Adults (15)**

   A. The client was encouraged to inform parents, school officials, or other supportive individuals when being bullied.

   B. The client identified several individuals they could inform if bullying occurred.

   C. The client was unwilling to inform adults when bullying occurs and was provided with feedback and encouragement.

16. **Develop List of Supports (16)**

   A. The client was assisted in developing a list of peers, adults, school officials, and members of the community who can provide emotional support after experiencing bullying/intimidation.

   B. The client was assisted in developing a list of peers, adults, school officials, and members of the community who can intervene effectively and prevent the client from experiencing further acts of bullying/intimidation.

   C. The client successfully compiled a list of trusted peers and adults who can provide support and intervene effectively to prevent the client from experiencing further acts of bullying/intimidation.

   D. The client was unable to identify any trusted peers or adults to go to for support and intervention in bullying/intimidation and was assisted in brainstorming during the session.

17. **Empower Client to Call Police (17)**

   A. The client and parents were empowered to contact police and authority figures at school when the client has been a victim of severe assault or seriously threatened with harm.

   B. The client and parents were provided with resources on how to contact police and authority figures in the event of a severe assault or serious threat of harm.

18. **Assign Peer Mentor (18)**

   A. The client was encouraged to use a peer mentor who can provide ongoing support, friendship, and coaching on effective ways to handle or avoid bullying.

   B. School officials were contacted to encourage the assignment of a peer mentor to provide the client with support, friendship, and coaching.

   C. The client identified a positive experience of having a peer mentor and feelings were processed.

   D. The client was uninterested in having a peer mentor and was redirected to consider this option.

19. Encourage Assertiveness (19)

A. The client and therapist brainstormed ways to identify when they should contact an appropriate authority figure and when they should be assertive with the bully.

B. The client was able to appropriately identify when they should contact an appropriate authority figure and when they can be assertive with the bully.

C. The client identified specific statements to use to be assertive against a bully.

20. Probe Feelings Associated with Bullying by Others (20)

A. The client was given the opportunity to express feelings about past incidents of being bullied by an older/stronger peer.

B. The client was given empathy and support in expressing feelings about incidents of being bullied by older/stronger peers.

C. The client was instructed to use a journal to record thoughts and feelings about incidents of being bullied by older/stronger peers.

D. The empty-chair technique was employed to facilitate the client's expression of feelings surrounding incidents of being bullied by older/stronger peers.

E. The client was instructed to draw pictures that reflect feelings about incidents of being bullied by older/stronger peers.

F. Despite several attempts to allow the client to explore feelings associated with the incidents of being bullied by older/stronger peers, the client has continued to be defensive and guarded about these types of feelings and was encouraged to express them as they feel able to do so.

21. Identify Feelings Through Art Techniques (21)

A. The client was asked to draw pictures of different feelings and was then asked to identify times when they experienced different feelings surrounding the bullying/aggression victimization.

B. The client was able to use drawing pictures to eventually express feelings verbally within the session, and these feelings were empathetically reflected back to the client.

C. The client was able to express different emotions about the bullying/aggression victimization to family members or significant others.

22. Explore Self-Talk (22)

A. The client was assisted in identifying the self-talk that mediates their fears and reluctance to assert self with aggressive/intimidating peers.

B. The client was taught the role of self-talk in precipitating emotional responses.

C. The client was assigned *Don't Pick on Me: Help for Kids to Stand Up to and Deal with Bullies* (Green).

D. The client was reinforced as they verbalized an understanding of the self-talk that mediates fears and reluctant responses.

E. The client was assisted in replacing biased messages with realistic cognitions.

F. The client failed to identify self-talk and was provided with tentative examples in this area.

23. Assign Homework on Self-Talk (23)

A. The client was assigned homework exercises to identify negative self-talk and replace it with more positive or affirming self-statements.

B. The client was assigned the exercise "Replace Negative Thoughts with Positive Self-Talk" from the *Child Psychotherapy Homework Planner* (Jongsma, Peterson, McInnis, & Bruce).

C. The client's use of self-talk techniques was reviewed and reinforced.

D. The client has struggled in implementation of self-talk techniques and was provided with corrective feedback.

E. The client has not attempted to use the self-talk techniques and was redirected to do so.

24. Assign Readings (24)

A. *The No More Bullying Book for Kids: Become Strong, Happy, and Bully-Proof* (Allen) was read to the client in today's therapy session to help teach effective ways to deal with aggressive and intimidating behavior.

B. *Speak Up and Get Along!* (Cooper) was read to help the client gain social skills and friends.

C. *How to Stop Being Teased and Bullied Without Really Trying* (Kalman) was assigned to the client.

D. *Bullies to Buddies—How to Turn Your Enemies into Friends* (Kalman) was assigned to the client.

E. The key concepts from the assigned readings were processed with the client.

F. The assigned reading(s) helped the client to identify and express feelings.

25. Assign Videos (25)

A. The client was assigned to watch videos to learn how to be assertive effectively with bullies.

B. The client was assigned to watch *How to Win the War Against Bullying* (Kalman) and *How to Stop a Bully* (Gibbs).

C. The client viewed the assigned videos, and key concepts were reinforced.

D. The client has not viewed the assigned videos and was encouraged to do so.

26. Assess Ego Strength (26)

A. The client was assessed as to whether they have the ego strength or self-confidence to deal effectively with bullying/intimidation behavior or if they will need support/intervention from adults.

B. The client was assessed as having enough ego strength and self-confidence to deal effectively with bullying/intimidation behavior and does not need additional support or intervention from adults.

C. The client was assessed to have low ego strength and low self-confidence and will likely need support/intervention from adults to deal with bullying.

27. Role Play Assertiveness Skills (27)

A. The client was taught assertiveness skills through role-playing.

B. In the session, the client was assisted in role-playing "I messages," maintaining good eye contact, and remaining calm.

    C. The client was assigned "Learn to Be Assertive" in the *Child Psychotherapy Homework Planner* (Jongsma, Peterson, McInnis, & Bruce).

    D. The client was reinforced for clear understanding of assertiveness skills and was instructed to practice this in everyday life.

    E. The client displayed a poor understanding of assertiveness skills and was provided with remedial feedback.

28. Teach Goal of Bully (28)

    A. The client was assisted in realizing that the goal of the bully is to get a reaction or cause them to be upset.

    B. It was emphasized to the client that they can win against the bully by staying calm and not getting upset.

    C. The client showed insight into the goal of the bully and the way to win by staying calm and was provided with positive reinforcement for this understanding.

29. Teach the Golden Rule Principle (29)

    A. The client was taught about the Golden Rule principle where they respond with calm and kindness or treat the bully the way the client would like to be treated.

    B. The client accurately role-played the Golden Rule principle in session and was provided with positive feedback.

    C. The client inaccurately role-played the Gold Rule principle in session and was provided with remedial feedback.

30. Explore Impact on Self-Perception (30)

    A. The client was assisted in exploring how bullying incidents affected their self-perception.

    B. The client was asked to draw pictures reflecting things they can do to feel more powerful.

    C. The client drew pictures of empowering actions, such as speaking assertively to the bullying or ignoring the bully and talking to a friend instead, and this insight was processed.

    D. The client drew pictures of unhelpful actions and was redirected with more positive empowering actions.

    E. The client was unwilling to draw pictures of empowering actions and this reluctance was reviewed.

31. Replace Powerlessness Self-Image (31)

    A. The client was asked to identify positive self-talk or statements that can replace the image of self as being weak or powerless.

    B. The client was given examples of positive self-talk or statements to replace weak or powerless images of self.

    C. The client was assigned "Show Your Strengths" in the *Child Psychotherapy Homework Planner* (Jongsma, Peterson, McInnis, & Bruce).

    D. The client completed the "Show Your Strengths" assignment and processed the answers.

    E. The client did not complete the "Show Your Strengths" assignment and was redirected do so.

32. Develop Awareness of Strengths (32)

A. The client was assisted in identifying their own physical competencies and strengths.

B. The client was celebrated for knowing their own physical competencies and strengths.

C. The client was encouraged to use physical skills and strengths in everyday life or at school with peers.

D. The client identified several instances where they used physical skills or strengths in everyday life and this positive step was processed.

33. Confront Client Blaming Self (33)

A. The client was asked to create and process a list of reasons why they were bullied.

B. Each time the client made an excuse for the bully's aggressive behavior, the client was confronted and reminded that they in no way deserved being hurt.

C. The message was given to the client that even though they are not perfect, the violence was not deserved.

D. The client was redirected when continuing to excuse the bully for the violent behavior and engaged in self-blame.

E. Positive feedback was provided as the client has begun to place clear responsibility for the violence on the bully and has discontinued self-blame.

34. Teach Problem-Solving Skills (34)

A. The client was taught tailored, age-appropriate social problem-solving skills.

B. The client was taught problem-solving skills, including specifying the problem, generating options, listing pros and cons of each option, selecting an option, implementing an option, and refining.

C. The client was asked to use client-tailored, age-appropriate social problem-solving skills on a regular basis.

35. Teach Calming Techniques (35)

A. Deep muscle relaxation, deep breathing, positive self-talk, and positive imagery techniques were taught to the client to enhance the ability to relax.

B. The client was assigned the "Deep Breathing Exercise" and "Replace Negative Thoughts with Positive Self-Talk" from the *Child Psychotherapy Homework Planner* (Jongsma, Peterson, McInnis, & Bruce).

C. The client was assigned the "Progressive Muscle Relaxation" from the *Adolescent Psychotherapy Homework Planner* (Jongsma, Peterson, McInnis, & Bruce).

D. Behavioral rehearsal was used to give the client opportunity to practice each relaxation skill.

E. The client was reminded of the benefits of deep muscle relaxation, deep breathing, and positive imagery and encouraged to use each on a regular basis.

F. The client has implemented the calming techniques and reports a reduction in stress and anxiety.

G. The client has failed to follow through with implementation of calming techniques.

36. Teach Conflict-Resolution Skills (36)

A. The client was taught conflict-resolution skills through modeling, role-playing, and behavioral rehearsal in order to minimize or manage aggressive or intimidating behaviors by peers.

B. The client was taught about empathy and active listening.

C. The client was taught about "I messages," respectful communication, assertiveness without aggression, and compromise.

D. The client was reinforced for clear understanding of the conflict-resolution skills.

E. The client displayed a poor understanding of the conflict-resolution skills and was provided with remedial feedback.

37. Refer to Peer Mediation Group (37)

A. For less severe cases, the client was referred to a peer mediation group where the client and bully share thoughts and feelings about each other's actions and select uncoerced solutions to prevent future reoccurrences of bullying behavior.

B. The client was willing to engage in a peer mediation group with the bully.

C. The client attended the peer mediation group with the bully and processed the thoughts and feelings experienced during this group.

D. The client did not attend the peer mediation group and was redirected to try this useful tool.

38. Select Exposures That Are Likely to Succeed (38)

A. Initial in vivo or role-played exposures were selected, with a bias toward those that have a high likelihood of being a successful experience for the client.

B. Cognitive restructuring was done within and after the exposure using behavioral strategies (e.g., modeling, rehearsal, social reinforcement).

C. A review was conducted with the client about the use of in vivo or role-played exposure.

D. The client was provided with positive feedback regarding the use of exposures.

E. The client has not used in vivo or role-played exposures and was redirected to do.

39. Assign Homework on Exposure (39)

A. The client was assigned homework exercises to perform sensation exposure and record their experience.

B. The client's use of sensation exposure techniques was reviewed and reinforced.

C. The client has struggled in implementation of sensation exposure technique and was provided with corrective feedback.

D. The client has not attempted to use the sensation exposure techniques and was redirected to do so.

40. Assign Overnight Visit with Friend (40)

A. The client was given the homework assignment to either invite a friend for an overnight visit or set up an overnight visit at the friend's home.

B. The client was given the opportunity to express and work through fears and anxiety about inviting a friend for an overnight visit or setting up an overnight visit at a friend's home.

C. The client complied with the directive to have an overnight visit with a friend, resulting in some anxiety but also pride of accomplishment.

D. The client failed to set up an overnight visit with a friend and was refocused on this task.

41. **Contact School Officials About Socialization (41)**

A. School officials were contacted about ways to increase the client's socialization (e.g., raising the flag with a group of peers, participating in school fundraising project, pair the client with a popular peer on a classroom assignment).

B. The school officials agreed to assign tasks or activities that will enable the client to socialize with peers.

C. The consultation with school officials was helpful in increasing the client's socialization with peers.

D. School officials have not implemented ways to increase the client's socialization, and additional consultation was provided to encourage the use of these helpful techniques.

42. **List Ways to Improve Self-Esteem (42)**

A. The client was assisted in listing positive peer group or extracurricular activities that can improve self-esteem and feelings of acceptance/belonging, and overcome feelings of insecurity related to bullying.

B. The client was provided with initial examples of appropriate ways to improve self-esteem.

C. The client listed realistic, appropriate ways to improve self-esteem.

D. The client was unable to list realistic, appropriate ways to increase self-esteem and was assisted in brainstorming this.

43. **Explore Attention-Seeking Behaviors (43)**

A. The client was provided with insight into how annoying, immature, or negative attention-seeing behaviors may set up the client for being teased, mocked, or bullied by older/stronger peers.

B. The client reported an understanding of the impact of annoying, immature, or negative attention-seeking behaviors on how others view and treat them.

C. The client identified specific annoying, immature, or negative attention-seeking behaviors that they can decrease.

D. The client displayed minimal insight into annoying, immature, or negative attention-seeking behaviors, and the contribution to their experiences of being teased, mocked, or bullied.

44. **Use "Finding Ways to Get Positive Attention" Exercise (44)**

A. The client was assigned the "Finding Ways to Get Positive Attention" exercise from the *Child Psychotherapy Homework Planner* (Jongsma, Peterson, McInnis, & Bruce) to help identify ways to seek positive attention from peers.

B. The client was encouraged to participate in extracurricular or positive peer group activities as a way to increase self-esteem.

C. The client reported that the "Finding Ways to Get Positive Attention" exercise helped the client realize how their acting-out behaviors are related to the emotional pain surrounding their parents' divorce.

D. The client failed to complete the "Finding Ways to Get Positive Attention" exercise and was asked to complete this task.

45. Conduct Family Therapy to Explore Dynamics (45)

A. Family-therapy sessions were held to explore the dynamics that contribute to the client's passivity and lack of assertiveness with peers.

B. The family was supported as they identified dynamics and stressors that support the client's passivity and lack of assertiveness with peers.

C. The family has not identified dynamics that contribute to the client's passivity and lack of assertiveness with peers and were provided with tentative examples in this area (e.g., parents who are distant and critical or overprotective and coddling; modeling of aggressive behavior by parents or siblings).

46. Assess Parents' Overprotectiveness (46)

A. A family therapy session was conducted to explore whether the parents' overprotectiveness of the client contributes to a lack of assertiveness.

B. The parents were helped to see how their pattern of overprotectiveness contributes to the client's lack of assertiveness.

C. The parents were assisted in differentiating between times when it is important to advocate for the client versus when it is appropriate to allow the client to be assertive independently with peers.

47. Teach Respectful Family Conflict-Resolution Techniques (47)

A. Family members were taught respectful conflict-resolution techniques, in which the parents' authority is recognized but not flaunted without regard to the feelings of others.

B. The family was provided with specific examples of how respectful conflict-resolution techniques can be used within a family.

C. Positive feedback was provided as the family displayed a clear understanding of respectful conflict-resolution techniques.

D. The family members failed to understand the use of respectful conflict-resolution techniques and the recognition of the parents' authority without sounding authoritarian; they were provided with additional information in this area.

48. Employ Play Therapy (48)

A. A play therapy approach was used to help the client begin to identify feelings related to painful emotions, passivity, and lack of assertiveness with peers.

B. The client was given unconditional positive regard, warm acceptance, and support while working through feelings related to painful emotions, passivity, and lack of assertiveness with peers.

C. The client's feelings were reflected as expressed in play, and these feelings were then related to their painful emotions, passivity, and lack of assertiveness with peers.

D. The child-centered play therapy sessions have helped the client begin to express feelings.

E. The child-centered play therapy sessions have helped the client work through many of their feelings.

49. Use Storytelling Technique (49)

A. The therapist used puppets, dolls, and stuffed animals to create scenarios that modeled and/or suggest constructive ways for the client to be assertive and remain calm with bullying behavior by peers.

B. A storytelling technique using puppets, dolls, and stuffed animals was used to model ways for the client to appear more assertive and calmer with bullying behaviors by peers.

C. The client was given the directive to practice what was taught in the stories using puppets, dolls, and stuffed animals.

D. The client has not used the skills learned through the storytelling and puppet techniques and was encouraged to use these effective strategies.

CONDUCT DISORDER/DELINQUENCY

CLIENT PRESENTATION

1. **Refusal to Comply (1)***
   A. The client has demonstrated a persistent refusal to comply with the rules or expectations at home, at school, and in the community.
   B. The client voiced opposition to the rules at home and school.
   C. The client has started to comply with the rules and expectations at home, at school, and in the community.
   D. The client verbalized willingness to comply with the rules and expectations at home, at school, and in the community.
   E. The client has consistently complied with the rules and expectations at home, at school, and in the community.

2. **Acting-Out/Antisocial Behaviors (2)**
   A. The parents reported that the client has an extensive history of engaging in acting-out or antisocial behaviors, such as fighting, intimidation, cruelty or violence toward people or animals, and/or destruction of property.
   B. The client has continued to act out and engage in antisocial behaviors.
   C. The client has a tendency to minimize the seriousness of their antisocial behaviors.
   D. The client verbalized an awareness of how acting-out and antisocial behaviors negatively affect self and others.
   E. The client and parents reported a significant reduction in the frequency and severity of acting-out and antisocial behaviors.

3. **Stealing (3)**
   A. The parents reported that the client has an extensive history of stealing from others at home, at school, and in the community.
   B. The parents reported that the client was recently caught stealing.
   C. The client has not engaged in any stealing in the recent past.
   D. The client has stopped stealing and found more effective ways to meet needs.

4. **Destructive Behaviors (4)**
   A. The client described a series of incidents where they became destructive when upset or frustrated.
   B. The client projected the blame for destructive behaviors onto other people.
   C. The client has begun to take steps to control destructive impulses.

---

*The numbers in parentheses correlate to the number of the Behavioral Definition statement in the companion chapter with the same title in the *Child Psychotherapy Treatment Planner*, Sixth Edition, by Jongsma, Peterson, McInnis, & Bruce (Wiley, 2023).

D. The client has recently demonstrated good self-control and has not engaged in any destructive behaviors.

E. The client has exhibited a significant reduction in the frequency and severity of destructive behaviors.

5. School Behavior Problems (5)

A. A review of the client's history revealed numerous acting-out and rebellious behaviors in the school setting.

B. The client has often disrupted the classroom with negative attention-seeking behaviors.

C. The client has missed a significant amount of time from school due to suspensions.

D. The client has started to exercise greater self-control in the classroom setting.

E. The client has recently demonstrated a significant reduction in the frequency of acting-out or rebellious behaviors at school.

6. Authority Conflicts (6)

A. The client displayed a negativistic attitude and was highly argumentative during today's therapy session.

B. The client has often tested the limits and challenged authority figures at home, at school, and in the community.

C. The client has often talked back to authority figures in a disrespectful manner when reprimanded.

D. The client has recently been more cooperative with authority figures.

E. The client has been cooperative and respectful toward authority figures on a consistent basis.

7. Impulsivity (7)

A. The client presented as a highly impulsive individual who seeks immediate gratification of needs and often fails to consider the consequences of their actions.

B. The client has engaged in impulsive/thrill-seeking behaviors in order to achieve a sense of excitement and fun.

C. The client has begun to take steps toward improving impulse control and delaying the need for immediate gratification.

D. The client has recently demonstrated good impulse control and has not engaged in any serious acting-out or antisocial behaviors.

E. The client has ceased engaging in acting-out behaviors because of improved ability to stop and think about the consequences of their actions.

8. Lying/Conning (8)

A. The client described a pattern of lying, conning, and manipulating others to meet needs and avoid facing the consequences of their actions.

B. The client appeared to be lying in the therapy session about misbehaviors or irresponsible actions.

C. The client was honest in the therapy session and admitted to wrongdoing or irresponsibility.

D. The parents reported that the client has been more honest and accepting of their decisions at home.

9. **Blaming/Projecting (9)**
   A. The client was unwilling to accept responsibility for poor decisions and behaviors; instead the client blamed others as the cause for their decisions and actions.
   B. The client has begun to accept greater responsibility for their actions and placed the blame less often for their wrongdoings onto other people.
   C. The client admitted to wrongdoings and verbalized an acceptance of responsibility for their actions.

10. **Lack of Remorse/Guilt (10)**
   A. The client expressed little or no remorse for irresponsible, acting-out, or aggressive behaviors.
   B. The client expressed remorse for their actions, but apparently only because they had been caught and suffered the consequences of their actions.
   C. The client appeared to express genuine remorse or guilt for misbehavior.

11. **Lack of Empathy/Insensitivity (11)**
   A. The client displayed little concern or empathy for the thoughts, feelings, and needs of other people.
   B. The client has often demonstrated a willingness to ride roughshod over the rights of others in order to meet needs.
   C. The client verbalized an understanding of how their actions negatively affected others.
   D. The client has demonstrated empathy and sensitivity to the thoughts, feelings, and needs of other people.

INTERVENTIONS IMPLEMENTED

1. **Establish Rapport (1)***
   A. Caring was conveyed to the client through support, warmth, and empathy.
   B. The client was provided with nonjudgmental support and a level of trust was developed.
   C. The client was urged to feel safe in expressing conduct issues.
   D. The client began to express feelings more freely as rapport and trust level have increased.
   E. The client has continued to experience difficulty being open and direct about the expression of painful feelings; the client was encouraged to use the safe haven of therapy to express these difficult issues.

2. **Focus on Strengthening Therapeutic Relationship (2)**
   A. The relationship with the client was strengthened using empirically supported factors.
   B. The relationship with the client was strengthened through the implementation of collaborative approach, agreement on goals, demonstration of empathy, verbalization of positive regard, and collection of client feedback.

---

*The numbers in parentheses correlate to the number of the Therapeutic Intervention statement in the companion chapter with the same title in the *Child Psychotherapy Treatment Planner*, Sixth Edition, by Jongsma, Peterson, McInnis, & Bruce (Wiley, 2023).

C. The client reacted positively to the relationship-strengthening measures taken.

D. The client verbalized feeling supported and understood during therapy sessions.

E. Despite attempts to strengthen the therapeutic relationship, the client reports feeling distant and misunderstood.

F. The client has indicated that sessions are not helpful and will be terminating therapy.

3. Assess Anger Dynamics (3)

A. The client was assessed for various stimuli that have triggered anger.

B. The client was helped to identify situations, people, and thoughts that have triggered anger.

C. The client was assisted in identifying the thoughts, feelings, and actions that have characterized anger responses.

4. Assess Prior Responses (4)

A. The parents were assessed in regard to how they have attempted to respond to the child's misbehavior.

B. Triggers and reinforcements that may have been contributing to the behavior were reviewed.

C. The parents were assessed for their consistency in their approach to the child.

D. The parents were assessed for whether they have experienced conflicts between themselves over how to react to the child.

5. Provide Psychological Testing (5)

A. A psychological evaluation was conducted to determine whether emotional factors or attention-deficit/hyperactivity disorder are contributing to the client's impulsivity and acting-out behaviors.

B. The client was uncooperative and resistant to engaging in the evaluation process.

C. The client approached the psychological testing in an honest, straightforward manner and was cooperative with any requests.

D. Feedback from the psychological testing was given to the client, parents, school officials, or criminal justice officials, and appropriate interventions were discussed.

6. Assess Level of Insight (6)

A. The client's level of insight toward the presenting problems was assessed.

B. The client was assessed in regard to the syntonic versus dystonic nature of their insight about the presenting problems.

C. The client was noted to demonstrate good insight into the problematic nature of the behavior and symptoms.

D. The client was noted to be in agreement with others' concerns and is motivated to work on change.

E. The client was noted to be ambivalent regarding the problems described and is reluctant to address the issues as a concern.

F. The client was noted to be resistant regarding acknowledgment of the problem areas, is not concerned about them, and has no motivation to make changes.

7. Assess for Correlated Disorders (7)

A. The client was assessed for evidence of research-based correlated disorders.

B. The client was assessed in regard to the level of vulnerability to suicide.

C. The client was identified as having a comorbid disorder, and treatment was adjusted to account for these concerns.

D. The client has been assessed for any correlated disorders, but none were found.

8. Assess for Culturally Based Confounding Issues (8)

A. The client was assessed for age-related issues that could help to better understand their clinical presentation.

B. The client was assessed for gender-related issues that could help to better understand their clinical presentation.

C. The client was assessed for cultural syndromes, cultural idioms of distress, or culturally based perceived causes that could help to better understand their clinical presentation.

D. Alternative factors have been identified as contributing to the client's currently defined "problem behavior," and these were taken into account in regard to treatment.

E. Culturally based factors that could help to account for the client's currently defined "problem behavior" were investigated, but no significant factors were identified.

9. Assess Severity of Impairment (9)

A. The severity of the client's impairment was assessed to determine the appropriate level of care.

B. The client was assessed in regard to impairment in social, relational, and educational endeavors.

C. It was reflected to the client that the impairment appears to create mild to moderate effects on the client's functioning.

D. It was reflected to the client that the impairment appears to create severe to very severe effects on the client's functioning.

E. The client was continuously assessed for the severity of impairment, as well as the efficacy and appropriateness of treatment.

10. Assess for Pathogenic Care (10)

A. The home, school, and community of the client were assessed for pathogenic care and concerns.

B. The client's various environments were assessed for the persistent disregard of the child's needs, repeated changes in caregivers, limited opportunities for stable attachment, harsh discipline, or other grossly inept care.

C. Pathogenic care was identified, and the treatment plan included strategies for managing or correcting these concerns and protecting the child.

D. No pathogenic care was identified and this was reflected to the client and caregivers.

11. Consult with Criminal Justice Officials (11)

A. The client's pattern of illegal behavior was assessed.

B. The exercise "Childhood Patterns of Stealing" from the *Child Psychotherapy Homework Planner* (Jongsma, Peterson, McInnis, & Bruce) was assigned.

C. Consultation was held with criminal justice officials about the need for appropriate consequences for the client's antisocial behavior.

D. The client was placed on probation for antisocial behaviors and instructed to comply with all the rules pertaining to probation.

E. The client was encouraged as they agreed to make restitution and/or perform community service for past antisocial behavior.

F. The client was placed in an intensive surveillance treatment program as a consequence of antisocial behavior.

12. Review Alternative Placement (12)

A. A consultation was held with parents, school officials, and criminal justice officials about placing the client in an alternative setting because of antisocial behavior.

B. It is recommended that the client be placed in a juvenile detention facility as a consequence of antisocial behavior.

C. It is recommended that the client be placed in a foster home to help prevent recurrences of antisocial behavior.

D. The recommendation was made that the client be placed in a residential program to provide external structure and supervision for the client.

E. After consultation with parents, school officials, and criminal justice officials, it was recommended that the client not be placed in an alternative setting.

13. Reinforce Legal Consequences (13)

A. The parents were encouraged and challenged not to protect the client from the legal consequences of the client's actions.

B. The parents agreed to contact the police or appropriate criminal justice officials if the client engages in any future antisocial behavior; they were reinforced for this decision.

C. The parents followed through and contacted the police or probation officer after the client engaged in antisocial behavior; they were supported for their decision.

D. The parents failed to contact the police and/or criminal justice officials after the client engaged in some antisocial behavior, and the reasons for this were processed.

14. Refer for Medication Evaluation (14)

A. The client was referred to a physician for an evaluation for psychotropic medication to help in controlling anger symptoms.

B. The client complied with the medication evaluation referral and has attended the appointment.

C. The client refused to attend an evaluation appointment with the physician for psychotropic medication; the client was encouraged to proceed with the evaluation as they feel willing to do so.

D. The issues of medication adherence and effectiveness were addressed with the parents and the client.

E. Information related to the client's medication adherence and its effectiveness was communicated to the physician.

F. The client's responsible adherence with medications was verbally reinforced.

G. The client reported that the use of the psychotropic medication has been effective in reducing the experience of anger.

15. Improve Motivation to Accept Responsibility (15)

A. Motivational interviewing techniques were used to assist the client in taking greater responsibility for their actions.

B. The client was consistently confronted and challenged to cease blaming others for their misbehaviors and accept greater responsibility for their actions.

C. The client was asked to list how poor decisions and irresponsible behavior resulted in negative consequences for self and others.

D. The client was praised as they identified ways to resolve conflict and/or meet needs that were more effective than acting out or behaving in an irresponsible manner.

E. The client was instructed to verbally acknowledge wrongdoing and apologize to others.

16. Confront Blame Statements (16)

A. The client was confronted for statements in which they lie or blame others for misbehaviors and fail to accept responsibility for their actions.

B. The client was assisted in identifying factors that contribute to a pattern of blaming others.

C. The client explored their pattern of blaming others and was praised for new insights.

D. The client was unable to accept confrontation for lies and blaming of others and was unable to explore factors that contributed to this pattern; remedial feedback was provided.

17. Connect Feelings and Behaviors (17)

A. The client was assisted in making a connection between feelings and reactive behaviors.

B. The client and parents were assigned the exercise "Risk Factors Leading to Child Behavior Problems" from the *Child Psychotherapy Homework Planner* (Jongsma, Peterson, McInnis, & Bruce).

C. The client was reinforced for their insight into the connection between feelings and reactive behaviors.

D. The client struggled to make a connection between feelings and reactive behaviors, and was provided with examples of such.

18. Reconceptualize Disruptive Behavior (18)

A. The client was assisted in reconceptualizing disruptive behavior as involving different components that go through predictable phases.

B. The client was taught about the different components of disruptive behavior, including cognitive, physiological, affective, and behavioral components.

C. The client was taught how to better discriminate between relaxation and tension.

D. The client was taught about the predictable phases of disruptive behavior, including demanding expectations that are not met, leading to increased arousal and anger, which leads to acting out.

E. The client displayed a clear understanding of the ways to conceptualize disruptive behavior and was provided with positive reinforcement.

F. The client has struggled to understand the ways to conceptualize disruptive behavior and was provided with remedial feedback in this area.

19. Teach Calming and Coping Strategies (19)

A. The client was taught calming techniques, such as muscle relaxation, paced breathing, and calming imagery.

B. The client was assigned the "Deep Breathing Exercise" from the *Child Psychotherapy Homework Planner* (Jongsma, Peterson, McInnis, & Bruce).

C. The client was assisted in developing specific ways to implement calming and coping strategies.

20. Explore Self-Talk (20)

A. The client's self-talk that mediates angry feelings was explored.

B. The client was assigned the exercise "Replace Negative Thoughts with Positive Self-Talk" from the *Child Psychotherapy Homework Planner* (Jongsma, Peterson, McInnis, & Bruce).

C. The client was assessed for self-talk (e.g., demanding expectations), reflected in "should," "must," or "have to" statements.

D. The client was assisted in identifying and challenging biases and in generating alternative self-talk that corrects for the biases.

E. The client was taught how to use correcting self-talk to facilitate a more adoptive behavioral response to frustration.

21. Assign Thought-Stopping Technique (21)

A. The client was directed to implement a thought-stopping technique on a daily basis between sessions.

B. The client's use of the thought-stopping technique was reviewed.

C. The client was provided with positive feedback for successful use of the thought-stopping technique.

D. The client was provided with corrective feedback to help improve use of the thought-stopping technique.

22. Teach Assertive Communication (22)

A. The client was taught about assertive communication through instruction, modeling, and role-playing.

B. The client was referred to an assertiveness training class.

C. The client displayed increased assertiveness and was provided with positive feedback in this area.

D. The client has not increased the level of assertiveness and was provided with additional feedback in this area.

23. Teach Conflict-Resolution Skills (23)

A. The client was taught conflict-resolution skills through modeling, role-playing, and behavioral rehearsal.

B. The client was assigned "Problem-Solving Exercise" from the *Child Psychotherapy Homework Planner* (Jongsma, Peterson, McInnis, & Bruce).

C. The client and parents were recommended to read *Cool, Calm, and Confident: A Workbook to Help to Kids Learn Assertiveness Skills* (Schab).

D. The client was taught about empathy and active listening.

E. The client was taught about "I messages," respectful communication, assertiveness without aggression, and compromise.

F. The client was reinforced for clear understanding of the conflict-resolution skills.

G. The client displayed a poor understanding of the conflict-resolution skills and was provided with remedial feedback.

24. **Construct Strategy for Managing Anger (24)**
    A. The client was assisted in constructing a client-tailored strategy for managing anger.
    B. The client was encouraged to combine somatic, cognitive, communication, problem-solving, and conflict-resolution skills relevant to needs.
    C. The client was reinforced for their comprehensive anger management strategy.
    D. The client was redirected to develop a more comprehensive anger management strategy.

25. **Select Challenging Situations for Managing Anger (25)**
    A. The client was provided with situations in which they may be increasingly challenged to apply new strategies for managing anger.
    B. The client was asked to identify likely upcoming challenging situations for managing anger.
    C. The client was urged to use strategies for managing anger in successively more difficult situations.

26. **Assign Anger Control Homework (26)**
    A. The client was assigned homework exercises to help practice newly learned calming, assertion, conflict-resolution, or cognitive-restructuring skills.
    B. The client has practiced the anger management skills, and the experience was reviewed and processed toward the goal of consolidation of such skills.
    C. The client has not regularly practiced anger control skills and was redirected to do so.

27. **Monitor/Decrease Outbursts (27)**
    A. The client's reports of angry outburst were monitored, toward the goal of decreasing their frequency, intensity, and duration.
    B. The client was urged to use new anger management skills to decrease the frequency, intensity, and duration of the anger outburst.
    C. The client was assigned the "Anger Control" or "Child Anger Checklist" exercise from the *Child Psychotherapy Homework Planner* (Jongsma, Peterson, McInnis, & Bruce); the client's progress in decreasing angry outbursts was reviewed.
    D. The client was reinforced for success at decreasing the frequency, intensity, and duration of an anger outburst.
    E. The client has not decreased the frequency, intensity, or duration of anger outbursts, and corrective feedback was provided.

28. **Encourage Disclosure (28)**

    A. The client was encouraged to discuss anger management goals with trusted persons who are likely to support their change.

    B. The client was assisted in identifying individuals who are likely to support their change.

    C. The client has reviewed anger management goals with trusted persons, and their response was processed.

    D. The client has not discussed anger management goals and was redirected to do so.

29. **Use Parent Management Training (29)**

    A. The parents were directed to read *Defiant Children* (Barkley) and "The Evolution of Oregon Model of Parent Management Training" (Forgatch & Gewirtz).

    B. The parents were taught how parent and child behavioral interactions can encourage or discourage positive or negative behavior.

    C. The parents were taught how changing key elements of parent–child interactions can be used to promote positive change.

    D. The parents were provided with specific examples of parent–child interactions (e.g., how prompting and reinforcing positive behaviors can be used to promote positive change).

    E. The parents were provided with positive feedback for the use of the Parent Management Training approach.

    F. The parents have not used the Parent Management Training approach and were redirected to do so.

30. **Read Parent Training Material (30)**

    A. The parents were asked to read material consistent with a parent training approach to managing disruptive behavior.

    B. The parents were assigned *The Kazdin Method for Parenting the Defiant Child* (Kazdin).

    C. The parents were assigned *Your Defiant Child* (Barkley & Benton).

    D. The parents have read the assigned material and key concepts were processed.

    E. The parents have not read the assigned material and were redirected to do so.

31. **Teach Parents to Define Aspects of Situation (31)**

    A. The parents were taught how to specifically define and identify problem behaviors.

    B. The parents were taught how to specifically identify their reactions to the behavior, and whether the reaction encourages or discourages the behavior.

    C. The parents were taught to generate alternatives to the problem behavior.

    D. Positive feedback was provided to the parents for their skill at specifically defining and identifying problem behaviors, reactions, outcomes, and alternatives.

    E. Parents were provided with remedial feedback as they struggled to correctly identify their child's problem behaviors and their own reactions, responses, and alternatives.

32. **Teach Consistent Parenting (32)**

    A. The parents were taught how to implement key parenting practices on a consistent basis.

    B. The parents were taught about establishing realistic, age-appropriate roles for acceptable and unacceptable behavior.

C. The parents were taught about prompting positive behavior and use of positive reinforcement.

D. The parents were taught about clear direct instruction, time out, and other loss-of-privilege techniques for problem behavior.

E. The parents were provided with positive feedback because they have been able to develop consistent parenting practices.

F. The parents have not developed consistent parenting practices and were redirected to do so.

33. Assign Home Exercises to Implement Parenting Techniques (33)

A. The parents were assigned home exercises in which they implement parenting techniques and record the results of the implementation exercises.

B. The parents were assigned "Clear Rules, Positive Reinforcement, Appropriate Consequences" in the *Adolescent Psychotherapy Homework Planner* (Jongsma, Peterson, McInnis, & Bruce).

C. The parents' implementation of homework exercises was reviewed within the session.

D. Corrective feedback was used to help develop improved, appropriate, and consistent use of skills.

E. The parents have not completed the assigned homework and were redirected to do so.

34. Conduct Parent–Child Interaction Therapy (34)

A. Parent–Child Interaction Therapy (McNeil & Hembree-Kigin; *Handbook of Parent–Child Interaction Therapy* by Niec) was described to teach appropriate child behavior and parent behavior management skills.

B. Child-directed sessions focused on teaching the child appropriate child behavior.

C. Parent-directed sessions focused on teaching parental behavior management skills (e.g., clear commands, consistent consequences, and positive reinforcement).

35. Refer to Parent Training Program (35)

A. The parents were referred to an evidence-based parent training program.

B. The parents were referred to a parent training program such as *The Incredible Years* or *Positive Parenting Program.*

C. The parents have utilized the evidence-based parent training program and were reinforced for their gains.

D. The parents have not used the evidence-based parent training program and were reminded to do so.

36. Design Contingency/Reward System (36)

A. A reward system was developed with the client.

B. A contingency contract was developed with the client.

C. A meeting was held with school officials to help reinforce identified positive behaviors.

D. The client was encouraged to participate in the reward system/contingency contract in order to deter impulsive or rebellious behaviors.

E. Fine-tuning was done to the reward system/contingency contract in order to reinforce identified positive behaviors at home and school.

37. **Explore Family Abuse History (37)**

   A. The client's family background was explored for a history of physical, sexual, or substance abuse that may contribute to the emergence of anger control problems.

   B. The client was assisted in developing a timeline in the therapy session where they identified significant historical events, both positive and negative, that have occurred in the family.

   C. The client's parents were confronted and challenged to cease physically abusive or overly punitive methods of discipline.

   D. The parents were asked to identify how physically abusive or overly punitive methods of discipline negatively affect the child and siblings.

   E. The parents were supported as they apologized to the client for abusive behaviors and overly harsh methods of discipline.

   F. The parents were taught how aggressive discipline promotes the client's aggression and poor anger management.

   G. The parents were referred to a parenting class.

38. **Protect Client from Abuse (38)**

   A. The abuse was reported to the appropriate agency.

   B. A recommendation was made that the perpetrator be removed from the home and seek treatment.

   C. A recommendation was made that the client and siblings be removed from the home to ensure protection.

   D. The client and family members were assisted in identifying the necessary steps to take to minimize the risk of abuse occurring in the future.

   E. The nonabusive parent was reinforced for verbalizing a commitment to protect the client and siblings from physical abuse in the future.

39. **Teach Empathy (39)**

   A. Role-playing and role-reversal techniques were used to increase client's sensitivity to how antisocial behaviors affect others.

   B. The "Apology Letter for Bullying" exercise from the *Child Psychotherapy Homework Planner* (Jongsma, Peterson, McInnis, & Bruce) was assigned to the client.

   C. The child was assigned the exercise "Building Empathy" from the *Child Psychotherapy Homework Planner* (Jongsma, Peterson, McInnis, & Bruce).

   D. The client was able to verbally recognize how their antisocial behaviors affect others through use of role-playing and role-reversal techniques.

   E. The client has not developed a greater understanding about the ways in which their antisocial behaviors affect others and was provided with additional feedback.

40. **Encourage Benevolent Acts (40)**

   A. The client was directed to engage in three altruistic or benevolent acts.

   B. The client was provided with examples of altruistic and benevolent acts (e.g., reading to a developmentally disabled student, mowing an elderly person's lawn).

   C. The client's experience of using altruistic or benevolent acts was reviewed.

    D. An emphasis on how the client can develop empathy and sensitivity to the needs of others through altruistic or benevolent acts was emphasized.

    E. The client has not done the assigned altruistic or benevolent acts and was redirected to do so.

41. Assign Empathy Homework (41)

    A. Homework assignments were developed to help increase the client's empathy and sensitivity toward the thoughts, feeling, and needs of others.

    B. The client was assigned the exercise "Building Empathy" from the *Child Psychotherapy Homework Planner* (Jongsma, Peterson, McInnis, & Bruce).

    C. The client was directed to specific tasks to help increase empathy and sensitivity toward others.

    D. The client was assigned to watch media presentations to help identify the thoughts, feelings, and needs of others.

    E. The client has completed the homework designed to increase empathy and sensitivity toward others, and the experience was reviewed and processed.

    F. The client has not done the assignments to increase empathy for others and was redirected to do so.

42. Encourage Allowing Client to Be in Charge of Tasks (42)

    A. The family was encouraged to allow the client to be in charge of tasks at home.

    B. Specific examples of areas in which the client might be able to be in charge of tasks at home were reviewed (e.g., preparing and cooking a special dish for a family get-together, building shelves, changing oil).

    C. The family was urged to demonstrate confidence in the client's ability to act responsibly.

    D. The family's experience of the client being in charge of tasks at home was reviewed and processed.

    E. The family has not allowed the client to be in charge of any significant tasks at home and was redirected to do so.

43. Conduct Specific Family Therapy (43)

    A. Functional Family Therapy was conducted with the family.

    B. Brief Strategic Family Therapy was conducted with the family.

    C. The family was assisted in assessing and intervening toward reducing the family contributions to the client's anger control problems.

44. Refer for Multisystemic Therapy (44)

    A. The client was seen to have severe conduct problems, and was referred to a multisystemic therapy program with cognitive, behavioral, and family interventions.

    B. The client has been involved in multisystemic therapy focusing on factors that are contributing to antisocial behavior and or substance use.

    C. Multisystemic therapy has focused on improving caregiver discipline practices, enhancing family affective relations, decreasing youth association with deviant peers, and increasing youth association with prosocial peers.

D. Multisystemic therapy has focused on improving youth's school and vocational performance, engaging prosocial recreational outlets, and developing an indigenous support network.

E. The client has fully engaged in the multisystem therapy program and the benefits of such were reviewed.

F. The client has not engaged well in the multisystemic therapy program and problems relating to this were reviewed.

45. Provide Rationale for Relapse Prevention (45)

A. A rationale for relapse prevention was introduced.

B. Discussions about risk situations and strategies for preventing relapse were reviewed.

46. Differentiate Between Lapse and Relapse (46)

A. A discussion was held with the client regarding the distinction between a lapse and a relapse.

B. A lapse was associated with an initial and reversible return of symptoms.

C. A relapse was associated with the decision to return to conduct disorder/delinquency patterns.

D. The client was provided with support and encouragement, as they displayed an understanding of the difference between a lapse and a relapse.

E. The client struggled to understand the difference between a lapse and a relapse, and the client was provided with remedial feedback in this area.

47. Discuss Management of Lapse Risk Situations (47)

A. The client was assisted in identifying future situations or circumstances in which lapses could occur.

B. The session focused on rehearsing the management of future situations or circumstances in which lapses could occur.

C. The client was reinforced for appropriate use of lapse management skills.

D. The client was redirected in regard to poor use of lapse management skills.

48. Encourage Routine Use of Strategies (48)

A. The client was instructed to routinely use the strategies learned in therapy (e.g., cognitive restructuring, assertiveness).

B. The client was urged to find ways to build new strategies into their life as much as possible.

C. The client was reinforced as they reported ways in which they have incorporated coping strategies into their life and routine.

D. The client was redirected about ways to incorporate new strategies into their routine and life.

49. Develop a "Coping Card" (49)

A. The client was provided with a coping card on which specific coping strategies were listed.

B. The client was assisted in developing the coping card on which to list helpful coping strategies.

C. The client was encouraged to use the coping card when struggling with anxiety-producing situations.

50. **Schedule Maintenance Sessions (50)**

A. Maintenance sessions were proposed to help the client maintain therapeutic gains and adjust to life without anger outbursts.

B. The client was reinforced for agreeing to the scheduling of maintenance sessions.

C. The client refused to schedule maintenance sessions and this was processed.

51. **Explore Feelings About Neglect or Abuse (51)**

A. The client was given the opportunity in session to express feelings about past neglect, abuse, separation, or abandonment.

B. The client was instructed to draw pictures that reflected feelings about neglect, abuse, separation, or abandonment.

C. The client was instructed to use a journal to record thoughts and feelings about past neglect, abuse, separation, or abandonment.

D. The empty-chair technique was employed to facilitate expression of feelings surrounding past neglect or abuse.

E. The client was assigned "The Lesson of Salmon Rock . . . Fighting Leads to Loneliness" from the *Child Psychotherapy Homework Planner* (Jongsma, Peterson, McInnis, & Bruce).

F. The client has been reluctant to explore feelings about neglect and abuse and was urged to process these feelings as they feel capable of doing so.

52. **Assess/Treat the Marital Dyad (52)**

A. The marital dyad was assessed for possible substance abuse, conflict, or triangulation.

B. Family therapy sessions were conducted to explore the dynamics that contribute to the emergence of the client's anger control problems.

C. The family therapy sessions identified several dynamics that contribute to the client's anger control problem.

D. Family dynamics were addressed within the family therapy session.

E. The family was referred for additional family therapy.

F. The parents were referred for couples therapy.

DEPRESSION

CLIENT PRESENTATION

1. **Sad, Depressed Moods (1)**[*]
   A. The parents and teachers reported that the client has appeared sad and depressed for a significant length of time.
   B. The client appeared visibly sad during today's therapy session and reported feeling depressed most of the time.
   C. The frequency and intensity of the client's depressed moods are gradually beginning to diminish.
   D. The client expressed happiness and joy about recent life events.
   E. The client's depression has lifted, and moods are much more elevated.

2. **Flat, Constricted Affect (1)**
   A. The parents and teachers reported that the client's affect often appears flat and constricted at home and school.
   B. The client's affect appeared flat and constricted, and they reported not feeling any emotion.
   C. The client appeared more animated in affective presentation and showed a wider range of emotions.
   D. The client has consistently appeared more animated in emotional presentation since the onset of treatment.

3. **Preoccupation with Death (2)**
   A. The parents and teachers reported that the client displays a strong preoccupation with the subject of death.
   B. The client displayed a preoccupation with the subject of death during today's therapy session and reported that death is often on their mind.
   C. The client's preoccupation with the subject of death is gradually beginning to decrease.
   D. The client did not talk about the subject of death in today's therapy session.
   E. The client's preoccupation with the subject of death has ceased, and they have demonstrated a renewed interest in life.

4. **Suicidal Thoughts/Actions (3)**
   A. The client reported experiencing suicidal thoughts on a number of occasions.
   B. The client made a recent suicide attempt.
   C. The client has made suicidal gestures in the past as a cry for help.
   D. The client denied that suicidal thoughts or urges are a problem any longer.

---

[*] The numbers in parentheses correlate to the number of the Behavioral Definition statement in the companion chapter with the same title in the *Child Psychotherapy Treatment Planner*, Sixth Edition, by Jongsma, Peterson, McInnis, & Bruce (Wiley, 2023).

5. **Moody Irritability (4)**

   A. The client has displayed a pervasive irritability at home and school.

   B. The client's angry, irritable moods have often masked deeper feelings of depression.

   C. The client appeared moody and irritable during today's therapy session.

   D. The frequency and intensity of the client's irritable moods are diminishing.

   E. The client's moods have stabilized, and the client has demonstrated significantly fewer irritable moods.

6. **Isolation from Family and Peers (5)**

   A. The client has become significantly more isolated and withdrawn from family members and peers since the onset of depression.

   B. The client appeared withdrawn in today's therapy session.

   C. The client's social isolation is diminishing, and the client is interacting more often with family members and peers.

   D. The client was much more talkative and spontaneous in today's therapy session.

   E. The client has become much more outgoing and has interacted with family members and peers on a regular, consistent basis.

7. **Academic Performance Decline (6)**

   A. The client has experienced a decrease in academic performance since the onset of depression.

   B. The client appeared visibly depressed when discussing lowered academic performance.

   C. The client's academic performance has increased since depression has lifted.

   D. The client expressed feelings of happiness and joy about improved academic performance.

8. **Lack of Interest (7)**

   A. The client reported experiencing little interest or enjoyment in activities that brought pleasure in the past.

   B. The parents and teachers reported that the client has shown little interest or enjoyment in activities at home and school.

   C. The client's depression has started to decrease, and the client has shown signs of interest in previously enjoyed activities.

   D. The client reported being recently able to experience joy or happiness in several activities.

   E. The client has developed a renewed interest in and zest for life.

9. **Lack of Communication About Painful Emotions (8)**

   A. The client has often suppressed and/or avoided talking about painful emotions or experiences with others.

   B. The client avoided talking about any painful emotions or topics during today's therapy session.

   C. The client's avoidance of, or refusal to talk about, painful emotions or experiences has been a significant contributing factor to depression.

D. The client has started to talk about painful emotions or experiences.

E. The client's willingness to talk about painful emotions or experiences has helped to lift depression.

10. Low Energy, Listless, and Apathetic (9)

A. The client's depression has been manifested in part by low energy level, fatigue, listlessness, and apathy.

B. The client appeared tired, listless, and apathetic during today's therapy session.

C. The client reported a mild increase recently in the level of energy.

D. The client reported experiencing a return to a normal level of energy.

11. Lack of Eye Contact (10)

A. The parents and teachers reported that the client displays very little eye contact during social interactions with others.

B. The client displayed poor eye contact during today's therapy session and acknowledged this to be a common practice.

C. The client has demonstrated satisfactory to good eye contact with individuals around whom they feel comfortable but has exhibited poor eye contact with unfamiliar people.

D. The client maintained good eye contact during today's therapy session and stated that they are also making more eye contact with others.

E. The parents and teachers reported that the client consistently maintains good eye contact.

12. Low Self-Esteem (11)

A. The client has been troubled by strong feelings of low self-esteem, inadequacy, and insecurity.

B. The client verbalized negative and disparaging remarks about self.

C. The client's low self-esteem, lack of confidence, and feelings of insecurity are significant concomitant aspects of their depression.

D. The client verbalized several positive self-descriptive statements during today's therapy session.

E. The client has taken active steps to improve self-esteem (e.g., reaching out to others, challenging self with new activities).

13. Appetite Disturbance (12)

A. The client reported experiencing a loss of appetite during depressive episodes.

B. The client has lost a significant amount of weight since becoming depressed.

C. The client reported that they have often turned to food to feel better about self during periods of depression.

D. The client reported a significant weight gain since the onset of depression.

E. The client's appetite has returned to a normal level since feelings of depression have decreased.

14. Sleep Disturbance (13)

A. The client reported having difficulty falling asleep and/or experiencing early morning awakenings since becoming depressed.

B. The client reported sleeping more than usual during the bout of depression.

C. The client reported sleeping well recently.

D. The client's sleep has returned to a normal level.

15. Poor Concentration and Indecisiveness (14)

A. The client reported having difficulty concentrating and making decisions since feeling depressed.

B. The client had trouble concentrating and staying focused during today's therapy session.

C. The client's low self-esteem, lack of confidence, and feelings of insecurity have contributed to difficulty in making decisions.

D. The client reported being able to concentrate and stay focused for longer periods of time now that they have ceased feeling depressed.

E. The client's ability to make some constructive decisions has helped to decrease feelings of depression.

16. Feelings of Hopelessness/Helplessness (15)

A. The client has developed a pessimistic outlook on the future and is troubled by feelings of hopelessness and helplessness.

B. The client expressed feelings of helplessness and voiced little hope that life will improve in the future.

C. The client expressed confidence about the ability to overcome problems or stress and improve life in the future.

D. The client has experienced a renewed sense of hope and feelings of empowerment.

17. Feelings of Guilt (15)

A. The client expressed strong feelings of guilt about past actions.

B. The client's strong feelings of irrational guilt are a significant contributing factor to depression and inability to move ahead with life.

C. The client made productive use of today's therapy session by exploring feelings of guilt about past actions.

D. The client denied being troubled by any significant feelings of guilt.

E. The client has successfully worked through and resolved feelings of guilt about past actions.

18. Unresolved Grief Issues (16)

A. The client's unresolved feelings of grief have been a significant contributing factor to the episode of depression.

B. The client expressed strong feelings of sadness and grief about past separations or losses.

C. The client was guarded and reluctant to talk about past losses or separations.

D. The client's depression has begun to lift as the client works through feelings of grief about past losses or separations.

E. The client has experienced a significant increase in the frequency and duration of their happy or contented mood since working through the issues of grief.

INTERVENTIONS IMPLEMENTED

1. **Establish Rapport (1)***
   A. Caring was conveyed to the client through support, warmth, and empathy.
   B. The client was provided with nonjudgmental support and a level of trust was developed.
   C. The client was urged to feel safe in expressing depression symptoms.
   D. The client began to express feelings more freely as rapport and trust level have increased.
   E. The client has continued to experience difficulty being open and direct about expression of painful feelings; the client was encouraged to use the safe haven of therapy to express these difficult issues.

2. **Focus on Strengthening Therapeutic Relationship (2)**
   A. The relationship with the client was strengthened using empirically supported factors.
   B. The relationship with the client was strengthened through the implementation of collaborative approach, agreement on goals, demonstration of empathy, verbalization of positive regard, and collection of client feedback.
   C. The client reacted positively to the relationship-strengthening measures taken.
   D. The client verbalized feeling supported and understood during therapy sessions.
   E. Despite attempts to strengthen the therapeutic relationship, the client reports feeling distant and misunderstood.
   F. The client has indicated that sessions are not helpful and will be terminating therapy.

3. **Assess Mood Episodes (3)**
   A. An assessment was conducted of the client's current and past mood episodes, including the features, frequency, intensity, and duration of the mood episodes.
   B. The Children's Depression Inventory (Kovacs) was used to assess the client's current and past mood episodes.
   C. The results of the mood episode assessment reflected severe mood concerns, and this was presented to the client.
   D. The results of the mood episode assessment reflected moderate mood concerns, and this was presented to the client.
   E. The results of the mood episode assessment reflected mild mood concerns, and this was presented to the client.

4. **Identify Depression Causes (4)**
   A. The client was asked to verbally identify the source of their depressed mood.
   B. The "Childhood Depression Survey" from the *Child Psychotherapy Homework Planner* (Jongsma, Peterson, McInnis, & Bruce) was assigned to help identify concerns that have contributed to the client's depression.
   C. Active listening skills were used as the client listed several factors that they believe contribute to feelings of hopelessness and sadness.
   D. The client struggled to identify significant causes for depression and was provided with tentative examples in this area.

---

*The numbers in parentheses correlate to the number of the Therapeutic Intervention statement in the companion chapter with the same title in the *Child Psychotherapy Treatment Planner*, Sixth Edition, by Jongsma, Peterson, McInnis, & Bruce (Wiley, 2023).

5. Administer Psychological Tests for Depression (5)

A. Psychological testing was arranged to objectively assess the client's depression and suicide risk.

B. The Beck Depression Inventory for Youth was used to assess the client's depression and suicide risk.

C. The Children's Depression Inventory was used to assess the client's depression and suicide risk.

D. The results of the testing indicated severe concerns related to the client's depression and suicide risk, and this was reflected to the client.

E. The results of the testing indicated moderate concerns related to the client's depression and suicide risk, and this was reflected to the client.

F. The results of the testing indicated mild concerns related to the client's depression and suicide risk, and this was reflected to the client.

6. Assess Level of Insight (6)

A. The client's level of insight toward the presenting problems was assessed.

B. The client was assessed in regard to the syntonic versus dystonic nature of their insight about the presenting problems.

C. The client was noted to demonstrate good insight into the problematic nature of the behavior and symptoms.

D. The client was noted to be in agreement with others' concerns and is motivated to work on change.

E. The client was noted to be ambivalent regarding the problems described and is reluctant to address the issues as a concern.

F. The client was noted to be resistant regarding acknowledgment of the problem areas, is not concerned about them, and has no motivation to make changes.

7. Assess for Correlated Disorders (7)

A. The client was assessed for evidence of research-based correlated disorders.

B. The client was assessed in regard to the level of vulnerability to suicide.

C. The client was identified as having a comorbid disorder, and treatment was adjusted to account for these concerns.

D. The client has been assessed for any correlated disorders, but none were found.

8. Assess for Culturally Based Confounding Issues (8)

A. The client was assessed for age-related issues that could help to better understand their clinical presentation.

B. The client was assessed for gender-related issues that could help to better understand their clinical presentation.

C. The client was assessed for cultural syndromes, cultural idioms of distress, or culturally based perceived causes that could help to better understand their clinical presentation.

D. Alternative factors have been identified as contributing to the client's currently defined "problem behavior," and these were taken into account in regard to treatment.

E. Culturally based factors that could help to account for the client's currently defined "problem behavior" were investigated, but no significant factors were identified.

9. **Assess Severity of Impairment (9)**

   A. The severity of the client's impairment was assessed to determine the appropriate level of care.

   B. The client was assessed in regard to impairment in social, relational, and educational endeavors.

   C. It was reflected to the client that the impairment appears to create mild to moderate effects on the client's functioning.

   D. It was reflected to the client that the impairment appears to create severe to very severe effects on the client's functioning.

   E. The client was continuously assessed for the severity of impairment, as well as the efficacy and appropriateness of treatment.

10. **Assess for Pathogenic Care (10)**

    A. The home, school, and community of the client were assessed for pathogenic care and concerns.

    B. The client's various environments were assessed for the persistent disregard of the child's needs, repeated changes in caregivers, limited opportunities for stable attachment, harsh discipline, or other grossly inept care.

    C. Pathogenic care was identified and the treatment plan included strategies for managing or correcting these concerns and protecting the child.

    D. No pathogenic care was identified and this was reflected to the client and caregivers.

11. **Explore History of Suicide (11)**

    A. The client's history of suicide urges was explored.

    B. The client's current state of suicide urges was explored.

    C. The client was noted to have experienced many previous urges regarding suicide.

    D. The client has not had many significant urges related to suicide, and this was reflected to them.

12. **Arrange for Hospitalization (12)**

    A. Because the client was judged to be uncontrollably harmful to self, arrangements were made for psychiatric hospitalization.

    B. The client cooperated voluntarily with admission to a psychiatric hospital.

    C. The client refused to cooperate voluntarily with admission to a psychiatric facility, and therefore commitment procedures were initiated.

13. **Refer to Prescriber (13)**

    A. The client was referred to a prescriber for an examination to rule out organic causes for depression.

    B. A referral to a prescriber was made for the purpose of evaluating the client for a prescription for psychotropic medication.

    C. The client has followed through on a referral to a prescriber and has been assessed for a prescription of psychotropic medication.

D. The client has been prescribed antidepressant medication.

E. The client has refused the prescription of psychotropic medication prescribed.

14. Monitor Medication Effects (14)

A. The client's response to medication was discussed.

B. The client and parents were assigned "Evaluating Medication Effects–Parent Form" in the *Adolescent Psychotherapy Homework Planner* (Jongsma, Peterson, McInnis, & Bruce).

C. The client reported that the medication has helped to decrease symptoms of depression and stabilize mood, and the client was encouraged to continue this treatment.

D. The client reported little to no improvement since starting to take the prescribed antidepressant medication, which was relayed to the prescriber.

E. The client has not complied with taking medication on a regular basis and was redirected to do so.

F. The client was encouraged to report the side effects of the medication to the prescriber.

G. Contact will be made with the prescriber regarding the lack of effectiveness and the need for an adjustment in the prescription.

15. Conduct Cognitive Behavioral Therapy (15)

A. The use of cognitive behavioral therapy concepts was utilized.

B. The client was helped to learn the connection between cognition, depressive feelings, and actions.

C. The client has responded well to cognitive behavioral therapy.

D. Cognitive behavioral therapy techniques have not been helpful to the client.

16. Arrange Meetings to Facilitate Skills (16)

A. The client's parents and family members were scheduled for ongoing/periodic meetings to learn about the skills that the client is learning.

B. The family members were assisted in identifying how to encourage and teach the ongoing use of newly learned skills.

C. The family was encouraged to use the skills to increase the frequency of positive family interactions.

17. Teach Rationale for Therapy (17)

A. The client was assigned material to help learn about cognitive-behavioral therapy and its rationale.

B. The client was led in a discussion regarding the use of therapy and the rationale behind it.

C. The client was assigned the portions of *The Children's Workbook for ACTION* (Stark).

D. The client was assigned the portions of *My Feeling Better Workbook: Help for Kids Who Are Sad and Depressed* (Hamil).

E. The parents were led in a discussion about the rationale for therapy.

18. **Educate About Cognitive Restructuring (18)**
   A. The client and parents were educated about cognitive restructuring.
   B. The client and parents were taught about self-monitoring of automatic thoughts reflecting depressogenic beliefs.
   C. The client and parents were taught about challenging depressive thinking patterns by examining evidence for and against them and replacing them with reality-based alternatives.
   D. The client was assigned the exercise "Replace Negative Thoughts with Positive Self-Talk" from the *Child Psychotherapy Homework Planner* (Jongsma, Peterson, McInnis, & Bruce).

19. **Assign Automatic Thought Journal (19)**
   A. The client was assigned to keep a daily journal of automatic thoughts associated with depressed feelings.
   B. The "Daily Record of Dysfunctional Thoughts" exercise from *Cognitive Therapy of Depression* (Beck et al.) was used to identify automatic thoughts associated with depressive feelings.
   C. The Socratic method was used to challenge the client's dysfunctional thoughts and to replace them with positive, reality-based thoughts.
   D. The client was reinforced for instances of successful replacement of negative thoughts within more realistic positive thinking.

20. **Conduct Behavioral Experiments (20)**
   A. The client was encouraged to do behavioral experiments in which depressive automatic thoughts are treated as hypotheses/predictions and are tested against reality-based alternative hypothesis.
   B. The client's automatic depressive thoughts were tested against the client's past, present, and/or future experiences.
   C. The client was assisted in processing the outcome of behavioral experiences.
   D. The client was encouraged by the experience of the more reality-based hypotheses/predictions; this progress was reinforced.
   E. The client continues to focus on depressive automatic thoughts and was redirected toward the behavioral evidence of the more reality-based alternative hypotheses.

21. **Conduct Attribution Retraining (21)**
   A. Attribution retraining was conducted, in which the client is taught to identify pessimistic explanations for events and generate more optimistic and realistic alternatives.
   B. The client was reinforced for positive, reality-based cognitive messages that enhance self-confidence and increase adaptive action.
   C. The client was assigned the exercise "Recognizing Your Abilities, Traits, and Accomplishments" from the *Adolescent Psychotherapy Homework Planner* (Jongsma, Peterson, McInnis, & Bruce).
   D. The client was assigned the exercise "Positive Self-Statements" from the *Child Psychotherapy Homework Planner* (Jongsma, Peterson, McInnis, & Bruce).

22. **Teach Calming Skills (22)**
    A. The client was taught cognitive and somatic calming skills.
    B. The client was taught about calming breathing, cognitive distancing, decatastrophizing, and distraction.
    C. The client was taught about progressive muscle relaxation and guided imagery.
    D. The client was assisted in rehearsing how to apply skills in daily life.
    E. The client was assigned "Deep Breathing Exercise" from the *Child Psychotherapy Homework Planner* (Jongsma, Peterson, McInnis, & Bruce).
    F. The client was assigned "Progressive Muscle Relaxation" from the *Adolescent Psychotherapy Homework Planner* (Jongsma, Peterson, McInnis, & Bruce).
    G. The client was assisted in reviewing and reinforcing successes.
    H. The client was assisted in providing corrective feedback toward consistent implementation of cognitive and somatic calming skills.

23. **Assign Reading on Progressive Muscle Relaxation (23)**
    A. The client was assigned to read information about progressive muscle relaxation.
    B. The client's parents were assigned to read information about progressive muscle relaxation.
    C. Information about calming strategies was assigned.
    D. The information from *The Relaxation and Stress Reduction Workbook for Kids* (Shapiro & Sprague) was reviewed.
    E. The information from the *Coping C.A.T. Series* (Kendall et al.) was reviewed.
    F. Assigned information has been read by the client and parents and key concepts were reviewed.
    G. Information assigned on progressive muscle relaxation and other calming strategies has not been reviewed by the client and parents and they were redirected to do so.

24. **Develop Personal Skills (24)**
    A. The client was assisted in developing skills that increase the likelihood of managing daily stressors and help alleviate depression.
    B. The client was taught problem-solving skills.
    C. The client was taught conflict-resolution skills.
    D. The client was reinforced for success in increasing personal skills.
    E. The client reported experiencing greater functionality in life and was reinforced for this.
    F. The client has not developed skills that will increase the likelihood of greater functionality and was redirected to do so.

25. **Engage in Behavioral Activation (25)**
    A. The client was engaged in behavioral activation by scheduling activities that have a high likelihood for pleasure and mastery.
    B. Rehearsal, role-playing, role reversal, and other techniques were used to engage the client in behavioral activation.
    C. The client and parents were assigned the exercise "Identify and Schedule Pleasant Activities" from the *Adult Psychotherapy Homework Planner* (Jongsma & Bruce).

D. The client was reinforced for successes in scheduling activities that have a high likelihood for pleasure and mastery.

E. The client has not engaged in pleasurable activities and was redirected to do so.

26. Increase Social and Communication Skills (26)

A. Instruction, role modeling, and role-playing techniques were used to help build the client's social and communication skills.

B. The client's social and communication skills were increased as described in *Social Effectiveness Therapy for Children and Adolescents* (Beidel et al.).

C. The client has increased social and communication skills, and this was positively reinforced.

D. The client has not displayed an increase in social and communication skills and was provided with additional feedback in this area.

27. Encourage Participation in Social/Recreational Activities (27)

A. The client was strongly encouraged to participate in social/recreational activities to decrease feelings of depression and enrich the quality of life.

B. The client was assisted in developing a list of social or recreational activities that will help to enrich the quality of life and provide an opportunity to establish meaningful friendships.

C. The "Greeting Peers" assignment from the *Child Psychotherapy Homework Planner* (Jongsma, Peterson, McInnis, & Bruce) was used to help the client develop social and recreational activities to enrich life.

D. The "Show Your Strengths" exercise from the *Child Psychotherapy Homework Planner* (Jongsma, Peterson, McInnis, & Bruce) was used to help the client develop social and recreational activities to enrich life.

E. The client reported that recent participation in social or recreational activities has helped to decrease feelings of depression.

F. The client has not participated in any recent social or recreational activities because of depression and feelings of low self-worth and was provided with additional support.

28. Use Therapeutic Feelings Games (28)

A. Therapeutic feelings games have been used to help the client become more verbal.

B. The "Talking, Feeling, Doing" game was used to help the client identify and express thoughts and feelings.

C. The therapeutic feelings games have helped the client identify feelings and unmet needs.

D. After playing a therapeutic feelings game, the client was helped to identify constructive ways to meet needs.

E. After playing a therapeutic feelings game, the client was encouraged to express thoughts and feelings directly toward significant others.

29. Clarify and Solve Current Conflicts (29)

A. A nondirective, client-centered approach was used to help the client clarify current conflicts and problems.

B. The client was assisted in generating solutions to current conflicts and problems.

C. The client was supported in efforts to generate and utilize solutions to identified conflicts and problems.

30. Conduct Individual Psychodynamic Psychotherapy (30)

A. Individual Psychodynamic Psychotherapy was used with a focus on interpersonal relationships, life stressors, and dysfunctional attachments.

B. Treatment was conducted in accordance with concepts as indicated in *Basic Principles and Techniques for Short-Term Dynamic Psychotherapy* (Davanloo).

31. Explore Unresolved Grief (31)

A. The client's history of losses that have triggered feelings of grief was explored.

B. The client was assisted in identifying losses that have contributed to feelings of grief that have not been resolved.

C. The client's unresolved feelings of grief are noted to be contributing to current feelings of depression and were provided a special focus.

32. Reinforce Physical Exercise (32)

A. A plan for routine physical exercise was developed with the client, and a rationale for including this in their daily routine was made.

B. The client and therapist agreed to make a commitment toward implementing daily exercise as a depression reduction technique.

C. The client has performed routine daily exercise and reports that it has been beneficial; these benefits were reinforced.

D. The client has not followed through on maintaining a routine of physical exercise and was redirected to do so.

33. Build Relapse Prevention Skills (33)

A. The client was assisted in building relapse prevention skills through the identification of early warning signs of relapse.

B. The client was directed to consistently review skills learned during therapy.

C. The client was assisted in developing an ongoing plan for managing routine challenges.

34. Assess Understanding About Self-Defeating Behaviors (34)

A. The client was assessed for their level of self-understanding about self-defeating behaviors.

B. The client was asked to explain their understanding of how self-defeating behaviors are linked to depression.

C. The client was asked to apply their understanding of self-defeating behaviors to their own experience of depression.

D. The client was reinforced for clear understanding of the issues related to self-defeating behavior and depression.

E. The client struggled in regard to their understanding of the connection between self-defeating behaviors and depression and was provided with remedial feedback in this area.

35. Identify Unmet Emotional Need (35)

A. The client was assisted in identifying unmet emotional needs.

B. The client's acting-out behaviors were interpreted as avoidance of the real conflict involving unmet needs.

C. Depression symptoms were noted to be a common reflection of the client's unmet needs and avoidance of the real conflict in life.

D. The client was reinforced as they displayed a clear understanding of how unmet emotional needs contribute to depression and acting-out behavior.

36. Teach Connection Between Surface Behavior and Inner Feelings (36)

A. The client was taught about the connection between angry, irritable behaviors (on the surface) and feelings of hurt or sadness (as inner feelings).

B. The client was assigned the "Surface Behavior/Inner Feelings" exercise from the *Child Psychotherapy Homework Planner* (Jongsma, Peterson, McInnis, & Bruce) to show the connection between angry, irritable, acting-out behaviors and feelings of hurt or sadness.

C. The client successfully completed the "Surface Behavior/Inner Feelings" homework and was assisted in identifying how angry, irritable behaviors are connected to underlying feelings of hurt and sadness.

D. The client successfully completed the homework assignment and reported being able to share feelings of hurt and sadness with other trusted individuals; the benefits of this closeness were reviewed.

E. The client did not complete the "Surface Behavior/Inner Feelings" homework and was asked again to do it.

37. Explore Fear of Loss (37)

A. Today's therapy session explored the client's fears of abandonment or the loss of love from significant others.

B. The client was helped to examine whether fears surrounding abandonment or loss of love from others are realistic or unrealistic.

C. The client was taught cognitive restructuring techniques to help challenge and overcome irrational fears about being abandoned or rejected by significant others.

D. Psychoanalytic therapy approaches were employed to explore the client's underlying fears of abandonment or loss of love from significant others.

E. The client acknowledged fear of loss and was provided with support and encouragement for verbalizing these feelings.

F. The client denied any fear of loss and was provided with tentative examples of how others have experienced these types of emotions.

38. Identify Missing Aspects of Life (38)

A. The client was asked to identify what is missing from life that contributes to personal unhappiness.

B. The client was assisted in identifying the missing aspects of life that contribute to feelings of unhappiness and depression.

C. The "Three Wishes Game" was assigned from the *Child Psychotherapy Homework Planner* (Jongsma, Peterson, McInnis, & Bruce).

D. A plan was developed with the client to attempt to find ways to satisfy those missing aspects of life.

E. The client was encouraged to use strengths and seek out the support of others to help cope with the missing aspects of life.

F. The client denied that any aspects of life are missing and was encouraged to continue to monitor this area.

39. Explore Emotional Pain from Past (39)

A. Today's therapy session explored the emotional pain from the client's past that contributes to feelings of hopelessness and low self-esteem.

B. The client was given empathy and support in expressing painful emotions about the past experiences that have contributed to current feelings of hopelessness and low self-esteem.

C. The client was encouraged to use positive self-talk as a means to offset the pattern of negative thinking and overcome feelings of hopelessness.

D. Guided imagery techniques were used to help the client visualize a brighter future.

E. The client consistently denied any emotional pain from the past and was provided with tentative examples of areas where they may have experienced emotional pain.

40. Identify Unmet Emotional Needs and Plans to Satisfy Needs (40)

A. The client was assisted in identifying unmet emotional needs.

B. The client was assisted in identifying specific ways in which unmet emotional needs could be met.

C. The client was assigned the "Unmet Emotional Needs—Identification and Satisfaction" exercise from the *Adolescent Psychotherapy Homework Planner* (Jongsma, Peterson, McInnis, & Bruce) to help identify unmet emotional needs and specific ways to meet those needs in the future.

D. The client completed the "Unmet Emotional Needs—Identification and Satisfaction" exercise and was helped to identify unmet emotional needs and several effective ways to meet them.

E. The client failed to complete the exercise and was again asked to work on it.

41. Utilize Art Therapy Techniques (41)

A. Art therapy techniques were used to help the client express depressive feelings.

B. The client's artwork was used as a springboard to help explore the causes of depression or other painful emotions.

C. The use of art therapy helped the client express feelings of depression and identify the causes.

D. The client's artwork was reviewed, but no interpretations were apparent.

42. Assign a Family Kinetic Drawing (42)

A. The client was asked to produce a family kinetic drawing to shed possible insight into the family dynamics that contribute to feelings of depression and hopelessness.

B. The family kinetic drawing was helpful in identifying the family dynamics that have contributed to the client's feelings of depression.

C. The client's family kinetic drawing revealed the client's sense of isolation and estrangement from other family members, which was reflected to the client.

D. The client's family kinetic drawing revealed the client's wish to establish closer family relations, which was reflected to the client.

E. The client's family kinetic drawing demonstrated how the client perceives parents as being overly critical and unavailable to meet emotional needs; the client was assisted in developing emotions in this area.

F. It was difficult to develop insight into the sources of the client's depression from the family kinetic drawing.

43. Facilitate Family Communication (43)

A. A family therapy session was held to give the client an opportunity to respectfully express emotional needs and conflicts with family members and significant others.

B. The family members were encouraged to respond with empathy and support for the client's expression of needs and conflicts.

C. The client and family members were helped to identify ways to meet the client's emotional needs.

D. The client and parents were helped to differentiate between respectful and disrespectful ways for the client to express thoughts, feeling, needs, and conflicts.

E. The parents were encouraged to ignore mild and occasional verbally aggressive or oppositional behaviors to help the client to become more assertive and less depressed.

F. The client and family members were helped to identify ways to meet the client's emotional needs.

G. The client's parents have not encouraged, supported, or tolerated the client's respectful expression of thoughts, feeling, needs, and conflicts and were redirected to do so.

44. Encourage Academic Effort (44)

A. The client was helped to establish academic goals to help lift depression and improve self-esteem.

B. The client was challenged and encouraged to achieve academic goals to offset feelings of depression and improve self-esteem.

C. The client and parents were assisted in developing a routine schedule of study times to mobilize the client and help achieve academic success.

D. The client and parents were assigned the exercise "Establish a Homework Routine" from the *Child Psychotherapy Homework Planner* (Jongsma, Peterson, McInnis, & Bruce).

E. A reward system was designed to reinforce the client for achieving academic goals.

F. The client and parents were encouraged to maintain regular communication with the teachers via phone calls or progress notes to help the client stay organized and achieve academic goals.

G. The client and parents were encouraged to work with a tutor to improve the client's academic performance.

45. Monitor Sleep Patterns (45)

A. Today's therapy session explored the factors that interfere with the client being able to sleep restfully through the night.

B. The client was trained in the use of guided imagery and relaxation techniques to help induce calm before attempting to sleep.

C. The client and parents were asked to track the client's sleep patterns to determine whether the client should be referred for a medication evaluation.

D. The parents were assigned the exercise "Childhood Sleep Patterns" from the *Child Psychotherapy Homework Planner* (Jongsma, Peterson, McInnis, & Bruce).

E. The client and parents were instructed to monitor the client's sleep patterns to help determine whether the medication needs to be changed or the dosage adjusted.

F. The client was administered electromyographic (EMG) biofeedback to reinforce a successful relaxation response to help the client sleep restfully at night.

46. Monitor Food Consumption (46)

A. The client and parents were instructed to keep a daily log of the client's food consumption.

B. The client was encouraged to eat nutritious, well-balanced meals to cease the pattern of weight loss.

C. The client was referred to a nutritionist to receive counseling about diet.

D. Today's therapy session explored the factors contributing to the client's overeating.

E. Encouragement was provided as the client verbally recognized that the pattern of overeating is related to unfulfilled dependency needs.

47. Arrange for Play Therapy (47)

A. Play therapy was begun to provide the client with the opportunity to express feelings about self and others.

B. The client was verbally reinforced as they made productive use of the play therapy sessions and have been able to express underlying feelings of depression, anxiety, and insecurity.

C. It was reflected that the client has been able to make productive use of the play therapy sessions and has expressed underlying feelings of anger through play.

D. It was noted that the client's play reflected little affect or emotional conflict.

48. Interpret Feelings in Play Therapy (48)

A. The client's feelings were interpreted in today's play therapy session and related to how the client feels about situations in their present life.

B. The client's play was noted to reflect feelings of sadness about previous separations, losses, and traumas.

C. The client's play was interpreted as reflecting underlying feelings of insecurity and helplessness relating to inability to overcome problems or conflicts.

D. The client's play was assessed to be reflecting underlying feelings of anger about past separations, losses, or traumatic experiences.

E. After interpreting the client's feelings expressed in play, the client was able to openly express feelings about significant life events.

49. Assign "Three Ways to Change the World" Exercise (49)

A. The client was given the "Three Ways to Change the World" exercise from the *Child Psychotherapy Homework Planner* (Jongsma, Peterson, McInnis, & Bruce) to identify ways to help bring increased feelings of joy, peace, and security into life.

B. The client was given the "Three Ways to Change the World" exercise to identify the stressors or unmet needs that contribute to feelings of depression.

C. The client was given the "Three Ways to Change the World" exercise to help the therapist establish rapport with them.

D. The client reported that the "Three Ways to Change the World" exercise was helpful in identifying constructive steps that they can take to cope with stress or overcome problems; the client was encouraged to put these steps into action.

E. The client identified the "Three Ways to Change the World" exercise as being a helpful way to identify the core conflicts contributing to depression; these were reviewed and processed.

DISRUPTIVE MOOD DYSREGULATION DISORDER (DMDD)

CLIENT PRESENTATION

1. **Severe Recurrent Temper Outbursts (1)***
   A. The parents report that the client engages in severe recurrent temper outbursts manifested verbally (e.g., verbal rages) or behaviorally (e.g., physical aggression toward people or property) that are grossly out of proportion in intensity or duration to the situation or provocation.
   B. The client behaved in a disruptive manner during today's therapy session by engaging in verbal or behavioral temper outbursts.
   C. The client has recently begun to exercise greater self-control and has not engaged in as many temper outbursts.
   D. The client demonstrated good self-control during today's therapy session and did not engage in any temper outbursts.
   E. The client has demonstrated a significant reduction in the frequency of temper outbursts.

2. **Developmentally Inappropriate Outbursts (2)**
   A. The client's temper outbursts are reported to be significantly below what would be expected for an individual with their developmental level.
   B. The client was observed to be having a temper outburst that was inconsistent with their developmental level during today's therapy session.
   C. The client has decreased temper outbursts, especially those that are inconsistent with their developmental level.
   D. The client has demonstrated a significant reduction in the frequency of temper outbursts.

3. **Multiple Outbursts Per Week (3)**
   A. The parents report that the client engages in temper outbursts three or more times per week.
   B. The client has decreased average weekly temper outbursts.
   C. The client has minimal temper outbursts per week.

4. **Irritable or Angry Mood (4)**
   A. The client and parents report the client's mood to be persistently irritable or angry most of the day, early every day, in between temper outbursts.
   B. The client's overall irritable or angry mood has been observable by others, including parents, teachers, and peers.

---

* The numbers in parentheses correlate to the number of the Behavioral Definition statement in the companion chapter with the same title in the *Child Psychotherapy Treatment Planner*, Sixth Edition, by Jongsma, Peterson, McInnis, & Bruce (Wiley, 2023).

C. The client's observable negative mood has decreased in intensity and duration.

D. The client and parents have identified a significant improvement in the client's mood throughout the day.

5. Irritable or Angry in Multiple Settings (5)

A. The client's irritable or angry mood and temper outbursts are present and occur in at least two settings and are severe in at least one setting.

B. The client's severe irritable mood and temper outbursts were observed in today's therapy session.

C. The client has reduced irritable or angry mood and temper outbursts in at least one setting.

6. Long-Term Presence (6)

A. The client's irritable or angry mood and temper outbursts have been present for at least 12 months with remission no longer than 3 consecutive months.

B. The client's irritable or angry mood and temper outbursts have decreased at times but have not extended for a period more than 3 consecutive months.

C. The client irritable or angry mood and temper outbursts have stopped for a significant period of time longer than 3 months.

INTERVENTIONS IMPLEMENTED

1. Establish Rapport (1)*

A. Caring was conveyed to the client through support, warmth, and empathy.

B. The client was provided with nonjudgmental support and a level of trust was developed.

C. The client was urged to feel safe in expressing mood concerns.

D. The client began to express feelings more freely as rapport and trust level have increased.

E. The client has continued to experience difficulty being open and direct about expression of painful feelings; the client was encouraged to use the safe haven of therapy to express these difficult issues.

2. Focus on Strengthening Therapeutic Relationship (2)

A. The relationship with the client was strengthened using empirically supported factors.

B. The relationship with the client was strengthened through the implementation of collaborative approach, agreement on goals, demonstration of empathy, verbalization of positive regard, and collection of client feedback.

C. The client reacted positively to the relationship-strengthening measures taken.

D. The client verbalized feeling supported and understood during therapy sessions.

---

*The numbers in parentheses correlate to the number of the Therapeutic Intervention statement in the companion chapter with the same title in the *Child Psychotherapy Treatment Planner*, Sixth. Edition, by Jongsma, Peterson, McInnis, & Bruce (Wiley, 2023).

E. Despite attempts to strengthen the therapeutic relationship, the client reports feeling distant and misunderstood.

F. The client has indicated that sessions are not helpful and will be terminating therapy.

3. **Identify Anger Sources (3)**

A. A nonjudgmental interview was used to encourage the client to discuss angry thoughts, feelings, and defiant actions and to identify sources for anger.

B. Play-therapy approaches were used to assist the client in expressing angry thoughts, feelings, and defiant actions

C. The client was given unconditional positive regard and warm acceptance when expressing angry thoughts, feelings, and defiant actions and when discovering sources of anger.

D. The individual play-therapy sessions have helped the client work through the angry thoughts, feelings, and defiant actions and identify the sources of anger.

E. Play-therapy sessions have been held with the client but have not been useful in helping the client work through angry thoughts, feelings, and defiant actions or find the sources of anger.

4. **Assign Behavior Log (4)**

A. The client was assigned to keep a log of each situation that produced angry feelings, the thoughts associated with the situation, and the actions taken.

B. The client was assigned to rate the level of anger in each situation on a scale from 1 to 100.

C. The client was assisted in processing the anger log, including uncovering the pattern of situations, thoughts, feelings, and actions that drive anger.

D. The client was assigned "Reasons for Negative Attention-Seeking Behaviors" in the *Child Psychotherapy Homework Planner* (Jongsma, Peterson, McInnis, & Bruce).

E. The client has not kept a log of angry feelings, thoughts, and actions and was redirected to do so.

5. **Assess Stimuli (5)**

A. The various stimuli that have triggered the client's anger were assessed.

B. The client was assigned the "Child Anger Checklist" from the *Child Psychotherapy Homework Planner* (Jongsma, Peterson, McInnis, & Bruce).

C. The client was helped to connect the situations, people, and thoughts to anger responses.

D. The client completed the "Child Anger Checklist" and processed new knowledge.

E. The client has not completed the "Child Anger Checklist" and was redirected to do so.

6. **Assess Prior Responses (6)**

A. The parents were assessed in regard to how they have attempted to respond to the child's misbehavior.

B. Triggers and reinforcements that may have been contributing to the behavior were reviewed.

C. The parents were assessed for their consistency in their approach to the child.

D. The parents were assessed for whether they have experienced conflicts between themselves over how to react to the child.

7. **Refer for Conduct/Psychological Testing (7)**

A. The client received a psychological evaluation to objectively assess features of DMDD and the parent–child relationship.

B. The client approached the psychological testing in an honest, straightforward manner and was cooperative with any requests presented to them.

C. The client was uncooperative and resistant to engage during the evaluation process.

D. The findings from the psychological testing were shared with the client and parents, and questions were answered.

8. **Assess Level of Insight (8)**

A. The client's level of insight toward the presenting problems was assessed.

B. The client was assessed in regard to the syntonic versus dystonic nature of their insight about the presenting problems.

C. The client was noted to demonstrate good insight into the problematic nature of the behavior and symptoms.

D. The client was noted to agree with others' concerns and is motivated to work on change.

E. The client was noted to be ambivalent regarding the problems described and is reluctant to address the issues as a concern.

F. The client was noted to be resistant regarding acknowledgment of the problem areas, is not concerned about them, and has no motivation to make changes.

9. **Assess for Correlated Disorders (9)**

A. The client was assessed for evidence of research-based correlated disorders.

B. The client was assessed in regard to the level of vulnerability to suicide.

C. The client was identified as having a comorbid disorder, and treatment was adjusted to account for these concerns.

D. The client has been assessed for any correlated disorders, but none were found.

10. **Assess for Culturally Based Confounding Issues (10)**

A. The client was assessed for age-related issues that could help to better understand their clinical presentation.

B. The client was assessed for gender-related issues that could help to better understand their clinical presentation.

C. The client was assessed for cultural syndromes, cultural idioms of distress, or culturally based perceived causes that could help to better understand their clinical presentation.

D. Alternative factors have been identified as contributing to the client's currently defined "problem behavior," and these were considered in regard to treatment.

E. Culturally based factors that could help to account for the client's currently defined "problem behavior" were investigated, but no significant factors were identified.

11. Assess Severity of Impairment (11)

A. The severity of the client's impairment was assessed to determine the appropriate level of care.

B. The client was assessed in regard to impairment in social, relational, and educational endeavors.

C. It was reflected to the client that the impairment appears to create mild to moderate effects on the client's functioning.

D. It was reflected to the client that the impairment appears to create severe to very severe effects on the client's functioning.

E. The client was continuously assessed for the severity of impairment, as well as the efficacy and appropriateness of treatment.

12. Refer for Medication Evaluation (12)

A. The client was referred for a medication evaluation to improve anger outbursts and stabilize moods.

B. The client and parents agreed to follow through with a medication evaluation.

C. Discussion with the client revealed that they are strongly opposed to being placed on medication to help improve anger outbursts and stabilize moods.

D. The parents were assigned "Evaluating Medication Effects–Parent Form" in the *Child Psychotherapy Homework Planner* (Jongsma, Peterson, McInnis, & Bruce).

E. The client and parents reported that the medication has helped to improve the client's anger outbursts and stabilize moods; they were encouraged to continue the use of the medication.

F. The client and parents reported that the medication has not produced the desired changes in behavior, and this was communicated to the prescribing clinician.

13. Utilize Motivational Interviewing (13)

A. Motivational interviewing techniques were used to help assess the client's stage of change.

B. The client was assisted in moving toward making a commitment to engage in therapy toward positive change.

C. The client was noted to be participating actively in treatment.

14. Utilize Cognitive-Behavioral Therapy Approach (14)

A. A cognitive-behavioral therapy approach was utilized to assist the client in conceptualizing anger.

B. The client was taught that anger involves different components that go through predictable phases that can be managed.

C. The client was provided with examples of the different components of anger and the predictable phases that result.

D. The client was understanding of this new knowledge and identified their own predictable phases that can be managed.

E. The client struggled to understand the components of anger or the resulting predictable phases and was provided with remedial information.

15. Teach Calming Techniques (15)

A. The client was trained in the use of muscle relaxation, paced breathing, and calming imagery.

B. The client was assigned "Progressive Muscle Relaxation" in the *Adolescent Psychotherapy Homework Planner* (Jongsma, Peterson, McInnis, & Bruce).

C. The client was assigned the "Deep Breathing Exercise" from the *Child Psychotherapy Homework Planner* (Jongsma, Peterson, McInnis, & Bruce).

D. The client reported a positive response to the use of calming techniques taught to help control anger.

E. The client appeared uncomfortable and unable to relax when being instructed in the use of calming techniques.

16. Explore Self-Talk (16)

A. The client's self-talk that mediates angry feelings was explored.

B. The client was assessed for self-talk (e.g., demanding expectations), reflected in "should," "must," or "have to" statements.

C. The client was assisted in identifying and challenging biases and in generating alternative self-talk to correct for the biases.

D. The client was assigned the exercise "Replace Negative Thoughts with Positive Self-Talk" from the *Child Psychotherapy Homework Planner* (Jongsma, Peterson, McInnis, & Bruce).

E. The client was taught how to use correcting self-talk to facilitate a more flexible and temperate response to frustration.

17. Assign Thought-Stopping Technique (17)

A. The client was directed to implement a thought-stopping technique on a daily basis between sessions.

B. The client was assigned "Thought Stopping" in the *Adolescent Psychotherapy Homework Planner* (Jongsma, Peterson, McInnis, & Bruce).

C. The client's use of the thought-stopping technique was reviewed.

D. The client was provided with positive feedback for helpful use of the thought-stopping technique.

E. The client was provided with corrective feedback to help improve use of the thought-stopping technique.

18. Teach Assertive Communication Skills (18)

A. The client was taught effective assertive communication skills.

B. Role-playing techniques were used to model effective ways to use assertive communication.

C. The client was assigned the exercise "Surface Behavior/Inner Feelings" from the *Child Psychotherapy Homework Planner* (Jongsma, Peterson, McInnis, & Bruce).

D. The client was encouraged to use "I messages" and assertive versus aggressive statements.

E. The client was helped to differentiate between being assertive and overly demanding.

F. The client has failed to use assertive communication skills and was provided with remedial information in this area.

19. **Teach Problem-Solving Skills (19)**

A. The client was taught problem-solving skills of defining a problem, listing options for solving it effectively, evaluating options, developing and implementing a plan, assessing effectiveness, and revising if needed.

B. The "Problem-Solving Exercise" assignment from the *Child Psychotherapy Homework Planner* (Jongsma, Peterson, McInnis, & Bruce) was assigned to help the client increase communication and problem-solving skills.

C. The client was reinforced for clear understanding of the problem-solving skills.

D. The client displayed a poor understanding of the problem-solving skills and was provided with remedial feedback.

20. **Teach Conflict-Resolution Skills (20)**

A. The client was taught conflict-resolution skills through modeling, role-playing, and behavioral rehearsal.

B. The client was taught about empathy and active listening.

C. The client was taught about "I messages," respectful communication, assertiveness without aggression, and compromise.

D. The "Learning to Be Assertive" assignment from the *Child Psychotherapy Homework Planner* (Jongsma, Peterson, McInnis, & Bruce) was assigned to help the client increase communication and conflict-resolution skills.

E. The client was reinforced for clear understanding of the conflict-resolution skills.

F. The client displayed a poor understanding of the conflict-resolution skills and was provided with remedial feedback.

21. **Teach Social Skills (21)**

A. The client was asked to list situations in which they have had social difficulties or find it hard to use appropriate social skills.

B. The client was assigned "Greeting Peers," "Social Skills Exercise," or "Show Your Strengths" from the *Child Psychotherapy Homework Planner* (Jongsma, Peterson, McInnis, & Bruce).

C. Difficult social situations that the client identified were modeled and role-played with them to teach appropriate social skills.

D. Behavioral rehearsal was used with the client to prepare for facing the identified difficult social situations.

22. **Construct Strategy for Managing Dysregulation (22)**

A. The client was assisted in constructing a client-tailored strategy for managing emotional and behavioral dysregulation.

B. The client was encouraged to combine somatic, cognitive, communication, problem-solving, and conflict-resolution skills relevant to needs.

C. The client was reinforced for comprehensive dysregulation management strategy.

D. The client was redirected to develop a more comprehensive dysregulation management strategy.

23. **Select Challenging Situations for Managing Anger (23)**

A. The client was provided with situations in which they may be increasingly challenged to apply new personal and interpersonal skills.

B. The client was asked to identify likely upcoming challenging situations where they can use new personal and interpersonal skills.

C. The client was urged to use strategies in successively more difficult situations.

24. **Assign Homework Exercises (24)**

A. The client was assigned homework exercises to help practice newly learned calming, assertion, conflict-resolution, or cognitive-restructuring skills.

B. The client has practiced the dysregulation management skills, and the experience was reviewed and processed toward the goal of consolidation of such skills.

C. The client has not regularly practiced dysregulation management skills and was redirected to do so.

25. **Teach Parent Management Approach (25)**

A. The parents were taught constructive skills for managing the child's anxiety.

B. The parents were taught about how to encourage or discourage positive or negative behavior and that changing key elements of those interactions can be used to promote positive change.

C. The parents were receptive to learning new skills and reported positive use.

D. The parents were resistant to using new skills with their child and were redirected to change elements of their interactions.

26. **Read Parent-Training Material (26)**

A. The parents were asked to read material consistent with a parent management training approach to managing disruptive behavior.

B. The parents were assigned *Parents and Adolescents Living Together: The Basics* (Patterson & Forgatch).

C. The parents were assigned *Parents and Adolescents Living Together: Family Problem Solving* (Forgatch & Patterson).

D. The parents were assigned *The Kazdin Method for Parenting the Defiant Child* (Kazdin).

E. The parents have read the assigned material and key concepts were processed.

F. The parents have not read the assigned material and were redirected to do so.

27. **Assign Homework (27)**

A. The parents were taught how to specifically define and identify problem behaviors, identify their reactions to the behavior, determine whether the reaction increases or decreases the frequency of the behavior, and generate alternative to the problem behavior.

B. The parents were assigned "Catch Your Teen Being Responsible" or "Clear Rules, Positive Reinforcement, Appropriate Consequences" in the *Adolescent Psychotherapy Homework Planner* (Jongsma, Peterson, McInnis, & Bruce).

C. The parents appropriately completed the assignments and were provided with positive feedback.

D. The parents did not complete the assignments and were redirected to use this as a way to show parent management skills.

28. Implement Key Parenting Practices Consistently (28)

A. The parents were taught how to implement key parenting practices consistently.

B. The parents were taught how to establish realistic age-appropriate rules for acceptable and unacceptable behavior.

C. The parents were taught about prompting of positive behavior in the environment and use of positive reinforcement to encourage behavior.

D. The parents were reminded about the use of calm, clear direct instruction, time out, and other loss-of-privilege practices for problem behavior.

E. The parents were assigned "Being a Consistent Parent" in the *Child Psychotherapy Homework Planner* (Jongsma, Peterson, McInnis, & Bruce).

29. Conduct DBT-C (29)

A. The client was oriented to dialectical behavioral therapy for children (DBT-C).

B. The multiple facets of DBT were highlighted, including mindfulness, distress tolerance, emotional regulation, and interpersonal effectiveness.

C. DBT topics were explained to the client and parents and appeared appropriate for this client.

30. Teach Mindfulness (30)

A. The client was taught mindfulness to encourage a present-focused, nonjudgmental approach to situations and interactions.

B. The client was asked to apply mindfulness to current situations and was asked to provide feedback of the experience.

C. The client was reinforced for use of mindfulness techniques.

D. The client struggled with mindfulness techniques, and obstacles were addressed.

31. Teach Distress Tolerance Skills (31)

A. The client was taught about how to apply DBT distress tolerance skills to recognize distress, stop, observe, and proceed mindfully when triggered.

B. The client was assisted in building an acceptance of what cannot be changed and effective responding to what can be.

C. The client was reinforced for using distress tolerance skills in current situations.

D. The client struggled to understand distress tolerance skills and was provided with remedial information.

32. Teach PLEASE and LAUGH (32)

A. The client was taught emotional regulation related to being able to "surf" emotional reactivity.

B. The client was taught the acronyms PLEASE (PhysicaL health, Eat healthy, Avoid drugs/alcohol, Sleep well, and Exercise) and LAUGH (Let go of worries, Apply oneself, Use coping skills, set Goals, and Have fun).

C. The client was asked to use these skills to encourage an adaptive, rewarding approach to daily activity.

D. The client was assisted in applying PLEASE and LAUGH principles through exercise and application in several situations.

33. Teach DEAR and FRIEND (33)

A. The client was taught interpersonal effectiveness skills to encourage getting what they want while getting along with others.

B. The client was taught the acronyms DEAR (Describing the situation, Expressing feelings and thoughts, Asking for what you want, Rewarding the other person) and FRIEND (be Fair, Respect the other person, act Interested, keep an Easy manner, Negotiate, and be Direct).

C. The client was asked to use these skills in several current situations and process outcomes.

D. The client reinforced for success in using DEAR and FRIEND skills.

E. The client was unable to use DEAR and FRIEND in current situations, and obstacles were addressed.

F. The client was assigned "Finding Ways to Get Positive Attention" in the *Child Psychotherapy Homework Planner* (Jongsma, Peterson, McInnis, & Bruce).

34. Teach Parents DBT-C (34)

A. The client's parents were taught the concepts of DBT-C including how dialectical principles relate to parent training, such as change as transactional and permissive versus restrictive parenting.

B. The parents were taught how to create a validating environment, how to target behavior, setting realistic expectations, flexibility in finding the specific approach to the child, and learning behavioral management techniques.

C. The parents were asked to practice DBT-C skills outside of session and process results.

D. The parents were reinforced for their gains in using DBT-C skills.

E. The parents struggled to use DBT-C skills, and obstacles were addressed.

35. Monitor Reports of Defiance (35)

A. The client and parents were asked to identify and report incidents of defiance in the client.

B. The clients and parents were provided with rational for reporting incidents of defiance, as a way to decrease their frequency, intensity, and duration.

C. The client and parents were asked to identify when the client used new anger management skills to reduce defiant behaviors.

D. The client was assigned "The Lesson of Salmon Rock . . . Fighting Leads to Loneliness" from the *Child Psychotherapy Homework Planner* (Jongsma, Peterson, McInnis, & Bruce).

36. Encourage Sharing Skills (36)

A. The client was encouraged to share new anger and conduct management skills with trusted peers, family, and significant others who are likely to support their change.

B. The client reported receiving positive feedback when sharing new anger and conduct management skills with others, and outcomes were processed.

37. Coach Parents in Supporting Change (37)

A. The parents and other supports of the client were met with in attempts to coach them in how to be supportive of the client's attempts to change.

B. The parents and other supports were receptive to coaching on how to support the client's attempts to change and were provided with positive feedback.

C. The parents and other supports struggle to understand their role in supporting the client's attempts to change and were provided with additional feedback.

38. Design Contingency/Reward System (38)

A. A reward system was developed with the client.

B. A contingency contract was developed with the client.

C. A meeting was held with school officials to help reinforce identified positive behaviors and deter impulsive oppositional behaviors.

D. The exercise was assigned "Clear Rules, Positive Reinforcement, Appropriate Consequences" from the *Adolescent Psychotherapy Homework Planner* (Jongsma, Peterson, McInnis, & Bruce).

E. The client was encouraged to participate in the reward system/contingency contract in order to deter impulsive or rebellious behaviors.

F. Fine-tuning was done to the reward system/contingency contract in order to reinforce identified positive behaviors at home and school.

39. Track Feelings and Behaviors (39)

A. The client and parents were asked to track the frequency and intensity of negative, hostile feelings and defiant behaviors.

B. After reviewing the frequency and intensity of feelings and behaviors, the client was assisted in brainstorming problem-solving solutions and developing a plan to reduce the feelings and behaviors, including by reinforcing competing behaviors.

C. The client's plan has resulted in a decrease in the frequency and intensity of negative, hostile feelings and defiant behaviors, and the client was encouraged for this positive step.

D. The client's plan to assist in reducing the frequency and intensity of negative, hostile feelings and defiant behaviors has not been useful, and new ideas were processed.

40. Teach Principle of Reciprocity (40)

A. The client was taught the principle of reciprocity in session.

B. The client was asked to agree to treat everyone in a respectful manner for a 1-week period to see if others will reciprocate by treating the client with more respect.

C. The client was assigned the exercise "Building Empathy" from the *Child Psychotherapy Homework Planner* (Jongsma, Peterson, McInnis, & Bruce).

D. The idea of how the client would like to be treated by others was explored, along with what they would need to do to make this possible.

41. Play Therapeutic Games (41)

A. "The UnGame" (The UnGame Company) and the "Talking, Feeling, and Doing" game (Gardner; available from Childswork/Childsplay) were played with the client to give them opportunities to express feelings respectfully.

B. Opportunities for feeling identification during games were seized to affirm the client's self-disclosure.

C. It was reflected to the client that they have become more adept at identifying and expressing emotions.

42. Videotape Family Session (42)

A. The client and parents were asked to agree to a videotaping of a family session.

B. Portions of the videotaped family session were shown to the family to exhibit family interaction patterns that are destructive.

C. The family was taught more respectful patterns through the use of role-playing, role reversal, and modeling.

43. Probe Family-of-Origin Patterns (43)

A. Patterns of violence, anger, and suspicion in the client's family of origin were identified as being prevalent.

B. The client was assisted in learning how family-of-origin problems can lead to present-day vulnerability and seeing people and situations as dangerous or otherwise threatening.

C. The client was understanding of the patterns and problems early in life that lead to current patterns and problems, and the specific situation was processed.

D. The client denied any family-of-origin patterns or problems that apply to them today, and remedial feedback was provided.

44. Explore Family Dynamics (44)

A. A family therapy session was held to explore dynamics within the family system that contribute to the development of the client's oppositional defiant behaviors.

B. The family members were asked to list the stressors that have had a negative impact on the family.

C. The family members were asked to identify the things that they would like to change within the family.

D. The family members were guarded about discussing family dynamics and were provided with feedback in this area.

45. Teach Anger Concepts (45)

A. The client was taught how anger blocks the awareness of pain, discharges uncomfortable feelings, deflects guilt or grief, and places blame for problems on someone else.

B. The client was assigned "The Lesson of Salmon Rock . . . Fighting Leads to Loneliness" from the *Child Psychotherapy Homework Planner* (Jongsma, Peterson, McInnis, & Bruce).

46. Educate on Forgiveness (46)

A. The client was assisted in identifying people they need to forgive.

B. The client was educated on the long-term process involved in forgiveness of another person.

C. The client was understanding of the reality of forgiveness as a long-term process and identified specific people they need to forgive.

D. The client struggled to understand the long-term process of forgiveness and was recommended to read material on forgiveness.

DIVORCE REACTION

CLIENT PRESENTATION

1. **Reduced Contact with a Parent (1)***
   A. The client has had infrequent or no contact with one of their parents since the separation or divorce.
   B. The client was guarded and reluctant to talk about the infrequent or loss of contact with one of their parents.
   C. The client expressed feelings of sadness, hurt, and disappointment about the infrequent or loss of contact with one of their parents.
   D. The client verbalized strong feelings of anger about the limited contact with one of their parents.
   E. The client has worked through many of their emotions surrounding the infrequent or loss of contact with one of their parents.

2. **Emotional Distress Around Separations (2)**
   A. The client has often exhibited a great deal of emotional distress when anticipating a separation from one of their parents.
   B. The client became visibly upset and began to protest vigorously when asked to separate from the parent in today's therapy session.
   C. The client has often displayed temper outbursts around separations from one of the parents.
   D. The client has gradually started to cope more effectively with separations and has not exhibited as much distress when anticipating separation from a parent.
   E. The client was able to separate effectively from the parent in today's therapy session without exhibiting a significant amount of distress.

3. **Emotional Distress Around Transfer from Home(s) (2)**
   A. The client has often exhibited a great deal of emotional distress when making the transfer from one parent's home to the other.
   B. The parents reported that the client frequently exhibits temper outbursts before and after they make the transfer from one home to the other.
   C. The client has often begged and pleaded to stay with one parent before making the transfer to the other parent's home.
   D. The client has gradually started to cope more effectively with the transfer between homes.
   E. The client has consistently been able to make the transition from one parent's home to the other without exhibiting any heightened emotional distress.

---

* The numbers in parentheses correlate to the number of the Behavioral Definition statement in the companion chapter with the same title in the *Child Psychotherapy Treatment Planner*, Sixth Edition, by Jongsma, Peterson, McInnis, & Bruce (Wiley, 2023).

4. **Fear of Abandonment/Separation (3)**

   A. The client has developed persistent fears about being abandoned or separated from parents.

   B. The client expressed fears of abandonment in today's therapy session.

   C. The client expressed worries about being separated from parents.

   D. The client has developed persistent worries about being separated from the custodial parent, in part because of the limited contact that they have with the noncustodial parent.

   E. The client has successfully worked through and resolved fears and worries about being abandoned or separated from parents.

5. **Feelings of Grief and Sadness (4)**

   A. The client has experienced strong feelings of grief and sadness since their parents' separation or divorce.

   B. The client was visibly sad when talking about their parents' separation or divorce.

   C. The client has begun to work through feelings of grief and sadness about the separation or divorce.

   D. The client's affect appeared happier and/or more contented in today's therapy session.

   E. The client reported a significant reduction recently in the frequency and severity of depressed mood.

6. **Low Self-Esteem (4)**

   A. The client's self-esteem has decreased significantly since their parents' separation or divorce.

   B. The client verbalized feelings of low self-esteem, inadequacy, and insecurity.

   C. The client has begun to take steps to improve self-esteem and develop a positive self-image.

   D. The client expressed positive self-descriptive statements during today's therapy session.

   E. The client has developed a healthy self-image after working through many of their feelings surrounding their parents' separation or divorce.

7. **Social Withdrawal (4)**

   A. The client has become significantly more withdrawn and isolated since their parents' separation or divorce.

   B. The client appeared very quiet and withdrawn during today's therapy session and initiated few conversations.

   C. The client has gradually started to socialize more often with peers.

   D. The client was more communicative and outgoing during today's therapy session.

8. **Feelings of Guilt/Self-Blame (5)**

   A. The client expressed feelings of guilt about having acted in some way to cause their parents' divorce.

   B. The client has continued to hold on to the unreasonable belief that they either behaved in some manner to cause their parents' divorce or failed to prevent the divorce from occurring.

C. The client has started to work through feelings of guilt about their parents' separation or divorce.

D. The parent(s) verbalized that the client is not responsible for the separation or divorce.

E. The client has successfully worked through feelings of guilt and no longer blames self for the parents' separation or divorce.

9. **Oppositional, Acting-Out, and Aggressive Behavior (6)**

A. The client has exhibited a significant increase in the frequency and severity of oppositional, acting-out, and aggressive behaviors since their parents' separation or divorce.

B. The client appeared angry and irritable when discussing the separation or divorce.

C. The frequency of the client's oppositional, acting-out, and aggressive behaviors has gradually started to diminish.

D. The client has recently demonstrated good self-control and has not engaged in a significant amount of oppositional, acting-out, or aggressive behavior.

10. **Decline in School Performance (7)**

A. The client's school performance has decreased markedly since their parents' separation or divorce.

B. The client verbalized that they have experienced a loss of interest or motivation to achieve academic success since the separation or divorce.

C. The client has experienced a renewed interest in schoolwork and has begun to take steps to improve academic performance.

D. The client reported completing school or homework assignments on a regular basis.

11. **Regressive Behaviors (8)**

A. The client has demonstrated an increase in regressive behaviors since their parents' separation.

B. The client exhibited regressive behaviors in today's therapy session.

C. The client spoke in a very immature or infantile (i.e., baby talk) manner when discussing their parents' separation or divorce.

D. The client did not engage in any regressive behaviors during today's therapy session.

E. The parent(s) reported that the client has demonstrated a significant reduction in the frequency of regressive behaviors.

12. **Bed-Wetting (8)**

A. The client has regressed and experienced problems with bed-wetting since their parents' separation or divorce.

B. The client verbalized feelings of shame and embarrassment about their bed-wetting problem.

C. The client has regained effective bladder control at night.

D. The client expressed feelings of happiness about overcoming their problems with bed-wetting.

13. **Pseudomaturity (9)**

A. The client has responded to their parents' separation or divorce by displaying an air of pseudomaturity.

B. The client presented with a facade of pseudomaturity and coolly denied being troubled by any painful emotions about their parents' separation or divorce.

C. The client has responded to the separation or divorce by often assuming parental roles or responsibilities.

D. The client verbalized an awareness of how their willingness to take on many parental roles or responsibilities has prevented the client from meeting their own emotional or social needs.

E. The client has achieved a healthy balance between fulfilling school or household responsibilities and meeting social and emotional needs.

14. **Psychosomatic Ailments (10)**

A. The client has demonstrated a significant increase in psychosomatic complaints since their parents' separation or divorce.

B. The client complained of not feeling well when the issue of their parents' separation or divorce was being discussed.

C. The client was resistant to the interpretation that their psychosomatic complaints are related to underlying painful emotions about the separation or divorce.

D. The client verbalized an understanding of the connection between psychosomatic complaints and anticipated separations, stress, or frustration related to the parents' marital conflict.

E. The client has demonstrated a significant reduction in the frequency of psychosomatic complaints.

15. **Anxiety (10)**

A. The client reported a significant increase in feelings of anxiety since their parents' separation or divorce.

B. The client appeared nervous, anxious, and tense during today's therapy session.

C. The client's feelings of anxiety have gradually started to decrease as they work through their feelings about the separation or divorce.

D. The client appeared more relaxed and comfortable in today's therapy session.

E. The client reported a significant reduction in the frequency of anxious moods.

16. **Reduced Support Due to Geographic Move (11)**

A. The client has had less frequent contact with one of their parents due to a geographic move.

B. The client has experienced a lack of support due to the distance between the client and the parent.

C. The client expressed feelings of sadness, hurt, disappointment and missing their geographically distant parent.

D. The client has worked through many of their emotions surrounding the loss of support from the parent.

17. **Grief Due to Disruption of Family Routine/Tradition (12)**

A. The client has experienced disruption in usual family routines or traditions.

B. The client's loss of routines or traditions has created feelings of sadness, grief, anxiety, or anger.

C. The client has begun to process the changes in routines and traditions that have created sadness, grief, anxiety, or anger.

D. The client has accepted the changes in routines and traditions and their feelings have eased in severity.

18. Parents' Heated Disputes (13)

A. The client reported that their parents often engage in heated disputes in their presence.

B. The client expressed feelings of anger, sadness, and frustration about their parents' pattern of heated disputes, feeling trapped and/or "caught in the middle."

C. The client verbalized a request for their parents to cease heated arguments in their presence.

D. The parents acknowledged that their heated disputes are upsetting to the client and siblings.

E. The client reported that their parents have ceased their heated disputes in the client's presence.

F. The client denied feeling trapped or "caught in the middle" of the disputes between their parents.

INTERVENTIONS IMPLEMENTED

1. Establish Rapport (1)*

A. Caring was conveyed to the client through support, warmth, and empathy.

B. The client was provided with nonjudgmental support, and a level of trust was developed.

C. The client was urged to feel safe in expressing their reaction to parental divorce.

D. The client began to express feelings more freely as rapport and trust level have increased.

E. The client has continued to experience difficulty being open and direct about the expression of painful feelings; the client was encouraged to use the safe haven of therapy to express these difficult issues.

2. Focus on Strengthening Therapeutic Relationship (2)

A. The relationship with the client was strengthened using empirically supported factors.

B. The relationship with the client was strengthened through the implementation of collaborative approach, agreement on goals, demonstration of empathy, verbalization of positive regard, and collection of client feedback.

C. The client reacted positively to the relationship-strengthening measures taken.

D. The client verbalized feeling supported and understood during therapy sessions.

E. Despite attempts to strengthen the therapeutic relationship, the client reports feeling distant and misunderstood.

F. The client has indicated that sessions are not helpful and will be terminating therapy.

---

*The numbers in parentheses correlate to the number of the Therapeutic Intervention statement in the companion chapter with the same title in the *Child Psychotherapy Treatment Planner*, Sixth Edition, by Jongsma, Peterson, McInnis, & Bruce (Wiley, 2023).

3. **Explore and Encourage Expression of Feelings (3)**

   A. Today's therapy session explored the client's feelings associated with their parents' separation or divorce.

   B. The client was given encouragement and support in expressing and clarifying their feelings associated with the separation or divorce.

   C. Client-centered therapy principles were utilized to assist the client in expressing thoughts and feelings about the parents' separation or divorce.

   D. The client was assigned the exercise "My Thoughts and Feelings About My Parents' Divorce" from the *Child Psychotherapy Homework Planner* (Jongsma, Peterson, McInnis, & Bruce).

   E. The client was assigned the exercise "Petey's Journey Through Sadness" from the *Child Psychotherapy Homework Planner* (Jongsma, Peterson, McInnis, & Bruce).

   F. The client made productive use of today's therapy session and was assisted in expressing a variety of emotions related to their parents' separation or divorce.

   G. The client remained guarded in sharing feelings regarding the separation or divorce, despite receiving encouragement and support.

4. **Create Photo Album (4)**

   A. The client was instructed to gather a diverse collection of photographs covering many aspects of their life and bring them to the next session to create a photo album.

   B. The client was assigned the exercise "Create a Memory Album" from the *Child Psychotherapy Homework Planner* (Jongsma, Peterson, McInnis, & Bruce).

   C. In today's therapy session, the client was assisted in placing the collection of photographs in a photo album.

   D. Creating the photo album has been noted to be helpful for the client to identify and express feelings about the changes within the family system.

   E. While creating the family photo album, the client was encouraged to express feelings of sadness about changes in the family system.

   F. While creating the photo album, the client expressed feelings of anger about the changes in the family system and was supported for this healthy expression of feelings.

   G. Despite creating a photo album displaying many aspects of the client's life, the client remained defensive about their feelings in this area; they were encouraged to express these emotions as they feel safe to do so.

5. **Assign Children's Books on Divorce (5)**

   A. During today's therapy session, children's books about divorce were read.

   B. In today's session, *What Can I Do?: A Book for Children of Divorce* (Lowry) was read to the client.

   C. In today's session, *My Parents Are Divorced Too* (Ford et al.) was read to help answer client questions about the parents' divorce and changes in the family system.

   D. In today's session, *Was It the Chocolate Pudding?: A Story for Little Kids About Divorce* (Levins) was read to the client and discussed.

   E. The client was assisted in processing the content of the readings in today's therapy session.

F. Reading the books on divorce was noted to help the client express and work through feelings about the parents' divorce.

G. After we read the book on divorce, the client was able to express thoughts and feelings about the changes that have occurred within the family system.

6. Use the "Color Your Life" Technique (6)

A. The "Color Your Life" technique (O'Connor) was used to help the client express feelings about the parents' separation or divorce.

B. The client was assisted in using the "Color Your Life" technique to identify and express ambivalent feelings toward both parents as a result of the parents' separation or divorce.

C. The "Color Your Life" technique was used to help the client identify and express feelings of sadness about the parents' separation or divorce.

D. The "Color Your Life" technique was used to help the client identify and express feelings of anger about the parents' separation or divorce.

7. Assign Feelings Exercise (7)

A. The client was asked to draw pictures of their emotions and share times when they experienced those emotions about their parents' separation or divorce.

B. The "Feelings and Faces" exercise from the *Child Psychotherapy Homework Planner* (Jongsma, Peterson, McInnis, & Bruce) was used to help the client express and work through ambivalent feelings about the parents' separation or divorce.

C. The "Feelings and Faces" exercise was employed to help the client work through feelings of grief about the parents' separation or divorce.

D. The "Feelings and Faces" exercise was used to enlist support of the parents in helping the client to identify and express thoughts and feelings about their separation or divorce.

E. The client identified the "Feelings and Faces" exercise as being a useful way to express feelings about the parents' separation or divorce; the client was reinforced for this healthy expression of feelings.

F. The client failed to complete the "Feelings and Faces" exercise and was asked to do it again to help work through feelings about the parents' separation or divorce.

8. Play Guess Which Hand Game (8)

A. The "Guess Which Hand" game (Lowenstein) was played with the client to promote expression of feelings.

B. The client was assisted in understanding different feelings through sharing times when they experienced each feeling.

C. The client engaged in the "Guess Which Hand" game and learned how to express their feelings more completely.

D. The client continued to struggle to express feelings despite playing the "Guess Which Hand" game in session.

9. Employ Empty-Chair Technique (9)

A. The empty-chair technique was used to help the client express the mixed emotions that they feel toward both parents because of their separation or divorce, and the changes in the family life.

B. The empty-chair technique was helpful in enabling the client to identify and express the emotions that they feel toward both parents because of their separation or divorce.

C. The empty-chair technique was useful in allowing the client to express thoughts and feelings about the custodial and noncustodial parent.

D. The client appeared uncomfortable with the use of the empty-chair technique and was reluctant to share the emotions that they feel toward both parents because of their separation or divorce.

10. **Assess Level of Insight (10)**

A. The client's level of insight toward the presenting problems was assessed.

B. The client was assessed in regard to the syntonic versus dystonic nature of their insight about the presenting problems.

C. The client was noted to demonstrate good insight into the problematic nature of the behavior and symptoms.

D. The client was noted to be in agreement with others' concerns and is motivated to work on change.

E. The client was noted to be ambivalent regarding the problems described and is reluctant to address the issues as a concern.

F. The client was noted to be resistant regarding acknowledgment of the problem areas, is not concerned about them, and has no motivation to make changes.

11. **Assess for Correlated Disorders (11)**

A. The client was assessed for evidence of research-based correlated disorders.

B. The client was assessed in regard to the level of vulnerability to suicide.

C. The client was identified as having a comorbid disorder, and treatment was adjusted to account for these concerns.

D. The client has been assessed for any correlated disorders, but none were found.

12. **Assess for Culturally Based Confounding Issues (12)**

A. The client was assessed for age-related issues that could help to better understand their clinical presentation.

B. The client was assessed for gender-related issues that could help to better understand their clinical presentation.

C. The client was assessed for cultural syndromes, cultural idioms of distress, or culturally based perceived causes that could help to better understand their clinical presentation.

D. Alternative factors have been identified as contributing to the client's currently defined "problem behavior," and these were taken into account in regard to treatment.

E. Culturally based factors that could help to account for the client's currently defined "problem behavior" were investigated, but no significant factors were identified.

13. **Assess Severity of Impairment (13)**

A. The severity of the client's impairment was assessed to determine the appropriate level of care.

B. The client was assessed in regard to impairment in social, relational, and educational endeavors.

C. It was reflected to the client that the impairment appears to create mild to moderate effects on the client's functioning.

D. It was reflected to the client that the impairment appears to create severe to very severe effects on the client's functioning.

E. The client was continuously assessed for the severity of impairment, as well as the efficacy and appropriateness of treatment.

14. **Assess for Pathogenic Care (14)**

A. The home, school, and community of the client were assessed for pathogenic care and concerns.

B. The client's various environments were assessed for the persistent disregard of the child's needs, repeated changes in caregivers, limited opportunities for stable attachment, harsh discipline, or other grossly inept care.

C. Pathogenic care was identified, and the treatment plan included strategies for managing or correcting these concerns and protecting the child.

D. No pathogenic care was identified, and this was reflected to the client and caregivers.

15. **Utilize Family Therapy to Facilitate Feelings Expression (15)**

A. A family therapy session was held to allow the client and siblings to express feelings and ask questions about the separation or divorce in the presence of the parent(s).

B. The client and siblings were assigned "My Thoughts and Feelings About My Parents' Divorce" from the *Child Psychotherapy Homework Planner* (Jongsma, Peterson, McInnis, & Bruce).

C. Each parent was prompted to affirm love for the children.

D. Each parent was provided with positive feedback for being supportive in allowing the client and siblings to express their feelings and ask questions about the separation or divorce.

E. Each parent was redirected when becoming defensive when the client and siblings began expressing their feelings and asking questions about the separation or divorce.

16. **Provide Opportunities at Home to Express Feelings (16)**

A. The parent(s) was (were) encouraged to provide opportunities at home to allow the client and siblings to express their feelings and ask questions about the separation or divorce and the subsequent changes in the family system.

B. The parent(s) was (were) encouraged to hold family meetings at home to allow the client and siblings an opportunity to express their feelings and ask questions about the separation or divorce and the subsequent changes in the family system.

C. The family members were helped to identify healthy and unhealthy ways to express their feelings about the separation or divorce and the subsequent changes in the family system.

D. The parent(s) was (were) encouraged to explore the client's feelings about the separation or divorce and the subsequent changes in the family system when they become more withdrawn or demonstrate an increase in emotional outbursts.

E. The client and siblings were asked to identify the specific, positive changes that they would like to see happen in the family.

F. The client's parents have not allowed the client to regularly express feelings (in a respectful manner) and were redirected to do so.

17. Discuss Importance of Routines/Traditions (17)

A. A family therapy session was conducted to discuss the importance of maintaining specific routines and traditions.

B. The family discussed routines and traditions that help provide stability for the client and siblings.

C. The family identified specific routines and traditions in which they will continue to engage.

D. The family was assisted in grieving specific routines and traditions that cannot be continued.

18. Assess Factors Contributing to Guilt (18)

A. Today's therapy session explored and identified the factors contributing to the client's feelings of guilt and self-blame about the parents' separation or divorce.

B. The client was supported as they expressed feelings of guilt about how their acting-out or rebellious behaviors may have contributed to the parents' separation or divorce.

C. The family was directed to read *It's Not Your Fault, Koko Bear: A Read-Together Book for Parents and Young Children During Divorce* (Lansky).

D. Today's therapy session did not reveal any specific events that have contributed to the client's feelings of guilt and self-blame about the parents' separation or divorce.

E. The client denied being troubled by any strong feelings of guilt about their parents' separation or divorce; the client was urged to identify any of these feelings if they become aware of them.

F. The client was helped to understand that their negative behaviors did not cause their parents' divorce to occur.

G. The client has continued to hold on to feelings of guilt about how their negative behaviors caused the parents' divorce, despite efforts to inform the client that they are not responsible.

19. Confront Belief About Getting Parents Back Together (19)

A. The client was gently confronted with the fact that they do not have the power or control to bring their parents back together.

B. The client was helped to realize how their negative behaviors will not bring the parents back together.

C. The client was provided with positive reinforcement as they acknowledged that they do not have the power to bring their parents back together.

D. The client continues to make comments about their belief that they can bring their parents back together and was reminded that they do not have the power to make this happen.

20. Affirm Client as Not Being Responsible for Separation/Divorce (20)

A. The custodial parent strongly affirmed the client and siblings as not being responsible for the separation or divorce, and the therapist emphasized this concept.

B. The noncustodial parent strongly affirmed the client and siblings as not being responsible for the separation or divorce, and the therapist emphasized this concept.

C. The parents were separated for verbalizing responsibility for the separation or divorce.

D. The client and siblings responded positively to the parents' affirmation that they are not responsible for the separation or divorce, and the meaning of this affirmation was elaborated.

E. The client has continued to be troubled by feelings of guilt about their parents' divorce despite the parents' statements that they are not responsible, and this was normalized.

21. **Confront Blaming by Parents (21)**

A. The custodial parent was challenged and confronted about making statements that place the blame or responsibility for the separation or divorce on the client or siblings.

B. The noncustodial parent was challenged and confronted about making statements that place the blame or responsibility for the separation or divorce on the client or siblings.

C. The custodial parent was reinforced for a verbalized commitment to stop making statements that place the blame or responsibility for the separation or divorce on the client or siblings.

D. The noncustodial parent was reinforced for a verbalized commitment to stop making statements that place the blame or responsibility for the separation or divorce on the client or siblings.

E. The parents have continued to make statements that place the blame or responsibility for the separation or divorce on the client or siblings, despite challenges to stop making such remarks.

22. **List Positive and Negative Aspects of Divorce (22)**

A. The client was given a homework assignment to list both the positive and negative aspects of their parents' divorce.

B. The client was reassured of the normalcy of feeling a variety of emotions while processing both the positive and negative aspects of their parents' divorce.

C. The client was supported as they expressed emotions about the negative aspects of their parents' divorce but was unable to identify any positive aspects.

D. The client's failure to complete the homework assignment of listing both the positive and negative aspects of their parents' divorce appeared to be due to the desire to avoid dealing with any painful emotions, and this was reflected to the client.

23. **Address Challenges (23)**

A. A family session was held to discuss challenges or difficult changes that have occurred because of the separation/divorce.

B. The client and family members were assisted in writing a list of specific challenges or difficult changes that have recently occurred.

C. The client and family were assisted in problem-solving and finding effective ways to adjust to new changes.

D. The client and family were unable to identify specific problem-solving techniques to assist their recent challenges or difficult changes.

24. Encourage Parents to Spend Time with Client (24)

A. The parents were given the directive to spend 10 to 15 minutes of one-on-one time with the client and siblings on a regular or daily basis, in order to identify the client's need.

B. It was noted that the one-on-one time spent with the parent(s) has helped the client to decrease their feelings of depression.

C. The client and parents reported that the one-on-one time spent together has helped to improve the client's anger control, and they were encouraged to continue this one-to-one time.

D. The client and parents reported that they have spent little time together because of their busy schedules, and a specific time to be together was identified.

E. The client and parents were strongly challenged to spend time together in order to help the client adjust to their parents' divorce.

25. Assist Transition from One Parent's Home to the Other (25)

A. A consultation was held with the client and parent(s) about establishing a routine or ritual to help decrease the client's emotional distress around periods of separation or transfer from one parent's home to the other.

B. The client and parent(s) reported that the client has made a smoother transition from one parent's home to the other by engaging in relaxing or enjoyable activities; they were encouraged to continue this practice.

C. The client has continued to find it difficult to make the transition from one parent's home to the other after visits, but has failed to follow through with the recommendation to engage in relaxing or enjoyable activities.

D. The client was helped to identify a list of activities that they could engage in to help cope with separations from parents.

E. The client was encouraged to play or interact with siblings or peers to help cope with separations from parents.

26. Reinforce Healthy Coping with Divorce (26)

A. The therapy session focused on empowering the client's ability to cope with their parents' divorce.

B. The client was asked to identify a list of behaviors or signs that would indicate they have made a healthy adjustment to the parents' divorce.

C. The client was reinforced for the positive steps that they have taken to adjust to their parents' divorce.

D. The client remains pessimistic and resistant to the idea that they can make a healthy adjustment to the divorce but was encouraged to keep this possibility open.

27. Connect Painful Emotions to Angry Outbursts (27)

A. The session was helpful in identifying how the client's underlying, painful emotions about their parents' divorce are related to an increase in the frequency of their angry outbursts or aggressive behaviors.

B. The client was helped to verbalize an understanding of how their aggressive behaviors are connected to underlying feelings of sadness, hurt, or disappointment about their parents' divorce.

C. The client was assigned "Surface Behavior/Inner Feelings" from the *Child Psychotherapy Homework Planner* (Jongsma, Peterson, McInnis, & Bruce).

D. Role-playing and modeling techniques were used to demonstrate appropriate ways for the client to express underlying painful emotions.

E. The client was asked to list more appropriate ways to express painful emotions about the divorce instead of reacting impulsively with anger or aggression.

F. The client denied any connection between painful emotions and angry outbursts and was encouraged to reconsider this connection.

28. Teach Appropriate Versus Inappropriate Anger Expressions (28)

A. The client was helped to identify appropriate and inappropriate ways to express anger about the parents' separation, divorce, or changes in the family.

B. The client was taught mediational and self-control strategies (e.g., relaxation, "stop, listen, think, and act") to help express anger through appropriate verbalizations and healthy physical outlets.

C. The client was encouraged to utilize active listening skills to delay the impulse or urge to react with anger or physical aggression when upset about their parents' separation, divorce, or changes in the family.

D. The client identified healthy physical outlets for strong feelings of anger and aggressive impulses, and positive feedback was provided.

E. Despite being taught appropriate anger expression, the client continues to use inappropriate means to express anger about the changes in the family structure and dynamics.

29. Use "Angry Tower" Technique (29)

A. The "Angry Tower" technique (Saxe) was used in today's therapy session to help the client identify and express feelings of anger about the parents' divorce.

B. The "Angry Tower" technique helped the client directly verbalize feelings of anger about the parents' divorce.

C. The client identified the "Angry Tower" technique as being an effective way to discharge angry feelings.

D. After playing the "Angry Tower" game, the client was assisted in processing whether they were willing to express feelings of anger toward the parent(s).

E. The client was encouraged to express feelings of anger in a direct and controlled manner toward their parents or significant others.

30. Utilize Feeling Angry Play-Doh Pounding Activity (30)

A. The client was provided with the opportunity to utilize the "Feeling Angry Play-Doh Pounding" activity (Lowenstein).

B. The client was assisted in creating with Play-Doh, then pounding it to express angry emotions while completing appropriate sentence starters.

C. The client was reinforced for expressing their angry emotions in useful ways during the "Feeling Angry Play-Doh Pounding" activity.

D. The client reported feeling heard regarding their angry emotions while utilizing the "Feeling Angry Play-Doh Pounding" activity.

31. Reinforce Parents Setting Consistent Limits (31)

A. The parents were strongly encouraged to set firm, consistent limits with the client's acting-out, oppositional, or aggressive behavior and not allow guilt feelings about the divorce to interfere with the need to impose consequences for such behaviors.

B. The parents acknowledged the failure to follow through with firm, consistent limits with the client's acting-out, oppositional, or aggressive behavior because of guilt feelings about the divorce; brainstorming techniques were used to implement consistent limits.

C. The parents reported that they have begun to set firm, consistent limits and were encouraged for not allowing their guilt feelings to interfere with the need to impose consequences.

D. The parents reported that the client has demonstrated improvements in behavior since they began to set firm, consistent limits with acting out, oppositional, or aggressive behavior, and the benefits of these limits were reviewed.

32. Encourage Parents to Establish Clear Rules (32)

A. The parents were helped to establish clearly defined rules and boundaries for the client.

B. The parents were assigned "Being a Consistent Parent" from the *Child Psychotherapy Homework Planner* (Jongsma, Peterson, McInnis, & Bruce).

C. The client and parents were helped to identify natural, logical consequences for the client's acting-out, oppositional, or aggressive behavior.

D. The client was asked to repeat the rules to demonstrate an understanding of the expectations of them.

E. The client verbally disagreed with the rules and expectations identified by the parents, but the right of the parents to set these rules was affirmed.

33. Use "Finding Ways to Get Positive Attention" Exercise (33)

A. The client was assigned the "Finding Ways to Get Positive Attention" exercise from the *Child Psychotherapy Homework Planner* (Jongsma, Peterson, McInnis, & Bruce) to help them recognize how acting-out behaviors are connected to the emotional pain surrounding the parents' divorce.

B. The client reported that the "Finding Ways to Get Positive Attention" exercise helped them realize how their acting-out behaviors are related to the emotional pain surrounding their parents' divorce.

C. The client failed to complete the "Finding Ways to Get Positive Attention" exercise and was asked to do it again.

34. Assign Readings on Disciplinary Techniques (34)

A. The parents were instructed to read *1-2-3 Magic: Effective Discipline for Children 2–12* (Phelan) to increase their knowledge of effective disciplinary techniques used to manage the client's acting-out, oppositional, and aggressive behaviors.

B. The parents were assigned *Bloom: 50 Things to Say, Think, and Do with Anxious, Angry, and Over-the-Top Kids* (Kenney & Young) to increase their knowledge of effective disciplinary techniques used to manage the client's acting-out, oppositional, and aggressive behaviors.

C. The assigned readings on effective disciplinary techniques were processed in today's therapy session.

D. The parent(s) reported that the assigned reading was helpful in learning about effective disciplinary techniques.

E. The parents reported improvements in the client's behavior after they began implementing the disciplinary techniques they learned from reading the assigned book; the benefits of these techniques were reviewed.

35. Design Reward System for Anger Control (35)

A. The client and parents identified a list of rewards to reinforce the client for demonstrating good anger control.

B. A reward system was designed to reinforce the client for demonstrating good anger control.

C. The client, parents, and therapist signed a contingency contract specifying the consequences for the client's acting-out, oppositional, or aggressive behavior.

D. The client, parents, and therapist verbally agreed to the terms of the contingency contract.

36. Assist Parents in Developing Homework Routine (36)

A. The parents were assisted in establishing a new routine to help the client complete their school or homework assignments.

B. The client and parents were assisted in identifying a list of rewards to reinforce the client for completing school or homework assignments on a regular basis.

C. The client and parents have developed a homework routine and reward system and report positive progress.

D. The client and parents were directed to sign a contingency contract specifying the consequences for the client's failure to complete school or homework assignments.

E. The parents have not developed a routine to help the client complete their school assignments and were redirected to do so. The client and parents have not used the reward system to improve academic performance and were redirected to do so.

37. Explore Relationship of Physical Complaints to Emotional Conflicts (37)

A. Today's therapy session focused on the relationship between the client's somatic complaints and underlying emotional conflicts associated with the parents' divorce.

B. Today's therapy session attempted to refocus the discussion away from the client's physical complaints onto the underlying emotional conflicts and the expression of feelings associated with the parents' divorce.

C. Today's therapy session explored the secondary gain that is achieved by the client's somatic complaints.

D. Positive feedback was provided as the client verbally acknowledged that their somatic complaints are associated with the stress and conflict surrounding their parents' divorce.

E. The client verbalized an understanding of how their somatic complaints are related to unfulfilled dependency needs and was assisted in developing these concepts.

38. Encourage Limit Setting by Noncustodial Parent (38)

A. The noncustodial parent was strongly encouraged to set firm, consistent limits on the client's misbehavior and to refrain from overindulging the client's desires during visits.

B. The noncustodial parent was helped to identify logical, natural consequences for the client's misbehavior.

C. The noncustodial parent verbally acknowledged how their pattern of overindulgence contributes to the client's immaturity and resistance to take on responsibilities and was urged to develop alternative behaviors.

D. The noncustodial parent acknowledged reluctance to set limits for the client's misbehavior because of feelings of guilt and desire to avoid conflict during visits and was assisted in developing alternative behaviors.

E. The noncustodial parent reported that the frequency of the client's misbehavior has decreased since the parent began setting firm, consistent limits on the client's acting out, and the benefits of this pattern of interacting were emphasized.

39. Emphasize Assignment of Responsibilities by Noncustodial Parent (39)

A. The noncustodial parent was given the directive to assign chore(s) to the client and siblings during their visits.

B. The noncustodial parent was encouraged to schedule times for the client and siblings to complete their homework.

C. The noncustodial parent acknowledged being reluctant to assign chores or require the children to complete homework because of the desire to avoid upsetting the client or siblings or creating potential conflict, and feedback about the long-term negative consequences of this pattern was emphasized.

D. The noncustodial parent was helped to develop a reward system to reinforce the client and siblings for completing chores and homework during visits.

E. The noncustodial parent was helped to identify consequences for the failure of the children to complete chores or homework.

40. Teach Enmeshed Parent(s) to Set Limits (40)

A. The enmeshed or overly protective parent was helped to see how failure to set limits reinforces the client's immature or irresponsible behavior.

B. The enmeshed or overly protective parent was helped to identify natural, logical consequences for the client's immature or irresponsible behavior.

C. The parent(s) was (were) encouraged to offer frequent praise and positive reinforcement for the client's responsible behaviors.

D. A reward system was designed to reinforce the client for behaving in a responsible manner.

41. Identify Age-Appropriate Ways to Meet Needs (41)

A. The client and parent(s) were helped to identify age-appropriate ways for the client to meet needs for affiliation, acceptance, and approval.

B. The client was given the homework assignment to engage in a specific, age-appropriate behavior three to five times before the next therapy session.

C. Role-playing and modeling techniques were used to demonstrate age-appropriate ways to gain affiliation, acceptance, and approval from others.

D. The client was taught effective communication skills to help meet needs for affiliation, acceptance, and approval.

E. Although the client has been taught age-appropriate ways to meet needs, they often fail to use these techniques; the client was redirected to increase use of these healthy, helpful techniques.

42. Urge Parent(s) to Stop Criticizing Ex-Spouse (42)

A. In today's therapy session, the parent(s) was (were) challenged and confronted about making hostile or overly critical remarks about the other parent in the presence of the client and siblings.

B. The client's parent(s) verbally recognized how hostile or overly critical remarks about the other parent are upsetting to the client and siblings, and positive feedback was provided.

43. Teach Effective Communication (43)

A. The client was taught effective communication and assertiveness skills.

B. Role-playing was used to teach the client ways to cope with parents' hostile or overly critical remarks about the other parent.

C. The client reported using effective communication and assertiveness skills to reduce their parents' remarks in their presence.

D. The client was unable to use effective communication and assertiveness skills to cope with their parents' remarks in their presence.

44. Teach Parent(s) to Avoid Placing Client in Middle (44)

A. The parent(s) was (were) challenged to cease the pattern of placing the client in the middle role by soliciting information about the other parent or sending messages through the client to the other parent about adult matters.

B. The parent(s) verbalized an awareness of how placing the client in the middle role is upsetting, and assistance was provided in developing alternative roles.

45. Confront Playing One Parent Against the Other (45)

A. The client was challenged and confronted about playing one parent against the other to meet the client's needs, obtain material goods, or avoid responsibility.

B. Today's therapy session explored the reasons for the client's attempt to play one parent against the other.

C. The parent(s) was (were) encouraged to deal directly with the client and set limits on manipulative behaviors.

D. The client was helped to identify more constructive ways to meet needs or obtain material goods than through the manipulation of parent(s).

E. The client acknowledged how their pattern of playing one parent against the other is aimed at trying to bring the parents back together, and the client was disabused of this notion.

46. Provide Opportunity for Questions (46)

A. The client and siblings were provided with the opportunity to ask questions to the parents about reasons for divorce.

B. The parents were counseled to give honest answers that are not critical of each other.

C. The client and siblings reported having their questions answered satisfactorily by their parents.

47. Encourage Noncustodial Parent to Maintain Visitation (47)

A. The noncustodial parent was challenged and encouraged to maintain regular visitation and involvement in the client's life.

B. The client asserted their wish in today's family-therapy session for the noncustodial parent to maintain regular visitation and involvement in the client's life.

C. Today's therapy session explored the factors contributing to the noncustodial parent's failure to maintain regular visitation and involvement in the client's life.

D. The noncustodial parent was supported verbally as they recognized how the lack of regular visitation has exacerbated the client's adjustment problems to the divorce.

E. The family-therapy session focused on developing a regular visitation schedule between the noncustodial parent and the client.

48. Assign Disengaged Parent to Increase Time with Client (48)

A. The disengaged parent was given a directive to spend more quality time with the client and siblings.

B. The disengaged parent was given a homework assignment of performing a specific task with the client.

C. The client and disengaged parent were assisted in developing a list of tasks or activities that they would like to do together.

D. The client reported that the increased time spent with the previously disengaged parent has helped them to establish a closer relationship, and the benefits of this involvement were reviewed.

E. The client was supported as they reported that their relationship with the disengaged parent remains distant, as the two have spent little time together.

49. Hold Family Theraplay Session (49)

A. A family Theraplay session (i.e., parental involvement) was held to facilitate the development of a closer parent–child bond.

B. The parent was instructed to allow the child to take the lead in expressing their feelings in today's Theraplay session.

C. The parent was encouraged to respond empathetically to the client's feelings and needs.

D. The family Theraplay sessions have helped the parent(s) gain greater insight into the factors contributing to the client's adjustment problems.

E. The family Theraplay sessions have helped to develop a closer parent–child relationship.

50. Employ Mutual Storytelling Technique (50)

A. The mutual storytelling technique using puppets, dolls, and stuffed animals was employed to model appropriate ways to express emotions related to the separation or divorce.

B. The client created their own story using puppets, dolls, and stuffed animals that modeled effective ways to express emotions related to the parents' separation or divorce; feedback was provided.

C. After using the mutual storytelling technique, the client was able to successfully identify effective ways to express emotions related to the parents' separation or divorce.

D. The client identified the mutual storytelling technique as being a useful way to learn effective ways to express feelings related to the parents' separation or divorce.

51. **Encourage Participation in Positive Peer Group Activities (51)**

A. The client was strongly encouraged to participate in school, extracurricular, or positive peer group activities to offset the loss of time spent with parents.

B. The client developed a list of school, extracurricular, or positive peer group activities that will help cope with the parents' divorce and establish meaningful friendships, and these were reviewed.

C. The client reported that the participation in school, extracurricular, or positive peer group activities has helped cope with the parents' divorce and feel less depressed or lonely, and they were encouraged to continue.

D. The client has continued to struggle to cope with their parents' divorce but has not yet taken many steps to become involved in school, extracurricular, or positive peer group activities; the client was redirected to be more socially involved.

52. **Refer to Children of Divorce Group (52)**

A. The client was referred to a children of divorce group to assist in expressing feelings and to understand that they are not alone in going through the divorce process.

B. The client was given the directive to self-disclose at least once about their parents' divorce during each group-therapy session.

C. The client's involvement in the children of divorce group has helped the client realize that they are not alone in going through the divorce process; the client was encouraged to continue using this resource.

D. The client's active participation in the children of divorce group has helped share and work through many of their emotions pertaining to the parents' divorce; the client was encouraged to continue using this resource.

E. The client has not made productive use of the group-therapy sessions and has been reluctant to share feelings about the divorce; the client was urged to make greater use of this resource.

53. **Identify Supportive Adults (53)**

A. The client was assisted in developing a list of supportive adults outside of the family whom they can turn to for support and guidance in coping with the divorce.

B. The client was given the homework assignment to seek guidance and support from at least one adult outside of the family before the next therapy session.

C. The client reported having talked with other significant adults outside of the family who have been helpful in offering support and guidance; their experience was processed.

D. The client has taken active steps to develop a network of significant adults outside of the family system to whom they can turn for guidance and support when needed; the client was urged to use this resource as needed.

E. The client has failed to follow through with the recommendation to make contact with significant adults outside of the family because of their mistrust and expectation of experiencing further disappointment; the client was urged to seek out these supports on a limited basis.

ENURESIS/ENCOPRESIS

CLIENT PRESENTATION

1. **Nocturnal Enuresis/Bed-Wetting (1)***
   A. The parents reported that the client has consistently wet the bed and has never achieved bladder control at night.
   B. The parents reported the client has regularly wet the bed in the recent past, after having previously achieved bladder control at night.
   C. The client and parents reported that the client has continued to wet the bed at night on a regular basis.
   D. The client and parents reported a moderate reduction in the frequency of the client's bed-wetting incidents.
   E. The client has achieved bladder control at night and is no longer wetting the bed.

2. **Daytime/Diurnal Enuresis (1)**
   A. The parents reported that the client frequently wets their clothing during the day and has never achieved bladder control.
   B. The parents reported that the client has recently regressed and started to wet their clothing during the day.
   C. The client has continued to wet their clothing during the day.
   D. The client has not recently wet their clothing during the day.
   E. The client's diurnal enuresis has been eliminated.

3. **Physiologically Caused Enuresis (1)**
   A. The client's problems with enuresis are related to a known health problem.
   B. The client's problems with enuresis are not related to any known physical or organic causes.

4. **Encopresis (2)**
   A. The parents reported that the client has never achieved consistent bowel control.
   B. The parents reported that the client has recently regressed and has begun to experience problems with encopresis, after having previously achieved bowel control.
   C. The client has continued to have problems with encopresis in the recent past.
   D. The client denied having any recent encopretic incidents.
   E. The client's encopresis has been successfully eliminated.

5. **Physiologically Caused Encopresis (2)**
   A. The client's problems with encopresis are related to a known health problem.
   B. The client's problems with encopresis are not related to any known physical or organic causes.

---

*The numbers in parentheses correlate to the number of the Behavioral Definition statement in the companion chapter with the same title in the *Child Psychotherapy Treatment Planner*, Sixth Edition, by Jongsma, Peterson, McInnis, & Bruce (Wiley, 2023).

6. **Feelings of Shame/Embarrassment (3)**

   A. The client expressed feelings of shame and embarrassment about problems with enuresis and/or encopresis.

   B. The client's feelings of shame and embarrassment have contributed to the pattern of avoiding situations (e.g., overnight visits with friends) that might lead to further embarrassment.

   C. The client's realization that they are not alone in having problems with enuresis and/or encopresis has helped to reduce feelings of shame and embarrassment.

   D. In today's therapy session, the client was able to talk about their problems with enuresis and/or encopresis without experiencing any feelings of shame or embarrassment.

   E. The client reported no longer being troubled by feelings of shame and embarrassment about enuresis and/or encopresis.

7. **Social Ridicule, Isolation, or Ostracism (4)**

   A. The client reported having been teased or ridiculed by peers at school or in the neighborhood because of their problem with enuresis.

   B. The client reported having been teased or ridiculed at school and in the neighborhood because of their problem with encopresis.

   C. The client reported that they have often responded to teasing or ridicule from peers by withdrawing and self-isolating.

   D. The parents and teachers reported that the client's problems with enuresis and/or encopresis have contributed to being ostracized.

   E. The client has increased social contacts and become more outgoing since overcoming the problem with enuresis and/or encopresis.

8. **Attempts to Hide Feces/Soiled Clothing (5)**

   A. The parents reported that the client has a persistent pattern of hiding soiled clothing and/or feces.

   B. The client acknowledged that they have often attempted to hide soiled clothing because of feelings of shame and fear of experiencing further teasing or ridicule.

   C. The client reported that they have often attempted to hide soiled clothing or feces because of fear of being punished harshly by parents.

   D. The client acknowledged that the pattern of hiding feces and/or soiled clothing is self-defeating because it only causes them to get into more trouble with parents.

   E. The client reported having stopped the pattern of hiding feces and/or soiled clothing.

9. **Excessive or Harsh Criticism by Parents (6)**

   A. The client described their parents as being very critical and harsh in their approach to their problems with enuresis and/or encopresis.

   B. In today's therapy session, the parents expressed strong feelings of anger about the client's problems with enuresis and/or encopresis.

   C. The parents have continued to be critical of the client because of their problem with enuresis and/or encopresis.

D. The parents acknowledged the need to cease making critical or hostile remarks about the client's bladder/bowel control problems.

E. The parents have stopped making hostile, critical remarks about the client's bladder/bowel control problems.

10. Rigid Toilet-Training Practices (6)

A. Today's therapy session revealed that the parents have established rigid toilet-training practices.

B. The client expressed feelings of anger and frustration about their parent's rigid toilet-training practices.

C. The parents' rigid toilet-training practices have contributed to the client's anxiety and fearfulness about not gaining bladder/bowel control.

D. The client reported experiencing less anxiety because their parents have become more relaxed and flexible in their toilet-training practices.

E. The client has assumed responsibility for toilet-training practices, and the parents have stopped imposing their rigid toilet-training practices.

11. Hostile-Dependent Cycle (6)

A. The client has established a hostile-dependent cycle with the parents whereby their wetting or soiling angers the parents; the parents respond in a critical or hostile manner; the client subsequently seeks to punish the parents for their strong displays of anger; and the cycle repeats.

B. The client and parents acknowledged the presence of a hostile-dependent cycle and agreed to take steps to reduce the anger between one another.

C. The client and parents continue to be locked in a hostile-dependent cycle.

D. The client and parents' hostile-dependent cycle has been terminated, and the client has started to assume responsibility for toilet-training practices.

12. Low Self-Esteem (6)

A. In today's therapy session, the client expressed feelings of low self-esteem and inadequacy about problems with enuresis.

B. In today's therapy session, the client expressed feelings of low self-esteem and inadequacy about problems with encopresis.

C. The parents' hostile or overly critical remarks about the client's problems with bladder/bowel control have contributed to feelings of low self-esteem.

D. The parents' overly punitive methods of discipline for the client's problems with enuresis and/or encopresis have caused the client to experience feelings of low self-esteem, inadequacy, and inferiority.

E. The client reported that self-esteem has increased significantly since gaining bladder/bowel control.

13. Fearfulness (7)

A. The client's anxiety and fears about toilet training have contributed to problems with enuresis.

B. The client's anxiety and fears about toilet training have contributed to problems with encopresis.

C. The client recognized that fears about toilet training are irrational or unrealistic.

D. The client's anxiety and fears about toilet training have started to decrease.

E. The client has successfully worked through the core conflicts contributing to anxiety and fearfulness and has recently demonstrated good bladder/bowel control.

14. **Anger/Hostility (7)**

A. The client's strong feelings of anger have been channeled into their problem with enuresis.

B. The client's strong feelings of anger have been channeled into their problem with encopresis.

C. The client has had much difficulty expressing their anger directly toward others.

D. The client has started to express their feelings of anger more openly and directly and, at the same time, has begun to assume greater responsibility for their toilet-training practices.

E. The client has achieved good bladder/bowel control since resolving the core conflicts that contributed to strong feelings of anger and resentment.

15. **Poor Impulse Control/Lack of Responsibility (8)**

A. The client's impulsivity and irresponsibility with toilet training has been a significant contributing factor to their problem with diurnal enuresis.

B. The client's impulsivity and irresponsibility with toilet training has been a significant contributing factor to their problem with encopresis.

C. The client has started to assume greater responsibility for toilet-training practices.

D. The client has developed good bladder/bowel control since improving impulse control and assuming greater responsibility.

16. **Smearing of Feces (9)**

A. The parents reported that the client has a history of smearing feces when angry or emotionally upset.

B. The client's pattern of smearing feces reflects the presence of a serious psychiatric disorder.

C. The client has smeared feces on the walls or their surroundings when in the midst of a psychotic break.

D. The client has recently not engaged in any smearing of feces.

E. The client has eliminated all incidents of smearing feces.

INTERVENTIONS IMPLEMENTED

1. **Establish Rapport (1)***

A. Caring was conveyed to the client through support, warmth, and empathy.

B. The client was provided with nonjudgmental support, and a level of trust was developed.

---

*The numbers in parentheses correlate to the number of the Therapeutic Intervention statement in the companion chapter with the same title in the *Child Psychotherapy Treatment Planner*, Sixth Edition, by Jongsma, Peterson, McInnis, & Bruce (Wiley, 2023).

C. The client was urged to feel safe in disclosing their elimination problem.

D. The client began to express feelings more freely as rapport and trust level have increased.

E. The client has continued to experience difficulty being open and direct about their expression of painful feelings; the client was encouraged to use the safe haven of therapy to express these difficult issues.

2. **Focus on Strengthening Therapeutic Relationship (2)**

   A. The relationship with the client was strengthened using empirically supported factors.

   B. The relationship with the client was strengthened through the implementation of collaborative approach, agreement on goals, demonstration of empathy, verbalization of positive regard, and collection of client feedback.

   C. The client reacted positively to the relationship-strengthening measures taken.

   D. The client verbalized feeling supported and understood during therapy sessions.

   E. Despite attempts to strengthen the therapeutic relationship, the client reports feeling distant and misunderstood.

   F. The client has indicated that sessions are not helpful and will be terminating therapy.

3. **Conduct Assessment (3)**

   A. A thorough assessment was conducted of the elimination problem, including its nature, frequency, environmental stimuli, responses, and management efforts.

   B. Other psychological or psychiatric conditions were assessed, which may account for the problems or warrant additional treatment attention.

   C. The results of the assessment were shared with the client and parents.

4. **Rule Out Medical Conditions (4)**

   A. The client was referred for a medical evaluation to rule out organic or physical causes that may be contributing to the client's enuresis.

   B. The client was referred for a medication evaluation to rule out organic or physical causes that may be contributing to the client's encopresis.

   C. The findings from the medical evaluation did not reveal the presence of any organic or physical causes for the client's problem with enuresis or encopresis, and this was reflected to the client and parents.

   D. The findings from the medical evaluation revealed that the client's problems with enuresis and/or encopresis are due to organic or physical causes, and this was reflected to the client and parents.

   E. The client was encouraged to comply with all the recommendations regarding medical interventions.

   F. The client has not been medically examined, and the parents were redirected to do so.

5. **Refer for Medication Evaluation (5)**

   A. The client was referred for a medication evaluation to help improve bladder control at night.

   B. The client and parents agreed to follow through with a medication evaluation.

   C. The parents objected to their child being placed on medication to help improve bladder control at night and were encouraged to discuss their concerns with the physician.

   D. The client was placed on medication to help improve bladder control at night.

6. **Refer/Conduct Psychological Testing (6)**

   A. The client received a psychological evaluation to help determine whether they have attention-deficit/hyperactivity disorder (ADHD) or an impulse-control disorder that may be contributing to the bladder/bowel control problems.

   B. The client received a psychological evaluation to help determine whether they have a serious underlying emotional problem that may be contributing to their problems with bladder/bowel control.

   C. The client and parents were provided feedback from the psychological testing, which revealed no serious emotional disorders.

   D. The findings from the psychological testing revealed the presence of ADHD and/or an impulse-control disorder that contributes to the client's problems with bladder/bowel control.

   E. The findings from the psychological testing revealed the presence of serious underlying emotional problems that contribute to the emergence of the client's problems with enuresis and/or encopresis.

7. **Assess Level of Insight (7)**

   A. The client's level of insight toward the presenting problems was assessed.

   B. The client was assessed in regard to the syntonic versus dystonic nature of their insight about the presenting problems.

   C. The client was noted to demonstrate good insight into the problematic nature of the behavior and symptoms.

   D. The client was noted to be in agreement with others' concerns and is motivated to work on change.

   E. The client was noted to be ambivalent regarding the problems described and is reluctant to address the issues as a concern.

   F. The client was noted to be resistant regarding acknowledgment of the problem areas, is not concerned about them, and has no motivation to make changes.

8. **Assess for Correlated Disorders (8)**

   A. The client was assessed for evidence of research-based correlated disorders.

   B. The client was assessed in regard to the level of vulnerability to suicide.

   C. The client was identified as having a comorbid disorder, and treatment was adjusted to account for these concerns.

   D. The client has been assessed for any correlated disorders, but none were found.

9. **Assess for Culturally Based Confounding Issues (9)**

   A. The client was assessed for age-related issues that could help to better understand their clinical presentation.

   B. The client was assessed for gender-related issues that could help to better understand their clinical presentation.

   C. The client was assessed for cultural syndromes, cultural idioms of distress, or culturally based perceived causes that could help to better understand their clinical presentation.

D. Alternative factors have been identified as contributing to the client's currently defined "problem behavior," and these were taken into account in regard to treatment.

E. Culturally based factors that could help to account for the client's currently defined "problem behavior" were investigated, but no significant factors were identified.

10. Assess Severity of Impairment (10)

A. The severity of the client's impairment was assessed to determine the appropriate level of care.

B. The client was assessed in regard to impairment in social, relational, and educational endeavors.

C. It was reflected to the client that the impairment appears to create mild to moderate effects on the client's functioning.

D. It was reflected to the client that the impairment appears to create severe to very severe effects on the client's functioning.

E. The client was continuously assessed for the severity of impairment, as well as the efficacy and appropriateness of treatment.

11. Assess for Pathogenic Care (11)

A. The home, school, and community of the client were assessed for pathogenic care and concerns.

B. The client's various environments were assessed for the persistent disregard of the child's needs, repeated changes in caregivers, limited opportunities for stable attachment, harsh discipline, or other grossly inept care.

C. Pathogenic care was identified, and the treatment plan included strategies for managing or correcting these concerns and protecting the child.

D. No pathogenic care was identified, and this was reflected to the client and caregivers.

12. Monitor Medication Adherence/Effectiveness (12)

A. The client and parents reported that the medication has helped the client gain effective bladder control at night, and they were encouraged to continue the medication as prescribed.

B. The client and parents reported little to no improvement while using the prescribed bladder control medication and were urged to report this to the physician.

C. Positive feedback was provided as the client has adhered with taking the medication prescribed.

D. The client has not adhered with taking the medication on a regular basis and was redirected to do so.

E. The client and parents were encouraged to report any side effects of the medication to the prescribing physician.

13. Explore Parent–Child Interactions (13)

A. Today's therapy session explored the parent–child interactions to assess whether the parents' toilet-training practices are excessively rigid.

B. Today's therapy session explored the parent–child interactions to assess whether the parents are making hostile, critical remarks about the client's bladder/bowel control.

14. **Teach Effective, Nonabusive Toilet-Training Practices (14)**

   A. The parents were taught effective, nonabusive toilet-training practices.

   B. The parents were supported as they verbalized their commitment to use nonabusive toilet-training practices.

   C. The parents were provided with positive feedback for their use of effective nonabusive toilet-training practices.

15. **Assess Family Dynamics (15)**

   A. Today's family therapy session explored the dynamics that contributed to the emergence or reinforcement of the client's enuresis, encopresis, or smearing of feces.

   B. The therapy session revealed how the parents' lack of consistency with toilet-training practices has contributed to the client's problems with enuresis or encopresis.

   C. We explored the reasons for the parents' lack of consistency with toilet-training practices.

   D. The family members were asked to identify the stressors that have negatively affected the family.

   E. The family members were asked to identify the positive changes they would like to see take place within the family.

16. **Use Alarm-Based Treatment (16)**

   A. The parents and child were educated about the trial use of an alarm-based biobehavioral treatment, with discussion about its features and rationale.

   B. The parents were requested to utilize an alarm-based biobehavioral treatment.

   C. An agreement was secured to have the parents and child use an alarm-based biobehavioral treatment.

17. **Teach Bell-and-Pad Conditioning Procedures (17)**

   A. The client and parents were trained on how to use bell-and-pad conditioning procedures to treat the client's nocturnal enuresis.

   B. The parents were assigned the "Dry Bed Training Program" from the *Child Psychotherapy Homework Planner* (Jongsma, Peterson, McInnis, & Bruce).

   C. The parents were taught to follow an alarm with a procedure of fully awakening the child, instructing the child to go to the bathroom, and show responsibility by changing bedding and pajamas.

   D. The parents were reminded to make certain that the alarm is able to be heard by both the child and parents.

   E. The use of the bell-and-pad conditioning procedure was reviewed.

18. **Use Measurement System (18)**

   A. The parents were taught to use a measurement system that measures the frequency of wetting and the size of the urine stain.

   B. The parents were taught about the rationale for measuring the frequency and severity of bedwetting.

   C. The results of the consistent measurement were reviewed with the parents.

19. **Continue Alarm-Based Treatment (19)**

    A. A criterion for improvement was identified (e.g., 14 consecutive "dry days").

    B. The alarm-based treatment is continued until the criteria for improvement has been met.

20. **Teach Overlearning Method (20)**

    A. The parents were encouraged to use the overlearning method (e.g., require client to drink a specific amount of fluid shortly before bedtime) during the latter stages of treatment to help prevent a relapse of nocturnal enuresis.

    B. The client and parents were encouraged to utilize the overlearning method, along with the bell-and-pad conditioning procedures.

    C. The parents reported that combining the bell-and-pad conditioning procedures with the overlearning method proved to be successful in eliminating the client's nocturnal enuresis.

    D. The overlearning method was not successful in preventing a relapse of the client's nocturnal enuresis.

    E. The parents have not used the overlearning method and were redirected to do so.

21. **Utilize Positive Reinforcement Procedures (21)**

    A. The parents were educated about the use of positive reinforcement procedures to increase the client's bladder or bowel control.

    B. A reward system was designed to reinforce the client for effective bladder control during the day.

    C. A reward system was designed to address the client's nocturnal enuresis.

    D. A reward system was designed to reward the client for demonstrating good bowel control.

    E. The reward system has helped the client to achieve good bladder/bowel control.

    F. The parents have not instituted a positive reinforcement procedure and were redirected to do so.

22. **Implement Medical Management (22)**

    A. The parents and client were taught to implement medical treatment, including initial bowel clean out, dietary changes, and medication use.

    B. The parents and client used medical treatment with success toward reducing retentive encopresis.

    C. The parents and client have attempted to use medical treatment but have not been successful, and challenges were addressed.

23. **Implement Behavioral Interventions (23)**

    A. The parents and client were taught to implement behavioral interventions, including physiological education, operant reinforcement techniques, consistent monitoring, toilet sitting schedules, cleanliness training, and positive feedback.

    B. The parents and client used behavioral treatment with success toward reducing retentive encopresis.

    C. The parents and client have attempted to use behavioral treatment but have not been successful, and challenges were addressed.

24. Teach Nonretentive Encopresis Techniques (24)

A. For nonretentive encopresis, the parent and clients were taught to implement treatment consisting of scheduled toilet sits, reinforcement for sitting and/or eliminating in the toilet, daily fiber supplements or laxatives to ensure frequent bowel movements, and prompts to clean up contingent on inappropriate soiling.

B. The parent and client used treatment techniques for nonretentive encopresis and were reinforced for their success.

C. The parents and client attempted to use treatment techniques for nonretentive encopresis but have not been successful, and challenges were addressed.

25. Teach Lifting Technique (25)

A. The lifting technique was taught to motivated parents.

B. The parents were taught to literally lift or walk the child to the bathroom to toilet during the night, then return the child to bed.

C. The parents were provided with support in weaning the child off the assistance.

D. The parents have reported that the child is self-sufficient in knowing and going to the bathroom at night as needed.

E. Despite using the lifting technique, the parents reported that the child is not yet self-sufficient in knowing and going to the bathroom at night as needed and were encouraged to continue this technique.

26. Conduct Biobehavioral Approach to Encopresis (26)

A. The biobehavioral approach was used in regard to the client's encopresis.

B. The client and parents were educated about the elimination process and the difficulties that can occur.

C. The components and rationale for treatment were explained to the parents.

D. Information consistent with principles from *Elimination Disorders in Children and Adolescents* (Christopherson & Friman) was provided to the parents.

27. Debunk Personality Myths (27)

A. The myth that personality characteristics such as stubbornness, immaturity, or laziness are the cause of encopresis was debunked.

B. Parents were discouraged from shaming or blaming the child for the encopresis.

C. A discussion was held about the typical reasons for encopresis.

28. Recommend Reading Materials (28)

A. Reading materials consistent with the therapeutic approach were recommended.

B. The client and parents were assigned to read portions of *It's No Accident* (Hodges & Schlosberg).

C. The client and parents were assigned to read portions of *Waking Up Dry* (Bennett).

D. The client and parents were assigned to read portions of *Toilet Training in Less Than a Day* (Azrin).

E. The client and parents were assigned to read portions of *Once Upon a Potty–Girl* or *Once Upon a Potty–Boy* (Frankel).

F. Internet-based resources, such as pottymd.com and encopresis.com, were recommended to the client and family.

G. Key concepts from the recommended resources were reviewed with the client and family.

29. Facilitate Bowel Cleansing (29)

A. The process of regular bowel movements was facilitated by first cleansing the bowel completely of fecal matter.

B. The client and parents were recommended to use supervised enemas.

C. The client and parents were recommended to use supervised laxative use.

D. The parents have assisted the client in fully cleansing the bowel of fecal matter.

30. Implement High Dietary Fiber (30)

A. With physician assistance, the client was assisted in implementing a diet with a high level of dietary fiber.

B. The client's diet was adjusted to increase colonic motility and moisture, thus facilitating easier and more regular bowel movements.

C. The parents' implementation of the dietary fiber changes was reviewed.

31. Develop Regular Bowel Movement Times (31)

A. The parents were assisted in choosing one or two regular times for the child to attempt bowel movements.

B. Timing of the child's attempted bowel movements was adjusted based on when they may be away at school and child and parent time constraints.

C. The parents were directed to have the child sit no longer than 10 minutes to avoid increasingly aversive properties of the toileting experience.

D. The use of the regular times for attempted bowel movements was reviewed and processed.

32. Transform Toileting to a Positive Experience (32)

A. The parents were assisted in making toileting a relaxed, pleasant experience by allowing the child to do pleasant activities.

B. The parents were encouraged to try options such as having the child listen to music, read, or talk with a parent while attempting to have a bowel movement.

C. The client and parents were assisted in troubleshooting ways to make toileting a relaxed, pleasant experience.

33. Utilize Praise and Rewards (33)

A. In the case of successful bowel movement, the parents were encouraged to praise the child or use other reward systems.

B. In the case of the child being unable to produce a bowel movement, the effort should be praised and another session rescheduled for later in the day.

C. The use of praise and rewards for the child's bowel movements was reviewed and processed.

34. Review Response to Accidents (34)

A. The parents were assisted in reviewing their typical response to accidents.

B. Parents were encouraged to respond to accidents without punishment or criticism, but to involve the child in age-appropriate clean-up.

    C. Because the child is older, they were expected to clean up the mess.

    D. Because the child is younger, they were directed to assist by bringing soiled clothing to the laundry.

35. Teach Parents Monitoring Techniques (35)

    A. The parents were encouraged to monitor progress using pants-check techniques.

    B. The parents were encouraged to provide praise for accident-free checks.

    C. The parents were encouraged to maintain ongoing recording of toileting successes, accidents, and size and consistency of both.

    D. The information recorded about the client's bowel movements was routinely reviewed, with reinforcement for successes and problem-solving for obstacles.

36. Encourage Client Responsibility (36)

    A. The client was encouraged and challenged to assume active responsibility for achieving bladder control.

    B. The client was encouraged and challenged to assume active responsibility for achieving bowel control.

    C. The client was assigned the "Bowel Control Training Program" from the *Child Psychotherapy Homework Planner* (Jongsma, Peterson, McInnis, & Bruce).

    D. The client was given the responsibility for cleaning soiled underwear or linens.

    E. The client was instructed to keep a record of wet and dry days or nights.

    F. The client was placed in charge of setting the alarm at night for voiding times.

37. Identify Periods of Good Bladder/Bowel Control (37)

    A. The client was assisted in identifying periods when they demonstrated good bladder control and did not experience any enuretic incidents.

    B. The client was assisted in identifying periods of time when they demonstrated good bowel control and did not experience any encopretic incidents.

    C. The client was encouraged to take the same positive steps taken in the past to achieve bladder control.

    D. The client was encouraged to take the same positive steps taken in the past to achieve bowel control.

    E. Today's therapy session revealed that the client demonstrated good bladder/bowel control during periods of time when they received strong family support and felt more self-confident.

38. Explore Irrational Cognitive Messages (38)

    A. Today's therapy session explored the client's irrational cognitive messages that produce fear or anxiety associated with toilet training.

    B. Today's therapy session helped identify the client's irrational cognitive messages that contribute to fear or anxiety about toilet training.

    C. The client was assisted in replacing unrealistic or irrational thoughts with positive, reality-based self-talk.

    D. The client was provided with positive feedback as they have been able to erase irrational cognitive messages and develop more positive, reality-based self-talk.

39. Help Client Realize Irrational Fears (39)

A. The client was helped to realize how their anxiety or fear surrounding toilet training is irrational or unrealistic.

B. The client was encouraged to replace irrational or unrealistic thoughts with positive, reality-based self-talk to help eliminate fears about toilet training.

C. Positive feedback was provided as the client has decreased anxiety and eliminated fears about toilet training.

40. Explore Secondary Gain (40)

A. A family therapy session was held to explore whether the client achieves any secondary gain from their problems with enuresis or encopresis.

B. The client and parents were assisted in identifying the secondary gain(s) that is (are) achieved from the client's enuresis or encopresis.

C. The therapy session showed how the client receives increased parental attention for their problems with enuresis or encopresis.

D. The client and parents were helped to realize how the client's enuresis or encopresis maintains or reinforces dependency on the parents.

E. The family therapy session failed to identify any secondary gain that is achieved from the client's enuresis or encopresis.

41. Utilize Strategic Family Therapy Intervention (41)

A. A strategic family therapy intervention was utilized where the therapist did not talk about the enuresis or encopresis, but, rather, discussed what might surface if the problem were resolved.

B. The strategic family therapy intervention helped bring to light underlying issues that contribute to the client's bladder or bowel control problem.

C. The client and family members were helped to identify more effective ways to resolve the core conflicts or problems that contribute to the client's problem with enuresis or encopresis.

42. Employ Paradoxical Intervention (42)

A. A paradoxical intervention was employed, whereby the client was instructed to pick out a specific night of the week when they were instructed to deliberately wet the bed.

B. The paradoxical intervention was successful as it allowed the client to control the enuresis by making the unconscious behavior a conscious maneuver.

C. The client and parents failed to follow through with implementation of the paradoxical intervention and were instructed to do so before the next therapy session.

43. Explore History of Separation, Loss, Trauma, or Rejection (43)

A. Today's therapy session explored whether the client's enuresis is associated with past separation, loss, traumatization, or rejection experiences.

B. Today's therapy session explored whether the client's encopresis or smearing of feces is associated with past separation, loss, traumatization, or rejection experiences.

C. It was noted that the client experienced a regression in bladder or bowel control after experiencing a major separation, loss, or rejection experience.

D. It was noted that the client experienced a regression with bladder or bowel control after experiencing a traumatic event.

E. It was noted that the client's problem with smearing feces began after they experienced a traumatic event.

44. **Encourage Expression of Feelings Related to Painful Event(s) (44)**

A. The client was given encouragement and support in expressing feelings associated with the past separation, loss, trauma, or rejection experience.

B. The client was instructed to draw pictures reflecting feelings about the past separation, loss, trauma, or rejection experience.

C. The empty-chair technique was employed to facilitate the expression of feelings surrounding the past separation, loss, trauma, or rejection experience.

D. The client was instructed to use a journal to record thoughts and feelings about the past separation, loss, trauma, or rejection experience.

E. A family therapy session was conducted to allow the client to express feelings about the past separation, loss, trauma, or rejection experience in the presence of the family.

45. **Employ Psychoanalytic Play Therapy (45)**

A. Using a psychoanalytic play therapy approach, the client was allowed to take the lead in exploring the issues that contribute to bladder or bowel control problem.

B. Today's session focused on interpreting the client's feelings that were expressed in play and related them to the client's feelings about the bladder or bowel control problem.

C. This session was focused on processing and working through the transference issues that emerged in today's psychoanalytic play therapy session.

D. The psychoanalytic play therapy sessions have helped identify the core issues or anxieties that contribute to the client's bladder or bowel control problem.

E. The psychoanalytic play therapy sessions have helped the client work through and resolve the issues contributing to the emergence of bladder or bowel control problem.

46. **Assign Drawings That Reflect Self-Esteem (46)**

A. The client was instructed to draw pictures reflecting how the enuretic or encopretic incidents affect self-esteem.

B. The client's drawings were noted to reflect feelings of low self-esteem, inadequacy, and shame.

C. The client's drawings were interpreted as reflecting how they feel ostracized from peers because of their bladder or bowel control problem.

D. Today's session processed the content of the client's drawings and related them to how the client feels in everyday life.

E. After completing the drawings, the client was helped to identify constructive ways to build self-esteem.

F. The client has not done the drawings on self-esteem and was reminded to do this homework.

47. Identify Positive Characteristics (47)

A. To help decrease feelings of shame or embarrassment, the client was asked to identify and list their positive characteristics.

B. The parents were strongly encouraged to provide frequent praise and positive reinforcement to help decrease the client's feelings of shame and embarrassment.

C. The client was encouraged to verbalize positive self-statements to offset feelings of shame and embarrassment.

D. To help improve self-esteem and decrease feelings of shame, the client was given the homework assignment of verbalizing three positive self-statements each night with their parents.

48. Assign Recording of Positive Self-Statements (48)

A. The client was directed to record one positive self-statement each day in a journal.

B. The client was instructed to verbalize at least one positive self-statement around peers each day.

C. The client reported that the assigned recording of positive self-statements helped to increase self-esteem and decrease feelings of shame.

D. The client failed to follow through with the homework assignment of recording the positive self-statements and was instructed to begin doing so.

49. Teach Communication/Assertiveness Skills (49)

A. The client was taught effective communication and assertiveness skills to learn how to express feelings through more appropriate verbalizations.

B. Role-playing techniques were used to model effective ways for the client to express feelings and meet needs.

C. The client and parents reported that the newly taught assertiveness and communication skills have helped the client to express feelings more directly and to begin to take greater responsibility for toilet-training practices.

D. The client was given the homework assignment to practice newly learned communication or assertiveness skills at home or school.

E. The client has not used the communication and assertiveness skills and was redirected to do so.

50. Teach Physical Outlets for Anger (50)

A. The client was encouraged to channel feelings of anger through appropriate physical outlets instead of through inappropriate wetting or soiling.

B. The client was helped to identify appropriate physical outlets for feelings of anger.

C. The client and parents reported that the client has been channeling anger effectively through appropriate physical outlets; positive feedback was provided.

D. The client recognized that they have channeled anger through inappropriate wetting or soiling and verbalized a commitment to cease this behavior.

E. The client has not channeled anger through appropriate means and was redirected to do so.

FIRE SETTING

CLIENT PRESENTATION

1. **Set One or More Fires in 6 Months (1)***
   A. It has been reported by others that the client has set several fires in the past several months.
   B. The client self-reported that they remember setting one or more fires in the past 6 months.
   C. The parents indicated that the client is suspected by them and other authorities of setting several recent fires in the community.
   D. There have been no reported incidents of fire setting by the client since they started treatment.

2. **Observed Play with Fire (2)**
   A. The client has consistently been observed playing with fire, fireworks, or other flammable substances.
   B. The parents indicated they are tired of and frustrated by the client's constant and continual requests to buy fireworks.
   C. Several neighbors have reported to parents and authorities that they have seen the client playing with fire and combustible substances.
   D. The client has honored the contract they signed not to play with fire or other combustible substances.

3. **Enjoys Being Around Fire (3)**
   A. The client indicated that they like to be around fire.
   B. The parents reported that the client seeks out any situation where fire is involved.
   C. The client talked excitedly about certain fires they have recently seen.
   D. The parents have seen a noticeable decrease in client interest in being wherever fire is present.

4. **Consistently Possesses Fire Articles (4)**
   A. The client has consistently been found with lighters, matches, and candles in their possession.
   B. The parents reported consistently finding matches, lighters, and so forth in the client's pockets or hidden in their room.
   C. The client has been caught stealing lighters from stores.
   D. The client has kept their agreement not to have any matches, lighters, or candles in their possession.

---

*The numbers in parentheses correlate to the number of the Behavioral Definition statement in the companion chapter with the same title in the *Child Psychotherapy Treatment Planner*, Sixth Edition, by Jongsma, Peterson, McInnis, & Bruce (Wiley, 2023).

5. Fascination/Preoccupation with Fire (5)

A. The client seemed to have a preoccupation with anything that has a connection to fire.

B. The client talked of being fascinated with fire and what it could do.

C. The parents indicated that the client has been very fascinated and preoccupied with anything that is related to fire for a long time.

D. The client's talk frequently referenced some aspect relating to fire.

E. It has been observed by the parents and others that the client's fascination and preoccupation with fire has diminished to the point that they hardly mention it.

F. The client showed a marked lack of interest now in talking about things related to fire.

6. History of Adverse Childhood Experiences (6)

A. The client has an identified history of multiple adverse childhood experiences.

B. The client has identified the symptoms they experience related to adverse childhood experiences.

C. The client has been involved in processing their history of adverse childhood experiences.

D. The client has experienced relief from symptoms related to adverse childhood experiences.

INTERVENTIONS IMPLEMENTED

1. Establish Rapport (1)*

A. Caring was conveyed to the client through support, warmth, and empathy.

B. The client was provided with nonjudgmental support, and a level of trust was developed.

C. The client was urged to feel safe in expressing fire setting issues.

D. The client began to express feelings more freely as rapport and trust level have increased.

E. The client has continued to experience difficulty being open and direct about the expression of painful feelings; the client was encouraged to use the safe haven of therapy to express these difficult issues.

2. Focus on Strengthening Therapeutic Relationship (2)

A. The relationship with the client was strengthened using empirically supported factors.

B. The relationship with the client was strengthened through the implementation of collaborative approach, agreement on goals, demonstration of empathy, verbalization of positive regard, and collection of client feedback.

C. The client reacted positively to the relationship-strengthening measures taken.

D. The client verbalized feeling supported and understood during therapy sessions.

---

*The numbers in parentheses correlate to the number of the Therapeutic Intervention statement in the companion chapter with the same title in the *Child Psychotherapy Treatment Planner*, Sixth Edition, by Jongsma, Peterson, McInnis, & Bruce (Wiley, 2023).

E. Despite attempts to strengthen the therapeutic relationship, the client reports feeling distant and misunderstood.

F. The client has indicated that sessions are not helpful and will be terminating therapy.

3. **Inquire About Fire Fascination (3)**

A. The client was asked to describe their history of fascination with fire.

B. The client was asked about how fire setting has been a part of their fascination with fire.

C. The client was provided with reflection and support as they processed their history of fascination with fire.

4. **Probe Thoughts and Feelings Regarding Fire (4)**

A. The client's thoughts and feelings that occur before, during, and after being close to a fire were probed.

B. The client was asked to identify thoughts and feelings that occur in association with setting a fire.

C. The role of anger in the client's fire-setting behavior was assessed.

5. **Assess Parents' Understanding of Fire Fascination and Behavior (5)**

A. The parents were interviewed as to their knowledge and understanding of the child's history of fire-setting behavior.

B. The parents were assessed in regard to their understanding of the child's history of fire fascination.

C. The parents' knowledge and understanding of the child's history was summarized and reflected.

6. **Assess Level of Insight (6)**

A. The client's level of insight toward the presenting problems was assessed.

B. The client was assessed in regard to the syntonic versus dystonic nature of their insight about the presenting problems.

C. The client was noted to demonstrate good insight into the problematic nature of the behavior and symptoms.

D. The client was noted to be in agreement with others' concerns and is motivated to work on change.

E. The client was noted to be ambivalent regarding the problems described and is reluctant to address the issues as a concern.

F. The client was noted to be resistant regarding acknowledgment of the problem areas, is not concerned about them, and has no motivation to make changes.

7. **Assess for Correlated Disorders (7)**

A. The client was assessed for evidence of research-based correlated disorders.

B. The client was assessed in regard to the level of vulnerability to suicide.

C. The client was identified as having a comorbid disorder, and treatment was adjusted to account for these concerns.

D. The client has been assessed for any correlated disorders, but none were found.

8. **Assess for Culturally Based Confounding Issues (8)**

   A. The client was assessed for age-related issues that could help to better understand their clinical presentation.

   B. The client was assessed for gender-related issues that could help to better understand their clinical presentation.

   C. The client was assessed for cultural syndromes, cultural idioms of distress, or culturally based perceived causes that could help to better understand their clinical presentation.

   D. Alternative factors have been identified as contributing to the client's currently defined "problem behavior," and these were taken into account in regard to treatment.

   E. Culturally based factors that could help to account for the client's currently defined "problem behavior" were investigated, but no significant factors were identified.

9. **Assess Severity of Impairment (9)**

   A. The severity of the client's impairment was assessed to determine the appropriate level of care.

   B. The client was assessed in regard to impairment in social, relational, and educational endeavors.

   C. It was reflected to the client that the impairment appears to create mild to moderate effects on the client's functioning.

   D. It was reflected to the client that the impairment appears to create severe to very severe effects on the client's functioning.

   E. The client was continuously assessed for the severity of impairment, as well as the efficacy and appropriateness of treatment.

10. **Assess for Pathogenic Care (10)**

   A. The home, school, and community of the client were assessed for pathogenic care and concerns.

   B. The client's various environments were assessed for the persistent disregard of the child's needs, repeated changes in caregivers, limited opportunities for stable attachment, harsh discipline, or other grossly inept care.

   C. Pathogenic care was identified, and the treatment plan included strategies for managing or correcting these concerns and protecting the child.

   D. No pathogenic care was identified, and this was reflected to the client and caregivers.

11. **Urge Structure and Supervision of Client (11)**

   A. Areas where structure and supervision were lacking with the client were explored and identified with the parents.

   B. The parents were assisted in developing specific ways to address the identified areas where the supervision and structure of the client's behavior were inadequate.

   C. The parents were taught the benefits of more effective structure and supervision for both them and the client.

   D. The parents have worked to develop more effective ways to supervise and structure the client's behavior and have verbally committed to implementing them; the parents were reinforced for this progress.

E. The parents were confronted regarding important issues of supervision where they were resistive to making vital changes.

12. **Monitor Parents' Efforts (12)**

   A. The parents' efforts to more effectively structure, set limits, and supervise the client were monitored for effectiveness, consistency, and follow-through.

   B. The parents were assigned "Being a Consistent Parent" from the *Child Psychotherapy Homework Planner* (Jongsma, Peterson, McInnis, & Bruce).

   C. Verbal encouragement and support were given to the parents' efforts to supervise and structure the client's behavior in new ways.

   D. The parents were given redirection when they were being lax or inconsistent in implementing and reinforcing new methods of supervision, limit setting, and structure.

   E. The parents have been very responsive to the encouragement, support, and redirection that were provided and have become effective in structuring, setting limits, and supervising the client's behavior.

13. **Develop Increased Impulse Control (13)**

   A. The parents were given several books, tapes, and other material on positive reinforcement to read/view to assist them in finding ways they could use behavior modification techniques to increase the client's impulse control.

   B. The parents were introduced to and educated in using positive reinforcement to increase the client's impulse control.

   C. The parents were trained to use positive reinforcement with the client at the times they demonstrate apparent impulse control.

   D. The parents verbally committed to implementing the positive reinforcement methods they had developed; they were provided with positive feedback.

   E. The parents have implemented positive reinforcement techniques with the client and report some initial increase in the client's impulse control; they were encouraged to continue the reinforcement.

14. **Assign Contrasting Fire Collages (14)**

   A. The parents and client were given the assignment and provided the materials to create two collages, one emphasizing the positive aspects of fire and the other the destructive aspects.

   B. The family process of creating the collages was observed and assessed to gain insight into key family dynamics and strengths.

   C. The completed collages were presented and discussed by the client and family; key destructive aspects of fire were identified and reinforced.

   D. The collages about fire were discussed; the client seemed to have gained an increased awareness of the destructive aspects of fire from this discussion.

15. **Assign Interview with Nurse/Firefighter (15)**

   A. The parents and client were asked to develop a list of questions to ask a nurse of a burn center or firefighter regarding the effects of fire that they have seen in their work.

   B. The parents were assisted in arranging an interview for themselves and the client with a firefighter/nurse.

C. The parents and client reported on their interview experience and processed the information they gathered about the effects of fire.

D. The client seemed to be affected by the information on the effects of fire on people that they obtained from the professional they interviewed; the client was assisted in processing this information.

E. The parents and client have not completed an interview with a professional about the effects of fire on people, and they were redirected to do so.

16. Provide Brain Development Psychoeducation (16)

A. The family was provided with psychoeducation on how the brain develops and works.

B. The family displayed an understanding of how the brain develops and works, and affect management skills were introduced.

C. The family struggled with understanding of how the brain develops and works and were provided with remedial feedback.

17. Provide Psychoeducation on Triggers (17)

A. The family was provided with psychoeducation on "triggers."

B. The family displayed an understanding of the concept of "triggers" and processed how these relate to impulsive actions.

C. The family struggled with understanding the concept of "triggers" and were provided with remedial feedback.

18. Complete *Whole Brain* Exercise (18)

A. The client was assisted in completing an exercise from the *Whole Brain Child Workbook* (Siegel & Bryson).

B. Ideas from the *Whole Brain Child Workbook* (Siegel & Bryson) exercise were processed and the client was able to identify one or two things learned.

C. The client was assisted in sharing new concepts learned with parents/caregivers.

D. The client struggled to understand new concepts and was provided with additional support.

19. Assign Operant-Based Intervention (19)

A. The concepts behind operant-based interventions were explained to the parents.

B. An operant-based intervention for fire setting was given to the parents and a commitment to implement it was elicited from them.

C. The client and parents were assigned "Fireproofing Your Home and Family" from the *Child Psychotherapy Homework Planner* (Jongsma, Peterson, McInnis, & Bruce).

D. The parents' implementation of the operant-based intervention was monitored with encouragement and redirection being given as needed.

E. The parents indicated they have done the operant-based intervention consistently for several weeks and are surprised by the decrease in the client's interest in playing with fire; the benefits of this progress were reviewed.

F. The parents indicated that they have done the operant-based intervention consistently for several weeks, but it has not been helpful in decreasing the client's interest in playing with fire; they were assisted in fine-tuning this intervention.

G. The parents have not used the operant-based intervention and were redirected to do so.

20. Assign Rewards for Turning in Fire-Setting Material (20)

A. The parent was assigned to give the child a monetary reward for turning in any fire-setting materials (e.g., lighters, matches, etc.).

B. The client was provided with rewards for not having fire-setting material in their room or in clothing.

C. The client was assigned the exercise "Fireproofing Your Home and Family" from the *Child Psychotherapy Homework Planner* (Jongsma, Peterson, McInnis, & Bruce).

D. The parent was directed to purposefully leave matches where they could be found by the child and keep a chart of how much money is earned.

21. Refer to Fire Prevention Program (21)

A. The client and parents were referred to a fire prevention program supported by a local fire department.

B. The client and parents attended a fire prevention program and new knowledge was processed.

C. The client and parents have not attended a fire prevention program and were redirected to do so.

22. Assign Parent to Teach Safely Building Fire (22)

A. The client's parent was asked to teach the client how to safely build a fire while emphasizing the need for strict control and respect for the power of fire.

B. The instruction session was monitored and afterward processed with the client and their parent.

C. The parent was asked to repeat the assignment at home with the client.

D. The parent reported that the client now seems to be quite responsible when the client is around or handles fire; the benefits of this progress were reviewed.

E. The client's parent has not repeated the assignment on safely building a fire and emphasizing the need for strict control and respect; he was redirected to do so.

23. Utilize Family Systems Approach (23)

A. The family was asked to agree on a number of sessions all members will attend and then make a verbal commitment to following through on that commitment.

B. Family roles, ways of communicating, and unresolved conflicts were explored and probed with the family.

C. Unresolved conflicts that were identified were processed and worked through to resolution.

D. Roles and communication patterns that were identified in the family as ineffective and destructive were confronted and restructured into new roles and patterns of communication that will increase the family's strength.

E. The family members were reinforced as they have kept their commitment to change destructive roles and patterns of communication within the family.

24. Assign Listing Negative and Positive Aspects of the Family (24)

A. Each family member was assigned to make a list of the positive or supportive and negative or conflicting aspects of the family.

B. The family was asked to complete and process the exercise "When a Fire Has No Fuel" from the *Child Psychotherapy Homework Planner* (Jongsma, Peterson, McInnis, & Bruce).

C. The family processed the no-fuel exercise and identified key unresolved issues within their nuclear family and families of origin.

D. Positive feedback was provided as the family worked to resolve the identified issue within the family and to start new, healthier patterns.

E. The family has struggled to reach some resolution of the unresolved conflicts that were identified by the exercise and were urged to resolve these issues.

25. Assist Family in Identifying Feelings (25)

A. The family members were provided with education on how to identify, express, and tolerate their feelings.

B. The family members were assisted in expanding their skills in identifying and expressing their feelings by taking part in feelings exercises in a family session.

C. Family members were affirmed and given positive verbal reinforcement when they identified and expressed their feelings.

D. It was reflected to the family members that they have increased their skills of identifying, expressing, and tolerating their own and others' feelings in healthy, constructive ways.

26. Explore Client's Feelings (26)

A. The client's emotions were probed gently to help the client become better able to identify and express these feelings.

B. The client received verbal affirmation and encouragement each time they identified and appropriately expressed feelings.

C. The client was gently confronted when they avoided either identifying or expressing emotions.

D. The client has exhibited skill in both the ability to identify and to express feelings; this was reflected to the client.

27. Assess Unmet Needs (27)

A. The client's unmet needs for attention, nurturance, and affirmation were assessed.

B. The family was assigned "Reasons for Negative Attention-Seeking Behaviors" from the *Child Psychotherapy Homework Planner* (Jongsma, Peterson, McInnis, & Bruce).

C. The therapist met with and assisted the client's caregivers in identifying and implementing actions that they could use to help meet the client's emotional needs.

D. The caregivers were given support, encouragement, and redirection in their effort to fill some of the client's unmet emotional needs.

E. It was noted that the client's acting-out behaviors (i.e., loud talk, showing off) have decreased as the client has responded positively to the nurturing actions of caregivers.

28. Brainstorm Meeting Emotional Needs (28)

A. The parents, child, and other caregivers were assisted in brainstorming ways to meet the child's unmet emotional needs.

    B. The emphasis was placed on meeting the child's unmet emotional needs in order to prevent the child's acting out in a maladaptive manner.

    C. The family was assigned the exercise "Unmet Emotional Needs—Identification and Satisfaction" from the *Adolescent Psychotherapy Homework Planner* (Jongsma, Peterson, McInnis, & Bruce).

29. **Assess Family Violence/Instability (29)**

    A. The family was assessed for the level of violence and chaos present and for what connection it has relative to the client's desire for power and control.

    B. The family members were assisted in identifying specific ways that they could improve the structure, predictability, and respectfulness within the family.

    C. Verbal support, encouragement, and guidance were provided to family members in their efforts to increase the structure, predictability, and respect within their family unit.

    D. The increased structure, predictability, and respect within the family were noted to have helped to stabilize the client's behavior and improve overall daily functioning.

30. **Develop Client–Parent Relationship (30)**

    A. The parent was worked with to increase his awareness of the positive value and impact that a closer relationship with the client could have.

    B. The parent was asked to identify three possible things he could do to relate more with the client, and then select two that he would be willing to implement.

    C. The parent was assisted in implementing the new ideas he had for expanding his relationship with the client.

    D. The parent's time spent with the client was monitored with encouragement, with redirection being given as needed.

    E. The parent's increased effort to relate more consistently and closely with the client has resulted in a marked decrease in the client's problem behaviors; the benefits of this change were reinforced.

    F. The client's parent has not increased his time with the client and was encouraged to use this as a way to build his relationship with the client.

31. **Facilitate the Big Brothers/Big Sisters Program (31)**

    A. The Big Brothers/Big Sisters program and its benefits were presented to the client and their parent.

    B. The client's parent was given direction and encouragement regarding making a request to the Big Brothers/Big Sisters program.

    C. The parent was assisted in making a referral for the client to the Big Brothers/Big Sisters program.

    D. The parent and client indicated that having a Big Brother/Big Sister has been a positive experience for the client; the benefits of this program were reviewed.

    E. The client's parent has not made a referral to the Big Brothers/Big Sisters program and was redirected to do so.

32. **Probe Rejection Feelings (32)**

    A. The client's feelings of hurt and anger over rejection by peers and family were probed and processed.

B. The client was assigned the "Child Anger Checklist" from the *Child Psychotherapy Homework Planner* (Jongsma, Peterson, McInnis, & Bruce).

C. The client and family were assigned portions of *Helping Your Angry Child* (Nemeth et al.).

D. The client was helped to connect feelings of hurt and anger to experiences of rejection in relationships with peers and family.

E. The client's fire setting was interpreted to the client as an expression of rage around the rejection of peers and family.

F. There have been no incidents of fire setting and a decreased interest in fire since the client started to process and resolve feelings of rage around the rejection that they experienced; the benefits of this hard work were emphasized.

33. Assess for Physical/Sexual Abuse (33)

A. The client was assessed for being a victim of physical and/or sexual abuse.

B. The parents were interviewed regarding the possibility of the client's being a victim of physical or sexual abuse.

C. The assessment substantiated that the client has been sexually abused.

D. The assessment substantiated that the client has been a victim of physical abuse.

E. The assessment ruled out that the client had been a victim of physical or sexual abuse.

F. The client's abuse was reported to the appropriate state or local authorities.

34. Complete A.C.E. Questionnaire (34)

A. The *Adverse Childhood Experiences Questionnaire (A.C.E.)* was conducted during today's session to establish a history of childhood traumas.

B. The rationale for the *A.C.E.* was accepted by the client and parents.

C. The results of the completed *A.C.E.* were processed with the client and parents.

D. The *A.C.E.* was not completed due to lack of information provided by the client and parents.

35. Assess for Severe Mental Illness (35)

A. The client was assessed for the purpose of establishing or ruling out the presence of a psychotic process or a major affective disorder.

B. The client cooperated fully with all aspects of the psychological assessment.

C. The results of the assessment ruled out the presence of a psychotic process or a major affective disorder.

D. The assessment established the presence of a psychotic process that will require treatment with medications.

E. The assessment established the presence of a major affective disorder that will need to be treated with psychotropic medications.

F. The client was referred for a psychiatric evaluation.

36. Assess for ADHD (36)

A. An attention-deficit/hyperactivity disorder (ADHD) assessment was conducted on the client.

B. The client was referred for a complete ADHD assessment.

C. The psychological assessment ruled out the presence of ADHD.

D. The psychological assessment concluded that the client has ADHD and needs to have a more complete ADHD workup and treatment.

E. A referral was made to a physician for a medication evaluation to treat ADHD.

37. **Facilitate ADHD Recommendations Implementation (37)**

A. The recommendations of the ADHD evaluation were presented and reviewed with the family, and any questions they had were answered and explained.

B. The family was assisted in implementing all the recommendations of the ADHD assessment.

C. The family was confronted and redirected when they failed to consistently implement the recommendations.

D. The family was given affirmation for its consistent implementation and follow-through on the recommendations of the evaluation.

E. The family's difficulty in implementing the recommendations was processed and resolved.

38. **Arrange for Residential Treatment (38)**

A. The need for the client to be placed in a residential setting for treatment of their serious psychiatric illness was explained to the family and processed with them.

B. Family resistance to the client's need for placement in a residential treatment program was addressed and resolved.

C. The various options in terms of residential treatment programs were discussed with the family.

D. The family was encouraged to tour several programs and make a decision on the program they feel is best for the client.

E. The family was assisted in obtaining a placement for the client in a residential treatment program.

F. Appropriate releases were signed by the parents to help expedite the procurement of a residential placement for the client.

G. The family was reinforced as they reported that the client has been accepted and has an admission date for placement in a residential treatment program.

GENDER DYSPHORIA

CLIENT PRESENTATION

1. **Desires to Be Opposite Sex (1)***
   A. The parents reported that the client frequently expresses the desire to be the opposite sex.
   B. The client expressed a desire in today's therapy session to be the opposite sex.
   C. The client verbalized positive remarks about their gender in today's therapy session.
   D. The client seems to be less certain about the desire to be the opposite sex.
   E. The client reported in today's therapy session that they no longer feel the desire to be the opposite sex.

2. **Dressing in Opposite-Sex Clothing (2)**
   A. The parents reported that the client frequently dresses in clothes typically worn by the opposite sex.
   B. The client expressed a preference to dress in clothes typically worn by the opposite sex.
   C. The client has continued to dress in clothes typically worn by the opposite sex.
   D. The client reports feeling most comfortable dressing in clothing traditionally worn by the opposite gender.
   E. The client reported that they no longer experience a desire to dress in clothes typically worn by the opposite sex.
   F. The client has consistently dressed in clothing typically worn by same-sex peers.

3. **Assumes Role of Opposite Sex in Play (3)**
   A. The parents reported that the client often assumes the role of the opposite sex in make-believe play.
   B. In today's play-therapy session, the client's play reflected strong identification with the opposite sex.
   C. The client has been teased by others for engaging in play that is perceived to be for the opposite sex.
   D. The client has gradually started to engage in play activities that are more typical of same-sex peers.
   E. The client has consistently engaged in play activities that are typical of same-sex peers.

4. **Participates in Pastimes Typical of the Opposite Sex (4)**
   A. The parents reported that the client often insists on participating in games or pastimes that are typical of the opposite sex.
   B. The client expressed interest in participating in games or activities that are typical of the opposite sex.

---

*The numbers in parentheses correlate to the number of the Behavioral Definition statement in the companion chapter with the same title in the *Child Psychotherapy Treatment Planner*, Sixth Edition, by Jongsma, Peterson, McInnis, & Bruce (Wiley, 2023).

    C. The client has remained firm in choosing to participate in activities that are culturally associated with children of the opposite gender.

    D. The client has started to participate in games or pastimes that are typical of same-sex peers.

    E. In today's therapy session, the client expressed an interest in participating in games or pastimes that are typical of same-sex peers.

    F. The client has consistently participated in games or pastimes that are typical of their gender.

5. Prefers Playmates of the Opposite Sex (5)

    A. The parents reported that the client often prefers to play with peers of the opposite sex.

    B. The client expressed greater interest and enjoyment in playing with opposite-sex peers.

    C. The client has started to play more often with peers of their gender.

    D. The client verbalized a desire to spend more time in play with same-sex peers.

    E. The client has consistently played with peers of their same gender.

    F. The client has established and maintained lasting same-sex peer friendships.

6. Frequently Passes as Opposite Sex (6)

    A. The client reported that they frequently pass as being of the opposite sex.

    B. The client expressed feelings of shame and embarrassment about others' frequently perceiving the client as being of the opposite sex.

    C. The client has attempted to present self to others as the opposite sex.

    D. The client expressed feelings of anger about others perceiving the client as being of the opposite sex.

    E. The client reported that they have recently not heard any comments or remarks from others about being of the opposite sex.

    F. The client has frequently passed as a member of the opposite sex because of their dress, preference for playing with members of the opposite sex, and participation in many games or activities that are typical of the opposite sex.

7. Insistence on Having Been Born the Wrong Sex (7)

    A. The parents reported that the client often insists that they were born the wrong sex.

    B. In today's therapy session, the client shared that they feel they were born the wrong sex.

    C. The client verbalizes feeling most comfortable when identifying as the opposite gender.

    D. The client has ceased making verbalizations about being born the wrong sex.

8. Disgust or Rejection of Sexual Anatomy (8)

    A. In today's therapy session, the client verbalized a disgust with or rejection of their sexual anatomy.

    B. The client verbalized a desire to change their sexual anatomy to that of the opposite gender.

    C. The client has reduced the frequency of critical and repulsive statements about their sexual anatomy.

D. The client has ceased making any critical or derogatory remarks about their sexual anatomy.

E. The client verbalized an acceptance of their sexual anatomy.

9. **Persistent Rejection of Same-Sex Activities (9)**

A. The parents reported that the client persistently rejects toys, games, or activities that are typical of same-sex peers.

B. The client expressed disinterest in engaging with toys and participating in games or activities that are typical of same-sex peers.

C. The client has started to engage with toys and participate in games or pastimes that are typical of same-sex peers.

D. In today's therapy session, the client expressed an interest in engaging with toys and participating in games or pastimes that are typical of same-sex peers.

E. The client has consistently engaged with toys and participated in games or pastimes that are typical of their sex.

10. **Emotional Distress Around Gender Discrepancy (10)**

A. The client has often exhibited a great deal of emotional distress connected to the discrepancy between assigned gender and expressed/experienced gender.

B. The client became visibly upset when discussing their assigned gender and expressed/experienced gender.

C. The client has often displayed temper outbursts regarding experiences related to their assigned gender and expressed/experienced gender.

D. The client has gradually started to cope more effectively when experiencing the discrepancy between assigned gender and expressed/experienced gender.

E. The client was able to discuss their assigned gender and expressed/experienced gender without exhibiting a significant amount of distress.

11. **Avoidance of Peers (11)**

A. The client's fears of being rejected, ridiculed, or criticized about gender identity issues have contributed to excessive shrinking from or avoidance of contact with peers in many social settings.

B. The client's fears of being rejected, ridiculed, or criticized about gender identity issues have decreased.

C. The client has recently started to socialize more with peers as fears of being rejected, ridiculed, or criticized about gender identity issues decreased.

INTERVENTIONS IMPLEMENTED

1. **Establish Rapport (1)***

A. Caring was conveyed to the client through support, warmth, and empathy.

B. The client was provided with nonjudgmental support, and a level of trust was developed.

---

*The numbers in parentheses correlate to the number of the Therapeutic Intervention statement in the companion chapter with the same title in the *Child Psychotherapy Treatment Planner*, Sixth Edition, by Jongsma, Peterson, McInnis, & Bruce (Wiley, 2023).

C. The client was urged to feel safe in expressing their gender identity issues.

D. The client began to express feelings more freely as rapport and trust level have increased.

E. The client has continued to experience difficulty being open and direct about the expression of painful feelings; the client was encouraged to use the safe haven of therapy to express these difficult issues.

2. Focus on Strengthening Therapeutic Relationship (2)

A. The relationship with the client was strengthened using empirically supported factors.

B. The relationship with the client was strengthened through the implementation of collaborative approach, agreement on goals, demonstration of empathy, verbalization of positive regard, and collection of client feedback.

C. The client reacted positively to the relationship-strengthening measures taken.

D. The client verbalized feeling supported and understood during therapy sessions.

E. Despite attempts to strengthen the therapeutic relationship, the client reports feeling distant and misunderstood.

F. The client has indicated that sessions are not helpful and will be terminating therapy.

3. Develop History (3)

A. A nonjudgmental interview was used to encourage the client to disclose the history and current status of their gender dysphoria.

B. Play-therapy approaches were used to assist the client in expressing thoughts, feelings, and desires about their gender identity, gender role behavior, and gender dysphoria.

C. A child-centered play-therapy session was held to explore the client's gender identity attitudes and causes for their gender dysphoria.

D. The client was given unconditional positive regard and warm acceptance when expressing thoughts and feelings about their gender identity.

E. The individual play-therapy sessions have helped the client work through the confusion surrounding their gender identity.

F. Play-therapy sessions have been held with the client but have not been useful in helping the client work through the confusion surrounding their gender identity.

4. Explore Reasons for Opposite-Sex Identity (4)

A. Today's therapy session explored the client's reasons for their attraction to an opposite-sex identity.

B. The client was asked to list reasons for their interest in the opposite gender identity.

C. The client maintains that their interest in living as an opposite-gender person stems from feeling that they were always wishing they were born as the opposite gender.

D. The therapy session was helpful in identifying the reasons or factors that have contributed to the client's attraction to an opposite-sex identity.

E. The therapy session did not produce insight into the factors contributing to the client's attraction to an opposite-sex identity.

F. A family-therapy session was held to assess the dynamics within the family system that contributed to the emergence of the client's confusion surrounding their sexual identity.

5. **Assess and Address Psychological Conditions (5)**
   A. The client was assessed for any clinically significant co-occurring psychological conditions.
   B. The client was assessed for depression, anxiety, attention-deficit/hyperactivity disorder, autism spectrum disorder, or oppositional defiant disorder.
   C. Co-occurring disorders were identified, and this was related to the client and caregivers, as well as treatment planning.
   D. No co-occurring disorders were identified, and this was related to the client and caregivers.
   E. Treatment plans were developed and implemented to address evident co-occurring psychological conditions.

6. **Assess Perception and Feelings Regarding Acceptance (6)**
   A. The client's perceptions and feelings were assessed in regard to acceptance on the part of social peers and family members.
   B. The client was assessed for possible bullying, rejection by peers, and criticism or punishment by the family members.
   C. The client was reviewed for potential stigmatization and labeling related to gender typicality in behavior, dress, or grooming.

7. **Assess Level of Insight (7)**
   A. The client's level of insight toward the presenting problems was assessed.
   B. The client was assessed in regard to the syntonic versus dystonic nature of their insight about the presenting problems.
   C. The client was noted to demonstrate good insight into the problematic nature of the behavior and symptoms.
   D. The client was noted to be in agreement with others' concerns and is motivated to work on change.
   E. The client was noted to be ambivalent regarding the problems described and is reluctant to address the issues as a concern.
   F. The client was noted to be resistant regarding acknowledgment of the problem areas, is not concerned about them, and has no motivation to make changes.

8. **Assess for Correlated Disorders (8)**
   A. The client was assessed for evidence of research-based correlated disorders.
   B. The client was assessed in regard to the level of vulnerability to suicide.
   C. The client was identified as having a comorbid disorder, and treatment was adjusted to account for these concerns.
   D. The client has been assessed for any correlated disorders, but none were found.

9. **Assess for Culturally Based Confounding Issues (9)**
   A. The client was assessed for age-related issues that could help to better understand their clinical presentation.
   B. The client was assessed for gender-related issues that could help to better understand their clinical presentation.

C. The client was assessed for cultural syndromes, cultural idioms of distress, or culturally based perceived causes that could help to better understand their clinical presentation.

D. Alternative factors have been identified as contributing to the client's currently defined "problem behavior," and these were taken into account in regard to treatment.

E. Culturally based factors that could help to account for the client's currently defined "problem behavior" were investigated, but no significant factors were identified.

10. **Assess Severity of Impairment (10)**

A. The severity of the client's impairment was assessed to determine the appropriate level of care.

B. The client was assessed in regard to impairment in social, relational, and educational endeavors.

C. It was reflected to the client that the impairment appears to create mild to moderate effects on the client's functioning.

D. It was reflected to the client that the impairment appears to create severe to very severe effects on the client's functioning.

E. The client was continuously assessed for the severity of impairment, as well as the efficacy and appropriateness of treatment.

11. **Assess for Pathogenic Care (11)**

A. The home, school, and community of the client were assessed for pathogenic care and concerns.

B. The client's various environments were assessed for the persistent disregard of the child's needs, repeated changes in caregivers, limited opportunities for stable attachment, harsh discipline, or other grossly inept care.

C. Pathogenic care was identified and the treatment plan included strategies for managing or correcting these concerns and protecting the child.

D. No pathogenic care was identified, and this was reflected to the client and caregivers.

12. **Explore Parents' Perception (12)**

A. The parents were assisted in exploring their perception of the client's gender-related thoughts, feelings, behaviors, and expressed desires.

B. The parents were assisted in identifying the time of onset as well as persistence, intensity, and pervasiveness of the client's gender dysphoria or transgender revelations.

C. The parents were assisted in summarizing their perceptions of the client's gender issues.

13. **Assess Parents' View of Gender Nonconformity (13)**

A. The parents were assessed for their attitude, behavior, and feelings regarding the client's nonconformity and gender identify behavior.

B. The parents were assisted in processing their feelings regarding the client's nonconformity in gender identity and behavior.

C. The parents were provided with nonjudgmental support in regard to their views on the client's gender nonconformity.

D. The parents were supported as they processed their feelings about the client's gender issues.

14. Encourage Parents' Support of Child's Exploration (14)

    A. The parents were encouraged to support and affirm their child's exploration of gender nonconformity.

    B. The parents were directed to reading material that may help them understand and be nonjudgmental about the client's gender dysphoria and transgender behavior.

    C. The parents were recommended to read *Transgender Identity & Gender Dysphoria in Children and Youth: A Practical Guide for Families and Professionals* (Jones) and *The Gender Identity Workbook for Kids: A Guide to Explaining Who You Are* (Storck).

    D. The parents have read information about supporting and understanding gender dysphoria and key concepts were processed.

15. Disclose Range of Treatment Options (15)

    A. A variety of treatment options were reviewed with the clients in regard to the client's continued development and gender dysphoria.

    B. The parents were taught about noninvasive social transitioning to a cross-gender role.

    C. The parents were taught about adolescent endocrine treatment to suppress puberty and secondary sex characteristics.

    D. Questions that the parents have about the options for treatment were answered.

    E. It was emphasized to the parents that research evidence is very limited to inform treatment decisions or predict treatment outcome.

    F. The parents were facilitated in decision-making from a position of neutrality and acceptance.

16. Offer Multidisciplinary Team Services (16)

    A. The parents and client were offered a multidisciplinary team of psychologists, physicians, endocrinologists, psychologists or social workers, and education specialists who treat children struggling with gender dysphoria.

    B. The family was directed to specialists that have been trained and are experienced in work with gender diverse and transgender children.

17. Teach Cognitive Restructuring Techniques (17)

    A. The client was taught cognitive restructuring techniques to give self positive and self-affirming messages to counteract social rejection.

    B. The client's positive self-talk was reviewed and reinforced.

    C. The client was encouraged to be patient and persistent in being true to self-identity.

18. Use "Positive Thinking" Game (18)

    A. The "Positive Thinking" game (Childswork/Childsplay) was played with the client to promote healthy self-talk and thought patterns.

    B. Today's session processed the "Positive Thinking" game experience with the client and identified specific ways to promote healthy self-talk and thought patterns.

    C. The client was assisted in selecting and implementing several suggestions from the "Positive Thinking" game into daily life.

D. The client was monitored, guided, and encouraged to follow through with using new healthy self-talk and thought patterns in daily life.

E. The parents were encouraged to play the "Positive Thinking" game at home with the client during the week.

19. **Replace Negative Cognitions with Positive Self-Talk (19)**

A. The client was encouraged to replace the negative cognitive messages regarding their gender identity with positive, realistic self-talk.

B. The client was encouraged to utilize positive self-talk as a means of decreasing their anxiety regarding gender identity and increase feelings of self-acceptance.

C. The client was assigned "Replace Negative Thoughts with Positive Self-Talk" in the *Child Psychotherapy Homework Planner* (Jongsma, Peterson, McInnis, & Bruce).

D. The cognitive therapy techniques have been helpful in revising the client's negative attitude regarding their gender identity.

E. The client has not replaced negative cognitions with positive self-talk and was provided with tentative examples in this area.

20. **Utilize Eye Movement Desensitization Reprocessing (20)**

A. Eye movement desensitization and reprocessing (EMDR) techniques were used to help reduce the client's emotional distress.

B. EMDR techniques were found to be useful in alleviating the client's emotional distress, and this was continued as necessary.

C. The client was unable to find usefulness through EMDR to alleviate their emotional distress, and therapy was continued as usual.

21. **Employ Mirror Exercise (21)**

A. The client was instructed to perform a mirror exercise at home where the client talks positively to self regarding gender identity.

B. The client performed the mirror exercise and reported that it was helpful in increasing feelings of self-esteem and self-worth; the client was encouraged to continue.

C. The client reported that the client followed through with performing the mirror exercise but continues to experience feelings of low self-esteem regarding their gender identity; the client was encouraged to continue this exercise.

D. Today's session processed the reasons for the client's inability to follow through with performing the mirror exercise.

22. **Reinforce Positive Self-Descriptive Statements (22)**

A. Today's therapy session reinforced the client's positive self-descriptive statements.

B. The parents were strongly encouraged to reinforce the client's positive self-descriptive statements at home.

C. The client was directed to verbalize at least one positive self-descriptive statement daily around others at school.

D. The client was encouraged to verbalize positive statements about self and others at school to help improve peer relationships in this setting.

    E. The client was given a homework assignment to record at least one positive self-descriptive statement daily in a journal.

    F. Journal entries reflecting the client's positive self-statements were reviewed and processed.

23. **Assign Reading (23)**

    A. The client was assigned books that promote awareness of gender identity issues and acceptance of self.

    B. The client was assigned to read *I Am Jazz* (Hethel & Jennings).

    C. The client was assigned to read *Who Are You?: The Kid's Guide to Gender Identity* (Pessin-Whedbee).

    D. The client was assigned *One of a Kind, Like Me* (Mayeno).

    E. Today's session focused on processing the content of the assigned reading material on gender identity issues and acceptance of self.

    F. The client reported that the books have helped them learn to effectively understand their gender identity issues and acceptance of self, and the benefits of this progress were reviewed.

24. **Affirm Nonjudgmental Neutralization (24)**

    A. Family sessions were used to affirm the client and nonjudgmentally neutralize their gender exploration.

    B. Individual sessions were used to affirm the client and nonjudgmentally neutralize their gender exploration.

    C. Care was used to avoid being critical and attempting to reverse or suppress the verbal or behavioral expressions of gender variance.

25. **Review Likely Reactions (25)**

    A. The client was assisted in understanding that their behavior may trigger reactions from others, including rejection, teasing, shunning, and criticism.

    B. The client was assisted in identifying the cultural and other reasons behind others' reaction to their behavior.

    C. Teach the client to use self-affirming statements in response to negative reactions from others.

    D. The client was directed to report peer rejection problems to trusted adults.

26. **Encourage Verbal Expression of Experiences (26)**

    A. The client was encouraged and supported in identifying and verbally expressing feelings pertaining to rejection and bullying experiences related to gender identity issues.

    B. The client was able to verbally express and clarify feelings pertaining to rejection and bullying experiences related to gender identity issues.

    C. The client struggled to verbally express feelings pertaining to rejection and bullying experiences related to gender identity; assistance was provided to help explore this area.

27. **List Supportive Peers and Adults (27)**

    A. The client was assisted in identifying a list of supportive peers and adults to whom they can turn for acceptance and belonging.

B. The client's list of supportive peers and adults was processed and discussed to identify each person's individual support.

C. The client was unable to identify many or any supportive peers and adults and was assisted in brainstorming ideas.

28. **Assign Strengths Exercise (28)**

A. The client was assigned a homework exercise to identify 5–10 of their strengths or interests that could be used to initiate social contacts with peers who hold similar interests.

B. The client was assigned the "Show Your Strengths" exercise from the *Child Psychotherapy Homework Planner* (Jongsma, Peterson, McInnis, & Bruce) to help identify their strengths or interests that could be used to initiate social contacts with peers who hold similar interests.

C. The client was instructed to use three strengths or interests in the upcoming week to initiate social contacts with peers who hold similar interests.

D. The client successfully completed the "Show Your Strengths" exercise and felt good about sharing the results with peers because they were receptive.

E. The client reported that the "Show Your Strengths" exercise helped to increase self-esteem and confidence; the benefits of this progress were reviewed.

F. The client reported that sharing their strengths with others helped them to feel accepted by peers at school or in the neighborhood and was encouraged to continue.

G. The client did not follow through with completing the "Show Your Strengths" exercise and was asked again to work on it.

29. **Direct Family's Acceptance (29)**

A. The client's family members were assisted in exploring their thoughts and feelings regarding the client's gender-variant behavior.

B. The family members were assisted in understanding that the client's gender identity cannot be altered by their reactions.

C. The family was assisted in identifying how their level of acceptance may affect the client's self-esteem.

30. **Encourage Patience (30)**

A. All family members were encouraged to be patient and affirming of the client.

B. The family was assisted in understanding the concept of living with the uncertainty about the client's gender and sexual identity development.

C. Information was provided to the family in regard to the likelihood that gender dysphoria will desist or continue (i.e., 12%–27% of cases of gender dysphoria lead to some degree of social or medical lesbian, gay, bisexual, transgender [LGBT] identity).

31. **Discuss Social Transitioning Experiment (31)**

A. Discuss with the parents whether they are open to allowing the client to engage in a social transitioning experiment.

B. If the parents and client are so inclined, a social transitioning experiment with opposite-gender behavior was developed.

C. The client was directed to engage in opposite-gender behavior (e.g., name, dress, actions, play) in a social setting apart from their regular neighborhood or school (e.g., while on vacation).

D. A family session was held to process the family member's thoughts and feelings.

32. Process Experiment in Social Transitioning (32)

A. The client was assisted in processing the experience of social transitioning while in a social setting apart from their neighborhood or school.

B. Family members' feelings about the social transitioning experiment were reviewed.

C. The comfort level of all family members was discussed, as well as ramifications for future gender-role behavior for the client.

33. Find Sensible Middle-of-the-Road Approach (33)

A. The parents were assisted in finding a sensible middle-of-the-road approach between an accepting and supportive attitude toward the client's dysphoria, while at the same time protecting their children against any negative reactions from others and remaining realistic about the actual situation.

B. The parents were able to identify and engage in a sensible middle-of-the-road approach to their child's dysphoria and were reinforced for this understanding.

C. The parent's approach to their child's dysphoria was identified as being impractical and they were provided with remedial feedback and support.

34. Encourage Meeting with School Personnel (34)

A. The parents were encouraged to meet with the client's school personnel to explain their child's gender identity struggles and transgender preferences.

B. The parents were urged to ask teachers to be accepting and affirming of a client's gender identity exploration.

C. The family was directed to find ways to nurture acceptance from the client's school peers.

D. School personnel were urged to be intolerant of any peer bullying.

E. The parents were informed of the willingness for clinicians to meet with the client's school personnel to explain gender dysphoria and transgender behavior.

F. The parents were advised that clinicians meeting with school personnel can help to increase understanding, reduce stigmatization, promote acceptance, sound an alert for social rejection or bullying, and encourage a supportive environment for the client.

35. Refer to Support Groups (35)

A. The client and parents were referred to support groups composed of others who are coping with gender identity variances and transgender preferences.

B. The client and parents were referred to PFLAG.com.

C. The client and parents were referred to TransYouth Family Allies (IMATYFA.org).

D. The client and family have attended support groups and their experiences were processed.

E. The family members have not attended support groups and were reminded about this useful resource.

36. Discuss Social Gender Transitioning (36)

A. The parents were engaged in a discussion regarding the possibility of supporting the client's persistent and intense desires for gender variance through allowing for a fully reversible social gender transition.

B. The parents were engaged in a discussion about allowing gender transitioning in school and neighborhood, including cross-gender clothing, name change, pronoun change, and hairstyle alteration.

C. The parents were assisted in processing their thoughts and feelings regarding implementing or not implementing this intervention in reversible steps.

37. Implement Social Gender Transitioning (37)

A. The client was assisted in implementing full reversible social gender transitioning in home, school, and neighborhood setting.

B. The client was assisted in processing and assessing feelings about implementation of the full reversible social gender transitioning.

C. Family members were assisted in processing their emotions related to the social gender transitioning.

38. Explore for Physical or Sexual Abuse (38)

A. The client's background was explored for a history of physical or sexual abuse that may have contributed to their gender confusion.

B. Today's therapy session revealed a history of physical abuse that has been a significant contributing factor to the client's gender confusion.

C. Today's therapy session revealed a history of sexual abuse that has contributed to the client's gender confusion.

D. The client verbally denied ever being physically or sexually abused, and this was accepted.

E. The client was given unconditional positive regard and warm acceptance in expressing feelings about the past abuse.

39. Explore Gay, Lesbian, or Transgender Identity (39)

A. The child was assisted in exploring whether their confusion over gender identity may be the beginning of a gay, lesbian, or transgender identity.

B. The client was assisted in processing their gender identity.

C. The client was assisted in processing knowledge of their sexual identity.

D. The client was reassured in regard to their self-worth as a gay person.

E. The client was assigned portions of *All I Want to Be Is Me* (Rothblatt).

F. The parents were assisted in accepting that their child may be at an early stage of LGBT identity.

GRIEF/LOSS UNRESOLVED

CLIENT PRESENTATION

1. **Parent Death Reaction (1)***
   A. The client presented as visibly upset and distressed over the recent loss of their parent.
   B. Teachers, friends, and others have reported that the client is exhibiting various grief reactions such as anger, depression, and emotional lability around the recent loss of their parent.
   C. The client indicated they cannot think of anything else but the death of their parent.
   D. The client frequently expressed that they still cannot accept that this parental death really happened.
   E. The client revealed that the feeling of being alone and helpless has been overwhelming since the parent's death.
   F. The client has started to talk about the loss of their parent and has begun to accept consolation, support, and encouragement from others.

2. **Termination of Parental Rights (2)**
   A. The client presented as sad and withdrawn after recently being told that their parents' rights are being terminated.
   B. The client indicated that they refuse to believe that they will not see their parents again.
   C. Foster parents reported that the client is continually angry and upset since receiving the news of their parents' rights being terminated.
   D. The client has made progress in coming to terms with their parents' loss of their rights and has started to look forward to a new home and family.

3. **Parental Incarceration Grief (3)**
   A. The client expressed feeling a big hole in their life since their parent went to prison.
   B. The client reported being angry most of the time since their parent was incarcerated.
   C. The client indicated that they have felt sad and embarrassed about the parent's imprisonment and have socially withdrawn from activities to avoid feeling more uncomfortable.
   D. The client has begun to accept and adjust to the parent's imprisonment and return to a normal level of functioning.

4. **Grief Due to Geographic Move (4)**
   A. The client presented as depressed and focused on the loss of their previous home and friends that have been left behind because of the geographic move.
   B. The client reported feeling angry and upset all the time now at parents for their decision to move them away from their neighborhood and friends.

---

*The numbers in parentheses correlate to the number of the Behavioral Definition statement in the companion chapter with the same title in the *Child Psychotherapy Treatment Planner*, Sixth Edition, by Jongsma, Peterson, McInnis, & Bruce (Wiley, 2023).

C. The parents indicated that the client is always sad and refuses to leave home except to go to school.

D. The client has started to accept the family's new location and is beginning to make new friends and becoming involved in other activities.

5. **Parent Emotional Abandonment (5)**

A. The client verbalized feeling abandoned emotionally since losing nearly all contact with the parent.

B. The client reported they have been cut off from nearly all contact with their other parent.

C. The client indicated they are devastated by the loss of nearly all meaningful contact with their parent.

D. The client has begun to openly grieve the emotional abandonment they have experienced from their parent.

6. **Emotionally Upset (6)**

A. The client presented in an upset, tearful, and distraught manner.

B. The client related that they are having a difficult time coming to terms with the recent loss they have experienced.

C. It appears the client is stuck in the grieving process and finding it difficult to move beyond being upset and distraught.

D. The client is gradually making progress in coming to terms and accepting their loss, as they report crying less and not being as upset as before.

7. **Depression Symptoms (7)**

A. The client described a lack of appetite, sleep disturbance, and other depression symptoms that have occurred since the experience of the loss.

B. The client's depression symptoms have diminished as they have begun to resolve the feelings of grief.

C. The client's depression symptoms have lifted.

8. **Tearful Spells (7)**

A. The client reported waves of depression and grief that result in tearfulness on a frequent basis.

B. The client's tearful spells have diminished somewhat in frequency.

C. The client reported better control over emotions and no incidents of spontaneous tearful spells.

9. **Social Withdrawal (7)**

A. The client presents as very withdrawn and nonverbal around past loss(es).

B. "I can't talk about it" is one of the few verbalizations coming from the client regarding past loss.

C. The client, with encouragement and support, has slowly moved from their withdrawn state and started to talk about the loss.

10. **Angry/Tense (8)**

   A. Anger and tension dominate the client's affect, mood, and manner.

   B. The client reports frequent verbal temper outbursts toward others and breaking things following the loss.

   C. The client's anger is freely vented toward God, doctors, and others that "had a hand" in the loss.

   D. The client's functioning in the school setting has decreased due to the pattern of angry outbursts when separating from parents.

   E. There is a decrease in the client's anger as they acknowledge and explain that now they are feeling more hurt and sadness about the loss.

11. **Academic Underachievement (8)**

   A. The client's teachers and parents reported a drop of academic performance that is below the expected level, given the client's measured intelligence or performance on standardized achievement tests.

   B. The client verbally admitted that current academic performance is below the expected level of functioning.

   C. The client has started to assume more responsibility for completing school and home-work assignments.

   D. The client has taken active steps (e.g., studying at routine times, seeking outside tutor, consulting with teacher before or after class) to improve academic performance.

   E. The client's academic performance has improved to the expected level.

12. **Guilty/Responsible (9)**

   A. The overall mood and manner of the client reflects a deep sense of guilt and responsibility for the recent loss.

   B. The client reported those things that make them feel guilty and responsible for the loss.

   C. To maintain control, the client appears to be stuck in their guilt and is either unwilling or unable to move beyond this point in the process of grieving.

   D. The client is moving toward letting go of guilt and accepting that they are not responsible for the loss.

13. **Avoidance of Loss (10)**

   A. The client presented with a high level of denial and strong resistance to acknowledging and accepting their loss.

   B. The client's family system has a definite pattern of denial and nonacceptance of losses.

   C. The client stated, "I don't believe this really happened; I won't accept this," and did not attend any part of the funeral process.

   D. Cracks are starting to show in the client's denial as they are now believing the loss is real.

   E. The client's denial has broken, and they are now being overwhelmed with feelings of anger, hurt, and sadness.

INTERVENTIONS IMPLEMENTED

1. **Establish Rapport (1)***
   A. Caring was conveyed to the client through support, warmth, and empathy.
   B. The client was provided with nonjudgmental support, and a level of trust was developed.
   C. The client was urged to feel safe in expressing feelings of grief.
   D. The client began to express feelings more freely as rapport and trust level have increased.
   E. The client has continued to experience difficulty being open and direct about the expression of painful feelings; the client was encouraged to use the safe haven of therapy to express these difficult issues.

2. **Focus on Strengthening Therapeutic Relationship (2)**
   A. The relationship with the client was strengthened using empirically supported factors.
   B. The relationship with the client was strengthened through the implementation of collaborative approach, agreement on goals, demonstration of empathy, verbalization of positive regard, and collection of client feedback.
   C. The client reacted positively to the relationship-strengthening measures taken.
   D. The client verbalized feeling supported and understood during therapy sessions.
   E. Despite attempts to strengthen the therapeutic relationship, the client reports feeling distant and misunderstood.
   F. The client has indicated that sessions are not helpful and will be terminating therapy.

3. **Assess Level of Insight (3)**
   A. The client's level of insight toward the presenting problems was assessed.
   B. The client was assessed in regard to the syntonic versus dystonic nature of their insight about the presenting problems.
   C. The client was noted to demonstrate good insight into the problematic nature of the behavior and symptoms.
   D. The client was noted to be in agreement with others' concerns and is motivated to work on change.
   E. The client was noted to be ambivalent regarding the problems described and is reluctant to address the issues as a concern.
   F. The client was noted to be resistant regarding acknowledgment of the problem areas, is not concerned about them, and has no motivation to make changes.

4. **Assess for Correlated Disorders (4)**
   A. The client was assessed for evidence of research-based correlated disorders.
   B. The client was assessed in regard to the level of vulnerability to suicide.

---

* The numbers in parentheses correlate to the number of the Therapeutic Intervention statement in the companion chapter with the same title in the *Child Psychotherapy Treatment Planner*, Sixth Edition, by Jongsma, Peterson, McInnis, & Bruce (Wiley, 2023).

C. The client was identified as having a comorbid disorder, and treatment was adjusted to account for these concerns.

D. The client has been assessed for any correlated disorders, but none were found.

5. **Assess for Culturally Based Confounding Issues (5)**

A. The client was assessed for age-related issues that could help to better understand their clinical presentation.

B. The client was assessed for gender-related issues that could help to better understand their clinical presentation.

C. The client was assessed for cultural syndromes, cultural idioms of distress, or culturally based perceived causes that could help to better understand their clinical presentation.

D. Alternative factors have been identified as contributing to the client's currently defined "problem behavior," and these were taken into account in regard to treatment.

E. Culturally based factors that could help to account for the client's currently defined "problem behavior" were investigated, but no significant factors were identified.

6. **Assess Severity of Impairment (6)**

A. The severity of the client's impairment was assessed to determine the appropriate level of care.

B. The client was assessed in regard to impairment in social, relational, and educational endeavors.

C. It was reflected to the client that the impairment appears to create mild to moderate effects on the client's functioning.

D. It was reflected to the client that the impairment appears to create severe to very severe effects on the client's functioning.

E. The client was continuously assessed for the severity of impairment, as well as the efficacy and appropriateness of treatment.

7. **Assess for Pathogenic Care (7)**

A. The home, school, and community of the client were assessed for pathogenic care and concerns.

B. The client's various environments were assessed for the persistent disregard of the child's needs, repeated changes in caregivers, limited opportunities for stable attachment, harsh discipline, or other grossly inept care.

C. Pathogenic care was identified and the treatment plan included strategies for managing or correcting these concerns and protecting the child.

D. No pathogenic care was identified, and this was reflected to the client and caregivers.

8. **Utilize Child-Centered Play Therapy (8)**

A. Child-centered play therapy was used to help the client work through their loss.

B. When the client expressed a feeling within the child-centered play therapy session, it was mirrored, reflected, and validated to them.

C. The client's feelings were reflected back to them in an affirming, nonjudgmental manner to promote working through the grieving process.

D. The child-centered play therapy approach has helped to support and encourage the client in working through the loss.

9. **Employ Individual Play Therapy (9)**

A. An individual play therapy session was conducted with the client to help them express and work through feelings about the loss.

B. The client actively participated in the play therapy session.

C. The feelings that were expressed through the client's play were affirmed and validated.

D. The supportive environment of the play therapy sessions has helped the client express and work through many of the feelings surrounding their loss.

E. The client's involvement in play therapy was rather cautious, and they did not disclose many emotions.

10. **Use Art Therapy Techniques (10)**

A. Various art therapy techniques were used to provide the client with an opportunity to creatively express feelings connected to the loss.

B. The client actively participated in the art therapy.

C. The client explained the artwork in detail, as requested.

D. The client's active participation in art therapy has helped them begin openly expressing feelings connected to the loss.

E. The client's involvement in art therapy was guarded.

11. **Employ Mutual Storytelling Technique (11)**

A. The client was engaged in a mutual storytelling exercise and encouraged to tell the story of their loss.

B. The client readily told their story, which was interpreted for its underlying meaning.

C. The client was told a story that used the same characters and settings as their story, but the new story was woven in healthy ways to adapt to and resolve the loss.

D. The client verbalized that the mutual storytelling technique was useful in giving them ways to cope with and resolve the loss.

12. **Utilize "Before and After Drawing Technique" (12)**

A. Using the "Before and After Drawing Technique" (Cangelosi), the client was asked to tell the story of their loss through drawings of how they were before and then after the loss.

B. The client explained the story told in the grief drawings, willingly filled in any gaps, and answered all questions that were asked.

C. Feelings connected to the loss events were identified, processed, and validated.

D. Drawing has opened the door to enable the client to tell the story of the loss and its effect on their life.

13. **Use Puppets or Felt Figures (13)**

A. The client was encouraged to act out or tell the story of their loss using puppets or a felt board.

B. The client acted out the story of their loss using puppets; their emotions were reflected.

C. The client used the felt board and figures to tell the story of the loss, which was reflected to them.

D. The client was given positive verbal affirmation for sharing the story of their loss.

14. **Use "Five Faces" Technique (14)**

A. The "Five Faces" technique (Jewett) was used to help the client move beyond their emotional block and become able to identify and express their feelings.

B. The client's ability to recognize feelings and express them has grown and been helpful in clarifying their many conflicting emotions connected to the grieving process.

C. The client continues to be blocked in their ability to identify and express grief-related feelings and was provided with tentative feedback in this area.

15. **Explore Grief Through Games (15)**

A. The "Goodbye Game" and the "Good Mourning Game" were played with the client to help explore the process of grief.

B. The client received positive verbal reinforcement for disclosing the thoughts and feelings connected to loss.

C. The client was resistive to using the therapeutic games as a springboard for expressing thoughts and feelings related to the grief experience and was encouraged to be open about this as they were able to do so.

16. **Identify Feelings Around Loss (16)**

A. The client was asked to write a letter to the lost loved one describing feelings, desires, and wishes connected to that person.

B. The client was assigned "Grief Letter" in the *Child Psychotherapy Homework Planner* (Jongsma, Peterson, McInnis, & Bruce).

C. The client read the letter that they had written to the lost loved one with appropriate affect and expression of feelings, and it was processed.

D. The client read the letter to the lost loved one with flat affect, showing no outward emotions either in voice or facial expression, and this was reflected to them.

E. The client has not developed a letter to the lost loved one and was redirected to do so.

17. **Use Art or Verbal Metaphor in Play Therapy (17)**

A. The client was requested to talk about what life was like before and after the loss using stories or drawings.

B. With encouragement, the client was able to talk about what life was like before and after the loss.

C. The client was assisted in identifying the specific changes in their life that have occurred since the loss.

D. The feelings expressed by the client through drawings or stories were mirrored, acknowledged, and validated.

E. The client was guarded about how life has changed due to the loss and was encouraged to be more open in this area.

18. **Identify/Clarify Feelings Connected to the Loss (18)**

A. The role of feelings and the way they work were explained to the client.

B. The client was assisted in identifying, labeling, and expressing feelings connected to the loss.

C. The client was assigned "Petey's Journey Through Sadness" from the *Child Psychotherapy Homework Planner* (Jongsma, Peterson, McInnis, & Bruce).

D. The client was supported with verbal affirmation and validation as they expressed feelings connected with the loss.

E. With assistance, the client was able to identify, express, and work through feelings connected to the loss.

F. The client was resistive to identifying or clarifying feelings connected to the loss and was provided with tentative examples of feelings they may be experiencing.

19. Assign Grief Journal (19)

A. The client was ask to keep a daily grief journal to record the thoughts and feelings associated with the loss.

B. The client's grief journal was reviewed and significant disclosures of thoughts and feelings were supported and reinforced.

C. The client's grief journal was reviewed, but it revealed that the client continues to distance self from struggling with the pain of grieving.

D. The client has not followed through with recording the thoughts and feelings related to grief in a journal and was reminded to do this homework.

20. Refer to Support Group (20)

A. The client was referred to and encouraged to attend a grief support group for children.

B. The client's experience of attending a grief support group was processed and continued attendance was supported and encouraged.

C. The client was resistive to a referral to a support group and has continued to refuse to attend such a group, but was once again encouraged to attend a grief support group.

21. Assign Reading on Death and Dying (21)

A. The client was assigned reading material on death and dying.

B. The client was assigned to read *The Fall of Freddy the Leaf* (Buscaglia).

C. The client was assigned to read *The Next Place* (Hanson).

D. The client was assigned to read *I Miss You: A First Look at Death* (Thomas).

E. The client's questions that arose from reading the material on death and dying were answered and supported.

F. The client's lack of questions was gently but firmly confronted as being avoidance of grieving.

22. Arrange for Answers to Grief Questions (22)

A. The client was assisted in identifying some peer or adult they know who has successfully worked through the grieving process and might be willing to talk with them about the experience.

B. The client was guided in developing a list of questions that they would like to have answered by the experienced person.

C. The client was directed to specific resources (e.g., books) to help answer questions related to grief.

D. The client was encouraged to set a date to talk with the experienced griever either at a time outside of a session or within a conjoint session.

E. The client has followed through with talking with the experienced griever, and the therapist and client processed this positive experience in today's session.

F. The client has not followed through with contacting an experienced griever and was redirected to do so.

23. **Read *The Empty Place: A Child's Guide Through Grief* (23)**

A. The book *The Empty Place: A Child's Guide Through Grief* (Temes) was used as a guide to help the client through the grieving process.

B. The client was supported, guided, and reassured while moving through the stages of grief.

C. The client was encouraged to share the book *The Empty Place: A Child's Guide Through Grief* with parents to help them understand and support them in the grieving process.

24. **Read *Don't Despair on Thursdays!* (24)**

A. Read *Don't Despair on Thursdays!* (Moser) with the client.

B. Suggestions from the *Don't Despair on Thursdays!* book were identified and processed with the client.

C. The client was assisted in selecting two ways to handle their grief feelings from the *Don't Despair on Thursdays!* book, and plans were developed for implementation in their daily life.

D. The client has reported positive results in using the suggestions from the *Don't Despair on Thursdays!* book to cope with their feelings of grief and was urged to continue to use these techniques.

E. The client has not used the grieving techniques from *Don't Despair on Thursdays!* and was encouraged to use these helpful techniques.

25. **Explore Thoughts of Guilt and Blame (25)**

A. The client's thoughts and feelings of guilt and blame for the loss were explored.

B. The client's irrational thoughts and feelings were identified and replaced with more realistic ones.

C. It was noted that the client's irrational thoughts and feelings regarding guilt and self-blame are no longer present.

D. Exercises from *Why Did You Die?: Activities to Help Children Cope with Grief and Loss* (Leeuwenburgh & Goldring).

26. **Help Client Communicate Self-Blame for the Loss (26)**

A. A Despart Fable was used with the client to help them begin expressing self-blame for the loss.

B. The client's active participation in the Despart Fable has assisted them in communicating the self-blame they feel for the loss.

C. The client has begun to openly express and communicate their feelings of self-blame for the loss.

D. The client resisted participation in the Despart Fable exercise as they did not know what to say.

27. Help Lift Self-Imposed Curse (27)

A. The therapist and client explored the client's belief in a self-imposed curse that makes them responsible for the death of the significant other.

B. The client was encouraged to ask the person who indicated that the death of the significant other was the client's fault to take the statement back.

C. A role-play phone conversation was done between the client and the deceased where the client had the opportunity to apologize for their behavior that caused the loss.

D. The client's unrealistic beliefs around the curse that caused the death of the significant other were confronted.

E. It was reflected to the client that they no longer believe that they are responsible for the death of the significant other through some curse phenomenon.

28. List Positive Things About Deceased (28)

A. The client was asked to construct a list of all the positive things about the deceased and how they plan to remember each.

B. The list was processed with the client and each positive thing/memory was affirmed, and the importance of remembering each was emphasized.

C. The client was noted to enjoy the experience of listing positive memories about the deceased significant other.

D. The client was overwhelmed with emotion when talking about positive memories of the deceased significant other and was provided with support.

E. It was reflected to the client that they can now recall positive things about the deceased significant other without becoming overwhelmed with sadness.

29. Talk About Pictures and Other Mementos (29)

A. The client was asked to bring pictures and mementos of the deceased significant other to the therapy session.

B. The client was assigned the exercise "Create a Memory Album" from the *Child Psychotherapy Homework Planner* (Jongsma, Peterson, McInnis, & Bruce).

C. The client followed through in bringing pictures and mementos of the deceased, and they were encouraged to talk about the memories attached to each in an open, free manner, making little probing necessary.

D. The client had to be encouraged and prodded to talk about pictures and mementos that they brought as requested.

E. It was reflected to the client that their grief appears to be lifting somewhat as they talk about positive memories attached to the deceased significant other.

F. The client has not connected their pictures and mementos of the deceased significant other to their emotions and was provided with tentative ideas in this area.

30. Encourage and Support Appropriate Anger (30)

A. The client was encouraged and reminded in sessions to look angry when feeling angry, act angry, and then to put their anger into words.

B. The client's fear of looking angry and expressing anger was explored with them.

C. The client was supported and given positive verbal feedback when they acted angry and expressed it.

D. The client was confronted when they appeared to be feeling angry but acted otherwise.

E. The client's feelings of anger toward God, self, and others have been noted to diminish as they were able to express them freely.

31. Use Physical Techniques to Release Anger (31)

A. Various acceptable physical techniques (e.g., kneading clay or kicking a paper bag) were used to help the client release repressed angry feelings.

B. The exercise was processed, and targets and causes for the anger were explored with the client.

C. The client only minimally participated in the physical techniques, despite encouragement and support being given to them to do so.

D. The use of behavioral techniques has helped the client express and externalize their repressed angry feelings.

32. Assign a Good-Bye Letter (32)

A. The client was asked to write a good-bye letter or draw a good-bye picture to the deceased.

B. The client was assigned the "Grief Letter" exercise from the *Child Psychotherapy Homework Planner* (Jongsma, Peterson, McInnis, & Bruce).

C. The client's completed grief letter or drawing was processed, and each feeling that they expressed or identified was affirmed.

D. Barriers that prevented the client from completing their grief letter or drawing were identified, processed, and resolved.

E. The client's completed grief letter or drawing was interpreted as indicating that they are making progress in the grieving process.

F. The client has not completed a good-bye letter and was redirected to do so.

33. Process Visit to Grave of Loved One (33)

A. The client was prepared to make their first visit to the grave of the deceased loved one and selected the adult they would like to accompany them.

B. The selected adult was prepared to be supportive of and provide guidance for the client's visit to the gravesite.

C. The client followed through with visiting the grave of the deceased loved one, said goodbye, and left their letter or drawing at the gravesite; their experience was processed.

D. The client declined to visit the grave of their loved one and was urged to use this grieving technique as they felt able to do so.

34. Identify Current Goals in Grief (34)

A. The client's parents were assisted in identifying the goals or tasks that the child has accomplished and which goals or tasks they are presently working through.

B. Goals such as acceptance of the death, expressing emotions, storing memories, reconstructing an identity, and creating a new normal were reviewed as to their status.

C. Positive feedback was provided to the client as they identified grief-resolution goals that they have accomplished.

D. The client was helped to develop a plan to move forward on tasks that have not been accomplished as yet.

E. The client struggled to clarify the current status of grief-resolving goals and was provided with feedback in this area.

35. Teach Question Answering (35)

A. The parents were educated on how to answer any of the client's questions considering the child's level of cognitive development.

B. The parents were recommended to read *Waterbugs and Dragonflies: Explaining Death to Young Children* (Stickney).

C. The parents were recommended to read *Caring for Your Grieving Child: A Parent's Guide* (Wakenshaw).

D. The parents were recommended to read *Good Grief* (Westberg).

E. It was emphasized with the family that grief is not a one-time event ("Just get over it") but an ongoing process.

F. The parents and child were noted to have a better understanding of the grieving process and, as a result, seem more capable of showing empathy and support toward one another.

G. The parents and/or child are resistant to any new information about grief and are in denial about the power of its impact on people's lives.

36. Teach Prominent Needs During Grieving (36)

A. The surviving parent was taught about the three prominent needs a child has during grieving: nurturance, support, and continuity.

B. The surviving parent was taught to gently encourage the child to express feelings about the loss.

C. The surviving parent was taught to show the child they will be cared for and safe.

D. The surviving parent was taught to remind the child that they did not cause the death due to anger or some other magical thinking.

E. The surviving parent has appropriately managed the child's needs during grieving, and progress was processed.

F. The surviving parent has been unable to manage the child's needs during grieving, and additional feedback was provided.

37. Teach Parents Supportive Methods (37)

A. The parents were taught various specific ways they could support and encourage the client in successfully working through the grieving process.

B. The parents' efforts to show love, consolation, and provide comfort were affirmed and reinforced.

C. The parents have been resistant to increasing behaviors that show comfort, consolation, and support for the client's grief; they were redirected to provide this support.

D. It was reflected to the parents that the client has responded favorably to the parents' showing more support and empathy for their grief.

38. Conduct Family Session to Express Grief (38)

A. A family session was conducted in which each family member was encouraged to talk about their experience related to the loss.

B. Family members who found it impossible to talk about their grief feelings were reminded of the importance of doing so in order to work through the loss.

C. Family members were encouraged to talk more about the loss at appropriate times outside of sessions.

D. The client felt reassured and understood when other family members shared their feelings of grief connected to the loss; this experience was processed.

39. Conduct Operational Mourning Family Session (39)

A. A family therapy session was conducted, with all members of the family expressing their experience related to the loss.

B. The child was allowed to observe others sharing strong emotions that are normalized before being asked to share their own feelings.

C. The child was able to express their feelings of grief during the family session.

D. The child continued to struggle to share their feelings of grief, and additional assistance was provided.

40. Conduct Integrated Grief Therapy for Children (40)

A. A family therapy session focusing on Integrated Grief Therapy for Children was conducted, combining cognitive-behavioral, family systems, and narrative approaches.

B. The family gained a greater understanding of grief through Integrated Grief Therapy for Children.

41. Use Family Systems Approach (41)

A. A family systems approach was used to mitigate dysfunctional family grieving such as avoidance of grieving, blaming others, or attempting to keep the deceased family member "alive."

B. Confronting dysfunctional grieving has led to understanding of negative aspects of problematic grieving.

C. The family has ended dysfunctional grieving and utilized more useful approaches to grief.

42. Refer Parents to Grief Group (42)

A. The client's parents were referred and encouraged to attend a grief/loss support group.

B. The client's parents were open to the suggestion of attending a support group and have committed themselves to attending the next meeting; positive feedback was provided.

C. The client's parents were resistant to the idea of attending a grief/loss support group and refused to follow through with this referral; they were urged to reconsider.

43. Encourage Involvement in Grieving Rituals (43)

A. The parents were encouraged to allow the client to be a part of all of the grieving rituals they request to participate in.

B. The parents were directed to be sensitive, supportive, and comforting to the client during the grieving rituals they attend.

C. The various grieving rituals were explained to the client, and they were given the choice of which they would like to attend.

D. It was noted that the client's attendance at the funeral and other grieving rituals was beneficial in sharing grief with others and saying good-bye to the deceased.

44. **Prepare Parents to Say Good-Bye (44)**

    A. The biological parents were prepared to say good-bye to the children over whom they are losing custody.

    B. The parents were assisted in identifying and expressing their feelings around losing permanent custody of their children.

    C. The parents were assisted in developing healthy, affirmative ways to say good-bye to the children over whom they are losing custody.

    D. The parents selected a healthy, affirmative way to say good-bye to their children, and they were assisted in developing plans to implement it.

    E. Role-play was used to give the parents exposure to saying good-bye to their children in a healthy, affirmative way.

    F. Unresolved issues around having to say good-bye were addressed, processed, and resolved.

    G. It was assessed that the parents have reached the point where they are ready to say good-bye to their children in a healthy, affirmative way.

45. **Facilitate Good-Bye Session (45)**

    A. A good-bye session was facilitated with the parents who were losing custody of their children so that the parents could give an appropriate message of permission to each child to move on.

    B. The parents were given affirmation and positive verbal feedback on their following through in saying good-bye to their children in a positive, healthy way.

    C. It was noted that the good-bye session was a conflictual one in that the parents left the child feeling guilty for the parents' grief and sadness.

    D. The parents were reinforced as they have written a letter of good-bye and affirmation to their children over whom they have lost custody.

46. **Create a Record of Life (46)**

    A. The client was asked to bring to a session pictures and other memorabilia that are associated with their life before and after the grief event.

    B. The client was assisted in creating a book or album of their life.

    C. The client's feelings associated with the loss were processed as they were expressed during the exercise of creating the album.

    D. The client was able to select magazine pictures to put in their album that represented future hopes and plans, indicating a beginning resolution of grief.

47. **Encourage Expression of Positive Memories (47)**

    A. The client was encouraged to express positive memories about the lost loved one.

    B. The story "Petey's Journey Through Sadness" from the *Child Psychotherapy Homework Planner* (Jongsma, Peterson, McInnis, & Bruce) was read with the client in today's session.

    C. The story was processed with the client, and they were encouraged to share positive memories of their lost loved one.

    D. The client's fears surrounding remembering the lost loved one were explored, addressed, and resolved using the story as an example.

    E. The client talked freely about the story "Petey's Journey Through Sadness," but was unwilling to express positive memories of their lost loved one; they were provided a tentative interpretation in this area.

INTELLECTUAL DISABILITY

CLIENT PRESENTATION

1. **Subaverage Intellectual Functioning (1)***

   A. The client has developed significant intellectual or cognitive deficits.

   B. The results from past intelligence testing revealed that the client's overall level of intellectual functioning lies in the mild intellectual developmental disorder range.

   C. The results from past intelligence testing revealed that the client's overall level of intelligence lies in the moderate intellectual developmental disorder range.

   D. The results from past intelligence testing revealed that the client's overall level of intelligence lies in the severe intellectual developmental disorder range.

   E. The results from past intelligence testing revealed that the client's overall level of intelligence lies in the borderline range of functioning.

2. **Speech/Language Delays (2)**

   A. The results from the past speech/language evaluation demonstrated that the client has developed significant speech/language deficits.

   B. The client's vocabulary and expressive language abilities are quite limited.

   C. The client often has difficulty understanding what is being said to them because of low receptive language skills.

   D. The client displayed noticeable speech articulation problems during today's therapy session.

   E. The client's speech articulation problems have improved through treatment.

3. **Poor Communication Skills (2)**

   A. The client has much difficulty communicating thoughts and feelings in an effective manner because of speech/language delays.

   B. The client had much difficulty expressing thoughts and feelings in today's therapy session.

   C. The client had difficulty comprehending what was being discussed in today's therapy session because of low receptive language abilities.

   D. The client was able to communicate thoughts and feelings in a simplistic but straightforward and effective manner in today's therapy session.

   E. The client has demonstrated improvements in the ability to identify and express basic thoughts and feelings.

4. **Inadequate Self-Care (2)**

   A. The parents or caregivers reported that the client's self-care skills are very low.

   B. The client has required a great deal of supervision when performing household chores or tasks at school.

---

*The numbers in parentheses correlate to the number of the Behavioral Definition statement in the companion chapter with the same title in the *Child Psychotherapy Treatment Planner*, Sixth Edition, by Jongsma, Peterson, McInnis, & Bruce (Wiley, 2023).

C. The client has recently started to perform simple chores at home.

D. The client has recently performed household chores or school responsibilities on a fairly consistent basis with prompting from caregivers.

5. Poor Personal Hygiene (2)

A. The parents or caregivers reported that the client's personal hygiene is often poor.

B. The client appeared unkempt during today's therapy session.

C. The client has a great deal of difficulty dressing independently even when clothes have been preselected for them.

D. The client appeared neatly groomed and attired during today's therapy session.

E. The client has recently been dressing independently.

6. Impaired Academic Functioning (2)

A. The client has performed significantly below their expected grade and age levels in all academic areas.

B. The client's academic performance has been commensurate with their overall level of intelligence.

C. The client has performed academically below their expected grade and age levels, even when considering the results from the past intellectual testing.

D. Academically, the client has performed above their expected levels, based on the results from the past intelligence testing.

7. Difficulty Following Instructions (3)

A. The client historically has had much difficulty comprehending and following instructions at home and school.

B. The parents and teachers reported that the client is capable of comprehending and following simple instructions but has trouble following through with multiple or complex instructions.

C. The teachers reported that the client is best able to follow instructions when they are presented in simple terms and are given one at a time.

D. The parents and teachers reported that the client has shown improvement in following simple instructions on a consistent basis.

8. Memory Impairment (4)

A. The results from past intellectual and cognitive assessments have shown that the client has developed significant short- and long-term memory impairments.

B. The client has often had difficulty retaining or recalling what has been said to them because of short-term memory deficits.

C. The client has had difficulty recalling significant past events because of long-term memory deficits.

D. The client had demonstrated improvements in everyday functioning by following a structured daily routine.

9. Concrete Thinking (5)

A. The client has much difficulty understanding psychological concepts because of their intellectual limitations and poor abstract reasoning abilities.

B. The client presented as very concrete in their thinking during today's therapy session.

C. The client's concrete thinking and poor abstract reasoning abilities have interfered with problem-solving abilities.

D. The client demonstrated an understanding of basic psychological terms or concepts during today's therapy session.

E. The parents report that the client has demonstrated improvement in the ability to resolve or manage everyday, routine problems by following specific, concrete steps that are outlined for them.

10. Poor Social Skills (6)

A. The client has developed poor social skills and frequently engages in immature or socially inappropriate behavior.

B. The client has often failed to pick up on important social cues or interpersonal nuances that are necessary to build and sustain meaningful relationships.

C. The client has started to develop the ability to differentiate between appropriate and inappropriate social behaviors.

D. The client displayed good social skills during today's therapy session.

11. Lack of Insight (7)

A. The client historically has shown very poor insight into the factors contributing to emotional, behavioral, or interpersonal problems.

B. The client demonstrated a lack of insight into the factors contributing to adjustment problems.

C. The client verbalized an awareness of the basic factors contributing to adjustment problems but had difficulty understanding the more complex factors.

12. Failure to Learn from Experience (7)

A. The client displayed a marked inability to learn from previous experiences or past mistakes because of intellectual limitations.

B. The parents or caregivers reported that the client repeatedly makes many of the same mistakes, without appearing to learn from their experiences.

C. Parents or caregivers reported that the client has started to show mild improvement in the ability to learn from past experiences or mistakes.

D. The client does not commit as many of the same mistakes when they are placed in a highly structured setting with an established routine.

13. Low Self-Esteem (8)

A. The client's intellectual limitations and learning problems have been a significant contributing factor to feelings of low self-esteem, inadequacy, and insecurity.

B. The client's low self-esteem has contributed to the hesitancy to try new tasks or make an effort at school.

C. The client verbalized self-derogatory remarks when discussing intellectual limitations or learning problems.

D. The client verbalized positive self-descriptive statements during today's therapy session.

E. The client has developed a healthy acceptance of intellectual and cognitive limitations as evidenced by the ability to consistently verbalize feelings of self-worth.

14. **Acting-Out Behaviors (9)**

    A. The client has demonstrated a persistent pattern of acting out when they become frustrated or upset because of intellectual limitations or learning problems.

    B. The client began to act in a silly and immature manner in today's therapy session when discussing intellectual limitations or learning problems.

    C. The client was helped to realize how they frequently begin to act out or engage in disruptive behaviors when frustrated or upset about not being able to perform a task.

    D. The client has started to seek help when frustrated about not being able to perform a task, instead of acting out or engaging in disruptive behaviors.

    E. The client has demonstrated a significant reduction in the frequency of acting-out or disruptive behaviors.

INTERVENTIONS IMPLEMENTED

1. **Establish Rapport (1)***

    A. Caring was conveyed to the client through support, warmth, and empathy.

    B. The client was provided with nonjudgmental support and a level of trust was developed.

    C. The client was urged to feel safe in expressing intellectual developmental disorder issues.

    D. The client began to express feelings more freely as rapport and trust level have increased.

    E. The client has continued to experience difficulty being open and direct about the expression of painful feelings; the client was encouraged to use the safe haven of therapy to express these difficult issues.

2. **Focus on Strengthening Therapeutic Relationship (2)**

    A. The relationship with the client was strengthened using empirically supported factors.

    B. The relationship with the client was strengthened through the implementation of collaborative approach, agreement on goals, demonstration of empathy, verbalization of positive regard, and collection of client feedback.

    C. The client reacted positively to the relationship-strengthening measures taken.

    D. The client verbalized feeling supported and understood during therapy sessions.

    E. Despite attempts to strengthen the therapeutic relationship, the client reports feeling distant and misunderstood.

    F. The client has indicated that sessions are not helpful and will be terminating therapy.

3. **Conduct Intellectual and Cognitive Assessment (3)**

    A. A comprehensive intellectual and cognitive assessment was conducted to determine the presence of intellectual developmental disorder and help gain greater insight into the client's learning strengths and weaknesses.

    B. The findings from the current intellectual and cognitive assessment revealed the presence of mild intellectual developmental disorder.

---

*The numbers in parentheses correlate to the number of the Therapeutic Intervention statement in the companion chapter with the same title in the *Child Psychotherapy Treatment Planner*, Sixth Edition, by Jongsma, Peterson, McInnis, & Bruce (Wiley, 2023).

C. The findings from the current intellectual and cognitive assessment revealed the presence of moderate intellectual developmental disorder.

D. The findings from the current intellectual and cognitive assessment revealed the presence of severe intellectual developmental disorder.

E. The findings from the current intellectual and cognitive assessment demonstrated that the client is currently functioning in the borderline range of intellectual abilities.

F. The results of the comprehensive intellectual and cognitive assessment were provided to the client and parents.

4. **Conduct Psychological Testing for Emotional/ADHD/ASD Factors (4)**

A. The client received a psychological evaluation to assess whether emotional factors. attention-deficit/hyperactivity disorder (ADHD), or autism spectrum disorder (ASD) are interfering with their intellectual functioning.

B. The findings from the psychological testing supported the presence of ADHD, which is interfering with the client's intellectual and academic functioning.

C. The findings from the psychological testing revealed the presence of serious emotional problems that are interfering with the client's intellectual and academic functioning.

D. The findings from the psychological testing supported the presence of ASD, which is interfering with the client's intellectual and academic functioning.

E. The findings from the evaluation did not support the presence of ADHD or ASD that could be interfering with the client's intellectual and academic functioning.

F. The findings from the psychological testing did not reveal any serious emotional problems that could be interfering with the client's intellectual and academic functioning.

G. The results of the psychological testing were provided for the client and parents.

5. **Refer for Neurological Examination/Neuropsychological Testing (5)**

A. The client was referred for a neurological examination and neuropsychological testing to rule out possible organic factors that may be contributing to the client's intellectual or cognitive deficits.

B. The findings from the neuropsychological evaluation revealed organic factors that may be contributing to the client's intellectual or cognitive deficits.

C. The findings from the neuropsychological evaluation did not reveal any organic factors that may be contributing to the client's intellectual or cognitive deficits.

D. The results of the neurological examination and neuropsychological testing were interpreted to the client and parents.

6. **Refer for Physical/Occupational Therapy (6)**

A. The client was referred to physical and occupational therapists to assess for the presence of perceptual or sensory-motor deficits and determine the need for ongoing physical and/or occupational therapy.

B. The evaluation revealed significant perceptual or sensory-motor deficits and the need for ongoing physical and/or occupational therapy.

C. The evaluation did not reveal any significant perceptual or sensory-motor deficits or the need for ongoing physical and/or occupational therapy.

D. The physical/occupational therapy assessment was reviewed with the client and parents.

7. **Refer for Speech/Language Evaluation (7)**
   A. The client was referred for a comprehensive speech/language evaluation to assess possible deficits in this area and determine the need for speech/language therapy.
   B. The comprehensive speech/language evaluation revealed a communication impairment and supported the need for speech/language therapy.
   C. The comprehensive speech/language evaluation did not reveal a communication impairment or the need for ongoing speech/language therapy.
   D. The results of the speech and language evaluation were interpreted to the client and parents.

8. **Assess Level of Insight (8)**
   A. The client's level of insight toward the presenting problems was assessed.
   B. The client was assessed in regard to the syntonic versus dystonic nature of their insight about the presenting problems.
   C. The client was noted to demonstrate good insight into the problematic nature of the behavior and symptoms.
   D. The client was noted to be in agreement with others' concerns and is motivated to work on change.
   E. The client was noted to be ambivalent regarding the problems described and is reluctant to address the issues as a concern.
   F. The client was noted to be resistant regarding acknowledgment of the problem areas, is not concerned about them, and has no motivation to make changes.

9. **Assess for Correlated Disorders (9)**
   A. The client was assessed for evidence of research-based correlated disorders.
   B. The client was assessed in regard to the level of vulnerability to suicide.
   C. The client was identified as having a comorbid disorder, and treatment was adjusted to account for these concerns.
   D. The client has been assessed for any correlated disorders, but none were found.

10. **Assess for Culturally Based Confounding Issues (10)**
    A. The client was assessed for age-related issues that could help to better understand their clinical presentation.
    B. The client was assessed for gender-related issues that could help to better understand their clinical presentation.
    C. The client was assessed for cultural syndromes, cultural idioms of distress, or culturally based perceived causes that could help to better understand their clinical presentation.
    D. Alternative factors have been identified as contributing to the client's currently defined "problem behavior," and these were taken into account in regard to their treatment.
    E. Culturally based factors that could help to account for the client's currently defined "problem behavior" were investigated, but no significant factors were identified.

11. **Assess Severity of Impairment (11)**
    A. The severity of the client's impairment was assessed to determine the appropriate level of care.

B. The client was assessed in regard to impairment in social, relational, and educational endeavors.

C. It was reflected to the client that the impairment appears to create mild to moderate effects on the client's functioning.

D. It was reflected to the client that the impairment appears to create severe to very severe effects on the client's functioning.

E. The client was continuously assessed for the severity of impairment, as well as the efficacy and appropriateness of treatment.

12. Assess for Pathogenic Care (12)

A. The home, school, and community of the client were assessed for pathogenic care and concerns.

B. The client's various environments were assessed for the persistent disregard of the child's needs, repeated changes in caregivers, limited opportunities for stable attachment, harsh discipline, or other grossly inept care.

C. Pathogenic care was identified and the treatment plan included strategies for managing or correcting these concerns and protecting the child.

D. No pathogenic care was identified, and this was reflected to the client and caregivers.

13. Attend an Individualized Educational Planning Committee (IEPC) Meeting (13)

A. An Individualized Educational Planning Committee meeting was held to determine the client's eligibility for special education services, design educational interventions, and establish goals.

B. The decision was made at the IEPC meeting that the client is eligible to receive special education services because of intellectual or academic deficits.

C. The decision was made at the IEPC meeting that the client is not eligible to receive special education services.

D. A consultation was held with the client's parents, teachers, and other appropriate professionals about designing educational interventions to help the client achieve their academic goals.

E. The client's academic goals were identified at the IEPC meeting.

14. Design Effective Teaching Programs (14)

A. Consultation was held with the client, parents, teacher, and other appropriate school officials about designing effective teaching programs or interventions that build on the client's strengths and compensate for weaknesses.

B. The client's learning strengths and weaknesses were identified in the consultation meeting with the client, parents, teachers, and other appropriate school officials.

C. Consultation was held with the client, parents, teachers, and other appropriate school officials about ways to maximize the client's learning strengths.

D. Consultation was held with the client, parents, teachers, and other appropriate school officials about ways to compensate for the client's learning weaknesses.

15. Process Placement Outside the Home (15)

A. Consultation was held with the client's parents, school officials, or mental health professionals about the need for placement in a foster home, group home, or residential program.

B. After consulting with the client's parents, school officials, or mental health professionals, the recommendation was made that the client should be placed in a foster home.

C. The recommendation was made that the client be placed in a group home or residential program to address their intellectual, academic, social, and emotional needs.

D. Placement of the client in a foster home, group home, or residential program was not recommended during the consultation meeting with parents, school officials, or mental health professionals.

16. Encourage Communication Between Home and School (16)

A. The parents, teachers, and school officials were encouraged to maintain regular communication with each other via phone calls or written notes regarding the client's academic, behavioral, emotional, and social progress.

B. Consultation with the teachers and school officials emphasized sending home daily or weekly progress notes informing the parents of the client's academic, behavioral, emotional, and social progress.

C. The client was informed of their responsibility to bring home daily or weekly progress notes, allowing for regular communication between parents and teachers.

D. The parents were helped to identify the consequences for the client's failure to bring home the daily or weekly progress notes from school.

17. Design Token Economy (17)

A. A token economy was designed for use in the classroom to improve the client's on-task behaviors, academic performance, impulse control, and social skills.

B. A token economy was designed for use in the residential program to improve the client's on-task behaviors, academic performance, impulse control, and social skills.

C. The client, parents, and teachers agreed to the conditions outlined in the token economy and pledged to follow through with the implementation of the program.

D. The conditions of the token economy were explained to the client in terms that they could understand.

18. Conduct Filial Therapy (18)

A. The parents were educated in the filial therapy approach and the possible benefits for the client of their involvement.

B. The client was encouraged in filial therapy sessions to express thoughts and feelings, and parents were coached to respond empathically.

C. The client openly expressed feelings, and parents responded appropriately with empathic statements.

D. The active participation of the client and parents in filial therapy sessions has resulted in increased awareness of the client's thoughts and feelings and a strengthening of the parent–child bond.

19. Praise Positive Behavior (19)

A. The parents were encouraged to provide frequent praise and positive reinforcement for the client's positive social behaviors and academic successes.

B. Positive feedback was provided as the parents praised the client's positive social behaviors and academic performance during today's therapy session.

C. The parents were assisted in identifying opportunities to praise the client's positive social behaviors and academic successes.

D. The client was strongly encouraged to engage in positive social behaviors and work hard to achieve academic goals to receive parents' approval and affirmation.

E. The client's parents have not used encouragement and praise for the client's positive social behaviors and academic successes and were redirected to do so.

20. **Utilize Reward System to Improve Prosocial Behaviors (20)**

A. The client and parents were assisted in identifying a list of rewards to be used to improve the client's adaptive and prosocial behaviors.

B. A reward system was designed to help improve the client's adaptive and prosocial behaviors.

C. The parents reported that the reward system has led to the desired improvements with the client's adaptive and prosocial behaviors and were encouraged to continue the reward system.

D. The parents were directed to use the reward system in the "Activities of Daily Living" program from the *Child Psychotherapy Homework Planner* (Jongsma, Peterson, McInnis, & Bruce) to improve the client's adaptive and prosocial behaviors.

E. The parents were strongly encouraged to praise and reinforce the client for improvements in adaptive and prosocial behaviors.

F. The parents reported that the "Activities of Daily Living" program has helped to improve the client's adaptive and prosocial behaviors.

G. The parents reported that the client has demonstrated little improvement in adaptive and prosocial behaviors since using the "Activities of Daily Living" program.

21. **Educate Parents About Intellectual Development Disorder (21)**

A. The client's parents were educated about the symptoms of intellectual development disorder.

B. The therapy session helped the client's parents gain a greater understanding of the symptoms and characteristics of intellectual development disorder.

C. The parents were given the opportunity to express their thoughts and feelings about raising a child with intellectual development disorder.

D. The parents were given support in verbalizing their feelings of sadness, hurt, anger, or disappointment about having a child with intellectual development disorder.

E. The parents were provided with resources, such as "Intellectual Disability" at the Center for Parent Information and Resources (www.parentcenterhub.org).

22. **Assess and Confront Parents' Denial of Client's Intellectual Deficits (22)**

A. A family-therapy session was held to assess the parents' denial surrounding the client's intellectual deficits.

B. The parents' denial about the client's intellectual deficits was confronted and challenged so that they will begin to cooperate with the recommendations regarding placement and educational interventions.

C. The therapy session was helpful in working through the parents' denial surrounding the client's intellectual deficits, and they agreed to follow through with recommendations regarding placement and educational interventions.

D. The parents have remained in denial about the client's intellectual deficits and are opposed to following through with the recommendations regarding placement and educational interventions.

23. Assess Excessive Parental Pressure (23)

A. A family-therapy session was held to assess whether the parents are placing excessive pressure on the client to function at a level that they are not capable of achieving.

B. The parents were asked to verbalize their expectations of the client's level of capabilities.

24. Confront Excessive Parental Pressure (24)

A. The parents were confronted and challenged about placing excessive pressure on the client to function at a level that they are not capable of achieving.

B. The parents acknowledged that they have placed unrealistic expectations and/or excessive pressure on the client to function at a level that they are not capable of achieving; this insight was reinforced.

C. The parents were reinforced as they agreed to cease placing excessive pressure on the client to perform at unrealistic levels.

D. The parents expressed resistance to the idea that they are placing excessive pressure on the client to function at unrealistic levels and were provided with specific examples of these pressures.

25. Assess Parental Overprotectiveness (25)

A. The parent-child interactions were observed in today's therapy session to assess whether the parent's overprotectiveness or infantilization of the client interferes with the client's intellectual, emotional, or social development.

B. The client and parents were given a task to perform in today's therapy session to assess whether the parents are overprotective of the client.

C. Active listening skills were used as the parents acknowledged that their pattern of overprotectiveness has interfered with the client's intellectual, emotional, and social development.

D. The therapy session was helpful in identifying various ways that the parents are overprotective of the client, and/or interfere with the client's intellectual, emotional, and social development.

E. The parents were recommended portions of the book *Life Skills Activities for Special Children* (Mannix).

F. The parents became defensive in today's therapy session when discussing their pattern of overprotectiveness.

26. Help Parents Develop Realistic Parental Expectations (26)

A. Today's therapy session focused on helping the parents or caregivers develop realistic expectations of the client's intellectual capabilities and level of adaptive functioning.

B. The parents and caregivers were recommended to read *Steps to Independence: Teaching Everyday Skills to Children with Special Needs* (Baker & Brightman).

C. The parents or caregivers were assisted in identifying a number of tasks that the client is capable of performing.

D. The therapy session helped the parents or caregivers identify several tasks that the client is not able to perform because of intellectual deficits and level of adaptive functioning.

E. The parents or caregivers were instructed to provide supervision initially on tasks that they are not sure that the client is capable of performing.

F. It was noted that the parents or caregivers have developed a good understanding of the client's intellectual capabilities and level of adaptive functioning.

G. The parents and caregivers have continued to have unrealistic expectations for the client and were redirected in this area.

27. Include Client in Family Outings (27)

A. The parents and family members were strongly encouraged to include the client in outings or activities on a regular basis.

B. A family-therapy session was held to explore the family member's resistance or objections to including the client in some outings or activities.

C. Positive feedback was provided as the parents and family members pledged to include the client in regular family outings or activities.

D. The client and family members were assisted in identifying a list of outings or activities that they would enjoy doing together.

E. The parents and family members were confronted about their failure to include the client in many outings or activities.

28. Assign Observation of Positive Behavior (28)

A. The parents and family members were instructed to observe and record positive behaviors by the client between therapy sessions.

B. The parents were encouraged to praise and reinforce the client for engaging in the positive behavior.

C. The client was praised in today's therapy session for positive behavior.

D. The client was strongly encouraged to continue to engage in the positive behavior to help improve self-esteem, gain parents' approval, and receive affirmation from others.

29. Assign Routine Tasks (29)

A. The client was placed in charge of a routine or basic task at home to increase feelings of self-worth within the family.

B. The parents were assigned the exercise "A Sense of Belonging" from the *Child Psychotherapy Homework Planner* by Jongsma, Peterson, McInnis, & Bruce.

C. A reward system was designed to reinforce the client for following through and completing their routine or basic task at home.

D. The client was placed in charge of another routine or basic task (appropriate to their level of adaptive functioning) after showing they could be responsible in performing the earlier assigned task.

E. Today's therapy session explored the reasons why the client did not follow through and complete the routine or basic task that was assigned to them.

30. Complete Kinetic Drawing (30)

A. The client was asked to complete a family kinetic drawing to assess how they perceive their role or place in the family system.

B. The client's perception of their role or place in the family was processed within a family session.

C. The family was open to understanding the client's perception of their role or place in the family, and their discussion was encouraged.

31. Encourage School/Residential Job Assignment (31)

A. Consultation was held with school officials about assigning a job to help build the client's self-esteem and provide them with a sense of responsibility.

B. Consultation was held with the staff at the residential program about assigning a job to help build the client's self-esteem and provide them with a sense of responsibility.

C. The client was given much praise in today's therapy session for being responsible in performing their job at school.

D. The client was given much praise in today's therapy session for being responsible in performing their job at the residential program.

E. Today's therapy session explored the reasons for the client's failure to comply with performing their job at school or the residential program.

32. Establish Allowance/Finance Management (32)

A. The parents were assisted in establishing an allowance plan to increase the client's responsibilities at home and help them learn simple money management skills.

B. The client and parents were directed to establish a budget whereby a certain percentage of the client's allowance money goes for both savings and spending.

C. The parents were encouraged to consult with schoolteachers about teaching the client basic money management skills.

D. The parents reported that the allowance plan has been successful in increasing the client's responsibilities around the home and teaching them simple money management skills.

E. The parents reported that, unfortunately, the allowance plan has not motivated the client to perform household chores or responsibilities on a consistent basis.

33. Utilize Reward System to Improve Personal Hygiene (33)

A. The client and parents were assisted in identifying a list of rewards to be used to improve the client's personal hygiene and self-help skills.

B. A reward system was designed to help improve the client's personal hygiene and self-help skills.

C. The parents reported that the reward system has led to the desired improvements with the client's personal hygiene and self-help skills and were encouraged to continue the reward system.

D. The parents were directed to use the reward system in the "Activities of Daily Living" program from the *Child Psychotherapy Homework Planner* (Jongsma, Peterson, McInnis, & Bruce) to improve the client's personal hygiene and self-care skills.

E. The parents were strongly encouraged to praise and reinforce the client for improvements in their personal hygiene and self-care skills.

F. The parents reported that the "Activities of Daily Living" program has helped to improve the client's personal hygiene and self-care skills.

G. The parents reported that the client has demonstrated little improvement in personal hygiene and self-care skills since utilizing the "Activities of Daily Living" program.

34. Teach Behavior Management Techniques (34)

A. The parents were taught effective behavior management techniques to decrease the frequency and severity of the client's temper outbursts, acting out, and aggressive behaviors.

B. The parents were encouraged to use techniques such as time-outs and removal of privileges to manage the client's behavior.

C. The parents reported effective use of behavioral management techniques to decrease the frequency and severity of the client's temper outbursts, acting out, and aggressive behaviors, and were provided with positive feedback.

D. The parents have not used the behavioral management techniques for the client's behaviors and were assisted in addressing barriers.

35. Utilize Natural Consequences (35)

A. The parents were instructed to use natural, logical consequences to help decrease the frequency and severity of the client's temper outbursts, acting out, and aggressive behaviors.

B. The parents were helped to identify natural, logical consequences for a variety of socially inappropriate or maladaptive behaviors.

C. The parents were trained in the use of time-out to manage the client's temper outbursts and aggressive behaviors.

D. The parents were instructed to remove privileges if the client engages in specific acting-out or aggressive behaviors.

E. The parents were challenged to follow through consistently with limits when the client displays temper outbursts, aggression, or acting-out behaviors.

F. The parents reported improvements in the client's behavior since they began consistently using time-outs and removal of privileges to deal with the client's temper outbursts, acting out, and aggressive behaviors; they were encouraged to continue this pattern and to consistently use positive reinforcement to strengthen adaptive behavior.

G. The parents have not used the behavior management techniques to help decrease the frequency and severity of the client's temper outbursts, acting out, and aggressive behaviors and were redirected to do so.

36. Teach Mediational/Self-Control Strategies (36)

A. The client was taught basic mediational and self-control strategies to help delay the need for immediate gratification and to inhibit impulses.

B. The parents were encouraged to establish a routine schedule for the client so that they postpone recreational or leisure activities until after completing homework or household responsibilities.

C. The client was encouraged to use active listening skills and talk with significant others before making quick, hasty decisions about important matters or acting out without considering the consequences of their actions.

D. The client was helped to develop an action plan that outlined specific, concrete steps that they could take to achieve identified long-term goals.

E. The client was helped to see the benefits of delaying the immediate need for gratification to achieve a longer-term goal.

F. The client has not used the mediational/self-control strategy of delaying the immediate gratification and was redirected to do so.

37. **Teach Guided Imagery/Relaxation (37)**

A. The client was trained in the use of guided imagery or deep-muscle relaxation techniques to help self-calm and improve anger control.

B. The client and parents were taught techniques from the *Relaxation and Stress Reduction Workbook for Kids* (Shapiro & Sprague).

C. The client and parents reported that the use of guided imagery and deep-muscle relaxation techniques has helped the client to self-calm and control anger more effectively.

D. The client and parents reported little to no improvement with the use of guided imagery and deep-muscle relaxation techniques to help the client self-calm and control anger.

E. The client failed to use the guided imagery and deep-muscle relaxation techniques to help them control anger and was redirected to do so.

38. **Teach/Reinforce Positive Social Skills (38)**

A. Role-play and modeling techniques were used to teach the client positive social behaviors.

B. The client was assigned the "Social Skills Exercise" and/or "Show Your Strengths" from the *Child Psychotherapy Homework Planner* by Jongsma, Peterson, McInnis, & Bruce.

C. A reward system was developed to reinforce specific positive social behaviors.

D. The parents were strongly encouraged to look for opportunities to praise and reinforce any emerging positive social behaviors.

E. The client was praised for the ability to correctly identify several positive social skills after engaging in the role-play or modeling exercises.

F. The client was instructed to practice newly learned social skills that were taught to them through role-playing, modeling, and mutual storytelling.

39. **Educate Client About Emotions (39)**

A. The client was helped to identify and label different emotions in today's therapy session.

B. Client-centered therapy principles were used to help the client identify and express emotions.

C. The parents were encouraged to reflect the client's feelings at home to help them express feelings more effectively.

D. The client has demonstrated improvements in the ability to identify and express basic emotions since the onset of therapy.

E. The client has continued to have difficulty identifying and labeling basic emotions and was provided with additional assistance in this area.

40. Express Emotions Through Art (40)

A. The client was instructed in today's therapy session to first draw faces of basic emotions and then was asked to share various times when they had experienced the different emotions.

B. The art therapy technique helped the client to identify and express different emotions.

C. An art therapy technique was employed, but the client had difficulty sharing times when they had experienced the different emotions in the past.

41. Teach Communication Skills (41)

A. The client was taught basic communication skills to improve the ability to express thoughts, feelings, and needs more clearly.

B. Role-playing, modeling, and behavioral rehearsal techniques were used to teach the client effective ways to express thoughts, feelings, and needs.

C. The client was taught the importance of displaying proper listening and maintaining good eye contact when communicating thoughts and feelings with others.

D. The client was taught to use "I messages" to communicate thoughts, feelings, and needs more clearly.

42. Model Appropriate Expression of Emotions (42)

A. The use of puppets, dolls, and stuffed animals was employed to model socially appropriate ways of expressing emotions or relating to others.

B. The therapist created a story that modeled socially appropriate ways of expressing emotions or relating to others.

C. The client created a story through the use of puppets, dolls, and stuffed animals that showed understanding of socially appropriate ways of expressing emotions or relating to others.

43. Use Feelings Poster (43)

A. The Feelings Poster (available from Childswork/Childsplay, LLC) was used to help the client identify and express basic emotions.

B. The parents were encouraged to use the Feelings Poster at home to help the client identify and express basic emotions.

C. The parents were encouraged to use the Feelings Poster at home when the client starts to become agitated or angry to help prevent an outburst.

D. The parents report that the Feelings Poster has helped the client identify and express basic emotions, and they were encouraged to continue to use this technique.

E. Use of the Feelings Poster has produced little to no improvement in the client's ability to identify and express feelings.

44. Promote Acceptance of Intellectual Limits (44)

A. The client was helped to gain greater understanding and acceptance of the limitations surrounding intellectual deficits and adaptive functioning.

B. A client-centered therapy approach was employed to reflect the client's feelings and move toward a greater acceptance of the limitations surrounding intellectual deficits and adaptive functioning.

C. The client was helped to identify their unique strengths or interests as well as individual weaknesses.

D. The client's self-worth was affirmed to help them come to a greater acceptance of the limitations surrounding intellectual deficits and adaptive functioning.

45. Explore for Depression and Insecurity (45)

A. Today's therapy session explored the underlying feelings of depression, anxiety, and insecurity related to the client's intellectual limitations.

B. The client was provided with support and unconditional positive regard as they worked through feelings of depression, anxiety, and insecurity related to their cognitive or intellectual limitations.

C. The client was strongly encouraged to use their unique strengths and engage in activities of interest to help cope with or offset feelings of depression, anxiety, and insecurity related to cognitive or intellectual limitations.

D. Positive feedback was provided to the parents for their support and affirmation of the client's self-worth.

46. Encourage Participation in Special Olympics (46)

A. The client was encouraged to participate in the Special Olympics to help build self-esteem.

B. The client and parents followed through with the recommendation to enroll the client in the Special Olympics.

C. The client expressed happiness about their participation and experiences in the Special Olympics; the experiences were reviewed.

D. The client and parents failed to follow through with the recommendation that the client participate in the Special Olympics and were redirected to do so.

47. Identify Components of Goal Accomplishment (47)

A. Today's therapy session identified periods of time when the client achieved success or accomplished a goal.

B. Today's therapy session was helpful in identifying the positive steps that the client took to successfully accomplish goals in the past.

C. The client was strongly encouraged to take steps similar to those that they had successfully taken in the past to accomplish present goals.

D. The therapy session revealed that the client achieved past success during periods of time when they received strong family support.

48. Express Loss Fears Through Art (48)

A. Art therapy techniques were utilized to help the client identify and verbalize feelings related to issues of loss, separation, or abandonment by parental figures or key staff figures in residential programs.

B. The client was instructed to draw a picture reflecting feelings about past losses, separations, or abandonment.

C. The client's artwork was interpreted as reflecting feelings of sadness about past losses or separations.

D. The client's artwork was interpreted, but did not provide any insight into feelings about past losses, separations, or abandonment.

LOW SELF-ESTEEM

CLIENT PRESENTATION

1. **Self-Disparaging Remarks (1)***
   A. The client's deep sense of inferiority was reflected in frequent self-disparaging remarks about their appearance, worth, and abilities.
   B. The lack of any eye contact on the client's part and negative self-remarks are evidence of how little the client thinks of self.
   C. The client reported feeling inferior to others and generally believes that they are a loser.
   D. The client has stopped making self-critical remarks and even has begun to acknowledge some positive traits and successes.

2. **Takes Blame Easily (2)**
   A. The client often explains their problems as being due to their own negative behavior.
   B. The client often takes responsibility for others' problems.
   C. The client has begun to make connections between low self-esteem and a tendency to take blame too easily.
   D. The client has been able to develop an appropriate level of personal responsibility.

3. **Lack of Accepting Compliments (3)**
   A. The client acknowledged their problem of not believing others when they say nice or complimentary things.
   B. The parents reported that the client discounts any praise from them or others.
   C. The client reported never hearing compliments from parents, so now they are unsure how to respond to accolades from anyone.
   D. The client has now begun to accept compliments at face value, feeling uncomfortable but good when these instances occur.

4. **Refusal to Try New Experiences (4)**
   A. The client's pervasive failure expectation was reflected in refusal to try new experiences.
   B. The client reported being frustrated with the pattern of never trying any new experiences.
   C. The client listed many experiences in which they experienced failure, but their perception was often slanted and distorted.
   D. The client expressed that failure is their greatest fear.
   E. The client has begun to take a few risks and try new experiences with encouragement and support.

---

*The numbers in parentheses correlate to the number of the Behavioral Definition statement in the companion chapter with the same title in the *Child Psychotherapy Treatment Planner*, Sixth Edition, by Jongsma, Peterson, McInnis, & Bruce (Wiley, 2023).

5. Avoidant/Quiet (5)

A. The client presented in a quiet, avoidant manner.

B. The client reported that they avoid more than brief contact with others and usually have little to say in social situations with peers.

C. The parents reported that the client has always been shy with adults and peers.

D. The client has gradually started to withdraw less and is feeling less tense around others.

6. Cautious/Fearful (5)

A. The client presented with a frightened affect and a very cautious manner.

B. From the earliest times the client can remember, others have always frightened them, and they always have been cautious not to upset anyone.

C. The client indicated that they are cautious and fearful of doing something wrong in social situations.

D. The client has started to be less cautious and now takes some carefully chosen social risks.

7. Pleasing/Friendly (6)

A. The client presented in a friendly, outgoing manner and seems eager to please others.

B. Everything was carefully checked out by the client to make sure what they are doing or saying is right or acceptable to others.

C. Past actions done to please others have gotten the client in trouble or left them feeling taken advantage of.

D. A noticeable decrease in the client's pleasing behaviors was observed as they are now starting to offer thoughts and opinions more assertively.

8. Inability to Accept/Recognize Positive Traits (7)

A. The client denied having any talents or positive attributes that others would admire.

B. The client struggled to identify any positive traits or talents about self.

C. The client rejected all the identified positive traits pointed out to them by others.

D. The client was able to recognize and accept positive things about self.

9. Insecure/Anxious (8)

A. There was visible insecurity and anxiousness to the client's affect and manner.

B. The client described several instances in which they did not say or do anything in front of peers because of fear of ridicule and rejection.

C. The client reported feeling anxious and insecure at home and in all social/peer situations, often believing that others may not like them.

D. As the session progressed, the client became less anxious and more able to open up to the therapist.

E. The client reported feeling more self-confident when in the presence of peers.

10. Attention-Seeking Behavior (9)

A. The client has often engaged in attention-seeking behavior to gain the acceptance of peers.

B. The client identified that they found it easier to feel accepted by peers when they engaged in negative behavior.

C. The client indicated that they have done various "bad acts" to gain the attention and acceptance of peers.

D. The client has dropped most of their attention-seeking behavior and has begun to work on self-acceptance.

11. **Difficulty Saying "No" (10)**

A. The client indicated they rarely say "no" to others out of fear of not being liked.

B. The client reported believing that they will not be liked unless they say "yes."

C. The client identified the paralyzing fear they experience when saying "no" to others.

D. The client has worked on starting to say "no" to others to be more true to their real beliefs, values, feelings, or thoughts.

12. **History of Adverse Childhood Experiences (11)**

A. The client has an identified history of multiple adverse childhood experiences.

B. The client has identified the symptoms they experience related to adverse childhood experiences.

C. The client has been involved in processing their history of adverse childhood experiences.

D. The client has experienced relief from symptoms related to adverse childhood experiences.

INTERVENTIONS IMPLEMENTED

1. **Establish Rapport (1)***

A. Caring was conveyed to the client through support, warmth, and empathy.

B. The client was provided with nonjudgmental support, and a level of trust was developed.

C. The client was urged to feel safe in expressing low self-esteem experiences.

D. The client began to express feelings more freely as rapport and trust level have increased.

E. The client has continued to experience difficulty being open and direct about the expression of painful feelings; the client was encouraged to use the safe haven of therapy to express these difficult issues.

2. **Focus on Strengthening Therapeutic Relationship (2)**

A. The relationship with the client was strengthened using empirically supported factors.

B. The relationship with the client was strengthened through the implementation of collaborative approach, agreement on goals, demonstration of empathy, verbalization of positive regard, and collection of client feedback.

C. The client reacted positively to the relationship-strengthening measures taken.

D. The client verbalized feeling supported and understood during therapy sessions.

---

*The numbers in parentheses correlate to the number of the Therapeutic Intervention statement in the companion chapter with the same title in the *Child Psychotherapy Treatment Planner*, Sixth Edition, by Jongsma, Peterson, McInnis, & Bruce (Wiley, 2023).

E. Despite attempts to strengthen the therapeutic relationship, the client reports feeling distant and misunderstood.

F. The client has indicated that sessions are not helpful and will be terminating therapy.

3. **Assess Self-Disparaging Comments (3)**

A. The client and parents were interviewed to assess the client's pattern of verbalization and other behaviors that are self-disparaging.

B. It was reflected that the client's comments and behaviors display a lack of self-confidence.

C. Information was collected on the types of behaviors and comments that the client makes that are self-disparaging and display a lack of self-confidence.

4. **Implement Psychoanalytic Play Therapy (4)**

A. A psychoanalytic play therapy approach was used that allowed the client to take the lead and explore unconscious conflicts and fixations.

B. A psychoanalytic play therapy approach was employed to establish trust with the client and assist them in letting go of negative thoughts, beliefs, and fears.

C. The client has been cooperative, but hesitant to build trust with the therapist or to take the lead in exploring unconscious conflicts or fixations; the client was encouraged to be more open.

D. Psychoanalytic play therapy approaches have helped the client build a level of trust with the therapist and begin to let go of negative thoughts, beliefs, and fears.

E. Despite the use of psychoanalytic play therapy techniques, the client has not been able to build a level of trust with the therapist.

5. **Use Puppets to Build Self-Esteem (5)**

A. Puppets were employed to assist the client in starting conversations and making friends to help build self-esteem.

B. Puppets were used to give the client practice in asking for things that they need.

C. Puppets were used in a nondirect way to allow the client to create their own scenes for building a more positive sense of self-esteem.

D. Use of puppets has helped the client learn skills to raise self-esteem and confidence.

E. Despite the use of puppets to help build self-esteem, the client has not increased skills in this area.

6. **Use Expressive Clay Technique (6)**

A. An expressive clay technique was used to assist the client in expressing and communicating issues and to facilitate increasing self-esteem.

B. The client was supported as they actively worked with clay to increase the ability to express and communicate issues.

C. The client's work with clay has facilitated the ability to express and communicate issues as well as increase self-esteem; the benefits of this progress were reviewed.

D. The client struggled with working with the clay and, despite assistance, was not able to express or communicate their issues.

7. Assess Level of Insight (7)

A. The client's level of insight toward the presenting problems was assessed.

B. The client was assessed in regard to the syntonic versus dystonic nature of their insight about the presenting problems.

C. The client was noted to demonstrate good insight into the problematic nature of the behavior and symptoms.

D. The client was noted to be in agreement with others' concerns and is motivated to work on change.

E. The client was noted to be ambivalent regarding the problems described and is reluctant to address the issues as a concern.

F. The client was noted to be resistant regarding acknowledgment of the problem areas, is not concerned about them, and has no motivation to make changes.

8. Assess for Correlated Disorders (8)

A. The client was assessed for evidence of research-based correlated disorders.

B. The client was assessed in regard to the level of vulnerability to suicide.

C. The client was identified as having a comorbid disorder, and treatment was adjusted to account for these concerns.

D. The client has been assessed for any correlated disorders, but none were found.

9. Assess for Culturally Based Confounding Issues (9)

A. The client was assessed for age-related issues that could help to better understand their clinical presentation.

B. The client was assessed for gender-related issues that could help to better understand their clinical presentation.

C. The client was assessed for cultural syndromes, cultural idioms of distress, or culturally based perceived causes that could help to better understand their clinical presentation.

D. Alternative factors have been identified as contributing to the client's currently defined "problem behavior," and these were taken into account in regard to treatment.

E. Culturally based factors that could help to account for the client's currently defined "problem behavior" were investigated, but no significant factors were identified.

10. Assess Severity of Impairment (10)

A. The severity of the client's impairment was assessed to determine the appropriate level of care.

B. The client was assessed in regard to impairment in social, relational, and educational endeavors.

C. It was reflected to the client that the impairment appears to create mild to moderate effects on the client's functioning.

D. It was reflected to the client that the impairment appears to create severe to very severe effects on the client's functioning.

E. The client was continuously assessed for the severity of impairment, as well as the efficacy and appropriateness of treatment.

11. **Assess for Pathogenic Care (11)**
    A. The home, school, and community of the client were assessed for pathogenic care and concerns.
    B. The client's various environments were assessed for the persistent disregard of the child's needs, repeated changes in caregivers, limited opportunities for stable attachment, harsh discipline, or other grossly inept care.
    C. Pathogenic care was identified and the treatment plan included strategies for managing or correcting these concerns and protecting the child.
    D. No pathogenic care was identified and this was reflected to the client and caregivers.

12. **Confront/Reframe Self-Disparaging Remarks (12)**
    A. The client's self-disparaging comments were confronted with the strong message that these comments were not an accurate reflection of reality.
    B. The client's self-disparaging comments were realistically reframed and given to the client to replace the negative comments.
    C. The client reported being more aware of their tendency to make self-disparaging remarks and has been more successful at reducing the frequency of this behavior; the client was encouraged to continue this progress.

13. **Explore How Negative Feelings Are Acted Out (13)**
    A. The client was asked to construct a list of ways that they see self expressing or acting out negative feelings about self.
    B. The client's self-awareness was increased by exploring how they express or act out negative feelings about self and how they could stop this habit.
    C. It was consistently pointed out to the client in a warm, respectful manner when they were projecting a negative self-image.

14. **Refer for Group Therapy (14)**
    A. The client was referred to group therapy that is focused on building self-esteem.
    B. Progress reports reflected that the client is actively taking part in group therapy and is slowly building some self-confidence.
    C. The client's fear of social interaction was given as a reason for refusal to attend group therapy; the client was redirected to attend the group.

15. **Identify Parents' Critical Interactions (15)**
    A. In family sessions, critical interaction patterns were identified with the family and redirected to supportive, affirming interaction patterns.
    B. A videotape of the family session was used to illustrate critical family interaction patterns.
    C. Negative parenting methods were discussed with the parents, and new affirming methods were recommended.
    D. The parents were supported as they have become more aware of their disparaging parenting methods and reported implementation of more affirming child-guidance techniques.

16. **Record Positive Aspects of Self (16)**
    A. The client was asked to identify one positive thing about self and record it in a journal.
    B. The client was assigned the exercise "Positive Self-Statements" from the *Child Psychotherapy Homework Planner* (Jongsma, Peterson, McInnis, & Bruce).

C. The client's journal was reviewed and positive traits or accomplishments were identified, affirmed, and supported.

D. The client reported feeling more positively about self and is more aware of their positive traits.

E. The client has not recorded positive aspects of self and was assisted in identifying and ameliorating barriers to this task.

17. Develop Positive Self-Talk (17)

A. Positive self-talk techniques were taught to the client to assist in boosting confidence and self-image.

B. Role-play was used to practice positive self-talk techniques.

C. A commitment was elicited from the client to employ positive self-talk on a daily basis.

D. The positive self-talk technique has been noted to be effective in increasing the client's self-esteem.

18. Develop Affirmations List (18)

A. The client was assisted in developing a list of positive affirmations for self.

B. A commitment was elicited from the client to read the affirmation list three times.

C. The client was assigned "Symbols of Self-Worth" from the *Child Psychotherapy Homework Planner* (Jongsma, Peterson, McInnis, & Bruce).

D. The client reported that regular reading of the self-affirmation list was beneficial in building self-esteem.

E. The client has not regularly used positive affirmations and was redirected to do so.

19. Use Helping, Caring, and Sharing Ball (19)

A. A Helping, Caring, and Sharing Ball (Childswork/Childsplay) was used to help the client identify and affirm positive things about self.

B. The positive things about the client that were identified through the use of the Helping, Caring, and Sharing Ball were verbally reinforced.

C. The client's statements that discounted the positive traits were confronted and the positive traits were verbally reaffirmed to them.

D. The client's identification of positive traits through the use of the Helping, Caring, and Sharing Ball has increased self-esteem.

20. Reinforce Positive Statements (20)

A. The client's statements of self-confidence and identified positive things about self were verbally affirmed and supported.

B. The frequency of the client's positive self-descriptive statements has been noted to be increasing.

21. Play Therapeutic Games (21)

A. "The UnGame" (The UnGame Company), "Let's See . . . About Me and My Friends" (Childswork/Childsplay), and the "Talking, Feeling, and Doing" game (Gardner; Childswork/Childsplay) were played with the client to give them opportunities for self-disclosure.

B. Opportunities for feeling identification during games were seized to affirm the client's self-disclosure.

C. It was reflected to the client that they have become more adept at identifying and expressing emotions.

22. **Enhance Ability to Identify Feelings (22)**

    A. Feelings charts and cards were used to teach the client how to identify specific feelings.

    B. The client was assigned the "Feelings and Faces Game" exercise from the *Child Psychotherapy Homework Planner* (Jongsma, Peterson, McInnis, & Bruce).

    C. The client was given positive verbal affirmation and reinforcement for identifying specific feelings during the session.

    D. The client's resistance to identifying feelings was confronted, addressed, and resolved.

    E. Through the work with feelings charts and cards, the client has developed the ability to identify specific feelings.

23. **Educate About Feelings Identification (23)**

    A. The client was educated in identifying, labeling, and expressing feelings.

    B. The client was given a feelings list and then given various scenarios and asked to identify what the individual in the scenario might be feeling.

    C. The client was asked to keep a daily feelings journal.

    D. The client was encouraged for showing how they have become more adept at identifying and expressing emotions.

24. **Encourage Eye Contact (24)**

    A. The client's lack of eye contact was focused on and discussed with the client.

    B. An agreement was obtained from the client to have regular eye contact with the therapist during sessions.

    C. The client was confronted by the therapist when they avoided or failed to make eye contact.

    D. The client reported an increase in the frequency of making eye contact with others outside of therapy sessions and was encouraged to continue this progress.

    E. Despite the use of support and encouragement, the client has very limited eye contact and was again encouraged to increase this eye contact.

25. **Broaden Eye Contact Experience (25)**

    A. The client was asked to make a commitment to increase eye contact with parents, teachers, and others.

    B. The client's experience of making eye contact with all adults was processed, with feelings specific to this experience being identified.

    C. The client reported an increase in the frequency of making eye contact with others outside of therapy sessions and was praised for this increase.

26. **Negate Self-Critical Messages (26)**

    A. *Don't Feed the Monster on Tuesdays!* (Moser) was read with the client, and the ideas for handling self-critical messages were explored.

    B. The client was assisted in identifying and implementing strategies for handling self-critical messages in daily life.

C. The client was helped to make a chart to record progress in building self-esteem.

D. Monitoring, encouragement, and affirmation were provided for the client's progress in building self-esteem.

27. Identify Good Qualities About Self (27)

A. The client was asked to read *Happy to Be Me!* (Adams & Butch) and then to make a list of their good qualities to process with the therapist.

B. The client's list of good qualities was processed and each quality was verbally affirmed and reinforced.

C. The client was instructed to read the list each morning and before bed.

D. The client's follow-through in reading the good qualities list was monitored and redirection was given, if needed.

E. It was noted that the client's list of positive qualities has helped build a more secure sense of self-esteem.

28. Assign New Experience Exercises (28)

A. The client was encouraged to try new activities and to see failure as a learning experience.

B. The client and parents were asked to complete the exercises "Dixie Overcomes Her Fears" and "Learn from Your Mistakes" from the *Child Psychotherapy Homework Planner* (Jongsma, Peterson, McInnis, & Bruce).

C. The completed new-experience exercises were processed with the client and parents, with emphasis on identifying new experiences the client could try.

D. The client was helped to select and verbally commit to several new activities to try.

E. The client was monitored, supported, and encouraged to try new experiences.

F. The message that "failure is a part of the learning experience" was reinforced at regular intervals with the client.

G. It was noted that the client has progressed to where they are willing to try new experiences and not be as afraid to fail.

29. Identify Emotional Needs (29)

A. The client was taught basic concepts of how to identify and verbalize emotional needs.

B. Ways to increase the client's emotional needs being met were explored.

C. The client failed to clearly identify and verbalize emotional needs or how to meet them and was provided with tentative examples in this area.

30. Share Emotional Needs (30)

A. A family session was conducted in which the parents and the client exchanged and identified their emotional needs.

B. The client and family were educated in ways to be sensitive to others' needs and to ask for their own emotional needs to be met.

C. The client and family were supported as they shared their emotional needs.

D. The client and family have not shared their emotional needs and were redirected to do so.

31. **Utilize Therapeutic Stories (31)**

   A. *Dr. Gardner's Fairy Tales for Today's Children* (Gardner) was read, and the client was helped to identify their feelings and needs.

   B. Each of the fairy tales was processed with the client, and they were assisted in identifying the feelings and needs of the characters in the stories.

   C. The client was helped, encouraged, and supported in verbalizing their feelings and needs.

   D. The client was given positive affirmation and reinforced for times when they verbally identified a feeling or need.

   E. Through the use of *Dr. Gardner's Fairy Tales for Today's Children* and verbal affirmation and reinforcement, the client increased their ability to identify their needs and feelings.

32. **Increase Physical Skills (32)**

   A. The parents and client were encouraged to begin or continue learning physical activities, such as learning to ride a bike, swim, tie shoes, and sign signature to develop skills.

   B. The parents were taught to provide positive feedback when the client masters a physical skill.

   C. The client was provided with positive feedback from their parents and mastered several physical skills.

33. **Record Accomplishments (33)**

   A. The client was asked to bring in an accomplishment that they have done in the past week, which was then written on a poster board with the client's name at the time.

   B. The client's list of accomplishments was reviewed with the client this week and insight was processed.

   C. The client expressed in increase in self-esteem through the review of their accomplishments.

   D. The client denied any increase in self-esteem when reviewing their accomplishments and this was processed.

34. **Teach Assertiveness and Social Skills (34)**

   A. The client was asked to list situations in which they have had social difficulties or find it hard to be asscrtive.

   B. The client was assigned the "Social Skills Exercise" from the *Child Psychotherapy Homework Planner* by Jongsma, Peterson, McInnis, & Bruce.

   C. Difficult social situations that the client identified were role-played with them to teach assertiveness.

   D. Behavioral rehearsal was utilized with the client to prepare them for facing the identified difficult social situations.

35. **Face Challenging Situations (35)**

   A. The client was taught the "Pretending to Know How" (Theiss) technique for facing new and uncomfortable situations.

   B. The "Pretending to Know How" technique was rehearsed using two different situations that the client might face, and the client was asked to commit to using the technique.

C. The experiences of using "Pretending to Know How" was processed, and the client was asked to try the technique on two additional situations/problems.

D. The client has successfully faced challenging situations using the new coping skills and has reported that their confidence is growing.

36. **Assign** *Good Friends Are Hard to Find* **(36)**

A. The parents were asked to read *Good Friends Are Hard to Find* (Frankel) with the client.

B. The parents were taught ways to help the client build and develop social skills using concepts from the Frankel book.

C. The client and parents were assisted in identifying suggestions/ideas from the Frankel book that could help increase the client's social skills.

D. The client's implementation and follow-through with the suggestions/ideas from the book have been noted to help them begin to increase their social skills and confidence.

E. The parents have not read the *Good Friends Are Hard to Find* book and were redirected to do so.

37. **Conduct Trauma-Specific Evaluation (37)**

A. A trauma-specific evaluation was conducted with the client and parents to obtain a more complete picture of the number of traumas experienced and how they have impacted the client.

B. The *Adverse Childhood Experiences Questionnaire (A.C.E.)* was conducted as a portion of this evaluation.

C. The rationale for the *Adverse Childhood Experiences Questionnaire (A.C.E.)* was accepted by the client and parents.

D. The *Adverse Childhood Experiences Questionnaire (A.C.E.)* was not completed due to lack of information provided by the client and parents.

38. **Identify Distorted Beliefs (38)**

A. The client was educated on how the brain works and how brains are triggered with positive and negative thoughts.

B. The client was asked to list their beliefs about self and the world.

C. The client's distorted, negative beliefs about self and the world were reframed.

D. The client struggled to identify any positive beliefs about self and the world and was provided with tentative examples of how others choose to see themselves and the world.

39. **Develop Positive Messages (39)**

A. The client was helped to identify and develop more positive, realistic messages about self and the world.

B. The client was assigned the exercise "Replace Negative Thoughts with Positive Self-Talk" from the *Child Psychotherapy Homework Planner* by Jongsma, Peterson, McInnis, & Bruce.

C. New positive, realistic life messages were implemented by the client and used on a daily basis.

D. The client was confronted when they failed to make positive, realistic statements about self or life events.

E. The client reported that they have developed a more positive outlook about self and the world, and the benefits of this positive outlook were reviewed.

40. **Complete *Yes Brain* Exercise (40)**

A. The client was assisted in completing an exercise from the *Yes Brain Workbook* (Siegel & Bryson).

B. Ideas from the *Yes Brain Workbook* (Siegel & Bryson) exercise were processed and the client was able to identify one or two things learned.

C. The client was assisted in sharing new concepts learned with their parents/caregivers.

D. The client struggled to understand new concepts and was provided with additional support.

41. **Use "Positive Thinking" Game (41)**

A. The "Positive Thinking" game (Childswork/Childsplay) was played with the client to promote healthy self-talk and thought patterns.

B. Today's session processed the "Positive Thinking" game experience with the client and identified specific ways to promote healthy self-talk and thought patterns.

C. The client was assisted in selecting and implementing several suggestions from the "Positive Thinking" game into their daily life.

D. The client was monitored, guided, and encouraged to follow through with using new healthy self-talk and thought patterns in their daily life.

E. The parents were encouraged to play the "Positive Thinking" game at home with the client several times per week.

42. **Use Responsibilities to Aid Esteem (42)**

A. The client was helped to identify daily tasks that when performed would increase their sense of responsibility and esteem.

B. The client's follow-through on daily tasks was monitored for consistency.

C. The client was given positive, verbal feedback for their follow-through on self-care responsibilities.

D. Positive feedback was provided as the client reported feeling better about self as they have become more active in performing daily responsibilities.

43. **Assign Telephone Contact About Accomplishment (43)**

A. The client was given the homework assignment to initiate a phone conversation with the therapist and relate a recent accomplishment of theirs.

B. The client was assigned the exercise "Three Ways to Change Yourself" from the *Child Psychotherapy Homework Planner* by Jongsma, Peterson, McInnis, & Bruce.

C. The client was requested to initiate a phone call to the therapist to relate a recent accomplishment of theirs.

D. The client received verbal praise, positive feedback, and compliments for their accomplishment.

E. The client was instructed in ways to receive and acknowledge praise, positive feedback, and compliments.

F. The feelings surrounding the experience of relating a recent accomplishment were processed with the client.

G. The client has not used the telephone contact to discuss accomplishments and was reminded to use this helpful resource.

44. Play "The Yarn Drawing Game" (44)

A. The client was asked to play "The Yarn Drawing Game" (Leben) to help them gain a sense of empowerment.

B. The client actively participated in playing "The Yarn Drawing Game," followed all the directives, and expressed satisfaction with the results.

C. "The Yarn Drawing Game" experience was processed and the empowerment gains achieved by the client were identified and reinforced.

D. It was noted that "The Yarn Drawing Game" experience has helped the client become more willing to take risks with new experiences.

E. Despite the use of "The Yarn Drawing Game," the client has not become more willing to take risks with new experiences and was provided with additional encouragement in this area.

45. Utilize Projective Art Exercise (45)

A. A projective art exercise, "Magic Art" (Walker), was utilized with the client in today's session.

B. The client actively participated in the projective art exercise.

C. Key points of trust and risk from the projective art exercise were processed with the client.

D. The client's resistance to trying new experiences was explored before they were willing to participate in the "Magic Art" exercise.

46. Teach Acceptance of Compliments (46)

A. Neurolinguistic and reframing techniques were used to alter the client's self-messages to make them able to receive and accept compliments.

B. Role-play techniques were used to give the client opportunities to practice accepting compliments.

C. The client reported a positive experience with accepting compliments from others recently.

D. The client has not ceased their pattern of refusing to accept compliments from others and was provided with remedial assistance in this area.

47. Refer for Positive Parenting Class (47)

A. The parents were asked to attend a parenting class that focuses on the issues of positive parenting.

B. The experience of positive parenting classes was processed along with key gains received.

C. The parents have not attended the parenting classes to focus on issues of positive parenting and were redirected to do so.

48. **Explore Parental Expectations (48)**
   A. Expectations that the parents hold for the client were explored and then affirmed where appropriate and adjusted when they were unrealistic.
   B. The parents were educated in what are age-appropriate and realistic developmental expectations for the client and what are realistic parental expectations, given the client's abilities.
   C. The parents were challenged in a respectful way when their expectations of the client seemed unrealistically high or age inappropriate.
   D. It was reflected to the parents that they have adjusted their expectations to a more realistic level, given the client's developmental stage.

49. **Teach Parents 3R Discipline Technique (49)**
   A. The 3R discipline technique was taught to the parents, and they were encouraged to read the book *Raising Self-Reliant Children in a Self-Indulgent World* (Glenn & Nelsen).
   B. The parents were assisted in implementing discipline that is respectful, reasonable, and related (3Rs) to the misbehavior and coached to offer support, guidance, and encouragement as they followed through.
   C. The parents have successfully implemented discipline that is respectful, reasonable, and related to the client's behavior.

50. **Increase Peer Group Activities (50)**
   A. The parents were presented with various options (e.g., scouting, sports, music) that could help boost the client's self-esteem, and they were encouraged to get them involved in at least one of them.
   B. The role of extracurricular activities in building the client's self-esteem was explored, with positive aspects being identified.
   C. The parents have followed through with enrolling the client in more peer group activities.
   D. The client's parents have not followed through with enrolling the client in more peer group activities and were redirected to do so.

LYING/MANIPULATIVE

CLIENT PRESENTATION

1. **Lying to Satisfy Personal Needs/Obtain Material Goods (1)***

   A. The client has displayed a repeated pattern of lying to satisfy personal needs.

   B. The client often lies to obtain some material goods or a desired object.

   C. The parents report that the client's lying to satisfy personal needs or obtain material goods has persisted on a frequent basis.

   D. The client has become more honest about satisfying personal needs or obtaining material goods or objects.

   E. The parents reported that the client has been more honest and has been able to accept when personal needs are not met or they do not obtain a desired object or material good.

2. **Lying to Escape Consequences/Punishment (2)**

   A. The client often lies in order to escape consequences or punishment for misbehavior.

   B. The client often attempts to divert consequences or punishment through telling a story that decreases the blame on them.

   C. The parents described frustration with the client's chronic pattern of lying in order to keep out of trouble.

   D. The client has become more honest and willing to accept the consequences and/or punishment for misbehavior.

   E. The client has ceased lying in order to escape punishment for misbehavior.

3. **Lying to Avoid Responsibilities/Work (3)**

   A. The client often lies in order to avoid facing responsibilities or performing work/chores.

   B. The client often indicates that their work has been completed when that is not accurate.

   C. The client often claims to have recently done work that is assigned to them, indicating that it is not their turn to do these responsibilities.

   D. The parents report that when they check on the truthfulness of the client's claims of having performed work or other responsibilities, they often find that they are untrue.

   E. The client has become more responsible in completing their work, which has decreased the need to lie.

   F. The client has ceased lying to avoid facing responsibilities or performing work.

4. **Lying to Avoid Punishment/Abuse (4)**

   A. The client has increased the pattern of lying after experiencing overly harsh punishments or abuse by parents/caregivers.

---

* The numbers in parentheses correlate to the number of the Behavioral Definition statement in the companion chapter with the same title in the *Child Psychotherapy Treatment Planner*, Sixth Edition, by Jongsma, Peterson, McInnis, & Bruce (Wiley, 2023).

B. The client often lies to decrease overly harsh punishments or abuse.

C. As the overly harsh punishments or abuse to the client have decreased, the pattern of lying has decreased as well.

D. The client has ceased lying as overly harsh punishments and abuse have stopped.

5. **Lying to Elevate Peer Status (5)**

A. The client often exaggerates their deeds or performance in order to boost self-esteem or elevate their status in the eyes of peers.

B. The client often makes up stories or tells outright lies about their deeds or performance in order to elevate their status in the eyes of peers.

C. The client often sticks to their story when caught in lies or exaggerations by peers.

D. As the client has developed better peer relationship skills, their pattern of lying or exaggeration has decreased.

E. The client has ceased lying or exaggerating about their deeds or performance in order to elevate their status in the eyes of peers.

6. **Manipulative/Exploitative to Meet Needs (6)**

A. The client often subtly manipulates others in order to satisfy needs or avoid consequences for misbehavior.

B. The client often exploits others without regard for the negative effects others may experience.

C. As the client has developed healthier ways to satisfy personal needs, their pattern of manipulation and exploitation has decreased.

D. As the client has taken greater responsibility for their behavior and its consequences, the desire to manipulate or exploit others has decreased.

7. **Triangulates Others Against Each Other (7)**

A. The client often makes attempts to pit parents and/or peers against each other in order to gratify personal needs or escape punishment.

B. The client is able to subtly switch discussions about inappropriate behavior into fights between parents.

C. The client often cajoles or lies to peers in order to turn them against each other, thereby gratifying personal needs or escaping punishment.

D. As the parents, family members, and/or peers have become more aware of the client's pattern of triangulation, they have decreased this pattern.

E. The client no longer attempts to manipulate or pit parents and/or peers against each other.

8. **Thrill Seeking (8)**

A. The client historically has presented as a highly impulsive individual who seeks immediate gratification of needs through acts of manipulation or deception and who often fails to consider the consequences of their actions.

B. The client has engaged in impulsive/thrill-seeking behaviors related to manipulating or deceiving others in order to achieve a sense of excitement and fun.

C. The client has begun to take steps toward improving impulse control and delaying the need for immediate gratification.

D. The client has recently demonstrated good impulse control and has not engaged in any serious manipulation or deception of others as a way to excite self.

E. The client has ceased engaging in acting-out or thrill-seeking behavior because of improved ability to stop and think about the possible consequences of their actions.

9. **Refusal to Accept Responsibility (9)**

A. The client persistently refuses to accept responsibility for deceitful or manipulative behavior.

B. The client often attempts to blame others as the cause for their decisions and actions.

C. The client has displayed little insight into the factors contributing to their behavioral problems.

D. The client has become more honest in the therapy session and has admitted to wrongdoing or irresponsibility.

E. The parents report that the client has become more honest and accepting of responsibility for behaviors.

10. **Low Self-Esteem (10)**

A. The client has displayed underlying feelings of insecurity or low self-esteem that contribute to the need to lie, falsify information, or manipulate others.

B. The client's deep sense of inferiority was reflected in the frequent self-disparaging remarks about appearance, worth, and abilities.

C. The lack of eye contact on the client's part and negative remarks about self are evidence of low self-esteem.

D. The client has made connections between insecurity, or low self-esteem, and the need to lie, falsify information, or manipulate others.

E. As the client's self-esteem has increased, the need to lie, falsify information, or manipulate others has decreased.

F. The client's parents report that they no longer tend to lie, falsify information, or manipulate others in order to raise self-esteem.

11. **Blurred Distinction Between Fantasy and Reality (11)**

A. The client's persistent lying and exaggerations have caused them to experience a blurred distinction between fantasy and reality.

B. The client often fails to realize that the lies or exaggerations they have made up are not the truth.

C. The client seems to have convinced self of the truthfulness of their lies and exaggerations.

D. The client has become more reality oriented and sees the difference between reality and their lies and exaggerations.

12. **Strained Family/Peer Relationships (12)**

A. The client's lying and manipulative behavior has been a significant contributing factor to strained interpersonal relationships with family and peers.

B. The client has often projected the blame for interpersonal problems onto peers and refused to acknowledge how their lying and manipulative behaviors contribute to the conflict.

C. The client has started to recognize how their lying and manipulative behavior interferes with the ability to establish and maintain peer friendships.

D. The client reported that decrease or cessation of lying and manipulating behavior has led to improved relations with peers.

INTERVENTIONS IMPLEMENTED

1. **Establish Rapport (1)***
   A. Caring was conveyed to the client through support, warmth, and empathy.
   B. The client was provided with nonjudgmental support, and a level of trust was developed.
   C. The client was urged to feel safe in expressing lying and manipulative behavior.
   D. The client began to express feelings more freely as rapport and trust level have increased.
   E. The client has continued to experience difficulty being open and direct about the expression of painful feelings; the client was encouraged to use the safe haven of therapy to express these difficult issues.

2. **Focus on Strengthening Therapeutic Relationship (2)**
   A. The relationship with the client was strengthened using empirically supported factors.
   B. The relationship with the client was strengthened through the implementation of collaborative approach, agreement on goals, demonstration of empathy, verbalization of positive regard, and collection of client feedback.
   C. The client reacted positively to the relationship-strengthening measures taken.
   D. The client verbalized feeling supported and understood during therapy sessions.
   E. Despite attempts to strengthen the therapeutic relationship, the client reports feeling distant and misunderstood.
   F. The client has indicated that sessions are not helpful and will be terminating therapy.

3. **Assess Level of Insight (3)**
   A. The client's level of insight toward the presenting problems was assessed.
   B. The client was assessed in regard to the syntonic versus dystonic nature of their insight about the presenting problems.
   C. The client was noted to demonstrate good insight into the problematic nature of the behavior and symptoms.
   D. The client was noted to be in agreement with others' concerns and is motivated to work on change.
   E. The client was noted to be ambivalent regarding the problems described and is reluctant to address the issues as a concern.
   F. The client was noted to be resistant regarding acknowledgment of the problem areas, is not concerned about them, and has no motivation to make changes.

---

*The numbers in parentheses correlate to the number of the Therapeutic Intervention statement in the companion chapter with the same title in the *Child Psychotherapy Treatment Planner*, Sixth Edition, by Jongsma, Peterson, McInnis, & Bruce (Wiley, 2023).

4. **Assess for Correlated Disorders (4)**

   A. The client was assessed for evidence of research-based correlated disorders.

   B. The client was assessed in regard to the level of vulnerability to suicide.

   C. The client was identified as having a comorbid disorder, and treatment was adjusted to account for these concerns.

   D. The client has been assessed for any correlated disorders, but none were found.

5. **Assess for Culturally Based Confounding Issues (5)**

   A. The client was assessed for age-related issues that could help to better understand their clinical presentation.

   B. The client was assessed for gender-related issues that could help to better understand their clinical presentation.

   C. The client was assessed for cultural syndromes, cultural idioms of distress, or culturally based perceived causes that could help to better understand their clinical presentation.

   D. Alternative factors have been identified as contributing to the client's currently defined "problem behavior," and these were taken into account in regard to treatment.

   E. Culturally based factors that could help to account for the client's currently defined "problem behavior" were investigated, but no significant factors were identified.

6. **Assess Severity of Impairment (6)**

   A. The severity of the client's impairment was assessed to determine the appropriate level of care.

   B. The client was assessed in regard to impairment in social, relational, and educational endeavors.

   C. It was reflected to the client that the impairment appears to create mild to moderate effects on the client's functioning.

   D. It was reflected to the client that the impairment appears to create severe to very severe effects on the client's functioning.

   E. The client was continuously assessed for the severity of impairment, as well as the efficacy and appropriateness of treatment.

7. **Assess for Pathogenic Care (7)**

   A. The home, school, and community of the client were assessed for pathogenic care and concerns.

   B. The client's various environments were assessed for the persistent disregard of the child's needs, repeated changes in caregivers, limited opportunities for stable attachment, harsh discipline, or other grossly inept care.

   C. Pathogenic care was identified and the treatment plan included strategies for managing or correcting these concerns and protecting the child.

   D. No pathogenic care was identified, and this was reflected to the client and caregivers.

8. **Gather History (8)**

   A. A detailed developmental history was obtained to help identify factors that contribute to the emergence of the client's lying and manipulative behavior.

B. A detailed family history was developed in order to gain insight into the family dynamics or environmental stressors that contribute to the emergence of the client's lying and manipulative behavior.

C. Insight was gained into the emotional factors, family dynamics, or environmental stressors that contribute to the emergence of the client's lying and manipulative behavior.

D. During the history-gathering process, the client was assisted in connecting feelings to developmental and family history factors.

E. The family gave only a vague, sketchy history of the factors that contribute to the emergence of the client's lying and manipulative behavior and were pressed for more specific details in this area.

9. **Develop Awareness of Previous Reinforcers (9)**

A. The client was assisted in developing an awareness of the prior life events or significant relationships that encouraged or reinforced lying or manipulative behavior.

B. The client was supported as they identified parents or family members who lie regularly.

C. Active listening skills were used as the client described an experience of overly rigid or punitive parenting.

D. It was reflected to the client that their affiliation with peers has often reinforced their lying behavior.

E. The client displayed an increased awareness of the prior life events or significant relationships that have encouraged lying and manipulative behavior and was provided with positive feedback regarding this insight.

F. The client has been guarded and defensive about connecting prior life events or significant relationships that have reinforced lying and manipulative behavior and was provided with tentative examples in this area.

10. **Explore Periods of Increased Lying/Manipulation (10)**

A. The client was assisted in identifying periods of time when they have demonstrated an increase in lying or acts of manipulation.

B. The periods of the client's increased lying and manipulation were investigated to identify factors that contributed to the emergence of such behavior.

C. Support and encouragement were provided as the client identified factors that contributed to the emergence of their lying and manipulative behavior.

D. The client was unable to identify specific factors that contributed to the emergence of their lying and manipulative behavior and was provided with tentative examples in this area.

11. **Identify Current Triggers (11)**

A. The client was assisted in identifying current life situations or people that trigger lying and manipulative behavior.

B. The client's parents were assisted in identifying current life situations or people that trigger lying and manipulative behavior for the client.

C. The client's and parents' description of current triggers were summarized, including situations of threats of being punished, failure experiences, or facing criticism.

12. Assist in Self-Disclosure of Behavior (12)

A. The client was assisted in identifying examples of their deceitful behavior.

B. The client was assigned the exercise "Truthful/Lying Incident Reports" from the *Child Psychotherapy Homework Planner* (Jongsma, Peterson, McInnis, & Bruce).

C. The client was assisted in identifying examples of their manipulative behavior.

D. The client was provided with positive feedback and encouragement for open discussion of deceitful and manipulative behaviors.

E. The client was guarded and defensive about deceitful and manipulative behaviors and was urged to be more open about this type of behavior as the client feels strong enough to do so.

F. The client was provided with tentative examples of deceitful and manipulative behaviors.

13. Assign Parent/Caregiver Log (13)

A. The parents/caregivers were assigned to keep a log of times when the client has been caught lying or engaging in manipulative behavior.

B. The parent/caregiver log of lying and manipulative behavior was processed in order to explore factors that contribute to the client's willingness to lie or manipulate.

C. The parents/caregivers have not kept a log of the client's lying or manipulative behavior and were redirected to do so.

14. Assign Reading for Parents (14)

A. The parents/caregivers were assigned to read *Why Kids Lie: How Parents Can Encourage Truthfulness* (Ekman) and *Telling the Truth: A Book About Lying* (Larson).

B. The parents/caregivers read the assigned books and key concepts about dealing with lying and manipulative behavior were processed.

C. The parents/caregivers have not read the assigned books about lying and manipulative behavior and were encouraged to do so.

15. Assign Videos (15)

A. The parents/caregivers were assigned to watch videos to learn how to effectively manage the client's lying.

B. The parents/caregivers were assigned *Why Kids Lie and How to End It Now* (Post) and *How to Stop a Child from Lying* (Jenkins).

C. The parents/caregivers viewed the assigned videos and key concepts were reinforced.

D. The parents/caregivers have not viewed the assigned videos and were encouraged to do so.

16. Counsel Effective Dealing with Lies (16)

A. The parents/caregivers were provided with education regarding appropriate ways to deal with the client's lies.

B. To effectively deal with the client's lie, the parents/caregivers were taught to remain calm, avoid asking "Why?" or set-up questions, identify what just happened, teach honesty, model positive behavior, and assign appropriate consequences.

C. The parents/caregivers have used appropriate ways to deal with the client's lies, and effects were processed.

D. The parents/caregivers continue to use unhelpful ways of dealing with the client's lies, and remedial education was provided.

17. Identify Irrational Thoughts (17)

A. The client was assisted in identifying irrational thoughts that contribute to the emergence of lying or manipulative behavior.

B. The client identified irrational or distorted thoughts that contribute to the emergence of lying or manipulative behavior, and these were processed.

C. The client was unable to identify irrational or distorted thoughts that contribute to the emergence of lying or manipulative behavior and was provided with tentative examples (e.g., "I deserve this toy, so it doesn't matter if I take advantage of anyone"; "Nobody will ever catch me lying"; "This person is weak and deserves to be taken advantage of").

18. Replace Irrational Thoughts (18)

A. The client was directed to replace irrational or distorted thoughts with reality-based or more adaptive ways of thinking.

B. The client was provided with examples of replacing irrational or distorted thoughts with reality-based thinking (e.g., "I could get caught lying, and it would only create more problems for me"; "It is best to be honest"; "My friends won't want to play with me if I lie or take advantage of them").

C. The client was praised as they replaced irrational or distorted thoughts with reality-based or more adaptive ways of thinking.

D. The client was unable to identify ways to change irrational or distorted thoughts for more adaptive ways of thinking and was provided with tentative examples in this area.

19. Confront Lying/Manipulation (19)

A. The client was firmly confronted about the impact of lying or manipulative behavior.

B. The client was assigned the exercise "Truthful/Lying Incident Reports" from the *Child Psychotherapy Homework Planner* (Jongsma, Peterson, McInnis, & Bruce).

C. The many consequences for self and others due to their lying and manipulative behavior were pointed out to the client.

20. Identify Negative Effects (20)

A. The client was directed to list the negative effects that lying and manipulative behavior have on self.

B. The client was directed to list the negative effects that lying and manipulative behavior have on others.

C. The client was provided with positive reinforcement as they identified many of the negative effects of lying and manipulative behavior for self as well as for others.

D. The client struggled to identify negative effects of lying and manipulative behavior and was provided with tentative examples in this area (e.g., creates mistrust, provokes anger or hurt in others, leads to social isolation).

21. Assign Books (21)

A. The client was assigned to read *The Lying King* (Beard), *Ruthie and the [Not So] Teeny Tiny Lie* (Rankin), or *A Children's Book About Lying* (Berry) to increase awareness of how lying affects self.

B. The client read the assigned books and processed new knowledge and awareness.

C. The client has not read the assigned books and was encouraged to do so before the next session.

22. Teach Value of Honesty (22)

A. The client was taught about the value of honesty as the basis for building trust and mutual respect in all relationships.

B. The client was assigned the exercise "The Value of Honesty" from the *Child Psychotherapy Homework Planner* (Jongsma, Peterson, McInnis, & Bruce).

C. The client was asked to verbally identify the benefits of honesty.

D. Positive feedback was provided to the client for identifying the ways in which honesty forms a basis for building trust and mutual respect in all relationships.

E. The client denied any value of honesty as a basis for relationships and was provided with specific feedback in this area.

23. Build Empathy (23)

A. The client was asked to express how they would likely feel if they were deceived or manipulated by others.

B. The client was recommended to read *Don't Tell a Whopper on Fridays!: The Children's Truth-Control Book* (Moser).

C. The client was assisted in identifying the emotional responses they would have to being deceived or manipulated.

D. The client's feelings about being deceived or manipulated were processed, with an emphasis on empathy for those they have deceived in the past.

E. The client was defensive about emotions that they would have if deceived or manipulated and was provided with tentative examples in this area.

24. Role-Play Impact of Deceit/Manipulation (24)

A. Role-reversal techniques were used to help the client become aware of how deceitful or manipulative behavior negatively affects others.

B. Situations in which others are deceived or manipulated were role-played.

C. As a result of the role-reversal and role-play techniques, the client became more aware of how deceitful or manipulative behavior negatively affects others.

D. Despite the use of role-play techniques, the client has not developed empathy for the negative effects of deceit and manipulation and was provided with remedial feedback in this area.

25. Assign Observation of Deceit/Manipulation (25)

A. The client was assigned the task of observing instances between others in which deceit/manipulation occurs.

B. The parents and client were assigned to work on the exercise "Bad Choice—Lying to Cover Up Another Lie" from the *Child Psychotherapy Homework Planner* (Jongsma, Peterson, McInnis, & Bruce).

C. The client was instructed to notice the feelings of individuals who have been taken advantage of or manipulated.

D. The client identified situations in which others were deceived or manipulated, but needed assistance in identifying emotions these individuals may have felt.

E. The client was provided with positive feedback as they identified situations in which others have been manipulated and the emotions that they may have experienced.

F. The client has not noticed situations in which others have been deceived or manipulated and was urged to continue to review these situations between sessions.

26. Teach Mediational and Self-Control Strategies (26)

A. The client was taught mediational and self-control strategies to help them resist the urge to lie or manipulate in order to meet needs or avoid consequences.

B. The client was taught the "stop, listen, think, and act" technique.

C. The client was taught about thought-stopping techniques.

D. The client was taught assertive communication techniques.

E. The client has regularly used the mediational and self-control strategies, and the benefits of these techniques were reviewed.

F. The client has not used the mediational and self-control strategies and was reminded about the use of these techniques.

27. Encourage Parents' Use of Praise and Reinforcement (27)

A. The parents were urged to use praise and reinforcement with the client whenever they accept "no" or another unfavorable response to their requests.

B. The parents were urged to reinforce the client whenever they do not attempt to lie or manipulate within the settings when they might usually do so.

C. The parents were reinforced for situations in which they observed and noted the client not being manipulative or deceitful.

D. The parents have not reinforced the client for honesty and were reminded about the essential nature of this parenting technique.

28. Establish Clear Rules (28)

A. The parents were assisted in establishing clearly defined rules and consequences for lying and manipulative behavior.

B. The parents gave rather vague rules and consequences for the client's lying or manipulative behavior and were assisted in making these more clear and specific.

C. The client was informed of the rules and consequences for lying or manipulative behavior.

D. The client was asked to repeat the rules and consequences in order to demonstrate understanding of these guidelines.

29. Develop Contingency Contract (29)

A. The client and parents were assisted in developing a contingency contract that clearly outlines the consequences if the client is caught lying or manipulating others.

B. The contingency contract was written out, and the therapist, client, and parents signed it.

C. The parents were directed to post the contract in a visible place in the home.

D. The client refused to sign the contingency contract outlining the consequences for lying/manipulative behavior; the parents were directed to sign and post the contract regardless of the client's refusal to sign.

30. Counsel Parents About Reinforcement Consistency (30)

A. The parents were counseled about how failure to follow through consistently with limits or consequences will reinforce the client's deceptive and manipulative behaviors.

B. The parents were assigned the exercise "Being a Consistent Parent" from the *Child Psychotherapy Homework Planner* (Jongsma, Peterson, McInnis, & Bruce).

C. The parents were assisted in developing insight into how failure to follow through consistently communicates a message to the client that they can possibly control the situation or get away with misbehavior.

D. Positive feedback was provided to the parents as they displayed acceptance of the need to follow through consistently in order to communicate an appropriate message to the client.

E. The parents continued to be inconsistent in their follow-through on limits and consequences for the client and were reminded about the unhealthy message this sends.

31. Instruct Parents on Requiring Undoing of Lies or Manipulation (31)

A. The parents were instructed to require that the client undo lies or manipulation by publicly acknowledging their wrongdoings to the individual(s) whom they have lied to or manipulated.

B. The parents have agreed with the requirement for the client to undo their lies and manipulation and were supported as they have implemented this expectation.

C. The parents have not been consistent in requiring the client to undo their lies and manipulation and were redirected about consistency in this area.

32. Assign Apologies (32)

A. The client was directed to verbally apologize to individuals whom they have lied to or manipulated.

B. The client was directed to write a written apology to those who they have lied to or manipulated.

C. Positive feedback was provided for the client's use of apologies.

D. The client has not made apologies to those whom they have lied to or manipulated and was redirected to follow through on this expectation.

33. Counsel About Withdrawing Attention (33)

A. The parents and family members were counseled about withdrawing attention from the client when they attempt to manipulate a situation in the home.

B. The parents were assisted in developing parameters for when they are able to withdraw their attention from the client in their attempts to manipulate a situation in the home.

C. The parents were reminded about the reinforcing nature of attention (even negative attention) on the client's lying and manipulative behavior.

D. Positive feedback was provided to the parents as they have regularly refrained from providing attention to the client for lying and manipulative behavior.

E. The parents continue to reinforce the client when they are attempting to manipulate a situation within the home and were redirected to refrain from this practice.

34. **Urge a United Front (34)**

A. The parents were urged to present a united front and prevent splitting by making each other aware of the client's attempts to deceive or manipulate (e.g., self-pity, somatic complaints, inappropriate jokes, lying).

B. The parents were urged to reach a mutually agreed-on consequence for the deceitful or manipulative behavior.

C. The parents were urged to use the same level of tolerance and consequence, regardless of their individual expectations or preferences in this area.

D. The parents were provided with positive feedback as they have presented a united front.

E. The parents were redirected after not displaying a united front with the client.

35. **Conduct Family Therapy to Explore Dynamics (35)**

A. Family-therapy sessions were held to explore the dynamics and stressors that promote or reinforce the client's deceptive or manipulative behavior.

B. The family was supported as they identified dynamics and stressors that support the client's deceptive or manipulative behavior.

C. The family has not identified dynamics or stressors that reinforce or promote the client's deceptive or manipulative behavior and were provided with tentative examples in this area (e.g., modeling of deception, severe criticism, harsh punishment, rejection of the client, substance abuse by parent).

36. **Challenge Parents to Cease Modeling Lying/Manipulation (36)**

A. The parents were confronted about ways in which they model inappropriate behavior to the client through their own acts of deception or manipulation.

B. The parents were challenged to cease modeling inappropriate behavior to the client.

C. The parents were supported as they identified how they have modeled inappropriate behavior to the client.

D. The parents denied any modeling of inappropriate behavior (e.g., deception or manipulation) and were provided with tentative examples of how this may have occurred.

37. **Connect Unmet Needs to Lying/Manipulation (37)**

A. Today's session explored the connection between the client's unmet needs related to past rejection experiences and their history of lying and manipulation.

B. The client was assigned the exercise "Unmet Emotional Needs—Identification and Satisfaction" from the *Child Psychotherapy Homework Planner* (Jongsma, Peterson, McInnis, & Bruce).

C. The client was supported as they identified how unmet needs and past rejection experiences have contributed to their history of lying and manipulation.

D. The client was provided with specific examples of how unmet needs may have led to lying and manipulative behavior.

E. The client was assisted in identifying more adaptive ways to meet needs for love, affection, or closeness, other than through lying or manipulating others.

F. The client endorsed many more adaptive ways to meet needs for love, affection, or closeness, other than through lying or manipulating others.

38. Encourage Emotional Expression (38)

A. The client was encouraged to express feelings of rejection or deprivation.

B. The client was supported as they expressed feelings of rejection or deprivation.

C. The client was provided with support as they verbalized the need for love and affection from parents or significant others.

D. Positive feedback was provided to the client for their ability to identify feelings and express needs.

E. The client has been guarded or otherwise unable to clearly identify feelings and needs and was provided with tentative feedback in this area.

39. Connect Painful Emotions to Lying and Manipulation (39)

A. The client was assisted in making the connection between underlying painful emotions (e.g., depression, anxiety, insecurity, anger) and lying or manipulative behavior.

B. The client was assigned "Surface Behavior/Inner Feelings" from the *Child Psychotherapy Homework Planner* (Jongsma, Peterson McInnis, & Bruce).

C. The client endorsed the connection between underlying painful emotions and lying or manipulative behavior and was supported for this insight.

D. The client denied any connection between underlying painful emotions and lying or manipulative behavior and was provided with examples from their history of how this might occur.

40. Probe Feelings Associated with Traumas (40)

A. The client was given the opportunity to express feelings about past neglect, abuse, separation, or abandonment.

B. The client was given empathy and support in expressing feelings about past neglect, abuse, separation, or abandonment.

C. The client was instructed to use a journal to record thoughts and feelings about past neglect, abuse, separation, or abandonment.

D. The empty-chair technique was employed to facilitate the client's expression of feelings surrounding past neglect, abuse, separation, or abandonment.

E. The client was instructed to draw pictures that reflect feelings about past neglect, abuse, separation, or abandonment.

F. Despite several attempts to allow the client to explore feelings associated with the traumas, they have continued to be defensive and guarded about these types of feelings and were encouraged to express them as they feel able to do so.

41. Teach Effective Communication and Assertiveness (41)

A. The client was taught effective communication skills to express painful emotions to others in a more direct and constructive fashion.

B. The client was taught assertiveness skills to express emotions and needs to others in a more direct and constructive fashion.

C. Positive feedback was provided to the client as they have become a more effective communicator and more assertive.

D. The client has not used the communication and assertiveness skills and was redirected to do so.

42. **Identify Trust Building Social Behaviors (42)**

A. The client was given the homework assignment to identify 5 to 10 positive social behaviors that can help them rebuild trust.

B. The client's list of 5 to 10 positive social behaviors was reviewed.

C. The client was encouraged to engage in the identified positive social behaviors.

D. The client has not completed the homework assignment of identifying and engaging in positive social behaviors and was redirected to do so.

43. **Instruct Parents to Observe and Reinforce Prosocial Behaviors (43)**

A. The parents were instructed to observe and record three to five prosocial or responsible behaviors by the client that help to rebuild trust.

B. The parents were directed to encourage, praise, and reinforce the client for use of prosocial or responsible behaviors.

C. Positive feedback was provided to the parents and client for the use, observation, and reinforcement of prosocial or responsible behaviors that help to rebuild trust.

D. The parents reported that although they have attempted to observe prosocial or responsible behavior by the client, the client has not completed these types of actions; they were encouraged to continue to look for these types of behaviors.

E. The parents reported that they have not been diligent in observing and recording the client's prosocial behaviors and were redirected to do so.

44. **Teach Honesty and Trust Through Assisted Stories (44)**

A. Stories were told to the client that teach the value of honesty, using puppets, dolls, and stuffed animals.

B. Puppets, dolls, and stuffed animals were used to create a story that teaches appropriate ways to rebuild trust.

C. The client was asked to create a story with similar themes to help teach the value of honesty and model appropriate ways to rebuild trust.

D. Positive feedback was provided to the client for displaying a clear understanding of the value of honesty and appropriate ways to rebuild trust, as evidenced through their story on this theme.

45. **Brainstorm Socially Appropriate Manipulation/Sneakiness (45)**

A. The client was introduced to the concept of the socially appropriate ways in which a person can be sneaky or manipulative.

B. The client was assisted in brainstorming socially appropriate ways in which they would like to be sneaky or manipulative.

C. The client identified socially appropriate ways to be sneaky or manipulative and was assigned the task of exercising this skill at least once before the next therapy session.

D. The client was unable to identify socially appropriate ways to be sneaky or manipulative and was provided with specific examples (e.g., learn a magic trick, ask peers to solve riddles, design a trick play for the basketball team).

E. The client's use of the socially appropriate ways of being sneaky or manipulative were reviewed.

46. Focus on Connection Between Low Self-Esteem and Exaggeration (46)

A. The client was assisted in realizing the connection between underlying feelings of low self-esteem and desire to lie or exaggerate about performance or deeds.

B. Support was provided as the client endorsed their own feelings of low self-esteem and how this creates a desire to lie or exaggerate about self.

C. The client denied any connection between underlying feelings of low self-esteem and desire to lie or exaggerate about performance or deeds and was provided of tentative examples of how this occurs.

D. The client was assisted in identifying more effective ways to improve self-esteem.

47. Note Self-Defeating Nature of Exaggerations (47)

A. It was pointed out to the client how lies or exaggerated claims are self-defeating as they interfere with the ability to establish and maintain close, trusting relationships.

B. Support and encouragement were provided as the client displayed an understanding of how exaggerated claims and lies are self-defeating and prohibit close, trusting relationships with others.

C. The client denied any connection between lies and exaggerated claims and problems establishing and maintaining close, trusting relationships and was provided with specific examples of this dynamic.

48. Symbolize Strengths (48)

A. The client was instructed to draw pictures of symbols or objects that reflect their interests or strengths.

B. The client was assigned the exercise "Symbols of Self-Worth" from the *Child Psychotherapy Homework Planner* (Jongsma, Peterson, McInnis, & Bruce).

C. The client was encouraged to use talents and strengths to improve self-esteem and meet needs for closeness and intimacy.

D. Positive feedback was provided as the client identified ways in which they have symbolized their interests and strengths.

E. The client has used talents and strengths to improve self-esteem and develop closeness and intimacy; the client was encouraged for this progress.

MEDICAL CONDITION

CLIENT PRESENTATION

1. **Diagnosis of a Chronic, Non-Life-Threatening Illness (1)***
   A. The client recently received a diagnosis of a chronic, non-life-threatening illness that will have a significant impact on their life.
   B. The client presented as upset and worried after they received confirmation of having a chronic, but non-life-threatening medical condition.
   C. The client was overwhelmed after they received the diagnosis of a chronic illness and the life changes it will require.
   D. The client has started to accept their medical condition and has begun to make the required life changes.

2. **Lifestyle Changes (1)**
   A. The client reported numerous lifestyle changes that need to be made in order to stabilize their medical condition.
   B. The client is struggling with letting go of certain things in their lifestyle that stand in the way of treating their medical condition.
   C. The client refused to consider making certain lifestyle changes that were recommended as part of treatment.
   D. Outside pressure from the family has moved the client to make the recommended lifestyle changes to improve their long-term physical health.

3. **Diagnosis of an Acute, Life-Threatening Illness (2)**
   A. The client presented as very upset after they received a diagnosis of having an acute, life-threatening illness.
   B. The client reported feeling an overwhelming sadness around having been diagnosed with an acute, life-threatening illness.
   C. The client indicated that they have not told any of their friends of the diagnosis and its seriousness.
   D. The client has begun to share their diagnosis and what it means with others close to them.

4. **Diagnosis of a Terminal Illness (3)**
   A. The client reported with hesitation and difficulty their diagnosis of having a terminal illness.
   B. The client failed to disclose their diagnosis of a terminal illness until they were asked.
   C. The client indicated that they find it impossible to talk about their diagnosis of a terminal illness.
   D. The client has begun to openly acknowledge their diagnosis and its terminal nature.

---

*The numbers in parentheses correlate to the number of the Behavioral Definition statement in the companion chapter with the same title in the *Child Psychotherapy Treatment Planner*, Sixth Edition, by Jongsma, Peterson, McInnis, & Bruce (Wiley, 2023).

5. **Anxious/Sensitive (4)**
   A. The client presented with anxious feelings related to their serious medical condition.
   B. The client reported that a discussion of anything related to their medical condition makes them feel anxious.
   C. The client has developed some peace of mind about their serious medical condition.

6. **Sad/Quiet (4)**
   A. The client presented in a sad, quiet manner.
   B. The client found it very difficult to talk about their medical condition.
   C. The client reported feeling overwhelming sadness around the loss of their health when the condition was diagnosed.
   D. The client's sadness has decreased as they have been willing to talk more openly about the medical diagnosis and prognosis.

7. **Social Withdrawal (4)**
   A. Recently the client has stopped associating with most of their friends.
   B. The client reported that they have been spending all of their spare time alone.
   C. The client appeared to be avoiding family and friends since learning of their medical condition.
   D. Due to their particular medical condition, the client has seen no reason to interact or have relationships with others.
   E. As the client has accepted their medical condition, they have begun to reconnect with others and receive their support.

8. **Depression (4)**
   A. The client's mood has been depressed since their medical condition was confirmed.
   B. The client presented in a depressed manner with low energy and little interest in life's activities.
   C. As the client's depression has lifted, they have started to have more energy and see some hope in living with their medical condition.

9. **Suicidal Ideation (5)**
   A. The client presented in a negative, despondent manner.
   B. The client reported feeling very hopeless and helpless regarding the future due to their medical condition.
   C. Suicidal thoughts and feelings seemed to dominate the client at the present time.
   D. The client revealed a plan along with a backup plan to take their own life.
   E. The client has gradually started to feel more hopeful and less despondent about their medical condition.

10. **Denial (6)**
    A. The client presented as if there was nothing wrong with them despite evidence to the contrary.
    B. The client reported that they did not agree with the seriousness of the condition as diagnosed by the physicians.

    C. The client seemed to vacillate between accepting and denying the diagnosed medical condition.

    D. The client refused to disclose or acknowledge having any medical condition.

    E. The client's denial has started to lessen and they are beginning to talk about their condition in a realistic manner.

11. Resistive to Treatment (7)

    A. The client presented in a resistive manner.

    B. The client reported that they are not open to treatment of any kind for their medical condition.

    C. The client's resistiveness to accepting treatment for their medical condition has had a deleterious effect on their general health.

    D. The client has refused to cooperate fully with the recommended medical treatments.

    E. The client has become more cooperative with medical treatment procedures.

INTERVENTIONS IMPLEMENTED

1. Establish Rapport (1)*

    A. Caring was conveyed to the client through support, warmth, and empathy.

    B. The client was provided with nonjudgmental support, and a level of trust was developed.

    C. The client was urged to feel safe in expressing their medical concerns.

    D. The client began to express feelings more freely as rapport and trust level have increased.

    E. The client has continued to experience difficulty being open and direct about the expression of painful feelings; they were encouraged to use the safe haven of therapy to express these difficult issues.

2. Focus on Strengthening Therapeutic Relationship (2)

    A. The relationship with the client was strengthened using empirically supported factors.

    B. The relationship with the client was strengthened through the implementation of collaborative approach, agreement on goals, demonstration of empathy, verbalization of positive regard, and collection of client feedback.

    C. The client reacted positively to the relationship-strengthening measures taken.

    D. The client verbalized feeling supported and understood during therapy sessions.

    E. Despite attempts to strengthen the therapeutic relationship, the client reports feeling distant and misunderstood.

    F. The client has indicated that sessions are not helpful and will be terminating therapy.

---

* The numbers in parentheses correlate to the number of the Therapeutic Intervention statement in the companion chapter with the same title in the *Child Psychotherapy Treatment Planner*, Sixth Edition, by Jongsma, Peterson, McInnis, & Bruce (Wiley, 2023).

3. **Gather History of Medical Condition (3)**

   A. A history of the client's medical condition that included symptoms, treatment, and prognosis was gathered.

   B. During the history-gathering process, the client was assisted in connecting feelings to aspects and stages of their medical condition.

   C. A sketchy, vague history of the client's medical condition was gathered due to their unwillingness to provide specific information.

4. **Obtain Additional Medical History (4)**

   A. Informed consent was obtained from the client so that their family and physician could be contacted for further information on their medical condition.

   B. Additional information regarding the client's diagnosis, treatment, and prognosis was gathered from their physician.

   C. Various family members contributed additional information when contacted on the client's medical condition and its progression, and this information was summarized.

   D. The client refused to give consent to have either their physician or family members contacted about their medical condition, and their wishes were accepted.

5. **Explore Fears Regarding Failing Health (5)**

   A. The client was asked to express fears around failing health, death, and dying through the use of interview or play therapy.

   B. The fear of death and dying expressed by the client was explored and processed.

   C. The concept of facing fears was presented to and processed with the client.

   D. The client was open in expressing fears regarding death and dying; this was reflected to them as a resolution of these fears, resulting in peace of mind.

6. **Normalize Anxious Feelings (6)**

   A. The client was assisted and supported in identifying and expressing feelings of anxiety connected to their medical condition.

   B. The anxious and sad feelings identified around the condition by the client were affirmed and normalized.

   C. The client was reminded of the value and benefit to their health and recovery of identifying and expressing feelings.

7. **Assess/Treat Depression and Anxiety (7)**

   A. The client was assessed for level of depression and anxiety, and appropriate treatment was recommended.

   B. It was determined that the client's level of depression was significant enough to merit focused treatment.

   C. The client's anxiety was explored, and appropriate interventions were implemented to assist the client in coping with these feelings.

   D. The client was assisted in recognizing their depression and in beginning to express the feelings associated with it.

8. **Assess Level of Insight (8)**
    A. The client's level of insight toward the presenting problems was assessed.
    B. The client was assessed in regard to the syntonic versus dystonic nature of their insight about the presenting problems.
    C. The client was noted to demonstrate good insight into the problematic nature of the behavior and symptoms.
    D. The client was noted to be in agreement with others' concerns and is motivated to work on change.
    E. The client was noted to be ambivalent regarding the problems described and is reluctant to address the issues as a concern.
    F. The client was noted to be resistant regarding acknowledgment of the problem areas, is not concerned about them, and has no motivation to make changes.

9. **Assess for Correlated Disorders (9)**
    A. The client was assessed for evidence of research-based correlated disorders.
    B. The client was assessed in regard to the level of vulnerability to suicide.
    C. The client was identified as having a comorbid disorder, and treatment was adjusted to account for these concerns.
    D. The client has been assessed for any correlated disorders, but none were found.

10. **Assess for Culturally Based Confounding Issues (10)**
    A. The client was assessed for age-related issues that could help to better understand their clinical presentation.
    B. The client was assessed for gender-related issues that could help to better understand their clinical presentation.
    C. The client was assessed for cultural syndromes, cultural idioms of distress, or culturally based perceived causes that could help to better understand their clinical presentation.
    D. Alternative factors have been identified as contributing to the client's currently defined "problem behavior," and these were taken into account in regard to treatment.
    E. Culturally based factors that could help to account for the client's currently defined "problem behavior" were investigated, but no significant factors were identified.

11. **Assess Severity of Impairment (11)**
    A. The severity of the client's impairment was assessed to determine the appropriate level of care.
    B. The client was assessed in regard to impairment in social, relational, and educational endeavors.
    C. It was reflected to the client that the impairment appears to create mild to moderate effects on the client's functioning.
    D. It was reflected to the client that the impairment appears to create severe to very severe effects on the client's functioning.
    E. The client was continuously assessed for the severity of impairment, as well as the efficacy and appropriateness of treatment.

12. Assess for Pathogenic Care (12)

A. The home, school, and community of the client were assessed for pathogenic care and concerns.

B. The client's various environments were assessed for the persistent disregard of the child's needs, repeated changes in caregivers, limited opportunities for stable attachment, harsh discipline, or other grossly inept care.

C. Pathogenic care was identified and the treatment plan included strategies for managing or correcting these concerns and protecting the child.

D. No pathogenic care was identified and this was reflected to the client and caregivers.

13. Encourage Learning About Medical Condition (13)

A. The client was encouraged to learn about their medical condition.

B. The client was asked to learn realistic information about the course of their illness.

C. The client was encouraged to learn about pain management and chances of recovery from their medical condition.

D. The client was reinforced for attaining information about their medical concern.

E. The client has not sought out information about their medical condition and was redirected to do so.

14. Monitor/Reinforce Treatment Adherence (14)

A. The client's adherence with the recommended medical treatment regimen was monitored.

B. The client's failure to adhere to medical treatment recommendations was confronted and addressed.

C. Positive affirmation and encouragement were given to the client for their consistent follow-through on all aspects of the medical treatment regimen.

D. Despite gentle confrontation and encouragement, the client still fails to adhere to the medical treatment recommendation for their medical condition.

15. Explore Factors Interfering with Treatment Adherence (15)

A. Misconceptions, fears, and situational factors were explored with the client for their possible interference with medical treatment adherence.

B. The client was assigned "Attitudes about Medication or Medical Treatment" in the *Adolescent Psychotherapy Homework Planner* (Jongsma, Peterson, McInnis, & Bruce).

C. The client's misconceptions, fears, and other situational factors were resolved to improve their follow-through with recommended medical treatment.

D. Since being helped to make the connection between their fears and misconceptions and avoiding medical treatment, the client has started to cooperate fully and responsibly with their medical treatment.

E. The client's resistance to adherence with the medical treatment regimen continues to be a problem; brainstorming techniques were used to increase adherence.

16. Utilize Motivational Interviewing (16)

A. Motivational interviewing techniques were used to help assess the client's stage of change.

B. The client was assisted in moving toward making a commitment to therapy toward positive change.

C. The client was noted to be participating actively in treatment.

17. Monitor Sleep Patterns (17)

A. Today's therapy session explored the factors that interfere with the client's ability to sleep restfully through the night.

B. The client was assigned the exercise "Childhood Sleep Problems" in the *Child Psychotherapy Homework Planner* (Jongsma, Peterson, McInnis, & Bruce).

C. The client was trained in the use of guided imagery and relaxation techniques to help induce calm before attempting to sleep.

D. The client was asked to track their sleep patterns to determine whether they should be referred for a medication evaluation.

E. The client was instructed to monitor their sleep patterns to help determine whether the medication needs to be changed or the dosage adjusted.

F. The client was administered electromyographic (EMG) biofeedback to reinforce a successful relaxation response to help them sleep restfully at night.

18. Monitor Eating Patterns (18)

A. Today's therapy session explored the factors that interfere with the client's ability to maintain a nutritious diet.

B. The client was trained in the use of a healthy diet plan.

C. The client was asked to track their eating patterns to determine whether they should be referred for a medication evaluation.

19. Explore Client's Feelings Regarding Medical Condition (19)

A. The client was assisted in identifying and verbalizing feelings connected to their medical condition.

B. The client was encouraged to recognize and express feelings related to the medical condition on a daily basis.

C. The "Gaining Acceptance of Physical Handicap or Illness" exercise from the *Child Psychotherapy Homework Planner* (Jongsma, Peterson, McInnis, & Bruce) was assigned to the client to help work through feelings generated by their medical condition.

D. The "Dealing with Childhood Asthma" exercise from the *Child Psychotherapy Homework Planner* (Jongsma, Peterson, McInnis, & Bruce) was assigned to the client.

E. Instances of the client recognizing, identifying, and expressing feelings were affirmed and reinforced verbally.

F. The client was not open with their feelings regarding the current medical condition and was urged to be more open as they feel ready to disclose.

20. Confront Denial of Need for Medical Treatment (20)

A. Gentle confrontation was used with the client regarding denial of the seriousness of their condition and of the need for adherence with recommended treatment.

B. Denial was normalized as part of the adjustment process, and barriers to acceptance of the need for treatment on the client's part were explored and addressed.

C. Despite gentle confrontation, the client continues to deny the seriousness of their condition and refuses to follow through with the recommended treatment.

D. The client was reinforced as their denial regarding the reality of the medical condition and the need for treatment has dissipated, resulting in consistent follow-through with medical recommendations.

21. **Reinforce Acceptance of Condition (21)**

A. The positive aspects of acceptance over denial of the medical condition were reinforced with the client.

B. The client's statements indicating acceptance of the condition were affirmed and reinforced.

C. Ambivalent statements by the client around their medical condition and its treatment were reframed to more positive ones and reinforced.

D. The client's denial regarding the reality of the medical condition and the need for treatment has dissipated, resulting in consistent follow-through with medical recommendations; the benefits of this reality focus were emphasized.

22. **Explore Family's Feelings Regarding Medical Condition (22)**

A. Feelings associated with a family member's medical condition were explored and normalized for the family.

B. Family sessions were conducted to help the family members clarify and share feelings they have experienced around the client's medical condition.

C. Family members were reminded that having a safe place to express feelings about the client's condition was helpful and healthy for all involved.

D. Family members were assigned "Coping with a Sibling's Health Problems" from the *Adolescent Psychotherapy Homework Planner* (Jongsma, Peterson, McInnis, & Bruce).

E. Family members expressed strong feelings of helplessness and fear of the client's medical condition deteriorating in the future.

F. The client's siblings expressed feelings of anger and jealousy regarding the attention focused on the client's medical condition.

23. **Explore Relationship Conflict (23)**

A. How the parents were dealing with the stress of the client's illness was explored individually with each parent.

B. The issue of increased conflicts between the parents because of the client's medical condition was addressed.

C. Specific ways that each parent could be supportive and accepting of the other were identified.

24. **Assess and Resolve Family Conflicts (24)**

A. The family conflicts were assessed.

B. Conflict-resolution techniques were used to help address family conflicts.

C. The family was reinforced for their willingness to address and resolve family conflicts.

D. Family members have not worked to resolve conflicts and were redirected to do so.

25. Increase Family Members' Spirit of Tolerance (25)

A. In family sessions, a spirit of tolerance for individually different responses to stress was facilitated and encouraged between members.

B. Family members were reminded of each person's individual differences regarding internal resources and response styles in the face of threat.

C. Tolerance was modeled to family members in sessions through active listening and warm acceptance of their feelings and thoughts.

26. Teach Power of Family's Involvement (26)

A. The family was educated in the potential healing power of members' involvement in all aspects of the client's care and recovery.

B. Assistance was provided to the family to help them make their care and home environment as warm, positive, kind, and supportive for the client as possible.

C. The family was provided with ongoing encouragement and reinforcement in providing warm, positive supportive care to the client.

27. List Limitations Caused by Medical Condition (27)

A. Using interview or play therapy techniques, the client was prompted to list all changes, losses, and limitations that have resulted from their medical condition.

B. The client was assisted in making a list of their losses, changes, and limitations that resulted from the medical condition, due to their difficulty in connecting the two things.

C. The client was assigned "Coping with Your Illness" in the *Adolescent Psychotherapy Homework Planner* (Jongsma, Peterson, McInnis, & Bruce).

D. The changes in the client's life brought on by the medical condition caused feelings of depression, frustration, and hopelessness.

E. The client tended to minimize the limitations caused by their medical condition and was provided with more accurate feedback in this area.

28. Teach Grieving Process (28)

A. The client was educated on the process of grief.

B. The client was asked to identify the types of grief that they have experienced.

C. Several books on grief and loss were suggested to the client to read alone or with parents.

D. In today's session, *Don't Despair on Thursdays!* (Moser) was read with the client to help them develop ideas for handling feelings of grief and loss.

E. The session focused on discussing and processing key ideas on grief and loss from the grief-related book with the client.

F. The client was assisted in identifying several ideas learned from reading the grief-related book and how they could use them to cope with feelings of grief and loss.

G. The client was resistive to discussing anything from the book on grief and loss and was encouraged to be more open.

29. Suggest Grief and Loss Books to Parents (29)

A. Books about the process of grief and loss were suggested to the client's parents.

B. *Good Grief* (Westberg) was recommended to the client's parents.

   C. The client's parents were encouraged to read *How Can It Be All Right When Everything Is All Wrong?* (Smedes).

   D. The client's parents were encouraged to read *When Bad Things Happen to Good People* (Kushner).

   E. The parents were encouraged to read *Caring for Your Grieving Child: A Parent's Guide* (Wakenshaw).

   F. The client's parents have read assigned material on grief and loss and were encouraged to use this information to help understand and support their child in the grieving process.

   G. The client's parents have not read the assigned books on grief and loss and were redirected to do so.

30. Assign a Grief Journal (30)

   A. The benefits of keeping a grief journal were explained, identified, and reinforced with the client.

   B. The client was asked to commit to keeping a daily grief journal to share in therapy sessions.

   C. Daily grief journal material that the client has recorded was shared in sessions and entries were processed.

   D. The client has not recorded feelings on a daily basis and was reminded of their commitment to keep a grief journal.

31. Assess Child-Rearing Practices (31)

   A. The parents were assessed in regard to their understanding of the use of positive reinforcement principles in child-rearing practices.

   B. The parents were taught about operant-based child management techniques.

32. Identify Distorted, Negative Thoughts (32)

   A. The client was assisted in identifying the cognitive distortions that contribute to a negative attitude and hopeless feeling regarding their medical condition.

   B. The client was assigned "Bad Thoughts Lead to Bad Feelings" from the *Adolescent Psychotherapy Homework Planner* (Jongsma, Peterson, McInnis, & Bruce).

   C. The connection between cognitive distortions and feelings of helplessness and negativity around the client's medical condition was established and made clear to them.

   D. The client was resistive to identifying, and is in denial of engaging in, cognitive distortion; tentative examples were identified and offered to the client.

33. Teach Positive, Realistic Self-Talk (33)

   A. The client was helped to generate a list of positive, realistic self-talk to replace the cognitive distortions and catastrophizing that accompany their medical condition.

   B. The client was assigned "Replace Negative Thoughts with Positive Self-Talk" from the *Child Psychotherapy Homework Planner* (Jongsma, Peterson, McInnis, & Bruce).

   C. The techniques of positive self-talk were taught to the client.

   D. Role-play situations around the client's medical condition were used for the client to practice using positive self-talk.

   E. The benefits of using positive self-talk reported by the client were reinforced.

   F. The client has not used positive, realistic self-talk to replace the cognitive distortions and catastrophizing and was assisted in identifying situations in which they could use these techniques.

34. **Assign Daily Mourning Time (34)**

   A. The client was educated on the value of mourning a loss.

   B. Ways for the client to daily mourn loss were explored, with several being selected and developed for implementation.

   C. The client was asked to commit to implementing their mourning ritual for a specific set amount of time daily and then getting on with other daily activities.

   D. The daily mourning ritual has been followed by the client and it has been effective in focusing grief feelings and increasing productivity during other times of the day.

   E. The client has failed to follow through on implementing the daily mourning ritual and has avoided the grieving process; the client was urged to use the mourning ritual.

   F. Instead of focusing and limiting the intense grieving to specific times of the day, the client continues to be preoccupied with grief throughout the day and was redirected about the use of the mourning ritual.

35. **Focus on Positive Life Aspects (35)**

   A. The client was assisted in listing all the positive aspects still present in their life.

   B. The client was challenged to focus on the positive aspects of life that they identified rather than the losses associated with the medical condition.

   C. The client was assigned "Replace Negative Thoughts with Positive Self-Talk" from the *Child Psychotherapy Homework Planner* (Jongsma, Peterson, McInnis, & Bruce).

   D. The client's focus on positive life aspects within sessions was reinforced.

   E. Gentle confrontation was used when the client refocused on their losses rather than positive life aspects.

36. **Teach Calming Techniques (36)**

   A. Deep muscle relaxation, deep breathing, and positive imagery techniques were taught to the client to enhance the ability to relax.

   B. The client was taught cognitive skills, such as distancing and decatastrophizing.

   C. The client was assigned the "Deep Breathing Exercise" from the *Child Psychotherapy Homework Planner* (Jongsma, Peterson, McInnis, & Bruce).

   D. The client was assigned the "Progressive Muscle Relaxation" from the *Adolescent Psychotherapy Homework Planner* (Jongsma, Peterson, McInnis, & Bruce).

   E. Behavioral rehearsal was used to give the client opportunity to practice each relaxation skill.

   F. The client was reminded of the benefits of deep muscle relaxation, deep breathing, and positive imagery and encouraged to use each on a regular basis.

G. The client has implemented the relaxation techniques and reports a reduction in stress and anxiety.

H. The client has failed to follow through with implementation of relaxation techniques.

37. Administer EMG Biofeedback (37)

A. Electromyographic (EMG) biofeedback was administered to the client to train and reinforce their successful relaxation response.

B. The client's response to EMG biofeedback was assessed and monitored for its effectiveness.

C. The client reported being able to relax more consistently and effectively since the EMG training, which has resulted in an improvement in their quality of sleep.

D. The client has not been able to consistently and effectively relax despite the use of EMG biofeedback training; the biofeedback training skills were reviewed to determine why this has failed.

38. Assign Reading on Relaxation and Calming Strategies (38)

A. The client was assigned to read about progressive muscle relaxation and other calming strategies in relevant books and treatment manuals.

B. The client was directed to read about muscle relaxation and other calming strategies in *The Relaxation and Stress Reduction Workbook for Kids* (Shapiro & Sprague).

C. The client was directed to read about calming strategies in *Coping C.A.T. Series* (Kendall et al.).

D. The client has read the assigned information on progressive muscle relaxation, and key points were reviewed.

E. The client has not read the assigned information on progressive muscle relaxation, and they were redirected to do so.

39. Teach Personal and Interpersonal Skills (39)

A. The client and parents were taught tailored, age-appropriate personal and interpersonal skills.

B. The client and parents were taught about problem-solving skills.

C. The client and parents were taught about conflict-resolution skills.

D. Modeling, role-playing, and behavior rehearsal were used to help develop skills and work through several current conflicts.

E. The client was assigned the "Problem-Solving Exercise" from the *Child Psychotherapy Homework Planner* (Jongsma, Peterson, McInnis, & Bruce).

40. List Pleasurable Activities (40)

A. The client was asked to list all the activities that they have enjoyed doing.

B. The client's list of activities was examined for the ones that can still be enjoyed alone and with others.

C. The client was encouraged to start again becoming involved in these pleasurable activities on a regular basis.

D. In spite of encouragement, the client continues to resist engagement in the pleasurable activities that they are capable of participating in.

41. Assess Social Network Impact (41)

A. An assessment was conducted of the effects of the medical condition on the client's social network.

B. The client was assigned "Effects of Physical Handicap or Illness on Self-Esteem and Peer Relations" from the *Adolescent Psychotherapy Homework Planner* (Jongsma, Peterson, McInnis, & Bruce).

C. The client was helped to realistically review the effects of their medical condition on their social networks, including both positive and negative effects.

D. Social support was facilitated for the client as available through the client's family and friends.

42. Solicit Commitment to Pleasurable Activities (42)

A. The client was asked to make a verbal commitment to increase their activity level in pleasurable social and physical activities.

B. "Show Your Strengths" from the *Child Psychotherapy Homework Planner* (Jongsma, Peterson, McInnis, & Bruce) was assigned to the client to help reinforce their use of engaging in enjoyable activities.

C. The client's involvement in activities was affirmed and reinforced.

D. The client's failure to keep their commitment to increase their activity level was gently confronted.

E. The client avoided the requested commitment by saying that they would give it a try and that's the best they could do.

F. In spite of encouragement, the client continues to resist engagement in the pleasurable activities that they are capable of participating in.

43. Engage in Behavioral Activation (43)

A. The client was engaged in "behavioral activation" by scheduling activities that have a high likelihood for pleasure and mastery.

B. The client was directed to complete tasks from the "Identify and Schedule Pleasant Activities" assignment from the *Adult Psychotherapy Homework Planner* (Jongsma & Bruce).

C. Rehearsal, role-playing, role reversal, and other techniques were used to engage the client in behavioral activation.

D. The client was reinforced for successes in scheduling activities that have a high likelihood for pleasure and mastery.

E. The client has not engaged in pleasurable activities and was redirected to do so.

44. Develop Physical Exercise Routine (44)

A. The client was assisted in developing a plan for a daily physical exercise routine within the limits of their medical condition.

B. The benefits of daily physical exercise were identified and reinforced.

C. Positive feedback was provided as the physical exercise plan was implemented by the client along with a commitment to follow the plan on a daily basis.

D. The client's follow-through with daily exercise and commitment was monitored and reinforced.

E. The client has not followed through with implementing any regular pattern of physical exercise, and they were redirected in this area.

45. Build Relapse Prevention Skills (45)

A. The client was assisted in building relapse prevention skills by identifying early warning signs of relapse into negative thoughts, feelings, and actions.

B. The client was assisted in reviewing skills learned during therapy and how to plan to manage challenges using these skills.

46. Refer to Support Group (46)

A. The client was educated on the various types of support groups available in the community.

B. The client was referred to a support group of others living with the same medical condition.

C. The benefits of the support group experience were identified and reinforced with the client.

D. The client's experience with attending the support group was processed, and continued attendance was encouraged.

E. The client has failed to follow the recommendation of attending a support group and was redirected to do so.

47. Refer to Family Support Group (47)

A. The purpose and benefits of attending a support group were identified and reinforced with the family.

B. Support group options were provided for the family.

C. The family was referred to a community support group associated with the client's medical condition.

D. The initial support group experience was processed with the family, and continued attendance was encouraged and reinforced.

E. The family has not followed through with attending the recommended support group and was redirected to do so.

48. Share Reading Material (48)

A. Family, friends, and caregivers were referred to reading material that is informative and supportive of their efforts in caring for the client.

B. Family, friends, and caregivers were provided with information about the *Families, Friends, and Caregivers* series (Keene et al.) to assist in their efforts in caring for the client.

49. Identify Resources for Support (49)

A. The parents' sources of emotional support were probed and assessed.

B. The parents were asked to identify their sources of emotional support.

C. The siblings' resources for support were reviewed.

D. The client's sources of emotional support were identified

50. Encourage Parents and Siblings Obtaining Support (50)

    A. The parents and siblings were assisted in identifying community resources for support.

    B. Barriers to accepting support were explored with the parents and siblings and addressed.

    C. The family's need for support was identified and reinforced.

    D. The family was praised as they have accepted their need for support and have followed through in making contact with potential resources for support.

51. Draw Out Parents' Fears (51)

    A. The parents were encouraged to express their underlying fears around the client's possible death.

    B. Empathy, affirmation, and normalization were used in responding to the fearful feelings that the parents verbalized.

    C. The parents were given the reassurance of God's presence as the giver and supporter of life.

    D. The parents were resistant to expressing their underlying fears about the client's possible death and were provided with additional support and empathy.

52. Identify Spiritual Support Resources (52)

    A. The client was assisted in identifying sources of spiritual support and how they could help them now.

    B. The client was encouraged to actively use their identified spiritual resources and support on a daily basis.

    C. The client has denied any interest in spiritual resources but was urged to keep this option open.

    D. The client's spiritual faith was noted to be deep and is a significant source of strength and peace during this time of pain and stress.

OBSESSIVE-COMPULSIVE DISORDER (OCD)

CLIENT PRESENTATION

1. **Recurrent/Persistent Thoughts (1)***
   A. The client described recurrent and persistent thoughts or impulses that are viewed as senseless, intrusive, and time consuming and that interfere with their daily routine.
   B. The intensity of the recurrent and persistent thoughts and impulses is so severe that the client is unable to efficiently perform daily duties or interact in social relationships.
   C. The strength of the client's obsessive thoughts has diminished and they have become more efficient in their daily routine.
   D. The client reported that the obsessive thoughts are under significant control and they are able to focus attention and effort on the task at hand.

2. **Failed Control Attempts (2)**
   A. The client reported failure at attempts to control or ignore obsessive thoughts or impulses.
   B. The client described many different failed attempts at learning to control or ignore obsessions.
   C. The client is beginning to experience some success at controlling and ignoring obsessive thoughts and impulses.

3. **Recognize Internal Source of Obsessions (3)**
   A. The client has a poor understanding that obsessive thoughts are a product of their own mind.
   B. The client reported that they recognize that the obsessive thoughts are a product of their own mind and are not coming from some outside source or power.
   C. The client acknowledged that the obsessive thoughts are related to anxiety and are not a sign of any psychotic process.

4. **Excessive Concern About Dirt and Disease (4)**
   A. The client displays excessive concern about dirt.
   B. The client has many unfounded fears about contracting a dreadful disease or illness.
   C. The client has frequently changed their behavior due to concerns and fears about germs and illnesses.
   D. The strength of the client's fears about dirt, germs, and illnesses has decreased, and the client has become more stable in their activities.
   E. The client reported that the excessive concerns about dirt and disease are under significant control and that they are able to focus attention and effort on their regular activities.

---

* The numbers in parentheses correlate to the number of the Behavioral Definition statement in the companion chapter with the same title in the *Child Psychotherapy Treatment Planner*, Sixth Edition, by Jongsma, Peterson, McInnis, & Bruce (Wiley, 2023).

5. **Aggressive/Sexual Obsessions (5)**
   A. The client described persistent obsessive thoughts about committing aggressive actions.
   B. The client has many troubling sexual thoughts and urges.
   C. The client described often imagining troubling aggressive or sexual actions.
   D. The client described that their aggressive, sexual thoughts are not compatible with their identifying values and morals.
   E. As treatment has progressed, the client reports a decreased pattern of obsessions regarding aggressive or sexual activity.
   F. The client reports that their aggressive, sexual thoughts, urges, or images are no longer occurring.

6. **Religious Obsessions (6)**
   A. The client described persistent and troubling thoughts about religious issues.
   B. The client described excessive concern about whether their actions are moral, right, or wrong.
   C. When under stress, the client turns the focus away from the stressor and on to religious/moral issues.
   D. The client described a decrease in persistent and troubling thoughts about religious issues.

7. **Compulsive Compensatory Behavior (7)**
   A. The client described repetitive and intentional behaviors that are performed in a ritualistic fashion.
   B. The client identified that their compulsive behaviors are in response to obsessive thoughts and increased feelings of anxiety and fearfulness.
   C. The client's compulsive behavior pattern follows rigid rules and has many repetitions to it.
   D. The client reported a significant decrease in the frequency and intensity of their compulsive behaviors.
   E. The client reports very little interference in their daily routine from their compensatory compulsive behavior rituals.

8. **Disconnected Behavioral Compulsions (8)**
   A. The client reports repetitive and excessive behaviors that are performed to neutralize or prevent discomfort or some dreadful situation.
   B. The client has identified that their behavior is not connected in any realistic way with what it is designed to neutralize or prevent.
   C. The client has identified their ritualistic behavior as unconnected to their actual fears.
   D. As treatment has progressed, the client's repetitive and excessive behaviors have decreased.

9. **Compulsions Seen as Unreasonable (9)**
   A. The client acknowledged that their repetitive and compulsive behaviors are excessive and unreasonable.
   B. The client's recognition of their compulsive behaviors as excessive and unreasonable has provided good motivation for cooperation with treatment and follow-through on attempts to change.

10. Cleaning/Washing Compulsions (10)

A. The client has had many cleaning compulsions, including cleaning and recleaning of many household items.

B. The client has engaged in washing compulsions, including excessive hand washing, bathing, and showering.

C. The client has had such severe hand-washing compulsions that skin breakdown is occurring.

D. As the client has participated in treatment, the frequency of cleaning and washing has decreased.

11. Hoarding/Collecting (11)

A. The client regularly engages in hoarding items that are unnecessary.

B. The client described the unnecessary collecting of innocuous items.

C. The client has become quite agitated when others have accidentally or purposefully threatened their hoarding or collecting.

D. As the client's functioning has improved, the desire to hoard or collect items has decreased.

E. The client's use of hoarding or collecting items has been eliminated.

12. Checking Compulsions (12)

A. The client identified that they frequently need to check and recheck basic tasks.

B. The client frequently checks and rechecks to see whether doors or windows are locked.

C. The client frequently checks and rechecks to make sure that homework has been done correctly.

D. The client has severe fears that others have been harmed and frequently checks and rechecks for no direct reason.

E. The client reports that they have significantly decreased the pattern of checking behaviors.

13. Arrangement Compulsions (13)

A. The client described frequently arranging objects to make certain that they are in "proper order," for no apparent reason (e.g., stacking coins in a certain order).

B. The client described being overly focused on arranging necessary objects (i.e., laying out clothes each evening at the same time or wearing only certain clothes on certain days).

C. As treatment has progressed, the client reports a decrease in their compulsion to order or arrange objects.

INTERVENTIONS IMPLEMENTED

1. Establish Rapport (1)*

A. Caring was conveyed to the client through support, warmth, and empathy.

B. The client was provided with nonjudgmental support and a level of trust was developed.

---

*The numbers in parentheses correlate to the number of the Therapeutic Intervention statement in the companion chapter with the same title in the *Child Psychotherapy Treatment Planner*, Sixth Edition, by Jongsma, Peterson, McInnis, & Bruce (Wiley, 2023).

C. The client was urged to feel safe in expressing their obsessive-compulsive disorder (OCD) issues.

D. The client began to express feelings more freely as rapport and trust level have increased.

E. The client has continued to experience difficulty being open and direct about the expression of painful feelings; the client was encouraged to use the safe haven of therapy to express these difficult issues.

2. **Focus on Strengthening Therapeutic Relationship (2)**

A. The relationship with the client was strengthened using empirically supported factors.

B. The relationship with the client was strengthened through the implementation of collaborative approach, agreement on goals, demonstration of empathy, verbalization of positive regard, and collection of client feedback.

C. The client reacted positively to the relationship-strengthening measures taken.

D. The client verbalized feeling supported and understood during therapy sessions.

E. Despite attempts to strengthen the therapeutic relationship, the client reports feeling distant and misunderstood.

F. The client has indicated that sessions are not helpful and will be terminating therapy.

3. **Assess OCD History (3)**

A. Active listening was used as the client described the nature, history, and severity of their obsessive thoughts and compulsive behaviors.

B. Through a clinical interview, the client described a severe degree of interference in their daily routine and ability to perform a task efficiently because of the significant problem with obsessive thoughts and compulsive behaviors.

C. The "Concerns, Feelings and Hopes About OCD" exercise from the *Child Psychotherapy Homework Planner* (Jongsma, Peterson, McInnis, & Bruce) was assigned to the client.

D. The client was noted to have made many attempts to ignore or control the compulsive behaviors and obsessive thoughts, but without any consistent success.

E. It was noted that the client gave evidence of compulsive behaviors within the interview.

4. **Conduct Psychological Testing (4)**

A. Psychological testing was administered to evaluate the nature and severity of the client's obsessive-compulsive problem.

B. The Children's Yale-Brown Obsessive-Compulsive Scale (Scahill et al.) was used to assess the client's frequency, intensity, duration, and history of obsessions and compulsions.

C. The psychological testing results indicate that the client experiences significant interference in their daily life from obsessive-compulsive rituals.

D. The psychological testing indicated a rather mild degree of OCD within the client.

E. The results of the psychological testing were interpreted to the client.

5. **Assess Level of Insight (5)**

A. The client's level of insight toward the presenting problems was assessed.

B. The client was assessed in regard to the syntonic versus dystonic nature of their insight about the presenting problems.

C. The client was noted to demonstrate good insight into the problematic nature of the behavior and symptoms.

D. The client was noted to be in agreement with others' concerns and is motivated to work on change.

E. The client was noted to be ambivalent regarding the problems described and is reluctant to address the issues as a concern.

F. The client was noted to be resistant regarding acknowledgment of the problem areas, is not concerned about them, and has no motivation to make changes.

6. Assess for Correlated Disorders (6)

A. The client was assessed for evidence of research-based correlated disorders.

B. The client was assessed in regard to the level of vulnerability to suicide.

C. The client was identified as having a comorbid disorder, and treatment was adjusted to account for these concerns.

D. The client has been assessed for any correlated disorders, but none were found.

7. Assess for Culturally Based Confounding Issues (7)

A. The client was assessed for age-related issues that could help to better understand their clinical presentation.

B. The client was assessed for gender-related issues that could help to better understand their clinical presentation.

C. The client was assessed for cultural syndromes, cultural idioms of distress, or culturally based perceived causes that could help to better understand their clinical presentation.

D. Alternative factors have been identified as contributing to the client's currently defined "problem behavior," and these were taken into account in regard to treatment.

E. Culturally based factors that could help to account for the client's currently defined "problem behavior" were investigated, but no significant factors were identified.

8. Assess Severity of Impairment (8)

A. The severity of the client's impairment was assessed to determine the appropriate level of care.

B. The client was assessed in regard to impairment in social, relational, and educational endeavors.

C. It was reflected to the client that the impairment appears to create mild to moderate effects on the client's functioning.

D. It was reflected to the client that the impairment appears to create severe to very severe effects on the client's functioning.

E. The client was continuously assessed for the severity of impairment, as well as the efficacy and appropriateness of treatment.

9. Assess for Pathogenic Care (9)

A. The home, school, and community of the client were assessed for pathogenic care and concerns.

B. The client's various environments were assessed for the persistent disregard of the child's needs, repeated changes in caregivers, limited opportunities for stable attachment, harsh discipline, or other grossly inept care.

C. Pathogenic care was identified and the treatment plan included strategies for managing or correcting these concerns and protecting the child.

D. No pathogenic care was identified, and this was reflected to the client and caregivers.

10. Refer for Medical Evaluation (10)

A. The client was referred to a physician for an evaluation for a medication prescription to aid in the control of their OCD.

B. The client has followed through with the referral for a medication evaluation and has been prescribed psychotropic medication to aid in the control of their OCD.

C. The client has failed to comply with the referral to a physician for a medication evaluation and was encouraged to do so.

11. Monitor Medication Adherence (11)

A. The client reported that they are taking the psychotropic medication as prescribed; the positive effect on controlling the OCD was emphasized.

B. The client reported adhering with the psychotropic medication prescription but that the effectiveness of the medication has been very limited or nonexistent; this information was relayed to the prescribing clinician.

C. The client has not consistently taken the psychotropic medication as prescribed and was encouraged to do so.

12. Provide Psychoeducation About OCD (12)

A. The client and parents were provided with initial psychoeducation about OCD.

B. The client and parents were provided with ongoing psychoeducation about OCD.

C. The client and parents were provided with a cognitive-behavioral conceptualization of OCD.

D. The client and parents were provided with information about the biopsychosocial factors influencing the development of OCD and how fear and avoidance serve to maintain the disorder.

E. The client and parents were asked to complete "Concerns, Feelings, and Hopes About OCD" in the *Child Psychotherapy Homework Planner* (Jongsma, Peterson, McInnis, & Bruce).

13. Discuss Usefulness of Treatment (13)

A. A discussion was held about how treatment serves as an arena to desensitize learned fear, reality-test obsessional fears and underlying beliefs, and build confidence in managing fears without compulsions.

B. Positive feedback was provided to the client as they displayed a clear understanding of the usefulness of treatment.

C. The client did not display a clear understanding of the usefulness of treatment and was provided with additional feedback in this area.

14. Confirm Motivation for Treatment (14)

A. The client was reviewed in regard to motivation to participate in treatment, and this was found to be significant.

B. The client's level of motivation to participate in treatment is fairly low, so motivational interviewing techniques were used to help unlock the client's motivation.

C. A pros-cons analysis was conducted to assist the client in increasing motivation.

D. The client was assisted in identifying their level of satisfaction with the status quo, understanding of the benefits of making a change, and level of optimism for being able to make a change.

15. Enroll in Exposure and Ritual Prevention Therapy (15)

A. The client was enrolled in intensive (e.g., daily) exposure and ritual prevention therapy for OCD.

B. The client was enrolled in nonintensive (e.g., weekly) exposure and ritual prevention for OCD.

C. The client was enrolled in individual exposure and ritual prevention therapy.

D. The client was enrolled in group or family exposure and ritual prevention therapy.

E. The client was asked to complete "Ritual Exposure and Response Prevention" in the *Child Psychotherapy Homework Planner* (Jongsma, Peterson, McInnis, & Bruce).

16. Develop Parents' Interventions (16)

A. A family-therapy session was held to identify specific, positive ways that the parents can help the client manage obsessions or compulsions.

B. The client's parents were reinforced for their identification of specific techniques to help the client manage obsessions or compulsions.

C. The client's parents were provided with tentative examples of ways to help the client manage obsessions or compulsions (e.g., parents refocus attention away from obsessions/compulsions by engaging in recreational activity or talking about other topics; parents encourage the client to participate in a feared activity).

D. The family was reinforced for the use of techniques to help the client manage obsessions or compulsions.

E. The family has not regularly prompted the client to use management techniques to control obsessions or compulsions and was redirected to do so.

17. Encourage Calmness and Support (17)

A. The client's parents were encouraged to remain calm, patient, and supportive when supporting the client in completing tasks of treatment.

B. The client's parents were instructed about specific ways in which they can display calmness, patience, and support when supporting the client.

C. The client's parents were assigned "Refocusing" in the *Child Psychotherapy Homework Planner* (Jongsma, Peterson, McInnis, & Bruce).

D. The client's parents were discouraged from reacting strongly with anger or frustration to the client.

E. The client's parents were reinforced for their calm, patient support of the client.

F. The parents have not consistently displayed calm, patient support of the client and were redirected to do so.

18. Teach Stress Management to Family (18)

A. The client's family members were taught about stress management techniques.

B. Family members were taught calming, problem-solving, and communication skills.

C. The family members were urged to use skills to resolve problems encountered by the family.

19. Monitor and Record Obsessions and Compulsions (19)

A. The client was instructed to self-monitor and record obsessions and compulsions.

B. The client was assisted in identifying triggers, specific fears, and mental or behavioral compulsions.

C. The parents were directed to assist the client in monitoring and recording obsessions and compulsions.

D. As treatment has progressed, the client's response to treatment was identified through their record of obsessions and compulsions.

E. The client was assisted in reviewing their record of obsessions and compulsions.

F. The client has not completed a regular record of obsessions and compulsions and was requested to do so.

20. Explore Self-Talk, Beliefs and Assumptions (20)

A. The client was assisted in exploring how their biased cognitive self-talk, beliefs, and underlying assumptions mediate their obsessional fears and compulsive behaviors.

B. The client's biased cognitive self-talk, beliefs, and underlying assumptions were reviewed.

C. The client was assigned "Replace Negative Thoughts with Positive Self-Talk" in the *Child Psychotherapy Homework Planner* (Jongsma, Peterson, McInnis, & Bruce).

D. The client was reinforced for their insight into their biased cognitive self-talk, beliefs, and underlying assumptions that support obsessional fears and compulsive behaviors.

E. The client struggled to develop insight into their own biased cognitive self-talk, beliefs, and underlying assumptions and was provided with tentative examples of these concepts.

21. Teach Cognitive Skills (21)

A. The client was taught cognitive skills, such as constructive self-talk, refocusing thoughts away from obsession, "bossing back" obsessions, distancing, and non-attachment.

B. The client was taught about letting obsessive thoughts, images, and/or impulses come and go.

C. The client was assigned "Refocusing" in the *Child Psychotherapy Homework Planner* (Jongsma, Peterson, McInnis, & Bruce).

D. The client was reinforced for use of cognitive skills such as constructive self-talk.

E. The client has not used cognitive skills very well and was redirected to do so.

22. Assign Media About OCD (22)

A. The client was assigned to review psychoeducational portions of books, videos, or treatment manuals on the rationale for exposure and ritual prevention therapy.

B. The client was assigned to review the psychoeducational media for the rationale for cognitive restructuring for OCD.

C. The client was assigned to review information from *It's Only a False Alarm Client Workbook* (Piacentini et al.).

    D. The client was assigned to review portions of *Parenting Kids with OCD* (Zucker).

    E. The client was assigned to read excerpts from *Up and Down the Worry Hill* (Wagner).

    F. The client has read the assigned material on the rationale for OCD treatment; key points were reviewed.

    G. The client has not read the assigned material on the rationale for OCD treatment and was redirected to do so.

23. Assess Cues (23)

    A. The client was assessed in regard to the nature of any external cues (e.g., persons, objects, and situations) that precipitate the client's obsessions and compulsions.

    B. The client was assessed in regard to the nature of any internal cues (e.g., thoughts, images, and impulses) that precipitate the client's obsessions and compulsions.

    C. The client was provided with feedback about their identification of cues.

24. Construct a Hierarchy of Fear Cues (24)

    A. The client was directed to construct a hierarchy of feared internal and external cues.

    B. The client was assisted in developing a hierarchy of internal and external fear cues.

    C. The client was assigned "Gradual Exposure to Fear" in the *Adolescent Psychotherapy Homework Planner* (Jongsma, Peterson, McInnis, & Bruce).

    D. The client has developed a useful hierarchy of feared internal and external cues, and positive feedback was provided.

    E. The client has struggled to clearly develop a hierarchy of feared internal and external cues and was provided with additional assistance in this area.

25. Select Likely Successful Imaginal Exposure (25)

    A. The client was assisted in identifying initial imaginal exposures with a bias toward those that have a likelihood of being successful experiences.

    B. Cognitive-restructuring techniques were used within and after the imaginal exposure of the OCD cues.

    C. The client was provided with feedback about their use of imaginal exposures.

26. Teach Coping Strategies (26)

    A. The client was taught to use coping strategies, such as constructive self-talk, distraction, and distancing.

    B. The client was directed to resist engaging in compulsive behaviors by using the coping strategies.

    C. The client was directed to record attempts to resist compulsions.

    D. The client was assigned the exercise "Reducing the Strength of Compulsive Behaviors" from the *Adult Psychotherapy Homework Planner* (Jongsma, Peterson, McInnis, & Bruce).

    E. The client was assisted in reviewing their attempts to use coping strategies to resist obsessions and compulsions, with reinforcement for success and corrective feedback toward improvement.

27. **Design Award System (27)**

   A. An award system was designed for the client for successful resistance of the urge to engage in compulsive behaviors.

   B. The client was rewarded for openly sharing obsessive thoughts with others.

28. **Assign Cue Exposure Practice (28)**

   A. The client was assigned a homework exercise in which they repeat the exposure to the internal and/or external OCD cues.

   B. The client was instructed to use restructured cognitions between sessions and to record responses.

   C. The client and the parents were assigned "Ritual Exposure and Response Prevention" from *Child Psychotherapy Homework Planner* (Jongsma, Peterson, McInnis, & Bruce).

   D. The client's use of the cue exposure homework was reviewed, and their success was reinforced.

   E. Corrective feedback was provided to the client for struggles in using restructured cognitions during exposure to OCD cues.

29. **Differentiate Between Lapse and Relapse (29)**

   A. A discussion was held with the client regarding the distinction between a lapse and a relapse.

   B. A lapse was associated with an initial and reversible return of symptoms, fear, or urges to avoid.

   C. A relapse was associated with the decision to return to fearful and avoidant patterns.

   D. The client was provided with support and encouragement as they displayed an understanding of the difference between a lapse and a relapse.

30. **Discuss Management of Lapse Risk Situations (30)**

   A. The client was assisted in identifying future situations or circumstances in which lapses could occur.

   B. The session focused on rehearsing the management of future situations or circumstances in which lapses could occur.

   C. The client was reinforced for appropriate use of lapse management skills.

   D. The client was redirected in regard to poor use of lapse management skills.

31. **Encourage Routine Use of Strategies (31)**

   A. The client was instructed to routinely use the strategies that they have learned in therapy (e.g., cognitive restructuring, exposure).

   B. The client was urged to find ways to build new strategies into their life as much as possible.

   C. The client was reinforced as they reported ways in which they have incorporated coping strategies into their life and routine.

   D. The client was redirected about ways to incorporate their new strategies into their routine and life.

32. **Schedule Maintenance Sessions (32)**

    A. Maintenance sessions were proposed to help maintain therapeutic gains.
    B. The client was reinforced for agreeing to the scheduling of maintenance sessions.
    C. The client refused to schedule maintenance sessions, and this was processed.

33. **Encourage Use of Coach (33)**

    A. The client was encouraged to involve a support person or coach who can help resist the urge to engage in compulsive behavior or to take their mind off obsessive thoughts.
    B. The client was reinforced as they have enlisted the assistance of a coach.
    C. The client was urged to regularly use their coach.

34. **Refer to Support Group (34)**

    A. The client was referred to a support group to help maintain and support the gains made in therapy.
    B. The client's parents were referred to a support group to help support and maintain the gains made in therapy.
    C. The client has attended the support group, and their experience was reviewed.
    D. The client's parents have attended the support group, and their experience was reviewed.
    E. The support group has not been attended, and the use of such support group was reinforced.

35. **Use ACT Approach (35)**

    A. Acceptance and Commitment Therapy (ACT) procedures were applied.
    B. The client was assisted in accepting and openly experiencing anxious or obsessive thoughts and feelings, without being overly impacted by them.
    C. The client was encouraged to commit their time and effort to activities that are consistent with identified personally meaningful values.
    D. The client has engaged well in the ACT approach and was reinforced for applying these concepts to their symptoms and lifestyle.
    E. The client has not engaged well in the ACT approach and remedial efforts toward engagement were applied.

36. **Assign Ericksonian Task (36)**

    A. The client was assigned an Ericksonian task of performing a behavior that is centered around the obsession or compulsion instead of trying to avoid it.
    B. As the client has faced the issue directly and performed a task, bringing feelings to the surface, the results of this were processed.
    C. As the client has processed feelings regarding the anxiety-provoking issue, the intensity of those feelings has been noted to be diminishing.
    D. The client has not used the Ericksonian task and was redirected to do so.

37. **Create Strategic Ordeal (37)**

    A. A strategic ordeal (Haley) was created with the client that offered a guarantee of cure for the obsession or compulsion.
    B. The client has engaged in the assigned strategic ordeal to help them overcome the OCD impulses.

C. It was noted that the strategic ordeal has been quite successful at helping the client reduce OCD symptoms and feelings of anxiety.

D. The client has not been successful at implementing the strategic ordeal consistently and was encouraged to do so.

38. Obtain Detailed Family History (38)

A. A detailed family history was obtained to identify other family members who have experienced OCD systems.

B. A variety of family members were identified to have experienced some level of OCD symptoms.

C. It was reflected to the client that their family tree did not include many relatives with OCD symptoms.

39. Address Contributing Factors to OCD Symptoms (39)

A. Family-therapy sessions were conducted to help address the factors contributing to the emergence, maintenance, or exacerbation of the client's OCD symptoms.

B. Factors contributing to the emergence, maintenance, and exacerbation of the client's OCD symptoms were directly treated.

C. The family was noted to decrease factors related to the client's OCD symptoms.

D. The family has not decreased factors related to OCD symptoms and were provided with remedial treatment in this area.

40. Conduct Psychodynamic Play Therapy (40)

A. Psychodynamic-oriented play therapy was conducted to address issues such as resistance, shame, and negative self-concept.

B. Psychodynamic-oriented play therapy was used to facilitate social adjustment.

OPPOSITIONAL DEFIANT

CLIENT PRESENTATION

1. History Persisting More Than 6 Months (1)*

A. The client's history of angry/irritable mood, argumentative/defiant behavior, or vindictiveness has persisted for more than 6 months.

B. The client's negative behavior has not reduced in severity in the past 6 months.

C. The client's behavior has begun to change and become easier to manage.

2. Negativistic/Hostile (2)

A. The client presented in a negative, hostile manner.

B. The client was negative regarding all matters great or small and hostile to all of the therapist's responses.

C. The client expressed hostile defiance toward their parents.

D. The client has noticeably reduced their level of hostility and defiance toward most adults.

3. Acts as If Adults Are the Enemy (3)

A. The client voiced that they have seen parents and other adults who have authority as the enemy.

B. The client verbalized a "me-versus-them" attitude when referring to interactions with most adults, especially those in authority.

C. The client has begun to see some adults, teachers, and even parents as possible allies as they have decreased their hostile attitude.

4. Temper Tantrums (4)

A. The client has erupted in temper tantrums in defiance of direction from an adult caregiver.

B. The client's temper tantrums include screaming, crying, throwing objects, thrashing on the ground and/or refusing to move.

C. The client has begun listening to their adult caregiver with less temper tantrums.

D. The client has ended use of temper tantrums as a way to get their way.

5. Temper Outbursts (5)

A. The parents report that the client engages in temper outbursts manifested verbally (e.g., verbal rages) or behaviorally (e.g., physical aggression toward people or property) that are grossly out of proportion in intensity or duration to the situation or provocation.

B. The client behaved in a disruptive manner during today's therapy session by engaging in verbal or behavioral temper outbursts.

---

*The numbers in parentheses correlate to the number of the Behavioral Definition statement in the companion chapter with the same title in the *Child Psychotherapy Treatment Planner*, Sixth Edition, by Jongsma, Peterson, McInnis, & Bruce (Wiley, 2023).

C. The client has recently begun to exercise greater self-control and has not engaged in as many temper outbursts.

D. The client demonstrated good self-control during today's therapy session and did not engage in any temper outbursts.

E. The client has demonstrated a significant reduction in the frequency of their temper outbursts.

6. **Touchy/Easily Annoyed (6)**

A. The client presented as being touchy or easily annoyed by others.

B. The client verbalized being annoyed with the therapist during today's session.

C. Overall, the client presented in a manner of being less annoyed with others and being somewhat tolerant of them.

D. The client is slowly coming to the point where they are not easily annoyed by others.

7. **Angry/Resentful (7)**

A. Anger and resentfulness dominate the client's affect, mood, and manner.

B. The client reports frequent verbal anger outbursts toward others.

C. The client's anger is freely vented toward others.

D. There is a decrease in the client's anger and resentment toward others.

8. **Authority Conflicts (8)**

A. The client displayed a negative attitude and was highly argumentative during today's therapy session.

B. The client has often tested the limits and challenged authority figures at home, at school, and in the community.

C. The client has often talked back to authority figures in a disrespectful manner when reprimanded.

D. The client has recently been more cooperative with authority figures.

E. The client has been cooperative and respectful toward authority figures on a consistent basis.

9. **Refusal of Requests (9)**

A. The client often defies or refuses to comply with requests from authority figures.

B. The client regularly fails to comply or actively refuses to comply with reasonable rules.

C. Others have become frustrated with the client's failure to comply in situations that would be socially expected.

D. As treatment has progressed, the client has become more compliant with typical expectations.

10. **Deliberate Annoying (10)**

A. The parents and teachers described a persistent pattern of the client engaging in deliberately annoying behaviors.

B. The client verbally acknowledged that they often deliberately annoy or frustrate others through their behaviors.

C. The client has started to verbalize thoughts and feelings instead of channeling thoughts and feelings into annoying behaviors.

D. The client has recently demonstrated a significant reduction in the frequency of deliberately annoying behaviors.

11. Blaming (11)

A. The client displayed an attitude of blaming others for their problems.

B. The client refused to take any responsibility for recent decisions and misbehavior, instead projecting it on to the parents and other authority figures.

C. The client carried the air that "I am not responsible or to blame for anything—it's all them."

D. The client has gradually started to take some responsibility for their decisions and behavior.

E. The client's general mood and manner reflect a noticeable decrease in blaming others for things that happen to them.

12. Vindictive/Spiteful (12)

A. The client's mood was vindictive and spiteful toward all persons who they perceived as being "against me."

B. There was a vindictive, spiteful edge in the client's attitude toward all key figures in daily life.

C. The client listed and vented acts of vengeance and spite that they would do to others.

D. The client has reduced their level of vindictiveness and spite toward others and has at times showed a little kindness in their speech.

13. Overreaction to Perceived Negative Circumstances (13)

A. The client seems to overreact to perceived disapproval, rejection, or criticism.

B. The client can become angry even when no disapproval, rejection, or criticism exists.

C. The client tends to have a bias toward the experience of disapproval, rejection, or criticism.

D. As treatment has progressed, the client has decreased their pattern of overreaction to disapproval, rejection, or criticism.

E. The client has decreased their angry overreaction to perceived disapproval, rejection, or criticism.

14. Passively Withholds Feelings (14)

A. The client passively withholds feelings from important individuals.

B. The client's inability to share feelings results in inappropriate reactivity and outbursts toward others.

C. Through significant work, the client has increased the ability to share feelings with important others.

D. The client has reduced their inappropriate reactivity to difficult situations or events.

15. Significant Impairments in Key Areas of Life (15)

A. The client reported impairments in social, academic, and occupational functioning.

B. The client indicated that according to most people they were not doing well socially and academically, but it did not concern them.

C. The client's social and academic functioning have improved as they have taken responsibility for their actions and been less defiant.

INTERVENTIONS IMPLEMENTED

1. **Establish Rapport (1)***

   A. Caring was conveyed to the client through support, warmth, and empathy.

   B. The client was provided with nonjudgmental support and a level of trust was developed.

   C. The client was urged to feel safe in expressing oppositional defiant concerns.

   D. The client began to express feelings more freely as rapport and trust level have increased.

   E. The client has continued to experience difficulty being open and direct about expression of painful feelings; the client was encouraged to use the safe haven of therapy to express these difficult issues.

2. **Focus on Strengthening Therapeutic Relationship (2)**

   A. The relationship with the client was strengthened using empirically supported factors.

   B. The relationship with the client was strengthened through the implementation of collaborative approach, agreement on goals, demonstration of empathy, verbalization of positive regard, and collection of client feedback.

   C. The client reacted positively to the relationship-strengthening measures taken.

   D. The client verbalized feeling supported and understood during therapy sessions.

   E. Despite attempts to strengthen the therapeutic relationship, the client reports feeling distant and misunderstood.

   F. The client has indicated that sessions are not helpful and will be terminating therapy.

3. **Assess Anger Dynamics (3)**

   A. The client was assessed for various stimuli that have triggered their defiant behavior.

   B. The client was helped to identify situations, people, and thoughts that have triggered their defiant behavior.

   C. The client was assisted in identifying the thoughts, feelings, and actions that have characterized their defiant responses.

   D. The *Child Behavior Checklist* (Achenbach) was used to help assess defiant dynamics.

   E. The *Eyberg Child Behavior Inventory* was used to help assess defiant dynamics.

   F. The *Sutter-Eyberg Student Behavior Inventory-Revised* was used to help assess defiant dynamics.

---

* The numbers in parentheses correlate to the number of the Therapeutic Intervention statement in the companion chapter with the same title in the *Child Psychotherapy Treatment Planner*, Sixth Edition, by Jongsma, Peterson, McInnis, & Bruce (Wiley, 2023).

4. **Refer/Conduct Psychological Testing (4)**

A. A psychological evaluation was conducted to determine whether emotional factors or attention-deficit/hyperactivity disorder (ADHD) are contributing to the client's behavior control problems.

B. The Parent-Child Relationship Inventory (PCRI) was used to help objectively assess the parent–child relational conflict.

C. The client was reinforced as they approached the psychological testing in an honest, straightforward manner and was cooperative with any requests presented to them.

D. The client was uncooperative and resistant to engage during the evaluation process and was encouraged to comply with the testing.

E. The client was resistive during the psychological testing and refused to consider the possibility of having ADHD or any serious emotional problems; support and redirection were provided.

F. Feedback was provided to the client and parents regarding the results of the psychological testing.

5. **Assess Level of Insight (5)**

A. The client's level of insight toward the presenting problems was assessed.

B. The client was assessed in regard to the syntonic versus dystonic nature of their insight about the presenting problems.

C. The client was noted to demonstrate good insight into the problematic nature of the behavior and symptoms.

D. The client was noted to be in agreement with others' concerns and is motivated to work on change.

E. The client was noted to be ambivalent regarding the problems described and is reluctant to address the issues as a concern.

F. The client was noted to be resistant regarding acknowledgment of the problem areas, is not concerned about them, and has no motivation to make changes.

6. **Assess for Correlated Disorders (6)**

A. The client was assessed for evidence of research-based correlated disorders.

B. The client was assessed in regard to the level of vulnerability to suicide.

C. The client was identified as having a comorbid disorder, and treatment was adjusted to account for these concerns.

D. The client has been assessed for any correlated disorders, but none were found.

7. **Assess for Culturally Based Confounding Issues (7)**

A. The client was assessed for age-related issues that could help to better understand their clinical presentation.

B. The client was assessed for gender-related issues that could help to better understand their clinical presentation.

C. The client was assessed for cultural syndromes, cultural idioms of distress, or culturally based perceived causes that could help to better understand their clinical presentation.

    D. Alternative factors have been identified as contributing to the client's currently defined "problem behavior," and these were taken into account in regard to treatment.

    E. Culturally based factors that could help to account for the client's currently defined "problem behavior" were investigated, but no significant factors were identified.

8. Assess Severity of Impairment (8)

    A. The severity of the client's impairment was assessed to determine the appropriate level of care.

    B. The client was assessed in regard to impairment in social, relational, and educational endeavors.

    C. It was reflected to the client that the impairment appears to create mild to moderate effects on the client's functioning.

    D. It was reflected to the client that the impairment appears to create severe to very severe effects on the client's functioning.

    E. The client was continuously assessed for the severity of impairment, as well as the efficacy and appropriateness of treatment.

9. Assess for Pathogenic Care (9)

    A. The home, school, and community of the client were assessed for pathogenic care and concerns.

    B. The client's various environments were assessed for the persistent disregard of the child's needs, repeated changes in caregivers, limited opportunities for stable attachment, harsh discipline, or other grossly inept care.

    C. Pathogenic care was identified, and the treatment plan included strategies for managing or correcting these concerns and protecting the child.

    D. No pathogenic care was identified, and this was reflected to the client and caregivers.

10. Refer for Medication Evaluation (10)

    A. The client was referred to a prescribing clinician for an evaluation for psychotropic medication to help in controlling the anger and behavior.

    B. The client adhered with a medication evaluation referral and has attended the appointment.

    C. The client refused to attend an evaluation appointment with the prescribing clinician for psychotropic medication; the client was encouraged to proceed with the evaluation as they feel willing to do so.

11. Monitor Medication Adherence/Effectiveness (11)

    A. The issues of medication adherence and effectiveness were addressed with the parents and the client.

    B. The client's resistance to taking medication was processed and addressed.

    C. Information related to the client's medication adherence and its effectiveness was communicated to the prescribing clinician.

    D. The client's responsible adherence with medications was verbally reinforced.

    E. The client reported that the use of the psychotropic medication has been effective in reducing the experience of anger.

12. Connect Feelings and Behaviors (12)

   A. The client was assisted in making the connection between their feelings and reactive behaviors.

   B. The "Risk Factors Leading to Child Behavior Problems" exercise from the *Child Psychotherapy Homework Planner* (Jongsma, Peterson, McInnis, & Bruce) was used to help make a connection between the client's feelings and reactive behaviors.

   C. The client completed the assigned exercise and was provided with positive feedback while processing this new knowledge.

   D. The client did not complete the assigned exercise and was asked to try to complete this again.

13. Teach Acceptance of Responsibility (13)

   A. The client was consistently confronted and challenged to cease blaming others for their anger control problems and accept greater responsibility for their actions.

   B. The client was assigned "Building Empathy" from the *Child Psychotherapy Homework Planner* (Jongsma, Peterson, McInnis, & Bruce).

   C. The client was assigned "The Lesson of Salmon Rock . . . Fighting Leads to Loneliness" from the *Child Psychotherapy Homework Planner* by Jongsma, Peterson, McInnis, & Bruce.

   D. The client was confronted with how the pattern of excessively blaming others for anger control problems places a strain on interpersonal relationships.

   E. The client was helped to identify more effective ways to resolve conflict and/or meet needs instead of expressing their anger through aggressive or destructive behavior.

   F. The client was strongly encouraged to apologize to others for their aggressive or destructive behavior.

14. Use Motivational Interviewing for Acceptance of Responsibility (14)

   A. Techniques derived from motivational interviewing were used to move the client away from externalizing and blaming and toward accepting responsibility.

   B. The client was asked to identify their level of satisfaction with current blaming and lack of acceptance of responsibility.

   C. The client was encouraged to identify the benefits of making a change to taking greater responsibility for their actions and motivation to change.

   D. The client was assisted in identifying their level of optimism for being able to change to become more responsible and accepting of their actions.

15. Identify Positive Consequences of Anger Management (15)

   A. The client was asked to identify the positive consequences they have experienced in managing anger.

   B. The client was assisted in identifying positive consequences of managing anger (e.g., respect from others and self, cooperation from others, improved physical health).

   C. The client was encouraged to learn new ways to conceptualize and manage anger.

16. Reconceptualize Anger (16)

   A. The client was assisted in conceptualizing oppositional behavior as involving different components that go through predictable phases.

B. The client was taught about the different components of oppositional behavior, including cognitive, physiological, affective, and behavioral components.

C. The client was taught how to better discriminate between relaxation and tension.

D. The client was taught about the predictable phases of oppositional behavior, including demanding expectations that are not met, leading to increased arousal and anger, which leads to acting out.

E. The client displayed a clear understanding of the ways to conceptualize oppositional behavior and was provided with positive reinforcement.

F. The client has struggled to understand the ways to conceptualize oppositional behavior and was provided with remedial feedback in this area.

17. **Discuss Rationale for Therapy (17)**

A. The client was led in a discussion regarding the use of therapy and the rationale behind it.

B. The client was assisted in learning about how a change in factors contributing to oppositional behavior can minimize negative consequences and increase positive ones.

18. **Teach Calming Techniques (18)**

A. The client was trained in the use of muscle relaxation, paced breathing, and calming imagery.

B. The client was assigned the "Deep Breathing Exercise" in the *Child Psychotherapy Homework Planner* (Jongsma, Peterson, McInnis, & Bruce).

C. The client was assigned "Progressive Muscle Relaxation" in the *Adolescent Psychotherapy Homework Planner* (Jongsma, Peterson, McInnis, & Bruce).

D. The client reported a positive response to the use of calming techniques taught to help control angry feelings.

E. The client appeared uncomfortable and unable to relax when being instructed in the use of calming techniques.

19. **Explore Self-Talk (19)**

A. The client's self-talk that mediates angry feelings and actions was explored.

B. The client was assessed for self-talk (e.g., demanding expectations), reflected in "should," "must," or "have to" statements.

C. The client was assisted in identifying and challenging biases and in generating alternative self-talk to correct for the biases.

D. The client was assigned the exercise "Replace Negative Thoughts with Positive Self-Talk" from the *Child Psychotherapy Homework Planner* (Jongsma, Peterson, McInnis, & Bruce).

E. The client was taught how to use correcting self-talk to facilitate a more flexible and temperate response to frustration.

20. **Assign Thought-Stopping Technique (20)**

A. The client was directed to implement a thought-stopping technique on a daily basis between sessions.

B. The client was assigned "Thought Stopping" in the *Adolescent Psychotherapy Homework Planner* (Jongsma, Peterson, McInnis, & Bruce).

C. The client's use of the thought-stopping technique was reviewed.

D. The client was provided with positive feedback for helpful use of the thought-stopping technique.

E. The client was provided with corrective feedback to help improve use of the thought-stopping technique.

21. **Teach Assertive Communication (21)**

   A. The client was taught about assertive communication through instruction, modeling, and role-playing.

   B. The client was referred to an assertiveness training group.

   C. The client displayed increased assertiveness and was provided with positive feedback in this area.

   D. The client has not increased their level of assertiveness and was provided with additional feedback in this area.

22. **Teach Conflict Resolution Skills (22)**

   A. The client was taught conflict resolution skills through modeling, role-playing, and behavioral rehearsal.

   B. The client was taught about empathy and active listening.

   C. The client was taught about "I messages," respectful communication, assertiveness without aggression, and compromise.

   D. The client and parents were assigned to read *Cool, Calm, and Confident* (Schab).

   E. "Learn to Be Assertive" and "Problem-Solving Exercise" from the *Child Psychotherapy Homework Planner* (Jongsma, Peterson, McInnis, & Bruce) were assigned to help the client increase communication and conflict resolution skills.

   F. The client was reinforced for clear understanding of the conflict resolution skills.

   G. The client displayed a poor understanding of the conflict resolution skills and was provided with remedial feedback.

23. **Construct Strategy for Managing Anger (23)**

   A. The client was assisted in constructing a strategy for managing anger.

   B. The client was encouraged to combine somatic, cognitive, communication, problem-solving, and conflict-resolution skills relevant to their needs.

   C. The client was reinforced for their comprehensive anger management strategy.

   D. The client was redirected to develop a more comprehensive anger management strategy.

24. **Select Challenging Situations for Managing Anger (24)**

   A. The client was provided with situations in which they may be increasingly challenged to apply new strategies for managing anger.

   B. The client was asked to identify likely upcoming challenging situations for managing anger.

   C. The client was urged to use strategies for managing anger in successively more difficult situations.

25. Monitor/Decrease Outbursts (25)

A. The client's reports of angry outburst were monitored, toward the goal of decreasing their frequency, intensity, and duration.

B. The client was urged to use new anger management skills to decrease the frequency, intensity, and duration of the anger outburst.

C. The client was assigned the "Anger Control" exercise in the *Child Psychotherapy Homework Planner* (Jongsma, Peterson, McInnis, & Bruce).

D. The client was assigned the "Child Anger Checklist" exercise in the *Child Psychotherapy Homework Planner* (Jongsma, Peterson, McInnis, & Bruce).

E. The client's progress in decreasing angry outbursts was reviewed.

F. The client was reinforced for success at decreasing the frequency, intensity, and duration of their anger outburst.

G. The client has not decreased frequency, intensity, or duration of anger outbursts, and corrective feedback was provided.

26. Encourage Disclosure (26)

A. The client was encouraged to discuss anger management goals with trusted persons who are likely to support their change.

B. The client was assisted in identifying individuals who are likely to support their change.

C. The client has reviewed anger management goals with trusted persons, and their response was processed.

D. The client has not discussed anger management goals and was redirected to do so.

27. Use Parent Management Training (27)

A. Parent Management Training was used.

B. The parents were taught how parent and child behavioral interactions can encourage or discourage positive or negative behavior.

C. The parents were taught how changing key elements of parent-child interactions can be used to promote positive change.

D. The parents were taught techniques as described in *Defiant Children* (Barkley) and *Parent Training for Disruptive Behavior* (Bearss et al.).

E. The parents were provided with specific examples of how prompting and reinforcing positive behaviors can be used to promote positive change.

F. The parents were provided with positive feedback for the use of the Parent Management Training approach.

G. The parents have not used the Parent Management Training approach and were redirected to do so.

28. Assign Parent Training Manuals (28)

A. The parents were directed to read parent training manuals.

B. The parents were directed to read *The Kazdin Method for Parenting the Defiant Child* (Kazdin).

C. The parents' study of pertinent parent training media was reviewed and processed.

D. The parents have not reviewed the assigned parent training media, and they were redirected to do so.

29. Teach Parents to Define Aspects of Situation (29)

A. The parents were taught how to specifically define and identify their child's problem behaviors.

B. The parents were taught how to identify their reactions to their child's behavior, and whether the reaction encourages or discourages the behavior.

C. The parents were taught to generate alternatives to their child's problem behavior.

D. Positive feedback was provided to the parents for their skill at specifically defining and identifying problem behaviors, reactions, outcomes, and alternatives.

E. Parents were provided with remedial feedback as they struggled to correctly identify their child's problem behaviors and their own reactions, responses, and alternatives.

30. Teach Consistent Parenting (30)

A. The parents were taught how to implement key parenting practices on a consistent basis, including establishing realistic, age-appropriate roles for their child's acceptable and unacceptable behavior.

B. The parents were taught about prompting positive behavior and use of positive reinforcement.

C. The parents were taught about clear direct instruction, time out, and other loss-of-privilege techniques for their child's problem behaviors.

D. The parents were taught about negotiation and renegotiation with children.

E. The parents were provided with positive feedback, as they have been able to develop consistent parenting practices.

F. The parents have not developed consistent parenting practices, and were redirected to do so.

31. Assign Home Exercises to Implement Parenting Technique (31)

A. The parents were assigned home exercises in which they implement parenting techniques and record results of the implementation exercises.

B. The parents were assigned "Clear Rules, Positive Reinforcement, Appropriate Consequences" in the *Adolescent Therapy Homework Planner* (Jongsma, Peterson, McInnis, & Bruce).

C. The parents' implementation of homework exercises was reviewed within the session.

D. Corrective feedback was used to help develop improved, appropriate, and consistent use of skills.

E. The parents have not completed the assigned homework and were redirected to do so.

32. Conduct Parent-Child Interaction Therapy (32)

A. Parent-child interaction therapy (McNeil & Humbree-Kigin) was implemented to teach appropriate child behavior and parent behavior management skills.

B. Child-directed sessions focused on teaching the child appropriate child behavior.

C. Parent-directed sessions focused on teaching parental behavior management skills (e.g., clear commands, consistent consequences, and positive reinforcement).

33. Refer to Parent Training Program (33)

A. The parents were referred to an evidence-based parent training program.

B. The parents were referred to the Incredible Years parent training program.

C. The parents were referred to the Positive Parenting Program.

D. The parents have used the evidence-based parent training program, and key concepts were reviewed.

E. The parents have not used the recommended parent training program and were reminded to do so.

34. **Design Contingency/Reward System (34)**

A. A reward system was developed with the client.

B. A contingency contract was developed with the client.

C. A meeting was held with school officials to help reinforce identified positive behaviors.

D. The exercise was assigned "Clear Rules, Positive Reinforcement, Appropriate Consequences" from the *Adolescent Psychotherapy Homework Planner* (Jongsma, Peterson, McInnis, & Bruce).

E. The client was encouraged to participate in the reward system/contingency contract in order to deter impulsive or rebellious behaviors.

F. Fine-tuning was done to the reward system/contingency contract in order to reinforce identified positive behaviors at home and school.

35. **Explore Family Abuse History (35)**

A. The client's family background was explored for a history of physical, sexual, or substance abuse that may contribute the emergence of their anger control problems.

B. The client was assisted in developing a timeline in the therapy session where they identified significant historical events, both positive and negative, that have occurred in their family.

C. The client's parents were confronted and challenged to cease physically abusive or overly punitive methods of discipline.

D. The parents were asked to identify how physically abusive or overly punitive methods of discipline negatively affect the client and siblings.

E. The parents were supported as they apologized to the client for abusive behaviors and overly harsh methods of discipline.

F. The parents were taught how aggressive discipline promotes the client's aggression and poor anger management.

G. The parents were referred to a parenting class.

36. **Protect Client from Abuse (36)**

A. The abuse of the client was reported to the appropriate agency.

B. A recommendation was made that the perpetrator be removed from the home and seek treatment.

C. A recommendation was made that the client and siblings be removed from the home to ensure protection.

D. The client and family members were assisted in identifying the necessary steps to minimize the risk of abuse occurring in the future.

E. The non-abusive parent was reinforced for verbalizing a commitment to protect the client and siblings from future abuse.

37. Provide Rationale for Relapse Prevention (37)

A. A rationale was reviewed with the client for relapse prevention.

B. The client was assisted in understanding the concepts of identifying risk factors and strategies for preventing them.

38. Differentiate Between Lapse and Relapse (38)

A. A discussion was held with the client regarding the distinction between a lapse and a relapse.

B. A lapse was associated with an initial and reversible return of angry outbursts.

C. A relapse was associated with the decision to return to the old pattern of anger.

D. The client was provided with support and encouragement as they displayed an understanding of the difference between a lapse and a relapse.

E. The client struggled to understand the difference between a lapse and a relapse, and the client was provided with remedial feedback in this area.

39. Discuss Management of Lapse Risk Situations (39)

A. The client was assisted in identifying future situations or circumstances in which lapses could occur.

B. The session focused on rehearsing the management of future situations or circumstances in which lapses could occur.

C. The client was reinforced for appropriate use of lapse management skills.

D. The client was redirected in regard to poor use of lapse management skills.

40. Encourage Routine Use of Strategies (40)

A. The parents/child were encouraged to routinely use strategies used in therapy.

B. Parent training techniques, problem-solving, and anger management techniques were encouraged to be used as a regular part of parent/child interactions.

C. The client and parent were encouraged to build strategies into their life as much as possible.

41. Develop a Coping Card (41)

A. The client was provided with a coping card on which specific coping strategies were listed.

B. The client was assisted in developing the coping card in order to list helpful coping strategies.

C. The client was encouraged to use the coping card when struggling with anger-producing situations.

42. Schedule Maintenance Sessions (42)

A. Maintenance sessions were proposed to help the client maintain therapeutic gains and adjust to life without anger outbursts.

B. The client was reinforced for agreeing to the scheduling of maintenance sessions.

C. The client refused to schedule maintenance sessions, and this was processed.

43. Emphasize Respect (43)

A. The client was taught about the basics of treating others respectfully.

B. The client was taught the principle of reciprocity, focusing on treating others the way that the client would wish to be treated.

C. The client was asked to conduct an experiment to treat everyone in a respectful manner for a one-week period to see if others will reciprocate by treating them with more respect.

D. The results of the client's experiment in treating others with respect were reviewed.

44. Play Checkers (44)

A. Checkers rules were established by the client and the therapist, and games were played with the client being confronted when they were violating or attempting to change the agreed-upon rules.

B. The importance of rules was reinforced with the client, by the therapist pointing out the chaos that would be present without them and the negative feelings that result when people break or bend rules.

45. Encourage Benevolent Acts (45)

A. The client was directed to engage in three altruistic or benevolent acts.

B. The client was provided with examples of altruistic and benevolent acts, such as reading to a developmentally disabled student, or mowing an elderly person's lawn.

C. The client's experience of using altruistic or benevolent acts was reviewed.

D. An emphasis on how the client can develop empathy and sensitivity to the needs of others through altruistic or benevolent acts was emphasized.

E. The client has not done the assigned altruistic or benevolent acts and was redirected to do so.

46. Encourage Allowing Client to Be in Charge of Tasks (46)

A. The family was encouraged to allow the client to be in charge of tasks at home.

B. Specific examples of areas in which the client might be able to be in charge of tasks at home were reviewed (e.g., preparing and cooking a special dish for a family get-together, building shelves, changing oil).

C. Techniques from "Share a Family Meal" from the *Child Psychotherapy Homework Planner* (Jongsma, Peterson, McInnis, & Bruce) were used to help the client take charge of tasks in the home.

D. The family was urged to demonstrate confidence in the client's ability to act responsibly.

E. The family's experience of the client being in charge of tasks at home was reviewed and processed.

F. The family has not allowed the client to be in charge of any significant tasks at home and was redirected to do so.

47. Explore Feelings About Neglect or Abuse (47)

A. The client was given the opportunity in session to express feelings about past neglect, abuse, separation, or abandonment.

B. The client was instructed to draw pictures that reflected feelings about neglect, abuse, separation, or abandonment.

C. The client was instructed to use a journal to record thoughts and feelings about past neglect, abuse, separation, or abandonment.

D. The empty-chair technique was employed to facilitate expression of feelings surrounding past neglect or abuse.

E. The client has been reluctant to explore feelings about neglect and abuse and was urged to process these feelings as they feel capable of doing so.

48. Reframe Complaints (48)

A. A family session was conducted during which complaints were reframed into requests for positive change.

B. The client was asked to complete the "Filing a Complaint" exercise from the *Child Psychotherapy Homework Planner* (Jongsma, Peterson, McInnis, & Bruce) to assist them in reframing complaints into requests.

C. The client was asked to complete the "If I Could Run My Family" exercise from the *Child Psychotherapy Homework Planner* (Jongsma, Peterson, McInnis, & Bruce).

D. The family was focused onto the pros and cons of reasonable suggestions for resolution of complaints/requests.

E. The client reported several instances of switching from making complaints to making requests of others around them, and the positive results from this change were highlighted.

49. Assess/Treat the Marital Dyad (49)

A. The marital dyad was assessed for possible substance abuse, conflict, or triangulation.

B. Family therapy sessions were conducted to explore the dynamics that contribute to the emergence of the child's anger control problems.

C. The family therapy sessions identified several dynamics that contribute to the client's anger control problem.

D. Family dynamics were addressed within the family therapy session.

E. The family was referred for additional family therapy.

F. The parents were referred for couples therapy.

OVERWEIGHT/OBESITY

CLIENT PRESENTATION

1. **High Body Mass Index (1)***

   A. The client reports an excess body weight relative to height that is attributed to an abnormally high proportion of body fat.

   B. The client reports a body mass index of 30 or more.

   C. As treatment has progressed, the client has decreased their body mass index to under 30.

2. **Binge Eating (2)**

   A. The client described a recurrent pattern of binge eating during times of stress or emotional upset.

   B. The client reported experiencing recent episodes of binge eating.

   C. The client has not experienced any recent episodes of binge eating.

   D. The client has terminated their pattern of binge eating.

3. **Eating to Manage Troubling Emotions (3)**

   A. The client described a pattern of eating in order to manage troubling emotions.

   B. The client reported their perception that they feel "comfort" from eating when upset.

   C. As the client has gained insight into the cyclical pattern of eating to manage troubling emotions, they have come to manage emotions in a healthier manner.

4. **Rapid Eating (4)**

   A. The client reports a history of eating much more rapidly than normal.

   B. The client is uncertain why they eat in a more rapid manner than would be expected.

   C. As treatment has progressed, the client's food intake is at a more measured pace.

5. **Uncomfortably Full (5)**

   A. The client reports that they eat until feeling uncomfortably full.

   B. The client has been able to identify cues toward the level of comfortable fullness.

   C. The client no longer experiences a sense of being uncomfortably full but is continuing to eat more moderately.

6. **Overeating When Not Physically Hungry (6)**

   A. The client reports eating large amounts of food when they do not actually feel physically hungry.

   B. The client identifies their use of food when not hungry as a compensatory behavior.

   C. The client has learned to eat when hunger cues are identified.

   D. The client no longer eats large amounts of food when not feeling physically hungry.

---

*The numbers in parentheses correlate to the number of the Behavioral Definition statement in the companion chapter with the same title in the *Child Psychotherapy Treatment Planner*, Sixth Edition, by Jongsma, Peterson, McInnis, & Bruce (Wiley, 2023).

7. **Eating Alone Due to Embarrassment (7)**
   A. The client reports that they often eat alone because of feeling embarrassed about how much they are eating.
   B. The client feels that they have alienated others from eating with them.
   C. The client has become more at ease with the social aspects of eating.
   D. As treatment has progressed, the client reports a more moderate food intake and feeling more at ease with the social aspect of eating with others.

8. **Low Self-Concept Due to Overeating (8)**
   A. The client reports that they feel disgusted, depressed, or guilty after eating too much.
   B. The client has explored their emotional reaction to overeating.
   C. The client reports that as they have decreased the pattern of overeating, their emotional well-being has improved.

9. **Hiding Food (9)**
   A. The client admits to hiding food in an effort to conceal their eating habits from others.
   B. Despite being urged by others to change eating habits, the client continues to consume high-calorie foods often.
   C. The client reports a reduction in hiding of food and has reduced the amount of high-calorie foods consumed.
   D. The client has desisted their habit of hiding food and has developed a healthy calorie consumption.

INTERVENTIONS IMPLEMENTED

1. **Establish Rapport (1)***
   A. Caring was conveyed to the client through support, warmth, and empathy.
   B. The client was provided with nonjudgmental support, and a level of trust was developed.
   C. The client was urged to feel safe in expressing their weight issues.
   D. The client began to express feelings more freely as rapport and trust level have increased.
   E. The client has continued to experience difficulty being open and direct about the expression of painful feelings; the client was encouraged to use the safe haven of therapy to express these difficult issues.

2. **Focus on Strengthening Therapeutic Relationship (2)**
   A. The relationship with the client was strengthened using empirically supported factors.
   B. The relationship with the client was strengthened through the implementation of collaborative approach, agreement on goals, demonstration of empathy, verbalization of positive regard, and collection of client feedback.
   C. The client reacted positively to the relationship-strengthening measures taken.

---

*The numbers in parentheses correlate to the number of the Therapeutic Intervention statement in the companion chapter with the same title in the *Child Psychotherapy Treatment Planner*, Sixth Edition, by Jongsma, Peterson, McInnis, & Bruce (Wiley, 2023).

D. The client verbalized feeling supported and understood during therapy sessions.

E. Despite attempts to strengthen the therapeutic relationship, the client reports feeling distant and misunderstood.

F. The client has indicated that sessions are not helpful and will be terminating therapy.

3. Gather Problem History (3)

A. Today's therapy session explored the factors contributing to the client's obesity.

B. The personal and family eating patterns, thoughts, attitudes, and beliefs about food and emotional status were assessed.

C. A complete history of the client's eating behavior was taken in today's therapy session.

D. Today's therapy session focused on the targets for treatment.

4. Assess for Psychopathology (4)

A. The child was assessed for psychopathology that may be contributing to overeating, including depression, anxiety, or other psychological conditions.

B. The parents were assessed for psychopathology that may be contributing to overeating, including depression, anxiety, or other psychological conditions.

C. Appropriate treatment was coordinated for the psychopathology uncovered within the family.

5. Provide Psychological Testing (5)

A. The client was referred for psychological testing to assist in forming the overall assessment, including confirming or ruling out psychopathology.

B. A psychological evaluation was conducted in order to assist in providing a clearer picture of the client's overall level of pathology.

C. The client was provided with feedback regarding the results of the assessment.

D. The psychological assessment instruments were readministered as needed to assess treatment outcome.

6. Assess Level of Insight (6)

A. The client's level of insight toward the presenting problems was assessed.

B. The client was assessed in regard to the syntonic versus dystonic nature of their insight about the presenting problems.

C. The client was noted to demonstrate good insight into the problematic nature of the behavior and symptoms.

D. The client was noted to be in agreement with others' concerns and is motivated to work on change.

E. The client was noted to be ambivalent regarding the problems described and is reluctant to address the issues as a concern.

F. The client was noted to be resistant regarding acknowledgment of the problem areas, is not concerned about them, and has no motivation to make changes.

7. Assess for Correlated Disorders (7)

A. The client was assessed for evidence of research-based correlated disorders.

B. The client was assessed in regard to the level of vulnerability to suicide.

C. The client was identified as having a comorbid disorder, and treatment was adjusted to account for these concerns.

D. The client has been assessed for any correlated disorders, but none were found.

8. **Assess for Culturally Based Confounding Issues (8)**

A. The client was assessed for age-related issues that could help to better understand their clinical presentation.

B. The client was assessed for gender-related issues that could help to better understand their clinical presentation.

C. The client was assessed for cultural syndromes, cultural idioms of distress, or culturally based perceived causes that could help to better understand their clinical presentation.

D. Alternative factors have been identified as contributing to the client's currently defined "problem behavior," and these were taken into account in regard to treatment.

E. Culturally based factors that could help to account for the client's currently defined "problem behavior" were investigated, but no significant factors were identified.

9. **Assess Severity of Impairment (9)**

A. The severity of the client's impairment was assessed to determine the appropriate level of care.

B. The client was assessed in regard to impairment in social, relational, and educational endeavors.

C. It was reflected to the client that the impairment appears to create mild to moderate effects on the client's functioning.

D. It was reflected to the client that the impairment appears to create severe to very severe effects on the client's functioning.

E. The client was continuously assessed for the severity of impairment, as well as the efficacy and appropriateness of treatment.

10. **Assess for Pathogenic Care (10)**

A. The home, school, and community of the client were assessed for pathogenic care and concerns.

B. The client's various environments were assessed for the persistent disregard of the child's needs, repeated changes in caregivers, limited opportunities for stable attachment, harsh discipline, or other grossly inept care.

C. Pathogenic care was identified and the treatment plan included strategies for managing or correcting these concerns and protecting the child.

D. No pathogenic care was identified, and this was reflected to the client and caregivers.

11. **Refer for Physical Examination (11)**

A. The client was referred for a thorough physical examination to assess the effects that the obesity has had on their health.

B. The client followed through by receiving a thorough physical examination.

C. The client is opposed to receiving a thorough physical examination to assess the effects of their obesity.

    D. The findings from the physical examination revealed that the client's obesity has had a detrimental effect on their health.

    E. The findings from the physical examination do not reveal any serious health problems.

    F. The client has not followed through on a physical examination and was redirected to do so.

12. Assess/Refer for Psychotropic Medication (12)

    A. The client's need for psychotropic medication was assessed.

    B. It was determined that the client would benefit from psychotropic medication, and a referral was made.

    C. A need for psychotropic medication was not found, and thus no referral was made.

    D. The client cooperated with the physician referral, and psychotropic medication has been prescribed.

    E. The client has failed to follow through on the physician referral and was encouraged to do so.

13. Monitor Medication (13)

    A. The effectiveness of psychotropic medication and its side effects were monitored.

    B. The client reported that the medication has been effective in stabilizing mood; the information is being relayed to the prescribing clinician.

    C. The client reported that the psychotropic medication has not been effective or helpful; this information is being relayed to the prescribing clinician.

    D. The client has not taken the medication on a consistent basis and was encouraged to do so.

14. Discuss Risks (14)

    A. A discussion was held with the client and parents about how the seeming short-term rewards of overeating increase the risk for more serious medical consequences.

    B. Medical consequences such as hypertension and heart disease were discussed with the client and parents.

    C. The positive health benefits of good weight management practices were reviewed.

15. Assess Motivation (15)

    A. The client and parents' motivation and readiness for change were assessed.

    B. The client appears to be unmotivated for treatment at this time, so motivational interventions were utilized to help clarify and uncover the client's hidden level of motivation.

    C. As the client remains unmotivated, treatment for these concerns was deferred for the time being.

    D. As the client appears motivated for entering treatment at this time, consent was obtained for continuing with treatment.

16. Assign Monitoring of Eating and Exercise (16)

    A. The client was assigned to self-monitor and record food intake and exercise.

    B. The parents were directed to assist the client in monitoring and recording food intake and exercise.

C. The client was assigned "My Eating and Exercise Journal" in the *Child Psychotherapy Homework Planner* (Jongsma, Peterson, McInnis, & Bruce).

D. The client's eating and exercise journal was processed with a focus on challenging maladaptive patterns.

E. The client was assisted in replacing maladaptive patterns with adaptive alternatives.

F. The client has not kept a journal record of food intake and exercise and the client was redirected to do so.

17. Conduct Behavioral Weight Management (17)

A. Treatment was conducted via the Behavioral Weight Management approach.

B. A discussion was held about obesity, factors influencing it, including lifestyle, exercise, attitudes, cognitions/beliefs, relationships, and nutrition.

C. The client was reinforced for regular engagement in the discussion about factors influencing obesity.

D. The client seemed to struggle to engage in a discussion about the factors relating to obesity and was provided with remedial feedback and support.

18. Assign Reading of Material About Obesity (18)

A. The client and parents were assigned to read psychoeducational information about obesity, factors influencing it, the rationale for treatment, and the emphasis for treatment.

B. The client and parents were assigned to read portions of *The LEARN Program for Weight Management* (Brownell).

C. The client and parents were assigned to read portions of *The Cognitive Behavioral Workbook for Weight Management* (LaLiberte et al.).

D. The client and parents have read the assigned material, and key concepts were processed.

E. The client and parents have not read the assigned material and were redirected to do so.

19. Review Emphasis of Program (19)

A. The primary emphasis of the treatment program was reviewed.

B. The emphasis was given to whether the client understands and agrees with the rationale and approach for treatment.

20. Discuss Challenges and Benefits of Treatment (20)

A. A discussion was held with the client and parents regarding realistic expectations for what therapy will entail, including the challenges and benefits.

B. An emphasis on adherence to the treatment program was maintained.

C. The discussion focused on the positive hope for success, as well as realistic expectations about the challenges.

21. Set Goals (21)

A. The client was assisted in establishing short-term goals, to be accomplished on a weekly basis.

B. The client was assisted in developing medium-term (monthly) goals.

C. The client was assisted in establishing long-term goals, to be accomplished in 6 months to a year.

D. The client was assisted in evaluating and updating their goals for treatment.

22. **Discuss Flexible Goal Setting (22)**

    A. Recognition that lapses may occur in behavioral change was given, and the need for flexible goals was emphasized.

    B. An emphasis was made on the problem-solving approach that should be taken should a lapse occur.

    C. Strategies for lapse situations, such as forgiving self, identifying triggers, generating and evaluating options for addressing risks, and getting back on track were emphasized.

23. **Monitor Weight (23)**

    A. The client was assisted in routinely measuring their weight.

    B. The client's weight was recorded on a chart/graph in order to represent their changes during treatment.

24. **Teach Healthy Nutritional Practices (24)**

    A. The client was taught healthy nutritional practices involving the concepts of balance and variety.

    B. The client was recommended to read portions of *The Monster Health Book* (Miller).

    C. The client was recommended to read portions of *Good Enough to Eat* (Rockwell).

    D. The client was assisted in outlining a healthy food diet consistent with good nutritional practices and aimed at attaining the client's weight goals.

    E. The client was assigned "Developing and Implementing a Healthier Diet" in the *Child Psychotherapy Homework Planner* (Jongsma, Peterson, McInnis, & Bruce).

25. **Refer to Nutritionist (25)**

    A. The client was referred to a nutritionist experienced in eating disorders for an assessment of nutritional rehabilitation.

    B. Recommendations were made by the nutritionist and these were coordinated into the care plan.

    C. The client has not followed through with the referral to a nutritionist and was reminded to do so.

26. **Develop Individualized Diet (26)**

    A. The client and parents were assisted in developing an individualized diet that includes the child's preferred food choices, while encouraging variety and allowing choice.

    B. The client and parents were taught the principle of portion control for managing total caloric intake.

    C. An emphasis was placed on the family approach to healthy eating.

    D. An emphasis was placed on not prohibiting certain foods, but that moderation of intake is the key to maintaining a healthy weight.

27. **Use Stimulus-Control Techniques (27)**

    A. Stimulus-control techniques were used to reduce exposure to triggers of spontaneous food buying, selecting, or eating.

    B. The client was taught to avoid buying and eating high-caloric snacks after school.

    C. The client was taught to eat prior to shopping for food, or going to a place where healthy food is not readily available.

  D. The client was taught to shop for food from a list.

  E. The family was asked to make a commitment to have nutritional snack foods openly available in the home.

  F. The family was encouraged to prepare foods from a preplanned menu.

28. Use Mealtime Stimulus-Control Techniques (28)

  A. The client was taught about mealtime stimulus-control techniques.

  B. The client was encouraged to serve food on a smaller plate and to eat slowly.

  C. The family was encouraged to create a pleasant mealtime ambiance to create an eating routine conducive to pleasurable, moderated eating.

29. Make Small Exercise Goals (29)

  A. The parents and client were encouraged to identify small, doable changes in activities consistent with therapeutic exercise goals.

  B. Lifestyle wellness techniques such as parking farther away to promote walking, taking the stairs, walking to school, and other activities was encouraged.

  C. The client was assigned "Increasing My Physical Activity" in the *Child Psychotherapy Homework Planner* (Jongsma, Peterson, McInnis, & Bruce).

  D. The client was reinforced for increased activity.

30. Encourage Physical Activity Games (30)

  A. The parents and child were encouraged to play games that require physical movement.

  B. The parents and child were encouraged that any computer games should be interactive, physically involved games.

  C. The child was reinforced for regular use of physical movement games.

31. Encourage Organized Physical Activities (31)

  A. The client was encouraged to participate in organized physical activities such as physical education, swimming, and youth club sports.

  B. The client was reinforced for regular participation in organized physical activities.

32. Explore Self-Talk (32)

  A. The client's self-talk and beliefs that mediate nontherapeutic eating habits were reviewed.

  B. The client was taught to challenge biases that promote nontherapeutic eating habits.

  C. The client was assisted in replacing biased messages with reality-based positive alternatives.

  D. The client has moved from overeating, eating to manage emotions, and poor self-concept to eating for health and using character/values to define self.

33. Assign Self-Talk Homework (33)

  A. The client was assigned homework exercises in which they identify self-talk and create reality-based alternatives.

  B. The client was assigned the exercise "Replace Negative Thoughts with Positive Self-Talk" from the *Child Psychotherapy Homework Planner* (Jongsma, Peterson, McInnis, & Bruce).

C. The client was assisted in reviewing self-talk replacement exercises, with corrective feedback for failure and reinforcement for success.

34. **Reinforce Positive Self-Talk (34)**
    A. Behavioral techniques such as modeling, corrective feedback, imagine rehearsal, and social reinforcement were used to teach the client positive self-talk.
    B. The client was taught to self-reward in order to facilitate new behavior change efforts.
    C. The client was assigned the exercise "Positive Self-Statements" from the *Child Psychotherapy Homework Planner* (Jongsma, Peterson, McInnis, & Bruce).

35. **Teach Calming Skills for High-Risk Situations (35)**
    A. The client was taught tailored calming skills to manage high-risk situations.
    B. The client was taught both cognitive and somatic calming skills.
    C. Modeling, role-playing, and behavior rehearsal were used to work through how to use calming skills in several current situations.
    D. The client was assigned the exercise "Deep Breathing Exercise" from the *Child Psychotherapy Homework Planner* (Jongsma, Peterson, McInnis, & Bruce).
    E. The client was assigned portions of *The Relaxation and Stress Reduction Workbook for Kids* (Shapiro & Sprague).
    F. The client displayed clear understanding of the calming skills for managing problematic situations and was positively reinforced for this.
    G. The client struggled to understand how to use calming skills to manage high-risk situations and was provided with remedial feedback in this area.

36. **Teach Problem-Solving Skills for High-Risk Situations (36)**
    A. The client was taught tailored problem-solving skills to manage high-risk situations.
    B. The client was taught about pinpointing the situation, generating options, listing pros and cons of each option, selecting an option, implementing an option, and refining.
    C. Modeling, role playing, and behavior rehearsal were used to work through how to use problem-solving skills in several current situations.
    D. The client was assigned the exercise "Problem-Solving Exercise" from the *Child Psychotherapy Homework Planner* (Jongsma, Peterson, McInnis, & Bruce).
    E. The client displayed clear understanding of the problem-solving skills for managing problematic situations and was positively reinforced for this.
    F. The client struggled to understand how to use problem-solving skills to manage high-risk situations and was provided with remedial feedback in this area.

37. **Teach Conflict-Resolution Skills for High-Risk Situations (37)**
    A. The client was taught tailored conflict-resolution skills to manage high-risk situations.
    B. The client was taught about empathy, active listening, and "I messages."
    C. Modeling, role-playing, and behavior rehearsal were used to work through how to use conflict-resolution skills in several current situations.
    D. The client was assigned the exercise "Negotiating a Peace Treaty" from the *Child Psychotherapy Homework Planner* (Jongsma, Peterson, McInnis, & Bruce).

E. The client was assigned the exercise "Problem-Solving Exercise" from the *Child Psychotherapy Homework Planner* (Jongsma, Peterson, McInnis, & Bruce).

F. The client displayed clear understanding of the conflict-resolution skills for managing problematic situations and was positively reinforced for this.

G. The client struggled to understand how to use conflict-resolution skills to manage high-risk situations and was provided with remedial feedback in this area.

38. Teach Assertiveness Skills for High-Risk Situations (38)

A. The client was taught tailored assertiveness skills to manage high-risk situations.

B. The client was taught about respectful communication, assertiveness without aggression, and compromise.

C. Modeling, role-playing, and behavior rehearsal were used to work through how to use assertiveness skills in several current situations.

D. The client was recommended to read portions of *Cool, Calm, and Confident* (Schab).

E. The client displayed clear understanding of the assertiveness skills for managing problematic situations and was positively reinforced for this.

F. The client struggled to understand how to use assertiveness skills to manage high-risk situations and was provided with remedial feedback in this area.

39. Teach Family Stress Management Skills (39)

A. All family members were taught stress management skills.

B. Family members were taught calming, problem-solving, communication, and conflict-resolution skills.

C. Family members were assigned "Deep Muscle Relaxation" in the *Adolescent Psychotherapy Homework Planner* (Jongsma, Peterson, McInnis, & Bruce).

D. The family members were encouraged to use stress management skills in order to manage stress and facilitate the client's progress in treatment.

40. Teach Parents About Prompting and Rewarding (40)

A. The parents were taught about how to prompt and reward treatment-consistent behavior.

B. The parents were taught about empathetically ignoring excessive complaining and modeling the behavior that is being prescribed for the client.

C. The parents were assigned "Being a Consistent Parent" in the *Child Psychotherapy Homework Planner* (Jongsma, Peterson, McInnis, & Bruce).

D. The parents were assigned "Clear Rules, Positive Reinforcement, Appropriate Consequences" in the *Adolescent Psychotherapy Homework Planner* (Jongsma, Peterson, McInnis, & Bruce).

E. The parents were reinforced for their success in prompting and rewarding treatment consistent behavior.

F. The parents were assisted in redirecting themselves about situations in which they have failed to reward treatment consistent behavior.

41. Reduce Enabling (41)

A. The family was assisted in identifying and overcoming the tendency to reinforce the client's poor eating habits and misplaced motivations.

B. The family members were taught constructive ways to reward the client's progress.

42. Encourage Ongoing Support (42)

A. The parents were encouraged to develop and coordinate ongoing support for the client in weight management efforts.

B. The parents were encouraged to use email messages, phone calls, texting, and postal mail notes to support the client in their changes.

C. The parents were encouraged to engage others in providing support to the client.

43. Differentiate Between Lapse and Relapse (43)

A. A discussion was held with the client regarding the distinction between a lapse and a relapse.

B. A lapse was associated with an initial and reversible return of poor eating habits.

C. A relapse was associated with the decision to return to the old patterns that contributed to and maintained obesity.

D. The client was provided with support and encouragement as they displayed an understanding of the difference between a lapse and a relapse.

E. The client struggled to understand the difference between a lapse and a relapse, and the client was provided with remedial feedback in this area.

44. Discuss Management of Lapse Risk Situations (44)

A. The client was assisted in identifying future situations or circumstances in which lapses could occur.

B. The session focused on rehearsing the management of future situations or circumstances in which lapses could occur.

C. The client was reinforced for appropriate use of lapse management skills.

D. The client was redirected in regard to poor use of lapse management skills.

45. Encourage Routine Use of Strategies (45)

A. The client was instructed to routinely use the strategies learned in therapy (e.g., cognitive restructuring, assertiveness).

B. The client was urged to find ways to build new strategies into their life as much as possible.

C. The client was reinforced as they reported ways in which they have incorporated coping strategies into their life and routine.

D. The client was redirected about ways to incorporate new strategies into their routine and life.

46. Develop a Coping Card (46)

A. The client was provided with a coping card on which specific coping strategies were listed.

B. The client was assisted in developing the coping card in order to list helpful coping strategies.

C. The client was encouraged to use the coping card when struggling with high-risk situations.

47. Refer to Group Weight-Loss Program (47)

A. The client and parents were referred to a group behavioral weight-loss program.

B. The use of a weight-loss program was emphasized, with an emphasis on changes in lifestyle, exercise, attitudes, relationships, and nutrition.

C. The client has been regularly engaged in a group behavioral weight-loss program and the experience and results were reviewed.

D. The client has not been involved in a group behavioral weight-loss program and was redirected to do so.

48. Investigate Emotional Needs (48)

A. Sensitive questioning, active listening, and unconditional regard were used to probe, discuss, and interpret positive emotional needs being met through eating.

B. The client was probed for possible emotional neglect or abuse.

49. Reinforce Insight (49)

A. The client was reinforced for their insight into past emotional pain and its connection to present overeating.

B. The client was assisted in developing greater insight into how past emotional pain has been connected to present overeating.

PARENTING

CLIENT PRESENTATION

1. **Feelings of Inadequacy in Limit Setting (1)***
   A. The parents expressed feelings of inadequacy in setting limits with their child.
   B. The parents described a sense of being overwhelmed by the child's behavior and unable to set effective limits with the child.
   C. As treatment has progressed, the parents have learned techniques to become more effective in setting limits with their child.
   D. The parents reported feeling much more effective in setting limits with the child.

2. **Difficulty in Managing Challenging Behaviors (2)**
   A. The parents reported frequent struggles to manage the challenging problem behaviors of the child.
   B. The parents reported that the responses to the child's challenging problem behaviors seem to have failed to help manage the problem behaviors.
   C. As treatment has progressed, the parents reported some success in managing the child's problem behaviors.
   D. The parents reported improvement and are typically able to manage the child's challenging behaviors with appropriate parenting interventions.

3. **Emotional Reactions to Misbehavior (3)**
   A. The parents often struggle to control their emotional reactions to their child's misbehavior.
   B. The parents tend to have extreme emotional reactions to their child's misbehavior.
   C. The parents' extreme emotional reaction to their child's misbehavior tends to prompt further misbehavior.
   D. As the parents have gained control over their emotional reactions to their child's misbehavior, they have become more effective in their parenting strategies.
   E. The parents regularly control their emotional reactions to their child's misbehavior.

4. **Conflict Regarding Parenting Strategies (4)**
   A. The parents described a lack of agreement regarding strategies for dealing with various types of negative child behaviors.
   B. One partner advocates for stricter control, while the other partner endorses a more permissive approach.
   C. The child's behavior seems to be unaffected by the parents' variable pattern of disciplinary response.

---

* The numbers in parentheses correlate to the number of the Behavioral Definition statement in the companion chapter with the same title in the *Child Psychotherapy Treatment Planner*, Sixth Edition, by Jongsma, Peterson, McInnis, & Bruce (Wiley, 2023).

D. The child's behavior is more out of control due to the parents' lack of agreement regarding limit setting.

E. As communication has increased, the parents have gained agreement regarding strategies for dealing with various types of negative child behavior.

5. **Deficits in Parenting Knowledge and Skills (5)**

A. The parents display deficits in parenting knowledge and skills.

B. The parents have a poor understanding of the use of basic techniques such as rewards, consequences, and time-outs.

C. As treatment has progressed, the parents have gained significant knowledge and skills in parenting.

6. **Inconsistent Parenting Styles (6)**

A. One parent seems to advocate for a more permissive discipline style, while the other partner endorses stricter control.

B. The child identified one parent as being overindulgent, and the other parent as too harsh.

C. Each parent's more extreme style seems to prompt the opposite extreme style in the other parent (e.g., the overindulgent parent becomes even more extreme, due to seeing the other parent as too harsh, and vice versa).

D. As the parents have achieved insight into the effects of their divergent pattern of parenting, they have become more balanced in their approach.

7. **Lax Supervision (7)**

A. The parents described a pattern of lax supervision over their child.

B. The parents described a pattern of setting inadequate limits on the child's behavior and privileges.

C. The parents reported that their child has had behavioral problems in other areas, due to the pattern of lax supervision and inadequate limit setting.

D. As the parents have developed a firmer pattern of supervision and limit setting, their relationship with their child has improved, with a commensurate improvement in the child's behavior.

8. **Overindulgence (8)**

A. The parents reported a pattern of overindulgence of the child's wishes and demands.

B. The parents often overindulge the child's wishes and demands in order to avoid a temper tantrum.

C. The parents have made a commitment to become more realistic regarding when to fulfill the child's wishes and demands.

D. As the parent's pattern of overindulgence of the child's wishes and demands has diminished, the overall relationship has improved.

9. **Harsh, Rigid, and Demeaning Behavior (9)**

A. The parents often treat the child in a rather harsh manner.

B. The parents are quite rigid in their rules and expectations for the child's behavior.

C. The parents act in a demeaning way toward their child.

D. As treatment has progressed, the parents have become more supportive and encouraging toward the child.

10. **Physical/Emotional Abuse (10)**

   A. The child has reported that their parents have been physically or emotionally abusive.

   B. The child's report of physical/emotional abuse has been confirmed through independent sources.

   C. The parents provided a detailed account of the physical/emotional abuse of the child.

   D. The reports of physical abuse have been referred to Child Protective Services as required by mandatory reporting statutes.

   E. The parents have ceased all physical and emotional abuse.

11. **Lack of Knowledge Regarding Developmental Expectations (11)**

   A. The client reported a lack of knowledge regarding reasonable expectations for a child's behavior at a given developmental level.

   B. The client often makes comments reflecting an unreasonable expectation for a child's behavior at a given developmental level.

   C. As treatment has progressed, the client has developed more realistic expectations for a child's behavior at a given developmental level.

12. **Parents Have Exhausted Their Options (12)**

   A. The parents reported that they have tried a variety of techniques to try to resolve the client's behavior problems.

   B. The parents have exhausted their repertoire of parenting techniques in an attempt to resolve the client's behavior problems.

   C. Despite the parents' use of many different techniques, the client continues to display a variety of behavioral problems.

13. **Outside Requests for Addressing Behavior (13)**

   A. School officials, court authorities, and/or friends have told the parents that their child's behavior needs to be addressed.

   B. The parents seem to disregard outside requests for addressing their child's behavior.

   C. The parents have been motivated by outside requests for addressing their child's behavior.

   D. Outside sources identify that the child's behavior has improved.

INTERVENTIONS IMPLEMENTED

1. **Establish Rapport (1)***

   A. Caring was conveyed to the client through support, warmth, and empathy.

   B. The client was provided with nonjudgmental support and a level of trust was developed.

---

*The numbers in parentheses correlate to the number of the Therapeutic Intervention statement in the companion chapter with the same title in the *Child Psychotherapy Treatment Planner*, Sixth Edition, by Jongsma, Peterson, McInnis, & Bruce (Wiley, 2023).

C. The client was urged to feel safe in expressing their concerns.

D. The client began to express feelings more freely as rapport and trust level have increased.

E. The client has continued to experience difficulty being open and direct about expression of painful feelings; the client was encouraged to use the safe haven of therapy to express these difficult issues.

2. Focus on Strengthening Therapeutic Relationship (2)

A. The relationship with the client was strengthened using empirically supported factors.

B. The relationship with the client was strengthened through the implementation of collaborative approach, agreement on goals, demonstration of empathy, verbalization of positive regard, and collection of client feedback.

C. The client reacted positively to the relationship-strengthening measures taken.

D. The client verbalized feeling supported and understood during therapy sessions.

E. Despite attempts to strengthen the therapeutic relationship, the client reports feeling distant and misunderstood.

F. The client has indicated that sessions are not helpful and will be terminating therapy.

3. Engage Parents (3)

A. Active listening techniques were used to establish a basis for a trust relationship with the parents.

B. The parents' struggles with parenting were normalized.

C. Information was gathered on the parent's marital relationship, child behavior expectations, and parenting style.

D. The parents appeared to place trust in the therapeutic relationship and were encouraged to provide full information.

4. Conduct Interview (4)

A. A clinical interview focusing on pinpointing the nature and severity of the client's misbehavior was conducted.

B. The clinical interview conducted assessed the parent's responses to the client's misbehavior.

C. Parents were given feedback regarding what possible triggers and reinforcements may be contributing to the client's behavior.

5. Assess Child Behavior Problems (5)

A. The client was assessed for emotional behavioral problems that may warrant an addition to the treatment plan.

B. The client's emotional behavioral problems were not of significant concern and no addition to the treatment plan was warranted.

C. The client's emotional behavioral problems are concerning enough to warrant an addition to the treatment plan.

D. The client was referred to additional psychological and/or pharmacological treatment for their emotional behavioral problems.

6. **Assess Marital Conflicts (6)**

   A. The information received from the parents about their relationship and parenting style was analyzed to assess the presence of marital conflict.

   B. It was reflected to the parents that they are experiencing significant marital conflicts that need to be resolved in order to address the parenting issues.

   C. It was reflected to the parents that their marriage appears to be strong and able to cope with the changes that may need to be made in order to become more effective parents.

7. **Conduct/Refer for Marital Therapy (7)**

   A. The parents were referred for marital/relationship therapy in order to resolve the conflicts preventing them from being effective parents.

   B. The focus of treatment was shifted to the parent's marital/relationship concerns and the need to resolve the conflicts preventing them from being effective parents.

   C. Through the use of marital therapy, the parents have been able to resolve the conflicts preventing them from being more effective parents.

   D. Despite the use of marital therapy, the parents continue to have conflict and were urged to resolve this in order to become more effective parents.

8. **Administer Testing Instruments (8)**

   A. The parents were directed to complete an objective assessment of their parenting status.

   B. The parents were administered the Parenting Stress Index (PSI).

   C. The parents were administered the Parent-Child Relationship Inventory (PCRI).

   D. The parents have not completed the objective testing instruments and were redirected to do so.

9. **Share Assessment Results (9)**

   A. The results of the objective parenting assessment instruments were shared with the parents.

   B. The parents were assisted in identifying issues to begin working on to strengthen the parenting team, based on the results of the assessment instruments.

   C. The parents were positively reinforced as they identified issues they need to work on.

   D. The parents denied needing to work on any issues to strengthen the parenting team, despite the results of the assessment instruments, and were urged to reconsider this.

10. **Identify Parental Strengths (10)**

    A. The results of the parenting status tests were used to identify parental strengths.

    B. The parental strengths were emphasized to the parents to help build confidence and effectiveness.

    C. As a result of the information from the assessments, the parents have increased their confidence and are more effective as a parenting team.

11. **Assess Level of Insight (11)**

    A. The client's level of insight toward the presenting problems was assessed.

B. The client was assessed in regard to the syntonic versus dystonic nature of their insight about the presenting problems.

C. The client was noted to demonstrate good insight into the problematic nature of the behavior and symptoms.

D. The client was noted to be in agreement with others' concerns and is motivated to work on change.

E. The client was noted to be ambivalent regarding the problems described and is reluctant to address the issues as a concern.

F. The client was noted to be resistant regarding acknowledgment of the problem areas, is not concerned about them, and has no motivation to make changes.

12. **Assess for Correlated Disorders (12)**

A. The client was assessed for evidence of research-based correlated disorders.

B. The client was assessed in regard to the level of vulnerability to suicide.

C. The client was identified as having a comorbid disorder, and treatment was adjusted to account for these concerns.

D. The client has been assessed for any correlated disorders, but none were found.

13. **Assess for Culturally Based Confounding Issues (13)**

A. The client was assessed for age-related issues that could help to better understand their clinical presentation.

B. The client was assessed for gender-related issues that could help to better understand their clinical presentation.

C. The client was assessed for cultural syndromes, cultural idioms of distress, or culturally based perceived causes that could help to better understand their clinical presentation.

D. Alternative factors have been identified as contributing to the client's currently defined "problem behavior," and these were taken into account in regard to treatment.

E. Culturally based factors that could help to account for the client's currently defined "problem behavior" were investigated, but no significant factors were identified.

14. **Assess Severity of Impairment (14)**

A. The severity of the client's impairment was assessed to determine the appropriate level of care.

B. The client was assessed in regard to impairment in social, relational, and educational endeavors.

C. It was reflected to the client that the impairment appears to create mild to moderate effects on the client's functioning.

D. It was reflected to the client that the impairment appears to create severe to very severe effects on the client's functioning.

E. The client was continuously assessed for the severity of impairment, as well as the efficacy and appropriateness of treatment.

15. **Assess for Pathogenic Care (15)**

A. The home, school, and community of the client were assessed for pathogenic care and concerns.

B. The client's various environments were assessed for the persistent disregard of the child's needs, repeated changes in caregivers, limited opportunities for stable attachment, harsh discipline, or other grossly inept care.

C. Pathogenic care was identified and the treatment plan included strategies for managing or correcting these concerns and protecting the child.

D. No pathogenic care was identified, and this was reflected to the client and caregivers.

16. Create a Compassionate Environment (16)

A. Empathetic listening, compassion, and support were provided to help the parents become more comfortable in the therapeutic setting.

B. The parents were urged to express the frustrations of parenting.

C. As the parents let their guard down and expressed the frustrations of parenting, they were provided with support and encouragement.

D. Despite a compassionate, empathetic environment, the parents have not been willing to express the frustrations of parenting and were redirected in this area.

17. Utilize Humor and Normalization (17)

A. Humor was injected into sessions when appropriate to help educate the parents on the full scope of parenting and to provide balance and perspective.

B. The parents were encouraged to use humor with each other to help express feelings of frustration, helplessness, and inadequacy that each experiences in the parenting role.

C. The parents' experiences were normalized.

D. Positive feedback was given to the parents as they have used appropriate humor and normalized their own experiences.

E. The parents have had extreme difficulty being humorous toward one another as tension levels are high and were encouraged to help each other use this release to express feelings.

18. Reduce Unrealistic Expectations (18)

A. The parents were assisted in reducing unrealistic expectations of themselves and of their child.

B. The parents were reinforced as they identified some of their unrealistic expectations, both for themselves and for their child.

C. The parents were confronted when they continued to have unrealistic expectations of themselves and their child.

D. The parents were unable to identify their own unrealistic expectations of themselves and their child and were provided with tentative examples in this area.

19. Explore Parents' Unresolved Issues (19)

A. Both parents were asked to describe their childhood.

B. Each parent's story of childhood and adolescence was reviewed for unresolved issues that might be present.

C. The parents were assisted in identifying any unresolved issues from their own childhood.

D. The parents were provided with tentative examples of the unresolved issues they may be experiencing.

E. The parents were assigned "Parents Understand the Roots of Their Parenting Methods" in the *Adolescent Psychotherapy Homework Planner* (Jongsma, Peterson, McInnis, & Bruce).

F. The parents were assisted in identifying how unresolved childhood issues from their own past are affecting their ability to effectively parent in the present.

G. Active listening skills were used as the parents described specific ways in which their unresolved childhood issues are affecting their ability to effectively parent.

H. The parents denied any connection between unresolved childhood issues and their ability to effectively parent and were provided with specific examples of how these two areas interact.

20. Work Through Parents' Issues (20)

A. The parents were assisted in working through their unresolved childhood issues.

B. The parents were supported as they worked through their childhood issues, and the benefits of their healthier functioning were emphasized.

C. The parents have declined to work through childhood issues and were urged to do this, as they are able.

21. Expand Repertoire of Intervention Options (21)

A. The parents' repertoire of intervention options was expanded by having them read material on parenting difficult children.

B. The parents were directed to read *The Difficult Child* (Turecki & Tonner).

C. The parents were directed to read *The Explosive Child* (Greene).

D. The parents were directed to read portions of *The Kazdin Method for Parenting the Defiant Child* (Kazdin).

E. The parents have failed to follow through on reading material to help expand their repertoire of parenting intervention options, and were redirected to complete this reading.

22. Assist in Implementing New Strategies (22)

A. Support, empowerment, and encouragement were provided to the parents in implementing new strategies for parenting their child.

B. The parents were monitored about how they implemented new parenting strategies for their child.

C. Feedback and redirection were provided to the parents as they implemented new strategies for parenting their child.

D. The parents have not used new strategies for parenting their child and were redirected to do so.

23. Evaluate Reactivity (23)

A. The parents' level of reactivity to the client's behavior was evaluated.

B. The parents were assisted in identifying situations in which they have been reactive to the child's misbehavior.

C. "Picking Your Battles" from the *Child Psychotherapy Homework Planner* (Jongsma, Peterson, McInnis, & Bruce) was assigned to help the parents learn to respond in a more modulated, thoughtful, planned manner.

D. The parents were assisted in learning how to respond in a more modulated, thoughtful, planned manner.

E. As treatment has progressed, the parents have become less reactive to the child's behavior and have responded in a more modulated, thoughtful, planned manner; the benefits of these interactions were identified.

F. The parents continue to respond to the child's behavior in a reactive manner and were provided with remedial feedback in this area.

24. Identify Hot Buttons (24)

A. The parents were assisted in becoming aware of any hot buttons they have that their child can push to get a quick negative response.

B. The parents were assisted in identifying how their overreaction to hot-button issues reduces their effectiveness as parents.

C. The parents identified several hot buttons, and these were processed.

D. As treatment has progressed, the parents have decreased their overreacting pattern of response, and these changes were processed.

E. The parents denied any hot buttons and were provided with tentative examples in this area.

25. Educate on Developmental Expectations (25)

A. The parents were educated about the appropriate developmental expectations of the child.

B. The parents were educated on a child's rate of development, perspectives, impulse control, temperament, and how these influence the parenting process.

C. Through a better understanding of the appropriate developmental expectations of the child, the parents reported a more appropriate parenting process.

D. The parents were unable to integrate new understanding of appropriate developmental expectations of the child, and additional education was provided.

26. Role-Play Thoughtful Responses (26)

A. Role-play techniques were used with the parents to practice responding in a thoughtful manner during a reactive situation.

B. The parents were coached on how to replace automatic reactions with thoughtful responses to their child's demands or negative behaviors.

C. Positive feedback was provided as the parents displayed the ability to thoughtfully respond to their child's demands or negative behaviors.

27. Use Parent Management Training (27)

A. Parent Management Training was used, as developed in *Parent Management Training* (Kazdin).

B. Techniques from *Parent Training for Disruptive Behavior* (Bearss et al.) were assigned to the parents.

C. The parents were assigned portions of *Your Defiant Child* (Barkley & Benton).

D. The parents were taught how parent and child behavioral interactions can encourage or discourage positive or negative behavior.

E. The parents were taught how changing key elements of parent–child interactions can be used to promote positive change in the child's behavior.

F. The parents were provided with specific examples as to how prompting and reinforcing positive behaviors can be used to promote positive change in the child's behavior.

G. The parents were provided with positive feedback for the use of the Parent Management Training approach.

H. The parents have not used the Parent Management Training approach and were redirected to do so.

28. Assign Parent Training Manuals (28)

A. The parents were directed to read parent training manuals.

B. The parents were directed to read *The Kazdin Method for Parenting the Defiant Child* (Kazdin).

C. The parents were directed to read *The Everyday Parenting Toolkit* (Kazdin).

D. The parents' study of pertinent reading was reviewed and processed.

E. The parents have not reviewed the assigned pertinent media and were redirected to do so.

29. Teach Parents to Define Aspects of Situation (29)

A. The parents were taught how to specifically define and identify their child's problem behaviors.

B. The parents were taught how to specifically identify their reactions to their child's behavior, and whether the reaction encourages or discourages the behavior.

C. The parents were taught to generate alternatives to their child's problem behavior.

D. Positive feedback was provided to the parents for their skill at specifically defining and identifying their child's problem behaviors, and their own reactions, outcomes, and alternatives.

E. Parents were provided with remedial feedback as they struggled to correctly identify their child's problem behaviors and their own reactions, responses, and alternatives.

30. Teach Consistent Parenting (30)

A. The parents were taught how to implement key parenting practices on a consistent basis.

B. The parents were taught about establishing realistic, age-appropriate roles for acceptable and unacceptable behavior.

C. The parents were taught how to prompt their child's positive behavior and to use positive reinforcement.

D. The parents were taught about clear direct instruction, time-out, and other loss-of-privilege techniques for their child's problem behavior.

E. The parents were taught about negotiation and renegotiation with children.

F. The parents were provided with positive feedback as they have developed consistent parenting practices.

G. The parents have not developed consistent parenting practices and were redirected to do so.

31. **Assign Home Exercises to Implement Parenting Technique (31)**

    A. The parents were assigned home exercises in which they implement parenting techniques and record the results of the implementation exercises.

    B. The parents were assigned "Clear Rules, Positive Reinforcement, Appropriate Consequences" in the *Adolescent Psychotherapy Homework Planner* (Jongsma, Peterson, McInnis, & Bruce).

    C. The parents' implementation of homework exercises was reviewed within the session.

    D. Corrective feedback was used to help develop improved, appropriate, and consistent use of skills.

    E. The parents have not completed the assigned homework and were redirected to do so.

32. **Teach Time-Out Technique (32)**

    A. The parents were taught to use the time-out technique as a consequence for inappropriate behavior.

    B. The parents were encouraged to use a signal seat, including a battery-operated buzzer that serves as both a timer and an alert that the child is not staying in the seat.

    C. The parents were reinforced for their regular use of the time-out techniques.

    D. The parents were provided with feedback about their use of the time-out technique; problematic interventions were redirected.

    E. The parents have not used the time-out techniques and were redirected to do so.

33. **Conduct Parent–Child Interaction Therapy (33)**

    A. Parent–Child Interaction Therapy (McNeil and Hembree-Kigin) was used to teach appropriate child behavior and parent behavior management skills.

    B. Child-directed sessions focused on teaching the child appropriate child behavior.

    C. Parent-directed sessions focused on teaching parental behavior management skills (e.g., clear commands, consistent consequences, and positive reinforcement).

34. **Refer to Parent-Training Program (34)**

    A. The parents were referred to a parent-training program

    B. The clients were referred to the *Incredible Years* program.

    C. The parents were referred to a group parent-training program teaching positive child-management practices and stress-management techniques.

    D. The clients have used the group parent-training program, and the benefits and difficulties were reviewed.

    E. The parents have not used the group parent training program and were redirected to do so.

35. **Teach Listening/Sharing Skills (35)**

    A. Modeling and role-play techniques were used to teach the parents to listen more than talk to their child.

    B. The parents were taught to use open-ended questions that encourage openness, sharing, and ongoing dialogue.

    C. The benefits of increased listening and helping the children to share more were reviewed.

36. Use Parent–Child Communication Materials (36)

A. The parents were asked to read material on parent–child communication.

B. The parents were directed to read *How to Talk So Kids Will Listen and Listen So Kids Will Talk* (Faber & Mazlish).

C. The parents were directed to read *Parent Effectiveness Training* (Gordon).

D. The parents have read the material on parent–child communication and were assisted in implementing the new communication style in daily dialogue with their children.

E. The parents were assisted in identifying the positive responses that the child has had to the new communication style.

F. The parents have not read the material on parent–child communication and were redirected to do so.

37. Design Contingency/Reward System (37)

A. A reward system was developed with the client.

B. A contingency contract was developed with the client.

C. A meeting was held with school officials to help reinforce identified positive behaviors.

D. The client was encouraged to participate in the reward system/contingency contract in order to deter impulsive or rebellious behaviors.

E. Fine-tuning was done to the reward system/contingency contract in order to reinforce identified positive behaviors at home and school.

38. Educate About Gender Differences (38)

A. The parents were educated about the numerous key differences between boys and girls (e.g., rate of development, perspectives, impulse control, and anger).

B. The parents were educated about how to handle the sex role differences in the parenting process.

C. The parents reported increased understanding of parenting issues related to a child's sex role; positive feedback was provided.

39. Complete "Parent Report Card" (39)

A. The children were requested to complete the "Parent Report Card" (Berg-Gross).

B. Feedback was provided to the parents based on the "Parent Report Card."

C. The parents were supported for areas of strength.

D. The parents were assisted in identifying weaknesses that need to be bolstered.

40. Identify Weaknesses/Encourage Skills (40)

A. The parental team was assisted in identifying areas of parenting weakness.

B. The exercise "Being a Consistent Parent" from the *Child Psychotherapy Homework Planner* (Jongsma, Peterson, McInnis, & Bruce) was assigned to help the parents improve their skills and boost their confidence and follow-through.

C. The parents were assigned "Parenting Report Card" in the *Adolescent Psychotherapy Homework Planner* (Jongsma, Peterson, McInnis, & Bruce).

D. The parents were assisted in improving their parenting skills and boosting their confidence and follow-through.

E. It was reflected to the parents that their increased parenting skill has remediated their areas of weakness.

F. The parental team has not attempted to improve their skills in the identified areas of weakness and was redirected in this area.

41. **Explore Family Abuse History (41)**

A. The client's family background was explored for a history of physical, sexual, or substance abuse that may contribute to the emergence of their anger control problems.

B. The client was assisted in developing a timeline in the therapy session in which they identified significant historical events, both positive and negative, that have occurred in their family.

C. The client's parents were confronted and challenged to cease physically abusive or overly punitive methods of discipline.

D. The parents were asked to identify how physically abusive or overly punitive methods of discipline negatively affect the child and siblings.

E. The parents were supported as they apologized to the client for abusive behaviors and overly harsh methods of discipline.

F. The parents were taught how aggressive discipline promotes the client's aggression and poor anger management.

G. The parents were referred to a parenting class.

42. **Protect Client from Abuse (42)**

A. The abuse of the client was reported to the appropriate agency.

B. A recommendation was made that the perpetrator be removed from the home and seek treatment.

C. A recommendation was made that the client and siblings be removed from the home to ensure protection.

D. The client and family members were assisted in identifying the necessary steps to minimize the risk of abuse occurring in the future.

E. The nonabusive parent was reinforced for verbalizing a commitment to protect the client and siblings from future abuse.

43. **Identify Support Opportunities (43)**

A. The parents were assisted in identifying and implementing specific ways that they can support each other as parents.

B. The parents were assisted in realizing the ways children work to keep the parents from cooperating in order to get their way.

C. The parents were assisted in brainstorming how they can support each other when the children work to keep them from cooperating.

D. The parents failed to identify specific ways they can support each other and were provided with remedial feedback in this area.

44. **Encourage Satisfying Stress Reducers (44)**

A. The parents were encouraged to use exercise, hobbies, social activities, entertainment, and relaxation techniques to reduce stress and increase feelings of life of satisfaction apart from parenting.

B. The parents were assigned the exercise "Identify and Schedule Pleasurable Activities" from the *Adult Psychotherapy Homework Planner* (Jongsma & Bruce).

C. The parents were recommended to read *Working Parents, Thriving Families* (Palmiter).

D. The parent use of auxiliary activities to increase satisfaction was reviewed and processed.

45. Give Permission to Decrease Activities (45)

A. The parents were encouraged to decrease outside pressures by choosing not to involve their child and themselves in too many activities, organizations, or sports.

B. Feedback was given to the family on how their involvement in activities, organizations, or sports can drain energy and time from the family.

C. The parents were assigned "One-on-One" in the *Adolescent Psychotherapy Homework Planner* (Jongsma, Peterson, McInnis, & Bruce).

D. The parents were provided with positive feedback as they indicated a need to decrease outside pressures, demands, and distractions (e.g., activities, organizations, and sports).

E. The parents were accepted for their decision to maintain the current level of activities, organizations, or sports.

46. Evaluate the Family's Level of Activity (46)

A. The parents were asked to provide a weekly schedule of their entire family's activities.

B. The parents were assisted in evaluating their family schedule, looking for valuable activities versus those that can possibly be eliminated to create a more focused and relaxed time to parent.

C. The parents were provided with encouragement as they identified activities that can be eliminated to create a more focused and relaxed time to parent.

D. The parents struggled with identifying activities that are most valuable versus those that can possibly be eliminated and were provided with tentative examples in this area.

47. Identify Unreasonable Expectations (47)

A. The parents were assisted in identifying any unreasonable and perfectionistic expectations of their child's behavior.

B. The parents were assisted in modifying their unreasonable and perfectionistic expectations of their child's behavior to those that are appropriate and reasonable.

C. The parents have identified their unreasonable and perfectionistic expectations, and modified these to more appropriate levels; the benefits of these changes were identified.

D. The parents denied any pattern of unreasonable and perfectionistic expectations and were urged to continue to consider this area.

48. Identify Negative Outcomes of Perfectionism (48)

A. The parents were assisted in identifying the negative consequences/outcomes that perfectionistic expectations have on a child.

B. The parents were assisted in identifying how perfectionistic expectations affect the relationship between the parents and the child.

C. The parents verbalized negative consequences/outcomes of perfectionistic expectations on their child and indicated that they would terminate this pattern; support and encouragement were provided in this area.

D. The parents were reluctant to admit to placing any perfectionistic expectations on their child and were provided with specific examples in this area.

49. Identify Connectedness Activities (49)

A. The parents were assisted in identifying activities that promote connectedness with their child.

B. The parents were encouraged to consistently introduce fun into their family routine.

C. The "Share a Family Meal" assignment from the *Child Psychotherapy Homework Planner* (Jongsma, Peterson, McInnis, & Bruce) was assigned to the family to help promote connectedness.

D. The parents were assigned "One-on-One" in the *Adolescent Psychotherapy Homework Planner* (Jongsma, Peterson, McInnis, & Bruce).

E. The parents were supported as they identified activities that they can use to promote connectedness with their child.

F. The parents' use of connectedness activities was reviewed, and they were provided with feedback about how they use this technique.

G. The parents struggled to identify activities that promote connectedness and were provided with tentative examples in this area (e.g., floor play, one-on-one specific activity).

50. Urge Routine Use of Strategies (50)

A. The parent and child were urged to routinely use strategies learned in therapy.

B. The parent and child were reminded to use parent training techniques, problem-solving, and anger management techniques.

C. The parent and child were urged to build these techniques into their lives as much as possible.

51. Develop Coping Card (51)

A. The clients were provided with a coping card on which specific coping strategies were listed.

B. The clients were assisted in developing their own coping card in order to list helpful coping strategies.

C. The clients were instructed to put important information on the coping card, including steps in problem-solving, positive coping statements, and reminders that were helpful to the client during therapy.

D. The clients were encouraged to use the coping card when struggling with anxiety-producing situations.

PEER/SIBLING CONFLICT

CLIENT PRESENTATION

1. **Angry/Tense (1)***
   A. The client described a pattern of frequent, intense conflict with peers and siblings.
   B. The client appeared angry at everything and everybody and was not willing to be very cooperative in the counseling process.
   C. The client denied responsibility for the frequent, overt verbal and physical fighting with both peers and siblings.
   D. The level of anger and fighting between the client and siblings has decreased as they have actively worked with the therapist in session.

2. **Projecting/Blaming (2)**
   A. The client displayed a propensity for blaming others for their problems.
   B. The client refused to take any responsibility for the ongoing verbal and physical conflicts they have with peers and siblings.
   C. The client viewed all problems or conflicts as the responsibility of others.
   D. The client has slowly started to take responsibility for some of the conflicts with which they are involved.

3. **Parents' Unfairness/Favoritism (3)**
   A. The client reported that the parents always treat siblings more favorably than they do them.
   B. The client cited instances of their perception of parents' unfairness toward them.
   C. The parents acknowledged that they find the other siblings easier to like than the client.
   D. The client's complaints about unfairness and favoritism have started to decrease, and the parents are beginning to be seen in a more favorable light.

4. **Defiant/Vengeful (4)**
   A. The client presented in a vengeful, defiant manner.
   B. The client reported a long list of people who have wronged or slighted them in some way and how they have gotten back at them.
   C. The client's level of bullying has caused them to be constantly at odds with peers and siblings.
   D. The client has gradually let go of some of their intimidation and vengeance and has started to have less conflict with peers and siblings.

5. **Isolated (5)**
   A. The client presented as a lonely, isolated individual.

---

*The numbers in parentheses correlate to the number of the Behavioral Definition statement in the companion chapter with the same title in the *Child Psychotherapy Treatment Planner*, Sixth Edition, by Jongsma, Peterson, McInnis, & Bruce (Wiley, 2023).

B. The client reported a history of aggressive relationships with peers that they have resolved by staying alone.

C. The client stated that they cannot get along with either peers or siblings without trouble, so they choose to stay alone.

D. Since taking part in the counseling process, the client has gradually started to relate at least superficially with others.

6. **Impulsive/Intimidating (6)**

A. The client showed a pattern of impulsiveness and intimidation within the session by not considering the consequences of their actions and by challenging the therapist.

B. The client described a pattern of relating with peers and siblings in an impulsive, intimidating manner.

C. The client reported a history of impulsive, intimidating actions toward peers that has caused them repeated social problems.

D. The client has gradually accepted that they are intimidating and this has been the reason for conflicts with peers and siblings.

7. **Aggressive/Mean (7)**

A. The client seems to have an aggressive, mean manner in which they relate with others.

B. The client indicated that they have been involved in encounters that resulted in physical injuries to others.

C. No remorse appeared evident on the client's part for the painful way they treat others.

D. All responsibility for the client's aggressive, mean acts are laid on others or given great justification.

E. As treatment has progressed, the client has displayed less aggressive and mean behavior.

8. **Insensitivity (7)**

A. The client did not appear to be bothered by the ongoing conflicts that they have with peers and siblings.

B. The hurtful impact on others of client's verbally hostile, aggressive behavior does not appear to have an effect on the client.

C. The client has started to understand the effect their conflictual behaviors have on others and their need to be more sensitive to them.

9. **Parents' Hostility (8)**

A. The client described instances in which severe and abusive punishment resulted whenever they were blamed for negative behavior.

B. The client described how parents always unfavorably compared them with peers and siblings, leading to feelings of anger, inadequacy, and resentment.

C. The parents' style of relating to the client is rude and hostile.

D. The client's home environment appears to be highly competitive, where one sibling is often pitted against the other to outdo them in a given area and thus win the parents' praise.

E. The client has begun to understand how their attitude and behavior toward others are connected to parents' treatment of them.

F. The parents have begun to treat the client in a more respectful and less hostile manner.

INTERVENTIONS IMPLEMENTED

1. **Establish Rapport (1)***
   A. Caring was conveyed to the client through support, warmth, and empathy.
   B. The client was provided with nonjudgmental support and a level of trust was developed.
   C. The client was urged to feel safe in expressing their sibling and peer conflicts.
   D. The client began to express feelings more freely as rapport and trust level have increased.
   E. The client has continued to experience difficulty being open and direct about the expression of painful feelings; they were encouraged to use the safe haven of therapy to express these difficult issues.

2. **Focus on Strengthening Therapeutic Relationship (2)**
   A. The relationship with the client was strengthened using empirically supported factors.
   B. The relationship with the client was strengthened through the implementation of collaborative approach, agreement on goals, demonstration of empathy, verbalization of positive regard, and collection of client feedback.
   C. The client reacted positively to the relationship-strengthening measures taken.
   D. The client verbalized feeling supported and understood during therapy sessions.
   E. Despite attempts to strengthen the therapeutic relationship, the client reports feeling distant and misunderstood.
   F. The client has indicated that sessions are not helpful and will be terminating therapy.

3. **Explore Relationships and Assess Denial (3)**
   A. The client's perception of how they relate with siblings and peers was explored.
   B. The client's degree of denial was found to be high regarding conflict and acceptance of responsibility for any part in it.
   C. The client was open in acknowledging the high degree of conflict between siblings and was supported as they accepted responsibility for their part in the conflict.

4. **Assess Level of Insight (4)**
   A. The client's level of insight toward the presenting problems was assessed.
   B. The client was assessed in regard to the syntonic versus dystonic nature of their insight about the presenting problems.
   C. The client was noted to demonstrate good insight into the problematic nature of the behavior and symptoms.
   D. The client was noted to be in agreement with others' concerns and is motivated to work on change.
   E. The client was noted to be ambivalent regarding the problems described and is reluctant to address the issues as a concern.
   F. The client was noted to be resistant regarding acknowledgment of the problem areas, is not concerned about them, and has no motivation to make changes.

---

*The numbers in parentheses correlate to the number of the Therapeutic Intervention statement in the companion chapter with the same title in the *Child Psychotherapy Treatment Planner*, Sixth Edition, by Jongsma, Peterson, McInnis, & Bruce (Wiley, 2023).

5. **Assess for Correlated Disorders (5)**

   A. The client was assessed for evidence of research-based correlated disorders.

   B. The client was assessed in regard to the level of vulnerability to suicide.

   C. The client was identified as having a comorbid disorder, and treatment was adjusted to account for these concerns.

   D. The client has been assessed for any correlated disorders, but none were found.

6. **Assess for Culturally Based Confounding Issues (6)**

   A. The client was assessed for age-related issues that could help to better understand their clinical presentation.

   B. The client was assessed for gender-related issues that could help to better understand their clinical presentation.

   C. The client was assessed for cultural syndromes, cultural idioms of distress, or culturally based perceived causes that could help to better understand their clinical presentation.

   D. Alternative factors have been identified as contributing to the client's currently defined "problem behavior," and these were taken into account in regard to treatment.

   E. Culturally based factors that could help to account for the client's currently defined "problem behavior" were investigated, but no significant factors were identified.

7. **Assess Severity of Impairment (7)**

   A. The severity of the client's impairment was assessed to determine the appropriate level of care.

   B. The client was assessed in regard to impairment in social, relational, and educational endeavors.

   C. It was reflected to the client that the impairment appears to create mild to moderate effects on the client's functioning.

   D. It was reflected to the client that the impairment appears to create severe to very severe effects on the client's functioning.

   E. The client was continuously assessed for the severity of impairment, as well as the efficacy and appropriateness of treatment.

8. **Assess for Pathogenic Care (8)**

   A. The home, school, and community of the client were assessed for pathogenic care and concerns.

   B. The client's various environments were assessed for the persistent disregard of the child's needs, repeated changes in caregivers, limited opportunities for stable attachment, harsh discipline, or other grossly inept care.

   C. Pathogenic care was identified and the treatment plan included strategies for managing or correcting these concerns and protecting the child.

   D. No pathogenic care was identified, and this was reflected to the client and caregivers.

9. **Employ Psychoanalytic Play Therapy (9)**

   A. A psychoanalytic play therapy session was conducted to explore and understand the reasons for the client's intense conflicts with peers and/or siblings.

   B. The client actively and freely participated in the psychoanalytic play therapy sessions.

C. Transference issues that emerged in the psychoanalytic play therapy sessions were worked through to resolution.

D. The client's feelings expressed during the psychoanalytic play therapy sessions were interpreted and connected to conflicts with peers and/or siblings.

E. The client's participation in psychoanalytic play therapy was noted to reduce the frequency and intensity of their peer and/or sibling conflicts.

F. The client has participated in psychoanalytic play therapy sessions, but this has not assisted in reducing the frequency and intensity of their peer and/or sibling conflicts.

10. Employ ACT Model of Play Therapy (10)

A. An ACT model play therapy session was conducted to acknowledge the client's feelings, communicate limits, and target appropriate alternatives to conflicts and aggression with peers/siblings.

B. Positive verbal affirmation was given to the client in the ACT play therapy session when they displayed or verbalized appropriate alternatives to conflict and aggression with others.

C. The client willingly and actively participated in the ACT play therapy session.

D. The client's involvement in an ACT play therapy session has helped them interact with peers and/or siblings with less conflict and aggression.

E. Although the client has been involved in the ACT play therapy sessions, they have not improved interactions with peers and/or siblings.

11. Interpret Feelings (11)

A. The client's feelings that emerged during the play therapy session were interpreted to them and related to conflicts with peers and/or siblings.

B. The client was assisted in increasing their understanding of the connection between feelings and conflicts with peers and/or siblings.

C. The parents were informed of the feelings the client was expressing in play therapy and how they connected with daily conflicts with peers and/or siblings.

D. The client's progress in connecting feelings with their peer/sibling conflicts has been noted to help reduce the daily frequency of conflict with peers and/or siblings.

12. Suggest Constructive Ways to Handle Conflicts (12)

A. Puppets were used to create scenarios to model and suggest to client constructive ways to handle conflicts with peers and/or siblings.

B. After each puppet scenario, the client was asked to identify how the conflict was constructively handled or resolved.

C. The client created several scenarios of conflict from their life using stuffed animals, to which the therapist suggested and modeled constructive ways of handling each one.

D. The client was encouraged to use the modeled means of reducing conflict in their daily life.

E. The client has used the suggested and modeled ways to handle conflicts constructively to decrease the amount of conflict in their daily life.

F. The client has not used the suggested and modeled ways to handle conflict constructively and was reminded about these helpful techniques.

13. Utilize the "Playing Baby" Game (13)

   A. The "Playing Baby" game (Schaefer) was explained to the parents, and plans were made to implement it with the client.

   B. The parents have consistently and effectively implemented the "Playing Baby" game with the client, and the results of this technique were processed.

   C. The parents' follow-through with using the "Playing Baby" game has been noted to reduce the level of conflict between the client and their siblings.

   D. The parents' failure to consistently use the "Playing Baby" game was addressed, processed, and resolved.

14. Utilize "Tearing Paper" Exercise (14)

   A. The "Tearing Paper" exercise (Daves) was given, and the guidelines explained, to the family.

   B. The family actively participated in the "Tearing Paper" exercise and followed all the guidelines set by the therapist.

   C. The family was observed and monitored as they participated in the "Tearing Paper" exercise.

   D. The "Tearing Paper" exercise was processed with the family members as they cleaned up and the positive feelings of releasing energy and doing activities without conflict were identified and reinforced.

15. Utilize "Stamping Feet" Method (15)

   A. The "Stamping Feet and Bubble Popping" method (Wunderlich) was used with the client to assist them in releasing feelings of anger and frustration.

   B. The appropriate release of feelings of anger and frustration was emphasized with the client.

   C. The client actively participated in the "Stamping Feet and Bubble Popping" method and the processing of it afterward.

   D. Possible ways for the client to appropriately release angry feelings were explored and identified.

16. Teach Social Learning Techniques (16)

   A. The parents and teachers were asked to identify all nonaggressive, cooperative, and peaceful behaviors of the client that they could praise and positively reinforce.

   B. Role-play and modeling techniques were used to show the parents and teachers how to ignore the client's nonharmful, aggressive behaviors and how to praise prosocial behaviors.

17. Teach an Understanding of Feelings (17)

   A. The client was taught to identify basic feelings using a feelings chart.

   B. The client was assigned the exercise "Building Empathy" from the *Child Psychotherapy Homework Planner* (Jongsma, Peterson, McInnis, & Bruce).

   C. The client was assigned the exercise "The Lesson of Salmon Rock . . . Fighting Leads to Loneliness" from the *Child Psychotherapy Homework Planner* (Jongsma, Peterson, McInnis, & Bruce).

   D. Aggressive actions were focused on with the client to assist them in identifying how others might feel when they were the object of such actions.

E. The idea of how the client would like to be treated by others was explored, along with what they would need to do to make this possible.

18. **Introduce Negotiation (18)**

   A. The client was urged to stipulate the problems that exist with siblings and suggest concrete solutions.

   B. The client and the parents were asked to complete the "Negotiating a Peace Treaty" exercise from the *Child Psychotherapy Homework Planner* (Jongsma, Peterson, McInnis, & Bruce) to introduce the concept of negotiation.

   C. The parents were asked to start negotiating key areas of conflict with the client.

   D. Role-play sessions involving negotiation were used with the client and the parents to build their negotiating skills.

   E. The positive aspects of negotiation versus winning and losing were identified and reinforced with the client.

19. **Play "Helping, Sharing, and Caring" Game (19)**

   A. The "Helping, Sharing, and Caring" game (Gardner) was played with the client to expose them to feelings of respect for self and others.

   B. The client was assisted in identifying how people feel when they show respect and receive respect from others.

   C. The client was reminded of how others feel when they are treated in a rude, disrespectful manner.

   D. The client reported success at more consistently showing respect for the feelings of others; they were encouraged to continue this pattern.

20. **Explain Attunement (20)**

   A. The client and parents were provided with education on the concept of attunement.

   B. The client and parents were taught the value of attunement for their family, such as understanding, concern, and closeness.

   C. The client and parents were willing to learn more about attunement.

   D. The client and parents were uninterested in attunement concepts.

21. **Conduct Attunement Exercise (21)**

   A. The family was invited to participate in an attunement exercise in which the therapist taps out three notes that each family member replicates in turn.

   B. The family found usefulness in this exercise and this was repeated at the start of all family sessions.

   C. The family did not find the attunement exercise to be useful and would not participate in this.

22. **Read Gardner's Therapeutic Stories (22)**

   A. Therapeutic stories were used to illustrate awareness of feelings and cooperation.

   B. Therapeutic stories from *Dr. Gardner's Fairy Tales for Today's Children* (Gardner) were read with the client to help increase awareness of feelings and to learn ways to cooperate with others.

   C. Verbal affirmation and reinforcement were given to the client when they identified possible feelings of characters in the therapeutic stories.

D. The client was assisted in identifying ways that they could increase cooperation with others and was asked to implement one in their daily life.

E. The client was redirected and verbally reinforced in implementing new cooperative behaviors.

F. Use of therapeutic stories has helped the client increase skills in identifying feelings and cooperating with others.

23. **Use Kindness Cards for Kids (23)**

A. *Kindness Cards for Kids* (Snitbhan) was used to emphasize and expend the importance of feelings of others and the client.

B. The client displayed a greater understanding of the importance of feelings of others and self through the use of *Kindness Cards for Kids*, and was provided with positive feedback.

C. The *Kindness Cards for Kids* were not useful in expanding the client's understanding of the importance of feelings, and other treatment techniques were used.

24. **Refer for Group Therapy (24)**

A. The client was referred to a peer therapy group to expand social sensitivity and behavioral flexibility.

B. The client accepted the referral to group therapy and has been attending regularly.

C. The client reported that the group therapy experience has taught them to be more sensitive to the feelings of others.

D. The client has been resistive to group therapy and has not attended on a regular basis; the client was encouraged to attend the group.

25. **Play the "Talking, Feeling, and Doing" Game (25)**

A. The "Talking, Feeling, and Doing" game (Gardner; available from Childswork/Childsplay) was played with the client to build and reinforce awareness of self and others.

B. After playing the "Talking, Feeling, and Doing" game, the client began sharing more about self and showing some sensitivity to others.

26. **Play the "Anger Control" Game (26)**

A. The "Anger Control" game (Berg) was played with the client to expose them to new ways of handling aggressive feelings.

B. The client was asked to make a commitment to try one of the new ways to handle aggressive feelings that were learned through playing the "Anger Control" game.

C. The client has reported that they have successfully implemented new anger control techniques; the benefits of this were reviewed.

D. The client reported that they continue to have problems managing anger; the client was encouraged to continue to use the techniques learned.

27. **Play the "Social Conflict" Game (27)**

A. The "Social Conflict" game (Berg) was played with the client to introduce them to prosocial behavioral skills.

B. The client was asked to list all of the negative consequences that have resulted from antisocial behaviors.

C. The client was reminded of the emotional and physical pain that their actions have caused others.

D. The client was assisted in identifying two positive consequences of showing respect and concern for others.

E. The client has used the skills learned in the "Social Conflict" game and was reinforced for success in this area.

F. The client has not used the skills learned in the "Social Conflict" game and was redirected to use these skills.

28. Conduct/Refer to Behavioral Group (28)

A. The client was asked to attend a behavioral contracting group that works to develop positive peer interactions.

B. The client's group goals for positive peer interaction were set and reviewed each week.

C. The client reported positive verbal feedback from peers on their interaction goals within the group.

D. The client's positive gains in peer interaction were verbally reinforced and rewarded.

E. The client has not consistently attended the behavioral contracting group and was redirected to do so.

29. Facilitate Involvement in Cooperative Activities (29)

A. The benefits of involving the client in cooperative activities were discussed with the parents.

B. Options for cooperative activities were presented to the parents, and they were asked to make a commitment to get the client involved.

C. The client was assisted in identifying positive gains they could make through participating in cooperative activities (e.g., sports, music, scouts).

D. It was noted that the client's involvement in cooperative activities with peers has increased significantly since the parents have encouraged this activity.

30. Refer to Camp (30)

A. The client was referred to a summer camp that focuses on building self-esteem and positive peer relationships.

B. The client was helped to identify a list of specific things they could do at camp to increase self-esteem.

C. Gains in self-esteem and peer relationships reported by the client as having been attained through the camp experience were affirmed and reinforced.

D. The client and parents have not followed through on enrolling the client in a summer camp focused on building self-esteem and peer cooperation and were encouraged to use this resource.

31. Read *Why Don't They Like Me? Helping Your Child Make and Keep Friends* (31)

A. The parents were asked to read *Why Don't They Like Me?* (Sheridan) to gain ideas for helping the client build connections to peers.

B. The parents were assisted in identifying several suggestions from the book and in making plans to implement each of their selections.

C. The parents were affirmed, encouraged, and reinforced in their efforts to help the client build social skills.

D. The parent's efforts to build the client's social skills have been noted to help them begin to form new friendships.

32. Teach Social Skills Through Modeling (32)

A. The client was taught social skills that include sustained eye contact, smiling, sharing toys, listening, empathy, and assertiveness without aggression.

B. The client was taught social skills through the use of modeling, role playing, reinforced feedback, and homework.

C. The client has increased use of appropriate social skills in the therapeutic setting.

33. Work Through Favoritism Perception (33)

A. The client was assisted in working through their perception that their parents have a favorite child.

B. The client was asked to complete the "Joseph, His Amazing Technicolor Coat and More" exercise from the *Child Psychotherapy Homework Planner* (Jongsma, Peterson, McInnis, & Bruce).

C. In processing the favoritism homework assignment, the client was assisted in identifying the negative as well as the positive aspects of being the parents' favorite child.

D. In processing the favoritism homework assignment, the client was reminded of the reality that even though nearly all parents love their children, they may still have favorites.

34. Teach Open Responses to Praise and Encouragement (34)

A. The client was assisted in identifying how they respond to praise and encouragement from others.

B. The client's barriers to being open to positive feedback were identified.

C. New ways to respond positively to praise and encouragement were taught to the client.

D. Role-play, modeling, and behavioral rehearsal were used to provide the client the opportunity to practice new accepting responses to praise and encouragement.

35. Teach Parents to Praise (35)

A. The parents were asked to list all the possible ways that they might give verbal affection and appropriate praise to the client.

B. The parents' resistance to giving affection and praise to the client for expected behavior was addressed and resolved.

C. The parents were asked to choose three ways to give verbal affection and appropriate praise and then were asked to implement each with the client when appropriate.

D. Affirmation and reinforcement were given to the parents for their reported use of verbal affection and praise with the client.

36. Explore Rejection Experiences (36)

A. The client's rejection experiences with family and friends were probed.

B. Active listening was provided as the client expressed numerous causes for their anger, which were based in rejection by family and friends.

C. The client denied any rejection experiences as being the basis for their anger, and this was accepted at face value.

37. Assign Reading Material on Siblings (37)

A. The parents and children were asked to read *Siblings* (Crist & Verdick) and to select several of the interventions to implement.

B. The family was assisted in implementing chosen techniques from the assigned book and role-play was used for the parents to increase their skills and confidence using the new techniques.

C. The family's resistance to trying new techniques was addressed, and the advantages of using new approaches were seeded with them.

D. The family has not read the material on siblings and rivalry and were redirected to do so.

38. Reduce Parental Aggression, Rejection, and Quarreling (38)

A. Parental patterns of aggression and rejection were identified in family session.

B. The parents were assisted in removing acts of aggression and messages of rejection from their parenting.

C. Various methods were modeled for the parents to respond to the client in a warm, firm, yet caring way.

D. Parent messages of rejection were blocked and confronted in family sessions.

39. Assign Reading (39)

A. The books *Siblings Without Rivalry* (Faber & Mazish) or *Peaceful Parents—Happy Kids* (Markham) were assigned to the parents to read and process with the therapist.

B. Based on their reading of *Siblings Without Rivalry* or *Peaceful Parents—Happy Kids* (Markham), the parents identified two new ways to reduce rivalry and began implementing them in their family.

C. The parents reported positive results from the new methods learned from reading *Siblings Without Rivalry* or *Peaceful Parents—Happy Kids* (Markham) that they have implemented to decrease the level of rivalry in the family.

D. The parents gave numerous excuses for their inconsistent use of new parenting methods and for the mixed results they experienced.

E. The parents have not read the material on siblings and rivalry and were redirected to do so.

40. Refer to Parenting Group (40)

A. The parents were referred and encouraged to attend a support group.

B. The parents reported attending a support group and receiving helpful feedback and encouragement.

C. The parents offered several reasons for not yet attending a support group; they were redirected to do so.

41. Utilize Behavior Modification Plan (41)

A. A behavior-modification plan targeting cooperative sibling interaction was developed by the parents and therapist for the client.

B. The parents were taught how to effectively implement and sustain a behavior-modification program focused on reinforcing positive sibling interaction.

C. The parents' administration of the behavior-modification plan was monitored and encouragement was given to the parents to continue their work.

D. The parents were confronted when they failed to immediately reinforce positive interactions by the client.

E. The behavior-modification plan focused on reinforcing positive sibling interaction has been successful in increasing such behaviors and reducing sibling conflicts.

42. Conduct Evaluation Session (42)

A. The effectiveness of the behavior modification plan was reviewed with the client and parents, with positive feedback given for implementing the plan.

B. Aspects of the behavioral modification plan focusing on reinforcing positive sibling interaction were modified with the client and the parents as expectations were set unrealistically high.

C. The parents and the client were confronted on their lack of follow-through with the behavioral modification plan and resistance issues were addressed and resolved.

43. Assess Dynamics and Alliances Underlying Conflicts (43)

A. The dynamics and alliances present in the family were assessed in a family session.

B. A structural intervention was implemented with the family to create new, healthier alliances between the members.

C. Key dynamics that create and promote sibling conflict were confronted in the family.

44. Confront Disrespect and Teach Conflict-Resolution Skills (44)

A. Family members' disrespectful interactions were highlighted and confronted in family session.

B. Conflict-resolution skills were taught to the parents and siblings.

C. Role-plays, behavioral rehearsal, and modeling were used with family members to teach effective conflict-resolution skills and to give them each opportunities to practice these new skills themselves.

D. The family was assigned the "Problem-Solving Exercise" from the *Child Psychotherapy Homework Planner* (Jongsma, Peterson, McInnis, & Bruce).

E. The family members have struggled to implement conflict-resolution techniques because they give up easily and fall back to old patterns of arguing and verbal abuse; this pattern was reflected to them.

45. Refer for Psychiatric/Psychological Evaluation (45)

A. Options for a psychiatric or psychological evaluation were explained to the client and family.

B. The client was referred for a psychiatric evaluation.

C. The client was referred for a psychological evaluation.

D. The parents were asked to make a verbal commitment to follow through with the evaluation and report results back to the therapist.

46. Monitor Implementation of Assessment Recommendations (46)

A. The parents and client were assisted in implementing the psychological/psychiatric evaluation's recommendations.

B. The importance of follow-through on the assessment recommendations for the client was emphasized with the parents.

C. The parents and the client were confronted for their inconsistent follow-through on the assessment recommendations.

D. The client and the parents reported following through on each of the recommendations of the evaluation and were given positive verbal affirmation for their efforts.

PHYSICAL/EMOTIONAL ABUSE VICTIM

CLIENT PRESENTATION

1. **Confirmed Report of Physical Abuse by an Adult (1)***
   A. The client's self-report of being assaulted by their parent has been confirmed by a Child Protective Services worker.
   B. The client's parent reported that the other parent has physically assaulted the client on more than one occasion.
   C. The client provided a detailed account of the assault by their parent and the resulting injuries.
   D. The physical abuse reported by the client was reported to Child Protective Services as required by mandatory reporting statutes.

2. **Evidence of Victimization (2)**
   A. Bruises were evident on the client's body.
   B. The client worked to explain away the injuries on their body, refusing to blame an adult for inflicting the injuries.
   C. Past records of bruises and wounds revealed the extent of the client's victimization.
   D. Since coming into treatment, the client has not reported receiving any bruises or wounds from caregivers.

3. **Fearful/Withdrawn (3)**
   A. The client appeared very fearful and withdrawn from others and avoided all but necessary interpersonal contacts.
   B. Fear seems to dominate the client's contacts with others.
   C. The client verbalized fear of further physical abuse by the caregiver.
   D. Since establishing trust in counseling, the client has started to be less fearful and withdrawn and a little more open about self.

4. **Recollections of the Abuse (4)**
   A. The client indicated they felt constantly haunted by the intrusive distressing memories of past emotional and physical abuse.
   B. The client reported that the memories of abuse intrude on their consciousness under a variety of circumstances.
   C. The client described a chaotic childhood in which they were the victim of ongoing emotional and physical abuse.
   D. The incidences of intrusive thoughts of the abuse have significantly diminished.
   E. The client has begun to verbalize some connections between past pain and present attitudes of detachment and fear of others.

---

*The numbers in parentheses correlate to the number of the Behavioral Definition statement in the companion chapter with the same title in the *Child Psychotherapy Treatment Planner*, Sixth Edition, by Jongsma, Peterson, McInnis, & Bruce (Wiley, 2023).

5. **Sleep Disturbance (5)**

   A. The client reported having difficulties with falling asleep, waking up frequently, and feeling tired and unrested in the morning.

   B. The client indicated they have been experiencing frequent night terrors and recurrent nightmares.

   C. The client has started to talk about the abuse that they experienced and is now reporting less night terrors and more restful sleep.

   D. The client has begun making connections between their sleeping difficulties and their history of being abused.

6. **Strong Feelings When Around Perpetrator (6)**

   A. The client indicated feeling intense anger and rage whenever they come into contact with the perpetrator of abuse.

   B. The caregivers have reported that the client becomes tearful and fearful immediately when the perpetrator of abuse is near.

   C. The client expressed that they experience mixed feelings of fear, anger, and rage whenever they encounter the perpetrator.

   D. The client indicated they noticed that since talking in therapy, their feelings are not as intense or scary when they come into contact with the perpetrator.

7. **Angry/Aggressive (7)**

   A. The client has an angry, aggressive manner that is obvious to nearly everyone.

   B. The client reported an increase in the frequency and severity of angry, aggressive behavior toward peers and adults.

   C. Client projected the blame for their aggressive behaviors onto others.

   D. The client described having a quick temper, which has resulted in destroying many of their own possessions.

   E. There has been a sharp decrease in the client's anger and aggressiveness since they started to disclose about their being physically and emotionally abused.

   F. The client has begun to realize how their anger and aggression are the result of what they saw and experienced in their home.

8. **Depressed/Irritable (8)**

   A. The client presented with a depressed mood and manner that contained an irritable edge.

   B. Between the client's depression and accompanying irritability, they were not willing or able to disclose about self in the counseling session.

   C. The client reported a pattern of social withdrawal and detachment from feelings.

   D. Since starting on antidepressant medication, the client's depression and irritability have decreased, and they are beginning to self-disclose in counseling sessions.

9. **Passive/Apathetic (8)**

   A. There was a strong passive, apathetic quality to the client that reflects little interest in what might happen to self or others.

   B. Because of their apathetic, passive manner, the client showed little interest in the counseling process.

C. The client reported that as far back as they can remember, they have not been concerned about what happens to them.

D. The client has exhibited less apathy and passivity since becoming more actively involved in therapy.

10. **Exaggerated Startle Response (9)**

A. The client has often displayed an exaggerated startle response when exposed to any sudden, unexpected stimuli.

B. The client displayed an exaggerated startle response in today's therapy session.

C. The client reported that they do not startle as easily or dramatically when exposed to unexpected stimuli.

11. **Guilt/Shame (10)**

A. The client has been troubled by strong feelings of guilt since the abuse first occurred.

B. The client expressed feelings of guilt about surviving, causing, or not preventing the abuse.

C. The client has begun to work through and resolve feelings of guilt about the abuse.

D. The client verbally denied experiencing any feelings of guilt about the abuse.

E. The client has successfully resolved feelings of guilt about the abuse.

12. **Regressive Behavior (11)**

A. The client presented with numerous regressive behaviors (e.g., baby talk and thumb sucking).

B. The client reported that they have begun to wet the bed since the abuse began.

C. Since beginning to share their physical and emotional abusive past, the client's regressive behaviors are reported to be decreasing.

13. **Running Away (12)**

A. The client reported running away from home on several occasions to escape from the physical abuse.

B. It seems the client has used running away as an attempt to draw attention to the abusiveness in their home.

C. There has not been an incident of running away since the abuse of the client started to be addressed.

14. **Closed/Detached (13)**

A. The client presented in a closed and detached manner with little visible interest in others or things.

B. The client showed little interest in the counseling process and was careful not to reveal anything significant about self.

C. The client seemed very closed and made a conscious effort to keep others at a safe distance and in the dark about self.

D. Since establishing a relationship with the therapist, the client has started to be less fearful and more open about self.

15. **Mistrustful/Anxious (13)**
    A. The client has a mistrustful, anxious manner when they interact with others.
    B. The client's body language and facial expressions seem to indicate a high level of mistrust of others, especially adults.
    C. The client reported a history of not being able to trust adults in their family because they rarely did what they said they would and often harmed them.
    D. The client has begun to verbalize some connections between childhood pain and present attitudes of detachment and fear of others.

INTERVENTIONS IMPLEMENTED

1. **Establish Rapport (1)***
    A. Caring was conveyed to the client through support, warmth, and empathy.
    B. The client was provided with nonjudgmental support, and a level of trust was developed.
    C. The client was urged to feel safe in expressing physical and emotional abuse symptoms.
    D. The client began to express feelings more freely as rapport and trust level have increased.
    E. The client has continued to experience difficulty being open and direct about the expression of painful feelings; the client was encouraged to use the safe haven of therapy to express these difficult issues.

2. **Focus on Strengthening Therapeutic Relationship (2)**
    A. The relationship with the client was strengthened using empirically supported factors.
    B. The relationship with the client was strengthened through the implementation of collaborative approach, agreement on goals, demonstration of empathy, verbalization of positive regard, and collection of client feedback.
    C. The client reacted positively to the relationship-strengthening measures taken.
    D. The client verbalized feeling supported and understood during therapy sessions.
    E. Despite attempts to strengthen the therapeutic relationship, the client reports feeling distant and misunderstood.
    F. The client has indicated that sessions are not helpful and will be terminating therapy.

3. **Clarify Facts of the Abuse (3)**
    A. The client was assisted in clarifying and expressing facts associated with the abuse.
    B. Support and encouragement were given to the client to increase their level of disclosure of the facts around the abuse.
    C. Even with support and encouragement being given to the client, they still had difficulty expressing and clarifying the facts about the abuse.
    D. The client openly outlined the facts associated with the most recent incident of their being a victim of abuse and was praised for their bravery.

---

*The numbers in parentheses correlate to the number of the Therapeutic Intervention statement in the companion chapter with the same title in the *Child Psychotherapy Treatment Planner*, Sixth Edition, by Jongsma, Peterson, McInnis, & Bruce (Wiley, 2023).

4. **Utilize Trauma-Focused Cognitive Behavioral Therapy (TF-CBT) (4)**
   A. The client was encouraged to share their trauma narrative through the use of Trauma-Focused Cognitive Behavioral Therapy.
   B. The client was assisted in building trusting relationships and recognizing their emotions to build self-empowerment.
   C. The client was taught to use coping strategies, such as deep breathing, use of physical activity, and art activities.

5. **Report Physical Abuse (5)**
   A. An assessment was conducted on the client to substantiate the nature and extent of the physical abuse.
   B. The client was sent to a physician to confirm and document the physical abuse.
   C. The physical abuse of the client was reported to the state child protection agency for further investigation.
   D. The parents were notified about the client's revelation of physical abuse and that, as required by law, it has been reported to the state child protection agency for investigation.

6. **Assess Veracity of Charges (6)**
   A. The client's family, physician, and criminal justice officials were consulted to assess the truthfulness of the client's allegations of physical abuse.
   B. The truthfulness of the client's allegations regarding physical abuse was confirmed by their family, physician, and the Child Protective Services worker.
   C. Consultation with the family, physician, and Child Protective Services worker resulted in divided opinions regarding the veracity of the client's allegations of abuse.

7. **Assess for Removal from Home (7)**
   A. The family environment was assessed to determine if it was safe for the client.
   B. The family environment was determined to be unsafe for the client, and they were moved to a safe, temporary placement outside the home.
   C. The perpetrator agreed to move out of the home and not visit until the nonabusive parent and protective service worker give their approval.
   D. After the family environment was assessed, a recommendation was made that a temporary restraining order be sought for the perpetrator.
   E. The nonabusive parent was assisted in obtaining a restraining order and implementing it on a consistent basis.
   F. The nonabusive parent was monitored and supported for consistent implementation of the no-contact agreement between the perpetrator and victim.
   G. The nonabusive parent was confronted on their inconsistent enforcement of the restraining order to keep the perpetrator from the presence of the client.

8. **Reassure Client of Protection (8)**
   A. The client was repeatedly reassured of concern and care of others in keeping them safe from further abuse.

B. The client was reassured by the nonabusive parent and others that they were looking out for their safety.

C. The client's anxiety level seems to be diminished as they have been reassured of their safety.

9. **Assess Level of Insight (9)**

A. The client's level of insight toward the presenting problems was assessed.

B. The client was assessed in regard to the syntonic versus dystonic nature of their insight about the presenting problems.

C. The client was noted to demonstrate good insight into the problematic nature of the behavior and symptoms.

D. The client was noted to be in agreement with others' concerns and is motivated to work on change.

E. The client was noted to be ambivalent regarding the problems described and is reluctant to address the issues as a concern.

F. The client was noted to be resistant regarding acknowledgment of the problem areas, is not concerned about them, and has no motivation to make changes.

10. **Assess for Correlated Disorders (10)**

A. The client was assessed for evidence of research-based correlated disorders.

B. The client was assessed in regard to the level of vulnerability to suicide.

C. The client was identified as having a comorbid disorder, and treatment was adjusted to account for these concerns.

D. The client has been assessed for any correlated disorders, but none were found.

11. **Assess for Culturally Based Confounding Issues (11)**

A. The client was assessed for age-related issues that could help to better understand their clinical presentation.

B. The client was assessed for gender-related issues that could help to better understand their clinical presentation.

C. The client was assessed for cultural syndromes, cultural idioms of distress, or culturally based perceived causes that could help to better understand their clinical presentation.

D. Alternative factors have been identified as contributing to the client's currently defined "problem behavior," and these were taken into account in regard to treatment.

E. Culturally based factors that could help to account for the client's currently defined "problem behavior" were investigated, but no significant factors were identified.

12. **Assess Severity of Impairment (12)**

A. The severity of the client's impairment was assessed to determine the appropriate level of care.

B. The client was assessed in regard to impairment in social, relational, and educational endeavors.

C. It was reflected to the client that the impairment appears to create mild to moderate effects on the client's functioning.

D. It was reflected to the client that the impairment appears to create severe to very severe effects on the client's functioning.

E. The client was continuously assessed for the severity of impairment, as well as the efficacy and appropriateness of treatment.

13. **Assess for Pathogenic Care (13)**

A. The home, school, and community of the client were assessed for pathogenic care and concerns.

B. The client's various environments were assessed for the persistent disregard of the child's needs, repeated changes in caregivers, limited opportunities for stable attachment, harsh discipline, or other grossly inept care.

C. Pathogenic care was identified, and the treatment plan included strategies for managing or correcting these concerns and protecting the child.

D. No pathogenic care was identified, and this was reflected to the client and caregivers.

14. **Assess for Acute Stress Disorder (14)**

A. The client was assessed as to whether their response to abuse has resulted in acute stress disorder or posttraumatic stress disorder (PTSD).

B. Acute stress disorder or PTSD was evident with the client, and treatment objectives and interventions were adjusted accordingly.

C. It was determined that the abuse has not resulted in acute stress disorder or PTSD for the client.

15. **Explore Expression of Feelings About Abuse (15)**

A. The client's feelings toward the perpetrator were identified and explored.

B. The client was asked to complete and process the "My Thoughts and Feelings" exercise from the *Child Psychotherapy Homework Planner* (Jongsma, Peterson, McInnis, & Bruce) to help them practice openness.

C. Encouragement and support were given to the client as they were assisted in expressing and clarifying their feelings associated with the abuse experiences.

D. The client expressed pain, anger, and fear as they told the story of the abuse; the client was supported through this difficult time.

E. The client was reminded that openness leads to health and secrecy leads to staying sick.

F. The client was reinforced for being open in expression of thoughts and feelings.

G. The client remains emotionally shut down and unwilling to express feelings openly, and their barriers to being more open were explored, identified, and removed.

16. **Utilize Eye Movement Desensitization Reprocessing (16)**

A. Eye movement desensitization and reprocessing (EMDR) techniques were used to help reduce the client's emotional distress.

B. EMDR techniques were found to be useful in alleviating the client's emotional distress, and this was continued as necessary.

C. The client was unable to find usefulness through EMDR to alleviate emotional distress, and therapy was continued as usual.

17. **Assign Reading (17)**

   A. The client was assigned books that promote expression of feelings connected to the abuse.

   B. The client was assigned to read *A Terrible Thing Happened* (Holmes).

   C. The client was assigned to read *Once I Was Very Scared* (Ghosh Ippen).

   D. The client was assigned *Brave Bart: A Story for Traumatized and Grieving Child* (Sheppard).

   E. The client was assigned to read *Angryman* (Dahle).

   F. Today's session focused on processing the content of the assigned reading material on feelings connected to the abuse.

   G. The client reported that the books have helped them learn to effectively understand feelings connected to the abuse, and the benefits of this progress were reviewed.

18. **Confront Denial of Family and Perpetrator (18)**

   A. Family sessions were conducted in which the family's denial of the client's abuse was confronted and challenged.

   B. The perpetrator was asked to list all of their rationalizations for the abuse.

   C. Confrontation was used to process the perpetrator's list of rationalizations for the abuse.

   D. Confrontation was used with the perpetrator to break through denial of abusing the client.

   E. The use of confrontation and challenge has been effective in breaking through the perpetrator's denial, and they are now taking ownership and responsibility for the abuse.

   F. The perpetrator remains in denial of abusing the client in spite of confrontation and challenge to their rationalizations.

19. **Confront Client Excusing Perpetrator's Abuse (19)**

   A. The client was asked to create and process a list of reasons why they were abused by the perpetrator.

   B. Each time the client made an excuse for the perpetrator's abuse, they were confronted and reminded that they in no way deserved being abused.

   C. The message was given to the client that even though they are not perfect, the abuse was not deserved.

   D. The client was redirected when they continued to excuse the perpetrator for the abuse and engaged in self-blame.

   E. Positive feedback was provided as the client has begun to place clear responsibility for the abuse on the perpetrator and has discontinued self-blame.

20. **Reassure That Abuse Was Not Deserved (20)**

   A. The client was reassured that the physical abuse they received was in no way deserved, no matter what they had done wrong, if anything.

   B. The message of not deserving the abuse no matter what happened was consistently given to the client.

   C. The client was educated regarding their deserving personal respect and controlled responses in punishment situations.

21. **Reinforce Holding Perpetrator Responsible (21)**

    A. All statements by the client that hold the perpetrator responsible for the abuse were reinforced.

    B. The client was asked to list all of the reasons why the perpetrator was responsible for the abuse.

    C. The client was reminded that regardless of any misbehavior on their part, it was still the perpetrator's fault for the abuse.

    D. Positive feedback was provided as the client has consistently made statements putting responsibility for the abuse firmly on the perpetrator.

22. **Support Confrontation of Perpetrator About Abuse (22)**

    A. The client was prepared in order to build their confidence to confront the perpetrator with the abuse in a family session.

    B. Role-play was used with the client to provide them with experience in confronting the perpetrator.

    C. Family sessions were conducted in which the nonabusive parent and client confronted the perpetrator with the abuse.

    D. Confrontation of the perpetrator with the abuse was modeled by the nonabusive parent in family sessions.

    E. In the family session, the client read a letter that they had written outlining the reasons why the perpetrator was responsible for the abuse.

    F. The client declined to confront the perpetrator in a family session, and their decision was accepted.

23. **Facilitate Perpetrator Apology (23)**

    A. The client was assessed as to their readiness to hear and accept an apology from the perpetrator.

    B. The perpetrator's apology was processed for genuineness and level of honesty.

    C. A family session was conducted in which the perpetrator apologized to the client and family for the abuse.

    D. The perpetrator's apology was assessed to be disingenuous and dishonest, and it was not accepted as appropriate for a family session.

24. **Refer Perpetrator to Group (24)**

    A. The perpetrator attended and participated in the required effective parenting and anger management groups.

    B. The gains made by the perpetrator in the group were monitored and reinforced.

    C. The perpetrator was confronted on their noncompliance with attending the required groups.

25. **Refer Perpetrator for Psychological Evaluation/Treatment (25)**

    A. The perpetrator was referred for a psychological evaluation.

    B. The perpetrator cooperated with all aspects of the evaluation.

    C. All treatment recommendations of the evaluation were given and explained to the perpetrator.

D. The perpetrator was asked to make a commitment to follow through on each of the treatment recommendations of the evaluation.

26. Evaluate Family for Substance Abuse (26)

A. Family sessions were conducted to assess issues of substance use and abuse within the family.

B. The parents were referred for a substance abuse assessment.

C. The parents cooperated and completed the requested substance abuse assessments.

D. Efforts to assess the issue of substance abuse and use within the family were met with denial and resistance.

E. The perpetrator was referred to a substance abuse program.

F. The perpetrator successfully completed a substance abuse program and is now involved in aftercare.

G. The perpetrator was referred but refused to follow through on completing a substance abuse program.

27. Counsel Parents on Boundaries (27)

A. The client's parents were counseled on what are and what are not appropriate discipline boundaries.

B. Past inappropriate disciplinary boundaries that allowed for abusive punishment were addressed and new appropriate boundaries established.

C. New appropriate boundaries for nonabusive, reasonable discipline were monitored for the parents honoring and enforcing them.

D. The parents reported that they have successfully implemented disciplinary measures that are nonabusive and reasonable.

28. Employ AF-CBT (28)

A. Alternatives for Families: Cognitive Behavioral Therapy (AF-CBT) was used with the family.

B. The parents were assisted in establishing a commitment to limit physical force, teach effective management skills, identify and manage reactions to abuse-specific triggers, identify cognitive contributors to abusive behavior, and learn to use disciplinary approaches to reduce risk of violent behavior in the family system.

C. The parents' list of appropriate disciplinary behavior was reviewed, with reasonable approaches being encouraged and reinforced.

D. The parents were monitored for their use of discipline techniques that reinforce reasonable, respectful actions and appropriate boundaries.

E. The parents were confronted and redirected when discipline was not reasonable and respectful.

29. Apply PCIT (29)

A. Parent/Child Interaction Therapy (PCIT) was used with the family.

B. The family was assisted in strengthening the parent–child relationship, teaching parent skills to effectively direct the child's difficult behaviors, set limits, establish a consistent approach to discipline, and restore warmth and positive feelings to their interactions.

   C. The family was encouraged for their effective understanding of PCIT concepts.

   D. The family struggled to use PCIT concepts, and remedial feedback was provided.

30. Construct Genogram That Identifies Abuse (30)

   A. A multigeneration family genogram was constructed with the family members.

   B. The family members were assisted in identifying patterns of physical abuse from the multigenerational family genogram.

   C. Positive feedback was provided as ways to begin breaking the physically abusive family patterns were identified and implemented by family members.

   D. The family members were supported as they acknowledged that the pattern of multigenerational physical abuse is existent and vowed to stop this pattern within their own family.

31. Assess Family Stress Factors (31)

   A. Family dynamics were assessed to identify stress factors and events that may have contributed to the abuse.

   B. The family members were assisted in identifying effective ways to cope with stress in order to reduce the probability of abuse.

   C. The family was directed to key community and professional resources that could assist in effectively coping with family stressors.

   D. The family members were assisted in identifying steps to take to reduce environmental stressors that may contribute to the precipitation of violence.

   E. Family members were asked to identify family stress factors and were urged to be more open in this area.

32. Reinforce Family Support and Nurture (32)

   A. Family members were taught the importance of emotional support and nurturing of the client and how they each could provide it for them.

   B. Positive reinforcement was given to family members for incidents of support and nurturing given to the client.

   C. The family position that the client should forget the abuse now and move on was confronted and processed, with members being reminded of the client's need for ongoing support and nurturing in order to fully heal.

33. Assign Letter to Perpetrator (33)

   A. The client was asked to write a letter to the perpetrator expressing feelings of hurt, fear, and anger.

   B. The completed letter to the perpetrator was processed, providing the client with assistance and support in expressing the feelings connected to the abuse.

   C. The client's inability to complete the assigned letter was explored with blocks being identified and processed.

   D. The client was asked to write the letter expressing feelings about the abuse to the perpetrator but refused to do so, saying that they did not want to experience those feelings again.

34. Interpret Anger and Aggression Triggered by Perpetrator (34)

   A. Expressions of anger and aggression by the client were interpreted as triggered by feelings toward the perpetrator.

B. Displays of seemingly unrelated anger and aggression were reflected to the client as indications of how angry they must be toward the perpetrator.

C. It was reflected that the client's general displays of anger and aggression have diminished as they have developed insight into their feelings of anger focused on the perpetrator.

D. The client rejected the concept that their anger and aggression have been triggered by feelings about the perpetrator and was urged to consider this as they are able.

35. Identify Sources of Help (35)

A. Various actions for the client to take to protect self from future abuse were identified and reinforced.

B. Efforts were made to empower the client to take necessary steps to obtain help against abuse if the situation warranted it.

C. The client was inundated with statements of empowerment regarding protecting self.

36. Complete "Letter of Empowerment" Exercise (36)

A. The client was assisted in writing out thoughts and feelings regarding surviving the abuse, coping with it, and overcoming it.

B. The client was asked to complete the "Letter of Empowerment" exercise from the *Child Psychotherapy Homework Planner* (Jongsma, Peterson, McInnis, & Bruce) to assist them in expressing thoughts and feelings around the abuse.

C. Unconditional positive regard and active listening were used to help the client express thoughts and feelings about the abuse.

D. Barriers and defenses of the client that prevent expression of thoughts and feelings about the abuse were identified, addressed, and removed.

E. Efforts to encourage the client to express thoughts and feelings about the abuse have not been effective, and the client remains closed regarding the abuse.

F. The client completed the "Letter of Empowerment" exercise and was helped to see that it has enabled them to express thoughts and feelings about the abuse.

G. The client has failed to complete the empowerment exercise and was redirected to do so.

37. Identify a Basis for Self-Esteem (37)

A. The client's talents, importance to others, and spiritual value were reviewed with them to assist in identifying a basis for self-worth.

B. The client was asked to verbally affirm each of their positive strengths and attributes that were identified.

C. Positive self-talk was developed around the client's strengths and attributes that they could use on a daily basis to affirm self.

38. Reinforce Positive Statements (38)

A. Every positive self-descriptive statement made by the client was affirmed and reinforced.

B. The client was assigned "Positive Self-Statements" in the *Child Psychotherapy Homework Planner* (Jongsma, Peterson, McInnis, & Bruce).

C. The client's negative self-statements were confronted and reframed.

D. The pattern of the client making more positive than negative self-statements was recognized, reinforced, and encouraged.

39. Assign Forgiveness Letter or Exercise (39)

A. The client was educated on the key aspects of forgiveness, with special emphasis being given to the power involved.

B. The client was asked to complete a forgiveness letter to the perpetrator while asserting the right to safety.

C. The client was given a forgiveness exercise to complete and to process in the next session.

D. The assigned letter of forgiveness was processed, and the evident empowerment provided by the experience was reinforced.

E. The client has not completed the forgiveness letter, and the reasons for this were processed.

40. Assign Letting Go Exercise (40)

A. The potential benefits of the process of letting go of anger and hurt were explored with the client.

B. A letting-go exercise was assigned in which the client would bury an anger list about the perpetrator.

C. The letting-go exercise was processed with the client and feelings were identified and expressed.

D. The client struggles with letting go of feelings of hurt and anger and is not able to reach this goal as yet; the client was encouraged to do this when they are ready.

E. The client reports that they have successfully let go of feelings of hurt and anger regarding being an abuse survivor, and this was processed and supported.

41. Formulate Future Plans (41)

A. The client was probed to determine what future plans they have developed that involve interaction with peers and family.

B. To assist and encourage the idea of future plans, the client was asked to complete the following fill-in-the-blank sentences: "I imagine that"; "I will"; "I dream that someday."

C. The client was assigned "Show Your Strengths" in the *Child Psychotherapy Homework Planner* (Jongsma, Peterson, McInnis, & Bruce).

D. The client was encouraged to include interaction with peers and family as part of their future plans.

E. The client struggled to envision any future plans despite assistance and encouragement to do so.

42. Refer to Victim Support Group (42)

A. The benefits of the client attending a support group were identified and discussed.

B. The client was referred to a support group for children who have been abused to decrease feelings of being the only one in this situation.

C. The client's experience of attending a support group with the others who are in the same situation was processed.

D. Active listening skills were used as the client indicated that they felt different from all the others in the support group.

E. The client reported feeling empowered and understood after having attended a support group of fellow survivors of abuse, and this was reinforced.

43. **Explore Loss of Trust in Adults (43)**

   A. The client was encouraged to express their loss of trust in adults.

   B. The client was assisted in connecting their loss of trust to the perpetrator's abuse and others' failure to protect them.

   C. The client rejected assistance in identifying and expressing loss of trust and stood firm when saying that they still trust adults.

44. **Teach Discriminating Trust Judgments (44)**

   A. The client was educated in the process of making discriminating judgments of trusting people.

   B. The client was assisted in identifying key factors that make some people trustworthy and those that make others untrustworthy.

   C. Various scenarios of individuals were presented to the client to practice trust-discrimination skills.

45. **Teach Share-Check Technique (45)**

   A. The share-check technique was taught to the client to increase skills in assessing an individual's trustworthiness.

   B. Role-play situations were used with the client to build skill and confidence in using the share-check technique.

   C. The client was asked to make a commitment to using the share-check technique and reporting results of the experience.

   D. The client reported success at using the share-check method of gradually building trust in others, and the benefits of this were processed.

46. **Employ Sand Tray Therapy (46)**

   A. The sand tray therapy approach was used to reenact trauma scenes, express emotions connected to trauma, and reflect and interpret feelings expressed through symbolic play.

   B. The client was able to use miniature toys, figurines, and objects to express self in a calming setting.

   C. The client used sand tray therapy to promote healing and was encouraged to continue this approach when appropriate.

   D. The client found sand tray therapy to be unhelpful and treatment was returned to status quo.

47. **Employ Child-Centered Play Therapy (47)**

   A. Child-centered approaches of genuine interest and unconditional positive regard were employed to provide the client with the supportive environment needed to resolve feelings of fear, grief, and rage surrounding the abuse.

   B. The feelings revealed during the play therapy session were consistently reflected back to the client.

   C. Consistent trust was communicated to the client that the direction of their play would promote the resolution of the fear and rage connected with abuse.

   D. The client's active participation in the child-centered play therapy sessions has resulted in them beginning to resolve feelings surrounding the abuse.

48. Assign Drawing Faces of Self (48)

A. The client was asked to draw pictures of their own face before, during, and after the abuse occurred.

B. The client drew three faces in detail and, as the drawings were explained, the feelings that they had experienced were processed.

C. The client attempted but could not draw the faces to reflect how they felt before, during, and after the abuse occurred, but they were supported for this effort.

49. Promote Technology Use (49)

A. The client and parents were encouraged to use available technology to teach mindfulness relaxation techniques to minimize anxiety, anger, or shame when experiencing memories or flashbacks connected to the abuse.

B. The client and parents were assisted in finding suitable technology to teach mindfulness relaxation techniques, such as the Calm App, Cosmic Kid Yoga YouTube channel, or Sesame Street Mindfulness video.

C. The client identified positive use of technological tools to develop mindfulness relaxation techniques.

D. The client was unable or unwilling to use technological tools to teach mindfulness relaxation techniques, and these techniques were taught in session instead.

50. Refer to Equine Therapy (50)

A. The client and parents were provided with the rationale for equine therapy of being able to practice asking and receiving help, regaining a sense of control, becoming more aware of body language, and developing more internal resources to reduce the impact of trauma on their life.

B. The client and parents were interested in equine therapy techniques, and a referral was made to an appropriate equine therapist.

C. The client and parents were uninterested in equine therapy, and concepts were practiced within a regular session.

POSTTRAUMATIC STRESS DISORDER (PTSD)

CLIENT PRESENTATION

1. **Traumatic Event (1)***
   A. The client described a traumatic experience in which they had exposure to threats of death.
   B. The client described a traumatic experience that resulted in serious injury to self and/or others.
   C. The client described a history of being physically and/or sexually abused.
   D. The client was open and talkative about the traumatic event(s).
   E. The client was guarded and reluctant to talk about the traumatic event(s).

2. **Intrusive, Distressing Thoughts (2)**
   A. The client reported that they have experienced frequent intrusive, distressing thoughts or images about the traumatic event.
   B. The client was visibly upset when describing the distressing images of the traumatic event.
   C. The client denied experiencing any recent intrusive, distressing thoughts or images about the traumatic event.
   D. The frequency and intensity of the client's intrusive, distressing thoughts or images have started to decrease as they work through thoughts and feelings about the traumatic event.

3. **Disturbing Dreams (3)**
   A. The client reported experiencing frequent nightmares or distressing dreams since the traumatic event first occurred.
   B. The client has continued to be troubled by disturbing dreams associated with the trauma.
   C. The client has experienced a mild reduction in the frequency of the disturbing dreams.
   D. The client has not experienced any disturbing dreams about the traumatic event since the last therapy session.

4. **Flashbacks or Illusions (4)**
   A. The client reported experiencing numerous flashbacks or illusions that the traumatic event is recurring.
   B. The client experienced a flashback or illusion during today's therapy session when discussing the traumatic event.
   C. The frequency of the client's flashbacks or illusions has started to decrease as they make productive use of therapy.
   D. The client denied experiencing any recent flashbacks or illusions.

---

*The numbers in parentheses correlate to the number of the Behavioral Definition statement in the companion chapter with the same title in the *Child Psychotherapy Treatment Planner*, Sixth Edition, by Jongsma, Peterson, McInnis, & Bruce (Wiley, 2023).

5. **Intense Emotional Distress (5)**

   A. The client has experienced a significant amount of emotional distress and turmoil since the traumatic event first occurred.

   B. The client was visibly distressed and upset when discussing the traumatic event.

   C. The intensity of the client's emotional distress when discussing the traumatic event has started to diminish.

   D. The client has been able to talk about the traumatic event without displaying a significant amount of emotional distress.

6. **Strong Physiological Reaction (6)**

   A. The client reported that they often exhibit an intense physiological reaction (e.g., trembling and shaking, palpitations, dizziness, shortness of breath, sweating) when reminded of the traumatic event.

   B. The client demonstrated a strong physiological reaction (e.g., trembling and shaking, shortness of breath, sweating) when discussing the traumatic event in today's therapy session.

   C. The client's negative physiological reactions have started to decrease in intensity when talking about the traumatic event.

   D. The client did not experience any negative physiological reaction when discussing the traumatic event.

7. **Avoidance of Talking About Trauma (7)**

   A. The client has avoided conversations about the trauma and tries also to avoid thinking about it.

   B. In an attempt to avoid the feelings associated with the trauma, the client has resisted talking about it.

   C. The parents report that the client refuses to discuss the traumatic event.

   D. The client's general avoidance of the subject of the trauma has waned, and they are willing to discuss it briefly.

   E. The client is now able to think about, talk about, and experience feelings about the trauma without fear of being overwhelmed.

8. **Avoidance of Activities Associated with Trauma (8)**

   A. The client has avoided engaging in activities, going places, or interacting with people associated with the traumatic event.

   B. The client acknowledged that they avoid activities, places, or people that remind them of the traumatic event because of the fear of being overwhelmed by powerful emotions.

   C. The client has started to tolerate exposure to activities, places, or people that remind them of the traumatic event without feeling overwhelmed.

   D. The client has returned to a pretrauma level of functioning without avoiding people or places associated with the traumatic event.

9. **Changes in Mood (9)**

   A. The client's mood has changed significantly since the traumatic event.

   B. The client verbalized feelings of distress and/or disability since the traumatic event.

   C. The client has begun to take steps to return their mood to more regular levels.

    D. The client verbalized a more positive mood during today's therapy session.

    E. The client has worked through many of their feelings surrounding the traumatic event and has developed a healthy mood.

10. **Limited Recall (10)**

    A. The client reported that they are unable to recall some important aspects of the traumatic event.

    B. The client's emotional distress has been so great that they are unable to recall many details of the traumatic event.

    C. The client has started to recall some of the important details of the traumatic event.

    D. The client recalled most of the important aspects of the traumatic event.

11. **Lack of Interest (11)**

    A. The client has displayed little interest in activities that normally brought them pleasure before the traumatic event.

    B. The client has significantly reduced participation in social or extracurricular activities since the traumatic event.

    C. The client verbalized little to no interest in socializing or participating in extracurricular activities.

    D. The client has started to participate in more social or extracurricular activities.

    E. The client has participated in social or extracurricular activities on a regular, consistent basis.

12. **Social Detachment (12)**

    A. The client has become more withdrawn since the traumatic event first occurred.

    B. The client appeared aloof and detached in today's therapy session.

    C. The client has started to socialize with a wider circle of peers.

    D. The client has become more outgoing and interacts with peers on a regular, consistent basis.

13. **Emotionally Constricted (13)**

    A. The client has generally appeared flat and constricted in emotional presentation since the traumatic event.

    B. The client's affect appeared flat and constricted when talking about the traumatic event.

    C. The client acknowledged that they are reluctant to share deeper emotions pertaining to the traumatic event because of the fear of losing control of emotions.

    D. The client has started to show a wider range of emotions about the traumatic event in the therapy sessions.

    E. The client has been able to express genuine emotions about the traumatic event without feeling overwhelmed.

14. **Pessimistic Outlook (14)**

    A. The client has developed a pessimistic outlook on the future and often feels overwhelmed by feelings of helplessness and hopelessness.

    B. The client verbalized feelings of helplessness and hopelessness during today's therapy session.

C. The client has gradually begun to develop a brighter outlook on the future.

D. The client expressed a renewed sense of hope for the future in today's therapy session.

E. The client's willingness to be assertive and assume healthy risks reflected their renewed sense of hope and feelings of empowerment.

15. Irritability (15)

A. The client has displayed irritability and moodiness since the trauma occurred.

B. The client's irritability has resulted in many incidents of verbal outbursts of anger over small issues.

C. The parents reported that the client reacts irritably to minor stimuli.

D. The client has become less irritable as the trauma is processed and underlying feelings are resolved.

16. Lack of Concentration (16)

A. The client has not been able to maintain concentration on schoolwork or other tasks.

B. The parents and teachers report that the client is having difficulty maintaining concentration since the traumatic event.

C. The client stated that their concentration is interrupted by flashbacks of the traumatic incident.

D. The client's concentration is becoming more focused as the feelings surrounding the trauma are resolved.

17. Hypervigilance/Mistrustfulness (17)

A. The client has developed a deep mistrust of others because of the traumatic event.

B. The client described self as being overly vigilant when they go out into public places because of fear of possible harm or danger.

C. The client appeared guarded and mistrustful during today's therapy session.

D. The client has slowly begun to develop trust and gain acceptance from several individuals.

E. The client's increased trust in others has helped to stabilize mood and allowed them to work through many of thoughts and feelings about the traumatic event.

18. Exaggerated Startle Response (18)

A. The client has often displayed an exaggerated startle response when exposed to any sudden, unexpected stimuli.

B. The client displayed an exaggerated startle response in today's therapy session.

C. The client reported that they do not startle as easily or dramatically when exposed to unexpected stimuli.

19. Guilt (19)

A. The client has been troubled by strong feelings of guilt since the traumatic event first occurred.

B. The client expressed feelings of guilt about surviving, causing, or not preventing the traumatic event.

C. The client has begun to work through and resolve feelings of guilt about the traumatic event.

D. The client verbally denied experiencing any feelings of guilt about the traumatic event.

E. The client has successfully resolved feelings of guilt about the traumatic event.

20. **Depression (19)**

A. The client reported experiencing a significant amount of depression and unhappiness since the traumatic event first occurred.

B. The client expressed strong feelings of sadness and hurt about the traumatic event.

C. The client's level of depression has begun to diminish as they work through many of their thoughts and feelings about the traumatic event.

D. The client did not appear sad or depressed when talking about the traumatic event.

E. The frequency and intensity of the client's depressed moods have decreased significantly.

21. **Sleep Disturbance (20)**

A. The client has experienced significant disturbances in their sleep pattern since the traumatic event.

B. The client reported having problems falling asleep.

C. The client has experienced frequent early morning awakenings.

D. The client reported recent improvements in sleep.

E. The client reported experiencing a return to their normal sleep pattern.

22. **Angry Outbursts/Aggression (21)**

A. The client described a persistent pattern of exhibiting intense outbursts of rage or becoming physically aggressive.

B. The client expressed strong feelings of anger and rage about the traumatic event.

C. The client has recently struggled to control hostile/aggressive impulses.

D. The client was able to talk about the traumatic event with much less anger and resentment.

E. The frequency and severity of the client's angry outbursts and aggressive behaviors have decreased significantly.

23. **Symptom Duration Over 1 Month (22)**

A. The symptoms that formed in reaction to the traumatic event have been present in the client for more than 1 month.

B. Although the traumatic event occurred many months ago, the symptom pattern has been present only for the past several weeks.

C. The parents reported that the client's symptoms seemed to have started immediately after the traumatic event several months ago.

D. The client's symptoms have been gradually improving since treatment began.

E. The client reported being free of all symptoms associated with the traumatic incident.

INTERVENTIONS IMPLEMENTED

1. **Establish Rapport (1)***
   A. Caring was conveyed to the client through support, warmth, and empathy.
   B. The client was provided with nonjudgmental support and a level of trust was developed.
   C. The client was urged to feel safe in expressing their PTSD concerns.
   D. The client began to express feelings more freely as rapport and trust level have increased.
   E. The client has continued to experience difficulty being open and direct about their expression of painful feelings; they were encouraged to use the safe haven of therapy to express these difficult issues.

2. **Focus on Strengthening Therapeutic Relationship (2)**
   A. The relationship with the client was strengthened using empirically supported factors.
   B. The relationship with the client was strengthened through the implementation of collaborative approach, agreement on goals, demonstration of empathy, verbalization of positive regard, and collection of client feedback.
   C. The client reacted positively to the relationship-strengthening measures taken.
   D. The client verbalized feeling supported and understood during therapy sessions.
   E. Despite attempts to strengthen the therapeutic relationship, the client reports feeling distant and misunderstood.
   F. The client has indicated that sessions are not helpful and will be terminating therapy.

3. **Assess Nature of PTSD Symptoms (3)**
   A. The client was asked about the frequency, intensity, duration, and history of their anxiety symptoms, fear, and avoidance.
   B. *The Anxiety Disorders Interview Schedule for Children—Parent Version or Child Version* (Silverman & Albano) was used to assess the client's anxiety symptoms.
   C. The exercises "PTSD Incident Report" from the *Child Psychotherapy Homework Planner* (Jongsma, Peterson, McInnis, & Bruce) and "Describe Your PTSD Symptoms" from the *Adolescent Psychotherapy Homework Planner* (Jongsma, Peterson, McInnis, & Bruce) were assigned to help develop an understanding of the PTSD symptoms.
   D. The assessment of the client's anxiety symptoms indicated that their symptoms are extreme and severely interfere with their life.
   E. The assessment of the client's anxiety symptoms indicates that these symptoms are moderate and occasionally interfere with daily functioning.
   F. The results of the assessment of the client's anxiety symptoms indicate that these symptoms are mild and rarely interfere with daily functioning.
   G. The results of the assessment of the client's anxiety symptoms were reviewed with the client.

---

*The numbers in parentheses correlate to the number of the Therapeutic Intervention statement in the companion chapter with the same title in the *Child Psychotherapy Treatment Planner*, Sixth Edition, by Jongsma, Peterson, McInnis, & Bruce (Wiley, 2023).

4. **Conduct Psychological Testing (4)**

   A. Psychological testing was administered to assess for the presence and strength of PTSD symptoms.

   B. The client was administered The Child PTSD Symptom Scale (CPSS) (Foa et al.).

   C. The client was administered The Child Post Traumatic Stress Reaction Index (CPTSRI) (Frederick et al.).

   D. The client was administered the Clinician-Administered PTSD Scale—Child and Adolescent Version (CAPS-C) (Nader et al.).

   E. The psychological testing indicated that the client's PTSD symptoms are extreme and severely interfere with their life.

   F. The psychological testing indicated that the client's PTSD symptoms are moderate and occasionally interfere with their life.

   G. The psychological testing indicated that the client's PTSD symptoms are mild and rarely interfere with their life.

   H. The client declined to complete the psychological testing, and the focus of treatment was changed to this resistance.

5. **Explore Recollection of Traumatic Event (5)**

   A. The client was gently encouraged to tell the entire story of the traumatic event.

   B. The client was given the opportunity to share what they recall about the traumatic event.

   C. Today's therapy session explored the sequence of events before, during, and after the traumatic event.

   D. "Describe the Trauma and Your Feelings" from the *Adolescent Psychotherapy Homework Planner* (Jongsma, Peterson, McInnis, & Bruce) was used to help recall the thoughts, feelings, and action of the traumatic incident.

   E. Despite encouragement, the client struggled to disclose the information about the traumatic event.

6. **Assess Depression/Suicide Risk (6)**

   A. The client's depression was assessed.

   B. The client's suicide risk was assessed.

   C. Appropriate treatment was indicated for the client's level of depression and suicide risk.

   D. Appropriate safety precautions were taken due to the client's high level of depression and suicide risk.

   E. The client was judged to have a very low level of depression and no significant suicide risk.

7. **Assess Level of Insight (7)**

   A. The client's level of insight toward the presenting problems was assessed.

   B. The client was assessed in regard to the syntonic versus dystonic nature of their insight about the presenting problems.

   C. The client was noted to demonstrate good insight into the problematic nature of the behavior and symptoms.

D. The client was noted to be in agreement with others' concerns and is motivated to work on change.

E. The client was noted to be ambivalent regarding the problems described and is reluctant to address the issues as a concern.

F. The client was noted to be resistant regarding acknowledgment of the problem areas, is not concerned about them, and has no motivation to make changes.

8. Assess for Correlated Disorders (8)

A. The client was assessed for evidence of research-based correlated disorders.

B. The client was assessed in regard to the level of vulnerability to suicide.

C. The client was identified as having a comorbid disorder, and treatment was adjusted to account for these concerns.

D. The client has been assessed for any correlated disorders, but none were found.

9. Assess for Culturally Based Confounding Issues (9)

A. The client was assessed for age-related issues that could help to better understand their clinical presentation.

B. The client was assessed for gender-related issues that could help to better understand their clinical presentation.

C. The client was assessed for cultural syndromes, cultural idioms of distress, or culturally based perceived causes that could help to better understand their clinical presentation.

D. Alternative factors have been identified as contributing to the client's currently defined "problem behavior," and these were taken into account in regard to their treatment.

E. Culturally based factors that could help to account for the client's currently defined "problem behavior" were investigated, but no significant factors were identified.

10. Assess Severity of Impairment (10)

A. The severity of the client's impairment was assessed to determine the appropriate level of care.

B. The client was assessed in regard to impairment in social, relational, and educational endeavors.

C. It was reflected to the client that the impairment appears to create mild to moderate effects on the client's functioning.

D. It was reflected to the client that the impairment appears to create severe to very severe effects on the client's functioning.

E. The client was continuously assessed for the severity of impairment, as well as the efficacy and appropriateness of treatment.

11. Assess for Pathogenic Care (11)

A. The home, school, and community of the client were assessed for pathogenic care and concerns.

B. The client's various environments were assessed for the persistent disregard of the child's needs, repeated changes in caregivers, limited opportunities for stable attachment, harsh discipline, or other grossly inept care.

C. Pathogenic care was identified and the treatment plan included strategies for managing or correcting these concerns and protecting the child.

D. No pathogenic care was identified, and this was reflected to the client and caregivers.

12. Refer for Medication Evaluation (12)

A. The client was referred for a medication evaluation to help stabilize mood and decrease the intensity of angry feelings.

B. The client and parent(s) agreed to follow through with the medication evaluation.

C. The client was strongly opposed to being placed on medication to help stabilize moods and reduce emotional distress.

13. Monitor Effects of Medication (13)

A. The client's response to the medication was discussed in today's therapy session.

B. It was noted that the medication has helped the client to stabilize mood and decrease the intensity of angry feelings.

C. It was noted that the client has had little to no improvement in mood or anger control since being placed on the medication.

D. The client was reinforced as they have consistently taken the medication as prescribed.

E. The client has failed to adhere with the medication as prescribed and was redirected to do so.

14. Conduct Trauma-Focused Cognitive Behavioral Therapy (14)

A. Individual sessions were conducted consistent with the trauma-focused cognitive-behavior therapy approach.

B. Group sessions were conducted consistent with the trauma-focused cognitive-behavior therapy approach.

C. Parents were involved in the trauma-focused cognitive-behavioral individual therapy, as needed.

15. Discuss PTSD Symptoms (15)

A. A discussion was held about how PTSD results from exposure to trauma and results in intrusion symptoms, hyperarousal, a tendency to avoid trauma-related stimuli, changes in mood and/or beliefs, and other vulnerabilities, such as fear, shame, anger, guilt, and hopelessness.

B. The client's experiences were normalized and hope was instilled through the promise of recovery through treatment.

C. The client was provided with specific examples of how PTSD symptoms occur and affect individuals.

D. The client displayed a clear understanding of the dynamics of PTSD and was provided with positive feedback.

E. The client has struggled to understand the dynamics of PTSD and was provided with remedial feedback in this area.

16. Assign Reading on Anxiety (16)

A. The parents and client were assigned to read psychoeducational chapters of books or treatment manuals on PTSD.

B. The parents and client have read the assigned information on PTSD, and key points were reviewed.

C. The parents and client have not read the assigned information on PTSD and were redirected to do so.

17. Discuss Treatment Rationale (17)

A. The client was taught about the overall rationale behind treatment of PTSD.

B. The client was assisted in identifying the appropriate goals for PTSD treatment.

C. The client was taught about coping skills, cognitive restructuring, and exposure techniques.

D. The client was taught about techniques that will help to build resilience, confidence, and see self, others, and the world in a less fearful and/or depressing manner.

E. The client was reinforced for clear understanding of the rationale for the treatment of PTSD.

F. The client struggled to understand the retinue behind the treatment for PTSD and was provided with additional feedback in this area.

18. Assign Written Information on PTSD (18)

A. The parents were assigned to read about stress inoculation, cognitive restructuring, and/or exposure-based therapy in chapters of books or treatment manuals on PTSD.

B. The parents were assigned specific chapters from *Prolonged Exposure Therapy for PTSD—Teen Workbook* (Chrestman et al.).

C. The parents were assigned specific chapters from *Think Good—Feel Good: A Cognitive Behaviour Therapy Workbook for Children* (Stallard).

D. The parents were assigned specific chapters from *The Relaxation and Stress Reduction Workbook for Kids* (Shapiro & Sprague).

E. The client has read the assigned information on PTSD; key concepts were reviewed.

F. The parents have not read the assigned information on PTSD, and were redirected to do so.

19. Use Parent Management Training (19)

A. Parent Management Training was used.

B. The parents were taught that parent–child behavioral interactions can encourage or discourage positive or negative behavior.

C. The parents were taught that changing key elements of parent–child interactions can be used to promote positive change.

D. The parents were provided with specific examples of how prompting and reinforcing positive behaviors can be used to promote positive change.

E. The parents were provided with positive feedback for the use of Parent Management Training approaches.

F. The parents have not used the Parent Management Training approach and were redirected to do so.

20. Read Parent-Training Material (20)

A. The parents were asked to read material consistent with a parent management training approach to managing disruptive behavior.

B. The parents were assigned *The Kazdin Method for Parenting the Defiant Child* (Kazdin).

C. The parents have read the assigned material, and key concepts were processed.

D. The parents have not read the assigned material and were redirected to do so.

21. **Teach Parents to Define Aspects of Situation (21)**

A. The parents were taught how to specifically define and identify problem behaviors.

B. The parents were taught how to specifically identify their reactions to the behavior and determine whether the reaction encourages or discourages the behavior.

C. The parents were taught to generate alternatives to the problem behavior.

D. Positive feedback was provided to the parents for their skill at specifically defining and identifying problem behaviors, reactions, outcomes, and alternatives.

E. Parents were provided with remedial feedback as they struggled to correctly identify problem behaviors, reactions, responses, and alternatives.

22. **Teach Consistent Parenting (22)**

A. The parents were taught how to implement key parenting practices on a consistent basis.

B. The parents were taught about establishing realistic, age-appropriate expectations and rules for acceptable and unacceptable behavior.

C. The parents were taught about prompting positive behavior and using positive reinforcement.

D. The parents were taught about clear, direct instruction as well as time-out and other loss-of-privilege techniques for problem behavior.

E. The parents were provided with positive feedback, as they have been able to develop consistent parenting practices.

F. The parents have not developed consistent parenting practices, and they were redirected to do so.

23. **Assign Home Exercises to Implement Parenting Techniques (23)**

A. The parents were assigned home exercises in which they implement parenting techniques and record the results of the implementation exercises.

B. The parents were assigned to read "Clear Rules, Positive Reinforcement, Appropriate Consequences" in the *Adolescent Psychotherapy Homework Planner* (Jongsma, Peterson, McInnis, & Bruce).

C. The parents' implementation of homework exercises was reviewed within the session.

D. Corrective feedback was used to help develop improved, appropriate, and consistent use of skills.

E. The parents have not completed the assigned homework and were redirected to do so.

24. **Teach Symptom Management Skills (24)**

A. Using discussion, play, drawing, and other skill-building techniques, the client was taught skills needed to prepare them for later work with memories of the trauma.

B. The client was taught skills such as identification, labeling, and management of emotions.

C. The client was taught emotional regulation techniques to teach tailored calming and coping skills, such as relaxation, breathing control, coping self-statements, covert modeling and role-playing.

D. The client was reinforced for clear understanding of the stress-management skills.

E. The client was provided with additional examples of relaxation, breathing control, coping self-statements, covert modeling, and other emotional regulation techniques.

F. Role-play was used to assist the client in the effective use of relevant skills.

25. Teach Interpersonal Skills (25)

A. The client was taught interpersonal skills such as assertive communication, problem-solving, and conflict resolution.

B. The client was urged to use skills to mitigate and manage interpersonal conflicts, with the focus on resuming negatively impacted developmental competencies.

C. Behavioral skills training methods were used to instruct, model, rehearse, develop skills in interpersonal relationships, review, reinforce, and address obstacles.

D. Reinforcement and supportive corrective feedback were used for refining and consolidating interpersonal skills usage.

26. Identify Distorted Thoughts (26)

A. The client was assisted in identifying the self-talk and beliefs that mediate anxiety responses.

B. The client was taught age appropriate techniques to identify and challenge biases and assist in generating appraisals that correct for the biases and promote resilience and confidence.

C. The client was assigned the exercise "Replace Negative Thoughts with Positive Self-Talk" from the *Child Psychotherapy Homework Planner* (Jongsma, Peterson, McInnis, & Bruce).

D. The client was reinforced as they verbalized an understanding of the cognitive beliefs and messages that mediate anxiety responses.

E. The client was assisted in replacing distorted messages with positive, realistic cognitions.

F. The client failed to identify distorted thoughts and cognitions and was provided with tentative examples in this area.

27. Assign Self-Talk Homework (27)

A. The client was assigned homework exercises in which they identify biased self-talk and create reality-based alternatives.

B. The client has completed homework related to biased self-talk and creating reality-based alternatives; the client was provided with positive reinforcement for success in this area.

C. The client has completed homework related to biased self-talk and creating reality-based alternatives; the client was provided with corrective feedback for inability to identify and replace self-talk with reality-based alternatives.

D. The client has not attempted homework related to fearful self-talk and reality-based alternatives and was assisted in problem solving.

28. Construct Anxiety Stimuli Hierarchy (28)

A. The client was assisted in developing a narrative to describe the traumatic event.

B. The client was assisted in constructing a hierarchy of anxiety-producing situations associated with the trauma narrative.

C. The "Finding My Triggers" exercise from the *Child Psychotherapy Homework Planner* (Jongsma, Peterson, McInnis, & Bruce) was assigned to the client to assist in developing imaginal exposures.

D. It was difficult for the client to develop a hierarchy of stimulus situations because the causes of their anxiety remain quite vague; the client was assisted in completing the hierarchy.

E. The client was successful at creating a focused hierarchy of specific stimulus situations that provoke anxiety in a gradually increasing manner; this hierarchy was reviewed.

F. The client was directed to develop a detailed narrative description of the trauma for imaginal exposure.

29. Use Imaginal Exposure (29)

A. The client was asked to describe a traumatic experience at an increasing, but client-chosen level of detail.

B. The client was asked to continue to describe their traumatic experience at their own chosen level of detail until trauma-driven beliefs shifted to more reality-based alternatives.

C. The client was provided with recordings of the session and asked to listen to it between sessions.

D. The client was reinforced for progress in imaginal exposure.

E. The client was assisted in problem-solving obstacles to imaginal exposure.

30. Assign Homework on Exposures (30)

A. The client was assigned homework exercises to perform exposure to environmental stimuli, and record the experience.

B. The client was assigned "Gradual Exposure to Fear" in the *Adolescent Psychotherapy Homework Planner* (Jongsma, Peterson, McInnis, & Bruce).

C. The client's use of exposure techniques was reviewed and reinforced.

D. The client has struggled in implementation of exposure techniques and was provided with corrective feedback.

E. The client has not attempted to use the exposure techniques and was redirected to do so.

31. Assess Traumatic Grief (31)

A. The level to which traumatic grief is a consequence of the trauma was assessed.

B. The client was assisted in expressing traumatic grief, working toward accepting and resolution.

32. Discuss Lapse Versus Relapse (32)

A. The client was assisted in differentiating between a lapse and a relapse.

B. A lapse was associated with the initial and reversible return of symptoms, fear, or urges to avoid.

C. A relapse was associated with the decision to return to a repeated pattern of trauma-driven thoughts, feelings, and actions.

D. The client was reinforced for ability to respond to a lapse without relapsing.

33. Identify and Rehearse Response to Lapse Situations (33)

A. The client was asked to identify the future situations or circumstances in which lapses could occur.

B. The client was asked to rehearse the management of potential lapse situations.

C. The client was reinforced as they identified and rehearsed how to cope with potential lapse situations.

D. The client was provided with helpful feedback about how to best manage potential lapse situations.

E. The client declined to identify or rehearse the management of possible lapse situations, and this resistance was redirected.

34. Encourage Use of Therapy Strategies (34)

A. The client was encouraged to routinely use strategies practiced in therapy.

B. The client was urged to use cognitive restructuring, social skills, and exposure techniques while building social interactions and relationships.

C. The client was reinforced for regular use of therapy techniques within social interactions and relationships.

D. The client was unable to identify many situations in which they have used therapy techniques to help build social interactions and social relationships and was redirected to seek these situations.

35. Develop a Coping Card (35)

A. The client was provided with a coping card on which specific coping strategies were listed.

B. The client was assisted in developing the coping card in order to list helpful coping strategies.

C. The client was encouraged to use the coping card when struggling with anxiety-producing situations.

36. Involve Family in Treatment (36)

A. Family members were taught about developmentally appropriate treatment goals for the client.

B. Family members were taught how to give support to the client as they face fears.

C. Family members were assisted in understanding how to prevent reinforcing the client's fear and avoidance.

D. Encouragement, support, and redirection were provided to the family for how they interact with the client about the pattern of symptoms.

E. Family members were provided with positive feedback regarding their involvement in the client's treatment.

37. Support Family Members Managing Their Own Emotions (37)

A. Support was provided to family members to help recognize their own difficult emotional reactions to the client's experience of trauma.

B. The family members were assisted in managing their own difficult emotional reactions to the client's experience of the trauma.

C. Family members were noted to be more capable of supporting the client's positive behavior changes as they have managed their own emotional reactions to the client's trauma.

D. Family members were provided with remedial feedback as they have struggled to manage their own emotions.

38. Encourage Modeling of Skills and Praise (38)

A. Family members were encouraged to model constructive skills that they have learned that will assist in the client's positive behavior change.

B. The family members were encouraged to praise the client when they use therapeutic skills.

C. Family members have been noted to model and praise the use of calming techniques.

D. Family members were reinforced for modeling and praising the client's use of cognitive-restructuring techniques.

E. Family members were encouraged to keep modeling and praising the use of nonavoidance of unrealistic fears.

F. The family members have not modeled and praised the client's use of therapeutic skills and were redirected to do so.

39. Review Shared Therapeutic Activities (39)

A. A conjoint session was led with the client and parent reviewing shared therapeutic activities.

B. Open communication was facilitated between the client and parent regarding the therapeutic activities that they have engaged in.

C. The client was positively reinforced for advancements.

D. Modeling was presented to the parents as a way to positively reinforce advancements for the client.

40. Utilize EMDR (40)

A. Eye movement desensitization and reprocessing (EMDR) techniques were used to help reduce the client's emotional reactivity to the traumatic event.

B. The EMDR techniques described in *Through the Eyes of a Child* (Tinker & Wilson) were used to help reduce the client's emotional reactivity to the traumatic event.

41. Encourage Physical Exercise (41)

A. The client was encouraged to consult a physician regarding the appropriate routine of physical exercise.

B. The client was referred to a fitness expert for an appropriate physical exercise regimen.

C. The client was encouraged to regularly exercise in order to keep fit and reduce stress.

D. The client was reinforced for regular use of exercise.

E. The client has not regularly exercised and was redirected to do so.

42. Employ Child-Centered Play Therapy (42)

A. A child-centered play therapy session was held to provide the client with the opportunity to identify and express feelings surrounding the traumatic incident.

B. The client was offered unconditional positive regard and warm acceptance to help them identify and express feelings surrounding the traumatic incident.

C. The feelings that were expressed in the client's play were reflected back to them in a nonjudgmental manner.

D. The child-centered play therapy session reinforced the client's capacity for growth and ability to cope with the pain surrounding the traumatic event.

E. The play therapy session has helped the client work through and resolve many of their painful emotions surrounding the traumatic incident.

43. Utilize Psychoanalytic Play Therapy (43)

A. A psychoanalytic play therapy session was held to provide the client with the opportunity to express and work through feelings surrounding the traumatic incident.

B. The client was allowed to take the lead in the psychoanalytic play therapy session to help them begin to explore painful emotions surrounding the traumatic incident.

C. The client's play was noted to reflect feelings of anger, hurt, and sadness about the past traumatic incident.

D. The client's play in today's therapy session was interpreted as reflective of the fear and vulnerability that they had experienced during the traumatic incident.

E. The client's feelings reflected in play were interpreted and related to their feelings about the traumatic incident.

44. Use Mutual Storytelling Technique (44)

A. The mutual storytelling technique using puppets, dolls, and stuffed animals was employed to help the client identify and work through feelings surrounding the past traumatic incident.

B. Using the mutual storytelling technique, the therapist created a story that modeled constructive steps that the client can take to protect self and feel empowered.

C. The client created a story through the use of puppets, dolls, and stuffed animals that was interpreted as being reflective of their emotions about the traumatic incident.

D. The client created a similar story to that of the therapists, which reflected ways to protect self and feel empowered.

E. The mutual storytelling technique has been a helpful way for the client to not only express feelings about the past traumatic incident, but also learn how to protect self and feel empowered.

45. Employ Art Therapy (45)

A. The client was provided with materials and asked to draw or paint a picture that reflected feelings of the past trauma.

B. The client's artwork was noted to reflect feelings of anger about the past traumatic incident.

C. The client's artwork was noted to reflect the fear, anxiety, and helplessness that they had experienced during the traumatic incident.

D. The client's drawings were noted to reflect feelings of sadness and hurt about the past traumatic incident.

E. The content of the client's drawings was processed, and the client was given the opportunity to directly verbalize feelings.

46. Monitor Sleep Patterns (46)

A. The client was encouraged to keep a record of how much sleep they get every night.

B. The client was trained in the use of relaxation techniques to help induce sleep.

C. The client was trained in the use of positive imagery to help induce sleep.

D. The client was referred for a medication evaluation to determine whether medication is needed to help them sleep.

47. Reinforce Reality-Based Cognitive Messages (47)

A. The client's positive, reality-based cognitive messages were reinforced.

B. The client was assisted in enhancing self-confidence and increasing adaptive action.

C. The client was noted to have an increase in positive, reality-based cognitive messages and subsequent self-confidence and adaptive action.

D. The client's level of positive, reality-based cognitive messages has not increased, and they were provided with remedial assistance in this area.

REACTIVE ATTACHMENT/DISINHIBITED SOCIAL ENGAGEMENT DISORDER

CLIENT PRESENTATION

1. **Removal from Abusive Family (1)***
   A. Reports and sources indicated that the client comes from a severely abusive and neglectful biological family.
   B. The client's affect and emotional distance were consistent with their history of an abusive and neglectful family background.
   C. The parents reported that the client seemed to be very unsure and confused in the structured, caring environment of their family.
   D. The parents have started to see signs that the client is overcoming their abusive and neglectful past and is becoming more of a part of the new family.

2. **No Bond to Any Caregiver (2)**
   A. The client has made no appreciative reference to any past caregivers.
   B. Reports and evaluations have indicated that the client was not attached to the biological mother or any other caregiver.
   C. It has been observed that the client does not look for or ask for parents when in a setting other than home.
   D. The client has started to show signs and indications of bonding with new parents.

3. **Raised in Unusual Settings (3)**
   A. The client has limited ability to establish secure attachments due to being raised in alternate or unusual settings.
   B. Reports indicated the client was raised in environments such as institutions with high child-to-caregiver ratios or frequent foster care home moves.
   C. The client continues to experience living situations that limit the ability to establish secure attachments.
   D. The client has been involved in a consistent living situation and has shown some ability to establish secure attachments.

4. **Absent Attachment with Caregiving Adults (4)**
   A. The client has little to no attachment to caregiving adults.
   B. The client has not gained an attachment to a caregiving adult by the age of 5.
   C. The client has difficulty managing emotions or interacting well with others.
   D. The client has begun to establish a secure attachment with one or more consistent caregivers.

---

*The numbers in parentheses correlate to the number of the Behavioral Definition statement in the companion chapter with the same title in the *Child Psychotherapy Treatment Planner*, Sixth Edition, by Jongsma, Peterson, McInnis, & Bruce (Wiley, 2023).

5. **Experienced Neglect of Emotional/Physical Needs (5)**
   A. Records of the client's background reflect that they were severely emotionally and physically neglected by the biomother and other caregivers.
   B. The parents reported that to date, the client has shown difficulty accepting or responding positively to their caring and supportive actions.
   C. The client indicated that they remember always taking care of and looking out for self.
   D. The client has started to respond positively to parents' efforts to meet emotional and physical needs.

6. **Resists Care and Help of Others (6)**
   A. The parents reported that the client does not seek comfort, support, nurturance, or protection from caregivers.
   B. The client reported in clear terms that they can and prefer to do things without help from others.
   C. The client has resisted or rejected all help from the teacher.
   D. Gradually, the client has come to allow others to help them and to accept their caring gestures.

7. **Does Not Initiate/Respond to Social Interactions (7)**
   A. The parents indicated that from the beginning the client has withdrawn from and rejected their attempts to be warm and affectionate.
   B. It has been observed by caregivers and professionals that the client relates in a detached manner to everyone.
   C. Both parents and teacher have noted that the client does not attempt to form relationships with peers or with adults.
   D. The client has begun to initiate some social contacts and has started to respond more warmly to contact with others.

8. **Becomes Friendly Too Quickly (8)**
   A. The parents reported that the client quickly becomes too friendly and affectionate with any adult.
   B. The client has rapidly become very friendly and affectionate with the therapist.
   C. The client has been observed becoming very friendly and somewhat affectionate with strangers they meet in public places.
   D. The client has stopped being overly friendly and affectionate to strangers.

9. **Strong Need for Control (9)**
   A. The client has displayed a strong need to be in control.
   B. The client has manifested the need to be in control through aggressive behaviors, manipulative acts, and stealing.
   C. The client has not decreased controlling behaviors.
   D. The client has reduced aggressive behaviors, manipulation, and stealing.
   E. The client is no longer engaging in aggressive behaviors, manipulation, or stealing.

10. **Hoarding or Gorging Food (10)**

   A. The parents have discovered that the client has stashes of food in various hiding places in their bedroom.

   B. It has been observed that the client eats quickly to ensure that they can get more.

   C. The parents reported that the client often eats so much that they become physically sick.

   D. The client has been seen sneaking food at home and at school to save for a later time.

   E. The parents indicate that the client now eats more normal amounts of food and no longer hides food for later consumption.

11. **No Sign of Conscience Development (11)**

   A. It is reported by caregivers that the client does not show any guilt or remorse for bad behavior.

   B. The parents reported that the client blames others for bad behavior and refuses to see it otherwise, even when confronted with solid evidence.

   C. Records of the client's behavior indicate that they showed little or no remorse when caught lying, cheating, or hurting another person.

   D. The client appeared to fail to see anything they did as bad or wrong.

   E. The client has started to show some concern and regret when caught doing something that is wrong.

12. **Aggressive Behaviors (12)**

   A. Records of the client reflect a long, clear history of aggressive acts toward siblings, peers, and caregivers.

   B. The parents indicated that they confront the client's aggressive actions toward siblings, peers, and/or themselves on a daily basis.

   C. School officials have reported intervening with the client on a frequent basis for aggressive actions toward peers.

   D. The client showed little, if any, concern about aggressive behaviors.

   E. The client has reduced the frequency and intensity of aggressive behavior toward siblings, peers, and parents.

13. **Clinginess to Primary Caregiver (13)**

   A. The parents reported that it is impossible to leave the client without the client becoming emotionally distraught.

   B. The client presented as being excessively clingy to parents.

   C. The client expressed becoming very afraid and worried when parents are out of sight.

   D. The client's excessive clinginess has made it difficult for parents to get the client to attend school.

   E. The client has gradually started to tolerate being away from parents without becoming emotionally distraught.

INTERVENTIONS IMPLEMENTED

1. **Establish Rapport (1)***
   A. Caring was conveyed to the client through support, warmth, and empathy.
   B. The client was provided with nonjudgmental support and a level of trust was developed.
   C. The client was urged to feel safe in expressing attachment concerns.
   D. The client began to express feelings more freely as rapport and trust level have increased.
   E. The client has continued to experience difficulty being open and direct about expression of painful feelings; the client was encouraged to use the safe haven of therapy to express these difficult issues.

2. **Focus on Strengthening Therapeutic Relationship (2)**
   A. The relationship with the client was strengthened using empirically supported factors.
   B. The relationship with the client was strengthened through the implementation of collaborative approach, agreement on goals, demonstration of empathy, verbalization of positive regard, and collection of client feedback.
   C. The client reacted positively to the relationship-strengthening measures taken.
   D. The client verbalized feeling supported and understood during therapy sessions.
   E. Despite attempts to strengthen the therapeutic relationship, the client reports feeling distant and misunderstood.
   F. The client has indicated that sessions are not helpful and will be terminating therapy.

3. **Conduct Session in Consistent Manner (3)**
   A. Session structure followed a consistent, predictable form to help the client feel more comfortable and trust the therapist.
   B. The session structure was explained to the client, and questions that they had were answered to the client's satisfaction.
   C. The client appears to have become very comfortable with the session's structure and has begun to self-express a little more freely.
   D. Despite the consistent, predictable structure of the session, the client has not become more comfortable and willing to trust the therapist; the client was reminded that sessions will continue to flow in a consistent, predictable manner.

4. **Conduct Celebrity-Style Interview (4)**
   A. A celebrity-style interview was conducted with the client to build a relationship and to help the client to learn more about self.
   B. After completing the celebrity-style interview, the client was encouraged to ask any of the same questions of the therapist or any other questions they wished answered about the therapist.
   C. Important information about the client that become evident from the interview was reflected back to help affirm things about self.

---

*The numbers in parentheses correlate to the number of the Therapeutic Intervention statement in the companion chapter with the same title in the *Child Psychotherapy Treatment Planner*, Sixth Edition, by Jongsma, Peterson, McInnis, & Bruce (Wiley, 2023).

    D. Active listening was used as the client was able to identify several specific things they had learned about self from the interview.

    E. The client was assigned "Some Things I Would Like You to Know About Me" from the *Child Psychotherapy Homework Planner* (Jongsma, Peterson, McInnis, & Bruce).

5. Conduct Psychosocial Evaluation (5)

    A. A psychosocial evaluation was conducted with the parents and the client.

    B. The parents and client cooperated with all aspects of the psychosocial evaluation, answering all questions in significant detail.

    C. The parents and client complied with the psychosocial evaluation but gave brief information with very little detail.

    D. Strengths of both the parents and the client that emerged from the psychosocial evaluation were identified and affirmed with them.

6. Arrange for Psychological Evaluation (6)

    A. The purpose of the psychological evaluation was explained to the client and parents, and any questions they had regarding it were answered.

    B. A psychological evaluation was conducted with the client to determine the level of behavioral functioning, cognitive style, and intelligence.

    C. The client cooperated with all aspects of the psychological evaluation.

    D. The psychological evaluation could be only partially completed due to the client's lack of focus and cooperation.

7. Assess for PTSD (7)

    A. A structured assessment was conducted to help identify the presence of symptoms of posttraumatic stress disorder (PTSD).

    B. No symptoms of PTSD were identified, and this has been reflected to the client and parents.

    C. Symptoms of PTSD have been identified and this was reflected to the family members.

    D. Treatment has been focused onto the client's PTSD symptoms.

8. Arrange for a Medication Evaluation/Monitor Adherence (8)

    A. The need for a psychiatric evaluation for medication was explained to the parents and the client, and any questions they had regarding it were answered.

    B. The client was referred for a psychiatric evaluation for medications and cooperated fully with all aspects of the psychiatric evaluation.

    C. The results of the evaluation were shared and discussed with the client and parents, and any questions they had were answered.

    D. The client's taking of medication as prescribed was monitored for adherence, effectiveness, and any possible side effects; the client and parents were asked to report any side effects they observed to either the therapist or the psychiatrist.

    E. The client and parents were confronted about the client's taking medication on an inconsistent basis.

    F. The overall effectiveness of the medication was communicated to the psychiatrist.

9. **Assess Level of Insight (9)**
   A. The client's level of insight toward the presenting problems was assessed.
   B. The client was assessed in regard to the syntonic versus dystonic nature of their insight about the presenting problems.
   C. The client was noted to demonstrate good insight into the problematic nature of the behavior and symptoms.
   D. The client was noted to be in agreement with others' concerns and is motivated to work on change.
   E. The client was noted to be ambivalent regarding the problems described and is reluctant to address the issues as a concern.
   F. The client was noted to be resistant regarding acknowledgment of the problem areas, is not concerned about them, and has no motivation to make changes.

10. **Assess for Correlated Disorders (10)**
   A. The client was assessed for evidence of research-based correlated disorders.
   B. The client was assessed in regard to the level of vulnerability to suicide.
   C. The client was identified as having a comorbid disorder, and treatment was adjusted to account for these concerns.
   D. The client has been assessed for any correlated disorders, but none were found.

11. **Assess for Culturally Based Confounding Issues (11)**
   A. The client was assessed for age-related issues that could help to better understand their clinical presentation.
   B. The client was assessed for gender-related issues that could help to better understand their clinical presentation.
   C. The client was assessed for cultural syndromes, cultural idioms of distress, or culturally based perceived causes that could help to better understand their clinical presentation.
   D. Alternative factors have been identified as contributing to the client's currently defined "problem behavior," and these were taken into account in regard to treatment.
   E. Culturally based factors that could help to account for the client's currently defined "problem behavior" were investigated, but no significant factors were identified.

12. **Assess Severity of Impairment (12)**
   A. The severity of the client's impairment was assessed to determine the appropriate level of care.
   B. The client was assessed in regard to impairment in social, relational, and educational endeavors.
   C. It was reflected to the client that the impairment appears to create mild to moderate effects on the client's functioning.
   D. It was reflected to the client that the impairment appears to create severe to very severe effects on the client's functioning.
   E. The client was continuously assessed for the severity of impairment, as well as the efficacy and appropriateness of treatment.

13. **Assess for Pathogenic Care (13)**
   A. The home, school, and community of the client were assessed for pathogenic care and concerns.
   B. The client's various environments were assessed for the persistent disregard of the child's needs, repeated changes in caregivers, limited opportunities for stable attachment, harsh discipline, or other grossly inept care.
   C. Pathogenic care was identified and the treatment plan included strategies for managing or correcting these concerns and protecting the child.
   D. No pathogenic care was identified, and this was reflected to the client and caregivers.

14. **Utilize Trauma-Focused Cognitive Behavioral Therapy (TF-CBT) (14)**
   A. The client was encouraged to share their trauma narrative through the use of Trauma-Focused Cognitive Behavioral Therapy.
   B. The client was assisted in building trusting relationships and recognizing emotions to build empowerment within self.
   C. The client was taught to use coping strategies, such as deep breathing, use of physical activity, and art activities.

15. **Employ Sand Tray Therapy (15)**
   A. The sand tray therapy approach was used to reenact trauma scenes, express emotions connected to neglect and abuse, and reflect and interpret feelings expressed through symbolic play.
   B. The client was able to use miniature toys, figurines, and objects to self-express in a calming setting.
   C. The client used sand tray therapy to promote healing and was encouraged to continue this approach when appropriate.
   D. The client found sand tray therapy to be unhelpful and treatment was returned to status quo.

16. **Assign *Life Book* (16)**
   A. The parents were educated about the key benefits to the client in having a *life book*.
   B. The parents and client were given instructions on how to create a *life book* and then were assigned to put one together.
   C. The parents were assigned the "Create a Memory Album" exercise in the *Child Psychotherapy Homework Planner* (Jongsma, Peterson, McInnis, & Bruce).
   D. The parents and client were monitored on their completion of the assignment of creating a *life book*.
   E. The completed *life book* was reviewed by the parents with the client in order to give the client perspective on and knowledge of their history; the results of this technique were reviewed.
   F. The parents have not completed a *life book* and were redirected to do so.

17. **Elicit Parents' Treatment Commitment (17)**
   A. The possible benefits of their active involvement in the client's treatment were discussed with the parents.
   B. Specific ways that the parents could be involved in treatment were explored and identified.

C. The parents were asked to make a verbal commitment to be an active part of the client's treatment, both in counseling sessions and in their home.

D. As their participation decreased, the parents were gently but firmly reminded of their commitment to the treatment process and the benefits of their involvement.

E. It was noted that the active participation by parents in the client's treatment, both in sessions and at home, has helped to build a bond between them and the client.

18. **Train Parents as Co-therapists (18)**

A. The parents were introduced to the concept of being co-therapists in the client's treatment process.

B. The benefits of the parents being co-therapists were identified and processed.

C. The parents were trained and empowered to be involved as co-therapists in the client's treatment.

D. The parents were guided and directed in their roles as co-therapists.

E. Positive verbal affirmation was given to the parents for their consistent commitment to being co-therapists in the client's treatment.

F. The client has shown strong positive gains in the ability to develop strong bonds, which has been aided by the parents' involvement as co-therapists.

G. Despite the parents' involvement as co-therapists in the client's treatment, the client has continued to be reluctant to develop strong bonds, but the parents were encouraged to continue with this treatment.

19. **Conduct Parent–Child Interaction Therapy (19)**

A. Parent–child interaction therapy was used to build warmth and security in the parent/child relationship.

B. Child-directed sessions focused on teaching the child appropriate child behavior.

C. Parent-directed sessions focused on teaching parental behavior management skills (e.g., clear commands, consistent consequences, and positive reinforcement).

20. **Provide Parents with Education Regarding Attachment (20)**

A. Education on the nature of attachment and the effect of trauma on it were provided to the parents.

B. The parents were assigned the "Attachment Survey" from the *Child Psychotherapy Homework Planner* by Jongsma, Peterson, McInnis, & Bruce.

C. The parents were asked to construct a list of questions they had regarding attachment and the effect of trauma.

D. The list of questions constructed by parents about the effects of trauma on attachment were answered and processed.

E. The parents now seem to have a better understanding of attachment.

21. **Process Parents' Expectations for Client (21)**

A. The parents were asked to list the expectations that they currently hold for the client and to indicate which expectation is most important to them.

B. The parents' list of expectations for the client was processed, and each unrealistic expectation was addressed and either modified or discarded.

C. The parents' insistence on holding on to unrealistic expectations for the client was addressed and the negative consequences of doing so were explained.

D. The parents were assisted in forming more realistic expectations and developing ways to help the client meet these expectations.

E. The parents' modified expectations were identified as resulting in a more relaxed relationship with the client.

22. Educate Parents on Attachment (22)

A. The parents were educated to understand the meaning and purpose of the client's attachment.

B. Issues and questions the parents had concerning attachment were discussed, answered, and resolved.

C. The parents were understanding that attachment in a relationship takes a long time.

23. Empathize with Parents' Frustration (23)

A. The parents were assisted in identifying the frustration they experience in living with a detached child.

B. The parents were encouraged to express the pain and disappointment they feel as a result of living with a detached child.

C. The parents' barriers to recognizing and expressing their frustrations, pain, and disappointment were identified, processed, and resolved.

D. After expressing their frustration with living with a detached child, the parents' commitment to keep trying to build a relationship with their child was affirmed and reinforced.

E. The parents' identification and expression of their feelings of frustration have helped them continue to work effectively with the client.

24. Suggest Books for Parents to Read (24)

A. Readings were suggested to the parents to help them better understand the client and give them ideas and encouragement in dealing daily with the client.

B. The parents were directed to read *The Difficult Child* (Turecki & Tonner), *The Challenging Child* (Greenspan), or *When Love Is Not Enough: A Guide to Parenting Children with RAD* (Thomas).

C. The parents were encouraged to implement one or more new approaches to their child that were gained from their reading.

D. The parents' questions that were stimulated by their reading were answered and processed.

E. It was noted that the parents seem to have gained increased understanding, fresh ideas, and encouragement from the parenting material they read.

F. The parents have not read the assigned books on attachment problems and were redirected to do so.

25. Utilize Theraplay Approach (25)

A. The parents were educated in the Theraplay approach to building a relationship with the client.

B. A verbal commitment was elicited from the parents to be active co-therapists using the Theraplay approach.

C. The Theraplay attachment-based approach was used as the focus of therapy to entice the client into a relationship and to steer away from intrapsychic conflicts.

D. The parents were given specific therapeutic assignments to do at home with the client between therapy sessions.

E. The parents' follow-through as co-therapists on assignments was monitored, and any needed redirection was given.

F. The Theraplay approach appears to be effective because the client has started to form a relationship with the therapist and parents.

G. The Theraplay approach does not appear to be effective because the client has continued to act out and does not seem to be forming a better relationship with parents and therapist.

26. **Conduct Filial Therapy (26)**

A. The parents were educated in the filial therapy approach and the possible benefits for the client of their involvement.

B. The client was encouraged in filial therapy sessions to express angry feelings, while parents were coached to respond empathically to the underlying feelings of hurt, fear, and helplessness.

C. The client openly expressed angry feelings, and parents responded appropriately with empathic statements reflecting underlying hurt, fear, and helplessness.

D. The active participation of the client and parents in filial therapy sessions has resulted in a major reduction in the client's angry feelings.

27. **Assign Parents One-on-One Play with Client (27)**

A. The value of spending time in one-on-one daily play was explored and processed with parents.

B. The parents were asked to commit to spending consistent one-on-one time playing with the client.

C. A daily schedule of one-on-one time, with each parent playing with the client, was developed and implemented.

D. The parents were monitored, encouraged, and redirected in their follow-through on one-on-one daily playtime with the client.

E. The parents reported seeing visible gains in client's bonding as they have been spending daily one-on-one time with the client.

F. The parents have not spent one-on-one time with the client and were redirected to do so.

28. **Encourage Verbal Reinforcement/Physical Affection (28)**

A. The positive value of providing large doses of genuine verbal reinforcement and physical affection was identified with the parents.

B. The parents were assisted in exploring ways they could give the client large doses of reinforcement or affection, and specific ways were selected for them to start implementing.

C. The parents were encouraged, supported, and monitored in their efforts to provide the client with large daily doses of genuine verbal reinforcement and physical affection.

D. The parents were reinforced for consistently providing the client with large doses of reinforcement and affection, to which the client has responded by showing signs of increased attachment.

E. The parents have not consistently provided the client with large doses of positive reinforcement and affection and were redirected to do so.

29. Assign Physical Touching (29)

A. The parents were assisted in identifying the potential benefits that physical touching could have on the client.

B. Barriers to providing increased physical touching to the client were explored, identified, and resolved.

C. The parents were assigned the exercise of 10 minutes of physical touching of the client twice daily for 2 weeks.

D. The experience of the exercise was processed with the parents, and positive outcomes were identified and reinforced.

E. The parents were encouraged to continue the increased physical touching of the client after completion of the assigned exercise.

F. The parents have not used the physical touching techniques, and the barriers to the use of this technique were processed and addressed.

30. Stress Importance of Regular Communication (30)

A. The importance of regular communication was stressed to the parents.

B. The parents were taught communication techniques in order to prevent the client from manipulating parents.

C. The parents were taught to corroborate stories told by the client in order to prevent the client from "pitting" parents against each other.

D. The parents displayed positive communication skills with each other.

E. The parents struggled to keep from being manipulated by their child and were provided with additional feedback.

31. Design Effective Behavioral Strategies (31)

A. Parents and teachers were consulted in order to design effective behavioral strategies such as the use of a reward system or use of natural consequences.

B. Parents and teachers were assisted in using strategies to effectively manage the client's concerning behaviors.

C. Parents and teachers have communicated regularly to prevent the client from "pitting" significant adults against each other, and positive outcomes were identified.

D. Parents and teachers were unable to come together to effectively manage the client's concerning behaviors and were provided with remedial feedback.

32. Utilize Reward System (32)

A. The client and parents identified a list of rewards to reinforce the client for prosocial or responsible behaviors at school.

B. A reward system was designed to reinforce the client for prosocial or responsible behaviors at school.

C. The client, parents, and therapist verbally agreed to the terms of the reward system.

D. The reward system has helped the client manage prosocial behaviors at school.

E. The client and parents have not used the reward system to reinforce the client for prosocial or responsible behaviors and were redirected to use this helpful technique.

33. **Design Preventive Safety Measures (33)**

A. The need for and value of preventive safety measures to be used if the client's behavior becomes dangerous were explained, emphasized, and reinforced with parents.

B. The parents were assisted in designing preventive safety measures to use if the client's behavior ever becomes dangerous to self or others.

C. The parents were trained to identify situations in which they should implement their preventive safety measures.

D. The parents' use of the preventive safety measures was monitored and reviewed at regular intervals in the client's treatment.

E. The parents were noted to have used preventive safety measures appropriately with client and have avoided the escalation of dangerous behaviors.

F. The parents have not regularly used preventative safety measures to avoid the escalation of the client's dangerous behavior and were provided with remedial information in this area.

34. **Teach Parents to Give Feedback of Expectations (34)**

A. The parents were trained in ways to give feedback, structure, and repeated emphasis of expectations to the client to reassure them that they are in control.

B. The parents were directed to consistently use feedback, structure, and repeated emphasis of expectations with the client to assert their control and to keep feelings in check.

C. Encouragement was given to the parents for following through with measures that reinforce their control with the client.

D. It was noted that the parents have consistently used measures that reassure the client that they are in control and that intense feelings will remain in check.

E. The parents have not regularly used measures to reassure the client that they are in control and that intense feelings will remain in check and were redirected in this area.

35. **Train Client in Meditation and Focused Breathing (35)**

A. The client was trained in meditation and focused breathing techniques to self-calm when tension, anger, and frustration are building.

B. The client was recommended techniques from *The Relaxation and Stress Reduction Workbook for Kids* (Shapiro & Sprague).

C. Role-play and behavioral rehearsal were used to give the client the opportunity to practice meditation and focused breathing techniques.

D. The client was helped to identify situations in which they could use the stress-reduction techniques and then was asked to implement them in these situations as they arise in daily life.

E. The client's use of meditation and focused breathing was monitored, with both redirection and encouragement being given.

F. The client's consistent implementation of meditation and focused breathing has reduced the level of tension, anger, and frustration.

G. The client has not regularly used meditation and focused breathing techniques to self-calm and was reminded to use these techniques.

36. **Utilize EMDR (36)**

   A. Eye movement desensitization and reprocessing (EMDR) techniques were used to help reduce the client's distress associated with traumatic memories, reduce physiological arousal, and reformat the client's aggressive or violent thoughts.

   B. The EMDR techniques described in *Eye Movement Desensitization and Reprocessing (EMDR) Therapy* (Shapiro) were used to help reduce the client's distress.

37. **Counsel Parents on Discipline (37)**

   A. The client's parents were counseled on what are and what are not effective disciplinary measures to decrease frequency of stealing, hoarding, or gorging of food.

   B. Past inappropriate disciplinary that allowed for abusive punishment were addressed and new appropriate boundaries established.

   C. New discipline measures were monitored for effectiveness.

   D. The parents reported that they have successfully implemented disciplinary measures that are useful for their child.

38. **Identify Healthy Sense of Control (38)**

   A. The client was assisted in identifying age-appropriate and healthy ways to achieve a sense of control.

   B. The client was assisted in identify healthy ways to get needs met other than through stealing, hoarding, or gorging of food.

   C. The client was able to identify a list of appropriate and healthy ways to achieve a sense of control.

   D. The client used the list of appropriate ways to achieve a sense of control to reduce stealing, hoarding, or gorging of food and was provided with encouragement.

   E. The client was unable to reduce stealing, hoarding, or gorging of food through the use of alternatives and was provided with remedial feedback.

39. **Assign Self-Esteem Exercise (39)**

   A. The client was assigned self-esteem exercises in order to help develop self-knowledge, acceptance, and confidence.

   B. The client was assigned self-esteem exercises from the *SEALS + PLUS* workbook (Korb-Khalsa et al.) to develop self-knowledge, acceptance, and confidence.

   C. The client's completed self-esteem workbook exercises were processed with all key points regarding self-knowledge, acceptance, and confidence being verbally affirmed.

   D. The *SEALS + PLUS* workbook exercise seemed to have noticeably increased the client's degree of self-knowledge, acceptance, and confidence.

   E. The client's resistance to completing, sharing, and taking the self-esteem workbook exercise seriously was gently confronted, processed, and resolved.

40. **Encourage Sharing of Fears for Self-Acceptance (40)**

   A. The client was encouraged to share fears in order to gain self-acceptance.

   B. The client was asked to complete and process the exercise "Dixie Overcomes Her Fears" or "Building Relationships" from the *Child Psychotherapy Homework Planner* (Jongsma, Peterson, McInnis, & Bruce) to help the client share fears and gain self-acceptance.

C. The completed exercise was processed with the client, and the client was able to specifically identify and share fears and gain self-acceptance.

D. Plans were made with the client to implement several of the ideas that were identified in the exercise as a way to continue to increase self-acceptance.

E. The client has effectively used the exercise to continue to share fears and boost self-acceptance; the benefits of this project were reviewed.

41. **Refer to Initiative- or Adventure-Based Summer Camp (41)**

A. The benefits of attending an initiative- or adventure-based summer camp were identified, explained, and processed with the client and parents.

B. The parents were given information on several camps and encouraged to choose one for the client to attend.

C. The parents were reinforced as they made the proper arrangements for the client to attend an initiative-based summer camp.

D. The client's camp experience was processed with the client and parents, and positive gains in self-confidence were identified and reinforced.

E. The client has not attended an initiative- or adventure-based summer camp, and parents were reminded about the use of this resource.

42. **Conduct Trust Walk (42)**

A. A family session was conducted in which the client, family, and therapist took part in a trust walk.

B. The trust-walk experience was processed with the client and family, with barriers to trusting being identified and resolved.

C. The trust-walk experience was repeated with the family and processed, with gains in trust by each member being recognized and affirmed.

D. The trust-walk experience reflected gains that family members have made in increasing their level of trust with each other.

E. The client had extreme difficulty participating in the trust-walk experience but was provided with encouragement to try to complete this type of experience.

43. **Assign Parents to Give Client Choices (43)**

A. The advantages of offering choices to the client were explored, identified, and reinforced with parents.

B. The parents were asked to give the client as many choices as is reasonable in order to impart a sense of control and empowerment.

C. The parents' use of choices was monitored with redirection being given as needed.

D. The parents have effectively given the client choices whenever it was reasonable, and the client has seemed to gain a sense of empowerment and control.

E. The parents' resistance to offering choices to the client was identified, processed, and resolved.

44. **Encourage Development and Use of Respite Care Providers (44)**

A. The role of respite care was discussed and processed with the parents.

B. The parents were assisted in developing a list of potential respite care providers.

C. The parents were assigned to arrange to visit and interview several respite care providers and to choose two they would like to use.

D. Barriers to parents' follow-through on the use of respite care were explored, identified, and resolved.

E. The parents' use of respite care was encouraged and monitored for their consistent follow-through.

F. The parents have started to use respite care on a consistent basis, and it has been beneficial for their energy and perspective in dealing with the client.

45. Encourage Parents' Venting of Frustrations (45)

A. Conjoint sessions were conducted in which the parents were given permission and encouraged to vent their concerns and frustrations in dealing daily with the client.

B. The parents were helped to identify difficult situations with the client in which they feel frustrated.

C. The difficult behavior-management situations identified by the parents were processed, and specific suggestions were given to them to try.

D. The parents have openly and freely expressed their frustrations and concerns in working with the client daily and have tried the suggestions given for situations in which they felt ineffective.

E. The parents were reluctant to express their negative emotions regarding the frustration of dealing daily with the client and were encouraged to do this as they felt capable.

46. Refer Parents to Skills-Based Marital Program (46)

A. The possible benefits of the parents attending a program to strengthen their marriage were identified and explored.

B. The parents were referred to a skills-based marital program that teaches personal responsibility, communication skills, and conflict resolution (e.g., "PREP" in *Fighting for Your Marriage* by Markman et al.).

C. The parents' follow-through on completing the recommended marriage enrichment program was monitored, and positive gains were reinforced.

D. The parents completed the recommended marital program and indicated that they gained many new skills that have improved their marital relationship.

E. The parents' dropping out of the recommended marriage enrichment program was addressed and processed.

47. Assist and Support Grieving Process (47)

A. The client was assisted in recognizing the stages of grieving and where they were in that process.

B. Consistent encouragement, support, and assistance were provided to the client as they worked through the stages of grief.

C. Barriers that arose in the client's grieving process were identified, addressed, and resolved.

D. Regular reassurance was given to the client that they would make it through the process of grieving the losses.

E. The client has been successfully assisted in working through each stage of the grieving process.

SCHOOL REFUSAL

CLIENT PRESENTATION

1. **Reluctance or Refusal to Attend School (1)***
   A. The client has demonstrated a persistent reluctance or refusal to attend school.
   B. The client has missed a significant amount of school because of separation anxiety and fearfulness about leaving home.
   C. The client appeared visibly anxious in today's therapy session when discussing their return to school.
   D. The client has recently started to attend school on a part-time basis.
   E. The client has attended school on a regular, full-time basis.

2. **Emotional Distress Before Attending School (2)**
   A. The client and parents report that the client often exhibits a great deal of emotional distress before leaving home to attend school.
   B. The client became visibly anxious and had difficulty separating from parents in today's therapy session.
   C. The intensity of the client's emotional distress before attending school in the morning has gradually started to diminish.
   D. The client reports that they have recently been able to get ready for school in the morning without exhibiting any significant amount of emotional distress.
   E. The client has consistently attended school without exhibiting distress before leaving home.

3. **Emotional Distress After Arriving at School (2)**
   A. The parents and teachers report that the client exhibits a significant amount of emotional distress after arriving at school.
   B. The client has often requested that they either be allowed to call their parents or go home after arriving at school.
   C. The intensity of the client's emotional distress after arriving at school has gradually started to diminish.
   D. The client reports that they have recently been able to remain relaxed and calm after arriving at school.
   E. The client has been able to remain relaxed and calm on a consistent basis after arriving at school.

4. **Crying and Pleading (2)**
   A. The client has demonstrated a persistent pattern of crying and pleading to stay home before leaving for school in the morning.

---

* The numbers in parentheses correlate to the number of the Behavioral Definition statement in the companion chapter with the same title in the *Child Psychotherapy Treatment Planner*, Sixth Edition, by Jongsma, Peterson, McInnis, & Bruce (Wiley, 2023).

B. The client has often cried and pleaded to go home after arriving at school.

C. The intensity and duration of the client's crying and pleading before leaving home or after arriving at school have gradually started to diminish.

D. The client reports that they have recently not exhibited any crying or pleading before leaving home or after arriving at school.

E. The client has attended school consistently without exhibiting any crying or excessive pleading.

5. **Temper Tantrums (2)**

A. The client has frequently exhibited intense temper tantrums before leaving home in the morning for school.

B. The client exhibited intense temper tantrums after arriving at school with the hope that they will be able to return home.

C. The frequency and intensity of the client's temper tantrums before leaving home or after arriving at school have gradually started to diminish.

D. The client has not exhibited any temper tantrums before leaving home or after arriving at school.

E. The client has attended school consistently without exhibiting any temper tantrums.

6. **Somatic Complaints (3)**

A. The parents report that the client frequently makes somatic complaints (e.g., headaches, stomachaches, nausea) before leaving home to attend school.

B. School officials report that the client often makes somatic complaints after arriving at school.

C. The client complained of not feeling well in today's therapy session when discussing school attendance.

D. The frequency and intensity of the client's somatic complaints have recently started to diminish.

E. The client has demonstrated a significant reduction in the frequency and intensity of somatic complaints.

7. **Excessive Clinging/Shadowing (4)**

A. The parents reported that the client often becomes very clingy when anticipating leaving home for school in the morning.

B. The client became very clingy in today's therapy session when asked to separate from parents.

C. The intensity and duration of the client's clingy behavior before leaving home or after arriving at school have gradually started to diminish.

D. The client has recently been able to separate from parents to attend school without exhibiting any excessive clinging or shadowing.

E. The client has consistently attended school without displaying any excessive clinging or shadowing of parents.

8. **Regressive Behaviors (4)**

A. The client has often regressed and behaved in an infantile manner before separating from their parents to attend school.

B. The client spoke in a very regressive and immature manner in today's therapy session when discussing school attendance.

C. The frequency of the client's immature and regressive behaviors has recently started to diminish.

D. The parents reported that the client has recently behaved in an age-appropriate manner before leaving home or after arriving at school.

E. The enmeshed family relationships have contributed to the emergence of the client's immature and regressive behaviors.

9. **Family Enmeshment (4)**

A. The client's enmeshed and overly dependent relationship with their parents has been a significant contributing factor to their reluctance or refusal to attend school.

B. The parents verbally recognized how they have reinforced the client's excessive dependency and in turn their reluctance to attend school.

C. The parents have encouraged the client to take steps to become more independent.

D. The parents have recently started to set limits on the client's overly dependent behaviors, excessive clinging, and temper tantrums.

E. The parents' improved ability to set limits on the client's overly dependent behaviors, excessive clinging, and temper tantrums has helped the client attend school on a full-time basis.

10. **Negative Comments About School (5)**

A. The parents and teachers reported that the client often verbalizes many negative comments about school.

B. The client verbalized several negative remarks about school during today's therapy session.

C. The frequency of the client's negative remarks about school experiences or performance has recently started to decrease.

D. The client verbalized several positive remarks about school during today's therapy session.

E. The client has consistently been able to verbalize positive remarks about school experiences or performance.

11. **Unrealistic Fears or Worries (6)**

A. The client has developed a persistent and unrealistic fear that some future calamity will separate them from their parents if they attend school.

B. The client shared their worry in today's therapy session about some future calamity separating them from their parents.

C. The client verbally recognized how fear of some future calamity occurring is unrealistic and irrational.

D. The client has recently not verbalized any unrealistic fears or worries about a future calamity separating them from parents.

E. The client has ceased experiencing any unrealistic fears or worries about some calamitous event separating them from parents.

12. **Separation/Loss (6)**
    A. The client has refused or been reluctant to attend school since experiencing a major separation or loss.
    B. The client appeared visibly anxious and upset in today's therapy session when talking about the separation or loss.
    C. The client was guarded and reluctant to discuss the past separation or loss.
    D. The client was open and talkative about the past separation or loss in today's therapy session.
    E. The client has been able to attend school on a regular, full-time basis since successfully working through many of their thoughts and feelings about the past separation or loss.

13. **Traumatic Event (6)**
    A. The client has had difficulty attending school since experiencing a traumatic event.
    B. The client appeared visibly anxious and upset in today's therapy session when talking about the traumatic event.
    C. The client was guarded and reluctant to discuss the past traumatic event.
    D. The client was open and talkative about the past traumatic event in today's therapy session.
    E. The client has been able to attend school on a regular, full-time basis since successfully working through many of their thoughts and feelings about the past traumatic event.

14. **Low Self-Esteem (7)**
    A. The client's low self-esteem and lack of confidence have been significant contributing factors to fear of attending school.
    B. The client expressed feelings of insecurity and strong self-doubts about their ability to succeed in school.
    C. The client verbalized positive self-statements in today's therapy session about their ability to succeed in school.
    D. The client's increase in school attendance has coincided with their increase in confidence and self-esteem.
    E. The client has confidently attended school on a regular basis and usually talked about school experiences in positive terms.

15. **Fear of Failure or Ridicule (8)**
    A. The client's strong fear of failure and anxiety about academic performance have been significant contributing factors to reluctance or refusal to attend school.
    B. The client has had problems attending school since experiencing failure, ridicule, or rejection.
    C. The client's fear of failure or ridicule has recently started to decrease, and they have been able to take healthy risks.
    D. The client has consistently been able to apply self at school without experiencing any strong fear of failure or ridicule.

16. **Shrinking from or Avoidance of Unfamiliar People (9)**
    A. The client has developed a persistent pattern of shrinking away from or avoiding contact with unfamiliar people in the school setting.

B. The client's social anxiety and fear of being ridiculed or scrutinized by others have been significant contributing factors to their school refusal.

C. In today's therapy session, the client verbalized feelings of anxiety about interacting with unfamiliar people at school.

D. The client has started to feel more confident in interacting with unfamiliar people at school.

E. The client has successfully overcome anxiety about interacting with unfamiliar people, and they socialize with others on a regular basis.

INTERVENTIONS IMPLEMENTED

1. **Establish Rapport (1)***
   A. Caring was conveyed to the client through support, warmth, and empathy.
   B. The client was provided with nonjudgmental support and a level of trust was developed.
   C. The client was urged to feel safe in expressing school refusal issues.
   D. The client began to express feelings more freely as rapport and trust level have increased.
   E. The client has continued to experience difficulty being open and direct about the expression of painful feelings; the client was encouraged to use the safe haven of therapy to express these difficult issues.

2. **Focus on Strengthening Therapeutic Relationship (2)**
   A. The relationship with the client was strengthened using empirically supported factors.
   B. The relationship with the client was strengthened through the implementation of collaborative approach, agreement on goals, demonstration of empathy, verbalization of positive regard, and collection of client feedback.
   C. The client reacted positively to the relationship-strengthening measures taken.
   D. The client verbalized feeling supported and understood during therapy sessions.
   E. Despite attempts to strengthen the therapeutic relationship, the client reports feeling distant and misunderstood.
   F. The client has indicated that sessions are not helpful and will be terminating therapy.

3. **Build Trust (3)**
   A. The objective of today's therapy session was to establish trust with the client so that they can begin to identify and express feelings associated with school attendance.
   B. Attempts were made to build a level of trust with the client through consistent eye contact, active listening, unconditional positive regard, and warm acceptance.
   C. The client's expression of thoughts and feelings during the therapy session was supported empathetically.

---

*The numbers in parentheses correlate to the number of the Therapeutic Intervention statement in the companion chapter with the same title in the *Child Psychotherapy Treatment Planner*, Sixth Edition, by Jongsma, Peterson, McInnis, & Bruce (Wiley, 2023).

D. The therapy session was helpful in building a level of trust with the client.

E. The therapy session was not successful in establishing trust with the client as they remained guarded when discussing thoughts and feelings about attending school.

4. Explore School Refusal Dynamics (4)

A. The client's feelings and behaviors regarding school attendance were explored.

B. Specific reasons for the client's refusal to attend school were examined.

C. The parents were interviewed regarding their perceptions of the child's pattern of school attendance and refusal, as well as the causes behind the refusal.

5. Conduct/Refer for Psychological Testing (5)

A. The client was referred for a psychological evaluation to assess the severity of their anxiety, depression, or gross psychopathology and to help gain greater insight into the underlying dynamics contributing to school refusal.

B. The client was very guarded and reserved during the psychological testing.

C. The client appeared visibly anxious about taking part in the psychological testing.

D. The client approached the psychological testing in an honest, straightforward manner and was cooperative with any test presented to them.

E. Feedback regarding the psychological testing was provided to the client and parents.

6. Conduct/Refer for Psychoeducational Evaluation (6)

A. The client received a psychoeducational evaluation to rule out the presence of a possible learning disability that may be contributing to their reluctance or refusal to attend school.

B. The client appeared anxious and seemed to lack confidence in their abilities during the psychoeducational evaluation.

C. The client was uncooperative during the psychoeducational evaluation and did not appear to put forth good effort.

D. Rapport was easily established with the client, and they appeared motivated to do their best during the psychoeducational testing.

E. Feedback from the psychoeducational testing was provided to the client, parents, and school officials.

7. Assess Level of Insight (7)

A. The client's level of insight toward the presenting problems was assessed.

B. The client was assessed in regard to the syntonic versus dystonic nature of their insight about the presenting problems.

C. The client was noted to demonstrate good insight into the problematic nature of the behavior and symptoms.

D. The client was noted to be in agreement with others' concerns and is motivated to work on change.

E. The client was noted to be ambivalent regarding the problems described and is reluctant to address the issues as a concern.

F. The client was noted to be resistant regarding acknowledgment of the problem areas, is not concerned about them, and has no motivation to make changes.

8. **Assess for Correlated Disorders (8)**
   A. The client was assessed for evidence of research-based correlated disorders.
   B. The client was assessed in regard to the level of vulnerability to suicide.
   C. The client was identified as having a comorbid disorder, and treatment was adjusted to account for these concerns.
   D. The client has been assessed for any correlated disorders, but none were found.

9. **Assess for Culturally Based Confounding Issues (9)**
   A. The client was assessed for age-related issues that could help to better understand their clinical presentation.
   B. The client was assessed for gender-related issues that could help to better understand their clinical presentation.
   C. The client was assessed for cultural syndromes, cultural idioms of distress, or culturally based perceived causes that could help to better understand their clinical presentation.
   D. Alternative factors have been identified as contributing to the client's currently defined "problem behavior," and these were taken into account in regard to treatment.
   E. Culturally based factors that could help to account for the client's currently defined "problem behavior" were investigated, but no significant factors were identified.

10. **Assess Severity of Impairment (10)**
   A. The severity of the client's impairment was assessed to determine the appropriate level of care.
   B. The client was assessed in regard to impairment in social, relational, and educational endeavors.
   C. It was reflected to the client that the impairment appears to create mild to moderate effects on the client's functioning.
   D. It was reflected to the client that the impairment appears to create severe to very severe effects on the client's functioning.
   E. The client was continuously assessed for the severity of impairment, as well as the efficacy and appropriateness of treatment.

11. **Assess for Pathogenic Care (11)**
   A. The home, school, and community of the client were assessed for pathogenic care and concerns.
   B. The client's various environments were assessed for the persistent disregard of the child's needs, repeated changes in caregivers, limited opportunities for stable attachment, harsh discipline, or other grossly inept care.
   C. Pathogenic care was identified and the treatment plan included strategies for managing or correcting these concerns and protecting the child.
   D. No pathogenic care was identified, and this was reflected to the client and caregivers.

12. **Refer for Medical Examination (12)**
   A. The client was referred for a thorough medical examination to determine whether their health problems are genuine or psychosomatic in nature.

B. A consultation was held with the client's physician about the results from the medical examination.

C. The medical examination revealed that the client is experiencing genuine health problems, and they have subsequently been placed on medication and/or received appropriate treatment.

D. The medical examination did not reveal the presence of any genuine health problems; rather, the client's physical complaints appear to be psychosomatic in nature.

E. The client was encouraged to take the medication as prescribed for their genuine health problems.

13. Refer/Monitor for Medication (13)

A. The client was referred for a medication evaluation to help decrease anxiety or emotional distress.

B. The client was strongly opposed to being placed on medication to help stabilize moods and/or decrease anxiety or fearfulness; their concerns were reviewed and processed.

C. Positive feedback was processed as the client reported that they have been taking their medication as prescribed.

D. The client has not adhered to a regular medication schedule, and this was relayed to the prescribing clinician.

E. The client reported that the medication has helped to decrease anxiety and emotional distress.

F. The client reported little to no improvement on the medication; the client was referred to the prescribing clinician.

G. The client reported experiencing side effects from the prescribed medication; the client was referred to the prescribing clinician.

14. Coordinate Parent/Teacher Training (14)

A. The parents were taught behavior management strategies to assist in consistent school attendance.

B. Parents were taught about reducing home-based reinforcement during school hours.

C. Parents were assisted in planning for the process for escorting the child to school.

D. Parents and teachers were assisted in identifying positive reinforcement of coping behavior and attendance.

15. Consult About School Return (15)

A. School personnel were consulted prior to returning the client to school to discuss preparations for the child's return.

B. The school personnel were assisted in identifying techniques to help the child settle into school on arrival.

C. The use of positive reinforcement and planned ignoring was emphasized to school personnel.

D. The school personnel were consulted in regard to accommodating the child academically, socially, and emotionally.

16. **Consult with Parents/School Officials (16)**

   A. A consultation was held with the parents and school officials to develop a plan to manage the client's emotional distress and negative outbursts after arriving at school.

   B. An action plan was developed in today's therapy session to help the parents effectively separate from the client after arriving at school.

   C. The parents were instructed to cease their lengthy good-byes with the client after arriving at school.

   D. The client was instructed to go to the principal's office to calm down if they begin to feel distressed after arriving at school.

   E. The parents were instructed to reinforce the client's ability to self-calm after arriving at school.

17. **Plan High-Success School Assignment (17)**

   A. A consultation was held with the client's teacher about planning an assignment that will provide them with an increased chance of success during the initial stages of treatment.

   B. The teacher was encouraged to give the client an assignment related to one of their interests.

   C. The teacher was encouraged to modify the length of the assignment to help decrease the client's anxiety.

   D. The teacher was encouraged to pair the client up with a friend or well-liked peer on a school assignment to help decrease their anxiety and provide them with the opportunity to achieve academic success.

18. **Utilize Teacher's Aide/Positive Peer Attention (18)**

   A. A consultation was held with school officials about assigning a teacher's aide to the client to help reduce fear and anxiety about attending school.

   B. A recommendation was made that the client work with a teacher's aide to help address learning problems.

   C. A consultation was held with school officials about pairing the client with a positive peer role model to help them manage fears and anxiety about attending school.

   D. A recommendation was offered that the client be paired with a positive peer role model on a school assignment to help provide the client with a sense of acceptance and belonging at school.

   E. The client reported that the support they have received from the teacher's aide or positive peer role model has helped to decrease fear and anxiety about attending school; the client was encouraged to continue using this resource.

19. **Explore/Confront Negative Cognitive Messages (19)**

   A. Today's therapy session explored the irrational, negative cognitive messages that contribute to the client's anxiety and fear about attending school.

   B. The client was helped to identify the irrational, negative cognitive messages that contribute to anxiety and fear about attending school.

C. The client was strongly encouraged to challenge the irrational thoughts that contribute to anxiety and fear about attending school.

D. Today's therapy session helped the client to realize that fears about attending school are irrational or unrealistic.

E. A cognitive-behavioral therapy approach was used to help the client realize how their fears about attending school are irrational or unrealistic.

F. The client was helped to realize how irrational or negative thinking is self-defeating and exacerbates feelings of anxiety or depression.

20. Develop Positive Cognitive Messages (20)

A. The client was encouraged to use positive self-talk to help them reduce or cope with the anxiety or fear.

B. The client was strongly encouraged to replace negative self-talk with positive cognitive messages that increase self-confidence and reinforce the ability to cope with anxiety or fear about attending school.

C. The parents were taught about how to be supportive about the client's cognitive changes.

D. The parents were encouraged to read portions of *When Children Refuse School: A Cognitive-Behavioral Therapy Approach—Parent Workbook* (Kearney & Albano).

E. The client reported that the use of positive cognitive messages has helped to increase confidence while decreasing anxiety and fearfulness; the client was encouraged to continue this progress.

F. The client has failed to follow through with using positive cognitive messages to help decrease anxiety and fearfulness and was reminded about how to use this technique.

21. Teach Relaxation/Guided Imagery (21)

A. The client was taught relaxation techniques and guided imagery to help reduce anxiety and fear about attending school.

B. The client was recommended to read portions of *The Relaxation and Stress Reduction Workbook for Kids* (Shapiro & Sprague).

C. The client was assigned the "Deep Breathing Exercise" from the *Child Psychotherapy Homework Planner* (Jongsma, Peterson, McInnis, & Bruce).

D. The client reported a positive response to the use of relaxation or guided imagery techniques to help decrease anxiety and fearfulness; the client was encouraged to continue these techniques.

E. The client has failed to consistently use the relaxation or guided imagery techniques and, as a result, has continued to experience anxiety and fearfulness about attending school; the conditions contributing to this failure were reviewed and problem-solved.

22. Teach Social Communication Skills (22)

A. The client was taught social communication skills.

B. The client was taught common social scripts and conversational, assertive, and conflict-resolution skills.

C. Predictable social encounters were practiced.

D. Homework exercises were assigned to help the client practice skills.

E. The client was assigned the exercise "Greeting Peers" from the *Child Psychotherapy Homework Planner* (Jongsma, Peterson, McInnis, & Bruce).

F. The client was assigned the exercise "Show Your Strengths" from the *Child Psychotherapy Homework Planner* (Jongsma, Peterson, McInnis, & Bruce).

23. **Play "Stand Up for Yourself" Game (23)**

A. In today's session, the "Stand Up for Yourself" game (Shapiro) was played to help establish rapport with the client.

B. Today's session used the "Stand Up for Yourself" game to help teach the client effective assertiveness skills that can be used to help them feel more confident at school.

C. After playing the "Stand Up for Yourself" game, the client was able to identify several assertiveness and communication skills that will help them feel more confident and relaxed around others at school.

D. The client was given the homework assignment of practicing the assertiveness skills that they learned from playing the "Stand Up for Yourself" game.

E. The client reported being able to successfully practice the newly acquired assertiveness skills; positive feedback was provided.

F. The client has not successfully practiced the newly acquired assertiveness skills and was redirected to do so.

24. **Assign Readings on Aggressive or Intimidating Peers (24)**

A. The client was assigned reading material to teach them effective ways to deal with aggressive or intimidating peers at school.

B. The client was assigned to read *Why Is Everybody Always Picking on Me? A Guide to Understanding Bullies for Young People* (Webster-Doyle) to help teach them effective ways to deal with aggressive or intimidating peers at school.

C. Today's session focused on processing the content of the assigned reading material on effective ways of dealing with aggressive or intimidating peers.

D. After reading the assigned material, the client was helped to identify effective ways to deal with aggressive or intimidating peers at school.

E. The client was encouraged to practice the coping strategies that they learned through reading the material assigned.

F. The client reported that the books have helped them learn to effectively deal with aggressive or intimidating peers at school, and the benefits of this progress were reviewed.

25. **Implement in vivo Systematic Desensitization (25)**

A. A consultation was held with the client, parents, and school officials about designing and implementing an in vivo systematic desensitization program to help the client manage anxiety and gradually attend school for longer periods of time.

B. The client was assigned the exercise "Gradual Exposure to Fear" from the *Adolescent Psychotherapy Homework Planner* (Jongsma, Peterson, McInnis, & Bruce).

C. The client and parents agreed to follow through with implementation of the in vivo systematic desensitization program that was present, which allows the client to attend school for gradually longer periods of time.

D. The in vivo systematic desensitization program has been implemented and has helped the client attend school for gradually longer periods of time.

E. The in vivo systematic desensitization program has proved to be successful in allowing the client to return to school on a regular, full-time basis.

F. It was noted that the client has not succeeded in attending school for the specified period of time because of anxiety and difficulty separating from parents.

26. Design/Implement Reward System/Contingency Contract (26)

A. The client and parents were assisted in identifying a list of rewards to be used to reinforce the client for attending school for increasingly longer periods of time.

B. A reward system was designed to reinforce the client for attending school for increasingly longer periods of time.

C. The client, parents, and therapist signed a contingency contract specifying the negative consequences for failure to attend school for the specified period of time.

D. The client, parents, and therapist verbally agreed to the terms of the contingency contract.

E. The reward system and/or contingency contract have helped the client attend school for increasingly longer periods of time.

F. The parents have not implemented the contingency contract and reward system and were redirected to do so.

27. Design/Implement Token Economy (27)

A. A token economy was designed to reinforce the client's school attendance.

B. The client, parents, and school officials agreed to the conditions outlined in the token economy program and agreed to follow through with their implementation.

C. Upon review, the token economy has proven to be successful in increasing the client's school attendance.

D. The token economy was reviewed and has not proven to be successful in increasing the client's school attendance.

E. The parents have not implemented the token economy and were redirected to do so.

28. Identify Times When Client Attended School (28)

A. Today's therapy session explored the days or periods of time when the client was able to attend school without exhibiting significant emotional distress.

B. The client was encouraged to use coping strategies similar to those that they had used in the past to attend school without displaying excessive fear or anxiety.

C. Active listening skills were used as the client shared their realization that talking with other peers or school officials helped to decrease anxiety and fearfulness after arriving at school.

D. Today's family therapy session revealed that the client has been able to attend school without exhibiting a significant amount of distress when the parents provide encouragement and set limits on temper outbursts, manipulative behavior, or excessive clinging.

29. Teach Parents Anticipation of Stressors (29)

A. The parents were told to anticipate possible stressors or events (e.g., illness, school holidays, vacations) that might cause the client's fear and anxiety about attending school to reappear.

B. The parents were informed that the client may regress and exhibit more distress shortly before and after the next school break or holiday.

C. The client and parents were encouraged to use coping strategies that were successful in the past to help the client attend school, in the event that they regress and experience fear or anxiety about attending school in the future.

D. The client and parents were helped to identify potential stressors that may appear in the future that could impact the client's school attendance.

E. The client and parents were assisted in identifying coping strategies and developing a contingency plan that can help them cope with stress in the future.

30. **Identify Accomplishments and Relationships (30)**

A. The client was encouraged to use positive self-talk as a means of managing anxiety or fear before leaving to attend school.

B. The client was encouraged to use positive self-talk as a means of managing anxiety or fear after arriving at school.

C. The client was directed to verbalize at least one positive statement about an accomplishment at school.

D. The client was given a homework assignment to record at least one positive school experience daily in a journal.

E. The client was encouraged to verbalize positive statements about others at school to help improve peer relationships.

F. The client has not implemented the use of positive statements about self, school, and others and was redirected to do so.

31. **Develop Contingency Plan for Somatic Complaints (31)**

A. A consultation was held with the parents and school officials to develop a contingency plan to manage the client's somatic complaints.

B. The parents and school officials were instructed to ignore the client's obvious psychosomatic complaints and redirect them to another task.

C. A contingency plan was developed where the client would go to the nurse's office at school and have their temperature taken to verify their illness before being allowed to call home.

D. The client was encouraged to use guided imagery and relaxation techniques to redirect their focus away from the somatic complaints.

E. The client has not used the guided imagery and relaxation techniques to direct their focus away from somatic complaints and was redirected to use this technique.

32. **Shift Focus from Physical Complaints to Emotional Conflicts (32)**

A. Today's therapy session refocused the client's discussion away from physical complaints to emotional conflicts and the expression of feelings.

B. Today's therapy session helped the client realize how their somatic complaints are related to underlying emotional conflicts and painful emotions.

C. The client was helped to identify more effective ways to cope with stress and conflict to help reduce the chances of them developing somatic ailments.

D. The client was taught effective communication and assertiveness skills to help them communicate feelings more directly.

33. Assess Family Dynamics (33)

A. A family therapy session was held to explore the dynamics within the family system that contribute to the emergence of the client's school refusal.

B. The family members were asked to list the stressors that have had a negative impact on the family.

C. The family members were asked to identify the things they would like to change within the family system.

34. Assign Drawing of House (34)

A. In today's therapy session, the client was first asked to draw a picture of a house, then instructed to make up a story identifying what it is like to live in that house.

B. The art therapy technique (i.e., asking client to draw picture of a house) helped reveal insight into the family dynamics that contribute to the emergence of the client's school refusal.

C. The art therapy technique revealed how the client has developed an overly enmeshed relationship with one of their parents.

D. The art therapy technique helped to reveal how the client has developed a distant relationship with the disengaged parent.

E. The art therapy technique led to a discussion about how to increase the involvement of the disengaged parent.

35. Assign School Transport to Disengaged Parent (35)

A. The disengaged parent was asked to transport the client to school each morning.

B. The overly enmeshed parent was instructed not to be present when transporting the client to school.

C. The disengaged parent was instructed to play games or converse with the client while driving to school to help reduce anxiety and fearfulness.

D. The family was assigned "A Pleasant Journey" from the *Child Psychotherapy Homework Planner* (Jongsma, Peterson, McInnis, & Bruce).

E. The therapist contacted the parent's employer to gain permission for the parent to adjust their work schedule to allow them to transport the client to school each morning.

F. The disengaged parent has not begun transporting the client to school each morning, and the reasons for this failure were reviewed and problem-solved.

36. Encourage Parents to Reinforce Autonomy (36)

A. The parents were strongly encouraged to praise and positively reinforce the client's autonomous behavior.

B. The parents were strongly encouraged to set limits on the client's overly dependent or regressive behavior.

C. The parents were encouraged to praise the client for attending school for the specified period of time.

D. The parents were encouraged to praise and reinforce the client for working alone on school assignments.

E. The parent was instructed to cease entering the classroom with the client in the morning.

F. The parents have continued to reward dependency and have not reinforced autonomy; the reasons for this pattern were reviewed and problem-solved.

37. **Encourage Parents to Remain Calm (37)**

A. Today's therapy session stressed the importance of the parents remaining calm and not communicating their anxiety to the client.

B. The parents were helped to realize how the client's anxiety increases when the client perceives them as being anxious or apprehensive.

C. The parents were instructed to remain firm and clearly communicate the expectation that the client is expected to go to school when they become distressed and beg or plead to stay home.

D. Role-playing and modeling techniques were used to teach the parents effective ways to manage the client's anxiety, fearfulness, or emotional distress.

E. The parents were instructed to verbalize confidence in the client's ability to manage their stress or anxiety at school.

F. The parents have continued to display anxiety, which has contributed to the client's school refusal; they were redirected to decrease the communication of their anxiety.

38. **Reinforce Positive Steps by Parents (38)**

A. The parents were praised and reinforced for taking positive steps to help the client overcome fear or anxiety about attending school.

B. The parents were helped to identify how the combination of encouragement and consistent limit setting has helped the client attend school regularly.

C. The parents identified the positive steps that they have taken to help the client attend school without exhibiting significant distress; they were reinforced for this progress.

D. The parents were strongly encouraged to take the same steps to help the client continue to attend school on a regular basis.

39. **Reinforce Parents' Limit Setting (39)**

A. The parents were encouraged to set firm, consistent limits on the client's temper outbursts and manipulative behavior.

B. The parents were encouraged to set firm, consistent limits on the client's excessive clinging or pleading.

C. The parents acknowledged that they have been reluctant to set firm, consistent limits because of their desire to avoid dealing with the client's temper outbursts or heightened emotional distress; they were encouraged to set these limits.

D. The parents were informed that the intensity of the client's temper outbursts, pleading, or clinging will likely increase at first when they begin to set limits.

E. The parents were instructed to remain calm and firmly in control when they first begin to set limits on the client's temper outbursts, manipulative behavior, or excessive clinging.

40. **Assign Parents to Write a Letter of Encouragement (40)**

A. The parents were instructed to write a letter (based on the "Letter of Encouragement" exercise from the *Child Psychotherapy Homework Planner* by Jongsma, Peterson, McInnis, & Bruce) to the client that sends a clear message about the importance of attending school and reminding them of coping strategies that they can use to calm fears or anxieties.

B. The parents were instructed to place the "Letter of Encouragement" in the client's notebook so that they can read the letter at appropriate times during the school day when the client begins to feel afraid or anxious.

C. The client reported that the parents' "Letter of Encouragement" helped them to calm down when beginning to feel anxious or afraid at school; the benefits of this technique were highlighted.

D. The "Letter of Encouragement" exercise helped the parents send a strong and clear message about the importance of attending school.

E. The parents failed to follow through with writing the "Letter of Encouragement" and were again asked to do it.

41. Identify Role of Enmeshed Parents (41)

A. Today's therapy session helped identify how the enmeshed or overly protective parents reinforce the client's dependency and irrational fear.

B. Today's therapy session explored the reasons why the enmeshed or overly protective parents have failed to set limits with the client's overly dependent and/or regressive behaviors.

C. The enmeshed or overly protective parents were helped to realize how they reinforce the client's excessive clinging or pleading when they begin to feel afraid.

D. The enmeshed or overly protective parents were taught more effective ways to deal with the client's overly dependent behaviors or irrational fears.

E. The parents were encouraged to redirect the client by engaging in activities or conversations that take their mind or attention off irrational fear.

42. Employ Paradoxical Intervention (42)

A. A paradoxical intervention was implemented to work around the family's resistance and to disengage the client from an overly protective parent.

B. The paradoxical intervention proved to be successful in working around the family's resistance and disengaging the client from the overly protective parent.

C. The paradoxical intervention helped increase the client's motivation to function more autonomously.

D. Today's session processed the family's resistance in following through with the paradoxical intervention.

43. Explore Trauma History (43)

A. Today's therapy session explored whether the client's anxiety and fear about attending school are associated with a previously unresolved separation, loss, trauma, or realistic danger.

B. The assessment revealed that the client began to have trouble attending school after experiencing a significant separation or loss.

C. The assessment revealed that the client began having trouble attending school after experiencing a traumatic event.

D. The assessment revealed that the client began having trouble attending school after being exposed to a realistic danger.

44. Reinforce Expressing Feelings About Trauma (44)

A. The client was given encouragement and support in expressing feelings associated with a past separation, loss, trauma, or realistic danger.

B. The client was helped to identify and clarify feelings associated with a past separation, loss, trauma, or realistic danger.

C. Client-centered therapy principles were used to encourage and support the client in expressing feelings surrounding a past separation, loss, trauma, or realistic danger.

D. The empty-chair technique was used to help the client express and work through feelings associated with a past separation, loss, trauma, or realistic danger.

E. The client was encouraged to use a journal to express thoughts and feelings associated with a past separation, loss, trauma, or realistic danger.

F. The client continues to have difficulty expressing feelings about their history of trauma and was encouraged to express these feelings as the client feels able to do so.

45. Assign Letter Writing About Trauma (45)

A. The client was assigned to write a letter to express thoughts and feelings about a previous separation or loss.

B. The client was given the homework assignment of writing a letter to express thoughts and feelings about a past traumatic or dangerous event.

C. Today's therapy session processed the content of the client's letter.

D. The client's letter was noted to reflect strong feelings of anger about a past separation, loss, trauma, or realistic danger.

E. The client's letter were noted to reflect feelings of sadness, hurt, and vulnerability about a past separation, loss, trauma, or realistic danger.

F. The client has not completed the homework assignment of writing a letter to express thoughts and feelings and was redirected to complete this assignment.

46. Encourage Participation in Peer Group Activities (46)

A. The client was strongly encouraged to participate in extracurricular or positive peer group activities at school to help them feel more comfortable and relaxed around others.

B. The client was assisted in developing a list of positive peer group activities that will help provide them with the opportunity to establish meaningful friendships at school.

C. The client was supported as they verbalized an understanding of how feelings of insecurity and inadequacy contribute to reluctance to become involved in extracurricular or peer group activities at school.

D. The client reported that recent participation in extracurricular or peer group activities helped them feel more comfortable and relaxed at school; the client was encouraged to continue this participation.

E. The client has continued to have problems separating from parents and has not participated in any extracurricular or positive peer group activities; the client was encouraged to do this on a smaller scale.

47. Assign Time Spent with Peers (47)

A. The client was given a directive to spend a specified period of time with peers after school or on weekends.

B. The client was helped to identify a list of activities that they would like to engage in with peers after school or on the weekends.

C. The client's increased involvement with peers after school or on weekends has helped manage separations from their parents in a more adaptive manner.

D. The client has remained resistant to socializing with peers after school or on weekends because of separation anxiety and fear of rejection or ridicule; the client was urged to try spending a smaller amount of time.

48. Assign Social Contact (48)

A. The client was given the directive of initiating three social contacts per week with unfamiliar people or when placed in new social settings.

B. Role-playing and modeling techniques were used to teach the client appropriate ways to initiate conversations.

C. The client's thoughts and feelings about initiating social contacts with unfamiliar people or when placed in new social settings were processed.

D. The client followed through with the directive to initiate at least three social contacts per week, and their experience in this area was reviewed.

E. The client failed to follow through with the directive to initiate at least three social contacts per week because of social anxiety and was redirected to do so.

49. Employ Psychoanalytic Play Therapy (49)

A. Using a psychoanalytic play therapy approach, the client was allowed to take the lead in exploring the unconscious conflicts or core anxiety that contribute to school refusal.

B. Using a psychoanalytic play therapy approach, the client's core conflicts and anxiety about attending school were identified and processed.

C. Today's session processed and worked through the transference issues that emerged.

D. The client's feelings and fear expressed in play were interpreted and related to fear about attending school.

E. The psychoanalytic play therapy sessions have helped the client work through and resolve the issues contributing to school refusal.

50. Use Mutual Storytelling Technique (50)

A. The client actively participated in the mutual storytelling exercise.

B. Using the mutual storytelling technique, the therapist modeled effective ways for the client to overcome anxiety or fear about attending school.

C. The client created a story using puppets, dolls, or stuffed animals that was noted to reflect fear about attending school.

D. The client was helped to create a story using puppets, dolls, or stuffed animals that showed effective ways to cope with fear or anxiety.

E. The client identified the mutual storytelling technique as being a fun and useful way to learn strategies on how to overcome anxiety or fear about attending school.

51. Employ Art Therapy Techniques (51)

A. The client was instructed to draw a picture or create a sculpture reflecting what they fear will happen when they go to school.

B. Today's session processed the content of the client's artwork and discussed whether their fears about attending school are realistic or unrealistic.

C. The client's artwork was noted to reflect fear about separating from parents to face stressors or responsibilities at school.

D. The client's artwork was noted to reflect anxiety or fear about experiencing rejection or failure at school.

E. After completing artwork, the client was helped to identify effective ways to overcome fear about attending school.

52. **Utilize "Angry Tower" Technique (52)**

A. The "Angry Tower" technique (Saxe) was used in today's therapy session to help the client identify and express underlying feelings of anger that contribute to refusal to attend school.

B. The "Angry Tower" technique helped the client to openly identify the target(s) of their anger.

C. After playing the "Angry Tower" game, the client explored whether they would be willing to express feelings of anger directly toward the target(s).

D. The therapeutic game led to a discussion about more effective ways for the client to express feelings of anger.

E. The client and parents were instructed to play the "Angry Tower" game at home when the client is experiencing strong feelings of anger.

53. **Refer Enmeshed Parent for Treatment (53)**

A. The overly enmeshed parent was assessed for the possibility of having either an anxiety or depressive disorder that may be contributing to the client's refusal to attend school.

B. The client's overly enmeshed parent was referred for a medication evaluation to help decrease anxiety or depression.

C. A recommendation was made that the overly enmeshed parent pursue individual therapy to help decrease feelings of depression or anxiety.

D. Positive feedback was provided as the overly enmeshed parent has followed through with seeking the medication evaluation.

E. Positive feedback was provided as the overly enmeshed parent has followed up with pursuing individual therapy to decrease feelings of depression or anxiety.

SEPARATION ANXIETY

CLIENT PRESENTATION

1. **Excessive Distress Anticipating Separation (1)**[*]
   A. The client has often exhibited a great deal of emotional distress when anticipating separation from parents or major attachment figures.
   B. The client became visibly upset and had difficulty separating from parents in today's therapy session.
   C. The client has gradually started to cope more effectively with separations and has not exhibited as much distress.
   D. The client was able to separate from parents or caregivers in today's therapy session without exhibiting any emotional distress.
   E. The client has consistently been able to separate from parents or caregivers without exhibiting emotional distress.

2. **Crying and Pleading (1)**
   A. The parents report that the client frequently begins to cry and plead to stay with them when anticipating separations.
   B. The client had much difficulty separating from parents or caregivers in today's therapy session and began to cry and plead to stay with them.
   C. The intensity and duration of the client's crying and pleading behavior have gradually started to diminish.
   D. The client was able to effectively separate from parents or caregivers without crying or pleading.
   E. The client has consistently been able to manage separations without crying or pleading to stay with the parents or caregivers.

3. **Regressive Behaviors (1)**
   A. The parents report that the client often regresses and behaves in an immature manner when anticipating separations from them.
   B. The client regressed and displayed immature behaviors in today's therapy session when asked to separate from parents/caregivers.
   C. The frequency of the client's regressive or immature behaviors has gradually started to decrease.
   D. The client was able to effectively separate from parents/caregivers in today's therapy session without regressing or engaging in immature behaviors.
   E. The client has ceased the pattern of engaging in regressive or immature behaviors when anticipating separations.

---

[*] The numbers in parentheses correlate to the number of the Behavioral Definition statement in the companion chapter with the same title in the *Child Psychotherapy Treatment Planner*, Sixth Edition, by Jongsma, Peterson, McInnis, & Bruce (Wiley, 2023).

4. **Temper Tantrums (1)**

   A. The parents report that the client frequently displays intense temper outbursts when anticipating separations from them.

   B. The client exhibited a temper tantrum in today's therapy session when asked to separate from parents or caregivers.

   C. The frequency and intensity of the client's temper tantrums around separation situations have gradually started to decrease.

   D. The client was able to separate from parents/caregivers in today's therapy session without displaying a temper tantrum.

   E. The client has demonstrated a significant reduction in the frequency and intensity of temper tantrums around separation situations.

5. **Unrealistic Worry About Possible Harm (2)**

   A. The client has experienced persistent and unrealistic worries about some possible harm befalling parents/caregivers.

   B. In today's therapy session, the client expressed worries about some possible harm befalling parents/caregivers.

   C. The frequency and intensity of the client's worries or anxiety about possible harm befalling parents/caregivers has gradually started to diminish as they recognize that the worries are unrealistic.

   D. In today's therapy session, the client did not verbalize any worries or fears about some possible harm befalling parents/caregivers.

   E. The client has overcome excessive or unrealistic worries about some possible harm befalling parents/caregivers.

6. **Irrational Fear About Future Calamity (3)**

   A. The client has developed persistent and unrealistic fears that some future calamity will separate them from parents/caregivers.

   B. The client expressed fear in today's therapy session that some future calamity will separate them from parents/caregivers.

   C. The client reported a slight reduction in the intensity of fears about a calamitous event separating them from parents/caregivers.

   D. The client did not express any irrational fears during today's therapy session.

   E. The client has ceased experiencing irrational fears about a future calamity separating them from parents/caregivers.

7. **Emotional Distress After Separation (4)**

   A. The client has often exhibited a great deal of emotional distress after experiencing a separation from home or major attachment figure.

   B. The client became visibly upset and protested vigorously after separating from parents/caregivers in today's therapy session.

   C. The client has gradually started to cope more effectively with separations and has not exhibited as much distress after separating from parents/caregivers.

   D. The client managed to separate from parents/caregivers in today's therapy session without exhibiting an excessive amount of emotional distress.

    E. The client has demonstrated a significant reduction in the intensity of emotional distress after separating from home or major attachment figures.

8. Excessive Clinging (5)

    A. The parents reported that the client often clings to them excessively when anticipating separations.

    B. The client began to cling to parents in today's therapy session when asked to separate from them.

    C. The intensity and duration of the client's clinging have gradually started to diminish.

    D. The client did not become clingy in today's therapy session when asked to separate from parents/caregivers.

    E. The client has consistently been able to manage separations effectively without exhibiting any excessive clinging.

9. Family Enmeshment/Overly Protective Parent(s) (5)

    A. The client has established a highly enmeshed relationship with their parents that contributes to separation anxiety.

    B. The parents verbally recognized how their overprotectiveness reinforces the client's excessive dependency.

    C. The parents have encouraged the client to become more independent and engage in play or socialize more often with peers.

    D. The parents have reinforced the client's positive social behaviors and have set limits on overly dependent behaviors.

    E. The client has achieved a healthy balance between socializing with peers and spending quality time with parents and family members.

10. Nighttime Fears (6)

    A. The client has demonstrated a significant amount of fearfulness and distress at night when it is time to separate from parents and sleep in their own room.

    B. The client has often refused to sleep without the parents being present in the same room at night.

    C. In today's therapy session, the client verbalized fears about sleeping alone.

    D. The client's nighttime fears have gradually diminished, and the client has exhibited less distress when having to separate from the parents at bedtime.

    E. The client has consistently slept in their own room at night without exhibiting any emotional distress or fearfulness.

11. Recurrent Nightmares (7)

    A. The client has experienced frequent nightmares centering around the themes of separation from major attachment figures.

    B. The client has often entered into their parents' room at night after experiencing a nightmare.

    C. The client has continued to experience nightmares centering around the theme of separation.

    D. The client has not experienced any recent nightmares.

E. The client reported that they have experienced a significant reduction in the frequency of nightmares.

12. Frequent Somatic Complaints (8)

A. The client has expressed frequent somatic complaints when anticipating separations from home or major attachment figures.

B. The client expressed somatic complaints in today's therapy session after separating from parents/caregivers.

C. The frequency and intensity of the client's somatic complaints have gradually started to decrease.

D. The client was able to separate from parents in today's therapy session without voicing any somatic complaints.

E. The frequency and intensity of the client's somatic complaints have decreased significantly since the onset of treatment.

13. Excessive Need for Reassurance (9)

A. The parents report that the client seeks frequent reassurance about their safety and protection from possible harm or danger.

B. In today's therapy session, the client sought reassurance from parents about their safety.

C. The client has slowly started to calm down and does not require as much reassurance as previously needed about their safety or protection from harm or danger.

D. The parents report that the client seldom needs reassurance about their safety or protection from possible harm or danger.

14. Low Self-Esteem (10)

A. The client's low self-esteem and lack of self-confidence have contributed to fears of being alone or participating in social activities.

B. In today's therapy session, the client expressed strong feelings of inadequacy and insecurity about having to socialize with others or participate in social activities.

C. During today's therapy session, the client expressed strong feelings of insecurity about separating from attachment figures.

D. In today's therapy session, the client verbalized confidence about the ability to socialize with others and participate in social activities.

E. The client has regularly participated in social activities without displaying any separation anxiety.

INTERVENTIONS IMPLEMENTED

1. Establish Rapport (1)*

A. Caring was conveyed to the client through support, warmth, and empathy.

B. The client was provided with nonjudgmental support, and a level of trust was developed.

---

*The numbers in parentheses correlate to the number of the Therapeutic Intervention statement in the companion chapter with the same title in the *Child Psychotherapy Treatment Planner*, Sixth Edition, by Jongsma, Peterson, McInnis, & Bruce (Wiley, 2023).

C. The client was urged to feel safe in expressing separation anxiety issues.

D. The client began to express feelings more freely as rapport and trust level have increased.

E. The client has continued to experience difficulty being open and direct about expression of painful feelings; the client was encouraged to use the safe haven of therapy to express these difficult issues.

2. **Focus on Strengthening Therapeutic Relationship (2)**

A. The relationship with the client was strengthened using empirically supported factors.

B. The relationship with the client was strengthened through the implementation of collaborative approach, agreement on goals, demonstration of empathy, verbalization of positive regard, and collection of client feedback.

C. The client reacted positively to the relationship-strengthening measures taken.

D. The client verbalized feeling supported and understood during therapy sessions.

E. Despite attempts to strengthen the therapeutic relationship, the client reports feeling distant and misunderstood.

F. The client has indicated that sessions are not helpful and will be terminating therapy.

3. **Build Therapeutic Trust (3)**

A. The objective of today's therapy session was to establish trust with the client so that they can begin to identify and express feelings.

B. Attempts were made to build the level of trust with the client through consistent eye contact, active listening, unconditional positive regard, and warm acceptance.

C. The "Expressions of Fear Through Art" exercise from the *Child Psychotherapy Homework Planner* (Jongsma, Peterson, McInnis, & Bruce) was assigned to promote the trusting expression of fearful thoughts and feelings.

D. The client's expression of thoughts and feelings during the therapy session was supported empathetically.

E. The therapy session was helpful in building a moderate level of trust with the client.

F. The therapy session was not successful in establishing trust with the client as they remained guarded when discussing the factors contributing to fears and anxiety.

4. **Assess Nature of Anxiety Symptoms (4)**

A. The client was asked about the frequency, intensity, duration, and history of anxiety symptoms, fear, and avoidance.

B. *The Anxiety Disorders Interview Schedule for Children—Parent Version or Child Version* (Silverman & Albano) was used to assess the client's anxiety symptoms.

C. The assessment of the client's anxiety symptoms indicated that their symptoms are extreme and severely interfere with life.

D. The assessment of the client's anxiety symptoms indicates that these symptoms are moderate and occasionally interfere with daily functioning.

E. The results of the assessment of the client's anxiety symptoms indicate that these symptoms are mild and rarely interfere with daily functioning.

F. The results of the assessment of the client's anxiety symptoms were reviewed with the client.

5. **Administer Objective Assessment Instrument (5)**
   A. An objective assessment instrument was administered to help assess the nature and degree of the client's fears, worries, and anxiety symptoms.
   B. *The Revised Children's Manifest Anxiety Scale* (Reynolds & Richmond) was used to help assess the client's level of fears, worries, and anxiety symptoms.
   C. *The Multidimensional Anxiety Scale for Children* (March et al.) was used to help assess the client's level of fears, worries, and anxiety symptoms.
   D. *The Screen for Anxiety Related Emotional Disorders: Child* and/or *Parent Version* (Birmaher et al.) was used to help assess the client's level of fears, worries, and anxiety symptoms.
   E. The objective assessment instrument was readministered to assess therapeutic progress.

6. **Assess Level of Insight (6)**
   A. The client's level of insight toward the presenting problems was assessed.
   B. The client was assessed in regard to the syntonic versus dystonic nature of their insight about the presenting problems.
   C. The client was noted to demonstrate good insight into the problematic nature of the behavior and symptoms.
   D. The client was noted to be in agreement with others' concerns and is motivated to work on change.
   E. The client was noted to be ambivalent regarding the problems described and is reluctant to address the issues as a concern.
   F. The client was noted to be resistant regarding acknowledgment of the problem areas, is not concerned about them, and has no motivation to make changes.

7. **Assess for Correlated Disorders (7)**
   A. The client was assessed for evidence of research-based correlated disorders.
   B. The client was assessed in regard to the level of vulnerability to suicide.
   C. The client was identified as having a comorbid disorder, and treatment was adjusted to account for these concerns.
   D. The client has been assessed for any correlated disorders, but none were found.

8. **Assess for Culturally Based Confounding Issues (8)**
   A. The client was assessed for age-related issues that could help to better understand their clinical presentation.
   B. The client was assessed for gender-related issues that could help to better understand their clinical presentation.
   C. The client was assessed for cultural syndromes, cultural idioms of distress, or culturally based perceived causes that could help to better understand their clinical presentation.
   D. Alternative factors have been identified as contributing to the client's currently defined "problem behavior," and these were taken into account in regard to treatment.
   E. Culturally based factors that could help to account for the client's currently defined "problem behavior" were investigated, but no significant factors were identified.

9. **Assess Severity of Impairment (9)**

   A. The severity of the client's impairment was assessed to determine the appropriate level of care.

   B. The client was assessed in regard to impairment in social, relational, and educational endeavors.

   C. It was reflected to the client that the impairment appears to create mild to moderate effects on the client's functioning.

   D. It was reflected to the client that the impairment appears to create severe to very severe effects on the client's functioning.

   E. The client was continuously assessed for the severity of impairment, as well as the efficacy and appropriateness of treatment.

10. **Assess for Pathogenic Care (10)**

    A. The home, school, and community of the client were assessed for pathogenic care and concerns.

    B. The client's various environments were assessed for the persistent disregard of the child's needs, repeated changes in caregivers, limited opportunities for stable attachment, harsh discipline, or other grossly inept care.

    C. Pathogenic care was identified and the treatment plan included strategies for managing or correcting these concerns and protecting the child.

    D. No pathogenic care was identified, and this was reflected to the client and caregivers.

11. **Refer for Medication Evaluation (11)**

    A. The client was referred to a prescriber for an evaluation for psychotropic medication to help control the anxiety symptoms.

    B. The client complied with the medication evaluation referral and has attended the appointment.

    C. The client refused to attend an appointment with a prescriber for a psychotropic medication evaluation; they were encouraged to proceed with the evaluation as they feel willing to do so.

12. **Monitor Medication Adherence/Effectiveness (12)**

    A. The issues of medication adherence and effectiveness were addressed with the parents and the client.

    B. The client's resistance to taking medication was processed and addressed.

    C. Information related to the client's medication adherence and its effectiveness was communicated to their physician.

    D. The client's responsible adherence with medications was verbally reinforced.

    E. The client reported that the use of the psychotropic medication has been effective in reducing their experience of anxiety.

13. **Discuss Separation Fears (13)**

    A. A discussion was held about how separation fears involve perceiving unrealistic threats, underestimating coping skills, feeling anxiety, and avoiding what is threatening.

B. The client was informed of how factors interact in a cycle of fear and avoidance that maintains the problem.

C. Examples were elicited from the client about how their fears cause a cycle of fear and avoidance.

14. Discuss Benefits of Exposure (14)

A. A discussion was held about how exposure serves to break the fear and avoidance cycle, lessen fear, build confidence, and lead to feeling safer.

B. The use of exposure to build a new history of successful experiences was emphasized.

C. The client and parents were reinforced for their understanding of the use of exposure to build a new history of successful experiences.

D. The client and parents displayed a poor understanding of the use of exposure to build successful experiences and were provided with additional feedback in this area.

15. Teach Anxiety Management Skills (15)

A. The client was taught anxiety management skills.

B. The client was taught to stay focused on behavioral goals and positive self-talk.

C. Techniques for muscular relaxation and paced diaphragmatic breathing were taught to the client.

D. The client was reinforced for clear understanding and use of anxiety management skills.

E. The client has not used new anxiety management skills and was redirected to do so.

16. Assign Calming Skills Exercises (16)

A. The client was assigned a homework exercise in which they practice daily calming skills.

B. The client was assigned the "Deep Breathing Exercise" from the *Child Psychotherapy Homework Planner* (Jongsma, Peterson, McInnis, & Bruce).

C. The client was assigned "Deep Muscle Relaxation" in the Adolescent Psychotherapy Homework Planner (Jongsma, Peterson, McInnis, & Bruce).

D. The client's use of the exercises for practicing daily calming skills was closely monitored.

E. The client's success at using daily calming skills was reinforced.

F. The client was provided with corrective feedback for failure to practice daily calming skills.

17. Use Biofeedback Techniques (17)

A. Biofeedback techniques were used to facilitate the client's success in learning relaxation skills.

B. The client was provided with consistent feedback about physiological responses to relaxation skill training.

C. The client was reinforced for their increase in relaxation skills through biofeedback training.

D. The client has not increased success at learning skills through biofeedback techniques, and remedial instruction was provided.

18. **Identify Biased Thoughts (18)**

    A. The client was assisted in identifying the biased schemas and related thoughts that mediate separation anxiety responses.

    B. The client was taught the role of biased thinking in precipitating emotional responses.

    C. The client was reinforced as they verbalized an understanding of the cognitive beliefs and messages that mediate anxiety responses.

    D. The client was assisted in replacing biased messages with reality-based alternative cognitions.

    E. The client failed to identify biased thoughts and cognitions and was provided with tentative examples in this area.

19. **Teach Positive Self-Talk Through Behavioral Techniques (19)**

    A. The client was trained in the use of self-talk that facilitates completing behavioral experiments and exposures realistically and successfully.

    B. Behavioral techniques were used to teach helpful self-talk.

    C. Modeling and imaginal rehearsal were used to train the client in positive self-talk.

    D. Corrective feedback and social reinforcement were used to train the client in positive self-talk to help endure anxiety symptoms.

    E. The client was reinforced for increased use of realistic self-talk.

    F. The client has not used realistic self-talk and was redirected to do so.

20. **Assign Exercises on Self-Talk (20)**

    A. The client was assigned homework exercises in which they identify fearful self-talk and create reality-based alternatives.

    B. The client was assigned the exercise "Replace Negative Thoughts with Positive Self-Talk" from the *Child Psychotherapy Homework Planner* by Jongsma, Peterson, McInnis, & Bruce.

    C. The client's replacement of fearful self-talk with reality-based alternatives was reviewed.

    D. The client was reinforced for successes at replacing fearful self-talk with reality-based alternatives.

    E. The client was provided with corrective feedback for failures to replace fearful self-talk with reality-based alternatives.

    F. The client has not completed assigned homework regarding fearful self-talk and was redirected to do so.

21. **Construct Anxiety Stimuli Hierarchy (21)**

    A. The client was assisted in constructing a hierarchy of separation anxiety–producing situations associated with two or three spheres of worry.

    B. It was difficult for the client to develop a hierarchy of stimulus situations because the causes of separation anxiety remain quite vague; the client was assisted in completing the hierarchy.

    C. The client was successful at creating a focused hierarchy of specific stimulus situations that provoke separation anxiety in a gradually increasing manner; this hierarchy was reviewed.

22. **Select Initial Exposures (22)**

   A. Initial exposures were selected from the hierarchy of anxiety-producing situations, with a bias toward likelihood of being successful.

   B. A plan was developed with the client for managing the symptoms that may occur during the initial exposure.

   C. The exercise "Gradually Facing a Phobic Fear" from the *Adolescent Psychotherapy Homework Planner* (Jongsma, Peterson, McInnis, & Bruce) was used to help develop a plan for managing the client's symptoms during exposures.

   D. The client was assisted in rehearsing the plan for managing the exposure-related symptoms within their imagination.

   E. Positive feedback was provided for the client's helpful use of symptom management techniques.

   F. The client was redirected for ways to improve symptom management techniques.

23. **Assign Information on Situational Exposure (23)**

   A. The client's parents were assigned to read about how exposure-based therapy can be beneficial.

   B. The parents were assigned to read excerpts from *The Coping C.A.T. Series* (WorkbookPublishing.com).

   C. The parents were assigned to read *Helping Your Anxious Child* (Rapee et al.).

   D. The parents have read the assigned information on exposure-based therapy techniques, and key points were reviewed.

   E. The parents have not read the assigned information on exposure-based therapy techniques and were redirected to do so.

24. **Encourage Processing of Fears (24)**

   A. The client was encouraged to cooperate with the process of facing fear, rather than using avoidance to cope.

   B. The client was assisted in implementing exposure in practice situations.

   C. The client was assigned "Maurice Faces His Fear" from the *Child Psychotherapy Homework Planner* by Jongsma, Peterson, McInnis, & Bruce.

   D. Graduated tasks, modeling, and reinforcement of the client's success were used to help the client gradually practice greater levels of exposure.

   E. The client and their attachment figures were coordinated for specific practice exposures.

   F. It was reflected to the client that they have gradually become less anxious when the attachment figure has not been as available.

   G. The client continues to have a great deal of anxiety in practice exposures sessions, and remedial techniques were implemented.

25. **Conduct Practice Exposure Sessions (25)**

   A. The client was assisted in practicing exposure within the session.

   B. Graduated tasks, modeling, and reinforcement of success were used during the practice exposures.

C. As practice exposures progress, refine learned coping skills toward success throughout the exposure hierarchy.

D. The client was assigned "Gradual Exposure to Fear" in the *Adolescent Psychotherapy Homework Planner* (Jongsma, Peterson, McInnis, & Bruce).

26. Assign Homework on Situational Exposures (26)

A. The client was assigned homework exercises to perform situational exposures and record the experience.

B. The client's use of situational exposure techniques was reviewed and reinforced.

C. The client has struggled in their implementation of situational exposure techniques and was provided with corrective feedback.

D. The client has not attempted to use the situational exposure techniques and was redirected to do so.

27. Involve Parents in Treatment (27)

A. Parent management skills were taught to the client's parents to assist in managing separation anxiety.

B. The client's parents were involved in developing appropriate treatment goals with the client.

C. The client's parents were taught how to provide support to the client as they face fears, how to prevent reinforcing the fear and avoidance, ways to offer encouragement and support, and how to give peaceful direction and redirection.

D. Family therapy was conducted in which parents implemented skills for coping with their child's separation anxiety to facilitate therapeutic progress.

28. Teach Parents Management of Child's Anxiety (28)

A. The parents were taught constructive skills for managing the child's anxiety.

B. The parents were taught about how to encourage or discourage positive or negative behavior and that changing key elements of those interactions can be used to promote positive change.

29. Read Parent-Training Material (29)

A. The parents were asked to read material consistent with a parent management training approach to managing disruptive behavior.

B. The parents were assigned *The Kazdin Method for Parenting the Defiant Child* (Kazdin).

C. The parents have read the assigned material, and key concepts were processed.

D. The parents have not read the assigned material and were redirected to do so.

30. Support Parents Managing Their Own Emotions (30)

A. Support was provided to parents to help recognize their own difficult emotional reactions to the client's experience of trauma.

B. The parents were assisted in managing their own difficult emotional reactions to the client's experience of the trauma.

C. Parents were noted to be more capable of supporting the client's positive behavior changes as they have managed their own emotional reactions to the client's trauma.

D. Parents were provided with remedial feedback as they have struggled to manage their own emotions.

31. **Encourage Modeling of Skills and Praise (31)**
    A. Parents were encouraged to model constructive skills that they have learned that will assist in the client's positive behavior change.
    B. The parents were encouraged to praise the client when they use therapeutic skills.
    C. Parents have been noted to model and praise the use of calming techniques.
    D. Parents were reinforced for modeling and praising the client's use of cognitive-restructuring techniques.
    E. Parents were encouraged to keep modeling and praising the use of nonavoidance of unrealistic fears.
    F. The parents have not modeled and praised the client's use of therapeutic skills and were redirected to do so.

32. **Teach Problem-Solving and Communication Skills (32)**
    A. Parents were taught problem-solving techniques to help the client progress through therapy.
    B. Specific communication skills were taught to the parents to help the client progress through therapy.
    C. Positive feedback was provided to parents for their use of problem-solving and communication skills.
    D. Parents frequently failed to use problem-solving and communication skills and were redirected to do so.

33. **Encourage Parents' Limit Setting (33)**
    A. Today's session focused on teaching the parents about the importance of setting firm, consistent limits on the client's temper tantrums and/or excessive clinging or whining.
    B. The parents acknowledged that they have been reluctant to set firm, consistent limits because of their desire to avoid dealing with the client's temper outbursts or heightened emotional distress; they were reminded to set these limits.
    C. The parents were instructed to remain calm and firmly in control when they first begin to set limits on the client's temper tantrums, excessive clinging, or whining.
    D. The parents have become firmer and more consistent in their limit setting.

34. **Develop Reward System/Contingency Contract (34)**
    A. The client and parents identified a list of rewards to reinforce the client for managing separations from parents without displaying excessive emotional distress.
    B. A reward system was designed to reinforce the client for managing separations from parents in a calm and confident manner.
    C. The client, parents, and therapist signed a contingency contract specifying the negative consequences for temper tantrums, excessive clinging, or whining that occurs around separation points.
    D. The client, parents, and therapist verbally agreed to the terms of the contingency contract.
    E. The reward system and/or contingency contract have helped the client manage separations from parents without exhibiting excessive emotional distress; they were encouraged to continue this system.

F. The client and parents have not used the reward system/contingency contract to reinforce the client for managing separations from parents in a calm and confident manner and were redirected to use this helpful technique.

35. Identify Past Successful Coping Mechanisms (35)

A. Today's session inquired into what the client does differently on days when they are able to separate from parents without displaying excessive clinging, pleading, crying, or protesting.

B. The exercise "Parents' Time Away" from the *Child Psychotherapy Homework Planner* (Jongsma, Peterson, McInnis, & Bruce) was assigned to help identify successful coping techniques for the client.

C. Today's therapy session was helpful in identifying the positive coping mechanisms that the client used in the past to successfully manage separations from parents.

D. The client was strongly encouraged to use coping mechanisms similar to those that they used in the past to effectively separate from parents without displaying excessive clinging, pleading, crying, or protesting.

E. Active listening skills were used as the client shared the realization that talking or playing with other peers helped to decrease anxiety or fearfulness around separation points.

F. Today's family-therapy session revealed that the client was able to manage separations effectively in the past when the parents provided encouragement and set limits on temper tantrums, pleading, crying, protesting, or excessive clinging.

36. Encourage Peer Group Activities (36)

A. The client was strongly encouraged to participate in extracurricular or positive peer group activities to help them feel more comfortable and relaxed around others.

B. The client was assisted in developing a list of extracurricular or positive peer group activities that will help provide them with the opportunity to establish meaningful friendships at school and in the neighborhood.

C. The exercise "Show Your Strengths" from the *Child Psychotherapy Homework Planner* (Jongsma, Peterson, McInnis, & Bruce) was used to help identify additional extracurricular or peer group activities for the client.

D. Active listening was used as the client verbally recognized how feelings of insecurity and inadequacy contribute to reluctance to become involved in extracurricular or positive peer group activities.

E. The client reported that recent participation in extracurricular or positive peer group activities has helped them cope more effectively with separations; the client was encouraged to continue.

F. The client has continued to have problems separating from parents/caregivers and has not recently participated in any extracurricular or positive peer group activities; the client was reminded to use these helpful techniques.

37. Teach Coping Skills via Behavioral Rehearsal/Role-Play (37)

A. Behavioral rehearsal and role-playing techniques were used to help teach the client positive social skills and coping strategies to reduce social anxiety.

B. The exercise "Greeting Your Peers" from the *Child Psychotherapy Homework Planner* (Jongsma, Peterson, McInnis, & Bruce) was used to help teach the client social skills that reduce social anxiety.

C. The client was assisted in identifying several positive social skills after engaging in the behavioral rehearsal and role-playing exercises.

D. After role-playing in the therapy session, the client expressed a willingness to practice the newly learned social skills in everyday situations.

E. The client was given the homework assignment to practice the newly learned social skills at least three to five times before the next therapy session.

38. **Assign Overnight Visit with Friend (38)**

A. The client was given a directive to invite a friend for an overnight visit and/or set up an overnight visit at a friend's home.

B. The client was helped to identify positive coping strategies that they can use to reduce anxiety when spending the night at a friend's house.

C. The parents were strongly encouraged to praise and reinforce the client for having a friend sleep over at their house or spending the night at a friend's home.

D. The client was praised and reinforced for having a successful overnight visit.

E. The clients' fears that contribute to reluctance to have an overnight visit with a friend were explored.

39. **Assign Time Spent in Independent Play (39)**

A. The client was directed to spend gradually longer periods of time in independent play or with friends after school.

B. An action plan was developed to help the client spend gradually longer periods of time in individual play or with friends after school.

C. A reward system was designed and implemented to reinforce the client for spending gradually longer periods of time in independent play or with friends after school.

D. The parents were strongly encouraged to praise and reinforce the client for engaging in independent play or spending time with friends after school.

E. The client is noted to be spending more time away from parents/caregivers in independent peer group play.

40. **Encourage Autonomy Through Exploring (40)**

A. The client was encouraged to explore their immediate neighborhood to foster autonomy.

B. The client was assigned the "Explore Your World" exercise from the *Child Psychotherapy Homework Planner* (Jongsma, Peterson, McInnis, & Bruce) to help foster greater autonomy and increase their time spent in independent play or activities outside of the home.

C. The client was assigned the "Explore Your World" exercise to help them tolerate separations from parents or attachment figures more effectively.

D. The client was assigned the "Explore Your World" exercise to help decrease the intensity of fears about the surrounding environment being a foreboding or ominous place.

E. The client and parents reported that the "Explore Your World" exercise helped the client tolerate separations from the parents more effectively; the benefits of this progress were reviewed.

F. The client reported that the "Explore Your World" exercise helped to decrease the intensity of their anxiety and fearfulness; the client was encouraged to continue this technique.

G. The client has not used the "Explore Your World" exercise, and the barriers to using this technique were reviewed, processed, and ameliorated.

41. **Assign Weekly Outing for Parents (41)**

   A. The parents were instructed to go on weekly outings without the client to help them learn to tolerate separations more effectively.

   B. The client was taught relaxation and deep-breathing techniques to help reduce separation anxiety while parents are away on their weekly outing.

   C. The client was instructed to call a friend or play with siblings to help reduce separation anxiety while parents are away on their weekly outing.

   D. The parents reported that they complied with the directive to go on a weekly outing without the client.

   E. Today's session explored the reasons for the parents' resistance to going on a weekly outing without the client.

42. **Differentiate Between Lapse and Relapse (42)**

   A. A discussion was held with the client regarding the distinction between a lapse and a relapse.

   B. A lapse was associated with an initial and reversible return of symptoms, fear, or urges to avoid.

   C. A relapse was associated with the decision to return to fearful and avoidant patterns.

   D. The client was provided with support and encouragement as they displayed an understanding of the difference between a lapse and a relapse.

   E. The client struggled to understand the difference between a lapse and a relapse and was provided with remedial feedback in this area.

43. **Discuss Management of Lapse Risk Situations (43)**

   A. The client was assisted in identifying future situations or circumstances in which lapses could occur.

   B. The session focused on rehearsing the management of future situations or circumstances in which lapses could occur.

   C. The client was reinforced for appropriate use of lapse management skills.

   D. The client was redirected in regard to poor use of lapse management skills.

44. **Encourage Routine Use of Strategies (44)**

   A. The client was instructed to routinely use the strategies learned in therapy (e.g., cognitive restructuring, exposure).

   B. The client was urged to find ways to build new strategies into their life as much as possible.

   C. The client was reinforced as they reported ways in which they have incorporated coping strategies into their life and routine.

   D. The client was redirected about ways to incorporate new strategies into their routine and life.

45. **Develop a Coping Card (45)**

   A. The client was provided with a coping card on which specific coping strategies were listed.

   B. The client was assisted in developing the coping card in order to list helpful coping strategies.

   C. The client was encouraged to use the coping card when struggling with anxiety-producing situations.

46. Assess Enmeshed Parent (46)

A. The overly enmeshed parent was assessed for having an anxiety or affective disorder.

B. The overly enmeshed parent was identified as having an anxiety or affective disorder and this information was shared with the parent.

C. The parent was referred for a medication evaluation for a psychiatric disorder.

D. The overly enmeshed parent was referred for individual therapy for a psychiatric disorder.

E. The overly enmeshed parent's improvement in regard to an anxiety or affective disorder was noted, as was that parent's decreased tendency to become enmeshed.

F. The overly enmeshed parent has not followed up on treatment for a psychiatric disorder and was redirected to do so.

47. Assess/Treat the Marital Dyad (47)

A. The marital dyad was assessed for possible conflict, or triangulation.

B. Family therapy sessions were conducted to explore the dynamics that contribute to the emergence of the child's separation anxiety problems.

C. The family therapy sessions identified several dynamics that contribute to the client's separation anxiety problem.

D. Family dynamics were addressed within the family therapy session.

E. The family was referred for additional family therapy.

F. The parents were referred for couple's therapy.

48. Assess Anxiety Connection to Past Experiences (48)

A. The client's anxiety and fears were assessed in regard to the association with a previous separation, loss, abuse, trauma, or dangerous situation.

B. It was reflected to the client that their fears seemed to be associated with their previous experiences.

49. Encourage Expression of Emotions About Past Experiences (49)

A. The client's experiences of separation, loss, trauma, or dangerous situation were explored.

B. The client was encouraged and supported as they described their experience of separation, loss, trauma, or danger.

C. The client was reinforced for expression of feelings related to past experiences.

D. The client has been reluctant to express emotions related to past experiences and was encouraged to do this as they feel safe.

50. Assign Letter About Emotions (50)

A. The client was assigned to write a letter to express feelings about a past separation, loss, trauma, or danger.

B. The client has completed the letter about emotions related to a past separation, loss, trauma, or danger, and this letter was processed with the therapist.

C. The client was supported as their letter about past experiences was reviewed.

D. The client has not completed the assigned letter about emotions regarding past experiences and was redirected to do so.

51. Use Child-Centered Play Therapy (51)

A. The use of child-centered play therapy principles was emphasized.

B. The client was assisted in gaining greater awareness of self through the use of genuine interest, unconditional positive regard, and a demonstration of trust in the client's capacity to grow.

C. The client was encouraged to increase motivation to overcome fears about separation through the reflection of feelings in a nonjudgmental manner.

D. It was noted that the child has responded positively to play therapy, with greater self-awareness and increased motivation to overcome fears.

52. Use Mutual Storytelling Technique (52)

A. The mutual storytelling technique was used to help express feelings and fears.

B. The therapist's story modeled an appropriate way to overcome fears and anxieties.

C. The client was encouraged to tell a story similar to the therapist's, using their own characters overcoming fears and anxieties.

53. Use Art Therapy Technique (53)

A. The client was instructed to draw a picture reflecting fears about what may happen upon separation from a major attachment figure.

B. After completing the drawing on what they fear, the client was assisted in identifying what is realistic or unrealistic.

54. Play the "Stand Up for Yourself" Game (54)

A. The "Stand Up for Yourself" game was used within the therapy session to teach the client assertiveness skills.

B. The client was reinforced for their increase in assertiveness skills after playing the "Stand Up for Yourself" game.

55. Refer to Group Therapy (55)

A. The client was referred to a small group for separation anxiety symptoms.

B. The client was enrolled in a group designed to increase social skills and assertion and decrease social anxiety.

C. As no group was available, the client was provided with individual therapy based on the group treatment model.

D. The client has participated in the group therapy for separation anxiety; their experience was reviewed and processed.

E. The client has not been involved in group therapy for social anxiety concerns and was redirected to do so.

SEXUAL ABUSE VICTIM

CLIENT PRESENTATION

1. **Self-Report of Sexual Abuse (1)***
   A. The client reported that they have been sexually abused.
   B. The client was guarded and evasive when being questioned about whether they have ever been sexually abused.
   C. The client has previously reported being sexually abused but has since recanted these earlier statements.
   D. The client has verbally denied being sexually abused, although there is other evidence to suggest that they have been abused.

2. **Physical Signs of Sexual Abuse (2)**
   A. The medical examination revealed physical signs of sexual abuse.
   B. The medical examination did not reveal any physical signs of sexual abuse.

3. **Strong Interest About Sexuality Issues (3)**
   A. The client has displayed a strong interest in or curiosity about issues related to sexuality since their sexual victimization.
   B. The client exhibited a strong interest in or curiosity about issues related to sexuality in the therapy session.
   C. The client's strong interest in or curiosity about issues related to sexuality has masked deeper feelings of sadness, hurt, and helplessness about their own sexual victimization.
   D. The client has demonstrated less of a preoccupation with issues related to sexuality since addressing their own sexual abuse issues.

4. **Advanced Knowledge of Sexuality (3)**
   A. The client has developed an advanced knowledge of sexuality for a child their age.
   B. The client has developed an advanced knowledge of sexuality because of their past sexual victimization.
   C. The client spoke about sophisticated sexual behaviors in today's therapy session.
   D. The client has developed an age-appropriate knowledge of sexuality.

5. **Sexualized Behaviors (4)**
   A. The client has displayed highly sexualized behaviors with family members, other adults, and peers.
   B. The client has engaged in inappropriate sexual behavior with younger or same-age children.
   C. The client's past sexual victimization has contributed to their highly sexualized behaviors.

---

*The numbers in parentheses correlate to the number of the Behavioral Definition statement in the companion chapter with the same title in the *Child Psychotherapy Treatment Planner*, Sixth Edition, by Jongsma, Peterson, McInnis, & Bruce (Wiley, 2023).

D. The client has engaged in sexualized behaviors with others in an attempt to meet dependency needs.

E. The client has not engaged in any recent sexual behaviors.

6. **Sexual Themes in Play/Artwork (4)**

A. The parent(s) and teachers reported that sexual themes often emerge in the client's play or artwork.

B. Sexual themes appeared in the client's play during today's therapy session.

C. The client's artwork reflected a strong sexual preoccupation.

D. The client has recently engaged in sexualized play with peers.

E. Sexual themes have not appeared in the client's recent play or artwork.

7. **Recurrent and Intrusive Recollections of Sexual Abuse (5)**

A. The client has experienced recurrent, intrusive, and distressing recollections of the past sexual abuse.

B. The client has reexperienced intrusive and distressing recollections of the past sexual abuse after coming into contact with the perpetrator and/or having exposure to sexual topics.

C. The client denied being troubled any longer by intrusive recollections of the sexual abuse.

8. **Recurrent Nightmares (5)**

A. The client has experienced recurrent nightmares of the past sexual abuse.

B. The client reported that they continue to be troubled by recurrent nightmares of the past sexual abuse.

C. The client has reexperienced nightmares of the sexual abuse since coming into contact with the perpetrator and/or being exposed to sexual topics.

D. The client stated that they are no longer troubled by nightmares of the past sexual abuse.

9. **Dissociative Flashbacks, Delusions, or Hallucinations (6)**

A. The client reported experiencing dissociative flashbacks of the past sexual abuse.

B. The client reported experiencing delusions and hallucinations related to the past sexual abuse.

C. The client reported reexperiencing dissociative flashbacks, delusions, or hallucinations since coming into contact with the perpetrator and/or being exposed to sexual topics.

D. The client stated that dissociative flashbacks, delusions, or hallucinations have ceased.

10. **Anger and Rage (7)**

A. The client expressed strong feelings of anger and rage about the past sexual abuse.

B. The client has exhibited frequent angry outbursts and episodes of rage since the onset of the sexual abuse.

C. The frequency and intensity of the client's angry outbursts have decreased since they have felt more secure and started to work through feelings about the sexual abuse.

D. The intensity of the client's anger has decreased whenever they talk about the past sexual abuse.

E. The client has demonstrated a reduction in the frequency and intensity of their angry outbursts and episodes of rage.

11. **Disturbance of Mood and Affect (8)**

A. The client has experienced frequent and prolonged periods of depression, anxiety, and irritability since the sexual abuse occurred.

B. The client appeared visibly depressed when talking about the sexual abuse.

C. The client appeared anxious when talking about the sexual abuse.

D. The client's moods have gradually started to stabilize as they work through feelings of sadness, anxiety, insecurity, and anger about the past sexual abuse.

E. The client's moods have stabilized and they report no longer being troubled by frequent or prolonged periods of depression, anxiety, or irritability.

12. **Suicidal Ideation (9)**

A. The client verbalized suicidal ideation.

B. The client reported feeling very hopeless and helpless regarding the future.

C. Suicidal thoughts and feelings seemed to dominate the client at the present time.

D. The client revealed a plan along with a backup plan to take their own life.

E. The client has gradually started to feel more hopeful and less despondent.

13. **Regressive Behaviors (10)**

A. The client has engaged in frequent regressive behaviors (e.g., thumb sucking, baby talk, bed-wetting) since the onset of the sexual abuse.

B. The client exhibited regressive behaviors in today's therapy session when they began talking about the past sexual abuse.

C. The client has engaged in more regressive behaviors since being removed from their home.

D. The client was able to talk about sexual abuse issues in today's therapy session without engaging in any regressive behaviors.

E. The client has demonstrated a significant reduction in the frequency of regressive behaviors.

14. **Fearfulness/Distrust (11)**

A. The client stated that they have felt strong feelings of fearfulness and a marked distrust of others since being sexually abused.

B. The client's fearfulness has slowly started to diminish, and they have begun to establish trust with significant others.

C. The strong support from family and individuals outside the family has helped to decrease the client's fearfulness and distrust.

D. The client has successfully worked through many of their feelings surrounding the sexual abuse and has established close, trusting relationships with significant others.

15. Social Withdrawal (11)

A. The client has become significantly more withdrawn from others since the onset of the sexual abuse.

B. The client appeared detached and withdrawn in today's therapy session when the topic of the sexual abuse was discussed.

C. The client acknowledged that they have become more withdrawn because of feelings of low self-esteem and distrust of others.

D. The client has started to become more assertive and outgoing in interactions with family members, other adults, and peers.

16. Feelings of Guilt and Shame (12)

A. The client expressed strong feelings of guilt and shame about the past sexual abuse.

B. The client has continued to experience strong feelings of guilt and shame about the past sexual abuse, despite being given reassurance that they are not responsible for the sexual abuse.

C. The client's feelings of guilt and shame have started to decrease as they now recognize that the perpetrator is responsible for the sexual abuse.

D. The client has successfully worked through and resolved feelings of guilt and shame about the past sexual abuse.

17. Low Self-Esteem (12)

A. The client expressed strong feelings of low self-esteem and insecurity about the past sexual abuse.

B. The client's self-esteem has started to improve as they work through feelings about the past sexual abuse.

C. Strong family support has helped to increase the client's self-esteem.

D. The client verbalized several positive self-descriptive statements during today's therapy session.

18. Exaggerated Startle Response (13)

A. The client has often displayed an exaggerated startle response when exposed to any sudden, unexpected stimuli.

B. The client displayed an exaggerated startle response in today's therapy session.

C. The client reported that they do not startle as easily or dramatically when exposed to unexpected stimuli.

19. Perfectionistic Behaviors (14)

A. The client displays strong perfectionist behavior, such as obsessive clinging or excessive studying.

B. The client reported using perfectionist behaviors to attempt to achieve control over their environment.

C. The client reported a reduction of obsessive or excessive behavior related to perfectionism and control.

D. The client has successfully worked through their need to control their environment.

INTERVENTIONS IMPLEMENTED

1. Establish Rapport (1)*

A. Caring was conveyed to the client through support, warmth, and empathy.

B. The client was provided with nonjudgmental support, and a level of trust was developed.

C. The client was urged to feel safe in describing their sexual abuse.

D. The client began to express feelings more freely as rapport and trust level have increased.

E. The client has continued to experience difficulty being open and direct about their expression of painful feelings; the client was encouraged to use the safe haven of therapy to express these difficult issues.

2. Focus on Strengthening Therapeutic Relationship (2)

A. The relationship with the client was strengthened using empirically supported factors.

B. The relationship with the client was strengthened through the implementation of collaborative approach, agreement on goals, demonstration of empathy, verbalization of positive regard, and collection of client feedback.

C. The client reacted positively to the relationship-strengthening measures taken.

D. The client verbalized feeling supported and understood during therapy sessions.

E. Despite attempts to strengthen the therapeutic relationship, the client reports feeling distant and misunderstood.

F. The client has indicated that sessions are not helpful and will be terminating therapy.

3. Develop Expression of Feelings (3)

A. The client was given encouragement and support to tell the entire story of the sexual abuse and to express feelings experienced during and after the abuse.

B. Support was provided as the client described the sequence of events before, during, and after the sexual abuse incidents, but they neither showed nor talked of any feelings.

C. Client-centered principles were used to encourage and support the client in expressing feelings surrounding the past sexual abuse.

D. The client was assigned "My Story" in the *Child Psychotherapy Homework Planner* (Jongsma, Peterson, McInnis, & Bruce).

E. The parents were encouraged to allow the client opportunities at home to express thoughts and feelings about the sexual abuse.

F. The client has not been able to tell the entire story of the sexual abuse and express feelings that they experienced during and after the abuse and was redirected to do so.

4. Utilize Trauma-Focused Cognitive Behavioral Therapy (TF-CBT) (4)

A. The client was encouraged to share their trauma narrative through the use of Trauma-Focused Cognitive Behavioral Therapy.

---

*The numbers in parentheses correlate to the number of the Therapeutic Intervention statement in the companion chapter with the same title in the *Child Psychotherapy Treatment Planner*, Sixth Edition, by Jongsma, Peterson, McInnis, & Bruce (Wiley, 2023).

B. The client was assisted in building trusting relationships and recognizing their emotions to build empowerment within self.

C. The client was taught to use coping strategies, such as deep breathing, physical activity, and art activities.

5. Use Anatomical Dolls (5)

A. Anatomically detailed dolls were used to assess whether the client has been sexually abused.

B. Anatomically detailed dolls or puppets were used to allow the client to tell and show how they were sexually abused.

C. Caution was exercised to not lead the client's description about the past sexual abuse.

D. Through the use of anatomically detailed dolls, the client was able to identify how they were sexually abused.

E. The use of anatomically detailed dolls helped the client verbalize feelings about the past sexual abuse.

6. Report Sexual Abuse (6)

A. The sexual abuse was reported to the appropriate child protection agency.

B. Criminal justice officials have been informed of the sexual abuse.

C. The client has been referred for a medical examination to determine whether there are any physical signs of the sexual abuse and/or evaluate any health problems that may have resulted from the sexual abuse.

D. The client and family members were supportive of the sexual abuse being reported to the appropriate child protection agency or criminal justice officials.

E. The client and family members objected to the sexual abuse being reported to the appropriate child protection agency or criminal justice officials.

7. Assess Veracity of Sexual Abuse Charges (7)

A. A consultation was held with the child protection case manager and criminal justice officials to assess the veracity of the client's sexual abuse charges.

B. A consultation was held with the physician who examined the client to assess the veracity of the sexual abuse charges.

C. A consultation held with the child protection case manager, criminal justice officials, and physician has provided strong support for the client's reports that they have been sexually abused.

D. A consultation held with the child protection case manager, criminal justice officials, and physician has provided inconclusive evidence as to whether the client has been sexually abused.

E. A consultation held with the child protection case manager, criminal justice officials, and physician has provided little or no support for the client's reports that they have been sexually abused.

8. Assess Level of Insight (8)

A. The client's level of insight toward the presenting problems was assessed.

B. The client was assessed in regard to the syntonic versus dystonic nature of their insight about the presenting problems.

C. The client was noted to demonstrate good insight into the problematic nature of the behavior and symptoms.

D. The client was noted to be in agreement with others' concerns and is motivated to work on change.

E. The client was noted to be ambivalent regarding the problems described and is reluctant to address the issues as a concern.

F. The client was noted to be resistant regarding acknowledgment of the problem areas, is not concerned about them, and has no motivation to make changes.

9. Assess for Correlated Disorders (9)

A. The client was assessed for evidence of research-based correlated disorders.

B. The client was assessed in regard to the level of vulnerability to suicide.

C. The client was identified as having a comorbid disorder, and treatment was adjusted to account for these concerns.

D. The client has been assessed for any correlated disorders, but none were found.

10. Assess for Culturally Based Confounding Issues (10)

A. The client was assessed for age-related issues that could help to better understand their clinical presentation.

B. The client was assessed for gender-related issues that could help to better understand their clinical presentation.

C. The client was assessed for cultural syndromes, cultural idioms of distress, or culturally based perceived causes that could help to better understand their clinical presentation.

D. Alternative factors have been identified as contributing to the client's currently defined "problem behavior," and these were taken into account in regard to treatment.

E. Culturally based factors that could help to account for the client's currently defined "problem behavior" were investigated, but no significant factors were identified.

11. Assess Severity of Impairment (11)

A. The severity of the client's impairment was assessed to determine the appropriate level of care.

B. The client was assessed in regard to impairment in social, relational, and educational endeavors.

C. It was reflected to the client that the impairment appears to create mild to moderate effects on the client's functioning.

D. It was reflected to the client that the impairment appears to create severe to very severe effects on the client's functioning.

E. The client was continuously assessed for the severity of impairment, as well as the efficacy and appropriateness of treatment.

12. Assess for Pathogenic Care (12)

A. The home, school, and community of the client were assessed for pathogenic care and concerns.

B. The client's various environments were assessed for the persistent disregard of the child's needs, repeated changes in caregivers, limited opportunities for stable attachment, harsh discipline, or other grossly inept care.

C. Pathogenic care was identified and the treatment plan included strategies for managing or correcting these concerns and protecting the child.

D. No pathogenic care was identified, and this was reflected to the client and caregivers.

13. Assess for PTSD (13)

A. A structured assessment was conducted to help identify the presence of symptoms of posttraumatic stress disorder (PTSD).

B. No symptoms of PTSD were identified, and this has been reflected to the client and parents.

C. Symptoms of PTSD have been identified, and this was reflected to the family members.

D. Treatment has been focused onto the client's PTSD symptoms.

14. Reveal Sexual Abuse to Family (14)

A. A conjoint therapy session was held to reveal the sexual abuse to key family member(s) or caregiver(s).

B. A family-therapy session was held to eliminate the secrecy about the client's sexual abuse.

C. A conjoint therapy session was held to reveal the nature, frequency, and duration of the sexual abuse to key family member(s) and/or caregiver(s).

15. Confront Denial Within Family System (15)

A. The family members' denial about the impact of the sexual abuse was confronted and challenged so that they can begin to provide the support the client needs in order to make a healthy adjustment.

B. The family members' denial of the sexual abuse was strongly challenged, and responsibility for the sexual abuse was placed on the perpetrator.

C. The therapy session was helpful in working through the family members' denial surrounding the sexual abuse, and they agreed to follow through with the necessary treatment and support.

D. The therapy session was not successful in working through the family members' denial of the sexual abuse.

16. Verbalize Belief of Abuse (16)

A. A family session was held with key members of the client's family.

B. The family session gave the family the time to provide support and verbalize their belief that the client had been abused.

C. The family members were able to provide support to the client and they were reinforced for this helpful step.

D. The family made statements of disbelief regarding the client's abuse and were redirected.

17. Protect Client and Other Children (17)

A. A consultation was held with the criminal justice officials and the child protection case manager about implementing the necessary steps to protect the client and other children in the home from future sexual abuse.

B. A family-therapy session was held to discuss and identify the appropriate steps that need to be taken to protect the client and other children in the home from future sexual abuse.

C. An individual-therapy session was held to provide the client with the opportunity to identify what steps they feel need to occur in order to feel safe.

18. Consider Placement of Client (18)

A. A consultation was held with the criminal justice officials and the child protection case manager to assess whether it is safe for the client to remain in the home or if they should be removed.

B. The decision was made that the client be allowed to remain in the home, while the perpetrator was required to leave.

C. The decision was made to allow the client to continue living in the home because it was felt that the nonabusive parent would take the necessary steps to protect them from further sexual abuse.

D. A recommendation was made that the client be placed in a foster home to ensure their protection from further sexual abuse.

E. A recommendation was made that the client be placed in a residential treatment program to ensure their protection from further sexual abuse and provide treatment for emotional/behavioral problems.

19. Empower Client (19)

A. Today's therapy session sought to empower the client by reinforcing the steps necessary to protect self.

B. Today's therapy session sought to empower the client by praising and reinforcing their decision to report the sexual abuse to the appropriate individuals or agencies.

C. The client was strongly encouraged to contact a child protection hotline, police, or the therapist if they are ever sexually abused in the future.

D. The client was helped to identify a list of safe places where they can go if feeling at risk of sexual abuse.

E. The client was taught effective assertiveness and communication skills to help them stand up for self and feel safe.

20. Establish Boundaries Within Family System (20)

A. The family members were counseled about establishing appropriate parent-child boundaries to ensure protection of the client and other children in the home from further sexual abuse.

B. The family members were counseled about establishing appropriate adult-child boundaries regarding privacy, physical contact, and verbal content.

C. An assessment of the family system revealed weak and blurred parent-child boundaries.

D. Today's therapy session sought to strengthen the roles and responsibilities of the nonabusive parent in enforcing appropriate privacy, physical contact, verbal content, and adult-child boundaries.

E. It was noted that appropriate boundaries have not been established within the family system, and the nonabusive parent was directed to enforce appropriate privacy, physical contact, verbal contact, and adult-child boundaries.

21. Explore Stress Factors or Precipitating Events (21)

A. Today's therapy session explored the stress factors or precipitating events that contributed to emergence of the sexual abuse.

B. Today's therapy session explored the family dynamics that have contributed to emergence of the sexual abuse.

C. Today's therapy session was helpful in identifying the stress factors or precipitating events that contributed to emergence of the sexual abuse.

D. Today's therapy session identified several family dynamics that have contributed to emergence of the sexual abuse.

E. The family members were taught positive coping strategies and effective problem-solving approaches to help them manage stress and overcome the identified problems.

22. Gather Detail Where Abuse Occurred in Home (22)

A. The client was given an assignment to draw a diagram of the house where the sexual abuse occurred, indicating where everyone slept and describing what it was like to live there, to provide greater insight into the factors or precipitating events that led up to the sexual abuse.

B. Active listening skills were used as the client recounted the story of the sexual abuse as they shared the diagram of the house where the sexual abuse occurred.

C. The client's drawing of where the sexual abuse occurred was reviewed and found to be helpful in identifying the precipitating events leading up to the sexual abuse.

D. The client shared a diagram of the house where the sexual abuse occurred but was guarded in talking about details or the precipitating events that led up to the sexual abuse; they were supported and encouraged.

E. The client refused to complete the assignment of drawing a diagram of where the sexual abuse occurred, and the reasons for this were reviewed.

23. Construct Family Sex Abuse Genogram (23)

A. The client and family members were assisted in constructing a multigenerational family genogram that identified the history of sexual abuse within the family.

B. The construction of the multigenerational family genogram helped the client to realize that other family members have been sexually abused and that they are not alone.

C. The construction of the multigenerational family genogram helped the perpetrator recognize the cycle of repeated boundary violations within the extended family.

D. The construction of a multigenerational family genogram helped the family members voice their commitment to taking the necessary steps to end the cycle of sexual abuse within their family.

E. The client and family tended to downplay any issues of multigenerational family sexual abuse issues and were directed to provide more complete information in this area.

24. Assign Letter to Perpetrator (24)

A. The client was given a homework assignment to write a letter to the perpetrator and bring it to the following therapy session for processing.

B. The client was assigned "Letter of Empowerment" in the *Child Psychotherapy Homework Planner* (Jongsma, Peterson, McInnis, & Bruce).

C. It was reflected that the client expressed strong feelings of sadness, hurt, and disappointment in their letter to the perpetrator.

D. It was reflected that the client expressed strong feelings of anger about the sexual abuse in their letter to the perpetrator.

E. The client was supported as they expressed a willingness to share the letter directly with the perpetrator.

F. After processing the letter, the client reported that they are not ready to share thoughts and feelings about the sexual abuse directly with the perpetrator.

25. Utilize "Angry Tower" Technique (25)

A. The "Angry Tower" technique (Saxe) was used to help the client express feelings of anger about the past sexual abuse.

B. The client was provided with support as they vented strong feelings of anger toward the perpetrator while playing the "Angry Tower" game.

C. Using the "Angry Tower" technique, the client expressed strong feelings of anger toward the nonabusive parent for failing to protect them from the sexual abuse.

D. The "Angry Tower" technique has helped the client to express and work through feelings of anger surrounding the past sexual abuse.

26. Teach Guided Fantasy and Imagery Techniques (26)

A. Guided fantasy and imagery techniques were taught to help the client identify and express thoughts and feelings associated with the sexual abuse.

B. The client reported a positive response to the use of guided fantasy and imagery techniques to help them identify thoughts, feelings, and unmet needs associated with the sexual abuse.

C. Guided fantasy and imagery techniques were used, but the client still had difficulty identifying and expressing thoughts, feelings, and unmet needs associated with the sexual abuse.

27. Assign Readings (27)

A. *A Very Touching Book. . .For Little People and for Big People* (Hindman) was read to the client in today's therapy session to help them verbalize feelings about the past sexual abuse and identify steps that they can take to feel protected or empowered.

B. *I Can't Talk About It* (Sanford) was read to help the client verbalize feelings about the past sexual abuse.

C. *It's Not Your Fault* (Jance) was read to reinforce that the client is not responsible for the sexual abuse.

D. *Healing Days: A Guide for Kids Who Have Experienced Trauma* (Farber Straus) was read to provide the client with a guide to talk about and process trauma.

E. The key concepts from the assigned readings were processed with the client.

F. The assigned reading(s) helped the client to identify and express feelings about the past sexual abuse.

28. Utilize Eye Movement Desensitization Reprocessing (28)

A. Eye movement desensitization and reprocessing (EMDR) techniques were used to help reduce the client's emotional distress.

B. EMDR techniques were found to be useful in alleviating the client's emotional distress, and this was continued as necessary.

C. The client was unable to find usefulness through EMDR to alleviate emotional distress, and therapy was continued as usual.

29. Teach Calming Skills (29)

A. The client was taught calming skills during today's session.

B. The client was taught about progressive muscle relaxation, guided imagery, and slow diaphragmatic breathing.

C. The client used calming exercises to help manage painful emotions when recalling or reminded of past abuse.

D. The client's success at using calming skills was reinforced.

30. Promote Technology Tools (30)

A. The client and parents were encouraged to use available technology to teach mindfulness relaxation techniques to minimize anxiety, anger, or shame when experiencing memories or flashbacks connected to the abuse.

B. The client and parents were assisted in finding suitable technology to teach mindfulness relaxation techniques, such as the Calm App, Cosmic Kid Yoga YouTube channel, or Sesame Street Mindfulness video.

C. The client identified positive use of technological tools to develop mindfulness relaxation techniques.

D. The client was unable or unwilling to use technological tools to teach mindfulness relaxation techniques, and these techniques were taught in session instead.

31. Explore/Resolve Guilt and Shame (31)

A. The client's feelings of guilt and shame connected to the sexual abuse were explored.

B. The client was given the "You Are Not Alone" exercise from the *Child Psychotherapy Homework Planner* (Jongsma, Peterson, McInnis, & Bruce) to help them express feelings connected to the sexual abuse and decrease feelings of guilt and shame.

C. The client reported that they found the "You Are Not Alone" exercise helpful in reducing feelings of guilt, shame, anger, and fear.

D. The grief/shame exercise helped the client talk about how the sexual abuse has affected their life.

E. The client did not follow through with completing the grief/shame exercise and the assignment was given again.

F. The "You Are Not Alone" story was read in today's group-therapy session to facilitate a discussion among group members about how sexual abuse has affected their lives.

32. Assign Reading Material Regarding Sexual Addiction and Recovery from Sexual Abuse (32)

A. The client's parents were assigned reading material to increase their knowledge of sexual abuse and recovery issues.

B. The client was assisted in reading *My Body Is Mine, My Feelings Are Mine: A Storybook About Body Safety for Young Children with an Adult Guidebook* (Hoke).

C. The parents were directed to read *When Your Child Has Been Molested: A Parent's Guide to Healing and Recovery* (Brohl & Potter).

D. The parents were directed to read *Helping Your Child Recover from Sexual Abuse* (Adams & Fey).

E. The client's parents and family members have read the assigned material and found it to be helpful in identifying ways they can help the client recover from the sexual abuse and in expanding their knowledge of sexually addictive behaviors.

F. The parents have failed to read the assigned material and were redirected to do so.

33. Facilitate Time Spent with Nonabusive Parent (33)

A. The disengaged, nonabusive parent was directed to spend more time with the client in leisure, school, or household activities.

B. The client and disengaged, nonabusive parent were assisted in identifying a list of activities that they would like to perform together.

C. The client was supported as they verbalized the need to spend greater time with the disengaged, nonabusive parent in leisure, school, or household activities.

D. The disengaged, nonabusive parent was reinforced for verbalizing a commitment to spend increased time with the client.

E. Today's therapy session explored the factors contributing to the distant relationship between the client and the nonabusive parent.

F. The disengaged, nonabusive parent has not increased time spent with the client in leisure, school, or household activities and was reminded about this necessary commitment.

34. Use Mutual Storytelling Technique with Nonabusive Parent (34)

A. The mutual storytelling technique was used in today's filial play therapy session to help establish a closer relationship between the nonabusive parent and the client.

B. Using a mutual storytelling technique, the client was able to share feelings about the past sexual abuse in the presence of the nonabusive parent.

C. Using a mutual storytelling technique, the nonabusive parent was helped to identify the client's feelings about the past sexual abuse.

D. The nonabusive parent was encouraged to give empathy and support for the client's expression of feelings about the past sexual abuse.

E. The client and nonabusive parent were encouraged to use the mutual storytelling technique to strengthen their relationship.

35. Confront Perpetrator (35)

A. The perpetrator's denial of the sexual abuse was confronted.

B. The client was helped to prepare to confront the perpetrator about the sexual abuse.

C. The client confronted the perpetrator about how the sexual abuse has negatively affected their life and feelings about self.

D. The perpetrator was confronted about minimizing the significance of the sexual abuse.

E. The perpetrator was confronted with the facts of the sexual abuse but continued to deny sexually abusing the client.

36. Conduct Apology Session (36)

A. The perpetrator was helped to prepare to apologize to the client and other family members about the sexual abuse.

B. Positive feedback was provided as the perpetrator apologized to the client and family members for the sexual abuse, taking full responsibility for the abuse.

C. The perpetrator listened appropriately to the client and family members' expressions of anger, hurt, and disappointment about the sexual abuse and then offered a sincere apology; the client, the family, and the perpetrator were supported through this task.

D. A decision was made to postpone the apology session because the perpetrator does not appear ready to offer a sincere or genuine apology to the client and family members.

37. Refer to Psychological Evaluation (37)

A. The perpetrator was referred to a psychological evaluation to rule out serious psychiatric disorder.

B. The perpetrator was referred to individual therapy with an experienced therapist working with those who have sexually harmed.

C. The perpetrator was referred to a sex offense specific group to address their inappropriate sexual behaviors.

D. The perpetrator has consistently attended the sex offense specific group, and their learning in this area was reviewed.

E. The perpetrator has been an active participant in the sex offense specific group and stated that it has helped them identify the factors contributing to their inappropriate sexual behaviors.

F. The perpetrator has failed to consistently attend the sex offense specific group and was redirected to do so.

38. Assign Forgiveness Letter/Forgiveness Exercise (38)

A. The client was given a homework assignment to write a forgiveness letter to the perpetrator and bring it to the following session for processing.

B. It was noted that the client's letter reflected readiness to offer forgiveness to the perpetrator and/or significant family member(s).

C. The client verbalized their forgiveness to the perpetrator and/or significant family member(s) in today's therapy session; they were supported for this growth.

D. After processing the client's letter, it was evident that the client is not ready to offer forgiveness to the perpetrator and/or significant family member(s).

39. Assign Letting Go Exercise (39)

A. The potential benefits of the process of letting go of anger and hurt were explored with the client.

B. A letting-go exercise was assigned in which the client would bury an anger list about the perpetrator.

C. The letting-go exercise was processed with the client and feelings were identified and expressed.

D. The client struggles with letting go of feelings of hurt and anger and is not able to reach this goal as yet; they were encouraged to do this when they are ready.

E. The client reports that they have successfully let go of feelings of hurt and anger regarding being an abuse survivor, and this was processed and supported.

40. Utilize Mutual Storytelling Technique (40)

A. The client actively participated in the mutual storytelling exercise.

B. The mutual storytelling technique was used to model constructive steps that the client can take to protect self and feel more empowered.

C. The client created a story using puppets, dolls, or stuffed animals that reflected feelings of helplessness and vulnerability.

D. The client was helped to create a story using puppets, dolls, or stuffed animals that taught them steps that they could take to feel safe and protected.

E. The client identified the mutual storytelling technique as being helpful in learning how to protect self.

41. Employ Child-Centered Play Therapy (41)

A. A child-centered play therapy approach was used to help the client begin to identify feelings surrounding the past sexual abuse.

B. The client was given unconditional positive regard, warm acceptance, and support while working through feelings surrounding the past sexual abuse in today's play therapy session.

C. The client's feelings were reflected as expressed in play, and these feelings were then related to feelings about the past sexual abuse.

D. The child-centered play therapy sessions have helped the client begin to express feelings about the past sexual abuse.

E. The child-centered play therapy sessions have helped the client work through many of feelings surrounding past sexual abuse.

42. Employ Sand Tray Therapy (42)

A. The sand tray therapy approach was used to reenact trauma scenes, express emotions connected to trauma, and reflect and interpret feelings expressed through symbolic play.

B. The client was able to use miniature toys, figurines and objects to express self in a calming setting.

C. The client used sand tray therapy to promote healing and was encouraged to continue this approach when appropriate.

D. The client found sand tray therapy to be unhelpful and treatment was returned to status quo.

43. Identify Emotions Through Art Techniques (43)

A. The client was asked to draw pictures of different emotions and was then asked to identify times when they experienced different emotions surrounding the sexual abuse.

B. The "Feelings and Faces" exercise from the *Child Psychotherapy Homework Planner* (Jongsma, Peterson, McInnis, & Bruce) was used to help the client express myriad emotions surrounding the past sexual abuse.

C. The client reported that the "Feelings and Faces" exercise helped them identify and express different emotions about the sexual abuse.

D. After completing the "Feelings and Faces" exercise, the client was able to express different emotions about the sexual abuse to family members or significant others.

E. The client failed to complete the "Feelings and Faces" exercise and was instructed again to do it.

44. Employ "Color Your Life" Technique (44)

    A. The "Color Your Life" technique (O'Connor) was employed to help the client identify and verbalize feelings about the sexual abuse.

    B. Using the "Color Your Life" technique, the client expressed strong feelings of sadness and hurt about the past sexual abuse.

    C. The "Color Your Life" technique helped the client identify and express feelings of anger about the past sexual abuse.

    D. The "Color Your Life" technique helped the client identify how the past sexual abuse made them feel anxious, fearful, and helpless.

    E. The results of the "Color Your Life" technique reflected the client's ambivalent feelings toward the perpetrator.

45. Play "Survivor's Journey" (45)

    A. The client was engaged in playing the game "Survivor's Journey" to help them feel empowered.

    B. It was reflected to the client that they made several empowering statements during the playing of "Survivor's Journey."

    C. The client's continued feelings of empowerment were supported and reinforced.

    D. Despite the use of the "Survivor's Journey" game, the client continues to display a lack of empowerment and was provided with remedial assistance in this area.

46. Refer to Equine Therapy (46)

    A. The client and parents were provided with the rationale for equine therapy of being able to practice asking and receiving help, regaining a sense of control, becoming more aware of body language, and developing more internal resources to reduce the impact of trauma on their life.

    B. The client and parents were interested in equine therapy techniques and a referral was made to an appropriate equine therapist.

    C. The client and parents were uninterested in equine therapy, and concepts were practiced within a regular session.

47. List Supportive People (47)

    A. The client was asked to develop a list of resource people outside of the family whom they can turn to for support, guidance, and affirmation.

    B. The client was given a homework assignment to seek support or guidance from at least one individual outside of their family before the next therapy session.

    C. Active listening skills were used as the client reported that they have benefited from receiving support, guidance, and affirmation from individuals outside of their family.

    D. It was noted that the support the client has received from resource people outside of the family has helped them cope with the trauma of the sexual abuse.

    E. The client has been hesitant to turn to resource people outside of the family for support, guidance, or affirmation because of their mistrust and was urged to do this in small steps.

48. **Refer to Survivor Group (48)**

   A. The client was referred to a survivor group with other children to assist them in realizing that they are not alone in having experienced sexual abuse.

   B. The client was given the directive to self-disclose at least once during the group-therapy session.

   C. The client's participation in the survivor group with other children has helped them realize that they are not alone in experiencing sexual abuse.

   D. The client has actively participated in the survivor group-therapy sessions and verbalized many of their feelings about the past sexual abuse.

   E. The client has offered support to other members of the survivor group when they have shared their thoughts and feelings about their own sexual abuse experiences.

   F. The client has not attended the sexual abuse survivor's group, and their reasons for not attending this group were processed.

49. **Reinforce Survivor Identification (49)**

   A. The client was provided with verbal reinforcement when they identified as a survivor.

   B. It was reflected to the client that they make many comments that display their identification as a survivor.

   C. The client rarely makes comments about seeing self as a survivor but was reinforced when they approximated these types of comments.

SLEEP DISTURBANCE

CLIENT PRESENTATION

1. **Emotional Distress and Demands About Sleep (1)**[*]
   A. The parents indicated that the client has difficulty falling asleep and makes repeated demands to sleep with them.
   B. The parents reported the client becomes emotionally distressed about their difficulty to fall or remain asleep.
   C. The client's incessant crying and leaving their bed has caused the parents to exceed their frustration tolerance level.
   D. The new strategies implemented by the parents and designed to reduce the client's distress have helped the client fall and stay asleep.

2. **Demands Made on Parents About Sleep (2)**
   A. The parents stated that they can only remember a few times when the client went to sleep without them making a long list of demands on them.
   B. The client's demands at bedtime have caused the parents to become sleep deprived and extremely frustrated.
   C. The parents reported a nightly listing of demands made by the client before they eventually fall asleep.
   D. The parents indicate that now the client falls asleep without difficulty or demands and remains asleep most nights.

3. **Distress About Frightening Dreams (3)**
   A. The parents indicated the client experiences frightening dreams that result in awakening, crying, heart racing, and then a fear of returning to sleep.
   B. The client reported details of dreams that caused them distress as the dreams involve threats to self or significant others.
   C. The client's frightening dreams have caused them to get very few good nights of rest, and therefore they are often tired and very irritable, which has negatively affected school performance.
   D. The parents report that the client is experiencing fewer frightening dreams and is getting more nights of uninterrupted rest.

4. **Walking in Apparent Sleep State (4)**
   A. Parents report that the client has repeatedly been found in a sleep state, walking about their house at different hours of the night.
   B. The parents expressed concern over the client's sleepwalking about the house.
   C. The client's walking about in an apparent sleep state has negatively affected parents' sleep and increased their fear about not being able to keep them safe.

---

[*]The numbers in parentheses correlate to the number of the Behavioral Definition statement in the companion chapter with the same title in the *Child Psychotherapy Treatment Planner*, Sixth Edition, by Jongsma, Peterson, McInnis, & Bruce (Wiley, 2023).

D. The client indicated that they cannot remember walking about in a sleep state, although parents tell them that it has happened.

E. The parents reported that the client has not had an incident of walking around in a sleep state for an extended period of time.

5. Abrupt Panicky Awakening Without Dream Recall (5)

A. The parents reported that the client frequently awakens abruptly with screaming and intense anxiety that they cannot comfort easily.

B. The client indicated they cannot recall any part of the dreams from which they awaken with screaming.

C. The intense anxiety and autonomic arousal caused by the client's unrecalled dreams have made them afraid to go to sleep at night.

D. The frequency of the client's abrupt awakening with panicky screaming has decreased as the client and parents have started addressing various issues in the family.

6. Prolonged Sleep or Excessive Day Napping (6)

A. The client's prolonged sleep pattern has not resulted in them feeling rested but instead very tired.

B. The parents indicated that the client's prolonged sleep at night and excessive daytime napping still leaves them continually tired.

C. Even though they sleep a lot, the client still indicates they feel tired all the time.

D. The parents indicate that the client has started to nap less and feel more rested and refreshed after their nighttime sleep.

INTERVENTIONS IMPLEMENTED

1. Establish Rapport (1)*

A. Caring was conveyed to the client through support, warmth, and empathy.

B. The client was provided with nonjudgmental support and a level of trust was developed.

C. The client was urged to feel safe in expressing sleep issues.

D. The client began to express feelings more freely as rapport and trust level have increased.

E. The client has continued to experience difficulty being open and direct about the expression of painful feelings; they were encouraged to use the safe haven of therapy to express these difficult issues.

2. Focus on Strengthening Therapeutic Relationship (2)

A. The relationship with the client was strengthened using empirically supported factors.

B. The relationship with the client was strengthened through the implementation of collaborative approach, agreement on goals, demonstration of empathy, verbalization of positive regard, and collection of client feedback.

---

*The numbers in parentheses correlate to the number of the Therapeutic Intervention statement in the companion chapter with the same title in the *Child Psychotherapy Treatment Planner*, Sixth Edition, by Jongsma, Peterson, McInnis, & Bruce (Wiley, 2023)

C. The client reacted positively to the relationship-strengthening measures taken.

D. The client verbalized feeling supported and understood during therapy sessions.

E. Despite attempts to strengthen the therapeutic relationship, the client reports feeling distant and misunderstood.

F. The client has indicated that sessions are not helpful and will be terminating therapy.

3. Assess Pre-Sleep and Sleep Patterns (3)

A. The client's pre-sleep and sleep patterns were explored with parents and client.

B. The client's pre-sleep and actual sleep patterns were assessed and key points for intervention were identified.

C. The client was assessed for latency to sleep onset, behaviors during the night, and number and duration of nighttime awakenings.

D. The client was assessed for their pattern of evening activities, bedtime fears and behavioral difficulties, bedroom environment, and abnormal events during sleep.

E. Strategies for intervening at the identified key points of the client's sleep behavior pattern were developed with the parent's assistance, and plans for implementation were made.

F. The parents' implementation of the strategies to aid the client's sleep induction was monitored, with redirection and encouragement being given as needed.

G. The client's sleep patterns have become more regular and less disturbing to the family routine; the benefits of this progress were reviewed.

4. Assess Daytime Lifestyle (4)

A. The client's daytime lifestyle was assessed in regard to its impact on their sleep pattern.

B. The client's activity level; school adjustment; and psychological, social, and family function were assessed.

C. Stressful life events were reviewed in regard to the impact that they may have had on the client's sleep pattern.

5. Assign Record of Sleep and Caregiver's Responses (5)

A. The parents were given a form and asked to chart data related to the client's presleep activity, sleep time, awakening occurrences, and the caregiver's response to the child.

B. The parents were assigned the exercise "Childhood Sleep Patterns" from the *Child Psychotherapy Homework Planner* (Jongsma, Peterson, McInnis, & Bruce).

C. The client's pre-sleep and sleep activity record was reviewed and assessed for overstimulation, caregiver reinforcement, and contributing stressors.

D. The assessment of the record was shared with the parents, noting incidents of overstimulation, caregiver reinforcement, and high stress.

E. Strategies to reduce the overstimulation, caregiver reinforcement, and contributing stressors were explored with parents.

F. The reduction in overstimulation, caregiver reinforcement, and stressors was noted to have resulted in a more consistent and less-disturbed sleep pattern for the client.

G. The parents' failure to consistently record data on the sleep behavior and response form was addressed and a commitment to do the charting thoroughly was elicited from them.

6. Refer for Sleep Study (6)

A. The client was referred for a sleep study involving polysomnography (PSG) to assess sleep architecture and physiologically based sleep disruptors.

B. The client has participated in a sleep study and the results were reviewed.

C. The client has not participated in the sleep study and the family was redirected to coordinate this.

7. Assess Role of Mental Health Disorder (7)

A. The client was assessed for the role of a possible mental health disorder as a contributor to the client's sleep disturbance.

B. The client's level of depression was assessed as a possible cause of their sleep disturbance.

C. The client's level of anxiety was assessed as a possible cause for their sleep disturbance.

D. The assessment concluded that a definite connection exists between the client's depression and sleep disturbance and recommended that the depression should be addressed in therapy.

E. The assessment concluded that depression does not play a significant role in the client's sleep disturbance.

F. The assessment strongly recommended that the client's depression should be treated as the primary problem because the sleep disturbance was a result of it.

8. Explore Recent Traumatic Events (8)

A. Recent traumatic events were explored with the client to determine the extent of their effect on sleeping.

B. No recent traumatic events were uncovered that could be the cause of the client's disturbed pattern of sleep.

C. The client's sleep disturbance was identified as being greatly affected by the recent traumatic events in their life.

D. The client and parents have reported less sleep disturbance since recent traumatic events have been processed.

E. The client was reluctant to talk about recent traumatic events and was encouraged to talk about them as they felt comfortable.

9. Explore for Sexual Abuse (9)

A. The issue of whether the client had been the victim of sexual abuse was gently explored.

B. The exploration of sexual abuse with the client uncovered several incidents where they were a victim of abuse.

C. The exploration of sexual abuse with the client and parents failed to uncover any past incidents of abuse.

D. The client was referred to a specialized program for victims of sexual abuse.

E. The sexual abuse was reported to the state's child protection services, as per local law and agency guidelines.

10. Probe Disturbing Dreams (10)

A. The client's disturbing dreams were probed for their possible relationship to life stressors.

B. The probing of the client's disturbing dreams established a connection between them and present stressors in their life.

C. No connection could be established between the client's disturbing dreams and stressors in their life.

D. It was noted that the client has begun to address their life stressors and now is experiencing less-disturbing dreams.

E. The client was reluctant to explore disturbing dreams and was encouraged to talk about these dreams as they are able to do so.

11. **Assess Level of Insight (11)**

A. The client's level of insight toward the presenting problems was assessed.

B. The client was assessed in regard to the syntonic versus dystonic nature of their insight about the presenting problems.

C. The client was noted to demonstrate good insight into the problematic nature of the behavior and symptoms.

D. The client was noted to be in agreement with others' concerns and is motivated to work on change.

E. The client was noted to be ambivalent regarding the problems described and is reluctant to address the issues as a concern.

F. The client was noted to be resistant regarding acknowledgment of the problem areas, is not concerned about them, and has no motivation to make changes.

12. **Assess for Correlated Disorders (12)**

A. The client was assessed for evidence of research-based correlated disorders.

B. The client was assessed in regard to the level of vulnerability to suicide.

C. The client was identified as having a comorbid disorder, and treatment was adjusted to account for these concerns.

D. The client has been assessed for any correlated disorders, but none were found.

13. **Assess for Culturally Based Confounding Issues (13)**

A. The client was assessed for age-related issues that could help to better understand their clinical presentation.

B. The client was assessed for gender-related issues that could help to better understand their clinical presentation.

C. The client was assessed for cultural syndromes, cultural idioms of distress, or culturally based perceived causes that could help to better understand their clinical presentation.

D. Alternative factors have been identified as contributing to the client's currently defined "problem behavior," and these were taken into account in regard to treatment.

E. Culturally based factors that could help to account for the client's currently defined "problem behavior" were investigated, but no significant factors were identified.

14. **Assess Severity of Impairment (14)**

A. The severity of the client's impairment was assessed to determine the appropriate level of care.

B. The client was assessed in regard to impairment in social, relational, and educational endeavors.

C. It was reflected to the client that the impairment appears to create mild to moderate effects on the client's functioning.

D. It was reflected to the client that the impairment appears to create severe to very severe effects on the client's functioning.

E. The client was continuously assessed for the severity of impairment, as well as the efficacy and appropriateness of treatment.

15. **Assess for Pathogenic Care (15)**

A. The home, school, and community of the client were assessed for pathogenic care and concerns.

B. The client's various environments were assessed for the persistent disregard of the child's needs, repeated changes in caregivers, limited opportunities for stable attachment, harsh discipline, or other grossly inept care.

C. Pathogenic care was identified and the treatment plan included strategies for managing or correcting these concerns and protecting the child.

D. No pathogenic care was identified, and this was reflected to the client and caregivers.

16. **Refer for Medication Evaluation (16)**

A. The client's need for antidepressant medication was discussed with the client's parents.

B. An evaluation for antidepressant medication was arranged for the client.

C. The client and parents cooperated and completed the evaluation for antidepressant medication.

D. The parents and client were asked to make a verbal commitment to follow through on all of the recommendations of the medication evaluation.

17. **Monitor Medication Adherence (17)**

A. The client's need to take the medication consistently as prescribed was explained and reinforced to the client and parents.

B. The client and parents were asked to report any side effects to the prescribing psychiatrist or to the therapist.

C. The client's medication was monitored for its effectiveness and for any possible side effects.

D. The client and parents were monitored for the client taking the medication consistently as prescribed.

E. The medication was noted to have a positive impact on the client's sleep pattern.

F. The medication has not been effective in improving the client's sleep pattern, and this was relayed to the prescribing clinician.

18. **Assess/Resolve Tension and Conflict Within Family (18)**

A. A family session was held to assess the level of conflict and tension present in the family unit.

B. The family members were asked to identify conflicts and areas of tension they see present in the family unit.

   C. The conflicts identified by family members were processed and resolved in the family-therapy session.

   D. Interventions were developed and implemented with the family to reduce the level of conflict and tension and their negative effect on the client's sleep.

   E. The reduction in family conflict was noted to help improve the client's sleeping pattern.

19. Assess Marital Dyad (19)

   A. Today's session was a meeting with the parents to assess the level of stress that is present in their marital relationship.

   B. The parents were assisted in exploring the possible impact their marital conflict has on the client's sleep behavior.

   C. The parents were given a referral for marital counseling.

   D. The parents' follow-through and progress in marital therapy were monitored, with progress being affirmed.

   E. Positive feedback was provided as the parents have worked to decrease the level of stress in their relationship, which has alleviated many of the client' sleep problems.

20. Implement Behaviorally Based Approach (20)

   A. A behaviorally based treatment approach was implemented.

   B. The parents were encouraged to use techniques as reviewed by Mindell in *Sleeping Through the Night*.

   C. Psychoeducation regarding good sleep hygiene was provided.

   D. A rationale for major treatment interventions toward helping the child learn to fall asleep independently was reviewed.

   E. The parents were taught about consistent sleep-wake cycle, inconsistent bedroom routine, bedroom environment conducive to sleep, and a reduction in stimulation.

21. Establish Consistent Sleep-Wake Cycle (21)

   A. The parents were assisted in establishing a consistent sleep-wake cycle for the client.

   B. The parents were consulted with in regard to age-appropriate bedtimes, regular naps for infants and toddlers, and no more than a 1- to 2-hour difference between weekday and weekend bedtimes and wake times.

   C. The parents have attempted to establish a consistent sleep-wake cycle and they were reinforced for this.

   D. The parents were assisted in resolving problems with establishing a consistent sleep-wake cycle.

22. Develop Positive Stimulus Control Technique (22)

   A. The parents were assisted in developing a positive stimulus control technique for the client's bedtime.

   B. The parents were encouraged to use the same activities each night.

   C. The parents were encouraged to develop a consistent, pleasurable, and calming night-time routine that lasts no more than 20 to 30 minutes.

23. Educate About Sleep Hygiene (23)

A. The parents were educated regarding good sleep hygiene.

B. The parents were advised about creating a bedroom environment that is conducive to sleep, including being comfortable, cool, dark, and quiet.

C. The parents were encouraged to remove all technology that could be potentially arousing (e.g., televisions, computers, and cell phones).

24. Review Use of Caffeine (24)

A. All potential caffeinated products consumed by the child were reviewed.

B. The parents were encouraged to eliminate afternoon and evening use of caffeinated products.

25. Assess Fears of Being Alone (25)

A. The nature, severity, and origin of the client's fear of being alone in the bedroom were explored with the client.

B. The client was assisted in identifying all the reasons for their fears.

C. As the client has explored and faced their fear of being alone, the fear has been reduced; they were supported for overcoming this fear.

26. Establish Nightly Ritual (26)

A. The client and parents were assisted in establishing a nightly ritual that will help reduce the client's fears and induce calm before going to sleep.

B. The parents were provided with specific examples of nightly rituals (e.g., parents tell bedtime story, build a fortress of stuffed animals around the client's bed, have the mother spray perfume on daughter's wrist to remind her of parent's close proximity).

C. The parents were assigned "Reduce Nighttime Fears" from the *Child Psychotherapy Homework Planner* (Jongsma, Peterson, McInnis, & Bruce).

D. The parents were directed to use the bedtime ritual on a nightly basis.

E. The parents were encouraged to gradually extinguish and remove "safety cues" over time as the child's fears are resolved.

27. Encourage Use of Family Pet (27)

A. The parents were encouraged to allow the family pet to sleep in the client's room to reduce nighttime fears and anxiety.

B. The parents agreed to allow the family pet to sleep in the client's room at night to reduce nighttime fears and anxiety and were supported for this decision.

28. Encourage Parents to Set Limits (28)

A. The parents were assisted in identifying specific areas where they were vulnerable to the client's manipulative behaviors.

B. The parents were helped to develop and implement ways to set firm limits on the client's manipulative behaviors.

C. Role-plays and behavioral rehearsal techniques were used to build the parents' skill and confidence in implementing the new firm behavioral limits.

D. The parents were monitored on their consistent implementation of the new firm limits and given encouragement and redirection as needed.

E. The client's manipulative behaviors have decreased as the parents have consistently followed through with setting new firm behavioral limits; they were encouraged to continue to set these limits.

F. The parents have not regularly set limits on the client's manipulative behavior and were redirected to do so.

29. Devise Reward and Contingency Contract (29)

A. A reward system was designed to reinforce the client for achieving goals regarding sleeping in their own bed and not entering their parents' bedroom at night.

B. The client and parents were helped to develop a list of possible rewards that could be used to reinforce the client for achieving sleep goals.

C. The parents were assigned "Clear Rules, Positive Reinforcement, Appropriate Consequences" in the *Adolescent Psychotherapy Homework Planner* (Jongsma, Peterson, McInnis, & Bruce).

D. The implementation of the reward system was noted to be helping the client achieve goals of sleeping alone at night.

E. The parents have not instituted regular use of the reward system for appropriate sleep patterns and were redirected to use this technique.

30. Brainstorm Negative Consequences (30)

A. The parents were helped to brainstorm a potential list of negative consequences the client will receive if they engage in manipulative behavior to avoid going to bed on time.

B. The parents struggled to identify a helpful list of negative consequences and were provided with specific examples (e.g., earlier bedtime next evening, removal of privileges such as television or video games).

C. The parents were assisted in selecting a specific consequence for the client's manipulative behavior to avoid going to bed on time.

D. The parents were encouraged to follow through consistently if the client engages in misbehavior.

E. Positive feedback was provided as the parents have regularly followed through on the negative consequences for the client's misbehavior.

F. The parents have not followed through on using the negative consequences for manipulative behavior, and the reasons for this were reviewed and processed.

31. Develop Checking Procedure (31)

A. The parents were assisted in reviewing the optimal checking procedure.

B. The parents were encouraged to check on the child at agreed-upon intervals until the child falls asleep.

C. The parents were allowed to start with as frequent checks as may be needed, based on parental tolerance and the child temperament.

D. After identifying the agreed-upon intervals at which the child will be checked, the parents were encouraged to maintain this pattern.

32. **Encourage Calm and Consistent Checking Procedure (32)**

   A. The parents were encouraged to calmly and consistently respond to the child during the checking procedure.

   B. The parents were reminded that the child will need to develop self-soothing skills without the parents using interventions to induce sleep.

   C. The parents were reinforced for their adherence to calm, consistent, regularly scheduled checking of the child.

   D. The parents reported that they have struggled with maintaining the frequency and demeanor of the checks on the child and were provided with additional assistance in this area.

33. **Teach About Progressive Time Delays (33)**

   A. The parents were taught about a gradual extinction procedure involving progressive time delays between responding to bedtime protests or refusals.

   B. The parents were taught to use increasingly shorter intervals of comfort when checking on a crying or protesting child.

   C. The parents were recommended to read portions of *Solve Your Child's Sleep Problems* (Ferber).

   D. The parents were reinforced for their use of gradual extinction procedures.

   E. The parents have struggled to appropriately use the gradual extinction procedures and were provided with corrective feedback in this area.

34. **Teach Nongraduated Extinction (34)**

   A. The parents were taught about an extinction procedure in which the parents put their child to bed at a designated time and ignore the child's protests.

   B. The parents were assisted with support regarding their struggles with ignoring the child's protests.

35. **Review Record of Response to Interventions (35)**

   A. The parents were assigned to keep a written record of the child's adherence to relevant therapeutic interventions.

   B. The parents' record of the child's adherence to relative therapeutic interventions was reviewed.

   C. The parents were reinforced for successful implementation of interventions.

   D. The parents were assisted in resolving obstacles to the interventions.

36. **Teach Scheduled Awakening Procedure (36)**

   A. The parents were taught about a scheduled awakening procedure in which the parents awaken the child approximately 15 minutes before their typical nightly awakening times.

   B. The parents were encouraged to continue with the scheduled awaking procedure for 7 days, then stop and assess effectiveness.

   C. The scheduled awakening procedure has been gradually tapered.

37. Teach Positive Self-Talk (37)

A. The client's irrational fears were identified and confronted.

B. The client was taught the technique of positive, realistic self-talk and assisted in developing ways that they could implement it with their irrational fears.

C. Role-play and behavioral rehearsal were utilized to give the client the opportunity to practice positive, realistic self-talk on fears.

D. The client was given encouragement and verbal affirmation when they used positive self-talk on their fears.

E. The client's use of positive, realistic self-talk was identified as helping to diminish the impact of fear on sleep.

38. Teach Relaxation Skills (38)

A. The client was trained in relaxation skills, both with and without the use of an audiotape.

B. The client was assisted in practicing relaxation to increase the ability to use the skill to induce sleep.

C. The client was recommended to read portions of *The Relaxation and Stress Reduction Workbook for Kids* (Shapiro & Sprague).

D. The client was assigned "Deep Breathing Exercise" in the *Child Psychotherapy Homework Planner* (Jongsma, Peterson, McInnis, & Bruce).

E. The client was assigned "Progressive Muscle Relaxation" in the *Adolescent Psychotherapy Homework Planner* (Jongsma, Peterson, McInnis, & Bruce).

F. The client's use of relaxation was monitored, with positive affirmation being given to them for using the skill on a consistent basis to induce sleep.

G. Consistent use of the relaxation exercise was reinforced because it has helped the client more effectively cope with fears and anxieties.

H. The client has not used the relaxation skill to help cope with fears and anxieties and was redirected to do so.

39. Train in Use of Relaxation Tapes (39)

A. The client was trained to use relaxation tapes to self-calm as preparation for sleep.

B. The client was reinforced as they made a commitment to using the tapes on a nightly basis as part of preparation for sleep.

C. The client's follow-through on using the relaxation tapes to induce sleep was monitored and redirection was given as needed.

D. The client's consistent use of the relaxation tapes in preparation for sleep was noted to have improved their ability to fall and stay asleep.

E. The client has not consistently used relaxation techniques in preparation for sleep and was redirected to do so.

40. Teach Redirection of Dream (40)

A. The client was taught to reduce anxiety and fear after awakening from nightmares by visualizing how the dream might end on a positive note.

B. The client was supported as they identified several ways to visualize a nightmare changing to a positive dream.

C. The client was provided with specific examples of how to change a nightmare to a positive dream (e.g., visualize their mother or father coming to the rescue; client calls the police who arrest intruder, robber, or perpetrator in the dream).

D. The client was positively reinforced for use of the technique of changing the nightmare into a positive dream.

E. The client has not used the positive dream technique and was assisted in developing ways to implement this technique.

41. Administer EMG Biofeedback (41)

A. Electromyographic (EMG) biofeedback was administered to the client to train and reinforce successful relaxation response.

B. The client's response to EMG biofeedback was assessed and monitored for its effectiveness.

C. The client reported being able to relax more consistently and effectively since the EMG training, which has resulted in an improvement in the quality of sleep.

D. The client has not been able to consistently and effectively relax despite the use of EMG biofeedback training; the biofeedback training skills were reviewed to determine why this has failed.

42. Utilize Play Therapy Techniques (42)

A. Client-centered play therapy techniques were utilized to help the client express and resolve feelings and emotional conflicts.

B. A psychoanalytic play therapy approach was used to access the client's emotional conflicts and to explore healthy ways to resolve them.

C. The client was supported as they took an active role in the play therapy session.

D. Play therapy techniques have helped the client explore and resolve emotional conflicts.

43. Interpret Play Therapy Behavior (43)

A. The client's play therapy behavior was interpreted as a reflection of feelings toward family members.

B. The client embraced the interpretation of play therapy behavior as a reflection of their feelings toward family members.

C. The client rejected the interpretation of play therapy behavior as a reflection of their feelings toward parents.

D. The client accepted the interpretation of play therapy behavior and identified feelings they have toward specific family members.

SOCIAL ANXIETY

CLIENT PRESENTATION

1. Lack of Eye Contact (1)*

A. The parents and teachers report that the client displays very little eye contact during social interactions with others.

B. The client displayed poor eye contact during today's therapy session.

C. The client demonstrated satisfactory to good eye contact with individuals around whom they feel comfortable but exhibits poor eye contact with unfamiliar people.

D. The client maintained good eye contact during today's therapy session.

E. The parents and teachers report that the client consistently maintains good eye contact.

2. Quiet and Reserved (1)

A. The client reported a history of being quiet and reserved in the majority of social interactions.

B. The client was very quiet in today's therapy session and initiated few conversations.

C. The client often does not respond to overtures from other people.

D. The client has started to appear more at ease in the therapy sessions, as evidenced by the increased number of conversations that they initiate.

E. The client was much more open and talkative in today's therapy session.

3. Shyness/Social Anxiety (2)

A. The client described self as being shy and anxious in many social situations.

B. The client appeared anxious (e.g., hand tremors, lack of eye contact, fidgeting, restless, stammering) and inhibited during today's therapy session.

C. The client's social anxiety has gradually started to diminish, and they report feeling more at ease in conversations with others.

D. The client reported feeling confident and relaxed in the majority of recent social interactions.

E. The client has interacted socially with peers on a regular, consistent basis without excessive fear or anxiety.

4. Avoidance of Unfamiliar People (2)

A. The client has consistently avoided contact with unfamiliar people.

B. The client expressed feelings of anxiety about interacting with unfamiliar people.

C. The client has started to initiate more conversations with unfamiliar people.

D. The client has initiated social contacts with unfamiliar people on a consistent basis.

---

*The numbers in parentheses correlate to the number of the Behavioral Definition statement in the companion chapter with the same title in the *Child Psychotherapy Treatment Planner*, Sixth Edition, by Jongsma, Peterson, McInnis, & Bruce (Wiley, 2023).

5. **Social Isolation/Withdrawal (3)**

   A. The client described a persistent pattern of withdrawing or self-isolating from most social situations.

   B. The client acknowledged that social withdrawal interferes with their ability to establish and maintain friendships.

   C. The client has gradually started to socialize with a wider circle of peers.

   D. The client has become more outgoing and interacts with peers on a regular, consistent basis.

6. **Excessive Isolated Activities (3)**

   A. The client has spent an excessive or inordinate amount of time involved in isolated activities, instead of socializing with peers.

   B. The client verbalized an understanding of how excessive involvement in isolated activities interferes with their chances of establishing friendships.

   C. The client reports spending less time in isolated activities and starting to seek out interactions with peers.

   D. The client has achieved a healthy balance between time spent in isolated activities and social interactions with others.

7. **No Close Friendships (4)**

   A. The client described a history of having few to no close friendships.

   B. The client does not have any close friends at the present time.

   C. The client expressed feelings of sadness and loneliness about not having any close friends.

   D. The client has begun to take steps (e.g., greet others, compliment others, make positive self-statements) to try to establish close friendships.

   E. The client has now established close friendships at school and/or in the community.

8. **Enmeshed Family Relationships (4)**

   A. The client has established an enmeshed relationship with parents that interferes with opportunities to socialize with peers.

   B. The parents verbally recognized how they reinforce the client's excessive dependency at the expense of establishing peer friendships.

   C. The parents have encouraged the client to become more independent.

   D. The parents have reinforced the client's positive social behavior and set limits on overly dependent behavior.

   E. The client has achieved a healthy balance between socializing with peers and spending time with family members.

9. **Hypersensitivity to Criticism/Rejection (5)**

   A. The client has been very hesitant to become involved with others for fear of being met by criticism, disapproval, or perceived signs of rejection.

   B. The client described a history of experiencing excessive or undue criticism, disapproval, and rejection from parental figures.

   C. The client acknowledged that they tend to overreact to the slightest sign of criticism, rebuff, or rejection and subsequently withdraw from other people.

D. The client has begun to tolerate criticism or rebuff from others more effectively.

E. The client has continued to interact with others even in the face of criticism, disapproval, or perceived slights from others.

10. Excessive Need for Reassurance (6)

A. The client has been very reluctant to become involved with others unless they receive strong signs of assurance that they are liked or accepted.

B. The client has often sought reassurance from others in order to feel positive about self.

C. The client has started to reassure self with positive self-talk instead of turning excessively to others for approval and affirmation.

D. The client has achieved a healthy balance between self-affirming and seeking affirmation from others.

11. Reluctance to Take Risks (7)

A. The client has been reluctant to engage in new activities or take personal risks because of the potential for embarrassment or humiliation.

B. The client verbalized a desire to engage in new activities or take healthy risks to help improve self-esteem and develop friendships.

C. The client has started to take healthy risks in order to find enjoyment, build self-esteem, and establish friendships.

D. The client has engaged in new activities and assumed healthy risks without excessive fear of embarrassment or humiliation.

12. Negative Self-Image (8)

A. The client's negative self-image and lack of confidence have interfered with the ability to establish friendships.

B. The client verbalized several self-derogatory remarks and compared self unfavorably to others.

C. The client shared their viewpoint of self as being socially unattractive.

D. The client's increased confidence in self has helped them be more outgoing.

E. The client has consistently verbalized positive statements about self in the presence of others.

13. Poor Social Skills (8)

A. The client has established poor social skills and presents as socially immature.

B. The client has lacked awareness and sensitivity to the social cues and interpersonal nuances that are necessary to build positive peer friendships.

C. The client has started to develop an awareness of the social skills needed to build meaningful friendships.

D. The client has displayed good social skills in recent interactions with peers and adults.

E. The client has developed a number of essential social skills that have enhanced the quality of interpersonal relationships.

14. Lack of Assertiveness (9)

A. The client historically has much difficulty being assertive in social situations where it is indicated.

B. The client has generally avoided any social situations that involve the potential for conflict.

C. The client is beginning to be assertive more often instead of withdrawing from interpersonal problems or conflicts.

D. The client has recently asserted self in an effective manner during conflict with others.

15. **Family History of Excessive Criticism (9)**

A. The client reported a history of receiving undue or excessive criticism from family members.

B. The client appeared sad, anxious, and upset when describing the criticism that they have received from family members in the past.

C. The parents acknowledged that their overly harsh or critical remarks have contributed to the client's social anxiety, timidity, and low self-esteem.

D. The client was assertive with parents about their making overly critical remarks and asked them to cease making derogatory remarks in the future.

E. The parents have increased the frequency of their positive statements toward the client and refrained from making any overly critical or hostile remarks about the client.

16. **Physiological Distress (10)**

A. The client's social anxiety has been manifested in heightened physiological distress (e.g., increased heart rate, profuse sweating, dry mouth, muscular tension, and trembling).

B. The client appeared visibly anxious (i.e., trembling, shaking, sweating, tense, and rigid) when talking about social relationships.

C. The client reported that they have recently experienced less physiological distress when interacting with others.

D. The client has been able to consistently interact with other people in a variety of social settings without experiencing any physiological distress.

INTERVENTIONS IMPLEMENTED

1. **Establish Rapport (1)***

A. Caring was conveyed to the client through support, warmth, and empathy.

B. The client was provided with nonjudgmental support, and a level of trust was developed.

C. The client was urged to feel safe in expressing social anxiety issues.

D. The client began to express feelings more freely as rapport and trust level have increased.

E. The client has continued to experience difficulty being open and direct about their expression of painful feelings; the client was encouraged to use the safe haven of therapy to express these difficult issues.

---

*The numbers in parentheses correlate to the number of the Therapeutic Intervention statement in the companion chapter with the same title in the *Child Psychotherapy Treatment Planner*, Sixth Edition, by Jongsma, Peterson, McInnis, & Bruce (Wiley, 2023).

2. **Focus on Strengthening Therapeutic Relationship (2)**
   A. The relationship with the client was strengthened using empirically supported factors.
   B. The relationship with the client was strengthened through the implementation of collaborative approach, agreement on goals, demonstration of empathy, verbalization of positive regard, and collection of client feedback.
   C. The client reacted positively to the relationship-strengthening measures taken.
   D. The client verbalized feeling supported and understood during therapy sessions.
   E. Despite attempts to strengthen the therapeutic relationship, the client reports feeling distant and misunderstood.
   F. The client has indicated that sessions are not helpful and will be terminating therapy.

3. **Assess Nature of Social Discomfort Symptoms (3)**
   A. The client was asked about the frequency, intensity, duration, and history of social discomfort symptoms, fear, and avoidance.
   B. The Anxiety and Related Disorders Interview Schedule for DSM-5 (Brown & Barlow) was used to assess the client's social discomfort symptoms.
   C. The assessment of the client's social discomfort symptoms indicated that their symptoms are extreme and severely interfere with their life.
   D. The assessment of the client's social discomfort symptoms indicates that these symptoms are moderate and occasionally interfere with daily functioning.
   E. The results of the assessment of the client's social discomfort symptoms indicate that these symptoms are mild and rarely interfere with daily functioning.
   F. The results of the assessment of the client's social discomfort symptoms were reviewed with the client.

4. **Explore Social Discomfort Stimulus Situations (4)**
   A. The client was assisted in identifying specific stimulus situations that precipitate social discomfort symptoms.
   B. The client could not identify any specific stimulus situations that produce social discomfort; the client was helped to identify that they occur unexpectedly and without any pattern.
   C. The client was helped to identify that social discomfort symptoms occur when they are expected to perform basic social interaction expectations.

5. **Administer Social Anxiety Assessment (5)**
   A. The client was administered a measure of social anxiety to further assess the depth and breadth of social fears and avoidance.
   B. The client was administered the Social Phobia and Anxiety Inventory for Children (Beidel et al.).
   C. The result of the assessment of the social anxiety indicated a high level of social fears and avoidance; this was reflected to the client.
   D. The result of the assessment of the social anxiety indicated a medium level of social fears and avoidance; this was reflected to the client.

E. The result of the assessment of the social anxiety indicated a low level of social fears and avoidance; this was reflected to the client.

F. The client declined to participate in an assessment of social anxiety; the focus of treatment was turned to this resistance.

6. **Assess Level of Insight (6)**

A. The client's level of insight toward the presenting problems was assessed.

B. The client was assessed in regard to the syntonic versus dystonic nature of their insight about the presenting problems.

C. The client was noted to demonstrate good insight into the problematic nature of the behavior and symptoms.

D. The client was noted to be in agreement with others' concerns and is motivated to work on change.

E. The client was noted to be ambivalent regarding the problems described and is reluctant to address the issues as a concern.

F. The client was noted to be resistant regarding acknowledgment of the problem areas, is not concerned about them, and has no motivation to make changes.

7. **Assess for Correlated Disorders (7)**

A. The client was assessed for evidence of research-based correlated disorders.

B. The client was assessed in regard to the level of vulnerability to suicide.

C. The client was identified as having a comorbid disorder, and treatment was adjusted to account for these concerns.

D. The client has been assessed for any correlated disorders, but none were found.

8. **Assess for Culturally Based Confounding Issues (8)**

A. The client was assessed for age-related issues that could help to better understand their clinical presentation.

B. The client was assessed for gender-related issues that could help to better understand their clinical presentation.

C. The client was assessed for cultural syndromes, cultural idioms of distress, or culturally based perceived causes that could help to better understand their clinical presentation.

D. Alternative factors have been identified as contributing to the client's currently defined "problem behavior," and these were taken into account in regard to treatment.

E. Culturally based factors that could help to account for the client's currently defined "problem behavior" were investigated, but no significant factors were identified.

9. **Assess Severity of Impairment (9)**

A. The severity of the client's impairment was assessed to determine the appropriate level of care.

B. The client was assessed in regard to impairment in social, relational, and educational endeavors.

C. It was reflected to the client that the impairment appears to create mild to moderate effects on the client's functioning.

D. It was reflected to the client that the impairment appears to create severe to very severe effects on the client's functioning.

E. The client was continuously assessed for the severity of impairment, as well as the efficacy and appropriateness of treatment.

10. **Assess for Pathogenic Care (10)**

A. The home, school, and community of the client were assessed for pathogenic care and concerns.

B. The client's various environments were assessed for the persistent disregard of the child's needs, repeated changes in caregivers, limited opportunities for stable attachment, harsh discipline, or other grossly inept care.

C. Pathogenic care was identified and the treatment plan included strategies for managing or correcting these concerns and protecting the child.

D. No pathogenic care was identified, and this was reflected to the client and caregivers.

11. **Refer for Medication Evaluation (11)**

A. Arrangements were made for the client to have an evaluation for the purpose of considering psychotropic medication to alleviate social discomfort symptoms.

B. The client has followed through with seeing a prescriber for an evaluation of any organic causes for the anxiety and for the need for psychotropic medication to control the anxiety response.

C. The client has not cooperated with the referral to a prescriber for a medication evaluation and was encouraged to do so.

12. **Monitor Medication Adherence (12)**

A. The client reported that they have taken the prescribed medication consistently and that it has helped to control the anxiety; this was relayed to the prescribing clinician.

B. The client reported that they have not taken the prescribed medication consistently and were encouraged to do so.

C. The client reported taking the prescribed medication and stated that they have not noted any beneficial effect from it; this was reflected to the prescribing clinician.

D. The client was evaluated but was not prescribed any psychotropic medication by the clinician.

13. **Refer to Group Therapy (13)**

A. The client was referred to a small (closed enrollment) group for social anxiety.

B. The client was enrolled in a social anxiety group.

C. As no group was available, the client was provided with individual therapy based on the group-treatment model.

D. The client has participated in the group therapy for social anxiety; the experience was reviewed and processed.

E. The client has not been involved in group therapy for social anxiety concerns and was redirected to do so.

14. **Discuss Cognitive Behavioral Model (14)**
    A. A discussion was held regarding how social anxiety derives from cognitive biases and leads to unnecessary avoidance that maintains the fear.
    B. The client was provided with examples of cognitive biases that support social anxiety symptoms.
    C. The client was reinforced as they identified their own cognitive biases.
    D. The client was unable to identify any cognitive biases that support their anxiety symptoms and was provided with tentative examples in this area.

15. **Discuss Cognitive Restructuring (15)**
    A. A discussion was held about how cognitive restructuring and exposure serve to desensitize learned fear, build social skills and confidence, and reality-test biased thoughts.
    B. The client was reinforced as they displayed a clear understanding of the use of cognitive restructuring, exposure to desensitize learned fear, build social skills and confidence, and reality-test biased thoughts.
    C. The client did not display a clear understanding of the use of cognitive restructuring and exposure and was provided with remedial feedback in this area.

16. **Assign Information on Social Anxiety, Avoidance, and Treatment (16)**
    A. The parents were assigned to read information on social anxiety that explains the cycle of social anxiety and avoidance and provides a rationale for treatment.
    B. The parents were assigned information about social anxiety, avoidance, and treatment from *Helping Your Anxious Child* (Rapee et al.).
    C. The parents were directed to read portions of *The Shyness and Social Anxiety Workbook* (Antony & Swinson).
    D. The client was assigned to read portions of *Saying Goodbye to Being Shy* (Brozovich & Chase).
    E. The parents read the information on social anxiety, avoidance, and treatment, and key concepts were reviewed.
    F. The parents have not read the assigned material on social anxiety, avoidance, and treatment and were redirected to do so.

17. **Teach Anxiety Management Skills (17)**
    A. The client was taught anxiety management skills.
    B. The client was taught about staying focused on behavioral goals and riding the wave of anxiety.
    C. Techniques for muscular relaxation and paced diaphragmatic breathing were taught to the client.
    D. The client was assigned "Deep Breathing Exercise" in the *Child Psychotherapy Homework Planner* (Jongsma, Peterson, McInnis, & Bruce).
    E. The client was assigned "Progressive Muscle Relaxation" in the *Adolescent Psychotherapy Homework Planner* (Jongsma, Peterson, McInnis, & Bruce).
    F. The client and parents were recommended to read portions of *The Relaxation and Stress Reduction Workbook for Kids* (Shapiro & Sprague).

G. The client was reinforced for clear understanding and use of anxiety management skills.

H. The client has not used new anxiety management skills and was redirected to do so.

18. **Identify Underlying Assumptions (18)**

A. The client was assisted in identifying the self-talk and underlying assumptions that mediate social anxiety responses.

B. The client was taught the role of self-talk and underlying assumptions in precipitating emotional responses.

C. The client was assigned the exercise "Replace Negative Thoughts with Positive Self-Talk" from the *Child Psychotherapy Homework Planner* (Jongsma, Peterson, McInnis, & Bruce).

D. The client was reinforced as they verbalized an understanding of the self-talk and underlying assumptions that mediate anxiety responses.

E. The client was assisted in replacing biased messages with realistic cognitions.

F. The client failed to identify their self-talk and underlying assumptions and was provided with tentative examples in this area.

19. **Assign Exercises on Self-Talk (19)**

A. The client was assigned homework exercises in which they identify fearful self-talk and create reality-based alternatives.

B. The client was directed to do assignments from *The Shyness and Social Anxiety Workbook* (Antony & Swinson).

C. The client was directed to complete assignments from *Helping Your Anxious Child* (Rapee et al.).

D. The client's replacement of fearful self-talk with reality-based alternatives was critiqued.

E. The client was reinforced for successes at replacing fearful self-talk with reality-based alternatives.

F. The client was provided with corrective feedback for failures to replace fearful self-talk with reality-based alternatives.

G. The client has not completed assigned homework regarding fearful self-talk and was redirected to do so.

20. **Build Social and Communication Skills (20)**

A. Instruction, modeling, and role-playing were used to build the client's general social and communication skills.

B. Techniques from *Social Effectiveness Therapy for Children and Adolescents* (Beidel et al.) and *Goodbye to Being Shy* (Brozovich & Chase) were used to teach social and communication skills.

C. The client was assigned "Developing Conversational Skills" in the *Adolescent Psychotherapy Homework Planner* (Jongsma, Peterson, McInnis, & Bruce).

D. The client was assigned "Show Your Strengths" in the *Child Psychotherapy Homework Planner* (Jongsma, Peterson, McInnis, & Bruce).

E. Positive feedback was provided to the client for increased use of social and communication skills.

F. Despite the instruction, modeling, and role-playing about social and communication skills, the client continues to struggle with these techniques and was provided with additional feedback in this area.

21. Teach Calming and Problem-Solving Skills (21)

A. The client was taught age-appropriate social problem-solving skills.

B. The client was taught calming skills, including cognitive and somatic techniques.

C. The client was taught problem-solving skills, including specifying the problem, generating solution options, listing pros and cons of each option, selecting an option, implementing an option, and refining.

D. The client was assigned "Problem Solving Exercise" in the *Child Psychotherapy Homework Planner* (Jongsma, Peterson, McInnis, & Bruce).

E. The client was asked to use client-tailored, age-appropriate social problem-solving skills on a regular basis.

22. Teach Conflict-Resolution Skills (22)

A. The client was taught conflict-resolution skills through modeling, role-playing, and behavioral rehearsal.

B. The client was taught about empathy and active listening.

C. The client was taught about "I messages," respectful communication, assertiveness without aggression, and compromise.

D. The client was assigned "Learn to Be Assertive" in the *Child Psychotherapy Homework Planner* (Jongsma, Peterson, McInnis, & Bruce).

E. The client was reinforced for clear understanding of the conflict-resolution skills.

F. The client displayed a poor understanding of the conflict-resolution skills and was provided with remedial feedback.

23. Assign Practice of Skills (23)

A. The client was assigned to practice assertion, problem-solving, and conflict-resolution skills.

B. Positive reinforcement was used to reinforce the client's use of coping skills.

C. The client has not regularly practiced coping skills and was redirected to do so.

24. Construct Anxiety Stimuli Hierarchy (24)

A. The client was assisted in constructing a hierarchy of anxiety-producing situations associated with their phobic fear.

B. It was difficult for the client to develop a hierarchy of stimulus situations because the causes of fear remain quite vague; the client was assisted in completing the hierarchy.

C. The client was successful at completing a focused hierarchy of specific stimulus situations that provoke anxiety in a gradually increasing manner; this hierarchy was reviewed.

25. Select Exposures That Are Likely to Succeed (25)

A. Initial in vivo or role-played exposures were selected, with a bias toward those that have a high likelihood of being a successful experience for the client.

B. Cognitive restructuring was done within and after the exposure using behavioral strategies (e.g., modeling, rehearsal, social reinforcement).

C. A review was conducted with the client about use of in vivo or role-played exposure.

D. The client was provided with positive feedback regarding use of exposures.

E. The client has not used in vivo or role-played exposures and was redirected to do.

26. Assign Homework on Exposure (26)

A. The client was assigned homework exercises to perform sensation exposure and record the experience.

B. The client's use of sensation exposure techniques was reviewed and reinforced.

C. The client has struggled in implementation of sensation exposure technique and was provided with corrective feedback.

D. The client has not attempted to use the sensation exposure techniques and was redirected to do so.

27. Increase Participation in Peer Group Activities (27)

A. The client was strongly encouraged to participate in extracurricular or positive peer group activities to provide opportunities to establish meaningful friendships.

B. The client was assisted in developing a list of positive peer group activities that will provide them with the opportunity to establish meaningful friendships.

C. The client was assigned the exercise "Greeting Peers" from the *Child Psychotherapy Homework Planner* (Jongsma, Peterson, McInnis, & Bruce).

D. Active listening skills were used as the client verbalized an understanding of how feelings of insecurity and inadequacy contribute to reluctance to become involved in positive peer group activities.

E. The client reported recently participating in positive peer group activities and was praised for this.

F. The client denied participating in any recent extracurricular or positive peer group activities and was encouraged to use this resource.

28. Assign Overnight Visit with Friend (28)

A. The client was given the homework assignment to either invite a friend for an overnight visit or set up an overnight visit at the friend's home.

B. The client was given the opportunity to express and work through fears and anxiety about inviting a friend for an overnight visit or setting up an overnight visit at a friend's home.

C. The client complied with the directive to have an overnight visit with a friend, resulting in some anxiety but also pride of accomplishment.

D. The client failed to set up an overnight visit with a friend and was refocused on this task.

29. Contact School Officials About Socialization (29)

A. School officials were contacted about ways to increase the client's socialization (e.g., write for the school newspaper, tutor a more popular peer, pair the client with another popular peer on a classroom assignment).

B. "School Fear Reduction" in the *Adolescent Psychotherapy Homework Planner* (Jongsma, Peterson, McInnis, & Bruce) was assigned.

C. The school officials agreed to assign tasks or activities that will enable the client to socialize with peers.

D. The consultation with school officials was helpful in increasing the client's socialization with peers.

E. School officials have not implemented ways to increase the client's socialization, and additional consultation was provided to encourage the use of these helpful techniques.

30. Differentiate Between Lapse and Relapse (30)

A. A discussion was held with the client regarding the distinction between a lapse and a relapse.

B. A lapse was associated with an initial and reversible return of symptoms, fear, or urges to avoid.

C. A relapse was associated with the decision to return to fearful and avoidant patterns.

D. The client was provided with support and encouragement as they displayed an understanding of the difference between a lapse and a relapse.

E. The client struggled to understand the difference between a lapse and a relapse and was provided with remedial feedback in this area.

31. Discuss Management of Lapse Risk Situations (31)

A. The client was assisted in identifying future situations or circumstances in which lapses could occur.

B. The session focused on rehearsing the management of future situations or circumstances in which lapses could occur.

C. The client was reinforced for appropriate use of lapse management skills.

D. The client was redirected in regard to poor use of lapse management skills.

32. Encourage Routine Use of Strategies (32)

A. The client was instructed to routinely use the strategies learned in therapy (e.g., cognitive restructuring, exposure).

B. The client was urged to find ways to build new strategies into their life as much as possible.

C. The client was reinforced as they reported ways in which they have incorporated coping strategies into their life and routine.

D. The client was redirected about ways to incorporate new strategies into their routine and life.

33. Develop a Coping Card (33)

A. The client was provided with a coping card on which specific coping strategies were listed.

B. The client was assisted in developing the coping card in order to list helpful coping strategies.

C. The client was encouraged to use the coping card when struggling with anxiety-producing situations.

34. Encourage Family Modeling of Constructive Skills (34)

A. The family was urged to model constructive skills that they have learned for dealing with social shyness.

B. The family was encouraged to model the therapeutic skills that the client is learning (e.g., calming, cognitive restructuring, non-avoidance of unrealistic fears).

C. The client reported that they have received constructive examples of how to use therapeutic skills.

35. Teach Problem-Solving and Communication Skills (35)

A. Family members were taught problem-solving techniques to help the client progress through therapy.

B. Specific communication skills were taught to the family members to help the client progress through therapy.

C. The family was assigned "Problem-Solving Exercise" in the *Child Psychotherapy Homework Planner* (Jongsma, Peterson, McInnis, & Bruce).

D. Positive feedback was provided to family members for their use of problem-solving and communication skills.

E. Family members frequently failed to use problem-solving and communication skills and were redirected to do so.

36. Encourage Modeling of Skills and Praise (36)

A. Family members were encouraged to model constructive skills that they have learned that will assist in the client's positive behavior change.

B. The family members were encouraged to praise the client when they use therapeutic skills.

C. Family members have been noted to model and praise the use of calming techniques.

D. Family members were reinforced for modeling and praising the client's use of cognitive-restructuring techniques.

E. Family members were encouraged to keep modeling and praising the use of non-avoidance of unrealistic fears.

F. The family members have not modeled and praised the client's use of therapeutic skills and were redirected to do so.

37. Identify Similarities with Peers (37)

A. The client was assisted in developing a list of why they like their peers.

B. The "Greeting Peers" exercise from the *Child Psychotherapy Homework Planner* (Jongsma, Peterson, McInnis, & Bruce) was used to help encourage the client to increase contact with peers who share their interests and abilities.

C. The client was assisted in developing a list of activities that they could engage in with peers.

D. The client was encouraged to share interests with peers who have similar interests.

E. The client has not shared interests with peers and was redirected to do so.

38. Assign Strengths Exercise (38)

A. The client was assigned a homework exercise to identify strengths or interests that could be used to initiate social contacts and establish friendships.

B. The client was assigned the "Show Your Strengths" exercise from the *Child Psychotherapy Homework Planner* (Jongsma, Peterson, McInnis, & Bruce) to help identify their strengths or interests that could be used to initiate social contacts and establish friendships.

C. The client successfully completed the "Show Your Strengths" exercise and felt good about sharing the results with peers because they were receptive.

D. The client reported that the "Show Your Strengths" exercise helped to increase self-esteem and confidence; the benefits of this progress were reviewed.

E. The client reported that sharing strengths with others helped them to feel accepted by peers at school or in the neighborhood and were encouraged to continue.

F. The client did not follow through with completing the "Show Your Strengths" exercise and was asked again to work on it.

39. **Explore History of Traumas (39)**

A. The client's background was explored for a history of rejection experiences, harsh criticism, abandonment, or trauma that may have contributed to low self-esteem and social anxiety.

B. The client was assisted in developing a timeline where they identified significant historical events, both positive and negative, that have occurred in their background.

C. The client identified a history of abandonment and/or traumatic experiences that coincided with the onset of feelings of low self-esteem and social anxiety, and this connection was highlighted.

D. Exploration of the client's background did not reveal any significant rejection or traumatic experiences that contributed to the onset of social anxiety.

40. **Probe Feelings Associated with Traumas (40)**

A. The client was given the opportunity to express feelings about past rejection experiences, harsh criticism, abandonment, or trauma.

B. The client was given empathy and support in expressing feelings about past rejection experiences, harsh criticism, abandonment, or traumatic events.

C. The client was instructed to use a journal to record thoughts and feelings about past rejection experiences, harsh criticism, abandonment, or trauma.

D. The empty-chair technique was employed to facilitate the client's expression of feelings surrounding past rejection experiences, harsh criticism, abandonment, or trauma.

E. The client was instructed to draw pictures that reflect feelings about past rejection experiences, harsh criticism, abandonment, or trauma.

F. The client was assigned "Maurice Faces His Fear" or Dixie Overcomes Her Fears" in the *Child Psychotherapy Homework Planner* (Jongsma, Peterson, McInnis, & Bruce).

G. Despite several attempts to allow the client to explore feelings associated with the traumas, the client has continued to be defensive and guarded about these types of feelings and was encouraged to express them as they feel able to do so.

41. **Employ Child-Centered Play Therapy (41)**

A. Child-centered play therapy principles were used to help the client overcome social anxieties and feel more confident in social situations.

B. The client was given unconditional positive regard and warm acceptance while expressing feelings of anxiety and insecurity.

C. The client's feelings expressed in play were reflected and related to fears, anxieties, and insecurities in everyday social situations.

D. The child-centered play therapy sessions have affirmed the client's capacity for self-growth and reinforced the ability to overcome social anxiety.

E. The child-centered play therapy sessions have helped the client overcome social anxiety and feel more confident in social situations.

42. Utilize Ericksonian Play Therapy Technique (42)

A. An Ericksonian play therapy technique was used whereby the therapist spoke through a "wise doll" (or puppet) to an audience of other dolls or puppets to teach the client positive social skills.

B. The client identified the puppet play or storytelling technique as being an enjoyable and beneficial way to learn about positive social skills.

C. After finishing the story, the client was helped to identify positive social skills that were taught by the "wise doll."

D. The client was encouraged to practice the social skills that they learned from the "wise doll" in everyday social situations.

E. The client was given the homework assignment to practice daily at least one positive social skill that was taught by the "wise doll."

43. Use Storytelling Technique (43)

A. The therapist used puppets, dolls, and stuffed animals to create stories that modeled positive social skills.

B. The therapist used puppets, dolls, and stuffed animals to create a story that modeled appropriate ways to introduce self and greet others.

C. Using puppets, dolls, or stuffed animals, the therapist created a story that taught the importance of making positive statements about self and others in everyday social situations.

D. A storytelling technique using puppets, dolls, and stuffed animals was used to model ways for the client to appear more confident and assured in social situations.

E. The client was given the directive to practice at least one positive social skill daily that was taught in the stories using puppets, dolls, and stuffed animals.

F. The client has not used the skills learned through the storytelling and puppet techniques and was encouraged to use these effective strategies.

44. Assign Artwork Reflecting Social Anxieties (44)

A. The client was instructed to draw a picture or create a sculpture that reflects how they feel around unfamiliar people or when placed in new social settings.

B. The client was assigned "Expressions of Fear Through Art" in the *Child Psychotherapy Homework Planner* (Jongsma, Peterson, McInnis, & Bruce).

C. After finishing their drawing or sculpture, the client's insecurities around unfamiliar people or in new social situations were discussed.

D. The client's artwork was noted to reflect fears about embarrassing or humiliating self in front of others.

E. The client's artwork was noted to reflect fears about being ignored or rejected by others.

F. The client's artwork led to a discussion about what they can do to feel more comfortable around unfamiliar people or in new social situations.

45. **Assign Drawing of Symbols of Positive Attributes (45)**

A. The client was instructed to draw objects or symbols on a large piece of paper or poster board that symbolize their positive attributes.

B. After identifying their positive attributes, the client discussed how they can use strengths to establish peer friendships.

C. The client was asked to share strengths or interests with peers three to five times during the next week.

D. The client reported that the art assignment helped them feel more positive about self.

E. The client has shared strengths and interests with peers on a regular basis and was verbally reinforced for this progress.

F. The client has not shared strengths and interests with peers during the previous week and was redirected to do so.

SPECIFIC PHOBIA

CLIENT PRESENTATION

1. Persistent and Unreasonable Fear (1)*

A. An immediate anxiety response has been exhibited by the client each time they encountered the phobic stimulus.

B. The client reported that the strength of their phobic response has been increasing in the past several months.

C. The client described the level of fear they experience around the phobic stimulus as paralyzing.

D. The client indicated that the phobia has been a recent occurrence but has quickly become very persistent and unreasonable.

E. As the client has become engaged in therapy, there has been a decrease in the intensity and frequency of the phobic response.

2. Avoidance and Endurance of Phobia (2)

A. The client reported that avoidance of the phobic stimulus has caused major interference in normal daily routines.

B. The client indicated that the intensity of their anxiety around the phobic stimulus has resulted in marked personal distress.

C. The client questioned whether or not they would ever be able to resolve the phobia.

D. The client has progressed to the point where the phobic stimulus does not create interference in their normal daily routine or cause them marked distress.

3. Fear Seen as Unreasonable (3)

A. The client acknowledged that their persistent fear is seen as excessive and unreasonable.

B. The client's recognition of their persistent fear as excessive and unreasonable has provided good motivation for cooperation with treatment and follow-through on attempts to change.

4. Sleep Disturbance (4)

A. The client reported that sleep has been disturbed by frequent dreams of the feared stimulus.

B. The client indicated their disturbed sleep pattern has started to affect daily functioning.

C. The client's sleep has improved as they have worked toward resolving the feared stimulus.

5. Dramatic Fear Reaction (5)

A. The client indicated that at the slightest mention of the phobic stimulus they have a dramatic fear reaction.

---

*The numbers in parentheses correlate to the number of the Behavioral Definition statement in the companion chapter with the same title in the *Child Psychotherapy Treatment Planner*, Sixth Edition, by Jongsma, Peterson, McInnis, & Bruce (Wiley, 2023)

B. The client's reaction to the phobic stimulus is so dramatic and overpowering that it is difficult to calm them down.

C. The client reported that their reaction to the phobic stimulus is rapidly becoming more and more dramatic.

D. There has been a marked decrease in the client's dramatic fear reaction to the phobic stimulus since they have started to work in therapy sessions.

6. **Parental Reinforcement (6)**

A. The parents have catered to the client's fear and have thus reinforced and increased it.

B. The parents' own fears seemed to be projected onto and acted out by the client.

C. The parents have worked to curb their reaction to the client's fears, which has resulted in a marked decrease in the client's level of fear.

INTERVENTIONS IMPLEMENTED

1. **Establish Rapport (1)***

A. Caring was conveyed to the client through support, warmth, and empathy.

B. The client was provided with nonjudgmental support and a level of trust was developed.

C. The client was urged to feel safe in discussing their phobias.

D. The client began to express feelings more freely as rapport and trust level have increased.

E. The client has continued to experience difficulty being open and direct about their expression of painful feelings; they were encouraged to use the safe haven of therapy to express these difficult issues.

2. **Focus on Strengthening Therapeutic Relationship (2)**

A. The relationship with the client was strengthened using empirically supported factors.

B. The relationship with the client was strengthened through the implementation of collaborative approach, agreement on goals, demonstration of empathy, verbalization of positive regard, and collection of client feedback.

C. The client reacted positively to the relationship-strengthening measures taken.

D. The client verbalized feeling supported and understood during therapy sessions.

E. Despite attempts to strengthen the therapeutic relationship, the client reports feeling distant and misunderstood.

F. The client has indicated that sessions are not helpful and will be terminating therapy.

3. **Assess Fear and Avoidance (3)**

A. An objective fear survey was administered to the client to assess the depth and breadth of their phobic fear.

B. *The Anxiety Disorders Interview Schedule for Children—Parent Version* or *Child Version* (Silverman & Albano) was used to assess the level of phobia symptoms.

---

*The numbers in parentheses correlate to the number of the Therapeutic Intervention statement in the companion chapter with the same title in the *Child Psychotherapy Treatment Planner*, Sixth Edition, by Jongsma, Peterson, McInnis, & Bruce (Wiley, 2023).

C. The fear survey results indicated that the client's phobic fear is extreme and severely interferes with their life.

D. The fear survey results indicate that the client's phobic fear is moderate and occasionally interferes with daily functioning.

E. The fear survey results indicate that the client's phobic fear is mild and rarely interferes with daily functioning.

F. The results of the fear survey were reviewed with the client.

4. Administer Client-Report Measure (4)

A. A client-report measure was used to further assess the depth and breadth of the client's phobic responses.

B. "Measures for Specific Phobias" (Antony) was used to assess the depth and breadth of the client's phobic responses.

C. The client-report measure indicated that the client's phobic fear is extreme and severely interferes with their life.

D. The client-report measure indicated that the client's phobic fear is moderate and occasionally interferes with their life.

E. The client-report measure indicated that the client's phobic fear is mild and rarely interferes with their life.

F. The client declined to complete the client-report measure, and the focus of treatment was changed to this resistance.

5. Assess Level of Insight (5)

A. The client's level of insight toward the presenting problems was assessed.

B. The client was assessed in regard to the syntonic versus dystonic nature of their insight about the presenting problems.

C. The client was noted to demonstrate good insight into the problematic nature of the behavior and symptoms.

D. The client was noted to be in agreement with others' concerns and is motivated to work on change.

E. The client was noted to be ambivalent regarding the problems described and is reluctant to address the issues as a concern.

F. The client was noted to be resistant regarding acknowledgment of the problem areas, is not concerned about them, and has no motivation to make changes.

6. Assess for Correlated Disorders (6)

A. The client was assessed for evidence of research-based correlated disorders.

B. The client was assessed in regard to the level of vulnerability to suicide.

C. The client was identified as having a comorbid disorder, and treatment was adjusted to account for these concerns.

D. The client has been assessed for any correlated disorders, but none were found.

7. Assess for Culturally Based Confounding Issues (7)

A. The client was assessed for age-related issues that could help to better understand their clinical presentation.

B. The client was assessed for gender-related issues that could help to better understand their clinical presentation.

C. The client was assessed for cultural syndromes, cultural idioms of distress, or culturally based perceived causes that could help to better understand their clinical presentation.

D. Alternative factors have been identified as contributing to the client's currently defined "problem behavior," and these were taken into account in regard to treatment.

E. Culturally based factors that could help to account for the client's currently defined "problem behavior" were investigated, but no significant factors were identified.

8. Assess Severity of Impairment (8)

A. The severity of the client's impairment was assessed to determine the appropriate level of care.

B. The client was assessed in regard to impairment in social, relational, and educational endeavors.

C. It was reflected to the client that the impairment appears to create mild to moderate effects on the client's functioning.

D. It was reflected to the client that the impairment appears to create severe to very severe effects on the client's functioning.

E. The client was continuously assessed for the severity of impairment, as well as the efficacy and appropriateness of treatment.

9. Assess for Pathogenic Care (9)

A. The home, school, and community of the client were assessed for pathogenic care and concerns.

B. The client's various environments were assessed for the persistent disregard of the child's needs, repeated changes in caregivers, limited opportunities for stable attachment, harsh discipline, or other grossly inept care.

C. Pathogenic care was identified and the treatment plan included strategies for managing or correcting these concerns and protecting the child.

D. No pathogenic care was identified and this was reflected to the client and caregivers.

10. Refer for Medication Evaluation (10)

A. Arrangements were made for the client to have a physician evaluation for the purpose of considering psychotropic medication to alleviate phobic discomfort symptoms.

B. The client has followed through with seeing a physician for an evaluation of any organic causes for the anxiety and the need for psychotropic medication to control the anxiety response.

C. The client has not cooperated with the referral to a physician for a medication evaluation and was encouraged to do so.

11. Monitor Medication Adherence (11)

A. The client reported that they have taken the prescribed medication consistently and that it has helped to control the anxiety; this was relayed to the prescribing clinician.

B. The client reported that they have not taken the prescribed medication consistently and was encouraged to do so.

C. The client reported taking the prescribed medication and stated that they have not noted any beneficial effect from it; this was reflected to the prescribing clinician.

D. The client was evaluated but was not prescribed any psychotropic medication by the prescribing clinician.

12. Normalize Phobias (12)

A. A discussion was held about how phobias are very common.

B. The client was focused on how phobias are a natural, but irrational expression of our fight or flight response.

C. It was emphasized to the client that phobias are not a sign of weakness but cause unnecessary distress and disability.

D. The client was reinforced as they displayed a better understanding of the natural facets of phobias.

E. The client struggled to understand the natural aspects of phobias and was provided with remedial feedback in this area.

13. Discuss Phobic Cycle (13)

A. The client was taught how phobic fears are maintained by a cycle of unwarranted fear and avoidance that precludes positive, corrective experiences with the feared object or situation.

B. The client was taught how treatment breaks the phobic cycle by encouraging positive, corrective experiences.

C. The client was taught information from *Helping Your Anxious Child* (Rapee et al.) regarding the phobic cycle.

D. The client was taught about the phobic cycle from information in *Exposure Therapy for Treating Anxiety in Children and Adolescents* (Raggi et al.).

E. The client was reinforced as they displayed a better understanding of the phobic cycle of unwarranted fear and avoidance, and how treatment breaks the cycle.

F. The client displayed a poor understanding of the phobic cycle and was provided with remedial feedback in this area.

14. Use Storytelling Techniques (14)

A. Storytelling techniques were used to help the client identify their fears, their origins, and their resolution.

B. The exercise "Maurice Faces His Fears" from the *Child Psychotherapy Homework Planner* (Jongsma, Peterson, McInnis, & Bruce) was used to help the client identify components of their fears.

C. The client was supported as they described their fears, their origins, and their resolution.

D. The client has not been able to resolve fears and was provided with additional support.

15. Discuss Unrealistic Threats, Physical Fear, and Avoidance (15)

A. A discussion was held about how phobias involve appraising threats unrealistically, bodily expressions of fear, and avoidance of what is threatening and that these interact to maintain the problem.

B. The client displayed a clear understanding about how unrealistic threats, bodily expression of fear, and avoidance combine to maintain the phobic problem; their insight was reinforced.

C. Despite specific information about factors that interact to maintain the problem, the client displayed a poor understanding of these issues; the client was provided with remedial information in this area.

16. **Discuss Benefits of Exposure (16)**

    A. A discussion was held about how exposure serves to desensitize learned fear, build confidence, and lead to feeling safer by building a new history of successful experiences.

    B. The client was taught about the benefits of exposure as described in *Helping Your Anxious Child* (Rapee et al.).

    C. The client was taught about the benefits of exposure as described in *Freeing Your Child from Anxiety* (Chansky).

    D. The client displayed a clear understanding about how exposure serves to desensitize learned fear, build confidence, and feel safer by building a new history of successful experiences; their insight was reinforced.

    E. Despite specific information about how exposure serves to desensitize learned fear, build confidence, and lead to feeling safer by building a new history of successful experiences, the client displayed a poor understanding of these issues; the client was provided with remedial information in this area.

17. **Teach Anxiety Management Skills (17)**

    A. The client was taught anxiety management skills.

    B. The client was taught about staying focused on behavioral goals and positive self-talk.

    C. Techniques for muscular relaxation and paced diaphragmatic breathing were taught to the client.

    D. The client was reinforced for clear understanding and use of anxiety management skills.

    E. The client has not used new anxiety management skills and was redirected to do so.

18. **Assign Calming Skills Exercises (18)**

    A. The client was assigned a homework exercise in which they practice daily calming skills.

    B. The parents and child were recommended to read *The Relaxation and Stress Reduction Workbook for Kids* (Shapiro & Sprague).

    C. The client was assigned "Deep Breathing Exercise" in the *Child Psychotherapy Homework Planner* (Jongsma, Peterson, McInnis, & Bruce).

    D. The client was assigned "Progressive Muscle Relaxation" in the *Adolescent Psychotherapy Homework Planner* (Jongsma, Peterson, McInnis, & Bruce).

    E. The client's use of the exercises for practicing daily calming skills was closely monitored.

    F. The client's success at using daily calming skills was reinforced.

    G. The client was provided with corrective feedback for failures at practicing daily calming skills.

19. Use Biofeedback Techniques (19)

A. Biofeedback techniques were used to facilitate the client's success in learning relaxation skills.

B. The client was provided with consistent feedback about physiological responses to relaxation skill training.

C. The client was reinforced for their increase in relaxation skills through biofeedback training.

D. The client has not increased success at learning skills through biofeedback techniques, and remedial instruction was provided.

20. Teach Applied Tension Technique (20)

A. The client was taught the applied tension technique to help prevent fainting during encounters with phobic objects or situations.

B. The client was taught to tense their neck and upper torso muscles to curtail blood flow out of the brain to help prevent fainting during encounters with phobic objects or situations involving blood, injection, or injury.

C. The client was taught specific applied tension techniques as indicated in the article titled "Applied Tension, Exposure *in vivo,* and Tension-Only in the Treatment of Blood Phobia" from *Behavior Research and Therapy* (Ost et al.).

D. The client was provided with positive feedback for use of the applied tension technique.

E. The client has struggled to appropriately use the applied tension technique and was provided with remedial feedback in this area.

21. Assign Daily Applied Tension Practice (21)

A. The client was assigned a homework exercise in which they practice daily use of the applied tension skills.

B. The client's daily use of the applied tension technique was reviewed.

C. The client was reinforced for success at using the daily applied tension skills.

D. The client was provided with corrective feedback for failure to appropriately use daily-applied tension skills.

22. Identify Self-Talk (22)

A. The client was assisted in identifying the anxious self-talk and beliefs that mediate anxiety responses.

B. The client was taught the role of anxious self-talk and beliefs in precipitating emotional responses.

C. The client was reinforced as they verbalized an understanding of the anxious self-talk and beliefs that mediate their anxiety responses.

D. The client was assisted in replacing anxious self-talk with positive, realistic cognitions.

E. The client failed to identify anxious self-talk and was provided with tentative examples in this area.

23. Assign Homework on Self-Talk (23)

A. The client was assigned homework exercises to identify fearful self-talk, create reality-based alternatives, and record the experience.

B. The client was assigned the exercise "Replace Negative Thoughts with Positive Self-Talk" from the *Child Psychotherapy Homework Planner* (Jongsma, Peterson, McInnis, & Bruce).

C. The client's use of self-talk techniques was reviewed and reinforced.

D. The client has struggled in implementation of self-talk techniques and was provided with corrective feedback.

E. The client has not attempted to use the self-talk techniques and was redirected to do so.

24. Model/Rehearse Self-Talk (24)

A. Modeling and behavioral rehearsal were used to train the client in positive self-talk that reassured them of the ability to work through and endure anxiety symptoms without serious consequences.

B. The client has implemented positive self-talk to reassure self of the ability to endure anxiety without serious consequences; the client was reinforced for this progress.

C. The client has not used positive self-talk to help endure anxiety and was provided with additional direction in this area.

25. Construct Anxiety Stimuli Hierarchy (25)

A. The client was assisted in constructing a hierarchy of anxiety-producing situations associated with two or three spheres of worry.

B. It was difficult for the client to develop a hierarchy of stimulus situations because the causes of their anxiety remain quite vague; the client was assisted in completing the hierarchy.

C. The client was successful at creating a focused hierarchy of specific stimulus situations that provoke anxiety in a gradually increasing manner; this hierarchy was reviewed.

26. Develop Contingency Contract (26)

A. The child and parents were assisted in developing a contingency contact that details the child's exposure tasks and rewards.

B. The steps in the hierarchy were used to identify the gradual exposure tasks.

C. The parents were consulted in regard to approval of rewards for the successful completion of each exposure task.

27. Teach Strategies to Facilitate Exposure (27)

A. The parents were taught strategies to facilitate the child's exposure or approach behavior toward feared objects or situations.

B. The parents were taught about positive reinforcement, shaping, extinction, following through, and consistency.

C. The parents were reinforced for their use of strategies to facilitate the child's exposure or approach behavior.

D. The parents have not embraced their role in facilitating the child's exposure or approach behavior, and were redirected to do so.

28. Assign Information on Situational Exposure (28)

A. The client's parents were assigned to read about how exposure-based therapy can be beneficial.

B. The parents were assigned to read *Helping Your Anxious Child* (Rapee et al.).

C. The parents have read the assigned information on exposure-based therapy techniques, and key points were reviewed.

D. The parents have not read the assigned information on exposure-based therapy techniques and were redirected to do so.

29. **Select Initial Exposures (29)**

A. Initial exposures were selected from the hierarchy of anxiety-producing situations, with a bias toward the likelihood of being successful.

B. The client was assigned the exercise "Gradually Facing a Phobic Fear" from the *Adolescent Psychotherapy Homework Planner* (Jongsma, Peterson, McInnis, & Bruce).

C. A plan was developed with the client for managing the symptoms that may occur during the initial exposure.

D. The client was assisted in rehearsing the plan for managing the exposure-related symptoms within their imagination.

E. Positive feedback was provided for the client's use of symptom management techniques.

F. The client was redirected for ways to improve symptom management techniques.

30. **Conduct Practice Exposure Sessions (30)**

A. The client was assisted in implementing exposure in practice situations.

B. Graduated tasks, modeling, and reinforcement of the client's success were used to help the client gradually practice greater levels of exposure.

C. The client continues to have a great deal of anxiety in practice exposures sessions, and remedial techniques were implemented.

31. **Assign Homework on Situational Exposures (31)**

A. The client was assigned homework exercises to perform worry exposures and record the experience.

B. The client was assigned situational exposures homework from *Mastering Your Fears and Phobias: Workbook* (Antony et al.)

C. The client was assigned situational exposures homework from *Helping Your Anxious Child* (Rapee et al.).

D. The client's use of worry exposure techniques was reviewed and reinforced.

E. The client has struggled in implementation of worry exposure technique and was provided with corrective feedback.

F. The client has not attempted to use the worry exposure techniques and was redirected to do so.

32. **Use Emotional Imagery Approach (32)**

A. An emotional imagery approach was used to overcome the fear of the dark, using systematic desensitization as a self-empowering story.

B. Hero images were used as a competing response to the anxiety.

C. The client was assisted in developing hero images as a way to compete with anxiety symptoms.

33. Conduct Family Anxiety Management Sessions (33)

A. The family was taught how to prompt and reward courageous behavior in the client.
B. The family was taught how to empathetically ignore the client's excessive complaining and other avoidant behaviors.
C. The family was taught to manage their own anxieties and model behavior being taught in session.
D. Family anxiety management sessions were held based on the FRIENDS Program for Children (Barrett, et al.).

34. Remove Family Reinforcers (34)

A. The family was assisted in overcoming the tendency to reinforce the client's phobia.
B. Family members were taught specific ways in which they may tend to reinforce the client's phobia and how to change this pattern.
C. As the client's phobia has decreased, the family members have been taught constructive ways to reward the client's progress.

35. Teach Problem-Solving and Communication Skills (35)

A. Family members were taught problem-solving techniques to help the client progress through therapy.
B. Specific communication skills were taught to the family members to help the client progress through therapy.
C. Positive feedback was provided to family members for their use of problem-solving and communication skills.
D. Family members frequently failed to use problem-solving and communication skills and were redirected to do so.

36. Assign Reading Material About Specific Phobias (36)

A. The parents were assigned to read about specific phobias.
B. The parents were directed to read excerpts from *Helping Your Anxious Child* (Rapee et al.).
C. The parents have read information regarding specific phobias, and key points were reviewed and processed within the session.
D. The parents have not read information about specific phobias and were redirected to do so.

37. Differentiate Between Lapse and Relapse (37)

A. A discussion was held with the client regarding the distinction between a lapse and a relapse.
B. A lapse was associated with a temporary and reversible return of symptoms, fear, or urges to avoid.
C. A relapse was associated with the decision to return to fearful and avoidant patterns.
D. The client was provided with support and encouragement as they displayed an understanding of the difference between a lapse and a relapse.
E. The client struggled to understand the difference between a lapse and a relapse and was provided with remedial feedback in this area.

38. Discuss Management of Lapse Risk Situations (38)

A. The client was assisted in identifying future situations or circumstances in which lapses could occur.

B. The session focused on rehearsing the management of future situations or circumstances in which lapses could occur.

C. The client was reinforced for appropriate use of lapse management skills.

D. The client was redirected in regard to poor use of lapse management skills.

39. Encourage Routine Use of Strategies (39)

A. The client was instructed to routinely use the strategies that they have learned in therapy (e.g., cognitive restructuring, exposure).

B. The client was assigned "Finding a Strategy to Minimize My Fear" in the *Adolescent Psychotherapy Homework Planner* (Jongsma, Peterson, McInnis, & Bruce).

C. The client was urged to find ways to build new strategies into their life as much as possible.

D. The client was reinforced as they reported ways in which they have incorporated coping strategies into their life and routine.

40. Develop a Coping Card (40)

A. The client was provided with a coping card on which specific coping strategies were listed.

B. The client was assisted in developing the coping card in order to list helpful coping strategies.

C. The client was encouraged to use the coping card when struggling with anxiety-producing situations.

41. Employ Stimulus Desensitization Interventions (41)

A. A session was conducted with the client in which they were surrounded with pleasant pictures, readings, and storytelling related to the phobic stimulus situation.

B. The client remained calm and relaxed while the phobic stimulus situation was depicted in pictures, informational material, and storytelling.

C. The client's ability to face the phobic fear was affirmed and their ability to cope was reinforced.

D. The client had an extreme reaction to the pictures, reading, and storytelling related to the phobic situation and was provided with support for use of coping techniques during this anxiety.

42. Interject Use of Humor (42)

A. Situational humor, jokes, riddles, and stories about the phobic stimulus were used to decrease the client's tension and seriousness regarding the fear.

B. The client was asked to start each day by telling the parents a joke, riddle, or silly story about the phobic stimulus.

C. A humorous side was pointed out for each issue/fear the client raised.

43. Probe Symbolic Meanings of Phobic Situation (43)

A. The possible symbolic meaning of the client's phobic stimulus was probed and discussed.

B. Selected interpretations of the phobic stimulus were offered to the client and each was processed with them.

44. Clarify/Differentiate Present Fear from Past Pain (44)

A. The client was asked to list present fears and also past emotionally painful experiences that may be related to current fear.

B. The client was assisted in clarifying and separating present irrational fears from past emotional/painful experiences.

C. It was noted that since the client was successful at separating past emotionally painful experiences from the present, they have reduced phobic fears.

45. Reinforce Expression of Feelings About Trauma (45)

A. The positive value of expressing feelings was emphasized with the client.

B. Using active listening and unconditional positive regard techniques, the client was encouraged to express feelings regarding past painful experiences.

C. Gentle questioning was used with the client to help them start sharing feelings from the past.

D. Feelings that the client shared regarding past painful experiences were affirmed and supported.

46. Link Past Pain with Present Anxiety (46)

A. The connection the client was making between past emotional pain and present anxiety was pointed out.

B. When talking about present fear, the client was reminded of how they connected it to past emotional pain.

C. It was noted that since the client was successful at separating past emotionally painful experiences from the present, they have reduced phobic fears.

SPEECH/LANGUAGE DISORDERS

CLIENT PRESENTATION

1. Low Expressive Language Test Results (1)*

   A. The results from the speech/language evaluation showed that the client's expressive language abilities are significantly below their expected level.

   B. The results from the speech/language evaluation showed that the client's expressive language abilities are moderately below their expected level.

   C. The results from the speech/language evaluation showed that the client's expressive language abilities are mildly delayed.

   D. The results from the speech/language evaluation did not reveal any significant problems with the client's expressive language abilities.

2. Expressive Language Deficits Manifested (2)

   A. The client's expressive language deficits are manifested in limited vocabulary, frequent errors in tense, and difficulty recalling words or producing sentences of developmentally appropriate length or complexity.

   B. The client had difficulty communicating thoughts and feelings in today's therapy session because of limited vocabulary.

   C. The speech/language pathologist reported that the client has difficulty recalling words or producing sentences of developmentally appropriate length or complexity.

   D. The client's expressive language abilities have recently begun to improve since they began receiving speech/language services.

   E. The speech/language services have helped to improve the client's expressive language abilities up to the expected level.

3. Low Receptive Language Test Results (3)

   A. The results from the speech/language evaluation showed that the client's receptive language abilities are significantly below their expected level.

   B. The results from the speech/language evaluation showed that the client's receptive language abilities are moderately below their expected level.

   C. The results from the speech/language evaluation showed that the client's receptive language abilities are mildly delayed.

   D. The results from the speech/language evaluation did not reveal any significant delays in the client's receptive language abilities.

4. Receptive Language Deficits Manifested (4)

   A. The client's receptive language deficits are manifested in difficulty understanding simple words or sentences and certain types of words such as spatial terms or longer, complex statements.

---

*The numbers in parentheses correlate to the number of the Behavioral Definition statement in the companion chapter with the same title in the *Child Psychotherapy Treatment Planner*, Sixth Edition, by Jongsma, Peterson, McInnis, & Bruce (Wiley, 2023).

B. The client had difficulty understanding key concepts in today's therapy session because of receptive language deficits.

C. The client had difficulty following and comprehending multiple, complex directions because of receptive language deficits.

D. The speech/language pathologist reported that the client's receptive language abilities have started to improve.

E. The speech/language pathologist reported that the client has improved their receptive language abilities to their expected level.

5. **Academic Problems Due to Expressive/Receptive Language Deficits (5)**

A. The client's expressive language deficits have interfered with academic performance.

B. The client's receptive language deficits have interfered with academic performance.

C. The client acknowledged that they are often reluctant to ask questions or seek out help in the classroom because of speech/language problems and fear that they will appear stupid in the eyes of peers.

D. The client's academic performance has started to improve since they began receiving speech/language services.

E. The client has improved academic performance to their level of capability.

6. **Communication Problems Due to Expressive/Receptive Language Deficits (5)**

A. The speech/language pathologist and teacher(s) reported that the client has difficulty communicating thoughts and feelings because of language delays.

B. The client had difficulty verbalizing thoughts and feelings in today's therapy session because of language deficits.

C. The client had difficulty identifying and expressing emotions because of language deficits.

D. The client's consistent failure to use or produce developmentally expected speech sounds significantly interferes with academic achievement and social communication.

E. The client has started to become more communicative in the classroom since they began receiving speech/language services.

F. The client communicated thoughts and feelings in an effective manner in today's therapy session.

7. **Speech Articulation Problems (6)**

A. The client has been diagnosed by a speech/language pathologist as having a significant speech articulation problem.

B. The client displayed speech articulation problems during today's therapy session.

C. The speech/language pathologist reported that the client has trouble producing the following letter sounds:_____, :_____, :_____, :_____ [fill in the blank].

D. The client's speech articulation problems did not interfere with ability to communicate thoughts and feelings in an effective manner during today's therapy session.

E. The client has achieved mastery of the expected speech sounds that are appropriate for their age and dialect.

8. **Stuttering (7)**

   A. The client and parents reported that the client stutters in many social situations.
   B. The client began to stutter in today's therapy session when talking about emotionally laden or anxiety-producing topics.
   C. The client reported that their stuttering increases when they feel anxious or insecure.
   D. The client did not stutter in today's therapy session.
   E. The client's stuttering has ceased, and they are able to speak fluently and at a normal rate on a regular, consistent basis.

9. **Selective Mutism (8)**

   A. The parents reported that the client refuses to speak in certain social situations.
   B. School officials reported that the client refuses to speak at school.
   C. The client refused to speak in today's therapy session.
   D. The client has gradually started to speak more often in a wider circle of social situations.
   E. The client spoke with the therapist for the first time in today's therapy session.
   F. The client's selective mutism has been eliminated, and they regularly communicate with others in a variety of social situations.

10. **Aphasia (9)**

    A. The parents reported that the client has problems with oral or written communication, verbalizing unrecognizable words, speaking in short or incomplete sentences, or has trouble following conversations.
    B. Aphasia symptoms were evident during today's therapy session.
    C. The client's aphasia symptoms have shown improvement over time.
    D. The client's aphasia symptoms are no longer evident in their communication.

11. **Presence of Auditory Processing Disorder (10)**

    A. The client has been diagnosed with an auditory processing disorder.
    B. The client's auditory processing disorder has contributed to speech/language deficits and/or a learning disability.
    C. The client and parents have managed the auditory processing disorder to reduce its influence on speech/language deficits and/or a learning disability.

12. **Intense Fear About Public Speaking (11)**

    A. The client reported having intense fear of speaking in public settings, due to speech/language problems.
    B. The client reported that fear and anxiety increase significantly when they have to speak in social situations.
    C. The client's high anxiety level has contributed to problems with stuttering.
    D. The client appeared at ease when discussing speech/language problems during today's therapy session.
    E. The client's improved speech/language abilities have coincided with a reduction in the level of anxiety.

13. **Social Withdrawal (12)**

   A. The client's expressive language deficits have contributed to social withdrawal and lack of assertiveness in many social settings.

   B. The client's receptive and expressive language deficits have contributed to social withdrawal and lack of assertiveness in many social settings.

   C. The client's speech articulation problems have contributed to withdrawal and lack of assertiveness in many social settings.

   D. The client's fear of stuttering has contributed to social withdrawal and lack of assertiveness in many social settings.

   E. The client has recently started to socialize more with peers.

14. **Low Self-Esteem (12)**

   A. The client's speech/language problems have contributed to feelings of low self-esteem, inadequacy, and insecurity.

   B. The client expressed feelings of inadequacy and insecurity about speech/language problems during today's therapy session.

   C. The client acknowledged that they have a tendency to give up easily on many school assignments because of difficulty understanding key concepts or terms.

   D. The client verbalized positive self-statements during today's therapy session about improved speech/language abilities.

   E. The client has gained a healthy acceptance of speech/language problems and actively participates in many discussions at home, school, and with peers.

15. **Acting-Out, Aggressive, and Negative Attention-Seeking Behaviors (13)**

   A. The client has displayed a recurrent pattern of engaging in acting-out, aggressive, or negative attention-seeking behaviors when they begin to feel insecure or frustrated about speech/language problems.

   B. The client expressed feelings of anger and frustration about speech/language problems during today's therapy session.

   C. The client expressed feelings of anger, hurt, and sadness about the teasing or criticism that they have received from peers about speech/language problems.

   D. The frequency and severity of the client's acting-out, aggressive, and negative attention-seeking behaviors have gradually started to decrease as the client is learning more effective ways to cope with speech/language problems.

   E. The client has ceased their pattern of engaging in acting-out, aggressive, and negative attention-seeking behaviors when feeling frustrated about speech/language problems.

INTERVENTIONS IMPLEMENTED

1. **Establish Rapport (1)***

   A. Caring was conveyed to the client through support, warmth, and empathy.

   B. The client was provided with nonjudgmental support, and a level of trust was developed.

---

*The numbers in parentheses correlate to the number of the Behavioral Definition statement in the companion chapter with the same title in the *Child Psychotherapy Treatment Planner*, Sixth Edition, by Jongsma, Peterson, McInnis, & Bruce (Wiley, 2023)

C. The client was urged to feel safe in expressing speech/language issues.

D. The client began to express feelings more freely as rapport and trust level have increased.

E. The client has continued to experience difficulty being open and direct about the expression of painful feelings; the client was encouraged to use the safe haven of therapy to express these difficult issues.

2. Focus on Strengthening Therapeutic Relationship (2)

A. The relationship with the client was strengthened using empirically supported factors.

B. The relationship with the client was strengthened through the implementation of collaborative approach, agreement on goals, demonstration of empathy, verbalization of positive regard, and collection of client feedback.

C. The client reacted positively to the relationship-strengthening measures taken.

D. The client verbalized feeling supported and understood during therapy sessions.

E. Despite attempts to strengthen the therapeutic relationship, the client reports feeling distant and misunderstood.

F. The client has indicated that sessions are not helpful and will be terminating therapy.

3. Refer for Speech/Language Evaluation (3)

A. The client was referred for a speech/language evaluation to assess the presence of a disorder and determine eligibility for special education services.

B. The findings from the speech/language evaluation show that the client is eligible to receive speech/language services.

C. The findings from the speech/language evaluation show that the client does not meet the criteria for a speech/language disorder and is not eligible to receive special education services.

D. The findings from the speech/language evaluation were shared with the client and parents.

4. Refer for Hearing/Medical Examination (4)

A. The client was referred for a hearing examination to rule out a possible hearing problem that may be interfering with speech/language development.

B. The client was referred for a medical examination to rule out possible health problems that may be interfering with speech/language development.

C. The findings from the hearing examination revealed the presence of a hearing loss that has interfered with the client's speech/language development.

D. The findings from the medical examination revealed the presence of health problems that have interfered with the client's speech/language development.

E. The findings from the hearing and/or medical examinations did not reveal the presence of any hearing or health problems that have contributed to the client's speech/language development.

F. The findings from the hearing/medical examination were shared with the client and parents.

5. **Refer for Neurological Examination/Neuropsychological Examination (5)**

   A. The client was referred for a neurological evaluation to rule out the presence of organic factors that may be contributing to the client's speech/language problems.

   B. The client received a neuropsychological evaluation to rule out the presence of organic factors that may be contributing to the client's speech/language problems.

   C. The findings from the neurological examination revealed the presence of organic factors that have interfered with the client's speech/language development.

   D. The findings from the neuropsychological examination revealed the presence of organic factors that have interfered with the client's speech/language development.

   E. The findings from the neurological and/or neuropsychological evaluation did not reveal the presence of any organic factors that may be contributing to the client's speech/language development.

   F. The findings from the neurological/neuropsychological examinations were shared with the client and parents.

6. **Refer for Psychoeducational Evaluation (6)**

   A. The client received a psychoeducational evaluation to assess their intellectual abilities to rule out the presence of other possible learning disabilities.

   B. The client was cooperative during the psychoeducational evaluation and appeared motivated to do their best.

   C. The client was uncooperative during the psychoeducational evaluation and did not appear to put forth good effort.

   D. The findings from the psychoeducational evaluation revealed the presence of a specific learning disability.

   E. The findings from the psychoeducational evaluation did not reveal the presence of a specific learning disability.

   F. The findings from the psychoeducational evaluation were shared with the client and parents.

7. **Refer for Conduct/Psychological Testing (7)**

   A. The client received a psychological evaluation to determine whether emotional factors or attention-deficit/hyperactivity disorder (ADHD) are interfering with speech/language development.

   B. The client approached the psychological testing in an honest, straightforward manner and was cooperative with any requests presented to them.

   C. The client was uncooperative and resistant to engage during the evaluation process.

   D. The findings from the psychological testing revealed the presence of ADHD, which has interfered with the client's development.

   E. The findings from the psychological testing revealed the presence of underlying emotional problems, which have interfered with the client's speech/language development.

   F. The findings from the psychological testing were shared with the client and parents.

8. **Refer for Medication Evaluation (8)**

   A. The client was referred for a medication evaluation to help stabilize moods.

   B. The client was referred for a medication evaluation to address symptoms of ADHD that interfere with speech/language development.

C. Positive feedback was provided as the client and parents agreed to follow through with the medication evaluation.

D. The client and parents voiced their opposition to medication being used to stabilize moods and/or address the symptoms of ADHD; these concerns were processed.

E. The client and parents were strongly encouraged to maintain regular communication with the psychiatrist or prescribing physician to monitor the effectiveness of the medication.

9. Assess Level of Insight (9)

A. The client's level of insight toward the presenting problems was assessed.

B. The client was assessed in regard to the syntonic versus dystonic nature of their insight about the presenting problems.

C. The client was noted to demonstrate good insight into the problematic nature of the behavior and symptoms.

D. The client was noted to be in agreement with others' concerns and is motivated to work on change.

E. The client was noted to be ambivalent regarding the problems described and is reluctant to address the issues as a concern.

F. The client was noted to be resistant regarding acknowledgment of the problem areas, is not concerned about them, and has no motivation to make changes.

10. Assess for Correlated Disorders (10)

A. The client was assessed for evidence of research-based correlated disorders.

B. The client was assessed in regard to the level of vulnerability to suicide.

C. The client was identified as having a comorbid disorder, and treatment was adjusted to account for these concerns.

D. The client has been assessed for any correlated disorders, but none were found.

11. Assess for Culturally Based Confounding Issues (11)

A. The client was assessed for age-related issues that could help to better understand their clinical presentation.

B. The client was assessed for gender-related issues that could help to better understand their clinical presentation.

C. The client was assessed for cultural syndromes, cultural idioms of distress, or culturally based perceived causes that could help to better understand their clinical presentation.

D. Alternative factors have been identified as contributing to the client's currently defined "problem behavior," and these were taken into account in regard to treatment.

E. Culturally based factors that could help to account for the client's currently defined "problem behavior" were investigated, but no significant factors were identified.

12. Assess Severity of Impairment (12)

A. The severity of the client's impairment was assessed to determine the appropriate level of care.

B. The client was assessed in regard to impairment in social, relational, and educational endeavors.

C. It was reflected to the client that the impairment appears to create mild to moderate effects on the client's functioning.

D. It was reflected to the client that the impairment appears to create severe to very severe effects on the client's functioning.

E. The client was continuously assessed for the severity of impairment, as well as the efficacy and appropriateness of treatment.

13. **Assess for Pathogenic Care (13)**

A. The home, school and community of the client were assessed for pathogenic care and concerns.

B. The client's various environments were assessed for the persistent disregard of the child's needs, repeated changes in caregivers, limited opportunities for stable attachment, harsh discipline, or other grossly inept care.

C. Pathogenic care was identified and the treatment plan included strategies for managing or correcting these concerns and protecting the child.

D. No pathogenic care was identified and this was reflected to the client and caregivers.

14. **Attend IEPC Meeting (14)**

A. The client's Individualized Educational Planning Committee (IEPC) meeting was held with the parents, teachers, speech/language pathologist, and school officials to determine the client's eligibility for special education services, design educational interventions, establish speech/language goals, and outline emotional issues that need to be addressed in counseling.

B. The recommendation was made at the IEPC meeting that the client receive special education services to address speech/language deficits.

C. It was decided at the IEPC meeting that the client is not in need of special education services because they do not meet the criteria for a speech/language disorder.

D. The IEPC meeting was helpful in identifying specific speech/language goals.

E. The IEPC meeting was helpful in identifying emotional issues that need to be addressed in therapy.

15. **Refer to Private Speech/Language Pathologist (15)**

A. The client was referred to a private speech/language pathologist for extra assistance in improving speech/language abilities.

B. The client and parents followed through with the recommendation to work with a private speech/language pathologist.

C. The client and parents failed to follow through with the recommendation to contact a private speech/language pathologist and were encouraged to use this resource.

D. It was noted that the client's speech/language abilities have improved since they began working with the private speech/language pathologist.

E. The client's work with the speech/language pathologist has helped them manage or overcome the stuttering problem; the benefits of this progress were reviewed.

F. The client's work with the speech/language pathologist has not helped them to overcome speech/language problems, and additional services were reviewed to maximize the client's functioning.

16. Maintain Communication Between Home and School (16)

A. The parents, teachers, and speech/language pathologist were encouraged to maintain regular communication with each other via phone calls or written notes regarding the client's speech/language development.

B. The client's teachers were asked to send home daily or weekly progress notes informing the parents of the client's academic progress, particularly in regard to speech/language development.

C. The speech/language pathologist was encouraged to send home regular progress reports informing the parents of the client's progress in speech/language therapy.

D. Communication between the home and school has been poor, and specific steps were taken to increase this communication.

17. Educate Parents About Speech/Language Disorder (17)

A. The client's parents were educated about the signs and symptoms of the client's speech/language disorder.

B. The client's parents were encouraged to read books to learn more about speech/language problems.

C. The therapy session helped the client's parents gain a greater understanding of the signs and symptoms of the client's speech/language disorder.

D. The parents were given the opportunity to express their thoughts and feelings about their child's speech/language disorder.

E. The parents were given support in verbalizing their feelings of sadness about the client's speech/language disorder.

F. Despite education efforts, the client's parents did not display a clear understanding of speech/language disorder concerns for the client and were provided with remedial information in this area.

18. Assess/Confront Parents' Denial of Speech/Language Problem (18)

A. A family therapy session was held to assess the parents' denial surrounding the client's speech/language problem.

B. The parents' denial of the client's speech/language problem was confronted and challenged so that they will begin to cooperate with the recommendations regarding placement and interventions for the client.

C. The therapy session was helpful in working through the parents' denial surrounding the client's speech/language problems, and they agreed to follow through with the recommendations regarding placement and interventions.

D. The parents have remained in denial about the client's intellectual deficits and are opposed to following through with the recommendations regarding placement and educational interventions; these concerns were processed.

19. Encourage Language Enriched Activities (19)

A. The client's parents were encouraged to read to their child regularly, tell or create stories, talk about and label things that the client sees and comment on what the client is doing, and engage in other language-enriched activities.

B. The client and parents brainstormed language-enriched activities they could likely engage in on their own.

C. The parents were provided with positive feedback for taking an active role in promoting the client's speech/language development.

D. The parents struggled to regularly engage in language-enriched activities with the child, and were provided with remedial feedback in this area.

20. **Assign Reading and Language Program (20)**

A. The client was instructed to read to the parents for 15 minutes, 4 times weekly, and then retell the story to them to help build vocabulary.

B. The "Home-Based Reading and Language Program" from the *Child Psychotherapy Homework Planner* (Jongsma, Peterson, McInnis, & Bruce) was used to help build the client's vocabulary.

C. The "Home-Based Reading and Language Program" was employed to help the client feel more comfortable and confident in verbalizing thoughts and opinions.

D. The client and parents were encouraged to use the reward system outlined in the "Home-Based Reading and Language Program" to maintain the client's interest and motivation in improving expressive and receptive language skills.

E. The client and parents reported that the "Home-Based Reading and Language Program" has helped the client feel more confident in expressing thoughts and opinions; they were encouraged to continue this program.

F. The client and parents have not used the reading and language program and were reminded to use this helpful technique.

21. **Encourage the Client to Verbalize Feelings About Family Outing (21)**

A. The client and family were given the directive to go on a weekly outing and afterward have the client share thoughts and feelings about the outing to increase expressive and receptive language abilities.

B. The parents reported that the client's retelling of the weekly outing has helped them feel more confident in expressing thoughts and feelings; they were encouraged to continue this practice.

C. The parents were instructed to provide frequent praise and positive reinforcement to the client for retelling the story of the family outing.

D. The client and parents were instructed to use the "Tell All About It" program from the *Child Psychotherapy Homework Planner* (Jongsma, Peterson, McInnis, & Bruce) to help the client increase their confidence in expressing thoughts and feelings.

E. The "Tell All About It" program was used to increase the parents' support and involvement with the client's speech/language development.

F. The client and parents have not regularly gone on family outings and then reviewed them to increase the client's expressive and receptive language abilities and were confronted about not using this helpful technique.

22. **Engage in Child-Directed Activities (22)**

A. The parents were instructed to engage in child-directed activities that involve labeling different objects for them and identifying what they are doing.

B. The parents reported engaging in the child-directed activities and outcomes were discussed.

C. The parents denied interest in engaging in the child-directed activities and were provided with feedback and rationale for this activity.

23. Assign Parents to Sing Songs (23)

A. The parents were instructed to sing songs with the client to help them feel more comfortable with verbalizations in the home.

B. The parents reported that the exercise of singing songs along with the client has helped the client feel more comfortable and confident in verbalizing thoughts and feelings at home; they were directed to continue this practice.

C. The parents reported that singing songs along with the client has helped the client feel less anxious about speech/language problems; they were encouraged to continue to use this easy, helpful technique.

D. The parents admitted that they have not used the song-singing technique to increase the client's confidence and decrease anxiety regarding speech and language concerns; they were redirected to use this technique.

24. Design Reward System for Speech (24)

A. A consultation was held with the speech/language pathologist about designing a reward system to reinforce the client for achieving goals in speech therapy and mastering new speech behaviors.

B. The parents were helped to develop a list of possible rewards that can be used to reinforce the client for achieving speech therapy goals.

C. The reward system was noted to be helping the client achieve goals in speech therapy.

25. Encourage Parental Positive Reinforcement (25)

A. The parents were encouraged to provide frequent praise and positive reinforcement regarding the client's speech/language development.

B. The parents were encouraged to praise the client for efforts in attempting to master new speech sounds.

C. The parents were strongly encouraged to praise and positively reinforce the client for achieving speech/language goals.

D. The parents were encouraged to praise and reinforce the client for speaking up and being assertive in new social situations.

E. Today's session explored the reasons for the parents' resistance in offering praise and positive reinforcement to the client.

F. The parents were assigned "Clear Rules, Positive Reinforcement, Appropriate Consequences" in the *Adolescent Psychotherapy Homework Planner* (Jongsma, Peterson, McInnis, & Bruce).

26. Develop Acceptance of Limitations (26)

A. Today's therapy session helped the client and parents develop an understanding and acceptance of the limitations surrounding the client's speech/language disorder.

B. The client and parents were given support in expressing their feelings about the limitations surrounding the client's speech/language disorder.

C. The parents were seen in today's therapy session to help them express and work through their feelings of sadness about the client's speech/language disorder.

D. Positive feedback was provided to the client and parents as they gained a healthy understanding and acceptance of the limitations surrounding the client's speech/language disorder.

27. Confront Excessive Parental Pressure (27)

A. A family therapy session was held to assess whether the parents are placing excessive or unrealistic pressure on the client to "talk right."

B. The parents were confronted and challenged about placing excessive or unrealistic pressure on the client to "talk right."

C. The parents were supported as they acknowledged that they have placed excessive or unrealistic pressure on the client to overcome speech/language problems.

D. Positive feedback was provided as the parents agreed to cease placing excessive pressure on the client to "talk right."

E. The parents became defensive in the therapy session when they were confronted about placing excessive or unrealistic pressure on the client to speak clearly or fluently.

28. Assess Parents Speaking for Client (28)

A. Today's therapy session explored whether the parents often speak or fill in the pauses for the client to protect them from feeling anxious or insecure about speech.

B. Active listening skills were used as the parents acknowledged that they often speak or fill in pauses for the client to protect them from feeling anxious or insecure about speech/language problems.

C. The parents were supported as they agreed to cease speaking or filling in the pauses when the client begins to feel insecure.

D. The client reported that they have started to feel more confident and less anxious since the parents ceased their practice of speaking or filling in the pauses for them; the benefits of this progress were reviewed with the client.

E. Today's session explored the reasons for the parents' resistance to cease speaking or filling in the pauses for the client when they begin to feel anxious or insecure.

29. Encourage Client to Initiate Conversation (29)

A. The parents were strongly encouraged to allow the client to take the lead more often in initiating and sustaining conversations.

B. The client and parents were instructed to spend 10 to 15 minutes together on a daily basis where the client takes the lead in initiating and sustaining the conversation.

C. A reward system was designed to reinforce the client for initiating conversations at home.

D. The factors that contribute to the client's resistance to initiate or sustain conversations at home were explored.

E. Positive feedback was given as the client and parents reported that they have taken the lead more often in initiating and sustaining conversations.

30. Teach Communication Skills (30)

A. The client and parents were taught effective communication skills (e.g., active listening, reflecting feelings, "I statements") to facilitate the client's speech/language development.

B. Role-playing techniques were used to teach the client effective communication skills.

C. The parents were encouraged to use active listening skills and reflect the client's feelings to help facilitate speech/language development.

D. The client was taught to use "I messages" to communicate thoughts, feelings, and needs more clearly and effectively.

31. Confront Withdrawal Gently (31)

A. The client was gently confronted about their pattern of withdrawing in social settings to avoid experiencing anxiety about speech/language problems.

B. The reasons for the client's pattern of withdrawing in social settings were explored.

C. The client was taught effective communication and assertiveness skills to help them feel more confident and less anxious in social settings.

D. Active listening skills were used as the client acknowledged that they often withdraw in social settings to avoid experiencing criticism or ridicule about stuttering.

E. Support and encouragement were provided as the client acknowledged that they often withdraw in social settings to avoid feeling embarrassed or anxious about speech articulation problems.

32. Assign One Comment in Classroom (32)

A. The client was assigned the task of contributing at least one comment to the classroom discussion each day to increase confidence in speaking with others.

B. The client reported that the homework assignment of contributing at least one comment to the classroom discussion per day has helped increase confidence in speaking with others; the client was encouraged to continue this practice.

C. The reasons were explored for the client's failure to follow through with contributing at least one comment to the classroom discussion per day.

D. A reward system was utilized to reinforce the client for contributing at least one comment during classroom discussion per day.

E. The client has not made comments during classroom discussion and was reminded to take this step.

33. Assign Show-and-Tell (33)

A. The client was assigned the task of sharing toys or personal objects during show-and-tell time at school to increase expressive language abilities.

B. The client reported on participation in show-and-tell at school and was helped to identify how this has increased confidence in expressing self around others.

C. The parents and teachers were strongly encouraged to praise and reinforce the client for sharing toys or personal objects during show-and-tell.

D. The reasons were explored for the client's resistance to participate in show-and-tell at school.

34. Design Oral Reading Program (34)

A. A consultation was held with the speech/language pathologist and teachers about designing a program in which the client orally reads passages of increasing length or difficulty in the classroom.

B. The client's anxieties and insecurities about reading in the classroom were processed.

C. The client was given much praise and positive reinforcement for reading passages in the classroom.

D. A reward system was designed to reinforce the client for reading in the classroom.

E. The client has experienced increased confidence in their ability to verbalize thoughts and feelings since they began orally reading passages in the classroom.

F. The client has not participated in the oral reading of passages in the classroom and was encouraged to participate in this technique in whatever (limited) manner they can.

35. Teach Positive Coping Mechanisms (35)

A. The client was taught deep-breathing and deep-muscle relaxation techniques to help them cope with the frustration surrounding speech/language problems.

B. The client was encouraged to utilize positive self-talk to help them cope with the frustration surrounding speech/language problems.

C. The client was taught cognitive-restructuring techniques to help them cope with the frustration surrounding speech/language problems.

D. The client reported that the positive coping mechanisms they have been taught (e.g., deep-breathing and deep-muscle relaxation techniques, positive self-talk, cognitive restructuring) have helped to decrease frustration with speech/language problems.

E. The client reported experiencing little or no reduction in the level of anxiety or frustration through the use of relaxation techniques, positive self-talk, or cognitive restructuring; this experience was processed and problem-solved.

F. The client has not used positive coping mechanisms and was redirected to use these helpful techniques.

36. Encourage Sharing Insecurities (36)

A. The client was encouraged to verbalize insecurities about speech/language problems.

B. The client was assigned to read "Shauna's Song" from the *Child Psychotherapy Homework Planner* (Jongsma, Peterson, McInnis, & Bruce) to help them identify and express feelings of insecurity about speech/language problems.

C. The client's responses to the review questions from the short story "Shauna's Song" were processed.

D. The client and parents were assigned to read "Shauna's Song" to help the client develop an awareness and acceptance of speech/language problems.

E. The client was supported as they reported that the short story "Shauna's Song" helped them realize how they withdraw when feeling anxious about speech/language problems.

F. The client was encouraged as they reported that the short story "Shauna's Song" helped them identify personal strengths that can be used to gain acceptance in peer group or school settings.

37. Use Mutual Storytelling Technique (37)

A. The client actively participated in the mutual storytelling exercise.

B. Using the mutual storytelling technique, the therapist modeled effective ways for the client to manage insecurities and frustrations surrounding speech/language problems.

C. The client was assisted in creating a story using puppets, dolls, or stuffed animals that reflects insecurities and frustrations about speech/language problems.

D. The client was helped to create a story using puppets, dolls, or stuffed animals that shows effective ways to cope with frustrations surrounding speech/language problems.

E. The client identified the mutual storytelling technique as being a fun and useful way to manage frustrations surrounding speech/language problems.

38. Teach Self-Control Strategies (38)

A. The client was taught deep-breathing and relaxation techniques to inhibit the impulse to act out or engage in negative attention-seeking behaviors when encountering frustration with speech/language problems.

B. The client was encouraged to use positive self-talk when encountering frustration with speech/language problems, instead of acting out or engaging in negative attention-seeking behaviors.

C. The client was taught mediational, self-control strategies (e.g., "stop, listen, think, and act") to inhibit the impulse to act out or engage in negative attention-seeking behaviors when encountering frustration with speech/language problems.

D. The client was taught cognitive-restructuring techniques to help them inhibit the impulse to act out or engage in negative attention-seeking behaviors when encountering frustration with speech/language problems.

E. The client reported that the self-control strategies have helped them cope with frustrations surrounding speech/language problems and reduce the frequency of their acting out or negative attention-seeking behaviors; they were encouraged to continue these strategies.

F. The client has not used the self-control strategies that they have been taught and were redirected to do so.

39. Assign Reading Related to Stuttering (39)

A. The client was assigned to read books that teach effective ways to manage stuttering.

B. The client was assigned to read *When Oliver Speaks* (Garvin).

C. The client was assigned to read *Wendi's Magical Voice* (Kohls).

D. The client was assigned to read *Ben Has Something to Say: A Story About Stuttering* (Leers).

E. The client has read books on stuttering, and insights were discussed.

F. The client has not read the assigned books on their own time, and a portion of today's therapy session was devoted to reading an assigned book about stuttering.

40. Teach Anxiety-Reduction Techniques (40)

A. The client was taught deep-breathing and relaxation techniques to decrease anticipatory anxiety in social settings and help control stuttering.

B. The client was encouraged to utilize positive self-talk when experiencing anticipatory anxiety in social settings to help control stuttering.

C. The client was taught cognitive-restructuring techniques to help decrease anticipatory anxiety in social settings and control stuttering.

D. The client was recommended to read portions of *The Relaxation and Stress Reduction Workbook for Kids* (Shapiro & Sprague).

E. The client reported that the anxiety-reduction techniques have helped to decrease anticipatory anxiety in social settings; the client was encouraged to continue these techniques.

F. The client has not used the anxiety-reduction techniques, and this failure was reviewed, processed, and problem-solved.

41. Assign Three Social Contacts per Day (41)

A. The client was given the homework assignment of initiating three social contacts per day with peers to help them face and work through anxieties and insecurities related to stuttering.

B. Role-playing and modeling techniques were used to teach the client appropriate ways to greet peers and initiate conversations.

C. The "Greeting Peers" exercise from the *Child Psychotherapy Homework Planner* (Jongsma, Peterson, McInnis, & Bruce) was used to help increase the frequency of the client's social interactions with peers and help them face and work through anxieties and insecurities related to stuttering.

D. The "Greeting Peers" exercise has helped reduce the client's social isolation and enabled them to face and work through anxieties related to their stuttering problem.

E. The client reported that the "Greeting Peers" exercise has helped them increase social contacts and overcome anxieties associated with their stuttering problem.

42. Use Role-Playing and Positive Coping Strategies (42)

A. Role-playing was used in today's therapy session to model effective ways for the client to extinguish anxiety that triggers stuttering in various social settings (e.g., reading in front of class, talking on phone, introducing self to unfamiliar peer).

B. The client was trained in the use of cognitive-restructuring techniques to extinguish the anxiety that triggers stuttering in various social settings.

C. The client was strongly encouraged to use positive self-talk as a means of reducing the anxiety that frequently triggers stuttering in various social settings.

D. The client reported that the role-playing exercises were helpful in reducing anxiety.

E. The client reported that the cognitive-restructuring techniques and positive self-talk helped to extinguish the anxiety that triggers stuttering.

43. Design in vivo Desensitization Program (43)

A. A speech/language pathologist was consulted about designing an in vivo desensitization program to help the client overcome anxiety associated with stuttering.

B. The client was trained in the use of deep-muscle relaxation techniques, as part of the in vivo desensitization program, to help decrease anxiety associated with stuttering.

C. The in vivo desensitization program was noted to have helped to decrease the client's anxiety associated with their stuttering problem.

D. The client reported that the in vivo desensitization program has helped to decrease the frequency and intensity of their stuttering; the client was encouraged to continue.

E. Thus far, the in vivo desensitization program has not proven to be successful in reducing the client's anxiety related to their stuttering problem; the technique was reviewed.

44. Use Psychoanalytic Play Therapy Approaches (44)

A. Using a psychoanalytic play therapy approach, the client was allowed to take the lead in exploring the unconscious conflicts or core anxieties that contribute to selective mutism.

B. A psychoanalytic play therapy approach was utilized to help the client work through feelings surrounding past loss, trauma, or victimization that have contributed to the emergence of selective mutism.

C. Interpretations were made about the client's feelings and fears expressed in play and related to the emergence of selective mutism.

D. The psychoanalytic play therapy approaches have helped the client work through and resolve the issues contributing to the emergence of the selective mutism.

45. Employ Art Therapy (45)

A. An art therapy approach was used in the early stages of therapy to help establish rapport and allow the client to begin to express feelings.

B. The art therapy sessions have helped the client begin to work through feelings.

C. The client's artwork was noted to reveal insight into the factors contributing to the emergence of selective mutism.

D. Today's session processed the content of the client's artwork and related it to the emergence of selective mutism.

E. The art therapy sessions have helped the client establish trust with the therapist so that now they have begun to directly verbalize thoughts and feelings.

46. Assess Family Dynamics (46)

A. A family therapy session was held to assess the dynamics that contribute to the client's refusal to speak in some situations.

B. The family members were asked to list the stressors that have had a negative impact on the family.

C. The family members were asked to identify the things that they would like to change within the family system.

D. The family therapy session was helpful in identifying the factors that contribute to the client's refusal to use speech in some situations.

47. Explore Past Loss, Trauma, or Victimization (47)

A. Today's therapy session explored the client's background for a possible history of loss, trauma, or victimization that may have contributed to the onset of selective mutism.

B. Today's therapy session revealed how the client's selective mutism emerged after they experienced a significant loss or traumatic event.

C. An individual play therapy session was held to help the client begin to express and work through feelings about the past loss, trauma, or victimization.

D. Although no specific past loss, trauma, or victimization was identified that may have contributed to the onset of the client's selective mutism, this dynamic was reviewed with the client's parents, and they were asked to be aware of how this may cause selective mutism.